The Glannon Guide
to Criminal Law

ASPEN PUBLISHERS

The Glannon Guide to Criminal Law

Learning Criminal Law Through Multiple-Choice Questions and Analysis

Second Edition

Laurie L. Levenson
Professor of Law
David W. Burcham Chair in Ethical Advocacy
Loyola Law School

Wolters Kluwer
Law & Business

AUSTIN   BOSTON   CHICAGO   NEW YORK   THE NETHERLANDS

Aspen Publishers
Attn: Permissions Department
76 Ninth Avenue, 7th Floor
New York, NY   10011-5201

To contact Customer Care, e-mail customer.care@aspenpublishers.com,
call 1-800-234-1660, fax 1-800-901-9075, or mail correspondence to:

Aspen Publishers
Attn: Order Department
PO Box 990
Frederick, MD 21705

Printed in the United States of America.

1 2 3 4 5 6 7 8 9 0

ISBN 978-0-7355-7955-2

Library of Congress Cataloging-in-Publication Data

Levenson, Laurie L., 1956-
     The Glannon guide to criminal law : learning criminal law through multiple-choice
     questions and analysis / Laurie L. Levenson.—2nd ed.
         p. cm.
     Includes index.
     ISBN 978-0-7355-7955-2
     1. Criminal law—United States—Examinations, questions, etc. I. Title.

KF9219.85.L477 2009
345.73076—dc22

                                                                        2009011272

About Wolters Kluwer Law & Business

Wolters Kluwer Law & Business is a leading provider of research information and workflow solutions in key specialty areas. The strengths of the individual brands of Aspen Publishers, CCH, Kluwer Law International and Loislaw are aligned within Wolters Kluwer Law & Business to provide comprehensive, in-depth solutions and expert-authored content for the legal, professional and education markets.

CCH was founded in 1913 and has served more than four generations of business professionals and their clients. The CCH products in the Wolters Kluwer Law & Business group are highly regarded electronic and print resources for legal, securities, antitrust and trade regulation, government contracting, banking, pension, payroll, employment and labor, and healthcare reimbursement and compliance professionals.

Aspen Publishers is a leading information provider for attorneys, business professionals and law students. Written by preeminent authorities, Aspen products offer analytical and practical information in a range of specialty practice areas from securities law and intellectual property to mergers and acquisitions and pension/benefits. Aspen's trusted legal education resources provide professors and students with high-quality, up-to-date and effective resources for successful instruction and study in all areas of the law.

Kluwer Law International supplies the global business community with comprehensive English-language international legal information. Legal practitioners, corporate counsel and business executives around the world rely on the Kluwer Law International journals, loose-leafs, books and electronic products for authoritative information in many areas of international legal practice.

Loislaw is a premier provider of digitized legal content to small law firm practitioners of various specializations. Loislaw provides attorneys with the ability to quickly and efficiently find the necessary legal information they need, when and where they need it, by facilitating access to primary law as well as state-specific law, records, forms and treatises.

Wolters Kluwer Law & Business, a unit of Wolters Kluwer, is headquartered in New York and Riverwoods, Illinois. Wolters Kluwer is a leading multinational publisher and information services company.

I dedicate this book to my children, Solly, Havi, and Daniela, and to my infinitely patient husband, Douglas Mirell.

Contents

Acknowledgments

I am extremely grateful to my research assistants, Shira Moses and Amanda Sherman, for their assistance in reviewing chapters of this manuscript. I greatly appreciate all of the administrative assistance of Byllie Richardson, as well as the ongoing support of the William M. Rains Foundation. Without their backing, this project would not have been possible.

I also owe a special debt of gratitude to the many reviewers of this book and to my many colleagues who have given me input, particularly Professors Samuel Pillsbury, Gerald Uelmen, and David Crump. Their suggestions and insights have been invaluable.

Finally, many thanks to all of the wonderful people at Aspen Publishers, particularly its publisher, Carol McGeehan, and editors Lynn Churchill and Christine Hannan. As always, you set the standard for professionalism.

The Glannon Guide
to Criminal Law

1

A Very Short Introduction

*There are few better measures of the concern a society has
for its individual members and its own well being than the way
it handles criminals.*

C riminal law is one of the most important classes you will take in law
school. For some students, it is important because they want to
become prosecutors, defense lawyers, or judges. However, a course
in criminal law is also important for those students who see their futures in
civil practice. Especially in today's society, it is not unusual for clients from
all walks of life to have problems that implicate the criminal justice system.
For example, a simple business transaction may trigger questions regarding
fraud, or a family law case can raise issues regarding criminal abuse. In the
final analysis, criminal law is important because it teaches you how to read
statutes, interpret them in light of hundreds of years of common law, and
argue their application in light of today's policy concerns.

This book provides a short, clear, efficient review of basic topics in
criminal law, organized around the format of multiple-choice questions. In
each chapter, the individual sections explain fundamental principles of a
topic — such as mens rea, homicide, or defenses — and illustrate them with a
series of multiple-choice questions. After each question, I explain which
answer is correct, and why the wrong answers are incorrect. These short
explanations allow me to discuss the black-letter rules in the context of the
questions. Hopefully, this format will engage you in the study process, so
you'll develop a stronger understanding of the basics of criminal law. This
process will also help you at the time of your criminal law exam, regardless of
whether your professor relies on multiple-choice or essay questions.

When working with this book, keep in mind that the individual criminal laws of jurisdictions may differ. However, in a basic law school course on criminal law, your professor's focus is on the general concepts of the law and how they operate. Therefore, the goal of this book is to assist you in learning these principles and knowing how to apply them in analyzing a fact pattern. In that regard, multiple-choice questions are not that different from essay questions. Both of these types of questions require you to understand a fact pattern and to analyze it using correct legal principles.

I have tried to make my multiple-choice questions as fair as possible in that they have only one correct answer. However, ambiguities inevitably arise. Therefore, it is important that you learn to analyze questions for the "best possible answer." Your professor's exam is sure to have ambiguities as well. The more comfortable you feel with analyzing multiple-choice questions, the better you will do even if there are ambiguities on the exam.

This book is designed to follow the order of topics ordinarily covered by criminal law professors. Of course, your professor may choose a different path. If he or she does, feel free to review the chapters in a different order than they are presented. Each chapter is self-sufficient. You should be able to understand the concepts of that chapter and integrate them to your overall understanding of the course.

In using this book, you have a choice. You can either read the introductory material and then attempt the multiple-choice questions, or you may try your hand at the multiple-choice questions (the answers are listed at the back of the chapter under **Levenson's Picks**) and then use the introductory material, in conjunction with the explanations after the questions, to learn the material. Either way, the questions will keep you honest by helping you focus on what you do and do not understand about the criminal law topic being discussed.

I welcome your comments on how this book worked for you. I hope it will be the one learning aid that helps you both master the material and learn how to take an exam so that you can display your mastery. Please let me know your thoughts. I can be reached at Laurie.Levenson@lls.edu.

2

Nature of Criminal Law

Without shared ideas on politics, morals, and ethics, no society can exist . . .
—from Lord Patrick Devlin, *The Enforcement of Morals*

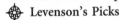

CHAPTER OVERVIEW
A. Criminal law versus tort law
B. Criminal law versus criminal procedure
C. Common law and statutory law
D. Purposes of punishment
E. Legality and overcriminalizing
F. The Closer: Proportionality and purposes of punishment
✦ Levenson's Picks

Criminal law is the study of offenses against society. A defendant who is convicted of a crime must make amends to society, as well as to his individual victim. Criminal laws are frequently designed to enforce the moral standards of society. While American criminal law is now governed primarily by statutory law, English common law forms the basis of much of our statutory law. The operation of criminal law, under either statutes or common law, is tied to its theoretical underpinnings — why do we punish?

A. Criminal law versus tort law

In law school, you will study both tort law and criminal law. At first glance, the topics may seem very similar. Both address what happens when a person harms another person. Both use similar terms, such as "recklessness," to describe the defendant's mental state when the harmful action is taken. However, there are key differences between criminal law and tort law. It is important to keep these differences in mind when studying criminal law.

First, a crime is an offense against the entire community, not just the victim who is directly hurt by the defendant's actions. For example, if a defendant hits a victim, the victim may sue the defendant for the tort of battery. However, the state or other governmental authority may also charge the defendant with the crime of assault because the defendant has violated society's code of conduct. Society, as well as the individual victim, has an interest in ensuring that the defendant is punished for his actions.

Second, if the defendant is found liable, the consequences of committing a tort are ordinarily that the defendant must compensate the victim for his injuries or loss by paying damages. However, in criminal prosecutions, the consequences are often more severe than monetary payments. The standard punishment for violating a criminal law is incarceration. A criminal defendant may also be ordered to pay a fine or restitution to the victim.

Third, violations of the criminal laws carry a stigma not ordinarily shared by being labeled a "tortfeasor." A criminal is marked as an individual who has violated the laws of society and should be morally condemned by others in the community.

The additional consequences of being convicted of a crime create differences in the meaning of terms that may also be used in your tort class. For example, criminal negligence is different from the negligence required for torts. Criminal negligence requires more than mere carelessness — it requires the type of carelessness for which society is willing to label the defendant a "criminal."

Finally, the labels affixed to someone who has been held responsible for harm are different under the criminal and tort systems. Under tort law, a defendant who has been found responsible for harm is "liable" for damages. Under criminal law, a guilty defendant is "culpable" for the crime.

In analyzing the question that follows, consider these differences between criminal and tort law in deciding which answer describes the defendant's culpability.

QUESTION 1. **Don't drink and drive.**   Eric was thrilled that he had just finished his first law school examination. He went out and celebrated with his friends. After several beers, Eric headed home to tell his parents the good news. Unfortunately, he hit Lynn's car on his drive home and totaled it. Eric's actions may make him

A. culpable of the tort of destroying Lynn's car, but not guilty of a crime because Lynn was not hurt.

> **B.** liable for destroying Lynn's car, but not guilty of a crime because Lynn was not hurt.
> **C.** subject to imprisonment for the tort of destroying Lynn's car.
> **D.** liable for damages for destroying Lynn's car and subject to imprisonment for the crime of drunk driving.

ANALYSIS. Don't be fooled by **A.** Although Eric may certainly be responsible for destroying Lynn's car, his tort responsibility would make him "liable" for damages. Moreover, if the criminal law prohibited drunk driving, it would not matter that Lynn was not hurt. Eric would also be culpable of the crime of drunk driving.

How about **B**? **B** sounds appealing because it used the right term, *liable,* to describe Eric's responsibility in tort for destroying Lynn's car. However, it is still wrong because it does not take into account that Eric's single act may cause both a civil and criminal cause of action.

C is just plain wrong because torts do not subject a defendant to imprisonment, no matter how bad they may be. At worst, and as discussed in more detail in your torts class, an intentional tort may subject the defendant to punitive damages. However, imprisonment is a punishment reserved for the criminal justice system.

D takes the prize. It accurately reflects that one harmful act may subject a defendant to both a tort lawsuit, and prosecution and punishment for a criminal offense.

B.   Criminal law versus criminal procedure

The study of criminal law focuses on the substantive law that defines what crimes are and what defenses there are to those crimes. Criminal procedure is a separate area of the law that examines the procedures by which a criminal case goes through the criminal justice system. Police investigative techniques and the handling of cases in the courtroom ordinarily are explored in a separate criminal procedure course. However, a basic understanding of the criminal justice system is important to comprehending criminal law.

There are many key participants in the criminal justice system. The police investigate cases. In doing so, they have considerable discretion in deciding whom to apprehend. Prosecutors decide which defendants they will charge and what charges they will bring against them. Prosecutors may seek formal charges either through the grand jury process or by filing a complaint. If the grand jury issues charges, the formal filing is called an indictment. If prosecutors file a complaint, a preliminary hearing is ordinarily held to determine if there is sufficient evidence (known as probable cause) to require the defendant to stand trial.

Most criminal cases are resolved by plea bargains. However, if a case proceeds to trial, the defendant is entitled to have a jury decide his guilt. In most states, a unanimous jury verdict is required. However, the U.S. Constitution only requires that a substantial majority of the jurors support the verdict. *Apodaca v. Oregon*, 406 U.S. 404 (1972). With the consent of the prosecution, the defendant may waive a jury trial and have the court decide the case.

In a criminal case, the burden of proof is on the prosecution to prove each element of a crime, including intent, beyond a reasonable doubt. *Patterson v. New York*, 432 U.S. 197 (1997). "[T]he presumption of innocence — that bedrock 'axiomatic and elementary' principle whose 'enforcement lies at the foundation of our criminal law' — the Due Process Clause of the United States Constitution requires the prosecutor to persuade the factfinder beyond a reasonable doubt of every fact necessary to constitute the crime charged." *In re Winship*, 397 U.S. 353 (1970). However, the burden of proof to prove an affirmative defense may be placed on the defendant without violating due process. *Leland v. Oregon*, 343 U.S. 790 (1952). As discussed in Chapters 16 to 20, typical affirmative defenses are insanity, self-defense, duress, necessity, intoxication, and entrapment.

Jurors have the inherent power to disregard the law and render a verdict contrary to it. This is referred to as *jury nullification*. Although jurors have this power, defendants are not entitled in most jurisdictions to a jury instruction advising jurors of their power to nullify. *United States v. Dougherty*, 473 F.2d 1113 (D.C. Cir. 1972).

If a jury returns a guilty verdict, the trial court has the power to overturn that verdict and enter an acquittal based upon insufficiency of the evidence. The trial court may also grant a new trial based upon procedural or evidentiary errors at trial. The most common errors relate to incorrect jury instructions. Jury instructions are the means by which the court advises the jurors of the requirements of the law related to the criminal charges in the case. They are, in essence, the "black-letter" criminal law.

The defendant may also appeal a guilty verdict. The appellate court reviews a case for legal errors. It does not have the power to reassess a witness's credibility. In determining whether there was sufficient evidence to convict the defendant, the appellate court must construe all inferences and make all credibility findings in favor of the government. It is only when no rational jury could have found the defendant guilty on the evidence presented that the appellate court may vacate or overturn a jury's verdict. *Jackson v. Virginia*, 443 U.S. 307 (1979).

The appellate court also reviews the trial to determine if the jury was properly instructed on the applicable law. If the jury was incorrectly instructed, the defendant is entitled to a new trial with proper instructions. For example, if the jury is given the wrong elements for a crime or incorrectly instructed that the defendant must prove he didn't intend to commit an offense, the defendant's conviction is likely to be reversed. Likewise, if the court has incorrectly precluded witnesses for the defense because it has wrongly decided that a proffered defense does not apply, the defendant is entitled to a new trial in which he can present evidence of that defense. While the defendant's conviction may be reversed, that does not mean that the defendant walks free. Rather, the defendant receives a new trial in which the law and evidence are correctly presented to the finder of fact.

The government does not have the right to appeal a not guilty verdict because of the Fifth Amendment's guarantee against double jeopardy. However, if the trial court dismisses a case because of an improper interpretation of the law, and the defendant has not yet been subjected to a trial, the government may appeal.

QUESTION 2. Bad verdict. Glenn was charged with helping with a bank robbery. Prosecutors claimed that Glenn knowingly loaned his car to Roger to use in the robbery. At trial, the prosecution called Roger as a witness. Roger had pled guilty and agreed to testify against Glenn in exchange for leniency at his own sentencing. At trial, Glenn tries to argue that Roger frequently borrows cars from friends for all his errands, not just bank robberies, but the trial court insists on instructing the jury that a person who loans his car is conclusively presumed to know the illegal purposes for which the car will be used. Which of the following is the best basis for Glenn's appeal?

A. No rational jury could believe an accomplice witness who has been given leniency in exchange for his testimony.

B. The police abused their discretion in arresting Glenn.

C. It was improper for the court to instruct the jury to presume Glenn's criminal intent.

D. There was insufficient evidence for Glenn's conviction.

ANALYSIS. Although you may be eager to help Glenn out of his predicament, it is important to remember the procedural limitations on a criminal defendant's right of appeal. Even if you personally do not believe Roger, it cannot be said that no rational jury could believe his testimony. Therefore answer **A** is incorrect. Appellate courts are stuck with the credibility decisions made by the jury.

Answer **B** goes too far. Remember that the police have broad discretion in arresting suspects. They need not have proof beyond a reasonable doubt to make an arrest. Mere probable cause — which roughly equates with a strong suspicion — is sufficient.

Answer **D** is incorrect for the same reason that Answer **A** was incorrect. It is not up to the appellate court to reweigh the evidence. If the jury believed the accomplice, as we must infer that they did, there was sufficient evidence for the guilty verdict.

Answer **C** is the best answer. Criminal intent is one of the elements of the offense that the prosecution must prove beyond a reasonable doubt. As such, a jury instruction directing the jury to presume that element unconstitutionally relieves the prosecution of its duty to prove intent. *Sandstrom v. Montana*, 442 U.S. 510 (1979). Glenn's best chance of success on appeal would be to challenge this instruction.

C. Common law and statutory law

U.S. criminal law is derived from English common law. The common law was established through a series of case decisions creating principles of law. This development of law is called *case precedent*.

Except in rare circumstances, the common law no longer governs in the United States. Statutory law now governs both state and federal courts. However, the common law remains important because U.S. statutes typically incorporate common law principles and terminology. For example, all U.S. jurisdictions prohibit "murder." The definition of murder is ordinarily set forth in common law terms, such as requiring that the defendant have acted with "malice."

Many jurisdictions have modeled their criminal laws on a model criminal code drafted by the American Law Institute (ALI). The Model Penal Code is a model statute drafted by the ALI that sets forth basic principles of criminal law. It is not binding on legislatures or courts, but is a tool frequently used to teach criminal law in law school.

Crimes were classified at common law according to their seriousness. Typically, crimes were divided into *felonies* and *misdemeanors*. Felonies were those offenses that carried serious punishment. Under federal law, felonies are now classified as crimes that carry a possible sentence of more than one year in jail. Less serious offenses are referred to as misdemeanors. There is also a third category of offenses that have developed since the common law. Referred to as regulatory offenses or infractions, they are the least serious types of crimes and typically carry only a fine as punishment.

Another way that crimes may be categorized is *malum in se* or *malum prohibitum*. *Malum in se* crimes are inherently immoral or dangerous, such as murder and fraud. *Malum prohibitum* crimes violate a specific prohibition of the law, but do not necessarily carry with them moral opprobrium. A traffic offense is a classic example of a *malum prohibitum* crime.

The classification of crimes is important in the criminal justice system in two ways. First, a crime's classification may help to identify the intent requirement, if any, required for that crime. Regulatory crimes, because they carry such minimum punishment, may not require a criminal intent and therefore may be classified as "strict liability" crimes. Second, a crime's classification may trigger certain procedural rights for a defendant. For example, a defendant who does not face jail time may not be entitled to a trial by jury.

QUESTION 3. Dr. Death. Assume that crimes in your jurisdiction are statutorily defined, but the legislature has thus far refused to pass a law making it a crime to assist another person in committing suicide. Dr. Death films himself handing poison to an ailing patient who then drinks it and dies. Viewers are appalled. Local law enforcement reacts by charging Dr. Death with assisting a suicide.

As to this charge, Dr. Death is

A. guilty because it is *malum in se* to help another person end his life.
B. guilty if the common law prohibited assisting a suicide.
C. guilty if the Model Penal Code prohibits assisting a suicide.
D. not guilty.

ANALYSIS. I know you are eager to convict Dr. Death, but be careful. Criminal law today is governed by statutory law. There is no law in the jurisdiction that prohibits assisting a suicide. Unless a jurisdiction has a "savings clause statute" prohibiting any offense that was illegal at common law, Dr. Death may be morally wrong by his conduct but not guilty of a criminal offense.

A is wrong because even though it may be inherently wrong to help someone end his life, Dr. Death is guilty only if there is a specific statute prohibiting his conduct. Likewise, **B** is wrong because the jurisdiction has expressly refused to adopt the common law on this issue.

C is not the correct answer because the Model Penal Code is not enforceable by itself. Although it has had a strong influence on jurisdictions that have redrafted their codes since 1962, it is not by itself a separate legal basis for finding a violation of the law.

D is therefore the best answer. Dr. Death is not guilty of the charge against him. As we will learn, in some jurisdictions, assisting in another's death may constitute murder. However, here Dr. Death was charged with "assisting a suicide," which was not a crime in that jurisdiction.

In addition to reviewing an area of criminal law, this question offers important hints on how to analyze a multiple-choice question.

- First, read the question very carefully. Do not presume facts. You must go with the facts as presented in the question. For example, if the question states that there is no statutory law prohibiting the defendant's behavior, you must answer your question based upon that fact.

- Second, do not look for the "right" answer when answering a multiple-choice question. Instead, analyze each possible answer for why it may be incorrect. By doing so, you will be forced to apply your knowledge of the law. This process of elimination is more likely to lead you to the correct answer than reacting quickly based upon your instincts.

D. Purposes of punishment

Warning! Many professors *love* to discuss purposes of punishment because they form the theoretical basis for all criminal law. Therefore, whether or not you are a theory person, it is imperative that you understand the basic purposes of punishment, including the problems with each theory.

Most books refer to the four purposes of punishment: retribution, deterrence, rehabilitation, and incapacitation. The *retributivist theory* holds that a defendant "deserves" to be punished because he has violated the rules of society. Punishment constitutes the defendant's "just desserts" or "payback" for having committed the offense. Retribution is often associated with the ancient concept of *lex talionis,* or "eye for an eye." This theory holds that a defendant should be punished regardless of whether other persons will be deterred because society must send a message that its moral norms cannot be violated.

Retributivism is criticized for legitimizing vengeance and inflicting pain even when it cannot be shown that punishment will promote the greater good. Philosophers like Immanuel Kant support a retributivist theory of punishment.

By contrast, *deterrence* is a *utilitarian* theory of punishment that holds that we must punish criminals to deter other individuals from committing the same crime. The deterrence theory is premised on the belief that criminals weigh the advantages and disadvantages of their acts before committing a crime. Punishment increases the costs of criminal behavior and thereby provides a disincentive to commit future crime. This theory is informed by philosopher Jeremy Bentham's principles of utilitarianism.

There are two types of deterrence: general and specific. General deterrence is punishment inflicted to deter others from committing the defendant's crime. Specific (or "special") deterrence is punishment inflicted to discourage that individual defendant from repeating his criminal behavior.

The deterrence theory is criticized for being ineffective in those cases in which a criminal is motivated by emotions, not rational decision. Moreover, it is questionable whether it is just to punish one person to control the behavior of others.

There are two other utilitarian purposes of punishment. *Rehabilitation* is a theory that calls for a defendant to be punished so that he can be trained not to commit crimes. Most jurisdictions have abandoned this theory because it is costly and proceeds on the assumption that human beings in prison can and will change their behavior if given the opportunity and incentive to do so. In reality, the prison setting can often teach inmates even more criminal behavior.

The final theory of punishment — *incapacitation* — also has a strictly utilitarian purpose. It holds that defendants should be incarcerated or executed to prevent them from doing further harm to society. The three strikes law that mandates life imprisonment for certain offenders is an example of a law based upon the theory of incapacitation. Incapacitation is a costly theory that presumes that defendants will not continue their criminal activities while incarcerated.

In any given case, one or more of the theories of punishment may be at play. At the time of sentencing, courts will try to gauge the application of these purposes of punishment by examining the severity of the offense, the defendant's prior history of criminal behavior, and other aggravating and mitigating factors that reflect on the need for punishment.

Importantly, the purposes of punishment not only form the basis for sentencing decisions, but are also the theoretical underpinnings determining what is classified as a crime and what defenses are allowed.

QUESTION 4. Fraternity party. James Chow, a 21-year-old college junior, is arrested for driving under the influence on his way home from a weekend fraternity party. James pleads guilty to the offense, but the judge sentences him to the maximum six months in the county jail. At the sentencing hearing, the judge addresses James regarding the sentence: "I'm doing this to teach you a lesson, so that for the rest of your life you'll never get behind the driver's wheel if you've been drinking."

Which of the following theories of punishment has the court primarily relied on in sentencing James Chow?

A. retribution.
B. general deterrence.
C. specific deterrence.
D. rehabilitation.
E. incapacitation.

ANALYSIS. Let's go through the answers in order. **A** is wrong because a truly retributivist sentence would not depend on whether the court was trying to control the defendant's future behavior. Rather, the court could have simply stated, "Mr. Chow, what you did was wrong and you must be punished for it, regardless of whether you or anyone else might make the same mistake again."

B is also wrong because the court's message is directed specifically at Mr. Chow, not other possible, future offenders. If the judge had stated,

"Mr. Chow, I'm going to use you to set an example for all your fraternity buddies so they'll think twice before they pull the same stunt as you," **B** would have been the correct answer.

C is the correct answer because the judge is trying to teach Chow a lesson. The court states that the punishment is meant to serve as specific deterrence so that Chow will not commit the same offense again in the future.

D is wrong because there is no mention by the court that having Chow serve time in jail will somehow make him a better person or less likely to drink and drive. If the court had stated, "Son, you need help with your alcohol problem and I know just the place to get it — jail," the applicable purpose of punishment would have been rehabilitation.

Finally, **E** is wrong because the court has not stated that Chow is being imprisoned specifically so he cannot hurt other people. Be careful about reading this into the answer. Instead, before you choose "incapacitation" as your answer, look for statements by the court such as, "Mr. Chow, you are a menace on the road and the only way I can keep us all safe is by keeping you in jail."

E.   Legality and overcriminalizing

It should come as no surprise that the criminal laws are based upon society's view of what is moral and immoral behavior. For this reason, there are so-called "victimless" crimes such as prostitution and drug use. However, not all harmful or immoral acts are crimes. The principle of legality requires that conduct be specifically prohibited by the criminal laws before it may be punished. Additionally, the principle of legality prohibits laws that are so vague that a person does not have fair notice as to when his behavior constitutes a crime.

The principle of legality serves many purposes: (1) It provides notice as to what conduct is unlawful; (2) it confines the discretion of the police in their enforcement of the laws; (3) it prevents judges and juries from arbitrarily creating new crimes; and (4) it ensures that the criminal law only operates prospectively. It is also a principle that has some constitutional roots in the prohibition against bills of attainder[1] and ex post facto laws.[2] (See U.S. Const. art. I, §§9 and 10, and the Due Process Clause, Fifth and Fourteenth Amendments.)

Without the principle of legality, the dangers of overcriminalizing behavior would become even more pronounced. Unused laws would engender disrespect for the laws, limited police and prosecutorial resources would be diverted to the wrong cases, there would be a serious invasion of

---

1. A bill of attainder is a legislative act that inflicts punishment without a criminal trial.
2. Ex post facto laws are laws that seek to make criminal an act that was innocent when done.

people's personal privacy, and there would be the increased possibility of discriminatory enforcement of the laws.

Typically, criminal law casebooks will use two other cases to illustrate the principle of legality. In *Commonwealth v. Mochan*, 177 Pa. Super. 454, 110 A.2d 788 (1955), the defendant was charged with intending to "debauch and corrupt, and [further embarrass and vilify the victim]" by making filthy, disgusting and indecent phone calls to her. No specific statute prohibits such conduct, but a savings clause in Pennsylvania law provided that all offenses punishable by common law remained punishable in Pennsylvania. Based upon that clause, the court upheld the conviction. The case illustrates the importance of the principle of legality. Without specificity in the laws, a broad range of conduct can be punished and defendants are not on notice as to whether their conduct is prohibited.

In a second case, *Keeler v. Superior Court*, 2 Cal. 3d 619 (1970), the defendant stomped on his ex-wife's pregnant stomach, causing her to deliver the fetus stillborn. He was charged with murder. Keeler successfully moved to block the prosecution, claiming that the law did not provide sufficient notice of what constituted a "human being" for California's murder law. Later, California amended its murder statute to provide that "Murder is the unlawful killing of a human being, or a fetus, with malice aforethought." Cal. Penal Code §187(b). Again, this case highlights how important it is that the legislature specifically defines the scope of criminal conduct so laws will not be applied in an arbitrary or vindictive manner.

With the principles of legality in mind, let's try the next question. Keep in mind that while common law continues to influence the interpretation of criminal laws, it is up to the legislature to define what constitutes a crime.

QUESTION 5. Sex directories. Mr. Shaw is accused of selling copies of his little black book that lists the phone numbers of all the prostitutes in town. He is charged with "conspiring to corrupt public morals." No statute details the meaning of "corrupting public morals." Prosecutors argue that the jury should decide whether Shaw's activities violated society's norms.

If Shaw argues that his case should be dismissed because it violates the principle of legality, his motion should be

A. denied because the jury has been given the responsibility to decide society's morals.
B. denied because all criminal laws are based upon public morals.
C. granted because imprecise statutory language violates principles of legality.
D. granted because the statute does not provide sufficient notice as to what behavior constitutes the corruption of public morals.

ANALYSIS.   Although all jury decisions somehow reflect society's morality, **A** is wrong because the principle of legality still requires that the defendant be given notice as to what specific behavior is considered criminal conduct.

Likewise, **B** is wrong because even though criminal laws are based upon public morals, the principle of legality still requires that the laws specify what public morality will be criminally enforced.

C is the wrong answer because it goes too far. Not all imprecise statutory language violates the principle of legality. For example, statutes commonly use common law terms, such as *negligently* and *recklessly*, without defining those terms. As long as there is a statute that identifies the prohibited criminal behavior and generally provides notice to the defendant as to what conduct crosses the line, the principle of legality does not bar the charge.

D is correct. Under basic principles of legality, a defendant may not be convicted unless his conduct was defined as criminal at the time it was committed so that the defendant could have notice that his behavior was illegal.

F.   The Closer: Proportionality and purposes of punishment

In each chapter I include a "Closer," a fairly challenging example to push the analysis and your understanding. For this first chapter, we look at the concept of "proportionality." The concept of proportionality plays a role throughout criminal law. For example, in deciding whether a defendant was permitted to use force in self-defense, the law looks at whether the force used by the defendant was proportional to the force with which he was threatened.

The doctrine of proportionality also arises in sentencing issues. Under current Supreme Court law, the test for determining whether a sentence violates the Eighth Amendment's prohibition against cruel and unusual punishment is whether the sentence imposed is "grossly disproportional" to the offense committed. In deciding whether a sentence is grossly disproportionate, the court examines three factors: (1) the gravity of the offense compared to the severity of the penalty; (2) penalties imposed for other crimes in that jurisdiction ("intra-jurisdictional" analysis); and (3) penalties imposed in other jurisdictions for that same offense ("inter-jurisdictional" analysis). See *Solem v. Helm,* 463 U.S. 277 (1983). See also *Harmelin v. Michigan,* 501 U.S. 957 (1991). Chapter 24 focuses on sentencing and analyzes this use of proportionality in more detail.

For now, however, let's try a final question to determine how firmly you understand the purposes of punishment and the role of proportionality in applying those standards.

QUESTION 6. Life in prison is a long time. Andretti was convicted of shoplifting six children's videotapes from Q-Mart Discount Store. The total value of the stolen videotapes was less than $100. Nonetheless, because Andretti has been convicted before of two relatively minor felonies (burglarizing a home when no one was present and using marijuana), he is sentenced under the jurisdiction's three strikes law to life imprisonment without parole. Andretti complains that his sentence is improper. He notes for the judge that under common law, petty theft did not result in lengthy prison terms. Moreover, he notes that he is not really a danger to the community and that he has already paid back Q-Mart Discount Store for its losses. What would Andretti's best argument be for overturning his sentence?

A. Andretti's sentence does not serve any purpose of punishment.
B. The victim has suffered no permanent injury from Andretti's actions.
C. Andretti's sentence does not comport with common law practices.
D. Andretti's sentence was per se cruel and unusual punishment.
E. None of the above.

ANALYSIS. **D** seems like a reasonable answer to this question: Life in prison for a few children's videotapes is a long time. However, **D** is not the correct answer. The Supreme Court held in *Lockyer v. Andrade,* 538 U.S. 63 (2003), and *Ewing v. California,* 538 U.S. 11 (2003), that three strikes sentences do not *per se* violate the Eighth Amendment. Applying purposes of punishment is a far more subtle exercise than just asking whether you would have imposed the same sentence. It requires discipline to critically analyze each purpose of punishment to determine whether there is an argument that the sentence was not disproportional to the crime. Therefore, it is best for us to start with the possible answers in order, since **A** requires us to examine the purposes of punishment as applied to this question.

Which, if any, purpose of punishment may Andretti's sentence serve? In fact, an argument could be made for all four purposes of punishment. First, if Andretti's crime is not characterized as simply shoplifting, but "shoplifting by a career criminal," there seems to be a stronger argument for a long sentence as retribution to Andretti for his life of crime. Second, it is important to deter people like Andretti who continue to commit crimes. Perhaps the only way such individuals can be deterred is by threatening them with extremely long sentences. Third, Andretti continues to pose a threat to society. Although he is only a shoplifter, he does not seem to be able to control his criminal impulses. Thus, incapacitation may be in order. Finally, Andretti definitely needs rehabilitation. He needs to change from his life of crime. Of course, there are problems with each of these theories of punishment. For example, even if retribution is warranted, how much jail time properly serves this purpose? Moreover, once he is sentenced to life imprisonment, rehabilitation will not matter. Despite these problems, an argument could be made that one or more of the purposes of punishment support Andretti's sentence. Therefore, **A** is the wrong answer.

B is also a wrong answer because criminal law does not require that there be an identifiable victim or that that victim suffer a permanent injury. Conspiracy and attempt are classic crimes in which a victim does not suffer an injury. Moreover, as Chapter 22 discusses, it is no defense to a theft crime that the defendant offers to pay back the victim after he is apprehended. Unlike tort law, the issue in criminal law does not focus heavily on what damage the victim suffered. Rather, the focus is on the defendant's actions and criminal intent.

C is wrong, as well. Common law can be used to interpret statutory law, but it does not supersede it. Thus, when the law is clear as to the nature of a crime and applicable sentence, it is the statutory law that governs.

Finally, we end the analysis the way we began it. A three strikes law, although harsh, is not per se cruel and unusual punishment. **D** is incorrect. It is up to the defendant to argue why the sentence is disproportionate to the crime. Therefore, for this closer problem, **E** is the correct answer.

Even though **E** is the best answer, you should be aware that the Supreme Court left open the possibility in *Ewing* that some three strikes sentences might violate the constitutional prohibition against cruel and unusual punishment. The Ninth Circuit made such a ruling in *Ramirez v. Castro*, 365 F.3d 755 (9th Cir. 2004). It found that a defendant who had shoplifted a video cassette recorder and then immediately returned it, and had no other prior offenses other than shoplifting offenses, could not be sentenced to 25-years to life imprisonment. What is the difference between *Ramirez* and the facts of Question 6? All of Ramirez's prior offenses were shoplifting. By contrast, Andretti, like the petitioner in *Andrade, supra,* had prior drug and burglary convictions.

In general, it is very rare for a court to overturn a sentence within the statutory maximum. A great deal of deference is given to the legislature to decide when the purposes of punishment dictate harsh sentences for repeat offenses. Only in the rare case, like that of *Ramirez,* is there a chance of having the court strike down the sentence for violating the Eighth Amendment.

✦ Levenson's Picks

1. Don't drink and drive		D
2. Bad verdict		C
3. Dr. Death		D
4. Fraternity party		C
5. Sex directories		D
6. Life in prison is a long time		E

3

Elements of a Crime

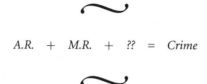

$$A.R. \quad + \quad M.R. \quad + \quad ?? \quad = \quad Crime$$

CHAPTER OVERVIEW
A. Actus reus: Culpable conduct
1. Voluntary affirmative acts
2. Omissions
3. Status crimes
4. Possession Crimes
B. Mens rea: Culpable mental state
1. Common law terminology
   a. Maliciously
   b. Intentionally
   c. Negligently
   d. Willfully
2. Model Penal Code terms
   a. Purposely
   b. Knowingly
   c. Recklessly
   d. Negligently
C. Specific intent versus general intent
D. The Closer: Euthanasia — Positive act or omission? Motive versus intent
◈ Levenson's Picks

C rimes are like mathematical formulas, although often not as precise. Before a defendant is found guilty, the prosecution must prove the required "elements" of the crime. All crimes require that the defendant engage in culpable conduct. "Conduct" is really a misnomer. Either the defendant engaged in affirmative misbehavior *or* failed to do something required by the law and is therefore guilty because of that omission. However, bad acts alone ordinarily are not enough for criminal culpability.

The heart of most crimes is the mens rea requirement. For a defendant to be found guilty, she must commit the wrongful act with a culpable mental state. Mere accidents may be enough to trigger tort liability, but they are rarely enough to make the defendant a criminal.

As you go through the next sections, keep in mind that the burden is on the prosecution to prove each of the elements of a crime. Therefore, if an element is missing, because, for example, the defendant was clueless, the defendant is not guilty of a crime. The challenge of mastering topics such as mistake of fact lies in discerning what a defendant must know or not know to be guilty of a crime.

The key to understanding criminal law is mastering how each of these elements of a crime work. Once you do, you should be able to analyze any criminal statute to determine what elements the prosecution must prove to show that the defendant is guilty of the crime.

A.   Actus reus: Culpable conduct

1. Voluntary affirmative acts

As a general rule, all crimes require that a defendant commit a voluntary criminal act — an actus reus. The actus reus may be a positive act, such as hitting another, or an omission, which is a failure to act when there is a legal duty to do so, such as when a parent fails to seek medical care for her child.

The purpose of the actus reus requirement is to ensure that people are not punished for bad thoughts alone. Each crime includes an actus reus. It is the "verb" of the crime. For example, homicide is defined as the "killing of another human being." The actus reus for this crime is killing.

There may be many different types of physical action that satisfy the actus reus of a crime. Think of all the ways you can kill someone. You can stab, poison, shoot, smother, choke, bomb, etc. All of these would qualify as the actus reus for a homicide charge.

How about words alone? Contrary to popular lore, words alone can constitute the "actus reus" of a crime. For example, the crimes of treason, sedition, solicitation, conspiracy, and aiding and abetting may all be accomplished by verbal conduct.

For a physical act to qualify as an actus reus, it must be voluntary. Be careful. The criminal law's notion of what is voluntary may be very different from your own. Under the criminal law, as long as the person is engaged in conscious and volitional movement, the act is considered voluntary. All this really means is that the person's brain was engaged at the time of the act. It doesn't mean that the defendant really wanted to do the act or got great satisfaction out of it. For example, a person who is forced with a gun at her head to rob a bank has a "voluntary" actus reus of robbing the bank, although she may have a separate defense of duress down the road.

Because most of our actions are considered voluntary for purposes of proving the actus reus, it is probably easier to remember what is considered an "involuntary" act. The Model Penal Code identifies four situations in which many jurisdictions are willing to say that the defendant did not act voluntarily. They are (1) reflex or convulsion; (2) bodily movement during unconsciousness or sleep; (3) bodily movement under hypnotic suggestion;[1] and (4) bodily movement not otherwise the product of the effort or determination of the actor, either conscious or habitual. In other words, when a person is acting like an automaton because her brain is not engaged with the body, the person may have a claim that her act was not voluntary. (MPC §2.01.)

As noted in the Model Penal Code, acts done out of habit are still considered to be voluntary, even though the defendant may not have given it much thought before engaging in the act. For example, some people routinely speed down the same street on the way to work because they know that the police never monitor that street. The defendant's act of speeding would still be voluntary because absentmindedness and habit are not the same as involuntary acts.

The trick in many criminal cases is to define when the period of the actus reus began and ended. Defendants want to limit the actus reus to a narrow period of time when the defendant may have unconsciously engaged in wrongful behavior. For example, an epileptic who has a seizure while driving and crashes into another person will claim that the act was involuntary. However, prosecutors want the period of time for the actus reus to be stretched out to include some period of voluntary action by the defendant, such as when the epileptic, knowing that he might have a seizure, nonetheless decided to drive the car. Under Model Penal Code §2.01(1), as long as the defendant's action "includes" a voluntary act, the defendant is culpable.

Here's a fairly straightforward question to illustrate these points.

---

1. Beware. Many jurisdictions have rejected this category of involuntary acts because they believe that a person who is under hypnosis still has the power to control her behavior.

QUESTION 1. **Home invasion.** Martin is sitting in his living room chair drinking his eighth beer of the night when the police arrive. They demand that he go outside to talk to them about a claim that he stole his neighbor's garden gnome. Martin has no recollection of taking the garden gnome. When Martin refuses to go outside with the officers, the police physically pick him up and carry him outside. While he is standing outside, Martin has a seizure. His body convulses and his arm hits one of the officers. Martin is charged with stealing his neighbor's garden gnome, being drunk in public, and assaulting an officer. Which of the following is false?

A. Martin cannot be guilty of stealing his neighbor's garden gnome because he acted involuntarily.

B. Martin cannot be guilty of being drunk in public because he was in public involuntarily.

C. Martin cannot be guilty of assaulting an officer because he acted involuntarily.

D. Martin cannot be guilty of assaulting an officer because his body acted convulsively.

ANALYSIS. Be careful. First, this is the type of multiple-choice question often included on exams that asks you to find the answer that is *un*true. Therefore, you must resist the temptation to jump at the "right" answer. By the very nature of the question, there will be several correct statements included among the answers. You want to find the statement that analyzes the problem incorrectly.

A is definitely an option. There are no facts to indicate that Martin was acting involuntarily when he allegedly stole his neighbor's garden gnome. Nothing indicates that at the time of that crime, Martin was not in control of his bodily motions. Therefore, **A** is an incorrect statement and the likely answer to choose. However, as is best when answering all multiple-choice questions, one must also review the other options to see if they are also possibilities.

B is a correct statement of the law. Martin is only in public because he was involuntarily carried there by the police officers. His body did not act of its own volition. Therefore, Martin would not have a voluntary actus reus for the crime of being drunk in public.

C is also a correct statement. When Martin hit the officers, he was not in control of his bodily movements. His body acted by convulsion, one type of involuntary act. It is not the same type of involuntariness that excuses his crime of being drunk in public, but it is nonetheless an involuntary act and therefore he cannot be guilty of the assault.

D is just another way of stating that Martin did not have a voluntary actus reus for the assault. **D** is a more detailed explanation of the answer in **C**. Sometimes professors will want the more detailed answer, but that is not the call of this question. The professor is looking for which option is an incorrect statement of the law, not a more specific statement of the law.

Given that **B**, **C**, and **D** are correct statements of the law, you can be even more certain that **A** is the correct answer; only **A** is an incorrect statement of the law as applied to this problem.

2. Omissions

The general rule in the United States is that there is no duty to help another or to rescue a person from harm. For many caring people, this rule does not sit well. It means that we are not a nation of Good Samaritans. However, it is the standard for criminal law. Therefore, a defendant ordinarily is not guilty simply for allowing harm to come to another, even if the defendant could easily have helped prevent that harm.

A tragic example of this rule occurred in New York in the famous Kitty Genovese case. In 1964, over the course of 35 minutes, Genovese was stabbed to death while numerous witnesses watched and failed to help. While morally troubling, the spectators' failure to assist was not a criminal actus reus.

Likewise, in the famous case of *Pope v. State*, 284 Md. 309 (Md. Ct. App. 1979), Mrs. Pope was charged with child abuse for failing to come to the rescue of an infant who was being severely beaten by its mother. The court held that Pope was not guilty because she had no specific duty to come to the child's aid.

Although the general rule is that omission is not an actus reus, an omission may satisfy the actus reus requirement for a crime if the defendant has a duty to act and fails to do so. *The duty to act may arise from several sources: (1) a statute; (2) a status relationship; (3) a contractual agreement; or (4) voluntarily assuming the care of another. In each of these situations, the failure to act may constitute an actus reus for a crime.*

Let's examine each of these duties. Statutes, criminal or civil, may create a duty to act. For example, tax statutes create a duty to file tax returns. Failure to file returns constitutes the actus reus for a tax offense. Similarly, a statute may require that educators help children who are being harmed. If a teacher fails in this duty, there may be criminal culpability. Moreover, some jurisdictions have gone so far as to create general Good Samaritan laws that require individuals to assist others or at least report crimes they see others commit. Failure to provide this assistance is considered in itself a criminal act.

A duty to help may also be created by a person's status relationship with the victim. It has been traditionally held that parents owe a duty of care to children, employers to employees, spouses to each other, owners to customers, innkeepers to guests, and captains to passengers. In these situations, the defendant does not have the freedom to ignore the victim's need for help. Thus, if a parent allows a child to starve to death, the parent may be guilty of homicide; the actus reus for that crime is failing to feed the child.

By contractual agreement, a defendant may assume the duty to help another. Two classic examples are babysitters and caretakers. In each of those situations, the defendant has agreed to assist another person. If the defendant fails in that agreement, the defendant may have criminal exposure because of her omission. Thus, if a babysitter watches a small child about to walk into traffic, the babysitter is responsible for harm to that child if she does nothing to stop the child.

Finally, a defendant has a duty to help if she has voluntarily assumed the care of another. In these situations, the defendant has often isolated the victim from the help of others. If the defendant indicates that she will care for the victim and then abandons that duty, the defendant has an actus reus for the crime. Consider, for example, a person who sees a person fall off his bicycle and then takes the injured person into her home, telling others that she will call for help. In fact, the defendant does not call for help or otherwise assist the victim. If the victim dies due to the defendant's neglect, the defendant may have criminal responsibility for the death.

Before we try a question related to the rule of omissions, let's examine two other aspects of the law of actus reus. First, although there may be a duty to help, a defendant is ordinarily excused from that duty unless she can fulfill it without harming herself. Thus, if a victim is in a burning house, the babysitter need not die trying to rescue the child if there is no safe way for the babysitter to assist.

Second, you should realize that some fact situations can be analyzed as either positive acts or omissions. For example, what if a defendant rapes a young girl who then jumps into the river out of despair? The defendant then watches the child drown instead of throwing her a life vest. See *Jones v. State,* 43 N.E.2d 1017 (Ind. 1942). There are two ways to analyze this situation. You can either stretch out the affirmative physical acts that led to the child's death to include the defendant's initial assault. In such a case, there is a voluntary act that constitutes the actus reus. Alternatively, this situation could be analyzed as one in which the defendant put the victim in peril and therefore had a duty to help the victim. In essence, this is a fifth category of situations in which the defendant must help the victim. Most of the time, the distinction between an affirmative act and the failure to fulfill a duty makes no difference. However, in the area of euthanasia, this distinction can be important. In many jurisdictions, only the affirmative act of "pulling the plug" constitutes euthanasia. By contrast, failure to continue to provide life support is considered passive euthanasia and not criminal conduct. See *Barber v. Superior Court,* 147 Cal. App. 3d 1006 (Cal. Ct. App. 1983).

Now you are ready for a hypothetical to test your understanding of omissions as a form of actus reus.

QUESTION 2. Save me.   John, Mike, Sue, and Roger are at a pool party. During the party, a toddler falls into the pool and starts to drown. Everyone sees what is happening, but no one stops to help. John is the toddler's father, Mike is the hired lifeguard, Sue is an off-duty police officer, and Roger is a guest at the party. The prosecution files criminal charges against all four defendants for failing to help the child. Which of the following is correct?

A. None of the defendants is guilty because there is no general duty to help another person.

B. Only John is guilty because he is the only defendant related to the child.

C. Mike and Roger are guilty if they were capable of saving the child without putting themselves at risk.

D. All of the defendants are guilty if they were capable of saving the child without putting themselves at risk.

E. John and Mike are guilty if they are capable of saving the child without putting themselves at risk.

ANALYSIS.   The easiest way to sort out the answer to this problem is to consider the culpability of each defendant before looking at the possible answers to the question. Go through each defendant — John, Mike, Sue, and Roger — and ask the question: "Did this defendant have a duty to try and help the toddler?"

John had a duty because he is the child's father. Students often ask whether it matters if the defendant knows he is related to the victim. In other words, what if the toddler was John's unknown illegitimate child? It does matter if the defendant knows. The duty based upon status relationship depends on the defendant knowing of that relationship. Assuming that John knows he is the child's father, he had a duty to help.

Mike has a contractual duty to help the child because he is a hired lifeguard. Sue may or may not have a duty to help the child. Many jurisdictions have a statute that requires even off-duty officers to assist others. If there is such a statute, Sue has a duty. Without it, it is much more questionable.

Roger has no duty to help. He is just a bystander. Although it would be a morally good thing for Roger to assist the child, without a duty, his failure to act does not constitute criminal conduct by omission.

Based upon this analysis, it is clear that John and Mike certainly have a duty to help; Sue may have a duty; Roger has no duty. Once this is ascertained, answering the question becomes easy. **A** is wrong because some defendants do have a duty to help. **D** is wrong because not all the defendants have a duty. That leaves us with **B**, **C**, and **E**. **B** is wrong because Mike also has a duty to rescue. **C** is wrong because Roger has no duty to rescue. The correct answer is **E**. From the facts, we know for sure that John and Mike had a duty to help and failure to do so was a criminal omission.

3. *Status Crimes*

In *Robinson v. California*, 370 U.S. 660 (1962), the United States Supreme Court held that the illness of drug addiction could not, by itself, be considered a criminal offense. Thus, it struck down the application of a California law making addiction an offense punishable by incarceration for 90 days to one year. The Court held that although a legislature could criminalize the manufacture, sale, purchase, and possession of narcotics, the mere status of being a drug addict could not be criminalized. It held that "even one day in prison" for a violation of California's statute would be a violation of the Eighth Amendment. Accordingly, *Robinson* is often cited for the principle that the mere status of an individual cannot be a criminal offense.

Yet *Robinson* should not be read too broadly. Six years later, in *Powell v. Texas*, 392 U.S. 514 (1968), the Supreme Court upheld a conviction for being intoxicated in public. The Court distinguished *Robinson* by noting that Powell was being punished for conduct — that is, being in public while drunk on a particular occasion — not for his status as an alcoholic.

Today, *Robinson* still stands for the principle that a person cannot be punished for her status alone. However, very little conduct is needed before criminal punishment may be imposed.

There is some conduct that is constitutionally protected and therefore cannot be punished. Recently, in *Lawrence v. Texas*, 539 U.S. 558 (2003), the Supreme Court overturned its previous decision in *Bowers v. Hardwick*, 478 U.S. 186 (1986), and held that there was a constitutional right to engage in private, consensual homosexual acts. Thus, neither the status of being a homosexual, nor private, consensual homosexual acts, may be considered to be a criminal offense.

> **QUESTION 3. The nymphomaniac.** Barbara admits that she is a nymphomaniac. A nymphomaniac is a person obsessed with having sex. The police arrest Barbara for solicitation for prostitution. Can she be prosecuted for this offense?
>
> **A.** Yes, because the Supreme Court has never held that the status of being a nymphomaniac is a protected status.
>
> **B.** Yes, because Barbara is being prosecuted for her conduct, not her status as a nymphomaniac.
>
> **C.** No, because Barbara has a constitutional right to engage in sexual conduct.

> **D.** No, because Barbara cannot be prosecuted for her status of being a nymphomaniac.

ANALYSIS. The difference between status and conduct becomes pretty clear in this question. If the authorities were coming after Barbara just because she is a known nymphomaniac, the prosecution would likely be barred. However, Barbara is engaging in the specific conduct of solicitation of prostitution. The criminal law can prohibit such behavior.

Let's look at the options to see which one most accurately answers the question. **A** is wrong. Although the Supreme Court has never specifically addressed the issue of nymphomania, it did hold in *Robinson* that status alone could not be criminalized. It is unlikely that courts would limit that ruling to just the status of being a drug addict.

By now, your instincts should be telling you that Barbara's actions go beyond a mere status offense. She is actually engaged in some conduct, that is, solicitation of prostitution. Under *Powell v. Texas,* the authorities can criminalize conduct, even if it is done by people with a particular status or condition. Therefore, **B** certainly looks like the correct answer.

Let's check **C** and **D** just to be sure. **C** is wrong because this question involves more than just engaging in sexual conduct. It involves soliciting money to engage in sexual conduct. Moreover, the Supreme Court still has not said that all consensual sexual acts are permissible. For example, sex with a minor and incest most likely can still be prohibited. **D** is also wrong because she is not being prosecuted just for her status. Therefore, **B** is the correct answer.

4. Possession Crimes

Possession itself may be a crime, but the Model Penal Code requires that the defendant at least be aware that she is in control of the item illegally possessed and have sufficient time to terminate possession. MPC §2.01(4). In a way, this rule of actus reus begins to incorporate mental state requirements that we will discuss in the next section. It is not enough for a defendant to be found with contraband. For the actus reus component, the defendant must be aware that she has the contraband and does not try to discard it.

Before we try the next question, let's consider a simple example. Defendant is charged with illegal possession of a counterfeit. Unknown to the defendant, someone has slipped some fake $100 bills into her purse. There will be two ways to analyze the defendant's guilt. First, under the Model Penal Code, one can argue that the defendant did not have a voluntary act for the crime because she was unaware of the counterfeit. Alternatively, as we will see in section B, even if the defendant possessed the counterfeit, she did not have a culpable mental state for the crime.

> **QUESTION 4. Alarm clock.** Obama hears a clicking in his luggage. He believes that it is the travel alarm clock that he packed. Little does he realize that someone has mysteriously substituted a ticking bomb for his alarm clock. When airport security inspects Obama's luggage, they discover the bomb. They charge him with illegally possessing an explosive device. Is Obama guilty of the offense?
>
> A. Yes, because Obama had a bomb in his luggage.
> B. Yes, because Obama owned the luggage with the bomb.
> C. No, because only the person who put the bomb into the luggage could have possessed it.
> D. No, because he was unaware that the illegal item was in his possession.

ANALYSIS. When it comes to possession crimes, the Model Penal Code does not even consider the defendant to have a voluntary act unless he is aware an item is in his possession. Thus, the mere fact that the bomb was found in Obama's luggage will be insufficient to convict him of a crime.

A is wrong because Obama is unaware that he actually has possession of the illegal item. It was slipped into his luggage.

B is wrong because it doesn't really matter who legally owns the luggage. What matters is that the person charged with possessing the item is aware that he has it.

C is wrong because it goes too far. Certainly, the person who put the bomb in the luggage would be guilty of possessing the explosive material, but so would anyone who realized he received it. The problem here is that Obama doesn't know he has the illegal article.

Therefore, **D** is the correct answer. The key word in the answer is "unaware." Again, under the Model Penal Code standard, there is no actus reus unless the person possessing the contraband is aware that he has it.

Now that you have a sense of how the actus reus for a crime works, it is time to examine the mens rea requirement for crimes. Instead of focusing on the defendant's actions, we focus on the defendant's intent. Instead of just focusing on whether the defendant was "aware" of certain facts, as we did when we discussed possession as a voluntary act, we will examine the various levels of culpable mental states defendants may have when committing crimes.

B.   Mens rea: Culpable mental state

Ordinarily, acts alone do not constitute a criminal offense, even if they cause harm. The classic maxim is *actus non facit reum, nisi mens sit rea*. It means "there is no crime without a vicious will." A vicious will is the mental state required for the crime. This mental state is also referred to as the "mens rea" for the crime. Culpability is the extent to which a defendant's mental state shows the defendant deserves to be punished for his acts.

Different crimes require different mental states. However, not all possible mental states are relevant under the law. For example, it is generally irrelevant whether a defendant acts regretfully or arrogantly. The mens rea requirement focuses on levels of awareness and intention with which the defendant acted, for example, did the defendant purposely cause a harm or was the harm the result of the defendant's carelessness?

The purposes of punishment that we reviewed in Chapter 2 rely heavily on the premise that the more a defendant intends to commit a wrongful act, the more that person should be punished. For example, the person who purposely harms another is most deserving of punishment under a retribution theory of punishment. Moreover, because that person is considering her acts before committing them, the person who acts purposefully should be subject to deterrence. Accordingly, the most serious crimes ordinarily require that the defendant acted intentionally in committing the crime; the less serious crimes may impose criminal responsibility for careless, but unintentional, conduct.

One of the most difficult things to master in criminal law is mens rea terminology. Common law developed a variety of terms to describe the mental state required for different types of crimes. These terms, however, were often confusing and used inconsistently by the courts. As a result, the Model Penal Code developed a set of terms to define more precisely the culpability/mental state required for different types of crimes. In some jurisdictions, both sets of terms are used throughout the statutes. Accordingly, it is important to learn both the common law and Model Penal Code terminology for describing the defendant's required mental state for a crime.

1. Common law terminology

At common law, courts used a variety of terms to describe the mental state required for crimes. Many of these terms have survived to the present. These terms are often puzzling because they don't mean in legal terms what their ordinary dictionary definitions would suggest. Rather, over the years, they have developed specialized legal meanings. Thus, many students feel like they are enrolled in a foreign language course while they are learning mens rea for their criminal law class. However, these terms can be mastered and the best way to do so is not only to learn a definition for the terms, but also to understand how they apply in different factual scenarios.

a. Maliciously. Let's start with the term *maliciously*. Older cases and statutes, especially in England, refer to a defendant acting *maliciously*. Although the term seems to suggest that the defendant must act in a wicked manner or with ill will, that is not the legal definition of the term. Rather, *maliciously* simply means that the defendant realizes the risks her conduct creates and engages in the conduct anyway. As we will see in the next section, the Model Penal Code term for this level of intent is *recklessness*.

Odds are that your casebook will use one of two cases to explain what maliciously means. The first is *Regina v. Cunningham*, 2 Q.B. 396 (1957). In *Cunningham*, a young man tore a gas meter off a wall to try to recover the coins that were in it. In those days, people would put money in a gas meter on the wall and it would dispense gas for heating and cooking in the apartment. Short of cash, Cunningham thought he would help himself to the money. When he tore the meter off the wall, he didn't realize gas would seep into the apartment next door. Well, it did, and almost asphyxiated the woman in that unit. The issue in the case was whether the defendant acted with the intent necessary for the crime, that is, did he "maliciously" asphyxiate the woman? Cunningham held no ill will toward the woman. He didn't really want to harm her. Nonetheless, his actions almost killed her. The court found that Cunningham did act maliciously because in criminal law the term simply means that the defendant foresaw that his acts might cause harm, but he nevertheless engaged in them.

Another classic case used to explain what maliciously means is *Regina v. Faulkner*, 13 Cox. Crim. Cas. 550 (1887). It is literally the story of a drunken sailor. Faulkner was a sailor who went into a ship's hold to steal some rum. While he was there, he lit a match to see where he was going, causing the rum and ship to catch fire. Did Faulkner act maliciously? Although he had no evil design to burn the ship, he would have been acting maliciously if he knew he was taking a risk of causing a fire and he disregarded it.

b. Intentionally.   Another confusing term is *intentionally*. The reason it is confusing is that courts have used it in different ways. In some situations, it has meant that the defendant had the purpose to cause a specific harmful result. For example, if a defendant wants to kill her competitor and she plants a bomb on his plane, the defendant has acted intentionally. However, the term *intentionally* can also refer to situations in which the defendant is aware of the harm she is likely to cause, although that harm is not her primary aim. For example, if a defendant wants to destroy the briefcase her competitor is carrying and she plants a bomb on the competitor's plane to do so, the defendant has still acted intentionally as to the competitor's death.

c. Negligently.   Even the term *negligently* can be confusing when used in the criminal context. Criminal negligence is different from civil negligence. Before someone is labeled a "criminal" by the law, the courts require a higher showing of carelessness than in tort law. Although the common law is vague as to what degree of negligence is required, it generally means not exercising the standard of care a reasonable person would under the circumstances, for example, letting a small child play with a boa constrictor. That could easily be considered criminal negligence if the child is killed. However, serving rancid sushi to one's guests, although not a good thing to do and something that may lead to a tort, may not be enough for criminal liability depending on why the mistake was made.

d. Willfully.   Finally, the word *willful* is often used at common law. Sometimes, it means doing an act with the purpose of violating the law. For example, the person who decides she doesn't believe in the tax laws, and wants to protest them, acts willfully if she does not file a tax return. However, willfully can also cover those situations in which the defendant doesn't necessarily want to protest the laws, but intentionally does an act that has illegal consequences. For example, the person who has no complaint against the tax laws, but knows that she should pay her taxes, also acts willfully if she does not file her tax returns.

Section C will discuss more common law terms, but it would be helpful to test our knowledge of the ones we have learned so far. Therefore, here is a hypothetical that sets forth problems relating to a defendant's mens rea for a crime.

QUESTION 5. Light my fire.   Stanley is charged with arson. The crime of arson requires that a defendant maliciously set fire and cause damage to property. Stanley's house caught fire when he was setting off fireworks in his yard. Part of the house burned before firefighters could extinguish the fire. What would the prosecution have to prove for Stanley to be guilty of arson?

A. Stanley knew he could set his house on fire but ignored the risk and set off the fireworks too close to his home.

B. Stanley's purpose in setting off the fireworks was to burn down his home.

C. Stanley always hated his home and therefore wanted to burn it down, so he set off the fireworks.

D. Stanley carelessly burned down his home.

ANALYSIS.   This problem requires that you understand what the common law term *maliciously* means. It does not mean, as suggested by **B**, that Stanley had to have as his goal or aim to burn down his home. Certainly, if Stanley did have that as his goal, he would be acting maliciously, but the standard of *maliciously* does not require that high level of intent. Therefore, **B** is the wrong answer.

Likewise, maliciously does not require that Stanley had an evil motive when he burned down his home. Therefore, **C** is a wrong answer. It is important to distinguish between motive and intent. Mens rea refers to a defendant's intent, not motive. Although each crime will require that the defendant act with a certain intent, it is generally not required that the defendant have a certain motive for his criminal behavior. Motive is the underlying reason a defendant engages in criminal behavior. Common motives include hatred, jealousy, and greed. A defendant may be guilty of a crime even with a good motive as long as the defendant has the necessary intent for the crime. For example, if a defendant's ailing wife begs him to kill her to end her misery and the defendant does so, the defendant has intentionally killed his wife, even if he did not act with a bad motive. Motive may help prove the defendant's intent, but it is not a separate element of a crime. It can become very relevant, however, in deciding on the appropriate sentence for the defendant once the defendant is convicted. Going back to this problem, it doesn't matter whether Stanley hated his house or loved it. If he acted with the necessary intent for arson, he is guilty.

Finally, **D** is a wrong answer because the legal standard of maliciously requires more than that the defendant acted carelessly. If a defendant acts in an unthinking manner, the defendant may act negligently or carelessly. However, the minimum intent required for most crimes is the standard of recklessly or maliciously. In other words, the defendant must actually consider the risk that she might burn property and disregard that risk. Therefore, the correct answer to this problem is **A**.

2. Model Penal Code terms

Because of the difficulty in interpreting and applying common law mens rea terms, many legislatures and courts have started using the Model Penal Code's language to describe a defendant's mens rea. Model Penal Code §2.02 refers to four levels of culpability. In essence, these four levels reflect four types of intent or mens rea: purposely, knowingly, recklessly, and negligently.

a. Purposely.   A person acts *purposely* if it is the defendant's goal or aim to engage in particular conduct or achieve a certain result. MPC §2.02(2)(a). For example, a defendant who points the trigger at a victim and shoots to kill him has purposely killed the victim. The phrase "intent to" is often used in criminal statutes to indicate that the defendant must have a specific purpose in mind when she commits an unlawful act. Burglary is one such crime. Burglary is often defined as "entering a building with the intent to commit a crime therein." Therefore, to be guilty of burglary the defendant must enter a building with the purpose of committing a crime in the building. If the defendant does not enter with that purpose, she may be guilty of trespass, but not burglary. If the phrase "specific intent to" is used in a statute, that is also a signal that the level of mens rea is purposely. Most crimes do not require the highest mens rea standard of purposely. A lower level of intent will satisfy. However, there are a few crimes, like premeditated murder or treason, that require that defendants have a specific purpose in mind when they commit their criminal acts.

b. Knowingly. *Knowingly* is the next highest level of intent. A person acts knowingly if she is virtually or practically certain that her conduct will lead to a particular result. MPC §2.02(2)(b). For example, if a defendant shoots at a car with the purpose of breaking its window, but knows that she is virtually certain to kill the occupant of the car, the defendant has acted knowingly with respect to the occupant's death. The mens rea standard of knowingly is often used in statutes prohibiting "knowing possession of narcotics." To prove this crime, prosecutors must show that the defendant knew that the substance in her possession was a narcotic. The issue often arises as to whether it is enough that the defendant suspects it is a narcotic, or whether the defendant must know for sure. For example, what if a stranger offers a defendant $10,000 to transport a suitcase to another country? The defendant suspects the suitcase contains cocaine, but intentionally does not look inside so that she can claim she did not "know" what she was transporting. The law has developed a doctrine to deal with this situation. It is called the *deliberate/ willful ignorance doctrine* or the *ostrich defense.* In such situations, the courts will often recognize that conscious avoidance of confirming the contents of the suitcase is the equivalent of knowing the contents and therefore the defendant's willful blindness is not a defense. See *United States v. Jewell,* 532 F.2d 697 (9th Cir. 1976).

c. Recklessly. *Recklessly* is the next level of intent. A person acts recklessly if she realizes that there is a substantial and unjustifiable risk that her conduct will cause harm but consciously disregards the risk. MPC §2.02(2)(c). For example, a defendant is late to work and therefore takes a shortcut by driving her car through a local playground. She hits one of the many children playing on the playground. It may not have been the defendant's purpose to kill a child; the defendant also may not have been virtually certain that she would do so. Nonetheless, the defendant subjectively realized that there was a risk of hitting a child and took that risk anyway. This gross deviation from the conduct of a law-abiding person when the defendant knew she was taking a risk makes the defendant's intent reckless. *Recklessness is the minimum mens rea standard for most crimes.* It is also referred to as "general intent" or, as we have seen, "maliciousness."

d. Negligently. Finally, some crimes, especially those that cause grave harm to other persons, only require that the defendant act *negligently.* A person acts negligently if she is unaware of and takes a risk that an ordinary person would not take. MPC §2.02(2)(d). For example, if a defendant is unaware that her child is suffering from a life-threatening illness, but an ordinary person would be aware, that defendant acts neg-ligently if she does not seek medical treatment for the child. Negligence is an objective standard. The focus is not on the defendant's state of mind, but on what an ordinary person would have known and done in the defendant's situation.

To test your understanding of the Model Penal Code's approach to mens rea, try the following problem.

QUESTION 6. Poisoning Mrs. Wade.   Consider again the case of *Regina v. Cunningham*, 2 Q.B. 396 (1957), where the defendant almost asphyxiated his neighbor by ripping a gas meter from the wall and thereby allowing gas to seep into the victim's room. If Cunningham claimed that he didn't realize that breaking a gas meter would cause gas to seep and the jury believed him, would he be guilty of the crime of recklessly asphyxiating his neighbor?

A. Yes, because an ordinary person would have realized that breaking a gas meter would allow the gas to seep into his neighbor's apartment.

B. Yes, because the defendant should have considered the risks to his neighbor when he broke the gas meter.

C. No, because the defendant did not have the purpose to kill his neighbor.

D. No, because the defendant never realized that he might harm his neighbor.

ANALYSIS.   Let's go through the answers in order. **A** is wrong because it describes the mens rea standard of negligently. The crime, however, requires that the defendant act recklessly. It is not enough that an ordinary person would have realized the risk. The recklessness standard requires that the defendant subjectively realize the risk to his neighbor and disregard it.

B is also wrong because it states the defendant "should have" considered the risk. Once again, that is the language of negligence. Recklessness requires that the defendant "did" consider the risk and disregarded it.

C is wrong because it sets too high a standard for the crime. The crime does not require that the defendant act purposely. Recklessly is enough. Certainly, if the defendant did act purposely, that would be enough to meet the lower standard of recklessly, but that is not demonstrated by the facts. Rather, the defendant argues that he not only didn't have the purpose to poison his neighbor, he didn't realize that he might do so.

D, then, is the correct answer. If the jury finds that the defendant did not consider the risk to his neighbor, the defendant has not acted recklessly. Accordingly, he has not met the mens rea (intent) requirement of the crime for which he was charged.

C. Specific intent versus general intent

Many jurisdictions attempt to distinguish crimes as requiring either specific or general intent. This distinction is particularly difficult because there is no precise definition of either specific or general intent. As a result, this area of the law can be extremely confusing. Nonetheless, there are some general principles you can keep in mind when trying to distinguish between the two types of mental states.

General intent crimes are those that only require that the defendant intend to commit the act that causes the harm. The defendant need not, however, intend the consequences of her acts. For example, consider the case of a defendant who has been charged with battery for hitting a victim. Battery is a general intent crime. Therefore, it is sufficient that the prosecution prove that the defendant intentionally swung her arms in a manner that might hurt someone. The prosecution need not prove that the defendant intended to inflict a particular harm on the victim when she swung her arms. By acting in a reckless manner, the defendant has satisfied the requirements of general intent.

Specific intent, by contrast, refers to crimes that require a higher level of intent. For these crimes, the prosecution must prove that the defendant acted either with the specific purpose to cause the harm or while knowing the harm would result. Many statutes use the words "with intent to" to describe the crime as a specific intent offense. A good example of a specific intent crime would be burglary. To be guilty of burglary, a defendant must enter a building with the intent to commit a felony inside. The requirement that the defendant have a specific purpose when she engages in her unlawful conduct makes the crime a specific intent crime.

The question of whether a crime is a specific or general intent crime becomes most important when the defendant raises a defense, such as intoxication or diminished capacity, in which the defendant claims she could not have formed the purposeful intent required to be guilty of the charged offense. For example, the defendant charged with burglary may claim that because she was drunk at the time she entered the building, she could not and did not form the specific intent for that crime. On the other hand, a defendant who assaults another person when she is drunk would not have a defense. Assault is a general intent crime and even the drunk can form the intent to engage in the physical act of swinging her arm.

Although the distinction between general and specific intent crimes is discussed in more detail under defenses (see Chapters 19 and 20), the following questions will help you reach a basic understanding of the distinction between general and specific intent crimes.

> **QUESTION 7. Felon with a firearm.** George is charged with being a felon in possession of a firearm. Under the applicable statute, "any person who has been convicted of a felony and who has in his possession, custody or control any firearm, is guilty of an offense." George is arrested when the police conduct a search of his home and find an old shotgun hanging on the mantel of George's fireplace. George tries to explain to the officers that the weapon is never loaded and that it is just a family heirloom left to him by his grandfather, but he is arrested anyway. The officers disregard George's argument that he should not be charged because he did not realize it was illegal for him to possess that particular weapon.
>
> Before trial, the court finds that in this jurisdiction, being a felon in possession of a weapon is a general intent crime. Given this ruling, George should be
>
> A. convicted because he knew he had a weapon.
> B. convicted because he knew he had a weapon and that he was a felon.
> C. convicted because he was required to and had the specific intent to violate the law.
> D. acquitted.

ANALYSIS. In analyzing this question, you must start with the definition of the crime and the court's ruling that it is a general intent crime. As we learned, general intent ordinarily means that the prosecution does not need to prove the defendant intended to violate the law. Rather, if George intended to do the act of possessing a firearm, knowing that he was a felon, that is sufficient intent for the offense. If the court had ruled it was a specific intent offense, the prosecution would have to prove that not only did George know he had the weapon and was a felon, but also that he knew it was illegal for a felon to have such a weapon. Since it appears that George did not have such knowledge, he would not be guilty if this were a specific intent crime. Unfortunately for George, the court has ruled it is a general intent, not specific intent offense.

Given this analysis, let's look at the choice of answers:

A seems on the right track, but it is only halfway there. One of the confusing things about general intent crimes is how much the defendant needs to know. Here, as in most jurisdictions, it may not be enough for the defendant to know he has a weapon. He also needs to know he is a convicted felon. While that won't be hard to prove, it is part of the general intent requirement here. For that reason, **A** is not correct.

B is a better answer because it includes all of the general intent that George needs for the crime. He may not need to know he is violating a law by being a felon in possession of a firearm, but he does need to know he is a felon and that he has a firearm. **B**, therefore, seems like the correct answer. Before making a final selection, it is always best to look at the other options.

C is incorrect on its face. The court has ruled that this is a general intent, not specific intent crime, and the evidence indicates that George did not intend to violate the law. Thus, on both legal and factual grounds, **C** is incorrect.

Finally, there is **D**. As is frequently the case, multiple-choice questions can be pared down to two possible answers. The ultimate choice depends on the student's confidence in her knowledge of this area of the law. Here, if you understand that George had all the intent he needs for a general intent crime, **B** is clearly the answer. If you think that a general intent crime requires more, you will pick **D**, which is incorrect.

Since the distinction between general intent and specific intent crimes is a particularly muddy area, let's try another example to see how the distinction works and what difference it may make in a case. Take a look at Question 8.

QUESTION 8. Ruling on the robber. Rick is charged with robbery. Robbery is defined as "taking money, by force or violence, from another person with the intent to permanently deprive that person of the property." At the time of the alleged robbery, Rick was under the influence of drugs. He claims that he is at most guilty of assault (defined as using unlawful force against another person), but that he never intended to keep the property he took. Assuming that the jury believes Rick, the court should rule that

A. Rick has a possible defense to both robbery and assault.
B. Rick has a possible defense to robbery only.
C. Rick has a possible defense to assault only.
D. Rick has no defense to the charges he faces.

ANALYSIS. This question requires that you differentiate between a specific intent and a general intent crime. Before looking at the answer options, examine each crime to determine whether it appears to require that the defendant have a specific intent or goal in mind when he committed the offense. The crime of robbery requires that the defendant act "*with the intent to* permanently deprive that person of the property." This language is a signal that robbery is a specific intent crime and that there may be a defense if Rick could not form the specific intent for that crime. On the other hand, assault only requires that the defendant use force against another person. No specific intent is required. Therefore, it is unlikely that the defendant will be able to argue that he could not form the general intent for the crime. Now, look at the options.

A and C are wrong because Rick's drug use is not a defense to assault. However, it is hypothetically a defense to robbery if the jury finds that the defendant was so under the influence that he did not intend to permanently deprive the victim of her property. If so, he could raise this defense. Therefore, **B** is the correct answer. **D** is wrong because the question includes a specific intent crime.

D.   The Closer: Euthanasia — Positive act or omission? Motive versus intent

This chapter focused on the fundamental elements of criminal law: actus reus and mens rea. Although these elements are the building blocks of criminal law, there is nothing simple about them. Sometimes, it is difficult to distinguish between an affirmative act and an omission. Likewise, there may be a thin line between the motive for a crime and the defendant's intent. A prime example of where the lines in these doctrines begin to blur is the crime of euthanasia.

QUESTION 9. Doctor Dearest.   Dr. Novak has worked at County General Hospital for 20 years. Throughout those years, he has seen people kept alive on machines for years, only to die in a painful, undignified manner. While he is on call, a patient is admitted who is in terrible condition. At the time the patient is admitted, the paramedics have already hooked her up to a simple ventilator. Dr. Novak would ordinarily switch her to a more sophisticated ventilator if he believed that she had a chance to survive. However, Dr. Novak believes the patient will die anyway and that switching her to the new ventilator will only prolong the agonizing process. Therefore, he simply disconnects the first ventilator and does not connect the patient to the more advanced ventilator. The patient dies.

Assuming no other statutes or ethical codes control Dr. Novak's conduct, if Dr. Novak is charged with "purposely taking the life of another human being," is he guilty?

A. No, because Dr. Novak's purpose was to save the patient from suffering a more painful death.
B. No, because Dr. Novak's failure to connect the patient to the more advanced ventilator was only an omission.
C. Yes, because Dr. Novak failed to connect the patent to the more advanced ventilator.
D. Yes, because Dr. Novak purposely removed the life-support device.

ANALYSIS.   In this chapter, we have sought to draw the line between acts and omissions, and between different levels of mental intent. However, in real life, such lines can become blurred. Consider, for example, euthanasia. Under traditional criminal law, the affirmative act of disconnecting the first ventilator would be construed as a positive act, thereby satisfying the actus reus requirements for the crime. By contrast, not putting the patient on the second ventilator would not fulfill the actus reus requirement unless Dr. Novak had a specific duty to use that ventilator. Both situations could lead to the patient's death, but the line between positive acts and omissions could spell the difference between a murder charge and no criminal culpability.

As for intent, this question also highlights the difference between motive and intent. Although the doctor may have had a good motive to help the patient avoid undue suffering, this good motive actually proved the defendant acted purposely. The statute simply requires that the defendant act purposely. It does not require that the defendant act with a particular motive.

With these principles in mind, let's look at the options for this final problem. **A** is wrong because it confuses motive with intent. Dr. Novak's motive may be a noble one, that is, to save the patient from suffering, but he is still acting purposely, as required by the statute.

B is also wrong, although it highlights one of the oddities of criminal law. Because the general rule is that an omission does not qualify as an actus reus, the law draws a line between affirmatively unplugging a patient and refusing to plug a patient into a life-saving device. Affirmatively unplugging a patient is a criminal act, whereas declining to connect a patient to a ventilator is only a criminal act if there is a specific duty to do so. In this problem, Dr. Novak takes the affirmative step of unplugging the patient. This is a much clearer example of actus reus than his omission. However, the omission could possibly qualify if there is a doctor-patient relationship requiring such care.

This leaves your choices to **C** or **D**. Between the two, **D** is the clearer choice. Without more facts indicating that the doctor had a duty to start the second ventilator, it is unclear whether Dr. Novak's omission would qualify as an actus reus. It is not clear in the problem, as it is often not clear in real life, whether doctors have a duty to extend all possible care to a patient, even if that additional care will not improve the quality of the patient's life. Therefore, **C** is a problematic answer. By contrast, the affirmative act of unplugging the patient is a much clearer example of a voluntary act that the law would recognize as a criminal actus reus. Because of the fine line between a affirmative and passive euthanasia, some courts have treated the unplugging of a patient as simply as omitting to provide further treatment. By doing so, they avoid finding the defendant guilty of the patient's death.

See *Barber v. Superior Court*, 195 Cal. Rptr. 484 (Ct. App. 1983) (treating unplugging as omission of further treatment).

 # Levenson's Picks

1. Home invasion	**A**
2. Save me	**E**
3. The nymphomaniac	**B**
4. Alarm clock	**D**
5. Light my fire	**A**
6. Poisoning Mrs. Wade	**D**
7. Felon with a firearm	**B**
8. Ruling on the robber	**B**
9. Doctor Dearest	**D**

4

Strict Liability Crimes

In the interest of the larger good [strict liability crime] puts the burden of acting at hazard upon a person otherwise innocent but standing in responsible relation to a public danger.
— *United States v. Dotterweich*, 320 U.S. 277, 281 (1943)

CHAPTER OVERVIEW
A. Introduction: Strict liability offenses
   1. Public welfare offenses
   2. Morality offenses
B. Determining whether a crime is a strict liability offense
C. Defenses to strict liability crimes
D. Vicarious liability
E. The Closer: "Good faith" defenses to strict liability offenses
  Levenson's Picks

A. Introduction: Strict liability offenses

As discussed in Chapter 3, criminal law is generally based upon the principle that a defendant may only be punished if he acted with a culpable intent. However, there is a narrow category of crimes in which there is no mens rea requirement for guilt. Strict liability crimes are those crimes in which the defendant is guilty, even if he honestly and reasonably believes his conduct was proper. The prosecution has no responsibility of proving a culpable mens rea. Rather, once the prosecution has established that the defendant committed a wrongful act, the defendant is automatically guilty regardless of whether he acted purposely, knowingly, recklessly, or even negligently. The Model Penal Code has rejected the concept of strict liability crimes, except for violations that cannot result in imprisonment or probation. MPC §1.04(5).

Where used, strict liability is typically imposed for two types of crimes: public welfare offenses and common law morality crimes.

1. Public welfare offenses

In response to the Industrial Revolution, legislatures enacted statutes to deal with the new, highly regulated industries. For example, new laws were passed to criminalize traffic violations, improper handling of food and pharmaceuticals, and unsafe conditions at power plants. A defendant charged with one of these crimes is guilty regardless of whether he intended any harm or even if a reasonable person would have made the same mistake. The defendant is automatically guilty simply by doing the criminal act.

In *United States v. Dotterweich*, 320 U.S. 277 (1943), the Supreme Court upheld the constitutionality of strict liability crimes. The defendant, the president of a pharmaceutical company, was convicted of shipping misbranded and adulterated products. Although there was no evidence that the defendant knew, or should have known, that the products had been misbranded, he was held criminally responsible because the crime did not require a mens rea.

The most common strict liability offense is speeding. To be guilty of speeding, it is sufficient that the defendant drove faster than the speed limit. The prosecution need not prove that the defendant realized he was going beyond the speed limit, nor is it a defense that the defendant did not intend to speed.

2. Morality offenses

There are also a number of morality offenses in which the defendant is guilty regardless of whether the defendant acted with a culpable mental state. These crimes include statutory rape, bigamy, and adultery. A defendant is guilty of statutory rape regardless of whether he honestly and reasonably believed the female was old enough to consent to sexual intercourse. Just having intercourse with a woman under the lawful age of consent is automatically a criminal offense.

Likewise a defendant was traditionally guilty of bigamy even if he didn't know that he was still married to his prior spouse when he remarried. Thus, a defendant who believed that he had been lawfully divorced, but his divorce was in fact invalid, would be guilty of bigamy. Similarly, a defendant would be guilty of adultery even if the defendant has an honest and reasonable belief that he is no longer married at the time he has an affair with another woman.

B.   Determining whether a crime is a strict liability offense

It should never be presumed that a crime is a strict liability offense. Strict liability offenses are the exception, not the rule. The Supreme Court held in *Morissette v. United States,* 342 U.S. 246 (1952), that common law crimes are presumed not to be strict liability crimes even if the statute codifying that offense does not expressly mention a mens rea requirement. In *Morissette,* the defendant was charged with stealing spent bomb casings that were government property. Defendant claimed that he believed the casings had been abandoned; the government claimed that the defendant was strictly liable if he took casings that turned out to still belong to the government. The Supreme Court held that even though the statute did not use any mens rea language, mens rea is a requirement of all crimes unless there is clear legislative intent not to require mens rea.[1]

To determine whether a crime is a strict liability offense, it is helpful to take the following approach. First, look at the language of the statute. If the statute expressly states that no mens rea is required, it is a strict liability offense. However, if the statute merely omits language of intent, you must move to step two. For step two, look at the legislative history of the offense. Some laws, such as child pornography laws, will have clear legislative history that states that a defendant who distributes such materials is guilty regardless of whether he knows the age of the child in the pornographic photographs. See, e.g., *United States v. United States District Court (Kantor),* 858 F.2d 534 (9th Cir. 1988). Third, look at the purpose of the law and the amount of penalty imposed. Except for offenses that were strict liability at common law (e.g., statutory rape, bigamy, and adultery), strict liability offenses generally carry very low penalties, such as fines or minimal jail time. If a crime carries a possible sentence of multiple years in jail, and the offense is not a holdover from common law, the defense has a strong argument that it should not be treated as a strict liability offense. Moreover, the more the crime seems like a regulatory offense, the easier it is for the prosecution to argue that it is a strict liability crime. Finally, look for signs that the legislature wanted to relieve the prosecution of the burden of proving mens rea, often because of the number of violations that occur under the questioned statute. If the

---

1. Under the Model Penal Code, if a mens rea is required and not otherwise specified, the defendant must act recklessly when committing the offense. MPC §2.02(3).

crime is like speeding, where it would nearly paralyze the system to require the prosecution to prove that each charged driver knew he was speeding, and the penalty is relatively low, it is likely that the crime is a strict liability offense.

QUESTION 1. Oil change. In an effort to protect the environment, Congress has passed a new statute making it a violation, punishable by 30 days in jail and a $10,000 fine, to discard used motor oil, except at specific recycling centers. During the congressional debates on the statute, the author of the bill expressly states that there are thousands of people improperly discarding their motor oil every day and "even if the average citizen doesn't know it is wrong, it still is." The law that passes states, "It is a violation of law to discard used motor oil except at designated recycling centers." Prosecutors are now arguing that the defendant, Mr. Goodwrench, violated the law because he improperly stored oil at his home, and that it accidentally drained out of the storage drum and into a local storm drain. There is no evidence that Goodwrench knew, or should have known, that the oil he stored would end up in a storm drain instead of a certified recycling center. Indeed, Goodwrench claims he is not guilty of violating the law because he thought the oil could be safely stored in the drums. Is the defense likely to be successful?

A. Yes, because Goodwrench did not act recklessly when he disposed of the oil.

B. Yes, because Goodwrench did not act negligently when he disposed of the oil.

C. Yes, because Goodwrench does not have the necessary mens rea for the offense.

D. No, because Goodwrench is charged with a strict liability offense.

ANALYSIS.   To answer this question, the first thing you need to do is to analyze the statute and legislative history to determine what, if any, mens rea requirement it has for the crime. On its face, the statute does not provide for any mens rea requirement. However, as the Supreme Court made clear in *Morissette*, the absence of mens rea language does not automatically mean the crime is a strict liability offense. One must instead examine the legislative history of the statute, as well as other indicia, to determine whether it requires the minimum mens rea of recklessness or no intent at all.

There are several indications that this statute is indeed a strict liability offense. The offense carries a minimum penalty, it relates to a highly regulated area of environmental crime, and the legislative history seems to dismiss defenses based upon intent. Armed with this analysis, take a look at the answer choices.

A is wrong because the statute does not require recklessness. As a strict liability offense, there is no requirement that the prosecution prove that the defendant considered and dismissed the risk of his actions. **B** is also wrong because the legislative history makes clear that the crime doesn't even require negligence. When the legislator states that the defendant's acts would be a crime regardless of whether the average person would have done the same thing, he is essentially stating that the defendant is strictly liable for his actions.

C is one of those tricky answers that many students would choose because it seems general enough to be true. The problem is that in a strict liability case, there is no necessary mens rea for the offense. Therefore, it makes no sense to state that the defendant did not have the necessary mens rea for the offense.

Ultimately, the correct answer is **D**. Defendant is charged with a strict liability offense and therefore is unlikely to have any defense based upon his argument that he didn't intend to cause harm by the manner in which he stored the oil.

C. Defenses to strict liability crimes

Because strict liability crimes do not require that the defendant act with a culpable mens rea, there are fewer ways to defend against such allegations. However, some defenses may apply. As discussed in later chapters, a defendant may have an affirmative defense, like entrapment, to such a crime. For example, if a government official repeatedly encouraged a defendant to dispose of his biohazardous material at a particular site even though the defendant did not want to do so, the defendant may be able to claim he was entrapped. Or, if a defendant was given specific legislative permission to dispose of the waste in the way that he did, but that permission was revoked after his acts, the defendant may have a mistake of law defense. All these defenses are explained in more detail later.

However, there is one defense you already know that may apply in strict liability crimes. Even though mens rea is not an element of a strict liability crime, actus reus is. In other words, a defendant must always voluntarily engage in an illegal act, even in strict liability crimes. Thus, a defendant who acts involuntarily may have a defense to a strict liability crime. For example, assume the defendant is charged with speeding. His defense is that he had an unexpected seizure and his foot hit the pedal. If the trier of fact believes that the defendant did not act voluntarily, there is no actus reus for the offense for the crime and the defendant is not guilty.

> **QUESTION 2. I'm stuck.** Baker is driving his new sports car. While he is driving, the accelerator sticks and his car begins to speed. Suddenly, he sees blue lights behind him. The only thing that Baker can do to stop is to turn off the engine. When he does, the police officer promptly comes over and gives him a ticket for speeding. Baker offers the following defenses to the charge. Which one is most likely to succeed?
>
> **A.** The car is new and Baker is unfamiliar with its features.
> **B.** Baker did not intend to violate the speeding laws.
> **C.** The car had an unexpected and uncontrollable mechanical failure.
> **D.** Baker was going the same speed as other drivers.

ANALYSIS.   As we have discussed, speeding is the paradigm strict liability crime. As such, it is irrelevant whether Baker intended to violate the law. The only question is whether he voluntarily committed the prohibited act. **A** is wrong because there is no requirement in a strict liability crime that the defendant intend or anticipate the wrong that occurred.

B is wrong for a similar reason. Because it is a strict liability crime, Baker's intent is irrelevant. It simply doesn't matter whether he wanted to be the safest or slowest driver. If he voluntarily did the criminal act, he is guilty.

Therefore, **C** is the answer most likely to succeed. Even though a strict liability crime does not require a culpable mens rea, it still requires a voluntary actus reus. If the accelerator's problem was truly unanticipated and uncontrollable, Baker may be able to argue that he did not commit a voluntary act that led to him speeding. Rather, he would argue that the accelerator is a mechanical device that literally moved on its own. If believed, this claim of no voluntary actus reus would be a legitimate defense to the strict liability crime.

Finally, **D** is incorrect because it is generally not a defense to a crime that other people are committing the same offense. If everyone is speeding, they are all guilty of the crime unless, of course, they have acted involuntarily.

D.   Vicarious liability

Another concept closely related to strict liability is the doctrine of vicarious liability. Vicarious liability is the responsibility of the defendant for the criminal acts of another person, ordinarily without a showing that the defendant has a culpable mens rea. It is most often a form of criminal, supervisory responsibility.

The classic vicarious liability situation occurred in *State v. Guminga*, 395 N.W.2d 344 (Minn. 1986). Guminga owned a restaurant where a waitress was caught serving alcohol to an underage customer. The statute imposed liability on the owner even though he wasn't present when the alcohol was served, nor did he know that his employee was selling to patrons under the legal age to drink. Under the doctrine of vicarious liability, Guminga would be guilty regardless of whether he knew or instructed his employees to act in an unlawful manner. Rather, his status alone would make him responsible for their behavior. In fact, carried to its extreme, the doctrine would not allow Guminga to argue that he had explicitly instructed his servers to check for identification and not to sell alcohol to underage customers. Vicarious liability would make him automatically guilty.

Many courts are troubled by the doctrine of vicarious liability because it automatically holds a defendant responsible for acts of another person. To get around the harsh application of these laws, courts will sometimes reevaluate a law and find it not to be strict liability. In fact, that is exactly what the court did in *State v. Guminga*. However, if the statute is strict liability, and does impose criminal liability on supervisors as well as the direct violator, the doctrine of vicarious liability would preclude the owner from claiming he was unaware of and did not condone his employee's improper acts.

QUESTION 3. **Rats in the vats.** Molly owns a pharmaceutical manufacturing plant. She tries to maintain the highest standards of production and cleanliness in her operation. Each of her employees goes through very detailed training on how to operate the machines that prepare the pharmaceuticals. The facility is routinely inspected for cleanliness. Molly personally tells her employees that their number one priority should be the safe production of pharmaceuticals. One night, when Molly is home asleep, a rat sneaks into the operating plant and finds its way into a vat of pharmaceuticals being produced. Unfortunately, an inspector finds the rat the next day doing the backstroke in the vat and charges Molly with a misdemeanor offense that holds an owner of a pharmaceutical manufacturing facility strictly liable for any contamination. Molly is fined $10,000 for the strict liability offense of operating a contaminated facility. If Molly claims that she was unaware of the rat and did everything she could to ensure her facility was not contaminated, her defense will

A. succeed because Molly generally operated a clean plant.
B. succeed because only the night watchman who could have spotted the rat should be responsible.
C. fail because Molly is automatically responsible for the violation.
D. fail because all crimes involving pharmaceutical plants are strict liability offenses.

ANALYSIS. Even though you may be sympathetic to Molly, she is likely to be responsible for her subordinates' acts under the doctrine of vicarious liability. Molly is operating in the highly regulated, high-risk industry of pharmaceutical production. Because of the threat to public welfare, the law imposes the burden on the defendant to ensure that the production of these drugs is absolutely safe. The doctrines of strict liability and vicarious liability are used to ensure that owners take responsibility for the operation of their facilities. Keeping these principles in mind, let's look at the possible answers.

A is wrong because it is no defense that Molly generally did not violate the law. Although that may be a factor at sentencing, it does not relieve Molly of criminal responsibility for this violation. **B** is also wrong. Even though she was not physically present at the plant at the time the vat was contaminated, Molly is the legal operator of the facility. Therefore, she is vicariously liable for the mistakes of her employees.

Even though the idea of automatic criminal responsibility may not sit well with you, if your analysis of the statute and situation indicates that Molly is charged with a strict liability crime that imposes vicarious liability on owners, Molly really is "automatically responsible" for the violation. This would make **C** the correct answer.

Finally, how about **D**? Be careful with statements in multiple-choice questions that are absolute or overly broad. We don't know from the question whether *all* crimes involving pharmaceutical plants are strict liability offenses. For example, what if a worker drowned in a vat? Some level of culpable mens rea may be required. We only know that because of the relatively low penalty assessed in this case ($10,000 fine) and the language of the statute, that Molly is charged with a strict liability, vicarious liability offense. That means that **C** is the better answer.

E. The Closer: "Good faith" defenses to strict liability crimes

Given the nature of strict liability offenses, courts and lawyers have assumed for years that there is no "mens rea" defense to a strict liability offense. After all, if a defendant is guilty regardless of whether he intended to commit the unlawful act, how can there be a mens rea defense?

In some limited areas, however, the courts have found a way to ameliorate the harsh effects of strict liability crimes. In essence, they do not require the prosecution to prove mens rea, but they allow the defense to prove a lack of culpable mens rea. In other words, they create a "good faith" defense to a strict liability crime. The closer question will give you an idea of how this works. This question is taken from *United States v. United States District Court (Kantor)*, 858 F.2d 534 (9th Cir. 1988).

QUESTION 4. Porn queen. Defendants are prosecuted for distributing child pornography. The legislative history of the criminal statute makes it absolutely clear that it is a strict liability offense to distribute pornographic videos featuring a minor under the age of 18 years old. Defendants claim that they were duped by pornography star Traci Lourdes into believing that she was over 18 years old at the time she made the movies. Among other things, Lourdes showed them false identification, had her parents verify she was an adult, and provided a curriculum vitae indicating that she had starred in porn films for years. Defendants file a motion in limine to require the prosecution to prove that they knew Lourdes was underage at the time they acquired the films. In response, the government files a motion in limine to preclude the defendants from introducing any evidence that they were duped into believing that Lourdes was an adult when she made the films.

Assume the court is troubled by the First Amendment implications of the law under which the defendants are being prosecuted. After all, as a strict liability crime, the law may chill producers from making lawful films that use youthful looking actors because they can never be sure as to whether the actors are representing their true age. Which of the following options does the court have if the statute has been designated a strict liability offense?

A. The court may require the prosecution to prove that the defendants knowingly used underage actors.

B. The court may shift the burden of proof to require that the defendants prove that they made all good faith efforts to determine the age of their actors.

C. The court may prohibit all strict liability crimes because they undermine the presumption of innocence.

D. The court may require the prosecution to prove that the defendants acted with the purpose to distribute child pornography.

ANALYSIS. Many courts disfavor the strict liability doctrine. It is contrary to the purposes of culpability to punish a defendant who has not acted with criminal intent. Moreover, for some crimes, such as the one referenced in this problem, the enactment of a strict liability crime may chill a defendant's exercise of his First Amendment rights. Accordingly, courts have struggled to find some way to consider a defendant's mens rea, but not convert a strict liability crime into a regular type of offense that requires the prosecution to prove mens rea.

One solution the courts use is to shift the burden of proof regarding mens rea onto the defendant in a strict liability case. Thus, in *Kantor, supra*, the court held that the prosecution does not have the burden in a strict liability crime to prove intent, even if the crime implicates the First Amendment. Nonetheless, in order not to chill a defendant's constitutional rights, the court may allow the defense to assume the burden of proving that the defendant acted in a good faith manner because he did not know, and a reasonable person would not have known, that the actor was underage. Can you see why this is a compromise? In a true strict liability case, a defendant's good faith intentions would be irrelevant. If the defendant committed the unlawful act, he is guilty. However, when the court has additional constitutional concerns, such as those prompted by the First Amendment, the good faith defense offers a compromise. It does not require the prosecution to prove intent, but it allows a way for the defendant to avoid the harsh impact of a strict liability law.

In this problem, **A** is a wrong answer because it is antithetical to the designation of a crime as a strict liability offense to require the prosecution to prove mens rea. **C** is also incorrect because the Supreme Court decided long ago, in the cases cited in this chapter, that strict liability crimes do not violate a defendant's due process rights. **D** is just another version of **A**. Therefore, **B** is the correct answer. In some jurisdictions, judges have accepted defense counsel's argument that even for strict liability crimes, some consideration of mens rea should be given, as long as the defense accepts the burden of proving the defendant acted in good faith in his constitutionally protected First Amendment activities.

One quick warning, however. Do not try to apply the good faith defense to all types of strict liability crimes. Thus far, the courts have only accepted it as applied to activities protected by the First Amendment. As for other types of strict liability crimes, the harsh law applies. A defendant's mens rea is simply irrelevant to the trier of fact's determination of the defendant's guilt or innocence.

✳ Levenson's Picks

1. Oil change	D
2. I'm stuck	C
3. Rats in the vats	C
4. Porn queen	B

5

Mistake of Fact

Everyone makes a mistake, but not all mistakes count.

CHAPTER OVERVIEW
A. Introduction to mistake of fact
B. No mens rea, no crime
C. Some mistakes matter, some do not
D. Material versus jurisdictional elements
E. Determining which is which: Analyzing a statute to determine whether an element is material or jurisdictional
F. Mistake of fact in rape cases
G. The Closer: Mistaken but still guilty
◈ Levenson's Picks

A. Introduction to mistake of fact

Before we examine how mens rea applies in specific types of crimes, such as homicide and rape, it is important to understand two defenses typically raised to rebut a claim that a defendant "intentionally" committed a crime. These two defenses are mistake of fact and mistake of law. This chapter discusses mistake of fact; Chapter 6 discusses mistake of law.

At its heart, mistake of fact is a claim that the defendant did not have the necessary mens rea for the crime because the defendant made a mistake or was ignorant of a fact she had to know to be guilty of the charged offense. It is a defense that may be raised either during the prosecution's presentation of its case (through cross-examination of prosecution witnesses) or in the defense's case. If successful, it is a complete defense.

Students often get caught up in whether to label a defense "mistake of fact" or "ignorance of fact." Don't worry about that. Whether a defendant is ignorant of a fact, or makes a mistake regarding it, the defendant may still have a mistake of fact defense if her ignorance or mistake precluded her from having the required mens rea for that offense. Rather than focusing on labels, focus on whether, despite her ignorance or mistake, the defendant knew enough to be guilty of the crime. If she does, mistake or ignorance of fact is not a defense; if she does not, mistake or ignorance is a defense.

A brief warning before you dive into this topic: Mistake of fact is one of the most challenging areas of criminal law. Common law cases are particularly notorious for providing convoluted and futile explanations as to why a defendant should or should not receive a mistake of fact defense. If the crime is labeled a specific intent offense, it is much more likely that the defendant will be entitled to a mistake of fact defense than if the crime has been labeled a general intent offense. Your professor may have you read some of these cases precisely so you can criticize the approaches they take. But keep your wits about you. Once you understand the basic function of the mistake of fact doctrine and its relationship to proving a defendant's mens rea, it is possible to master this topic.

To assist in that effort, many professors introduce their students to the Model Penal Code approach for dealing with mistake of fact issues. Although working with the Model Penal Code is also a challenging exercise, it can give clearer direction as to when mistake or ignorance of fact is an available defense. This chapter analyzes both approaches. Just take it step by step. You, too, will master the law of mistake of fact.

B.   No mens rea, no crime

The first step toward understanding mistake of fact is to understand how a defendant's mistake may affect whether the defendant had the necessary mens rea for the offense. Sometimes a defendant will complain that she did not have the necessary mens rea because she was confused regarding the facts of the situation. For example, consider the defendant charged with "knowingly receiving stolen goods." If the definition of that crime requires that the defendant know that she has received *stolen* goods, the defendant is not guilty if she makes a mistake and does not realize that the goods she has received are in fact stolen. She is not guilty because her mistake or ignorance has prevented her from having the necessary mens rea for the offense.

The Model Penal Code states the basic rule as follows: "[I]gnorance or mistake . . . is a defense when it negatives the existence of a state of mind that is essential to the commission of an offense . . . ." Model Penal Code §2.04(1). In other words, the Model Penal Code asks the basic question of whether the mistake has caused the defendant not to have the required mens rea for the offense. If so, it is a defense. If the defendant has the required mens rea regardless of the mistake, it is no defense.

One question that may have arisen in your mind is whether the "stolen" nature of goods is an issue of fact or law. The good news is that it does not matter. As discussed both in this chapter and Chapter 6, either type of mistake (mistake of fact or mistake of law) is a defense if it means that the defendant did not have the necessary mens rea for the offense. See also *People v. Navarro*, 160 Cal. Rptr. 692 (Cal. Super. App. 1979) (defendant not guilty of theft if he mistakenly believed beams stolen from construction site were abandoned).

Finally, as discussed in Chapter 3(B)(2)(b), don't forget that a defendant who strongly suspects certain facts to be true, but intentionally avoids confirming her suspicions, would still "know" those facts under the deliberate ignorance doctrine. Such a defendant cannot claim a mistake of fact defense. So, a defendant who strongly suspects that the suitcase she has grabbed from the airport baggage carousel belongs to someone else, but intentionally does not confirm that suspicion, cannot claim mistake of fact if she is charged with taking someone else's suitcase.

To get over the initial jitters, let's look at a fairly typical mistake of fact issue that arises in U.S. courtrooms every day. It will give you a concrete sense of how mistake of fact is tied to mens rea.

QUESTION 1. Strange powder. Margaret is stopped at the border as she returns from a recent visit to Tijuana, Mexico. Seeing a small jar of white powder on the seat next to her, the police ask Margaret what is in the jar. She tells them that it is some special talcum powder her friends gave her to deal with her terrible skin condition. When the police test the contents in the jar, it turns out to be cocaine. Margaret is charged with "knowingly possessing a controlled substance." If the jury at trial believes Margaret's story, she is

A. guilty because she should have known the jar contained cocaine.
B. guilty because she knew she was transporting a powder.
C. guilty because her mistake was unreasonable.
D. guilty because of the deliberate ignorance defense.
E. not guilty.

ANALYSIS. No matter how guilty you might think Margaret really is, you must use the facts as they are presented. As given, the facts establish a mistake of fact defense. Start by analyzing what the defendant must know to be guilty of the crime charged. Here, Margaret needs to know that the powder she possesses is a controlled substance. If she honestly doesn't know that, she is not guilty of the crime charged. With those principles in mind, let's look at the choices.

A is wrong because the charged offense requires that Margaret actually know that she has cocaine. It is not a negligence standard under which she is guilty if she "should have" known. You are told in the question to answer it as "if the jury believes Margaret's story." According to Margaret's story, she did not know the powder was cocaine. She honestly believed it was powder for her skin. Even though you might not believe her story, all that is important is that the jury did. According to her story, Margaret did not know that she possessed a controlled substance.

B is also wrong because it is insufficient that Margaret knew she was transporting a powder. This crime requires that the defendant also know that the powder she possesses is a controlled substance. Because Margaret does not know that crucial fact, she is not guilty of the crime.

C is the answer that many students instinctively choose, but it is also incorrect. Except in some rare circumstances, *the mistake of fact defense does not require that the defendant's mistake be reasonable.* An honest mistake is sufficient because it negates the defendant's mens rea for the crime. Put in simpler language, if Margaret honestly doesn't know she has cocaine, it doesn't matter that a reasonable person might have realized that the powder was a controlled substance. Of course, the more unreasonable Margaret's explanation is, the more unlikely it is that the jury will believe it. However, if the jury does believe the explanation, it is sufficient for a mistake of fact defense even if a hundred other people would have realized they were carrying cocaine.

Like **C**, many students see **D** as an attractive answer. As discussed in Chapter 3, a defendant who has a strong suspicion that she is engaged in an illegal activity but intentionally takes steps to avoid confirming the truth is presumed to be acting knowingly. Under the *Jewell* or deliberate ignorance doctrine, a high suspicion of the truth combined with efforts to avoid knowing it for sure is sufficient to prove the crime. While this may be true, nothing in the facts presented shows that Margaret suspected the powder was a controlled substance and deliberately avoided discovering the truth. Unless you are given such facts, the deliberate ignorance doctrine cannot be applied.

Therefore, **E** must be the correct answer. If the jury believes that Margaret honestly did not know that the powder was some type of controlled substance, she is not guilty of the crime charged.

As you have probably come to realize, to apply the mistake of fact doctrine one must determine what a defendant is required to know to be guilty of a crime. Some mistakes count and others do not. As the next section discusses, if the defendant makes a mistake with regard to something that is not an element of the crime, the mistake is irrelevant. However, if the mistake undermines the defendant's mens rea for the offense, it can form the basis for a defense.

C.   Some mistakes matter, some do not

There are many mistakes that do not create a mistake of fact defense. This is because the defendant already knows enough to be guilty of the crime. Therefore, the defendant's mistake is considered immaterial.

For example, assume that Margaret in Question 1 is charged with possessing a controlled substance, but this time she claims that the mistake she made was in believing that the powder she carried was heroin, not cocaine. Margaret is still guilty of possessing a *controlled substance* because the statute does not require that the defendant know exactly what type of controlled substance she possesses. As long as Margaret knows it is some type of controlled substance, she has met the requirements of the statute.

Another example is a defendant charged with murder. Murder is defined as "killing another human being with malice aforethought." Assume the defendant admits she intentionally and maliciously killed a person. However, she offers as a defense that she thought she was killing a Yankees fan but killed a Dodgers fan instead. Under the definition of the crime, the mistake is irrelevant. The defendant intentionally killed "another human being."

Therefore, a mistake of fact only matters if it shows that the defendant didn't know something she needed to know to be guilty of the crime. Once she knows these facts, other mistakes do not matter. The next question illustrates this point.

> **QUESTION 2. Charge it!** Mickey is charged with "knowingly using the credit card of another person." The charges arose when Mickey stole the wallets of a couple of customers shopping at an upscale department store. Upon reflection, Mickey felt badly about stealing the credit cards. Therefore, he decided that he would only charge items on the credit card of the customer who looked like she could afford it the most. While on his shopping spree, Mickey accidentally gave the sales clerk the credit card of the less-affluent customer. Does Mickey have a mistake of fact defense?
>
> **A.** Yes, because he honestly intended to use the credit card of a different customer.
>
> **B.** No, because he violated the charged statute.
>
> **C.** Yes, because he would not have used that credit card if he knew it belonged to the less affluent customer.
>
> **D.** No, because mistake of fact is never a defense to a common law crime.

ANALYSIS. Mickey has made a mistake that doesn't matter. Carefully examine the crime charged. As stated, as long as Mickey knows he is using the credit card of "another person," it does not matter if Mickey correctly identifies that person. The mistake he made is without legal consequence.

Therefore, **A** is the wrong answer. Mickey may have made an honest mistake, but it simply doesn't matter. He still knew that he was using the credit card of another person. For similar reasons, **C** is also incorrect. Perhaps Mickey's motives were not quite as bad because he thought the customer he was hurting could afford his purchases, but motive is not an element of the crime. As long as Mickey knew he was using someone else's credit card, he is guilty.

That leaves a choice between **B** and **D**. A good lesson to learn about taking multiple-choice exams is that an absolute answer is rarely the correct answer. Here, **D** incorrectly states that mistake of fact is "never" a defense to a common law crime. This statement is not true. Although we have been working with statutes, common law crimes work the same way once you know their definitions. For example, the common law crime of "theft" requires that the defendant knowingly take the property of another person without permission and with intent to permanently deprive that person of her property. Assume that after a hard day of criminal law classes, Sally picks up what she believes to be her book and leaves the classroom. Unbeknownst to her, Sally has made a mistake. In fact, she has picked up Billy's book. In that case, Sally would have a mistake of fact defense. Even common law crimes would allow such a defense.

Therefore, **B** is the correct answer. Even with his mistake, Mickey still violated the statute charged. He knowingly used another person's credit card without permission. It is irrelevant that he mistakenly thought he was using a different victim's card.

At common law, the courts struggled over how to decide which mistakes mattered, and which did not, in deciding whether the defendant had committed a crime. The classic case on point is *Regina v. Prince*, L.R. 2 Cr. Cas. Res. 154 (1875) (see the detailed discussion in Section E below). In *Prince*, the defendant was convicted of taking an unmarried girl under 16 years of age out of her father's possession without his permission. Prince claimed he made a mistake. He claimed, and the court assumed as true, that he did not know the girl was underage. To decide whether Prince was guilty of the offense, the court needed to decide whether Prince's mistake mattered and could excuse his otherwise criminal behavior.

The *Prince* court held that Prince's mistake as to the girl's age did not support a mistake of fact defense because Prince already knew everything he needed to know to be guilty of the offense. Based upon the morality of the day, the court held that any man taking an unmarried girl out of her father's possession without the father's permission deserved punishment, regardless of whether he realized the girl was underage. His mistake of fact as to her age did not matter because he already knew everything the court believed was important in holding him responsible for the offense. While prosecutors may have had to prove that the girl was of a certain age to fit the act within the definitional confines of the crime, *they did not need to prove that Prince was aware of her young age.*

Obviously, the crucial questions for mistake of fact cases are: Which facts does the defendant need to know to be found guilty, and which facts, although part of the definition of a crime, do not require the defendant's knowledge? How do we determine which mistakes of fact trigger the defense and which do not?

Before analyzing the approach to determining which facts may give rise to a mistake of fact and which do not, it is probably helpful to become familiar with the Model Penal Code nomenclature in this area. The Model Penal Code distinguishes between "material" and "jurisdictional" facts as a way of deciding which facts can form the basis of a mistake of fact defense and which cannot.

D.   Material versus jurisdictional elements

Under the Model Penal Code, a fact the defendant needs to know is considered to be a "material" element. Material elements are elements that relate to the harm or evil the offense is designed to prevent. Model Penal Code §1.13(10). They are the type of elements that help us judge whether a defendant should be punished for her behavior. For example, if a defendant is charged with possessing stolen goods, it would undoubtedly be a material element that the defendant knew the goods were stolen. It is only if the defendant knows the goods are stolen that she really deserves to be punished.

However, crimes may also contain elements that are considered to be "jurisdictional only." These elements do not relate directly to the harm or evil the offense addresses. Rather, jurisdictional elements simply dictate which court has jurisdiction to decide the case. If a defendant makes a mistake as to a jurisdictional element, there is no mistake of fact defense.

A classic case demonstrating this principle is *United States v. Feola*, 420 U.S. 671 (1975). In *Feola*, the defendants were charged with assaulting federal officers. The defendants conceded that they knew they were assaulting officers. However, they argued that they did not know that their victims were "federal" officers. The Supreme Court found that the requirement that the officers be federal was jurisdictional only. Although prosecutors would have to prove at trial that the victims were federal officers, they did not have to prove that the defendants knew that the officers were federal officials. Thus, any mistake the defendants made as to this fact was immaterial and not a defense.

Similarly, in *United States v. Yermian*, 468 U.S. 63 (1984), the defendant was charged with submitting false statements to an agency of the United States. Yermian had submitted a false personnel security form to his employer, a defense contracting firm. Then, unbeknownst to Yermian, his employer forwarded the form to the Defense Department. When Yermian's misrepresentations were discovered he was prosecuted. He claimed a mistake of fact defense because he did not know his form would be submitted to a federal agency. The Supreme Court rejected the defense. It held that submission of the statement to a federal agency was a jurisdictional element that did not require Yermian's knowledge.

As these cases make clear, if the defendant makes a mistake regarding a fact that only goes to a jurisdictional element, mistake of fact is no defense. In other words, it is a mistake that does not matter.

Under common law, many courts characterize offenses as general intent crimes if they don't require that the defendant have the specific intent to defraud a particular type of agency or injure a particular type of officer. If the crime is classified as a specific intent offense, it is much more likely that the defendant will need to know all the circumstances of the offense to be guilty.

QUESTION 3. 1,000 feet. Falu is arrested when he is caught selling heroin to an undercover drug agent. If he is charged in state court, his possible punishment is only three years. However, the authorities charge him in federal court because he sold drugs within 1,000 feet of a school. Falu wants to introduce evidence that he honestly did not know he was within 1,000 feet of a school when the sale took place. The court will not allow this testimony. The statute under which Falu has been charged states, "Any person who knowingly [sells drugs] within one thousand feet of a public or private elementary or secondary school is guilty of a federal crime punishable by twenty years in prison." Falu is convicted under this statute. Falu appeals his conviction. His conviction should be

A. affirmed because Falu was within 1,000 feet of a school.
B. affirmed because the offense has no mens rea requirement.
C. reversed if Falu honestly did not know he was within 1,000 feet of a school.
D. reversed if Falu reasonably did not believe he was within 1,000 feet of a school.

ANALYSIS. The best way to start answering this question is by analyzing the statute to see which elements are material and which are jurisdictional. The requirement that the sale be within 1,000 feet of a school to establish federal jurisdiction is a quintessentially jurisdictional element. As such, it doesn't matter whether Falu knew he was that close to a school as long as he knew he was selling drugs. With this analysis in mind, let's look at the options.

A is a definite possibility. The trial judge was not required to allow evidence of a mistake if the requirement that Falu was within 1,000 feet of a school is jurisdictional only. The distance from the school is a classic jurisdictional element. Regardless of whether Falu knew he was that near to a school, as long as he knew he was selling drugs, he has sufficient mens rea for the offense. Selling drugs anywhere is wrong. The fact that a particular court asserts jurisdiction only when drug sales are within a particular distance of a school does not change the basic fact that Falu knew his conduct was socially wrong. Unless there is more information indicating that the law was passed only to punish defendants who were intentionally selling within proximity of a school, it is unlikely that the 1,000-foot requirement is anything other than a jurisdictional element. Yet it is always dangerous to select an answer without reviewing the other possibilities.

How about **B**? **B** is a little trickier. Although the requirement that Falu be within 1,000 feet of a school is a strict liability element because Falu need not know it, this does not make the complete offense a strict liability crime. As the language of the statute makes clear, there is a mens rea requirement — the defendant must at least know that he is selling drugs. Therefore, **B** is the wrong answer.

C and **D** are also wrong because it doesn't matter whether the defendant honestly or reasonably made a mistake of fact if the mistake relates only to a jurisdictional element. Even if every other person in the world would have made the same mistake, it doesn't make a difference. It is irrelevant whether the defendant knew he was within 1,000 feet of the school at the time of the sale. He knew all he needed to know to be guilty — he knew he was selling the drugs. Therefore, the trial judge did not err in precluding the defendant's evidence and **A** is the correct answer. Under the common law, if the crime is labeled a general intent offense, you can expect the same result.

By the way, if you picked **A**, you agree with the Second Circuit's analysis in *United States v. Falu,* 776 F.2d 46 (2d Cir. 1985).

E.   Determining which is which: Analyzing a statute to determine whether an element is material or jurisdictional

By now you have probably realized that the key step in deciding whether a mistake of fact defense applies is deciding whether the defendant's mistake related to a material element or merely a jurisdictional element. But exactly how is this done?

There is actually a fairly simple approach you can use to decide whether an element is material (and therefore subject to a mistake of fact defense) or jurisdictional (and therefore the defendant cannot claim mistake of fact). Consider it a three-step process.

Step #1: Read the Statute

First, look at the language of the statute. Some statutes make it very clear what the defendant must know to be guilty of a crime. For example, assume a statute states, "It is a crime to knowingly apply for a building permit knowing that the information in the application is false." In this situation, it is quite clear that the defendant must know both that she is applying for a building permit and that she is using false information on that application. If the defendant doesn't know either of these things, she is not guilty. For example, if the defendant honestly believes the statements on the form are correct, the defendant is not guilty even if the statements turn out to be false because she does not "know" the information is false as the statute requires.

Conversely, assume the statute stated, "It is a crime to knowingly submit an application with false information regardless of whether the applicant knows the information is false." That hypothetical statute makes it clear on its face that a mistake of fact defense could not be raised. The defendant is guilty regardless of whether she knows the information on the application is false. She is strictly liable for any information she submits.

The problem is that in codifying laws, especially for common law offenses, legislators are not particularly careful to use drafting language that identifies which elements the defendant must know. Therefore, the statute may be written as follows: "It is a crime to knowingly submit an application with false information." On the face of this statute, it is unclear whether the defendant need only know he is submitting an application or whether he also needs to know the information on it is false. In other words, we need to find out how far down the statute the mens rea requirement travels.

Think of the statute in this way:

Knowingly   submit application   with false information

There are two possible ways to interpret this statute:

#1:   *Knowingly   submit application   with false information*

#2:   *Knowingly   submit application   with [knowingly] false information*

If option #1 is correct, the defendant does not have a mistake of fact defense if she didn't know the information was false because it is not something she needs to know. On the other hand, if option #2 is correct, the defendant has a mistake of fact defense if she didn't realize the information was false.

To determine how to interpret this statute, you often need to look beyond the statutory language. In some jurisdictions, the courts will affix labels such as general intent and specific intent offense to indicate whether a mistake defense is allowed. However, these labels are not always used consistently. Therefore, it is best to look to other tools to help decide which facts the defendant needs to know to be guilty of the crime: step 2 (legislative history) and step 3 (common sense and public policy). Before we take those steps, let's try another problem.

QUESTION 4. Spy versus spy. Boris is charged with illegally passing classified documents. Boris works as a telephone receptionist at a government agency. One day, his friend Natasha asked him if he had a good telephone directory of the Washington, D.C. area because she always had a hard time getting correct telephone numbers. Boris decided to give her a copy of the telephone directory he used at work. When he does so, Boris is charged with "willfully passing information the defendant knows to be classified." Boris claims that he honestly didn't realize that the telephone directory was classified. In support of his defense, he offers the book itself, which does not contain the word "classified." He also calls several witnesses to testify that they saw other people at the agency taking copies of the telephone directory home. Does Boris have a mistake of fact defense?

A. Yes, because he did not act willfully.
B. Yes, because he didn't realize the information in the telephone directory was classified.
C. No, because the crime involves national security.
D. No, because the evidence Boris offered was irrelevant to the charged offense.

ANALYSIS. No need to guess at the answer; just look at the statute. The statute makes clear that the defendant must know the information he is passing is classified. The statute states that it is a crime to "willfully pass information the defendant *knows* to be classified." If the defendant does not know this, he is not guilty. When Boris makes a mistake and doesn't realize the information is classified, he doesn't have the mens rea required for this crime. Therefore, he has a full defense. The goal is to identify the answer option that reflects this analysis.

Look first at **A**. It is close, but not close enough. Boris willfully passed the telephone directory. The problem is that he didn't know it contained classified information. Therefore, even though **A** focuses the reader on mens rea language in the statute, its focus is on the wrong mens rea language given the facts of this case. **A** is a wrong answer.

Skip to **C** and **D** for a moment. Both of these options reject the possibility that there is a mistake of fact defense in this case. **C** summarily states there is no mistake defense because the crime involves national security. While it is true that the crime involves national security, one need only look at the statute to see that there can be some crimes involving national security that do have detailed mens rea requirements. Therefore, **C** is wrong.

Finally, **D** is wrong because evidence of the mistake is not irrelevant if the prosecution must prove that the defendant knew the information was classified. It is evidence that goes to the heart of the case. **B** recognizes this and is therefore the correct answer. If the defendant didn't realize for any reason, including a mistake, that the information he gave was classified, he didn't have the mens rea for the crime and is not guilty.

Step #2: Legislative History

Sometimes, the legislative history makes clear whether the court should allow a mistake of fact defense. For example, let's go back to our friend Boris. Assume that the statute just read, "It is a crime to willfully pass classified information." On its face, that statute does not state whether Boris must know the information is classified. However, the legislative history may make clear that Congress intended that the statute only apply if the defendant knows he is passing classified information. If the legislative history is clear, Boris will have a mistake of fact defense.

The same is true for our prior hypothetical in step #1. That statute read, "It is a crime to knowingly submit a false application." Assume the legislative history reads as follows:

> Congressman Sniff: "There are so many documents that people must submit these days to the government. Surely not everyone who makes a mistake on those papers is a criminal, are they? Like everyone else here, I intend that this statute only apply to those who would try to trick the government by submitting information when they know it is untrue."

This legislative history makes it clear that a defendant is not guilty of this crime unless he knows he is submitting false information. If the defendant makes a mistake of fact, and doesn't know the information is false, the defendant is not guilty of the crime.

QUESTION 5. Exotic birds. Simon is charged with "knowingly capturing an American eagle." Simon claims that he intentionally captured the bird, but only because he believed that it was a large hawk. He says he had no idea that the bird he caught was an American eagle. Prosecutors argue that Simon's mistake is irrelevant. In making this argument, prosecutors draw upon the following legislative history.

> Congresswoman Hall: "Nothing is more precious than the aviary emblem of our country. I am gratified that Congress has decided to criminalize any capture of these magnificent birds, regardless of whether the defendant intends to nab an eagle. Any defendant who is out there trying to capture large birds takes his chances. He should have to live with his mistake because society will have to live without that precious bird."

Should Simon be able to argue his mistake of fact defense to the jury?

A. Yes, because Simon did not intend to harm the eagle.
B. No, because an eagle is a precious bird.
C. Yes, because generally it is not a crime to capture birds.
D. No, because Simon is guilty regardless of whether he knew the bird he captured was an American eagle.

ANALYSIS. As in all mistake of fact problems, we need to determine what facts the defendant must know to be guilty. If the defendant needs to know a fact to be guilty, he has a mistake of fact defense. However, if the defendant doesn't need to know that fact, and he can still fit the definition under the statute, mistake of fact is not a defense.

In this case, the language of the statute is ambiguous. Is it enough that the defendant knows that he has captured a large bird, or does he need to know he has captured an American eagle? Here is where the legislative history comes in to help. Congresswoman Hall's comments make it clear that the defendant is guilty even if he does not intend to capture an American eagle. If the defendant is out capturing birds, he has no defense if he mistakenly captures an American eagle. Given that legislative history, let's see which of the answers makes the most sense.

A is a red herring and wrong. The statute criminalizes capturing American eagles even if a defendant does not intend to harm them. Be very careful when reading a multiple-choice question. Make sure you know the nature of the crime charged. Don't assume that you know what the crime is — read the statute.

As for **B**, while it is certainly true that the eagle is a precious bird, there is probably a better answer that addresses the legal issues in the question. In law school exams, you are often asked to select the "best" answer. The best answer will address the legal issue at hand. **B** doesn't really answer why the court should deny a mistake of fact defense.

C is a wrong answer because it speaks of crimes in general, not the crime charged in this case. For a mistake of fact problem, it is critical that you analyze the specific crime alleged in the problem, not just crimes in general.

D is the best answer because it uses the facts and the law to explain why no mistake of fact defense should be permitted. No defense should be permitted because the legislative history makes clear that the drafters did not intend that there be a mistake of fact defense for this particular crime.

Step #3: Common Sense and Public Policy

In most situations, the question of whether a mistake of fact defense should be allowed will depend on a common sense analysis of the crime. Ordinarily, a defendant must know those facts that make her conduct morally and socially wrong. If the defendant does not know those facts because she has made a mistake, the defendant is entitled to a mistake of fact defense.

Go back to our earlier example of the statute prohibiting "knowing submission of a false application." How do we decide whether the defendant has a mistake of fact defense if the defendant claims she mistakenly thought the information on her form was true? If the language of the statute does not make the answer clear and there is no clarifying legislative history, don't be afraid to rely on your common sense. What makes the defendant's conduct bad? Submitting forms is not harmful or socially wrong behavior. It is only when the forms contain false information that the defendant is blameworthy. The basic principle of criminal law is that the defendant must know that which makes her conduct wrong. In this situation, the defendant would need to know that she was submitting *false* information on this form. If she doesn't know this because she made a mistake, the defendant is not guilty.

Take another easy example. Assume the defendant is charged with stealing. As we discussed earlier in this chapter, stealing is "knowingly taking the property of another person." How do we know whether the defendant has a mistake of fact defense if she accidentally picks up someone else's property? Using our common sense, the answer is obvious. There is nothing morally wrong with picking up your own property. It is only wrong when you take someone else's property. Under basic principles of criminal law, you need to know that which makes your conduct wrong. Therefore, unless the defendant knows she is picking up someone else's property, she is not guilty. If she doesn't know this because she made a mistake, she has a mistake of fact defense.

This approach becomes a little trickier when it is hard to judge what society would designate as the morally wrong behavior by the defendant. To make this point, recall the classic case of *Regina v. Prince*, L.R. 2 Cr. Cas. Res. 154 (1875), discussed earlier in the chapter. In *Prince*, the defendant was convicted of taking an unmarried girl under 16 years of age out of the possession and against the will of her father. Prince claimed that he mistakenly believed that the girl was 18, when in fact she was only 14 years old. He knew, however, that he did not have the father's permission in any case to take the girl. Does Prince get a mistake of fact defense?

The court answered no. Why? Because in that society, at that time, what made the defendant's conduct morally wrong was to take any girl, no matter what her age, out of her father's possession without his permission. Prince admitted that he did that. Once he crossed the line into socially prohibited behavior, it didn't matter whether he knew the girl's age. That extra element was more akin to a jurisdictional element. It only limits the universe of cases the prosecution could charge when a defendant has taken a girl out of her father's possession. However, Prince was not required to know anything more than what made his behavior socially wrong.

Part of the fun of criminal law (yes, I said "fun") is to argue over what makes a defendant's behavior socially wrong. It is only when this dispute is settled that the court can decide whether a defendant will have a mistake of fact defense. However, you'd be surprised how easy it is to use your common sense to resolve these issues. Prove it to yourself by trying the next two problems.

QUESTION 6. What a cad! Mike White is charged with abandoning his pregnant wife. Even though he admits he ran out on his wife, he claims that he is not guilty because he didn't know she was pregnant. The year is 1933 and the judge believes that it is wrong to run out on any wife, let alone a pregnant one. Given the court's conclusion as to what makes White's conduct morally culpable, is White entitled to a mistake of fact defense?

A. Yes, because Mike was unaware his wife was pregnant.

B. No, because Mike's mistake is irrelevant.

C. Yes, because the burden is on the prosecution to prove every element of the crime.

D. No, because Mike's mistake was unreasonable.

ANALYSIS.   In the problem, you are told that the social judgment has been made that it is wrong to run out on any wife, let alone one that is pregnant. If that is the case, it doesn't really matter whether the defendant knew she was pregnant. As long as he knew he was leaving his wife, he is guilty.

A is wrong because Mike does not need to know his wife is pregnant. As long as he knows he is leaving her, he is morally culpable. The jurisdiction may have added the requirement that the wife be pregnant just so it could limit the number of cases of this type that it prosecutes, but White can be guilty even if he does not know that his wife is pregnant.

C is also wrong. Although the burden is on the prosecution to prove every element of a crime, **C** doesn't really answer the question. While the prosecution may have to prove that White's wife was indeed pregnant, the real issue is whether White needs to know that fact. Given the judge's view of what made White's behavior morally culpable, as long as the prosecution proves she was pregnant, it does not have to prove defendant knew it.

As for **D**, this answer falls back into the trap of believing that a mistake must be reasonable to qualify for the mistake of fact defense. In fact, in most instances, even an honest but unreasonable mistake will work if the defendant is entitled to a mistake of fact defense.

B is the correct answer. Mike's mistake is irrelevant because once he knew he was leaving his wife, he knew all of the material elements of his crime. Not knowing that his wife was pregnant was irrelevant because that element was akin to a jurisdictional element. For a full explanation of this problem, see *White v. State*, 44 Ohio App. 331, 185 N.E. 64 (1933).

QUESTION 7. Crack cocaine. Defendant Collado-Gomez is charged with possessing cocaine and he faces a penalty enhancement because the cocaine is in crack form. Collado-Gomez claims that he knew that he possessed cocaine, but that he did not know the cocaine was crack cocaine. Can he claim a mistake of fact defense?

A. Yes, because the punishment is greater for selling crack cocaine than other types of cocaine.

B. Yes, because Collado-Gomez is entitled to show that he is not morally culpable for this crime.

C. No, because Collado-Gomez could not show he was engaged in an activity that would have been blameless absent his knowledge that the cocaine was crack.

D. No, because it is immaterial whether Collado-Gomez knew he possessed cocaine.

ANALYSIS. This problem is a little tougher, but it uses the same analysis as Question 6. The issue is whether Collado-Gomez, who knows he possesses some type of cocaine, needs to know that he possesses crack cocaine. Predictably, the answer is no. Once a defendant is engaged in an activity that is criminally and morally culpable, the defendant's mistake as to the details of that crime is likely to be irrelevant.

Therefore, **A** is incorrect even though there is a certain unfairness in punishing the defendant more for possessing crack cocaine than regular cocaine, especially when he does not know it is crack cocaine. Judges ordinarily do not require that the prosecution prove mens rea as to elements that merely increase the defendant's criminal punishment. For this reason, **B** is also incorrect.

That leaves you with a choice between **C** and **D**. To make this choice, just read carefully. Do you see the difference between the two? **D** goes too far. Collado-Gomez would have a mistake of fact defense if he didn't know he possessed any controlled substance. However, **C** is correct when it states that in this particular case the defendant cannot claim mistake of fact because even absent this mistake, he had enough knowledge to be guilty of the crime.

If you want to know more about this hypothetical, see *United States v. Collado-Gomez*, 834 F.2d 280 (2d Cir. 1987).

F.   Mistake of fact in rape cases

Recall that we learned that a defendant generally has a mistake of fact defense even if her mistake is unreasonable. The reason for this is that even an honest mistake negates the defendant's mens rea for the crime. However, this rule can lead to troublesome results. For example, consider the famous case of *Regina v. Morgan* (1976) A.C. 182. In *Morgan*, several men were charged with rape after the victim's husband told them that she liked "kinky" sex and struggling was the way she got excited. The men argued that they honestly, albeit mistakenly, believed she had consented. If an honest mistake is a full defense, these defendants could walk free. In recognition of this problem, courts now require in rape cases that the mistake be both honest and reasonable.

By requiring that a mistake be reasonable, the court essentially makes negligent commission of an act sufficient for criminal liability because the standard is no longer what the defendant actually knew, but what a reasonable person would have known in his situation. To avoid acquitting the heedless man who says that he thought the woman's "no, no, no" meant "yes, yes, yes," the court may require that the mistake of fact in a rape case be reasonable.

There are even some rape cases in which the defendant gets no mistake of fact defense. In statutory rape cases, it is generally no defense that the defendant did not realize that his sexual partner was legally incapable of consenting because she was underage. For these crimes, the defendant is strictly liable for knowing the victim's age and even a reasonable mistake is no defense.

Finally, the requirement that a mistake be reasonable is not just limited to rape crimes. Legislatures can also require for other crimes that the mistake be honest and reasonable. This requirement will be set forth in the language of the statute.

Let's end this section with a question related to these types of mistake of fact cases.

QUESTION 8. Bar mate. Barclay is surprised to find that he has been charged with rape. The night before, he met a woman in a bar who asked him for a ride home. When they got to her place, he assumed she wanted him to stay the night. Even though he never asked her if he could stay, he claimed that from the look in her eye he could see that she really wanted to have sex with him. Almost immediately, the woman started crying. However, she never actually said the words "no" or "stop." Barclay honestly believed that she was crying because she was so emotional over her good fortune to be with Barclay. In that jurisdiction, a defendant has a defense to rape if he honestly and reasonably believes the victim has consented to sexual intercourse. Does Barclay have a reasonable mistake of fact defense?

A. Yes, because he honestly believed that his victim consented to have sex with him.
B. Yes, because the woman assumed the risk by asking him for a ride home.
C. No, because rape is a strict liability crime.
D. No, if Barclay's mistake is not reasonable.

ANALYSIS.   Don't forget that this is a problem about rape, an offense that now usually requires that the defendant both honestly and reasonably believe that his victim is consenting to sex. If that is the standard, as is stated in the facts of this problem, a mere honest mistake will not be enough for a defense; the mistake must also be reasonable.

Therefore, **A** is the wrong answer. An honest mistake may be enough for many crimes, but it is not enough for this crime because the jurisdiction requires that the mistake be honest and reasonable. **B** is one of those red-herring answers. Victims don't assume the risk, nor is there a concept of contributory negligence in criminal law.

Stay away from **C**. It is also a wrong answer. Rape is not a strict liability crime. It requires that the defendant intend to have sex with the victim without her consent. Only statutory rape is a strict liability crime. In those situations, it doesn't matter if a reasonable person would have believed the girl was old enough to consent; if she isn't, the defendant is still criminally responsible.

D is the correct answer. For Barclay to have a defense to this rape, his mistake must be reasonable. It will be up to a jury to decide both whether he honestly believed his victim was consenting and whether that belief, given all the circumstances, was reasonable.

G.   The Closer: Mistaken but still guilty

Sometimes the issue arises as to whether a defendant can assert a mistake of fact defense if she genuinely made a mistake as to the charged crime, but would still be guilty of another offense. Should the defendant be held responsible for the criminal act she intended or the one she committed?

The common law and the Model Penal Code take different approaches to this problem. As discussed in the Comment to Model Penal Code §2.04, a defendant is only subject to punishment for the lesser offense she committed. At common law, however, the defendant would be guilty of the higher offense.

Consider, for example, a defendant who believes that she is killing her landlord. In fact, she ends up killing the President, a crime carrying a more severe punishment. At common law, the defendant would be responsible for the harm she actually caused, regardless of her mistaken belief. However, under the Model Penal Code, she would only be punished for the lesser crime. An even better example of this doctrine is set forth in the following question.

QUESTION 9. Open house? In many jurisdictions, there are different degrees of burglary. Unlawful entry of residence is punished more severely than unlawful entry of a nonresidential building. Assume that the defendant intended to burglarize a store. She didn't realize, however, that the owner lived in a back room of the store. If the defendant asserts a mistake of fact defense, which of the following is true?

A. Under the Model Penal Code, the defendant would only be punished for the degree of burglary she intended, that is, burglary of a nonresidential building.

B. Under the Model Penal Code, the defendant is still guilty of burglarizing a residence because she knew she was making an illegal entry, regardless of whether she knew the owner lived in the store.

C. Under the common law, the defendant is only guilty of the burglary she intended, that is, burglarizing a nonresidential building.

D. Under the common law and the Model Penal Code, the defendant cannot assert a mistake of fact defense because she still intended to commit an illegal act.

ANALYSIS. The Model Penal Code takes a more lenient view of mistake of fact defenses in those situations in which the defendant intended to commit an offense, but ended up committing a worse offense than the one she intended. Unlike the common law approach, the defendant is only punished at the level of the intended offense. Accordingly, **B** is a wrong answer. **B** actually states the common law rule. **C** is also wrong because the common law punishes the defendant for the higher degree offense. **D** is wrong because it is only partially correct. A defendant cannot assert a mistake of fact defense to avoid all culpability when she still intended to commit some criminal offense; however, she can mitigate her punishment under the Model Penal Code approach. For that reason, **A** is the correct answer. In essence, even though the defendant has committed the actus reus of a more serious offense, she is punished for the mens rea of the lesser offense. By contrast, the common law would punish the defendant according to the level of crime associated with her actus reus.

Levenson's Picks

1. Strange powder	E
2. Charge it!	B
3. 1,000 feet	A
4. Spy versus spy	B
5. Exotic birds	D
6. What a cad!	B
7. Crack cocaine	C
8. Bar mate	D
9. Open house?	A

6

Mistake of Law

~

Ignorantia legis neminem exusat.
(Ignorance of the law is no excuse.)

~

A. General rule: Mistake of law is no defense

It is often said that "mistake of fact is a defense, mistake of law is not a defense." While that may be a good general rule, there are exceptions to both parts of this rule. As we saw in Chapter 5, mistake of fact is only a defense if the defendant doesn't know something he must know to be guilty under the law. Thus, there are times when mistake of fact is not a defense.

Similarly, while the general rule is that mistake of law is not a defense, there are exceptions to that rule. There are three categories of cases in which mistake of law is a defense. Each is detailed in this chapter. The first category is when mistake of law operates just like mistake of fact. There are some occasions when a statute requires that a defendant "knowingly violate the law." If the defendant doesn't know what the law requires, the defendant is not guilty of violating that law.

The second type of mistake of law defense is when a defendant has been misled by a judicial authority or official misstatement of the law. In those situations, the government is estopped from claiming that the defendant's legal error is not a defense.

Finally, there is a very narrow category of crimes in which the defendant may claim ignorance or mistake of law because there has been insufficient notice of the defendant's legal duty.

Despite these exceptions, the general rule is that mistake or ignorance of the law is no defense. This rule makes sense for many reasons. The primary reason is that if ignorance of the law were a defense, every defendant would just claim he didn't know that his conduct was against the law. The rule would encourage people to avoid learning their legal duties. Another good reason for the general rule is that most common law crimes are based upon society's consensus as to what is proper behavior. Just by living in society, a person is on notice of what conduct is expected of him.

Therefore, it ordinarily is not a defense for a defendant to claim he didn't know what the law required or that he checked the law but misread or misunderstood its requirements. Ignorance of the law, except in limited situations, is no excuse.

QUESTION 1. Concealed weapon.   Officer Marrero is charged with illegally possessing a concealed weapon. He claims that he checked the law before he concealed his weapon and that he honestly believed that he fell under an exception for "correctional officers." Although Marrero is a federal correctional officer, the fine print of the statute provides that only state correctional officers are allowed to carry concealed weapons. Does Marrero have a mistake of law defense?

A. No, because misreading the law is not a defense.

B. No, because mistake of law is never a defense.

C. Yes, because Marrero made a good faith effort to learn the law.

D. Yes, because Marrero should have fallen within the law's exception and been permitted to carry a concealed weapon.

ANALYSIS.   If you have mastered the general rule, you should be able to answer this question. Misreading the law is not a defense. Otherwise, everyone would just claim that he had misread the law. Thus, Marrero is not likely to have a mistake of law defense, but let's look at the options.

A seems right on point. Misreading the law is not a defense. Unless the remaining options clearly put Marrero within an exception, **A** is likely to be the correct answer.

B we know is a wrong answer. The rule that mistake of law is not a defense is not an absolute rule. There are exceptions. Once again, beware of answers that are phrased in terms of absolutes ("never," "always," etc.).

C has a certain appeal because we want to encourage people to learn their legal responsibilities. However, the law is harsh on this point. A good faith effort to learn the law is not enough for a defense. Even if the defendant makes a good faith effort to learn the law, he is still guilty if he doesn't get it right.

D is also wrong. Even if you feel that the law is unreasonable or harsh, that is the law and the defendant is bound by it. The fact that you or the defendant might have drafted the law differently does not constitute a mistake of law defense.

Given these other answers, it becomes apparent that **A** is the correct answer. Misreading the law is not a defense and the defendant, although somewhat sympathetic, is still guilty of the offense.

For the story of the real-life Officer Marrero and why his case was not quite as sympathetic, see *People v. Marrero*, 69 N.Y.2d 382, 507 N.E.2d 1068 (1987).

B.   Exception #1: When mistake of law is just like mistake of fact

Although the general rule is that mistake of law is no defense, there are occasions when a defendant does have a mistake of law defense. One such occasion is when the elements of the crime require that the defendant know what the law requires, but the defendant lacks the mens rea for this element because of his ignorance or mistake of the law. In this situation, mistake of law acts just like mistake of fact.

As the Model Penal Code puts it, "[I]gnorance or mistake as to a matter of fact *or law* is a defense if . . . the ignorance or mistake negatives the purpose, knowledge, belief, recklessness, or negligence required to establish a material element of the offense. . . ." MPC §2.04(1) (emphasis added). In other words, if the law requires that the defendant know that he is acting contrary to the law, and he doesn't know that fact, he does not have the mens rea for the crime.

Consider the classic example of *Liparota v. United States*, 471 U.S. 419 (1985). Liparota was charged with "knowingly using food stamps in an unauthorized manner." As a defense, Liparota claimed that he did not know that the manner in which he was using food stamps was unauthorized by the law. While ordinarily mistake of law is not a defense, the Supreme Court recognized the defense in this case because the statute specifically required that the defendant knowingly use the stamps in an unauthorized manner. In other words, the defendant needed to know the law to know that he was using the food stamps in a way that the law did not permit.

Most statutes do not have a requirement that the defendant know that he is engaging in behavior unauthorized by the law. However, when a statute does make this an element of the crime, the defendant has a mistake of law defense if he does not know what the law authorizes or prohibits.

QUESTION 2. Kidnapping with authority. Defendant Weiss is charged with kidnapping. He and his buddies decided to help law enforcement by personally apprehending a person they believed committed a murder. It turns out that Weiss was wrong in his assessment and he and his friends were charged with kidnapping. Kidnapping is defined in that jurisdiction as "knowingly confining a victim without authority of the law." Weiss claims that he honestly believed that he was acting within the authority of the law when he apprehended the wrong suspect. Prosecutors argue that Weiss's mistake of law is no defense. Does Weiss have a mistake of law defense?

A. No, because mistake of law is no defense.
B. No, because mistake of law is only a defense if a defendant really was authorized to seize the victim.
C. Yes, because Weiss did not know that he was without lawful authority to seize the victim.
D. Yes, because Weiss had a good motive for seizing the victim.

ANALYSIS. Start with the general rule that mistake of law is no defense. Then start going through the exceptions to see if they apply in this hypothetical. The first exception is when the crime itself requires that the defendant know that he is engaging in unauthorized conduct. If Weiss doesn't know what the law authorizes, or makes a mistake as to what is authorized, he is not guilty of the crime of kidnapping as it is defined in that jurisdiction.

A is the wrong answer because it only states the general rule and does not consider the exceptions to that rule. While it is true that mistake of law is generally not a defense, there are exceptions, the first of which seems to apply in this case.

B is also a wrong answer. In fact, if you think about it, it makes no sense at all. If Weiss really was authorized by law to seize the victim, he would not be guilty of violating the statute and would not need to raise a mistake of law defense.

How about **C** and **D**? Let's start with **D**. Even defendants with good motives can be guilty of violating the law. The issue is not the defendant's motive, but whether he had the intent for the crime. In other words, did the defendant have all the necessary mens rea for the crime, that is, did he know the seizure was unauthorized by the law? If he knew this, a good motive (such as to help law enforcement) will not save him from being convicted. However, if he didn't know what the law authorized, he has a defense even if he had a bad motive in seizing the victim.

Therefore, **C** is the correct answer. The terms of the statute require that Weiss know that he is not authorized to seize the victim. Since he doesn't know this, he is not guilty of the crime charged. This situation is just like mistake of fact, except the "fact" that the defendant does not know is what the law does and does not authorize.

This exception is the toughest one so it is definitely worth another practice problem.

QUESTION 3. Who owns the property? David is charged with "knowingly damaging the property of another person" because he punched holes in his apartment's wall while installing his stereo system. David claims that he didn't realize that the wall was still the legal property of his landlord when he installed the stereo because David honestly believed that a tenant has the right to alter his walls. As it turns out, David is wrong regarding the property laws. Tenants cannot legally punch holes in their apartment walls, even if they pay their rent. Does David have a mistake of law defense?

A. Yes, because he reasonably believed he could punch a hole in his wall.
B. Yes, because he honestly believed he was only damaging his own property.
C. No, because mistake of law is not a defense.
D. No, because he should have known that it was against the law to punch a hole in the wall.

ANALYSIS. If you remember how to analyze mistake of fact problems, you'll breeze through this problem. The issue raised is whether David, who mistakenly believes he can punch a hole in his wall because it is his property, has a mistake of law defense. Here, the statute requires that he "knowingly" damage the property of another person. If David does not know that the wall is the property of another person, he does not meet the requirements of the statute. Thus, it looks like he may have a defense, but let's check the answers.

Be careful not to jump at **A**. Remember from our mistake of fact discussion in Chapter 5 that an honest mistake is ordinarily enough for a defense, even if it is not reasonable. Therefore, **A** is an incorrect answer, even though it would let David off the hook. However, if we changed the question to charge David with a violation of "negligently destroying another person's property," **A** might be a good answer. When a negligence crime is charged, the defendant's mistake must be both honest and reasonable. In this hypothetical, however, David is charged with knowing that the property belongs to another person. If he doesn't know this fact, even if his belief is unreasonable, he has a mistake defense. Of course, the more unreasonable his mistake, the less likely the jury is to believe it, but technically his mistake need not be reasonable.

Given that our analysis of the problem tells us that David probably has a defense, you should be a little suspicious of **C** and **D** when you consider them as answers. As it turns out, both are incorrect. **C** is wrong because it is too absolute. Sometimes mistake of law is a defense. In fact, it is in this case. **D** is wrong because it assumes that David is charged with negligently punching a hole in another person's wall. Once again, the negligence standard relies upon what the defendant "should have known" as opposed to what he actually knew.

B is the correct answer. As in Question 2, David has a defense to a crime that requires him to knowingly violate the law, if he does not understand the legal aspects of his actions. Because David did not know that his wall legally belonged to his landlord, he is not guilty of "knowingly" damaging the property of another person. However, if his lease put him on notice that he did not own the property, or he otherwise knew the law, he would not have a mistake of law defense.

For more information on David's case, see *Regina v. Smith (David)* [1974] 2 Q.B. 354.

C. Exception #2: When the defendant is misled by official authority

There is a second category of cases in which mistake of law may be a defense. Consider the situation in which a defendant has been misled by an official authority, for example, when a defendant relies on a recently posted law that states, "the sale of tobacco to a person over the age of 16 is permitted." As it turns out, the law was incorrectly posted. It should have read, "the sale of tobacco to a person over the age of 18 is permitted." However, before the law on the books can be corrected, the defendant has sold tobacco to a 17-year-old patron. If the authorities come after the defendant for that sale, he has a mistake of law defense because he relied upon the official statement of the law at the time it was posted and he committed his act. Once the official statement of the law is corrected, the defendant would no longer have a mistake of law defense.

A defendant may be misled either by reliance on a judicial decision, reliance on an invalid statute, reliance on an administrative order, or, in rare situations, reliance on an official interpretation of the law. (*See generally* MPC §2.04(3)(b)(i-iv).) In each of these cases, if the defendant is misled by the law as expressed (not as the defendant "interprets" the law), the defendant has a mistake of law defense because the government is estopped from prosecuting the defendant for an act that he reasonably believed was lawful when committed.

However, there are only a couple of tricks to using this category of exception. First, when it comes to relying on a judicial decision, make sure that the decision was issued by the controlling jurisdiction. A defendant cannot claim mistake of law when he incorrectly relied upon a decision from another jurisdiction or a higher court in his jurisdiction has overruled the decision upon which he relies.

Second, if the defendant claims he is relying upon an official interpretation of the law, he can only make this defense if he is receiving that interpretation from the highest official charged with interpreting that law. For example, the defendant cannot claim that the neighborhood cop told him that it was okay to park cars on his lawn without a license. However, if the defendant has the same official opinion from the state attorney general, the defendant may have a mistake of law defense.

Finally, this exception can trigger a discussion of whether a change in the law that occurred *after* the defendant committed an act that was lawful at the time can put the defendant at risk of being prosecuted. For example, many years ago, the United States Supreme Court held that it is legal to perform an abortion for a patient in her first trimester of pregnancy. Dr. Smith, relying on the Court's decision, performs abortions daily. However, the Supreme Court reverses its decision and holds that states may criminalize even first trimester abortions. Dr. Smith is then prosecuted in his state, not only for the abortions he performs after the reversal, but also for the abortions he performed before the law was changed.

Following the lead of the Ex Post Facto Clause of the U.S. Constitution (art. I, §9(3)), the law would permit Dr. Smith a defense because he relied upon the law in existence at the time he performed his acts. The state may not retroactively prosecute him for acts that were legal at the time they were committed. Technically, Dr. Smith has not made a mistake of law at all. Rather, the law has changed since his conduct.

With these basic rules and warnings in mind, let's try the following problems.

QUESTION 4. Off limits. Albert is charged with unlawfully entering a military base to conduct a demonstration against the war in Iraq. In defense of the charge, Albert claims that he was relying upon a decision by the court of appeals that held that the military base was a public forum and that there was a First Amendment right to demonstrate on the base. He also claims that he checked with the sentry at the guard post to the military base and confirmed with that individual that he had a right to enter the base to protest. Since the time of his protest, the sentry has been demoted and the Supreme Court has held that there is no constitutional right to protest on military bases. Does Albert have a mistake of law defense?

A. No, because every person is presumed to know what the law requires.
B. No, because his mistake was based upon a faulty interpretation of the law.
C. Yes, because the sentry had given him permission to protest.
D. Yes, because he relied upon a governing judicial decision.

ANALYSIS. This question raises the question of when reliance upon bad law is a defense. Out of fairness, if a defendant relies upon an official pronouncement of the law that later turns out to be wrong, the defendant may claim mistake of law. However, the courts like to keep this category narrow. It is only when the defendant's reliance is based upon a misinterpretation from a court or official at the highest level that the defendant can claim mistake of law.

Here, Albert has two separate claims of mistake of law. First, he claims that he relied upon the governing court of appeals decision at the time of his conduct. Additionally, he claims that he relied upon the opinion of the sentry who allowed him access to the base. The courts are likely to treat these claims separately. The first meets the stringent requirement of mistake of law defense; the second does not.

As for the possible answers offered to this question, this time the answers start with options that reject the mistake of law defense. Because the general rule is that mistake of law is no defense, your instincts may tell you to jump at one of the first two answers. However, never jump at an answer in a multiple-choice question. Instead, carefully evaluate the validity of each answer presented. This is especially the case when there are exceptions to the rule and specific requirements for each exception.

As it turns out, both **A** and **B** are incorrect answers. While it is true that every person is presumed to know what the law requires, that doesn't mean there aren't exceptions to that rule. Namely, if a person has been misled by the law, there can be a mistake of law defense. Therefore, **A** is a bit of a red herring. It is a correct statement of the law, but it doesn't really address the problem in this case.

B is also incorrect. While ordinarily a faulty interpretation of the law is not a defense, if that interpretation was provided by a governing court, the defendant does have a mistake of law defense. Once again, beware of choosing the answer that is correct in the abstract, but incorrect in the context of the problem you are solving.

How about **C**? Don't go overboard on Albert's behalf. The sentry is like the neighborhood cop. Albert is not entitled to rely upon his advice. There is a good reason for this rule. We don't know the sentry's legal training, motivation for his advice, or authority to make the statement he made. If a neighborhood cop were allowed to officially interpret the law, we could end up with thousands of different interpretations of the law. Thus, the exception for reliance upon an official interpretation of the law does not apply when the interpretation comes from someone low on the totem pole. It only applies when someone at the highest level, who has the authority to give an official interpretation, gives the legal advice.

D is the correct answer. The reason that Albert has a mistake of law defense is that he relied upon a governing appellate court decision. However, if the appellate court's decision had been stayed, or a different panel of that same appellate court had issued a conflicting decision, the defendant would not have been entitled to rely upon the judicial interpretation for his mistake of law defense. It is only during that very narrow period of time, when the law governing his behavior allows people to enter the base to protest, that Albert has a mistake of law defense. Once the Supreme Court rules against him, he can no longer assert the defense.

If you want to see what happened to the real Albert, see *United States v. Albertini*, 830 F.2d 985 (9th Cir. 1987).

Sometimes this category of mistake of law exception arises when the official interpretation is given by an administrative agency. Let's consider a problem that raises that issue.

QUESTION 5. Dog catcher. LeeAnn really loves dogs. She takes in any stray dog she finds. Currently, she is caring for 12 pathetic pooches. LeeAnn's neighbors have warned her that city ordinances limit the number of dogs per household to three. LeeAnn is not worried, however, because the dog catcher in her city sent her a letter last year congratulating her on being "citizen of the year" for her outstanding work in helping to shelter stray animals. LeeAnn interprets this as the dog catcher's approval of her activities. City officials recently issued LeeAnn a citation for violating the ordinance that prohibits more than three dogs per household. Not worried, LeeAnn marches to court with the letter of commendation she has from the city dog catcher. Does LeeAnn have a mistake of law defense?

A. Yes, because LeeAnn relied upon the dog catcher's letter.
B. Yes, because LeeAnn reasonably relied upon an official interpretation of the law.
C. Yes, because an official interpretation of the law by an administrative official is a valid mistake of law defense.
D. No.

ANALYSIS. Sometimes the trickiest multiple-choice questions are those in which the most obvious answer is the correct answer. The law applying to this situation is not particularly tricky. In some jurisdictions (careful, not all!), reliance on an official interpretation of the law by an administrative official provides a mistake of law defense. However, for this exception to trigger, there must be an official interpretation of the law by an administrative official. A letter of commendation does not qualify as an official interpretation of the law. LeeAnn may use it to ask for leniency in sentencing, but it is not a defense to the crime.

Therefore, **A** is incorrect because LeeAnn relied upon information from a governmental official that wasn't an official interpretation of the law. It was a commendation letter and nothing more.

B is also incorrect because the letter was not an official interpretation of the law. If it was an official statement of the law, and a top official issued it, a reasonable reliance on that statement might be a defense. However, those were not the facts in this case.

By now you have guessed that **C** suffers from the same defect. It is a correct statement of the law, but it incorrectly assumes that the dog catcher's letter was an official interpretation of the law. Don't abandon your common sense when answering multiple-choice questions. When you read that the dog catcher had sent a letter, did you honestly view it as an "official interpretation of the law"? If not, then **A-C** cannot be the correct answers.

D is the correct answer. Even though it provides no explanation, it reflects a correct evaluation of both the facts and law of this problem. LeeAnn does not get a mistake of law defense because she does not have an official interpretation of the law by a high enough governmental official. As for as what constitutes a "high enough" governmental official, this depends on the jurisdiction. Some jurisdictions reject this exception altogether. For example, in *Hopkins v. State*, 69 A.2d 456 (Md. 1940), the court refused to overturn a conviction simply because the state's attorney general had advised the defendant that his conduct would not be illegal. However, in other jurisdictions, there are state or local officials who are empowered to give official advisory opinions regarding the applicability of the law.

D. Exception #3: When there has been no reasonable notice of the law (the *Lambert* defense)

There is one other narrow category of exception to the general rule that mistake of law is no defense. The premise of this third exception is that due process requires that the defendant have sufficient notice as to what acts constitute a violation of the law. See MPC §2.04(3)(a). The courts have interpreted this exception as narrowly as possible.

In *Lambert v. California*, 355 U.S. 225 (1957), the defendant was charged with failing to register as a convicted person upon her arrival in Los Angeles. She had no actual notice of the reporting requirement and claimed ignorance of the law. The Supreme Court held that in the narrow circumstances of that case, due process required that the defendant be afforded a defense. The Supreme Court identified three circumstances that triggered Lambert's mistake of law defense: (1) her conduct was wholly passive; (2) she had no actual notice of the law; and (3) Lambert's violation involved a regulatory offense.

In his dissent in *Lambert*, Justice Felix Frankfurter predicted that the Court's decision would become "a derelict on the waters of the law." He turned out to be right. By and large, defendants are not able to claim mistake or ignorance of the law because of lack of notice because there are so many ways that a defendant can receive notice of what the law requires. When laws are enacted, notice of the law is routinely published in the public registry. As for defendants like Lambert, courts now routinely advise defendants who are sentenced of any reporting or registration requirements they become subject to because of their convictions. Once there is actual notice of these requirements, a defendant can no longer rely upon the *Lambert* exception. However, the exception hypothetically exists and some jurisdictions adopt the approach set forth in the Model Penal Code — if a law-abiding and prudent person would not have learned of the law's existence, the defendant may argue ignorance of the law.[1]

Don't get carried away with the *Lambert* exception. The general rule is still that a person is presumed to know what the law requires. However, if you are in one of those narrow circumstances when the defendant is charged with an omission, and it involves only a regulatory crime, there may be a defense if the defendant could not have reasonably known of his legal obligations.

QUESTION 6. Registered shoplifter. Rupa was recently convicted of shoplifting shoes from a local department store. It was her third conviction for shoplifting. Under a recent state law, all shoplifters must register with their local police departments as compulsive shoplifters once they have been convicted of three shoplifting offenses. Rupa is unaware of this requirement. The next time she goes shopping, she is spotted by the local sheriff. He checks the database and determines that Rupa is not registered as a shoplifter, as the law requires. Rupa is arrested for failing to comply with the reporting law. Does Rupa have an ignorance of the law defense?

---

1. For example, in New Jersey, the defendant may claim mistake of law if he "diligently pursues all means to ascertain the meaning and application" of the laws. N.J. Stat. Ann. tit. 2C, §2-4(c)(3).

A. Yes, because Rupa did not have notice that she was required to register as a shoplifter.

B. No, because post-conviction registration requirements have become quite common in our society.

C. Yes, because shoplifting is a crime of omission.

D. No, because Rupa was a repeat offender for shoplifting.

ANALYSIS. This question raises the issue of whether Rupa gets the benefit of the narrow *Lambert* defense. Remember, if Rupa had received actual notice of the reporting law, she could never claim this defense. It is only because she doesn't have notice of the law that she has a chance of invoking it. However, for the defense to apply, all three requirements must be met. First, was Rupa's conduct (with regard to not registering) wholly passive? Yes, it was. Certainly, if Rupa was caught again for shoplifting, she could never raise this defense. It only applies to the new registration requirement. Second, did she have actual notice of the registration requirement? Apparently not. Finally, did the violation involve a regulatory offense? Yes, it did. Therefore, as constructed, this problem probably recreates as closely as possible the fact scenario in *Lambert*. The goal is to find the answer that best reflects this analysis.

Before we consider **A**, let's look at **B**, **C**, and **D**. **B** is half-right. Post-conviction registration requirements have become quite common in our society. For that reason, if Rupa was required to register as a convicted child molester, the government might have more of an argument that the recent publicity regarding these registration requirements gave the defendant sufficient notice of her legal obligations. Even then, however, the defense might have a contrary argument. However, registration requirements for shoplifters are not common. Therefore, it would not be reasonable to believe that all residents generally have notice of this requirement just by living in society. Therefore, **B** is incorrect as applied to this fact scenario.

C is not the best choice because it only covers one of the three requirements for the exception to apply. While the offense must be a crime of omission, there are two other requirements as well. Beware when answering multiple-choice questions of selecting the answer that only contains part of a multipart standard.

D is incorrect because simply being a repeat shoplifter doesn't necessarily mean that Rupa has notice of the reporting requirement law. Rupa certainly has notice that she cannot shoplift again. If she did, she would of course be guilty and not have a mistake of law defense. However, **D** does not answer whether Rupa has a mistake of law defense this time.

A turns out to be the best answer. As written, the question poses a classic *Lambert* situation. Rupa does not have notice of her legal obligations, just like Mrs. Lambert did not have notice. Rupa may be one of those defendants lucky enough to use the *Lambert* defense.

A few words of warning. The *Lambert* defense is rarely recognized by the courts (or law professors) because there are so many ways that people can get notice of what the law requires. The primary way we know what the law requires is simply by living in our community. When it comes to reporting requirements, courts routinely advise defendants of their post-conviction disabilities and reporting requirements at the time they are sentenced. If a defendant is so advised, the *Lambert* defense will not work.

E. Advice of counsel defense

A question that often arises is whether the bad advice of a lawyer constitutes a defense to a criminal charge. The answer is sometimes.

The general rule remains the same — mistake of law is no defense. Thus, even if a defendant could convince a jury that his lawyer said it was okay to murder someone, don't expect a mistake of law defense.

However, there are some crimes in which the mistaken advice of counsel will negate the defendant's mens rea for the crime. If this sounds familiar, it should. In this situation, we are focusing on Exception #1 from earlier in this chapter. If a crime requires a specific intent in order to violate the law, and a defendant does not have that intent because his lawyer has misinterpreted the law for him, the defendant is not guilty of the crime.

Consider the crime of "willfully failing to file tax returns." Although the term willfully can mean different things in the law, for tax crimes it means that the defendant intentionally violated a known legal duty. In other words, the defendant knew he was required by law to file tax returns, but he purposely chose not to do so. As a specific intent offense, this statute requires that the defendant know that he has a legal duty to file a tax return. Assume that the defendant checked with his lawyer who erroneously told the defendant that he did not have to file tax returns. If the defendant failed to file those returns because of the bad legal advice, the defendant has not acted willfully, as required by the statute. The lawyer's bad legal advice created a mistake of law defense for the defendant because the defendant no longer had the required mens rea for the crime.

This type of defense is very similar to the defense the Supreme Court recognized in *Cheek v. United States*, 498 U.S. 192 (1991). In *Cheek*, the defendant relied upon bad legal advice, although not even from a lawyer, to decide not to file his tax returns. The Court held that because the government had the burden to prove that Cheek willfully failed to file tax returns, the bad advice could be a defense if the jury believed that Cheek honestly did not know he had a legal duty to file his tax returns. Of course, that is not always such an easy thing to show because there may be facts that show that the defendant, notwithstanding the bad advice, still knew he had a legal duty. For example, in *Cheek,* the evidence showed that the defendant had filed tax returns several times before and had talked about how he disagreed with the duties imposed by the tax laws. Since he disagreed with the laws, Cheek demonstrated that he in fact knew what those laws were. As discussed in the next section, disagreement with the law is not a defense. It is only a defense if the defendant honestly believes, based upon bad advice, that he does not have a legal duty.

Bad advice by counsel is sometimes raised as a defense in white-collar crimes, particularly in complex cases in which a defendant would not be presumed to know the law just by living in society. There are often practical difficulties in raising this defense — such as getting the lawyer to admit that he gave bad advice — but the defense could apply if it negates the defendant's mens rea for the crime.

Consider this illustration.

QUESTION 7. Who's listening? Cynthia is charged with a violation of 18 U.S.C. §545 for her recent importation of digital eavesdropping devices. Section 545 prohibits anyone from "fraudulently or knowingly importing any merchandise contrary to law, or receiving . . . such merchandise, knowing the same to have been imported or brought into the United States contrary to law." Cynthia runs an export/import business. Before importing the eavesdropping devices, Cynthia checked with her sales manager who said that there should be no legal problems with the importation. She also asked for advice from her regular lawyer. He told Cynthia that he had just checked the law for another client and he believes there should be no problem with importing the devices. Sure enough, Cynthia's sales manager and lawyer are wrong. The law does prohibit the importation of such devices. Cynthia believes she has a defense to the charges against her. Which of the following would best support her defense?

A. Testimony from her sales manager that he has regularly imported the eavesdropping devices without any legal problems.

B. Testimony from her sales manager that he told Cynthia that it was legal to import the eavesdropping devices.

C. Testimony from Cynthia's lawyer that he agreed that it was a good business decision to import the eavesdropping devices.

D. Testimony from Cynthia's lawyer that he told her that the law permits the importation of the eavesdropping devices.

E. None of the above because Cynthia cannot have a mistake of law defense to the charges against her.

ANALYSIS. This multiple-choice question is a little different in style than the other ones we have done in this chapter. Instead of asking whether the defendant has a defense, it asks what testimony is most likely to help the defendant at trial. Of course, that is just another way of asking for the same information. You need to examine the information to determine whether it could constitute a defense to the crime charged. Let's look at each proffered testimony to see if, assuming it is believed, it would constitute a defense.

A is incorrect because even if the sales manager has never gotten into trouble before, he is not a lawyer and has not given Cynthia advice that it is legal to import the eavesdropping devices. At most, he has suggested that he hasn't gotten into any trouble for doing so. That is not the same as legal advice that the importation is permissible. It may just be a sign that he has been able to stay under law enforcement's radar screen.

B is also incorrect because the sales manager does not have the credentials to give legal advice. He can give business advice, but that is different from legal advice. To give legal advice, the advisor must at least be someone who the defendant has reasonable grounds to believe is a lawyer. Here, there is no indication that the sales manager is anything other than a sales manager.

C is wrong, even though the advice is coming from Cynthia's lawyer. According to that answer, her lawyer does not pretend to give legal advice; rather, he is giving business advice. Business advice is different. It does not negate Cynthia's mens rea for the crime. It does not tell her what her legal duties are or are not with regard to the importation laws.

D is correct. The particular statute in this case, section 545, requires that a defendant actually know that he or she is acting contrary to the law. If Cynthia doesn't know that because she has been misinformed about the law, she is not guilty of violating that statute. Her lawyer gave her bad advice regarding the law. That advice negates her mens rea for the crime and would be the only testimony in this list of possible answers that would support her defense.

Because **D** is right, **E** is wrong. Once again, beware of answers that are absolute. The general rule may be that mistake of law is no defense, but it requires a closer examination of the specific charges against a defendant to determine whether there is an exception in that case.

F. Disagreement with the law is no defense

As suggested in Section E, even if mistake of law can be a defense under some circumstances, disagreement with the law is *never* a defense. Common sense shows why this is true. If everyone were free to disagree with the law, there would be no law. Everyone could just pick which statutes he wanted to comply with and ignore the rest. Thus, if the defense is disagreement with the law, rather than ignorance of the law, there are no exceptions that apply. In fact, a defendant's disagreement with the law is often the best evidence that the defendant knew what his legal duty was and intentionally ignored that duty.

The difference between disagreement with the law and unfamiliarity with the law arose in the *Cheek* case, *supra*. Cheek was a member of a tax protester group that opposes the tax laws. The Supreme Court made a special point in *Cheek* of drawing the distinction between disagreeing with the law and not knowing one's legal duties. If a defendant disagrees with the law, the defendant must comply with the law and use other legal alternatives to change that law. However, if a defendant honestly does not know his legal obligations, and the statute requires that he know them, he is not guilty. The task for prosecutors is to show that the defendant knows his legal obligations, but just disagrees with them.

Here is a hypothetical that is designed to make this point:

> **QUESTION 8. Supplying terrorists.** Ralph is charged with "knowingly providing material support to a foreign terrorist organization." Ralph is incensed by the charge because he considers himself a humanitarian, not an accomplice to terrorists. Ralph thinks the government has gone off the deep end in labeling so many world aid organizations as "foreign terrorist organizations," and that it is unconscionable to deny aid to these designated organizations. Does Ralph have a defense to the charges against him?
>
> A. Yes, because he did not willfully violate the statute.
> B. Yes, because he sincerely believes the law is unconscionable.
> C. No, because disagreement with the law is not a defense.
> D. No, because Ralph is strictly liable for his contributions to the terrorist organizations.

ANALYSIS. Ralph may disagree with the law, but he still must comply with it. In this hypothetical, Ralph appears to know what the law requires of him. He simply disagrees with the law and the government's interpretation of it. That is not a defense. Therefore, as we go through the possible answers, consider whether each answer undermines Ralph's mens rea for the crime or only shows his disagreement with the law. As far as the required mens rea for the crime, by its terms the law only requires that Ralph know he is giving support to an organization designated as a "foreign terrorist organization." The statute does not require that Ralph agree with that designation.

Be careful not to jump at **A** as the answer. There might be a natural tendency to do so since the term *willfully* in *Cheek* landed him a mistake of law defense. But this hypothetical is not *Cheek*. Cheek could claim that he did not act willfully because he did not know his legal duties. In this hypothetical, the statute does not include a requirement that the defendant act willfully and there is no indication that Ralph does not know his legal duty. Therefore, **A** is not the correct answer.

B is also incorrect because disagreement with the law, even if incredibly sincere and sympathetic, is not a defense. It is a form of civil disobedience. Ralph can disagree with the law, but if he doesn't comply with it, he will have to suffer the consequences.

By now, you should have a natural suspicion of **C** because it seems so absolute. Previously, we have noted that rules rarely turn out to be absolute. However, this is a situation where the rule is absolute. Disagreement with the law is never a defense. It is only when a disagreement with the law blinds the defendant into really believing that his conduct does not violate the law that he might have a shot at a defense, and that depends on the mens rea requirements of the statute. Certainly, in this case, mere disagreement with the law would be insufficient. Therefore, **C** is looking very promising.

But, let's look at **D**. It turns out to be a red herring. Even though Ralph may end up being guilty of this crime, it is not because it is a strict liability crime. In fact, on the face of the statute, it requires that Ralph act "knowingly" in providing the material support. Thus, **D** is wrong in its statement of the law.

C does turn out to be the correct answer. Ralph has no defense because he knows that he is acting contrary to the law, but chooses to do so because he disagrees with the law and the government's actions. Disagreement with the law is not a defense.

G.   Cultural defenses

The issue occasionally arises as to whether a defendant from another culture has a defense because he was unfamiliar with U.S. practices and laws. Some of these cases can be somewhat sympathetic. For example, consider the situation in which a defendant kills and eats his dog because dogs are considered a delicacy in his culture. Should that defendant be punished as a criminal?

On the other hand, there are cases that evoke much less sympathy for the defendant, even if the defendant is unfamiliar with U.S. laws and culture. Consider, for example, the case of a recent immigrant from Southeast Asia who was charged with kidnapping when he forced a young girl to submit to him after he paid her father for her hand in marriage. Can the defendant just claim that he was following the practices of his culture?

It is not just immigrants who may seek to invoke a cultural defense. For example, a polygamist may claim that he should not be judged under U.S. laws because he comes from a different religion or culture.

There is no formal "cultural defense" under U.S. law. If a person chooses to live in the United States, he agrees to behave according to U.S. law. However, there are plenty of ways that a person's individual culture can affect his culpability. To the extent that a specific intent law requires that a defendant willfully violate the law, it is easier for a person from a different culture to claim that he did not know enough about his duty to violate the law. Moreover, as we will see in the discussion of affirmative defenses in Chapters 16 to 20, cultural differences may also affect whether the defendant acted reasonably when acting in self-defense or when provoked.

Finally, differences in culture can have an impact on the sentence that a defendant receives. However, arguing a cultural defense can be a two-edged sword. Some judges will sentence a defendant more harshly to send the message that the defendant must learn to operate under U.S. social standards. Other judges, however, will show leniency and give the defendant a lesser sentence because the defendant did not intend to violate U.S. laws.

Here is an idea of how a cultural defense might be raised. You will see other examples in later chapters.

QUESTION 9. **Home remedies.**   Roland is charged with illegal possession of narcotics because he was caught using opium for his repeated migraines. He claims that he recently immigrated to the United States and that in his prior homeland in Asia, opium was a recognized treatment for his condition. In fact, he cannot understand why the United States would have criminalized it. Does Roland have a defense?

A. Yes, because he did not intend to violate U.S. law.
B. Yes, because he has a verifiable medical condition for which he is using the opium.
C. No, because Roland is presumed to know what U.S. law prohibits.
D. Yes, if Roland had an honest and reasonable disagreement with U.S. laws.

ANALYSIS.   This is a fairly straightforward question. Regardless of Roland's prior practices, he cannot use opium in the United States because its use is illegal here. There is no general cultural defense Roland can use to justify his actions and nothing about his culture would negate any of the elements of his crime. Therefore, to answer this question, you merely need to pick the answer that best expresses that Roland's cultural defense should be rejected.

A is wrong because it suggests that Roland needed to specifically intend to violate U.S. law to be guilty of illegally possessing a narcotic. Intent to violate the law is not a crime with which Roland has been charged. It is enough for a violation that he used the narcotic. If the law did require such intent, Roland might have a defense because he didn't realize his conduct was against the law.

However, as a general intent offense, it is irrelevant whether Roland thought his conduct was legal because of his cultural differences.

B is also wrong because it assumes that there is some general defense for using a narcotic when a person has a medical illness. Although the issue of medicinal use of marijuana has been in the news lately, there is no general defense for those whose background or culture says that the use of narcotics is permissible. *See United States v. Oakland Cannabis Buyers' Coop*, 532 U.S. 483 (2001). Thus far, U.S. society has rejected such a defense and Roland is stuck following the rules of this culture because he has chosen to live here.

The choice comes down to **C** and **D**. **C** correctly states the general rule that there is no cultural defense to criminal violations; defendants are presumed to know what the law prohibits. **D** is wrong because even an honest and reasonable disagreement with the law is not a defense. If Roland wants to treat his headache with opium, he needs to live elsewhere. In the United States, his conduct violates the law.

H.   The Closer: Mistake of law and strict liability offenses

Occasionally, the issue arises as to whether a defendant may argue mistake of law to a strict liability offense. By now, you should be able to derive an answer to this issue through your understanding of strict liability crimes and mistake of law. Recall that strict liability offenses are those that do not require a defendant's mens rea. As such, it is unlikely that the mistake of law doctrine will apply given that it cannot be used to negate the defendant's mens rea. Thus, unless the defendant can show that he reasonably relied on an official decision or that the state has violated the notice requirements of *Lambert v. California*, the defendant will not have a mistake of law defense to a strict liability crime. Using these general principles, try your hand at the following question.

> **QUESTION 10. All in the family.** Jerome falls in love with his first cousin, Cindy. Before marrying Cindy, Jerome asks his family whether it is appropriate for him to marry a first cousin. Jerome's uncle Harry, a family law lawyer, tells Jerome that the marriage is permitted. As it turns out, Harry is wrong. In fact, not only is it illegal for Jerome to marry Cindy, but such a marriage is also considered a strict liability offense.[2] Which, if any, of the following defenses are available for Jerome?

---

2. Assume for purposes of this question that the court has rejected any challenge to the statute under *Lawrence v. Texas, supra*, Chapter 2.

A. Jerome reasonably relied upon the advice of counsel.
B. Jerome had an honest and reasonable mistake of law.
C. Jerome did not receive sufficient notice that marrying Cindy was illegal.
D. None of the above.

ANALYSIS. The first thing to focus on is that Jerome has been charged with a strict liability offense. As such, the general rule is that mistake is not a defense because there is no mens rea to negate. It really doesn't matter if the mistake is reasonable or unreasonable. It simply is not a defense. Given this general rule, be careful not to jump too quickly at an answer giving Jerome a defense just because you personally feel it is unfair to prosecute him.

A is wrong because it doesn't matter for strict liability offenses whether the defendant relied upon the advice of counsel. Because the defendant need not have a mens rea for this offense, it really doesn't matter who gave the defendant bad advice, unless the defendant has one of the estoppel defenses set forth earlier in this chapter. Likewise, **B** is wrong because it doesn't matter whether Jerome has an honest and reasonable mistake of law. The unique aspect of a strict liability crime is that it imposes culpability even if a reasonable person might have made the same choice as the defendant. **C** does not apply in this case because the facts of this question do not fall under the limited *Lambert* doctrine whereby a crime of omission is not punished if there has been insufficient notice to the defendant and the public.

In fact, **D** is the correct answer to this problem. Jerome does not have a mistake of law defense. Even though he never intended to do anything unlawful, he is still guilty of the offense charged.

 # Levenson's Picks

1. Concealed weapons	A
2. Kidnapping with authority	C
3. Who owns the property?	B
4. Off limits	D
5. Dog catcher	D
6. Registered shoplifter	A
7. Who's listening?	D
8. Supplying terrorists	C
9. Home remedies	C
10. All in the family	D

Causation

The buck stops here.
—Harry S Truman

CHAPTER OVERVIEW

A. Causation: General concept
B. Comparison with tort law
C. Step #1: Actual cause ("But for" cause)
D. Step #2: Proximate cause ("Legal" cause)
  1. Direct cause
  2. Intervening causes
    a. Acts of nature
    b. Victim's acts
    c. Victim's conditions
    d. Medical maltreatment
    e. Acts of other perpetrators
    f. Omissions
E. Model Penal Code approach
F. Transferred intent
G. The Closer: Causation for strict liability crimes
⊕ Levenson's Picks

Another key building block for criminal law is the concept of causation. For some crimes, in order for the defendant to be found guilty, the prosecution must prove that the defendant's actions caused a harmful result.

$$\text{Actus Reus} + \text{Mens Rea} \rightarrow \text{Result} = \text{Crime}$$
$$[\text{Causation}]$$

As you may already realize, causation is also a major issue in your torts class. You will likely spend many weeks pondering the subtleties of proximate cause. In criminal law, causation can also be an important issue, but less time is usually spent on it in most criminal law courses because in the "real world," causation issues are relatively rare. Ordinarily, it is obvious how the defendant's actions caused the crime with which the defendant is charged. Nonetheless, because causation is still a very important concept in criminal law, and it is not always evident how the defendant is responsible for the harm caused, this chapter provides an approach and vocabulary for dealing with causation issues.

In general, causation refers to the connection between the defendant's acts and resulting harm. Some crimes, but certainly not all or most, require that a defendant's conduct cause a particular result. For example, homicide requires that the defendant's acts result in the death of the victim. What happens if the defendant's acts only indirectly lead to the victim's death? What if the defendant intends to kill another person, but an unexpected intervening act leads to the victim being killed in a different manner? What if the defendant starts the ball rolling, but the victim ends up taking her own life? When is the defendant responsible for the harm caused? In other words, what is needed to show that the "buck" stops with the defendant? This is the basic issue addressed by causation.

Some criminal law courses address causation early in the term when students are learning the basic elements of crimes. However, other courses introduce causation after a discussion of homicide because it is the crime for which causation is most relevant. Whichever approach your professor adopts, you should be able to use this chapter to master the basic concepts of causation.

As in other areas of the law, learning about causation is really an exercise in learning a new vocabulary. The language of causation helps to express the criminal justice system's judgments as to when the defendant's actions are related enough to the harm caused to hold the defendant responsible. This chapter goes step by step through the approaches and vocabulary used both in the common law and by the Model Penal Code in evaluating causation issues.

A.   Causation: General concept

Causation is NOT an issue in every criminal case. Rather, it is an issue that generally arises only in the context of those crimes requiring a specific result.

There are some crimes that don't depend on whether a defendant causes a particular result. For example, a defendant charged with conspiring to distribute drugs need not have actually caused drugs to be distributed.

However, there are other crimes, such as homicide, for which causation is an issue. In many situations, proving causation will not be difficult. For example, if the defendant shoots his victim through the heart, it will not be hard to show that the defendant "caused" the victim's death.

Yet, there are situations in which the defendant's acts may be viewed as too attenuated or distant from the harm that results. For example, consider the defendant who poisons his boss's coffee. The boss takes a sip, but before the poison can work, a co-worker shoots the boss. Who is responsible for the boss's death — the defendant or the co-worker? Or, consider the defendant who falsely tells the police they can find a kidnap victim in a certain cave. While the police are searching the cave, an earthquake strikes and the police officers are killed. Is the defendant's act the cause of the officers' death? As you can see, in some odd situations, causation can be a critical and difficult issue.

At its essence, finding causation is a policy decision that the defendant has done enough to be criminally punished for the harm that has resulted, regardless of what natural events or actions of others led to that harm. As Professor Joshua Dressler aptly phrases it, "It is the basis that links the actor to the social harm."[1] By establishing who caused a harm, society can decide who deserves to be punished. The very concept of retribution depends on showing that the defendant is personally responsible for the harm that she has caused.

To determine when a defendant has caused a criminal result, both the common law and Model Penal Code developed approaches for analyzing causation issues. Although the vocabulary they use is slightly different, the approaches are really quite similar. Essentially, it is a two-step process:

Step #1:   Is there *actual cause* ("but for" cause)?
           *Was the defendant a link in the chain of causation?

Step #2:   Is there *proximate cause* ("legal" cause)?
           *Were the defendant's actions a sufficiently direct cause of
           the harm to warrant imposing criminal liability?

Although there is an approach for examining causation issues, it would be wrong to believe there is a formula for mechanically deciding whether the defendant caused the harm charged. Ultimately, as with other key issues in the trial, it is a question the jury must decide. Studying causation equips you to argue for the appropriate jury instructions to direct the jury's decision, as

---

1. Joshua Dressler, Understanding Criminal Law (3d ed. 2001).

well as gives you arguments to make as to why they should or should not find that there was sufficient causation.

To get us started, here is a basic question to help you identify when there is a causation issue in a case.

QUESTION 1. Lightning bolts. John won't give up. For the last three months, he has asked Miriam to date him. She has steadfastly refused. He demands that she come out of her house and discuss the issue with him in private. When she agrees, he gently leads her out of the house to the porch. As they are standing there, a lightning bolt comes out of the blue and strikes Miriam dead. John is charged with murder.

Is John legally responsible for Miriam's death?

A. Yes, because she would not have been standing on the porch but for John's demand that she do so.
B. Yes, because he had no right to demand that Miriam date him.
C. No, because John's actions were not the legal cause of Miriam's death.
D. No, because Miriam should be responsible for the acts that led to her death.

ANALYSIS.   Even though you have not learned causation law yet, there is a good chance that your common sense helped you answer this question carefully. Let's consider the various answers.

First, your gut sense may have told you from the beginning that there is something odd about holding John responsible for freak acts of nature, especially when all he has done is to escort Miriam on to the porch. Also, you have already learned that "but for" is only one-half of the causation analysis. While it is true that John did something in the link of causation (i.e., but for him leading her to the porch, she would not have been hit by the lightning), it is not enough unless we also say that he is the "proximate cause" of Miriam's death. Here, **A** states only that John is a but for cause of her death. Without more, that is not enough. **A** is incorrect.

B seems to beg the question. Regardless of whether John had a right to demand that Miriam date him, there is the question of whether he has really done anything to cause her death. Beware of answers that don't really address the issue at hand. **B** is a red herring because it doesn't truly address the causation issue at all.

Let's look at **D** for a moment before examining **C**. Once again, your common sense probably has you wondering, "Why should we hold Miriam responsible for her own death?" In fact, as you learn in the upcoming sections, the law is reluctant to hold victims responsible for their own deaths. Criminal law, unlike tort law, does not embrace the concept of contributory negligence. In other words, it ordinarily does not blame the victim for harm that occurs to her. **D** is incorrect.

C is the correct answer. The bottom line is that John is not responsible because his acts were not a direct enough cause of Miriam's death. Two important principles can be gleaned from this answer. First, there is a relation between actus reus and causation. In fact, the concept of actus reus incorporates two aspects: (1) a voluntary act (or omission) by the defendant; and (2) an act that results in social harm. It is the second part of this actus reus concept that causation addresses.

The second principle to be learned from **C** is that not every act by a defendant is a direct enough cause of harm, even if it is a link in the chain of causation. It is very important to know what other factors lead to the victim's death and how we choose to evaluate these intervening or contributing acts. In studying causation, it is important to focus most of your attention on the concept of "proximate cause" and how it is used to define when the defendant's acts are sufficiently related to the harm caused to hold the defendant responsible for that crime. Most of this chapter (Section 7(D)) focuses on just that issue.

However, before we jump into steps 1 and 2 of the causation analysis, it is important that we spend a moment considering how causation for criminal law is different from causation for tort law. It is important to make this distinction so that you will not automatically assume that just because there is causation under tort law, the defendant is also criminally responsible for a harmful act. Although the terms used under tort law and criminal law may be quite similar, their meanings can be different because of the different consequences of holding someone civilly liable, as opposed to criminally responsible.

B.   Comparison with tort law

Causation can be an issue in both tort and criminal law. However, causation issues occur less frequently in criminal law. There are two reasons for this. First, many crimes do *not* require a harmful result. Consider, for example, the crimes of conspiracy and attempt. A defendant is responsible whether or not he has caused any actual harm. Second, causation issues are relatively rare in criminal cases because prosecutors tend not to bring cases in which causation is questionable. Instead, they frequently leave such cases for the tort system to resolve.

Yet, challenging causation issues do occasionally arise in criminal cases. Although the language used to resolve these issues is often the same as in tort law (words like *but for* cause or *proximate* cause), they have very different meanings. "As a matter of historical fact, the rules of causation in criminal cases are not tied to the rules of causation in civil cases." *People v. Tims*, 534 N.W.2d 675, 684 (Mich. 1995). Because the consequences of being criminally charged and convicted are far more severe than those of being held civilly liable, a term such as *proximate cause* can have very different meanings in the two contexts.

As you study criminal causation, keep in mind that the consequences for being held civilly liable are that the defendant is financially responsible for the harm to the victim. However, if a criminal defendant is found to have caused harm, she may end up going to jail and may be labeled a "criminal." Because the stakes are higher, the criminal law is ordinarily more exacting in its causation requirements. In criminal law, proximate cause generally requires more direct involvement by the defendant in causing harm than may be required to prove civil liability.

Test your understanding of the difference between civil and criminal causation by answering the following question.

QUESTION 2. Bad aspirin.   Regal Pharmacy sells over-the-counter cold medications. One day, there is a flood in the pharmacy. Although the store owner, Henry, cleans up the dirty water, he doesn't check to see if all the containers have remained sealed. As it turns out, one of the cold medications is contaminated. Customer Suzy buys the contaminated container, takes a pill, and dies.

Which of the following is true?

A. If Henry is civilly liable for the death of Suzy, he is also automatically criminally liable for her homicide.

B. Henry may be civilly liable for the death of Suzy, but not criminally liable for homicide.

C. The question of whether Henry is civilly liable for Suzy's death requires the same analysis as deciding whether Henry is criminally liable for Suzy's death.

D. The term *proximate cause* is used identically in criminal and civil cases.

E. None of the above.

ANALYSIS.   This question was designed to drive home the lesson that causation is approached slightly differently for criminal cases than civil cases. Even though the vocabulary used for each may be similar, criminal cases usually require a stricter standard of causation because of the severe consequences of being found guilty of a crime.[2]

---

2. Of course, the higher standard for causation is consistent with the higher requirements for mens rea in criminal cases. See Section G *infra*.

Therefore, **A** is incorrect. A defendant can be civilly liable without being criminally liable for a related offense. For example, a defendant may be found to be civilly liable for hitting another person's car and causing severe injuries. However, that defendant is not automatically responsible for a criminal assault charge. Criminal liability requires a higher level of proof (beyond a reasonable doubt) than civil cases (by a preponderance) and often sets forth a stricter standard for causation.

On its face, **B** appears to be a correct answer. It is absolutely true that a person may be civilly liable, without being criminally liable, for harm that results from the defendant's actions. However, before jumping at this answer, it is always best to consider the other options.

C is also incorrect. Criminal and civil liability should be considered separately. Although similar issues may be raised, the approach taken by the criminal law and civil law can be quite different given the different consequences to the defendant.

D is incorrect. Although proximate cause is a concept used in both criminal and civil cases, the interpretation is slightly different because it entails a policy decision of whether a defendant should be held responsible, either financially or punitively, for harm she has caused.

Beware of **E** (none of the above). Here, it is incorrect because there is a perfectly valid answer. **B** is the correct answer.

Now that we have reviewed some general issues regarding causation, it is time to analyze step by step how causation is determined in criminal cases. The first step — but for or "actual" cause — is set forth in the next section.

C.   Step #1: Actual cause ("But for" cause)

The first step in determining causation is to establish whether the defendant's conduct was a link in the chain of events that led to the harmful result. Actual cause is also referred to as "cause in fact" or "but for" cause. Traditionally, courts have determined actual cause by asking: But for defendant's conduct, would the harmful result have occurred when it did? If the answer is no, there is actual cause.

As you can see, this is a very minimal test. It essentially asks whether the defendant's acts were a link in the chain of causation. It doesn't answer whether the defendant's act was a sufficient enough link for criminal culpability. That issue will be decided when we examine the concept of proximate cause.

Consider this classic example of but for cause. In *People v. Acosta*, 284 Cal. Rptr. 117 (Cal. Ct. App. 1991) (unpublished), police officers began chasing a suspect in a car theft. Two helicopters joined in the pursuit. While they were following Acosta, the helicopters collided and three of the occupants in one of the helicopters died. The threshold question for the court was whether Acosta's act of fleeing the police was the actual cause of the deaths. In other words, but for Acosta's flight, would the injury have occurred? The court found that "but for Acosta's conduct of fleeing the police, the helicopters would never have been in position for the crash." Therefore, Acosta's actions were an actual cause of the crash.

The but for test serves a critical, but limited, purpose in deciding whether the defendant's actions were part of the chain of causation. It does not answer, however, whether the defendant sufficiently caused the harm to be held criminally liable. That decision can only be made after proximate cause is examined.

The defendant's actions will almost always be a but for cause of an accident because of the limited meaning of that phrase. *The but for test does not require that the defendant be the sole or exclusive factor in the victim's death.* Nor must the defendant's actions be the first link in the chain of causation. A defendant's actions can be one of many causes. When there are multiple causes for a harm, the causes are called *concurrent causes.* For example, assume that defendant *A* puts poison in the victim's food. While the victim is swallowing the poisoned food, defendant *B* stabs her. Both defendants are "causes in fact" of the victim's death even though death would have occurred if either had acted alone.

A defendant who accelerates a death that would have occurred anyway may also be an actual cause of the death. Remember: The issue for but for causation is whether "but for the defendant's acts, the victim would have died *when he did.*" In some situations, a defendant may merely hasten a victim's death. Technically, that defendant still is a but for cause of the victim's death. Known as the *acceleration theory,* a defendant who hastens death has still met the but for test, so long as there is sufficient evidence that the defendant's acts actually hastened the victim's demise. See generally *Oxendine v. State,* 528 A.2d 870 (Del. 1987) (insufficient evidence of causation reduced manslaughter conviction to assault).

Sometimes, it becomes awkward to apply the but for causation test too literally. For example, imagine that two people inflict mortal blows on the victim at exactly the same time. Although we tend to say the actions of both are causes in fact, technically it would be difficult to state that but for one defendant's actions, the victim would never have died when she did. In these situations, the but for test is relaxed and the law tends to view both defendants as having met the first part of the causation standard—actual cause.

The next question focuses on the issue of but for (actual) causation. Try applying the first step of causation analysis that you have just learned.

> **QUESTION 3. Moving target.**   Renee has been despondent. Nothing
> has been going right in her life. She decides to take her own life by jumping
> off a bridge. Renee drives to a bridge, climbs on a railing, and says her
> final words. However, before she can jump, defendant Jones shoots her.
> Renee falls to her death. The coroner cannot get a definitive answer as to
> whether the main cause of Renee's death was the fall or the gunshot.
>
> Can Jones be prosecuted for murder?
>
> **A.** Yes, Jones was a cause in fact (but for cause) of Renee's death.
> **B.** No, Renee caused her own death.
> **C.** No, Renee would have died anyway, even if Jones had never shot her.
> **D.** Yes, Jones had the intent to kill Renee.

ANALYSIS.   The issue in this problem is whether Jones is a link in the
chain of causation. In other words, but for Jones's actions, would Renee have
died when she did? Although there is some tendency for all of us to assume
that Renee would have died anyway because she would have jumped from
the bridge, there is no way we can know this for sure. Maybe she would have
changed her mind. Maybe she would have chosen just that moment to
embrace life. All we know is that by shooting her, Jones played a definite role
in the chain of causation.

   In this situation, **A** appears to be the correct answer. Although the
gunshot may not have been the only cause of Renee's death, it was a cause in
fact. But for Jones shooting her, we cannot state with any certainty that
Renee would have plunged at that moment to her death. Even if there were
additional causes for Renee's death, Jones's act is sufficient for actual cause.

   The other answers are therefore incorrect, but let's examine why. First,
B is wrong for several reasons. It is factually incorrect to state that Renee
caused her own death. Perhaps she was planning to do so, but at the moment
of her death, it was Jones's action, not hers, that precipitated the harm
to her.

   C is another version of **B**. It argues a point that can never be proved. We
will never know if Renee would have jumped anyway. All we do know is that
Jones shot her and she fell. It does not matter that Renee had prepared to
jump. Recall that the defendant's acts need not be the sole cause or the first
step in the chain of causation to satisfy the but for requirement.

   Finally, **D** is incorrect because mens rea and actual causation are
separate elements, although they can both be key issues in a case. For
example, in *People v. Acosta*, discussed above, the court reversed Acosta's
conviction for murder, even though it found sufficient evidence of causation.
In reversing the conviction, the court held that there was insufficient
evidence of malice. (See Chapters 8 and 9.)

As separate elements, there can be sufficient evidence of mens rea without sufficient evidence of causation, and vice versa. For example, a defendant intends to kill his victim, but does nothing more than look at her. At just the moment when the defendant is staring down the victim, a bolt of lightning hits the victim and the victim is killed. In this situation, there is mens rea, but no actual cause. However, imagine that a defendant is driving down the street and does not see the victim. The victim darts out in front of the defendant's car and is killed. In this situation, there is certainly actual cause, but no culpable mens rea.

The lesson here is that causation must be treated as a separate element and that the first step in the analysis is actual or but for cause. If the defendant had nothing to do with the death, the defendant will not satisfy this first step in the analysis and should be acquitted. However, even if the defendant does satisfy the first step, it does not mean that the causation analysis is complete. Now it is time to tackle the concept of proximate cause.

D.   Step #2: Proximate cause ("Legal" cause)

After the defendant's conduct is established as an actual cause of the harm, the next step is to decide whether it is a sufficiently direct cause to warrant imposing criminal liability. *Proximate cause* is the term historically used to designate those situations in which a defendant is held responsible. In the Model Penal Code, the term *legal cause* is used in lieu of the common law term *proximate cause.*

No specific legal formula exists for determining proximate cause. Causation is frequently viewed as a matter of common sense. Proximate cause is essentially the jury's determination that the defendant should be held criminally responsible for the harm that her actions caused.

Although there is no set formula for proximate cause, there are factors that guide courts and juries in determining whether a defendant should be held criminally responsible. First, courts consider whether the harm was foreseeable. Second, they determine whether intervening acts should break the chain of causation and relieve the defendant of criminal responsibility.

1. Direct cause

The simplest situation is one in which the defendant is the *direct cause* of the harm caused. For example, if a defendant takes a gun and shoots a victim in the head and the victim dies, there can be little dispute that the defendant is the direct cause of the victim's death. The harm to the victim is foreseeable (under an objective and subjective standard) and there are no intervening acts to account for the death. Proximate cause is clearly established in this sort of situation.

2. Intervening causes

However, there are other situations that are not so simple. For example, what about the helicopters colliding in the *Acosta* case? Although the helicopters were in the air because of Acosta, the actual collision occurred because of negligent flying by the helicopter pilots. Should their negligence break the chain of causation started by Acosta?

In making that determination, there are several factors the jury may consider:

1. What was the nature of the intervening cause? (That is, was it an act of nature or a deliberate harmful act by another perpetrator?)
2. Was the intervening cause foreseeable?
3. Who had control over the intervening cause?
4. How much harm did the intervening cause contribute?
5. What policy arguments are there in favor of having the intervening cause break or not break the chain of causation?

Using these factors, we can examine how courts tend to resolve several different types of recurring proximate cause issues.

a. Acts of nature   Imagine the following two scenarios:

Scenario 1. Defendants rob a man and leave him in his underwear on the side of a country road in a blizzard. The victim freezes to death.

Scenario 2. Defendants rob a man and leave him in his underwear on the side of a road, where he is swallowed up by an earthquake.

In which of these situations are the defendants most likely to be held responsible for the victim's death? The obvious choice is the first scenario. However, the question is why?

In both situations, the defendants are a but for cause of the victim's death. They were definitely a link in the chain of causation. However, when we examine proximate cause, we can see a difference. First, when is death by nature foreseeable? In the first scenario, it is foreseeable that the victim might succumb to the elements. However, in the second scenario, by definition we are dealing with a freak act of nature. Therefore, it is less likely that the defendants will be found to be the proximate cause of the victim's death. Second, we might ask to what extent the defendants could have controlled the impact of nature. In the first scenario, it would have been fairly easy for the defendants to prevent the victim from freezing to death. However, no one has control over an earthquake.

Although the defendants are still responsible in the second scenario for robbing the victim, and perhaps kidnapping him, the earthquake may be seen as a *superseding, intervening cause.* Of course, what we mean by superseding, intervening cause is simply that some event has happened that relieves that defendant of responsibility for the victim's death. It is a label that is imposed when we have adjudged that the chain of causation has been broken.

b. Victim's acts   What about acts by victims? Do they break the chain of causation? Ordinarily, acts by a victim, even fatal acts, do not break the chain of causation. There are two reasons for this determination. First, it is foreseeable that victims will do desperate things to escape from a difficult situation, even if it means harming themselves. For example, what if a defendant has assaulted a woman and she jumps out of a window to escape? Is the defendant the proximate cause of her death? Ordinarily, the defendant's act is still the proximate cause even though it was the intervening act by the victim that was the most immediate cause of her death. It is foreseeable that victims will do desperate things to escape, such as jumping out of a window. See, e.g., *Rex v. Beech*, 23 Cox. Crim. Cas. 181 (1912). Second, when we ask who had control over the situation and whom we want to punish, proximate cause points clearly in the direction of the defendant. Accordingly, acts by victims (unless clearly of their own "free will") ordinarily do not break the chain of causation. Intervening acts that do not break the chain of causation are often referred to as *responsive or dependent intervening causes*.

There are two famous cases that illustrate how this principle operates. Consider, for example, *People v. Kern*, 545 N.Y.S.2d 4 (App. Div. 1989). In *Kern*, three white youths, wielding bats and clubs, chased two black youths. To escape, the black youths ran onto a highway, where they were struck and killed by a passing car. Despite the victims' desperate acts, the defendants were held to be the proximate cause of the deaths. Neither the victims' actions, nor that of the passing car, broke the chain of causation.

In *Stephenson v. State*, 205 Ind. 141 (1932), the victim was kidnapped and sexually molested. To end her horrible situation, she swallowed poison. She died as a result of both the injuries inflicted by the defendant and the effect of the poison. Once again, the victim's acts did not break the chain of causation. Not only is it foreseeable that a victim will do desperate things to escape her situation, but she was under the control of the defendant and his henchmen when she took the poison. Her actions were not independent or autonomous. Rather, they were a dependent, intervening act.

c. Victim's conditions   A related issue that sometimes arises is whether the defendant is responsible for injuries that are caused because the victim is particularly vulnerable or fragile. For example, what if the defendant assaults a person with brittle bones? The ordinary victim might not have been seriously hurt by the defendant's assault, but the "eggshell victim" dies as a result of the defendant's assault.

Generally, a defendant "takes his victim as he finds him." Thus, a defendant need not foresee that a victim's peculiar frailties or vulnerabilities may aggravate the harm resulting from the defendant's conduct. The defendant remains the proximate cause of those injuries. See, e.g., *State v. Cummings*, 46 N.C. App. 680 (1980) (defendant beat victim who died of asphyxiation due to impaired gag reflex).

This principle plays a role in the so-called Jehovah's Witness cases in which a victim refuses medical treatment that could save her life. See, e.g., *Regina v. Blaue* (1975) 1 W.L.R. 1411 (victim refused blood transfusion based on her religious beliefs; defendant's attack constituted proximate cause of death). Neither a victim's physical or emotional condition, nor a victim's religious beliefs, are likely to break the chain of causation.

Before we move on to discussing other issues of proximate cause, here is a question to review the principles we have already covered.

QUESTION 4. Fiery night.   Monty is furious at his boss, Devon, so he decides to throw a stink bomb in Devon's house during the middle of the night. When the bomb goes off, Devon thinks his house is on fire. He runs out of the house and jumps into his unheated swimming pool. By the time emergency help arrives, Devon is dead. The coroner's report indicates that Devon died of hypothermia from the cold water. Devon was particularly susceptible to hypothermia because he was extremely underweight. Monty is charged with murder.

In his defense, Monty claims he did not cause Devon's death. Monty's defense is likely to

A. fail because he was the actual and proximate cause of Devon's death.
B. fail because he was the actual cause of Devon's death.
C. succeed because Devon's actions were a superseding, intervening cause of death.
D. succeed because Monty did not have control over the temperature and Devon's sensitivity to cold broke the chain of causation.

ANALYSIS.   This question tests your understanding of acts and conditions of a victim that contribute to the victim's death, as well as an understanding of how acts of nature affect the proximate cause analysis.

Let's start the analysis with **A**. It requires that we undertake a full causation analysis of this question. First, was Monty an actual cause (but for) cause of Devon's death? The answer is clearly yes. But for Monty throwing the stink bomb, Devon would never have fled his house and jumped into his unheated pool. How about proximate cause? That is a trickier issue. Several questions can be asked to help us analyze the issue: (1) Was it foreseeable that the victim would take drastic action to escape his circumstances? (2) Who had more control over the situation? (3) Who do we want to hold responsible for the harmful consequences? (4) Is there any reason to find a break in the chain of causation? These are all weighty considerations. While theoretically each causation problem needs to be analyzed on its own facts, we know that there are some general principles that the court will apply.

First, victims are ordinarily not held responsible for causing their own deaths, especially when they are reacting to a situation caused by the defendant. Thus, it is foreseeable that Monty would flee his house and do something drastic like jump into the pool. Likewise, ordinary phenomena of nature (e.g., heat, cold, etc.) generally do not break the chain of causation. Thus, it is unlikely that the cold temperatures would be viewed as an independent, intervening act. Finally, we must consider Monty's delicate condition. Once again, defendants generally take their victims as they find them. Thus, there does not appear to be an act or condition that breaks the chain of causation in this situation. Accordingly, Devon would be the proximate cause of Monty's death and **A** is a correct answer.

As always, however, it is important to examine why the other alternatives are not suitable answers. **B** is wrong because it addresses only half of the causation analysis. It is insufficient for a defendant to be just an actual cause of the victim's death. He must also be the proximate cause.

C is wrong because a victim's actions in trying to escape from harm generally do not break the chain of causation. Not only is it expected that a victim will try to escape harm, but it is also foreseeable that a victim will take drastic measures in his escape.

Finally, **D** is wrong because ordinary conditions of nature do not break the chain of causation. This is not a situation in which an earthquake or lightning strike kills the victim. Rather, it is like a victim being left to freeze in a blizzard or swelter in a desert. In such situations, nature generally does not break the chain of causation. Additionally, the special vulnerabilities of the victim do not break the chain of causation. For policy reasons, we insist that the defendant take his victim as he finds him. It is important that the most vulnerable in our society be protected. Accordingly, a victim's condition does not break the chain of causation.

Now, let's explore how other types of intervening acts are generally treated in the proximate cause analysis. Once again, remember these rules are not set in stone, but are guidelines for how these types of proximate cause analyses are often resolved. In any given case, the jury is ultimately asked to decide whether to hold the defendant responsible for the harm. A good lawyer will engage the jury in the process of analyzing the foreseeability of the harm, the foreseeability of the intervening cause, and a policy discussion of who, if anyone, has the most control over that intervening act and should be held responsible for the harm caused.

d. Medical maltreatment One situation that frequently arises is a victim who dies because she has received bad medical treatment. Is the defendant who caused the initial injury responsible for the death or does the medical maltreatment break the chain of causation? Unless it is intentional, or grossly incompetent, bad medical treatment does not break the chain of causation. In general, "ordinary" medical malpractice does not constitute a super-seding, intervening cause. See *Hall v. State*, 199 Ind. 592 (1928). But see *Regina v. Jordan*, 40 Crim. App. 152 (1956) (rare case finding gross medical negligence sufficient to break the chain of causation).

In light of this, consider the situation in which the defendant stabs a victim. The victim goes to a hospital and receives care for her wound. While at the hospital, an infection sets in because of unclean hospital conditions. Although the hospital may have been negligent, its acts are unlikely to break the chain of causation. Whether we believe it is foreseeable that there will be some unhealthy conditions or mistreatment at a hospital, or we feel that for policy reasons we still want to hold the defendant responsible for the death, ordinary negligence generally does not break the chain of causation. See *Bush v. Commonwealth*, 78 Ky. 268 (1880) (rare disease contracted from doctor may relieve the defendant of responsibility).

Compare the above situation with a case in which a victim goes to a hospital only to encounter a doctor who does not like the victim and either recklessly or intentionally gives her the wrong treatment. In such situations, the mistreatment may break the chain of causation. Not only is it unforeseeable that a doctor would act in such a manner, but in this situation the doctor seems to have more control over the harm than the defendant who inflicted the original injury. Accordingly, the doctor's acts would be viewed as an *intervening, superseding cause* of death.

It is time for a problem on medical maltreatment to test your causation analysis skills when the treatment or lack of treatment of the victim contributes to the victim's death.

QUESTION 5. A deadly delay.   Barney, a drunk driver, strikes and severely injures Ellis. When Ellis is taken to the hospital, he is mistakenly left in the corner of an overcrowded emergency room. Tragically, he dies of internal bleeding before doctors can treat him. According to the defense experts, if Ellis had been treated in a more timely manner, he could have been saved. Prosecutors charge Barney with murder. Is Barney the proximate cause of Ellis' death?

A. No, because the hospital officials were negligent in not treating Ellis sooner.

B. No, because Ellis could have been saved if he had been treated in a timelier manner.

C. Yes, because Barney started the chain of causation by striking and injuring Ellis.

D. Yes, because the hospital staff's actions did not break the chain of causation.

ANALYSIS.   Although Ellis's survivors may have a civil malpractice action against the hospital, the hospital's failure to treat Ellis in a timely manner does not necessarily constitute a superseding, intervening act that relieves Barney of criminal responsibility for Ellis's death. Medical maltreatment is rarely treated as a superseding, intervening act. Rather, the defendant who originally caused the injury remains responsible for the victim's death notwithstanding the medical maltreatment. Thus, **A** is the wrong answer. Even if the hospital officials were negligent, mere negligence does not break the chain of causation.

B is also incorrect. Even if proper treatment could have saved the victim, the defendant is not relieved of responsibility for the harm that is caused. Unless this was an egregious case of malpractice, which does not seem to be the case given the number of patients in the emergency room that night, medical maltreatment does not ordinarily act as a superseding, intervening act.

At first, **C** may seem like an appealing answer because it keeps Barney on the hook. However, it is not as good of an answer as **D**. It is not merely because he started the chain of causation that Barney is criminally responsible, but because that chain was not broken by the actions or omissions of the hospital staff. Accordingly, **D** is the better answer.

e. Acts of other perpetrators   One of the most frequently raised issues with regard to proximate cause is how causation laws should treat the acts of multiple perpetrators. Consider, for example, the problem that arises if two defendants are drag racing and one of them hits and kills a bystander. Are both defendants responsible or only the one who actually struck the victim? What if the defendant who struck the victim is also killed in the crash? Does that defendant's death change the causation analysis? Is the surviving drag racer responsible for the death of her fellow racer, the innocent bystander, neither, or both?

In examining the actions of other perpetrators, it is sometimes helpful to separate intentional acts by other perpetrators from unintentional acts.

i. Multiple perpetrators   One of the easier causation scenarios is when there are multiple actors intending to cause harm. For example, if defendant *A* stabs victim *X*, but before *X* bleeds to death, defendant *B* shoots *X*. Who is the cause of *X*'s death?

Some courts will hold that both *A* and *B* caused *X*'s death, especially if the evidence demonstrates that the wound inflicted by either *A* or *B* would have been enough to cause *X*'s death. However, many courts take a different approach. They look to see if *B* accelerated the victim's death. If so, they will hold that *B* was the cause of *X*'s death, but that *A* should be convicted of attempted murder.

Finally, if *A* and *B* are intentionally working together to kill *X*, they are responsible for each other's actions and are therefore both the proximate cause of *X*'s death.

ii. Complementary actors   The more difficult scenario arises when neither *A* nor *B* intend to kill the victim, but their joint activity nonetheless leads to death. Consider a drag racing scenario in which *A* and *B* are racing. *B* spins out of control and dies. Is *A*, by engaging in reckless activity with *B*, the proximate cause for *X*'s death?

In *Commonwealth v. Root*, 170 A.2d 310 (Pa. 1961), the court held that *A* was not responsible for *B*'s death because *B* voluntarily created the risk of his own injury. While we ordinarily do not blame victims for the harm that befalls them, some courts will relieve a defendant of responsibility if the victim is another actor in the criminal scheme. See also *Velazquez v. Florida*, 561 So. 2d 347 (Fla. 1990) (a driver-participant in an illegal drag race cannot be criminally responsible for the death of another driver-participant when the deceased, in effect, kills himself by his own reckless driving).

Other courts reject this approach. See, e.g., *State v. McFadden*, 320 N.W.2d 608 (Iowa 1982) (*A* was proximate cause because he participated in the series of acts that led to *B*'s death). For example, in *Commonwealth v. Atencio*, 189 N.E.2d 233 (Mass. 1963), the defendant played Russian roulette with the victim. The court held that the defendant's mutual encouragement in the joint criminal enterprise was sufficient to prove proximate cause.

Ordinarily, when the reckless or negligent conduct of complementary actors leads to the death of an innocent person, all surviving participants are held responsible. It is foreseeable that their careless activity will lead to serious injury or death and there is no good policy reason to hold that the contributory actions of fellow participants should break the chain of causation. The harm to the victim is reasonably foreseeable, as well as how the other party's intervening acts will lead to that harm.

iii. Blameless intervening actors   Finally, there are the scenarios in which the defendant puts in motion a series of acts that causes the victim's death, but other actors inadvertently contribute to the result. For example, what if a person wants to poison her enemy but the actual poison is administered by an individual who does not realize the vial contains poison? The defendant will be the proximate cause, notwithstanding the actions of others who unwittingly lead to the victim's harm.

There are an infinite number of scenarios in which proximate cause issues may arise. Use the following question to test your ability to analyze a problem involving multiple actors.

QUESTION 6. **The sky's the limit.** Arnold and Maria have had a tumultuous marriage. Arnold decides he wants to get rid of Maria. Accordingly, he takes Maria skydiving and intentionally packs her parachute in a faulty manner. When Maria jumps out of the plane, another skydiver, Diane, accidentally knocks Maria on the head. Maria is temporarily knocked out. She regains consciousness before hitting the ground, but she cannot get her parachute to open. When government officials inspect Maria's parachute pack and discover it was incorrectly packed, they charge Arnold with Maria's murder. Arnold claims he was not the cause of Maria's death.

Arnold's defense will most likely

A. succeed because Maria took her own life by engaging in the risky activity of skydiving.
B. succeed because Diane's act was a superseding, intervening act.
C. fail because Diane's act did not break the chain of causation.
D. succeed because Diane was an additional perpetrator.

ANALYSIS. Causation issues do not lend themselves particularly well to multiple-choice questions because there are so many factors to discuss, including foreseeability of harm, foreseeability of an intervening act, and the policy implications of finding proximate cause. Nonetheless, when faced with a multiple-choice causation problem, the answers can often guide you through the proper analysis for the problem. One can come to the correct answer almost by process of elimination.

Let's examine **A** first. **A** is incorrect because we rarely allow a victim's actions to break the chain of causation. While you might have initially thought of this like the drag racing case, it is different because Maria was not killed by a standard mishap in skydiving. Rather, affirmative efforts by others led to her death.

B raises a slightly tougher issue. Certainly, if Diane had intentionally knocked Maria on the head, we might be more inclined to shift blame from Arnold to her. But there are no good policy reasons to blame an intervening actor who unintentionally places a victim in harm's way, particularly when that victim would have died anyway. Therefore, **B** is incorrect.

If **B** is incorrect, **C** looks like a possible answer. If Diane's act did not break the chain of causation, Arnold would still be the actual and proximate cause of Maria's death.

Finally, **D** can be eliminated because Diane would ordinarily not be considered an additional perpetrator. Even though her actions gave Maria less time to react, the facts indicate that Maria would have died anyway from Arnold's actions. Accordingly, **C** would be the best answer.

f. Omissions Third-party omissions rarely serve as a superseding, intervening cause. Thus, if a victim is attacked in the streets, and no one comes to her aid, the attacker is still the actual and proximate cause of the victim's injuries or death. This is the case even if a third party was legally required to help. For example, if a parent saw a child being attacked and could have, but failed to, assist the child, the attacker would still be responsible for the assault. The parent may also be responsible, but the parent's omission is not a superseding, intervening cause.

This straightforward principle is reflected in the next question.

QUESTION 7. Surf's up. Annette is swimming at the beach. While she is swimming, she is attacked by Frankie. The lifeguard sees the assault, but does not come to Annette's aid. Annette drowns. When charged with her murder, Frankie claims that the lifeguard's failure to do his duty relieves Frankie of responsibility for the drowning. Frankie's argument will most likely

A. fail because there is no duty to rescue others under U.S. law.
B. fail because the lifeguard's inaction did not constitute a superseding, intervening act.
C. succeed because the lifeguard should have saved Annette.
D. succeed because Frankie was not the proximate cause of Annette's death.

ANALYSIS. This is a fairly easy question, especially in comparison with some of the earlier causation questions. Clearly, Frankie is both the actual and proximate cause of Annette's death. Although the lifeguard may also have some responsibility, his omission did not break the chain of causation. It was still completely foreseeable that Annette would drown and there are no good policy reasons to shift the blame completely from Frankie to the lifeguard.

A is wrong because it incorrectly states the law of omissions in the United States. Although the general rule is that there is no duty to rescue, there are exceptions to that general rule. One of those exceptions is when there is a contractual or statutory duty. A classic situation in which there is a duty to help is when someone is hired as a lifeguard. (See Chapter 3.)

B seems like the better answer. The lifeguard's inaction, although wrong, is unlikely to break the chain of causation. Rather, it would just make both Frankie and the lifeguard responsible for Annette's death. For the reasons that **B** is correct, **C** is wrong. Yes, the lifeguard should have saved Annette. However, failure to do so did not create a superseding, intervening act.

D is also wrong. Not only was Frankie an actual cause of Annette's death, but he is also the proximate cause. Frankie's act led directly to

Annette's death and there was no intervening act that would shift the blame from him. Therefore, **B** is the correct answer.

E. Model Penal Code approach

Few states have adopted a statutory approach for defining causation. Accordingly, the Model Penal Code is not as influential in causation issues as it is in other areas.

Under Model Penal Code §2.03(1)(a), to be guilty of an offense, the defendant's conduct must be the cause-in-fact of the prohibited result. *Cause* is defined as "an antecedent but for which the result in question would not have occurred." As in the common law, if the defendant's acts were a link in the chain of causation, the defendant may be charged with being an "actual cause" of the harm.

However, instead of discussing "proximate cause," Model Penal Code §§2.03(2)(b) and (3)(b) focus on determining whether the defendant was the "legal cause" of the harm. These sections examine the facts of the case to determine whether any other events make it no longer possible to find that the defendant caused the prohibited result with the level of culpability required by the offense. Only if a defendant's actions are not "too remote or accidental in occurrence to have a [just] bearing on the actor's liability or the gravity of his offense" is the defendant the cause of the harm. Thus, if some unusual act or condition makes it so that the defendant did not act with the requisite culpability for the actual result, the defendant is not the cause of the harm.

Thus, consider a situation in which a defendant has accidentally hit a bicyclist with her car when she accidentally ran a stop sign. The bicyclist was only stunned, but could have walked away if he had not been intentionally run over by another car that instantly killed him. If the first motorist were charged with murder, the prosecution's case would fail the Model Penal Code's causation test. The first motorist did not have the intent to murder the victim. Even though under other circumstances it might not be too remote to have a bicyclist killed by a car, the manner in which the killing occurred here — by an intentional killing by another car — make the result too remote and accidental to hold the first motorist culpable. The second motorist, not the first motorist, would be the cause of the bicyclist's death.

Under the common law approach, you would take the same problem and argue that the first motorist was a but for cause of the death. Then, the analysis would focus on whether the motorist was the proximate cause, or whether the second motorist's actions were a superseding, intervening act.

If a defendant is charged with recklessly or negligently causing a particular result, the Model Penal Code holds that causation is not established unless the actual result is within the risk of which the actor was aware or, in the case of negligence, of which she should be aware. However, if the only difference between the actual harm caused and the probable harm that could be anticipated was that the defendant caused less harm than was probable or hurt a different person, the defendant is still considered the legal cause.

QUESTION 8. Double trouble. Jane and Sydney both hate Paula. While Paula sleeps, Jane stabs her and Sydney shoots her. Both Jane and Sydney are charged with murdering Paula. Under the Model Penal Code

A. neither is guilty because there can be only one cause of a criminal harm.
B. both are guilty because they were the actual and legal cause of Paula's death.
C. only Jane is guilty because she acted first against Paula.
D. only Sydney is guilty because her acts broke the chain of causation for Jane.

ANALYSIS. This is also a straightforward question and leads to the same result as the common law test for causation. Both Jane and Sydney inflicted mortal wounds. Their actions were the actual and legal cause of Paula's death. In fact, the Commentary to the Code states that this situation should be treated as one of concurrent sufficient causes. See American Law Institute, Comment to §2.03, at 259. There is no problem with culpability because nothing about the other person's acts made Paula's death too remote or undermined the intent of the defendants to have her die at that time.

Therefore, **A** is wrong. Under the Model Penal Code, there can be multiple, concurrent causes of criminal harm. **C** is wrong because the test is not simply who acted first. Even though Sydney did not shoot until after Jane had stabbed Paula, Sydney still acted with the culpability required for murder.

D is also wrong. Jane is not excused from criminal culpability just because Sydney is also culpable. There was nothing about Paula's death that was so remote or accidental that it would have a just bearing on Jane's culpability.

Accordingly, **B** is the correct answer. Both Jane and Sydney are the legal cause of Paula's death.

F.   Transferred intent

Although labeled as an issue of "transferred intent," the issue of whether the defendant is responsible if she harms someone other than her initial target is actually a causation issue because the focus is still on whether the defendant is responsible for the harm she causes, or only the harm she intends.

Under both common law and the Model Penal Code, the transferred intent doctrine is used to address "bad aim" situations in which the defendant intends to harm *A*, but accidentally injures *B*. Under both approaches, the defendant is still culpable. See Model Penal Code §§2.03(2), (3). For example, if *A* shoots at *X*, but accidentally hits *Y*, *A* is still the cause of *Y*'s death.

However, an issue can arise as to whether a defendant is responsible for the harm she intended or the harm she actually caused. For example, assume that *A* shoots at a person she believes to be her neighbor. Instead, she accidentally shoots the President of the United States. The penalty for shooting the President is far greater than for shooting the neighbor. In some common law jurisdictions, *A* would be responsible for the harm she caused and punished according to the rules for shooting the President. However, under the Model Penal Code, the defendant may only be responsible for the harm she intended because the Model Penal Code requires the trier of fact to determine "whether the harm is too remote or accidental in its occurrence to have a [just] bearing on the . . . gravity of the offense." Model Penal Code §§2.03(2)(b), (3)(b).

Furthermore, under the Model Penal Code, if a defendant causes less harm than she intended, she is only responsible for the harm that resulted. Model Penal Code §211.1(2)(a).

QUESTION 9. **Bad aim.** Tim is furious at his boss, Susan. When Susan tells Tim he is fired, Tim throws a book at her. Just then, Susan's assistant, Marcy, walks in front of Susan. The book hits Marcy in the stomach. Marcy is pregnant and the impact of the blow causes her to lose the baby. The penalty for assaulting an adult is five years in jail; however, the penalty for causing the death of a fetus is 20 years in jail.

Which of the following statements is true?

A. Under the Model Penal Code, Tim is automatically subject to the increased penalty for injuring the fetus.
B. Under the Model Penal Code, Tim is only responsible for harming the mother if the injury to the fetus was too remote to have a just bearing on his liability.
C. Under both the Model Penal Code and common law, Tim is automatically responsible for the harm to the fetus and the mother.
D. Under both the Model Penal Code and common law, Tim is only responsible for the harm to the mother.

ANALYSIS. To answer this question, you must understand how the Model Penal Code analyzes injuries that can be traced back to a defendant's actions, but that the defendant did not specifically intend to cause. **A** is wrong because it incorrectly states the Model Penal Code's position. A defendant is not automatically subject to an increased penalty for the additional harm that he causes. Rather, the trier of fact must also consider "whether the harm is too remote or accidental . . . to have [just] bearing on the actor's liability or gravity of his offense." Thus, **B** is the better answer.

Under common law, Tim may very well have been punished for the additional harm to the unintended victim. Under the doctrine of transferred intent, Tim's intent to injure the mother would transfer to the victim he actually injured, the fetus. However, the Model Penal Code does not automatically find such liability. Thus, **C** is incorrect.

D is also incorrect because both the common law and the Model Penal Code leave open the possibility that Tim will be responsible for the additional harm. Harming the fetus may not be too remote to have just bearing on the defendant's liability, although the defendant may argue that it is unfair to impose the increased penalty. **B** is the best answer.

G. The Closer: Causation for strict liability crimes

As we have seen, causation is a separate element for crimes, although it has a link to the other standard elements of a crime: actus reus and mens rea. Causation traces how far a defendant's actus reus travels toward the actual result in the case and whether any events, conditions, or actions by others along the way break the chain of causation. But causation is also related to mens rea. Under the Model Penal Code, the preference is to punish the defendant for his culpability and, therefore, the focus is much more on the harm the defendant intended or believed she took the risk of causing. Likewise, under the common law and in many states, courts would often be willing to find causation, but might reverse a defendant's conviction for lack of mens rea. This happened, for example, in *People v. Acosta, supra,* when the California court of appeal held that Acosta was the actual and proximate cause of a helicopter crash that killed the pilots, but that the murder conviction needed to be reversed because the accident was so unforeseeable that the court could not find that Acosta acted with the malice ("gross recklessness") required for murder.

One interesting issue that arises is whether causation is necessary for strict liability crimes. The closer illustrates the rule that causation *is* required for all crimes that have a result as an element, even strict liability offenses.

To fully understand this closer, it is helpful for you to study felony murder, which imposes strict liability on felons for any deaths that occur during the course of a felony. (See Chapter 11.) However, even if you haven't yet studied felony murder, you can answer this question as long as you remember that felons are guilty of murder for any deaths that occur during their participation in a felony, even if they don't intend any harm to their victims. All that must be proved is that a felon *caused* the death of the victim.

QUESTION 10. A shocking result.   Barbara is charged with felony murder. Barbara entered a bank and demanded money from the teller. When the teller heard the demand, she pushed the emergency button. Because of a freak electrical storm, the teller was shocked and killed. Is Barbara guilty of the teller's murder?

A. Yes, because a felon is guilty of all deaths occurring during the commission of a felony.

B. Yes, because Barbara's participation in the robbery was the but for cause of the teller's death.

C. No, because Barbara never intended for the teller to be executed.

D. No, because the felon's actions were not the but for and proximate cause of the death.

ANALYSIS.   The rule is that causation is required for all crimes that have a result element, including felony murder. Although mens rea may not be required because felony murder is a type of strict liability offense (see Chapter 11), causation is still required. Accordingly, **A** is incorrect. A felon is only guilty of felony murder if she or a co-felon caused the victim's death. If there is a superseding act of causation, even a felon is not guilty.

B is incorrect because but for cause is not enough. Proximate cause is also required and freak acts of nature are ordinarily seen as independent, intervening acts. **C** is incorrect because it misstates the law of felony murder. All felons are responsible for deaths resulting during the course of a felony, regardless if they are present at the time of the death.

For this question, **D** is the best answer. Although there was but for causation, there was not proximate cause. Even for a strict liability crime like felony murder, there must be causation, as shown by but for and proximate cause.

 # Levenson's Picks

1. Lightning bolts	C
2. Bad aspirin	B
3. Moving target	A

 4. Fiery night   A
 5. A deadly delay   D
 6. The sky's the limit   C
 7. Surf's up   B
 8. Double trouble   B
 9. Bad aim   B
10. A shocking result   D

8

Homicide — An Overview

It isn't right to gloat over the dead.
—Homer's Odyssey

CHAPTER OVERVIEW
A. The actus reus: Killing
B. The mens rea: Preview of things to come
C. The circumstance: Defining a "human being"
D. Suicide versus homicide
E. The Closer: Procedural issues and study tip
✦ Levenson's Picks

The most popular crime in law school is homicide. I can almost guarantee you that someone will die on your criminal law examination. Don't let it be you. Homicide is the one crime you must know well to excel in the typical criminal law course.

Professors love to teach homicide because it challenges students to understand the relationship between modern homicide statutes and common law homicide crimes. Moreover, it is one of the few crimes in which there are gradations of the crime. In other words, not all killings are treated the same. There are murders and manslaughters and accidental killings. Even at common law, there were distinctions made in the type of killing, even though early on all homicides were punishable by death. Now, the distinctions make more difference than ever. While the range of sentence varies by jurisdiction, murder can typically carry a lengthy sentence of 15 years to life in prison. By contrast, manslaughter may result in only a few years of imprisonment. Thus, it is critical to understand the differences in the different kinds of homicide.

Like other crimes, homicide is composed of several elements. These elements are as follows:

Actus reus	=	Killing
Mens rea	=	Depends on the grade of homicide
Circumstances	=	Another human being
Result	=	Death

This chapter takes a close look at all these elements, *except for mens rea*. Because the defendant's mens rea tends to define the type of homicide charged, that issue is dealt with separately in the chapters on murder, manslaughter, negligent homicide, and felony murder.

Before we begin, keep in mind that different jurisdictions define their levels of homicide differently. We study the common terms and concepts all these jurisdictions share. However, to keep you on track, here are some charts of the major jurisdictions and most common approaches.

California Penal Code §§189, 192

Level of Homicide	*Mens Rea Requirement*
First-degree murder	Premeditation or occurring during the commission of certain felonies
Second-degree murder	All other killings with malice
Voluntary manslaughter	Heat of passion killings
Involuntary manslaughter	Killings during an unlawful act not constituting a felony or during a lawful act performed with gross negligence
Vehicular manslaughter	Killings committed with gross negligence or during unlawful operation of a motor vehicle

Pennsylvania Penal Code §§2502-2505

Level of Homicide	*Mens Rea Requirement*
First-degree murder	Intentional
Second-degree murder	Felony murder
Third-degree murder	All other killings with malice
Voluntary manslaughter	Provocation or imperfect self-defense
Causing suicide	Intentionally with duress or deception (felony)
Aiding suicide	Intentionally (misdemeanor)

New York Penal Code §§125.25–125.27

Level of Homicide	Mens Rea Requirement
First-degree murder	Intentionally committed against certain types of victims or while defendant in custody or during escape
Second-degree murder	Intent to kill or felony murder
First-degree manslaughter	Intent to cause serious bodily injury or intent to kill because of extreme emotional disturbance
Second-degree manslaughter	Reckless or intentionally aiding suicide
Negligent homicide	Criminal negligence

A. The actus reus: Killing

The actus reus for homicide is very simple—it is to kill. Let your imagination run wild. There are so many ways to kill another human being. The defendant can stab, shoot, poison, beat, smother, bleed, electrocute (you get the idea!) the victim. The law doesn't really care which method the defendant chooses, if it causes the victim's death.

It is also possible to cause another person's death by an omission. For example, assume that a mother allows her child to starve to death. In this situation, the actus reus for the murder is the failure to feed the child when there was a duty to do so. Remember, however, that there must be a duty by the defendant to provide for or help the victim. As we reviewed in Chapter 3, there is generally no duty to help another person, even if he is faced with extreme harm. However, when there is such a duty, failure to fulfill it may satisfy the actus reus requirement for homicide.

A slightly tougher question that arises is when does death occur? It might surprise you to learn that there is no one answer to this question. It depends on the jurisdiction. Each jurisdiction gets to define when life ends. In most jurisdictions, death occurs when the brain ceases to function. See, e.g., *Barber v. Superior Court*, 147 Cal. App. 3d 1006 (1983); *People v. Eulo*, 63 N.Y.2d 341 (1984). A minority of jurisdictions define death as the moment the victim's heart stops.

One last issue can arise with regard to the actus reus for a homicide. In some jurisdictions, prosecutors need to worry about the "year-and-a-day" rule. Under this common law rule, death must occur within a year and a day of the defendant's acts to constitute a "killing." Therefore, imagine that the defendant strangles the victim, but instead of dying, the victim lies in a coma for more than a year. Under the common law rule, the defendant could not be charged with homicide. Instead, the defendant might be charged with attempted murder. Today, most jurisdictions have abandoned the year-and-a-day requirement. However, it remains in force in federal courts.

The actus reus requirement is not usually the difficult issue on an exam, but it is important not to overlook it. Take a look at the next question to see how an actus reus issue may arise on a homicide problem.

QUESTION 1. Gang killings. Punchy and Mickey are rival gang members. One day, Punchy hears a fellow gang member, Jimmy, say that he plans to kill Mickey at his first opportunity because he heard Mickey was planning to attack him. Punchy knows it's not true but doesn't say anything to Jimmy. As a result, the next day Jimmy goes out and stabs Mickey. If Punchy is charged with murder for Mickey's death, he is

A. guilty because he knew that Jimmy was going to kill Mickey.
B. guilty because he could have prevented Mickey's stabbing.
C. guilty because he is in the same gang as Jimmy.
D. not guilty.

ANALYSIS. At first glance, this question is a little tricky. Your gut instincts may be telling you that Punchy should be guilty of something, but you must force yourself to evaluate the question to determine whether Punchy had the essential elements to be guilty of murder. The first element is actus reus. Did Punchy fulfill the actus reus requirement for the crime? Although Punchy may have been delighted that someone was going to kill Mickey, Punchy is only guilty if he did something, or failed to do something he had a duty to do, that helped cause Mickey's death.

There is no positive act by Punchy that caused Mickey's death. Punchy never encouraged Jimmy and he never physically helped him. There is also no actus reus by omission in this situation. You are given no facts to indicate that Punchy had a duty to warn Mickey or let Jimmy know that it wasn't true that Mickey was going to attack him. Therefore, Punchy's failure to warn Mickey is not an actus reus for the crime. Thus, as we see when we evaluate the answer options, Punchy may not be a good guy, but he is unlikely to be legally responsible for Mickey's death.

By the way, in evaluating this problem, we are assuming that there are no separate anti-gang laws that would impose criminal responsibility and that there was no conspiracy among the gang members to have Mickey killed. Rather, we are evaluating the question from the perspective of whether Punchy has done an act that directly caused Mickey's death.

Many students jump at **A** because their personal morality tells them that Punchy should have done something to stop the killing. However, **A** incorrectly assumes that Punchy is guilty so long as he has the intent for the victim to die. It completely ignores the fact that Punchy hasn't done anything that caused Mickey's death. For similar reasons, **B** is an incorrect answer. Punchy was under no duty to prevent the stabbing.

A full understanding of **C** requires that you learn about co-conspirator and accomplice liability (see Chapters 14 and 15 *infra*); however, it too is incorrect. Generally, mere membership in a gang, without a specific anti-gang statute, is insufficient to make gang members criminally responsible for each other's criminal acts.

Therefore, **D** is the correct answer. Punchy lacked the actus reus for Mickey's murder.

B.   The mens rea: Preview of things to come

As detailed in the next two chapters, most jurisdictions label the type of homicide committed by the defendant by the level of intent the defendant had at the time of the killing. Thus, purposeful killings are considered to be murder, whereas negligent killings are usually classified as manslaughter or negligent homicide.

The key common law mens rea terms to understand in homicide law are *malice, premeditation, provocation,* and *criminal negligence.* As with other terms derived from common law, it is important to keep in mind that these terms may have legal meanings that are quite different from their ordinary meanings. For example, murder is legally defined as a killing committed with "malice aforethought." The term *aforethought* is actually superfluous. All it suggests is that the defendant must have given some thought to the harm he would cause another before he killed. However, the key word in the phrase is *malice.* Malice refers to killings committed with callous disregard of human life. It may be proven by direct or circumstantial evidence. It also encapsulates several different types of killings.

The term *malice* can describe any of the following mindsets of the defendant:

- intent to kill the victim;
- intent to cause grave bodily harm to the victim; or
- gross indifference to the risk of death or great bodily harm to the victim.

Moreover, as discussed in Chapter 11, under the felony-murder doctrine, malice is artificially provided by the fact that the death occurred during the commission of a felony.

The confusing thing about murder law is that judges and statutes often use a variety of terms to describe the malice required for murder. For example, at common law, a synonym for malice was a killing committed with an "abandoned and malignant heart." Some statutes still retain this language. Or they refer to a "depraved heart" killing. All of these phrases are attempts to describe a heinous and callous killing.

Premeditation is also a term of art associated with homicide law. As discussed in Chapter 9, most jurisdictions classify premeditated killing as the most serious type of homicide — that is, first-degree murder. Yet, there is no one accepted definition of premeditation. In some jurisdictions, such as federal court, premeditation only refers to a purposeful killing. No particular amount of time is needed to form the purpose to kill, nor do the circumstances of the killing need to suggest that the defendant had a well-thought-out plan to kill. Yet, other jurisdictions, such as California, have more detailed requirements for premeditation. Those courts are looking for a "preconceived plan" that demonstrates by manner, motive, or planning that the defendant coolly formed the intent to kill.

Provocation is another legal term used in discussing a particular type of homicide, namely manslaughters committed in the "heat of passion." Chapter 10 reviews in detail these types of homicides. Yet, as a preview, it is important to understand that provocation is a doctrine that relates to an intentional killing that is not formed in a cool, deliberative process like premeditation. Rather, it is a hot-headed reaction to acts that caused the defendant to kill. If that provocation was legally sufficient, the defendant's intentional killing is not seen as it ordinarily would be — that is, as a murder. Rather, the defendant may be guilty of a lower level of homicide, such as voluntary manslaughter.

Finally, there is a category of negligent homicides, sometimes known as "involuntary manslaughter," that includes accidental killings for which the defendant is still morally culpable. Recall that the minimum standard for criminal culpability is ordinarily recklessness. Yet, because the harm is so serious in a homicide case, the law dips down to the level of criminal or "gross" negligence. As discussed in Chapter 10, there are some accidental deaths that are so preventable and troublesome that we hold the perpetrator criminally responsible.

You will be tested in more detail on these concepts in later chapters. Those chapters also focus on the Model Penal Code approach that does not distinguish between degrees of murder and uses Model Penal Code culpability terminology to distinguish among murder, manslaughter, and negligent homicide.

Model Penal Code §§210.0 et seq. and Non-Degree States

Level of Homicide	Mens Rea Requirement
Murder	Purposely, knowingly, or acting with grossly reckless regard for human life
Manslaughter	Recklessly or under extreme emotional disturbance
Negligent homicide	Negligently
Causing or aiding suicide	Purposely with force, duress, or deception

Later chapters distinguish in detail the common law approach from the Model Penal Code approach. However, for purposes of this introductory chapter, see if you have the basic common law concept of malice and premeditation under your belt.

QUESTION 2. **The mad scientist.** Marcus lives next to Jerry, the neighborhood "mad scientist." Jerry is always fooling around with different experiments and creating obnoxious odors and noises in the neighborhood. Marcus is determined to drive Jerry out of the neighborhood so that everyone else can be rid of his disturbances. Therefore, he wanders over to Jerry's yard when Jerry is not home and mixes up his own surprise for Jerry. In the container that is marked "H2O" for water, Marcus substitutes nitroglycerin, an extremely explosive compound. Sure enough, Jerry comes home from his job as a convenience store clerk and starts again with his home experiments. Soon thereafter, the neighbors hear a loud boom. Not knowing about the switch, Jerry has accidentally mixed the nitroglycerin into his other compound and caused a huge explosion that kills him instantly. Marcus is charged with Jerry's death.

A. Marcus is guilty of murder because he negligently caused Jerry's death.

B. Marcus is guilty of murder because he acted with callous disregard for Jerry's life.

C. Marcus is not guilty of murder because he did not premeditate Jerry's killing.

D. Marcus is not guilty of murder because he did not use a dangerous weapon to kill Jerry.

ANALYSIS.   Don't forget, this is just a preview of some of the issues covered in Chapters 9 and 10. However, it is never too early to develop your instincts as to the meaning of common law terms associated with homicide. This question tests your understanding of several of the basic terms, including premeditation, criminal negligence, and malice.

Let's start with **A**. Even without a detailed understanding of homicide law, the one thing you need to be very clear on is that a negligent killing will not be murder. By definition, murder requires malice. Negligence means that the defendant did not consider the risk that he would hurt someone, but a reasonable person would have. If, as is the case here, the defendant actually knows the risks of his actions and takes those risks anyway, he has not acted negligently. More likely, he has acted intentionally or recklessly. While either of those intents may be sufficient for malice, negligence is not. Therefore, **A** is an incorrect answer.

Skip **B** for a moment and move to **C**. They say that a "little bit of knowledge is a dangerous thing." That is particularly true in law school. While it is true that certain types of murder (namely, first-degree murder) require premeditation, other types of murder do not require premeditation. They only require malice. Therefore, **C** is wrong for two reasons. First, it suggests that premeditation is always required for any type of murder conviction. That is incorrect. Second, it suggests that Marcus's actions would not be sufficient for premeditation. They might be. Remember what Marcus did. He had a plan. He snuck into his neighbor's yard and intentionally put nitroglycerin in the water container. He had a motive to kill — he found his neighbor to be obnoxious. And, he chose a manner of killing that had a high possibility of success. Thus, he may very well have acted with premeditation. In that case, Marcus would be guilty of murder and **C** is factually wrong as well.

Now, return to **B** as an answer. Some students would skip over this answer because it doesn't have the magic word malice in it. Yet, your professor will often do what the courts do. He will substitute one of the common phrases used to describe malice to see if you understand what the underlying mens rea standard is for murder. As we discussed, malice may refer to a callous disregard for human life. It is not always a premeditated or intentional killing. At minimum, Marcus acted in callous disregard of Jerry's life. This is a form of malice and Marcus could therefore be guilty of murder. Therefore, **B** is the correct answer.

How about **D**? **D** is the red herring. Harking back to our discussion on actus reus, there are many ways a defendant can kill another person. Sometimes, the defendant uses a dangerous weapon, such as a gun or knife. However, murder does not require that a dangerous weapon be used so long as the instrument the defendant chooses to kill gets the job done. It is not that unusual, therefore, to have killings committed with everyday items such as frying pans or baseball bats. **D** is wrong because it suggests that unless a killing is done with a weapon that is by its nature dangerous, it is not murder.[1]

---

1. Don't get tripped up here by the "dangerous instrumentality" doctrine that we discuss in Chapter 10.

C.   The circumstance: Defining a "human being"

Not every killing, no matter how heinous, is a homicide. Rather, homicide requires the killing of another human being. Thus, if your despicable neighbor viciously kills your favorite pet, Fido, you might be very upset but you couldn't press charges for homicide.

Pet killings are not the real problem in this area. Rather, the question sometimes arises as to whether a fetus should be considered a human being. For example, what if a man kicks a pregnant woman and the woman survives, but the fetus dies? Is the man guilty of homicide? Or what if a pregnant woman intentionally does not receive needed medical care and thereby causes the death of her own fetus? Can she be charged with homicide?

Your first instinct might be that a fetus cannot be considered a human being because abortion is permitted in this country. However, a fetus may be a human being for one purpose under the law, but not for another. Thus, a jurisdiction may decide that outside of the abortion scenario a fetus is a human being. See *Keeler v. Superior Court*, 470 P.2d 617 (Cal. 1970) (fetus not considered a human being unless the laws of the jurisdiction expressly state otherwise). In designating a fetus as a human being, the law need not require that the prosecution prove the fetus was viable. See *People v. Davis*, 872 P.2d 591 (Cal. 1994) (viability not element of California fetal murder; fetus only need be beyond the eight-week embryonic stage). Moreover, it need not be proved that the fetus died inside the mother as a result of the defendant's acts. Injuries inflicted upon a child while in the mother's womb may be the basis for a homicide charge if the child is then born alive but subsequently dies as a result of the in utero injuries. *Williams v. State*, 561 A.2d 216 (Md. 1989).

Ordinarily, once the law has designated someone as a human being, it doesn't matter if the victim is old, young, or related to the defendant. However, some jurisdictions use special terms to describe certain types of homicides. For example, the killing of a fetus may be referred to as *feticide*. Similarly, killing a young child is often called *infanticide* and killing one's parents is referred to as *patricide*. All these are simply examples of homicide.

> **QUESTION 3. The Addams family.** Natasha and Gomez Addams have been married for several years. However, their relationship has not been a happy one. They frequently fight with each other. One day, Natasha tells Gomez she is four months pregnant. Gomez has just lost his job and isn't thrilled with the news. He tells her to have an abortion, but Natasha refuses. Gomez then kicks Natasha in the abdomen. Natasha agrees she will get an abortion, but before she does, the fetus dies from the injuries inflicted by Gomez. In their jurisdiction, a fetus is considered a human

being once it is beyond the eight-week embryonic stage. Can Gomez
be charged with murder?

A. No, because the fetus was going to be aborted anyway.
B. No, because there was no proof that the fetus was viable.
C. Yes, because a fetus is always considered a human being under the law.
D. Yes, because the fetus was beyond the eight-week embryonic stage.
E. No, because the fetus was never born alive.

ANALYSIS. First, a warning: Criminal law hypotheticals are often very
troubling, especially in the homicide area. The questions frequently include
scenarios in which people do terrible things to each other, including to
children. It is important to remain objective and analytical when you evaluate
a question. Just like in other areas, analyze each response to determine
whether it correctly states the legal standard and applies it to the facts of that
question.

In this question, the key issue is whether the fetus was legally considered
a human being at the time of Gomez's kick. Don't forget, this is controlled
by state law. In this state, the law defines any fetus beyond the eight-week
embryonic stage as a human being, regardless of whether the mother could
have legally aborted the fetus. Therefore, **A** is wrong. The fact that the
mother could have legally aborted the fetus does not mean that another
person, including the father, has the right to terminate the fetus's life.

B is also wrong because the law does not require proof that the fetus be
viable to be considered a human being for purposes of the murder law. As in
People v. Davis, 872 P.2d 591 (Cal. 1994), the legislature can define the fetus
as a human being even before the fetus is viable.

C looks good at first but it has one of the words that are always
dangerous in a multiple-choice exam. It states that a fetus is "always"
considered a human being under the law. As we have seen, that is not always
true. It depends on the jurisdiction. Beware of choosing answers that are too
far-sweeping or absolute.

D is the better answer because it fits the definition of a human being in
this jurisdiction. Once the fetus is beyond eight weeks, regardless of whether
it is viable, it is considered a human being. In this jurisdiction, it doesn't
matter whether the fetus was ever born alive. Therefore, **E** is a wrong answer.

D. Suicide versus homicide

One issue that can arise in homicide law is whether it is a crime to help
another person take his life. The person who kills himself has committed
suicide. Even if there is a law against suicide, that person is not around to

prosecute. Therefore, the authorities often look to prosecute the person who may have assisted in the suicide.

Assisting a suicide is still illegal in many jurisdictions. The jurisdictions that prohibit it may classify the crime as assisting a suicide or simply refer to it as a form of homicide. Consent is not a defense to the crime of homicide. Therefore, the defendant cannot claim that he was free to take the victim's life.

In recent years, the most famous defendant charged with illegally assisting a suicide is Dr. Kevorkian. See *People v. Kevorkian*, 205 Mich. App. 180 (1994). At his patients' request, Dr. Kevorkian would use a number of methods, including carbon monoxide poisoning, to help end the terminally ill patients' lives. Even though he was arguably following the patients' wishes, he was still guilty of homicide and/or assisted suicide.

In the last ten years, there have been legal challenges to state laws prohibiting physician-assisted suicide. However, the Supreme Court has refused to strike down these laws. Rather, in *Washington v. Glucksberg*, 521 U.S. 702 (1997), the Court held that it is up to the states to decide whether physician-assisted suicides will be permitted. Where it is permitted, there are typically many procedural protections to ensure that the patient is indeed terminally ill and consents to the procedure.

QUESTION 4. Goodbye, dear friend. Harry and Sally have been the best of friends for years. Tragically, Harry has developed a fatal disease and has been told by his doctors that he has only six months to live. He expects that his condition will continue to deteriorate during that six months and that when he finally dies, he will be incapable of caring for himself and in constant pain. Sally cannot stand to see her friend's suffering. Therefore, she agrees to help with Harry's plan to "end it all." At Harry's request, she makes him a chocolate milkshake (his favorite) that is spiked with enough sedatives to kill him. Sally leaves it for Harry near his bed. Harry thanks her, says goodbye, and drinks the shake. He dies peacefully in five minutes. Assuming the law in that jurisdiction prohibits assisting a suicide, which of the following is true?

A. Harry may be charged with suicide and Sally with assisting his suicide.
B. Neither Harry nor Sally may be charged with suicide because Harry voluntarily decided to end his life.
C. Harry may have been guilty of suicide, but Sally is not guilty of a crime because she did not administer the poison to Harry.
D. Sally is not guilty because Harry was guaranteed the constitutional right to end his life in a dignified manner.
E. Sally may be charged with assisting Harry's suicide.

ANALYSIS. Be careful with problems like this not to lapse in deciding what you think the law *should* be. Rather, you must answer the question according to the state of the law now.

At first, **A** looks like a good answer until you pause and realize that Harry is not around to be charged with any crime. Even if he committed suicide, he cannot be charged because he is deceased. Therefore, **A** is only half right. By contrast, **B** is all wrong. Unless the problem tells you so, you cannot assume that it is legal to help someone voluntarily end his life. Don't forget, consent is not a defense to homicide.

C is a little trickier. You will understand this question better after we discuss accomplice liability in Chapter 14. However, it is important in the meantime to understand that any act that helps another commit a crime, if it is done with the purpose for the crime to be completed, will also make the person who helps guilty of the crime. Therefore, it doesn't matter whether Sally physically administered any poison to Harry. She purposely helped him end his life and therefore may be guilty of assisting a suicide.

D is wrong because the Supreme Court has never held that there is a constitutional right to end one's life. See *Washington v. Glucksberg, supra*. Therefore, Sally may be charged with assisting a suicide and **E** would be the correct answer, unless that jurisdiction has specifically held that offering poison is insufficient to help another person with suicide.

E.   The Closer: Procedural issues and study tip

You might be wondering, Why does my professor spend so much time on homicide law and not as much time on other crimes? In fact, in some criminal law courses, the *only* crime covered during the semester is homicide. There are at least two reasons why your professor may focus so much on homicide law. First, it is an area of criminal law in which the offenses are "graded." In other words, not all homicides are treated the same under the law, nor do they all have the same legal requirements. Rather, there are more serious and less serious homicides. You will learn what factors are used to determine which homicides are considered the most serious and punished accordingly. Second, homicide law is an excellent example of an area where modern statutes often still rely on common law terms to delineate the type of homicide. Thus, a typical murder statute may simply state that a "killing with malice is murder." In order to understand malice, the professor can take you through the wonderful world of common law murder.

You also need to keep in mind some of the procedural aspects of homicide law. As you learn in later chapters, there may be several different theories by which a defendant is guilty of a homicide. For example, a defendant who kills a victim during a bank robbery may be guilty of murder either because he acted with malice or because the law artificially assigns him as acting with malice because the death occurred during the commission of a felony. Prosecutors may charge a defendant in the alternative with murder and felony murder. Likewise, the court may give alternative jury instructions by which a jury may find the defendant guilty of murder.

In analyzing homicide problems, I suggest that you work methodically through the various levels of homicide, from most serious to least serious. By doing so, you will train yourself to consider all arguments in favor and against each level. If you just jump at the type of homicide you first think the situation describes, you will often miss arguments in favor of other levels of homicide.

Finally, keep in mind that all the legal standards you will study are attempts by the court to guide the discretion of the jury. In real life, jurors are free to disregard the formal legal distinctions and vote by instinct. Thus, you will likely read cases in your criminal law class in which the jury's verdict does not comport with your academic understanding of how the law *should* work. However, you should still discipline yourself to analyze the case correctly and then try to understand why the jury may have rejected the formal legal principles.

QUESTION 5. The blundering kidnapper. Charles decides to kidnap his high school teacher, and hold her for ransom. The victim was always his favorite teacher. In fact, she is everyone's favorite teacher, so he is fairly sure he can secure a high ransom for her return. Charles intends to return the teacher unharmed as soon as he gets the money he needs to cover some drug debts. A week after the kidnapping, the police find the victim dead in the trunk of Charles's car. In charging Charles with homicide

A. prosecutors cannot charge Charles with murder because it is clear he did not act with malice.

B. prosecutors can charge Charles with murder and manslaughter for the death of his teacher.

C. prosecutors can charge Charles with murder if there is malice or felony murder.

D. prosecutors cannot charge Charles with murder because he did not premeditate his victim's death.

ANALYSIS. This problem is a good preview of the upcoming chapters. Once again, don't presume your everyday understanding of key words will get you through a homicide problem. You must know exactly what terms like malice, premeditation, murder, and manslaughter mean. Also, you need to keep in mind that the prosecutor may use alternative theories to convict a defendant.

If you picked **A**, it is probably because you misunderstand the principle of malice. As discussed in this chapter, a defendant can act with malice even though he adores his victim. Malice is a term of art that refers to intentional killings or those done with a certain level of recklessness. **A**, therefore, is a wrong answer because it is absolutely possible that Charles acted with malice.

B is wrong for procedural reasons. A defendant is not charged with both murder and manslaughter. Rather, a defendant will typically be charged with the more serious offense and the defense may ask for jury instructions on a lesser-included offense. Thus, Charles would be charged with murder. However, if the evidence during trial could support a manslaughter instruction, the court would be free to instruct the jury on the lesser-included offense of manslaughter.

If you picked **D**, it is because you assume you know a lot more about criminal law than you probably do at this point. Murder does not necessarily require premeditation. Only certain types of murders, that is first-degree murder, require premeditation. Otherwise, all that murder requires is malice. Accordingly, **D** is wrong because it incorrectly states the law of murder.

C is the correct answer. Prosecutors can charge Charles with murder and use various theories, including felony murder, to argue why he is guilty. In this scenario, Charles may be guilty of murder if he acted with reckless indifference to his victim's life, or if her death occurred during the commission of the felony of kidnapping.

As you can see, it is time to jump into the details. Accordingly, the next three chapters methodically walk you through the law of murder, manslaughter, felony murder, and misdemeanor manslaughter.

 # Levenson's Picks

1. Gang killings	**E**
2. The mad scientist	**B**
3. The Addams family	**D**
4. Goodbye, dear friend	**E**
5. The blundering kidnapper	**C**

9

Homicide — Murder

Murder, she wrote . . .

CHAPTER OVERVIEW
A. Definition of malice
B. Types of malice
    1. Intent to kill
    2. Intent to cause serious bodily harm
    3. Extreme recklessness
C. First-degree murder
    1. Premeditated murder
    2. Murder committed by specific statutory means
    3. First-degree felony murder
D. Second-degree murder
    1. Catch-all murder
    2. Second-degree felony murder
E. Model Penal Code approach to murder
F. The Closer: Delighted afterthoughts
✦ Levenson's Picks

From the previous chapter, you know that homicides are broken down into different types of killings. The more serious homicides are referred to as murder; the less serious receive the label of manslaughter or negligent homicide. While the victim is equally dead in either case, the defendant's culpability may differ. Jurisdictions are free to choose those factors by which they will distinguish categories of homicide. The one feature that classically distinguishes murder from other types of killings is "malice." In fact, murder is typically defined as "the unlawful killing of another human being with malice aforethought."

That sounds like an easy rule, but the devil is in the details. Malice has a myriad of definitions. At common law, phrases like "depraved heart" or "malignant heart" were used to describe a defendant who acted with malice. Although graphic, these terms do little to help the modern criminal law practitioner understand what malice really means. Therefore, it is important to get beyond the common law labels to a deeper understanding of the requirement of malice. This chapter takes you down the path of murder to a clearer understanding of today's concept of malice.

As you go through this chapter, keep in mind that words that are used in nonlegal discussions can have distinct meanings in homicide law. For example, as this chapter discusses, not every defendant who intentionally kills acts with premeditation. Intent to kill and premeditation are separate legal standards.

Most of this chapter focuses on common law approaches to homicide. However, Section E focuses on the Model Penal Code approach. The Model Penal Code does not recognize degrees of murder. Rather, as set forth in the chart in Chapter 8, the Model Penal Code recognizes all killings that are done purposely, knowingly, or with extreme indifference to human life as murder. See Model Penal Code §210.0. Differences in culpability can be addressed by the court at sentencing.

This chapter also uses the Model Penal Code culpability vocabulary you learned in Chapter 3 to help you understand the meaning of some common law terms. For example, one modern definition of malice includes a type of *recklessness*, a term we studied at length in that earlier chapter.

Finally, felony murder is an important topic when discussing homicide law. It is an alternative approach for holding defendants responsible for murder without having to prove malice. Because of its scope, felony murder has earned its own chapter in this book (Chapter 11). This initial chapter on murder law is devoted instead to approaches to proving murder that do not rely on felony-murder principles.

A.   Definition of malice

As we've been discussing, murder is ordinarily defined as a killing done with malice. The $64,000 question is: What is malice? Is it different from "malice aforethought"? Exactly what does a "depraved and malignant heart" look like and how are we supposed to know, since we chose law school instead of medical school?

Don't be thrown off by the colorful language used to describe malice. The language is a remnant of the past—repeated attempts by courts to describe the type of mindset of a person who intentionally or callously causes the death of another person. In fact, the common law language is often awkward and redundant. In truth, "malice aforethought" and "malice" mean the exact same thing. Likewise, "depraved heart" means the same as "malignant and uncaring heart." The words are a search for a way to describe the mindset of someone who uncaringly or intentionally kills another person.

Before we try to define malice in more detail, let's start by describing what it is not. Malice is not what you might have thought before you went to law school. Malice does *not* mean that the defendant killed the victim out of spite or because she harbored ill will toward the victim. A person may murder her best friend by reckless behavior. An adoring and dedicated spouse might murder his ailing wife because she is severely ill and wants to be freed from her misery. In other words, the motive for a murder need not be malevolent. Malice generally focuses on the intent of the defendant.

In most jurisdictions, malice can be demonstrated by any of the following:

1. Intent to kill
2. Intent to cause serious (grave) bodily harm
3. Callous or wanton disregard for human life (i.e., gross recklessness)
4. Killing during the commission of a felony (felony murder)[1]

B. Types of malice

1. Intent to kill

The first type of malice—intent to kill—is known as "express malice" and is fairly self-explanatory. Your job is to use the evidence regarding the killing to determine whether the defendant purposely killed her victim. You can use circumstantial or direct evidence to make that determination. Direct evidence is rare in a homicide case. It would entail an eyewitness's account, the defendant's admission that she committed the killing, or a videotape of the incident. More frequently, prosecutors must make their case from circumstantial evidence. Circumstantial evidence is all the other evidence regarding the killing that is used to prove the case. Contrary to what you might have seen on television or in the movies, circumstantial evidence is every bit as valuable as direct evidence. Most cases are proved with circumstantial evidence. In order to prove that the defendant had intent to kill, the prosecution could rely on circumstantial

---

1. Discussed in detail in Chapter 11.

evidence of the defendant's motive to kill, her use of a dangerous weapon to commit the killing, and her bragging about the killing after she committed it.

The best way to understand each type of malice is to see it in action. Therefore, try the following problem and how it defines malice.

QUESTION 1. Bad sport. Andre hates to lose. For the last five years, he has enjoyed the spotlight as the world's greatest chess player and a wonderful humanitarian and philanthropist. However, there is a new chess competitor coming up the ranks quickly. The new whiz kid is Nicolai. He is now the darling of the chess world and he has been bragging that he is better and smarter than Andre. Andre tells a friend that Nicolai's days are numbered. The next day, he shoots Nicolai in the head during a tournament. As Nicolai collapses, Andre simply smiles and says, "check-mate, game over." Andre is charged with murder. He claims that he did not act with malice. He is likely to be found

A. guilty because he had the intent to kill Nicolai.

B. guilty because he had a motive to kill Nicolai.

C. not guilty because the prosecution's case is based on circumstantial evidence.

D. not guilty because Andre is a man with a good and generous heart.

ANALYSIS. Andre has been charged with murder. Therefore, the government must prove malice. The first way to prove malice is by proving intent to kill. As an exercise, look at this problem to determine what evidence, direct or circumstantial, might be used to prove an intent to kill. It seems obvious, doesn't it? Shooting another person in the head is a darn good way of demonstrating intent to kill. Moreover, we know in this problem that Andre had a strong motive for killing Nicolai. Although the prosecution is not required to prove motive to prove a homicide case, motive is often helpful in proving the defendant's intent to kill. Even Andre's words after the shooting tend to show that he killed Nicolai intentionally, and not by accident. With this analysis of the problem in mind, let's look at the options for answers.

A seems right on the nose, but we can't be sure until we evaluate the other possible answers. Start with **B**. B is a wrong answer because it only focuses on Andre's motive. While motive may be used to prove intent to kill, the key issue in deciding whether Andre acted with malice is whether he had intent to kill. Therefore, **A** is a better answer than **B**, even though motive would be one factor in deciding whether Andre had intent to kill.

C is wrong because it suggests that the prosecution cannot succeed in proving malice with circumstantial evidence. As we know, that is a popular, but false, perception of the law. Circumstantial evidence can be sufficient to prove malice, as this question demonstrates. Although Andre never states, "I intend to kill you," his actions and words clearly demonstrate that intent.

If you picked **D**, it is probably because you are stuck on an old common law definition of malice as a killing done with a "depraved and malignant heart." However, that historical definition is misleading. Even a person who is generally good and generous can act with malice if he intentionally kills another person. Let's assume that Andre is nice to everyone else in the world. If he intentionally killed Nicolai, he has acted with malice. Therefore, **D** is a wrong answer.

The best answer turns out to be **A**. Sometimes the most straightforward answer is the correct answer for multiple-choice tests. If you know your first definition of malice — that is, intent to kill — this problem should have given you little trouble.

2. Intent to cause serious bodily harm

A second way to prove malice is to prove that the defendant acted with intent to cause serious (or grave) bodily harm to the victim. While the defendant may not have intended to kill the victim, the defendant intended to injure the victim in a manner that could easily lead to the victim's death. Consider, for example, a situation in which the defendant shoots an arrow at the victim's shoulder. The defendant doesn't intend to kill the victim, only to incapacitate her. As it turns out, defendant is not a great shot and the arrow goes straight into the victim's heart. For purposes of murder law, the defendant has acted with malice even though he did not intend to kill the victim. It is sufficient if he intended to cause serious bodily harm.

Test your understanding of this second type of malice with the following question.

QUESTION 2. The enforcer. Bruno works as a collector for the local mafia. He has been given the assignment to collect on a loan made to Mr. Brando. Unfortunately for Brando, he doesn't have the cash that Bruno wants. As a result, Bruno slams Brando against a wall, gives Brando a few strong punches to the gut, and then walks away while saying, "next time, you'll remember to pay on time." Brando staggers home. A few days later, he dies of a ruptured spleen caused by Bruno's blows. Is Bruno guilty of murder?

A. No, because he never intended to kill Brando, as evidenced by the fact that Bruno told Brando that he would be collecting from him in the future.

B. No, because a punch to the stomach is not necessarily a fatal blow.

C. No, because the killing was not premeditated.

D. Yes, because he acted with malice.

E. Yes, because he intended to kill Brando.

ANALYSIS.   You'll be fine with this question so long as you remember that there is more than one way to prove malice. Prosecutors are not required to prove that the defendant intended to kill. Rather, it is sufficient to prove that the defendant intended to cause serious bodily harm.

A sounds like the most complete answer, but it is actually wrong. While Bruno didn't intend to kill, he may still be guilty of murder. As long as Bruno intended to cause serious bodily harm, he acted with malice. For similar reasons, **B** is also a wrong answer. **B** suggests that unless Bruno wanted his blow to be fatal, he cannot be guilty of murder. In fact, that is not true. Malice includes situations in which the defendant only intends to harm his victim, but the victim dies instead.

As for **C**, we will learn about premeditation as it relates to first-degree murder. However, it is *not* a basic requirement for all murders. Rather, a defendant may act with malice even if he did not plan in advance to kill the victim. It is enough if the defendant intended to gravely harm the victim or was callously indifferent to the fact that he might severely injure the victim.

Skip **D** for a moment and move to **E**. At first, **E** seems correct because if Bruno intended to kill Brando, he would be guilty of murder. However, the answer is wrong because it doesn't reflect the facts as stated in the question. We know that Bruno did not intend to kill Brando because he believes there will be a next time when Brando will have to pay. You need to pick the answer that not only reflects a correct statement of the law, but also accurately reflects the facts of the question.

D is the right answer. Bruno has acted with implied malice because even though he did not intend to kill Brando, he still intended to cause serious bodily injury. That intent is enough to prove malice and, therefore, murder.

3. Extreme recklessness

There is yet another state of mind that qualifies as malice under murder law. At common law, phrases like "depraved heart" and "abandoned and malignant heart" were used to describe a category of malice. It is the state of mind of a defendant who demonstrates extreme indifference to the value of human life. In some jurisdictions, this type of extreme recklessness is referred to as *gross recklessness*. In other jurisdictions, the term *implied malice* is used for this type of malice.

To demonstrate that a defendant acted with extreme recklessness, the prosecution must show two things: (1) the defendant realized that her conduct posed a risk to human life; (2) the defendant's recklessness was particularly extreme or "gross." A simple example would be a defendant who drives his car down a crowded sidewalk. The defendant may not intend to kill or even seriously injure the pedestrians, but he is certainly showing an extreme disregard for human life.

Here are a couple of problems that provide more examples of this type of malice and murder.

QUESTION 3. Bad dog. Brian owns a pitbull named "Killer." Brian received Killer as a gift from his parents. He has no idea why his parents named the dog "Killer," but Brian thinks it is a funny name for such a wonderful, gentle pet. Killer has always been very tame with Brian. At most, he has barked at the postal carrier, but Killer is usually very well tempered. One day, Brian takes Killer to his local playground and lets him run loose among the small children. When one of the children, little Sammy, decides to pet Killer, the dog suddenly turns on Sammy and tears him to shreds. Brian is charged with murder.

A. Brian is guilty of murder because he should have known Killer was a dangerous dog.

B. Brian is guilty of murder because he knew his dog was likely to kill.

C. Brian is guilty of murder if he realized that Killer was a dangerous dog.

D. Brian is guilty of murder because he is strictly liable for the acts of his dog.

E. Brian is not guilty because he did not command the dog to kill the child.

ANALYSIS. Hopefully, you didn't fall into the trap of thinking that just because a terrible thing has happened, the defendant is automatically guilty of murder. You must analyze the defendant's state of mind to determine whether there is malice. From the fact pattern, it is clear that Brian didn't intend for his dog to kill or maul the young child. Therefore, he lacks the first two types of malice: intent to kill or intent to cause serious bodily harm. However, if Brian was aware the dog posed a serious risk, and he callously took that risk, he may still have implied malice by acting with gross recklessness. Keep these principles in mind as we evaluate each of the possible answers.

A is wrong because the standard for malice is not that the defendant "should have known" that his dog was dangerous, but that "he did know and took the risk." "Should have known" is the language of negligence, not recklessness. Recklessness requires that the defendant actually realize that he is taking risks that could harm another person. As we see in Chapter 10, gross negligence may be enough for some types of manslaughter, but it is not enough to prove malice for murder. Therefore, even if Brian should have known the dog was dangerous (although it is hard from the facts to even make that conclusion), he is still not guilty of murder.

B correctly states the right standard for a type of malice, but it doesn't accurately analyze what happened in the facts of this question. Did Brian know his dog was likely to kill? All the facts indicate that Brian sincerely believed that he had a wonderful, gentle dog. If he honestly believed that, he did not realize that the dog posed a danger to other people. Therefore, it cannot be said that he knowingly acted in callous disregard for human life. Once again, he may be a bit clueless. However, being naïve is not the same as acting with malice.

C focuses on what is really important for this question. The issue is whether Brian realized that Killer was a dangerous dog. If he did, there may be an argument for gross recklessness. If he didn't, he didn't act with malice. **C** is phrased in a manner that states "if he realized," then he would be guilty of murder. That is a true statement. So, even though **C** doesn't initially look like the right answer because it doesn't conclude what Brian's actual state of mind was, it is a correct statement. However, before selecting it, let's discuss the other two possible answers.

D is way off base, but for reasons that you should understand. *There is no such thing as a strict liability homicide,* except in cases of felony murder, which are not suggested in this problem. The lowest mens rea level for any homicide is criminal negligence. Due to the severity of the crime, the law does not find people guilty of homicide unless they or a reasonable person would have realized the risk to human life. There may be strict liability for other types of crimes, but not for homicide.

E is also incorrect. If Brian knew that the dog posed a danger, it wouldn't matter whether he ordered the dog to attack or not. Malice can also be demonstrated by an omission, such as failing to keep your dog from harming another person. Brian is not guilty of murder, but not because he didn't command the dog to attack. He is not guilty of murder because he didn't realize that Killer was a dangerous dog.

Therefore, **C** is the correct answer. In order to have malice, Brian needed to at least realize the risk that his dog would seriously hurt or kill someone. If he realizes that risk, he has malice and is guilty of murder; if he doesn't realize that risk, he is not guilty of murder.

QUESTION 4. Russian roulette. Bobby and Molly Malone decide to play a friendly game of Russian roulette. They play the game by placing one bullet in a five-chambered gun and spinning the cylinder. Then, they take turns pointing the gun at their temples, pulling the trigger, and seeing if the gun goes off. Bobby goes first. He spins the cylinder, pulls the trigger, but nothing happens. Molly then takes her turn. She spins the cylinder again. This time, the gun fires. Molly loses. She is killed instantly by the bullet and Bobby is charged with murder.

A. Bobby is guilty of murder because his participation in the game showed extreme disregard for human life.

B. Bobby is not guilty of murder because he didn't intend for Molly to die.

C. Bobby is guilty of murder because he should have known Molly might die.

D. Bobby is not guilty of murder because he couldn't know for sure whether the gun would fire.

E. Bobby is not guilty of murder because Molly consented to playing the dangerous game.

ANALYSIS. Here we go again. The goal here is to determine whether Bobby has acted with malice and is therefore guilty of murder. One thing might be on your mind before we jump into that analysis. How can Bobby be guilty at all if Molly pulled the trigger and shot herself? Isn't this suicide, not homicide? As we learned in Chapter 7, a person can indirectly cause the death of another person by jointly participating in a deadly activity. Therefore, for purposes of this question, you should assume that Bobby's mutual participation and encouragement is sufficient to prove causation for a charge of homicide. Now, did he have the malice necessary for murder?

The facts seem to indicate that Bobby realized the risk of playing Russian roulette (after all, if there isn't a risk of dying, what's the point of the game?) and that those risks were egregious. In other words, Bobby demonstrated malice by his "wanton and willful disregard of the likelihood that the natural tendency of [his] behavior [was] to cause death or great bodily harm." *People v. Goecke,* 579 N.W.2d 868, 879 (Mich. 1998).

To make life easier, you can use a two-step process to determine whether the risk taken by the defendant was so extreme (i.e., gross) that it should constitute malice.

Step #1:   Did the defendant realize the risk to human life?
— If yes, the defendant acted with recklessness.

Step #2:   Was the defendant's recklessness particularly egregious or gross?
— To make this determination you need to consider whether there was any good reason the defendant took the risk and how extreme the risk was.
— Although you can argue a variety of factors, it may be helpful to keep in mind the Learned Hand approach in evaluating how reckless the defendant's behavior was. Take a look at the costs of the defendant's behavior versus its benefits.

Magnitude of Risk	versus	Social Utility
Likelihood of harm		Societal benefit of activity
Seriousness of harm		Cost of alternative activity

For those of you who like flow charts, think of it this way:

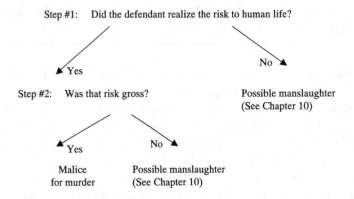

Step #1:   Did the defendant realize the risk to human life?

Yes

No

Step #2:   Was that risk gross?

Possible manslaughter
(See Chapter 10)

Yes   No

Malice
for murder

Possible manslaughter
(See Chapter 10)

If we apply this process to our question, it quickly becomes apparent that Bobby realized the risks of the game and that taking that risk was particularly egregious or wanton. Although the risk of being shot was only 20 percent, that seems a fairly high gamble when there is no true benefit, other than the thrill, in taking the risk.

Of course, this is a very stilted approach to what is still a gestalt approach by the jury in determining whether the defendant acted with gross or extreme recklessness. However, keeping these factors in mind gives the lawyer something to argue regarding the issue. The prosecutor will argue that it was outrageous for Bobby to take the risk that Molly would be killed just for the thrill of a silly game. Defense counsel might argue that the risks weren't that high so it wasn't extreme recklessness. Based on past cases, see *Commonwealth v. Malone*, 47 A.2d 445, 447 (Pa. 1946), Bobby is likely to be found guilty of murder.

Where does all this leave us with our possible answers. Skip **A** for the moment. By process of elimination, you can probably get to the right answer. **B** is wrong because it takes too limited a view of what is required to prove malice for murder. While Bobby may not have intended Molly to die, he is still guilty of murder if he acted with extreme recklessness.

As in the prior problem, **C** is also wrong because it provides the wrong standard for extreme recklessness. It is not enough that the defendant should have realized the risk of death; prosecutors must prove that he did realize the risk.

D is wrong because it suggests that a defendant must be 100 percent sure of the risks he takes in order for him to have acted with malice. There is no requirement that the defendant be sure that the victim will die. The essence of extreme recklessness is taking the risk. Even a 20 percent risk may be enough if there isn't any good reason to take the risk and the consequences are grave.

E, too, is wrong because consent or assumption of the risk are not defenses to homicide. Think about it this way. Your life doesn't just belong to you. Society also has an interest in ensuring that you do not die. As such, even if the victim consented to taking the risk, the defendant is still responsible if his conduct shows an extreme indifference to the value of human life.

Therefore, **A** is the correct answer. Bobby's actions showed extreme disregard of human life and is sufficient to prove malice for murder.

QUESTION 5. Danger below. Harry decides to clean off the top of a building that is cluttered with construction materials. He heads up to the roof during rush hour. The crowd is streaming by the building below, but Harry starts cleaning the roof anyway by tossing large pieces of timber and cement over the side of the building. At first, he tries to throw the pieces off the side only when people are not walking below. Then, he decides, "What the heck? I'm in a hurry and I don't know any of these people anyway." Alexis is walking by the building on her way to work. Suddenly, she gets hit in the head by a piece of cement and is killed instantly.

A. Harry is not guilty of murder because he had no motive to harm Alexis.
B. Harry is not guilty of murder because he did not intend to kill or harm Alexis.
C. Harry is guilty of murder because a reasonable person would have realized that there was an extreme risk in tossing debris off the building.
D. Harry is guilty of murder because he must have realized the risk that his actions would seriously injure or kill someone.
E. Harry is not guilty of murder because Alexis's death was accidental.

ANALYSIS.   This is our third question on malice by extreme recklessness. By now, your instincts should be steering you to the right answer. Moreover, you can easily go through the two-step process to determine whether this is an example of extreme recklessness.

Step 1: Did Harry seem to realize the risk that he could seriously harm someone? Yes, the evidence shows that Harry knew there was a risk to others because he saw the crowds below and initially tried to avoid hitting someone. Then, he basically said that he would take a risk because he didn't know them anyway. In other words, he acted recklessly.

Step 2: Did Harry act with extreme or gross recklessness? Once again, the answer would seem to be yes. There was little social utility to Harry's behavior and no good reason he couldn't wait to clean the roof until there were no pedestrians. On the other side of the balance, there is a fairly high likelihood of hitting someone if you start throwing things off a building during rush hour. And, if you hit someone with lumber or cement, there is a strong likelihood you will kill or seriously harm the victim. Therefore, it appears that Harry did act with extreme or gross recklessness.

To put it in common law parlance, Harry acted with a wanton and depraved heart. He had extreme indifference toward the persons below, regardless of whether he knew them or had a motive to harm them. Harry was certainly on notice that his actions posed tremendous risks to other people as he was cleaning the building.

Let's go through the options for this question. **A** is wrong because a defendant does not need a motive to commit murder. In fact, for murders caused by extreme recklessness, sometimes it is the defendant's very indifference that is the underlying reason the defendant commits the crime.

B is clearly wrong because it only covers two out of the three types of malice. Even if Harry did not have the intent to kill or harm, he could still be guilty of murder if he acted with callous disregard of the risk his acts posed to other people.

C is wrong because it misstates the standard for the third type of malice. The standard is *not* whether a reasonable person would have realized the risk. In order for there to be malice, the defendant needs to know and disregard the risk. It is a subjective standard for intent. We don't label someone a murderer unless he at least knows that he is taking risks with other people's lives.

Skip **D** for a moment and look at **E**. **E** is wrong because if the deaths were truly accidental (i.e., the defendant didn't foresee that his actions would harm anyone), this would not be a murder case. Rather, as we will learn in Chapter 10, such killings are either not criminal or, depending on the circumstances, manslaughter or negligent homicide. Of course, the difficult issue is how to draw the line between murder and manslaughter. That is an issue we will tackle soon.

D is the correct answer. After one considers all the facts of this problem, it becomes apparent that Harry must have known that there was a substantial risk that he would seriously hurt or kill the pedestrians near his building. In casually disregarding their safety, he acted with malice and is therefore guilty of murder for Alexis's death.

C.   First-degree murder

At common law, all murders were capital offenses. Gradually, jurisdictions came to recognize that not every murder should be treated so harshly.

Accordingly, they reformed their laws to provide for degrees of murder. In 1794, Pennsylvania became the first jurisdiction to distinguish between first- and second-degree murder. Defendants who were convicted of first-degree murder received the death penalty; defendants convicted of second-degree murder received a lesser sentence.

Jurisdictions can take different approaches in defining what constitutes first-degree murder. Many jurisdictions use a model that classifies various types of murder as first-degree murder. Typically, these include: (1) murders committed in a statutorily specified manner (e.g., by poison or lying in wait) or of certain types of victims (e.g., police officers); (2) "willful, deliberate, and premeditated" killings; and (3) certain types of felony murders.[2]

First-Degree Murder

1. Specific types of intentional killings or intentional killings of certain types of victims
2. Premeditation
3. Certain types of felony murder

It is easy to discern from reading a statute what specified manner of killings constitute first-degree murder. Most often, it includes killings conducted in a particularly heinous manner, like torture or lying in wait. Likewise, it is easy to identify when a murder involves a certain type of vicitim, such as a child or law enforcement officer. It is more difficult, however, to ascertain when a defendant has acted with sufficient premeditation to be guilty of first-degree murder. Therefore, the questions here focus on the meaning of premeditation and how premeditated murder differs from second-degree murder.

1. Premeditated murder

Most states that grade murder provide that "willful, deliberate, and premeditated" murders are first-degree murder. The first thing to keep in mind is that the phrase "willful, deliberate, and premeditated" is redundant, redundant, and redundant. Generally, courts focus only on whether the killing was premeditated. If it was, it was also willful (intentional) and deliberate.

Courts use different standards to decide whether a murder was premeditated. Some courts classify any willful murder as premeditated. As long as the defendant had a cool moment of thought, even for a second, and then purposely killed the victim, the defendant will be guilty of a premeditated killing. See, e.g., *Commonwealth v. Carroll*, 194 A.2d 911, 917 (Pa. 1963).

However, other courts require evidence of more deliberate thought and planning by the defendant. This can be viewed as an intent standard requiring "purpose plus preconceived plan." In addition to proving that the

---
2. For a discussion of felony murder, see Chapter 11.

defendant had the purpose to kill the victim, the prosecution must also prove that the defendant's killing was by "prior calculation and design." See *State v. Guthrie*, 461 S.E.2d 163 (W. Va. 1995). This type of premeditation is typically proved by three categories of evidence, either individually or in combination: (1) planning activity; (2) motive; and (3) manner of killing. See *People v. Anderson*, 447 P.2d 942 (Cal. 1968). The first two of these categories—planning and motive—are self-explanatory. As for manner of killing, the courts try to distinguish between killings that show cool, deliberate thought, such as a single stab wound to the heart, and killings that demonstrate more frantic, chaotic behavior, such as multiple, indiscriminate stab wounds.

The difference between the two approaches to premeditated killings is more qualitative than temporal. For the first type of premeditated killings, the barest purposeful conduct will satisfy. However, for the "purpose plus preconceived plan" type of premeditated killing, there must be more evidence of the defendant's cool deliberation before the killing. The following questions focus on the difference in how the courts view premeditation.

QUESTION 6. Punchy strikes again. Punchy is serving 20 years in prison for a violent felony. To put it mildly, he has not adjusted well to prison. He has repeatedly attempted to kill the correctional officer who guards him, and has lashed out at fellow inmates who don't give him enough respect. One day, Punchy attacks the trustee who brings him the afternoon meal. A trustee is a prison inmate who works for the warden and receives extra benefits for his work. Typically, inmates become trustees by snitching on their fellow inmates. At the time Punchy attacks the trustee, Punchy is wearing a heavy jacket (even though it is mid-summer), tennis shoes (rather than prison flip-flops), and has a homemade prison knife under his jacket. He kills the trustee with one stab wound directly to the heart. After the stabbing, Punchy hides the knife in the prison commode but it is found by the authorities. Punchy is charged with first-degree murder.

A. He is guilty of first-degree murder because he acted with malice.

B. He is guilty of first-degree murder under any standard for premeditation.

C. He is guilty of first-degree murder only in those jurisdictions that require purposeful conduct, but not in those jurisdictions that require purpose plus a preconceived plan.

D. He is guilty of first-degree murder because he used a dangerous weapon.

E. He is not guilty of first-degree murder.

ANALYSIS. To answer this question, you must evaluate the facts to determine whether Punchy deliberately killed the trustee and, if so, how much planning and preparation he made for his attack. If it was an on-the-spot killing, with only a brief moment of cool deliberation, the intent may be sufficient for first-degree murder, but only under the broader standard demonstrated by the *Carroll* case. However, if there is evidence of planning, motive, and deliberate means to kill, Punchy's actions may satisfy the requirements for premeditation under the more vigorous standard of the *Anderson* case.

It seems as if Punchy has done plenty of planning. He is wearing a jacket on a hot day to conceal the murder weapon. Instead of wearing flip-flops that would make it difficult for him to maneuver, he is wearing tennis shoes that give him more traction and a firm step. He even seems to have worked out a plan to hide the murder weapon in the commode. Additionally, Punchy has a motive to kill. The victim is a snitch. It would not be surprising if Punchy wanted to send a message to other inmates by killing the snitch. Finally, Punchy chose an effective manner to kill. One stab wound to the heart is consistent with a premeditated killing. Accordingly, Punchy appears to have killed in a premeditated manner, no matter what standard of premeditation is applied. With that analysis in mind, let's look at the possible answers.

A is incorrect because it does not cover the complete requirements for first-degree murder. Whereas malice alone may be enough for murder in general, in this situation first-degree murder requires premeditation. Malice alone is insufficient.

B seems like the right answer, but let's check the other possibilities just to be sure. Some students will pick **C** because they think it is safer to split the baby and they don't yet have a strong sense of how the standard of premeditation applies. However, the facts in this question are about as compelling for premeditation as you can get. The only other thing we could add is that Punchy sent a note to his friend saying that he planned to kill the snitch. Yet I think we can comfortably say that the facts as presented would be sufficient for premeditation under either standard. Therefore, **C** is too limited an answer and is incorrect.

D is also incorrect. In fact, if you think about it, it is actually a pretty silly answer. The fact that the victim was killed indicates that the defendant used a dangerous weapon. The real question is what was going on in the defendant's head before and at the time of the attack. Was that dangerous weapon part of a plan to kill the victim?

Finally, **E** is not correct because **B** is the right answer. This question presents a fairly straightforward set of facts demonstrating premeditation. Punchy is likely to be found guilty of first-degree murder.

> **QUESTION 7. Have some mercy.** Wilma and Bernie have been married for 50 years. Tragically, Wilma is dying a painful death from an incurable disease. Every day, she asks Bernie to help her die so that she can be relieved of her misery. Bernie can't bear to see her suffer. He finally takes matters into his own hands and gives Wilma an overdose of sedatives. Wilma dies peacefully in her sleep.
>
> A. Bernie is not guilty of murder because he killed Wilma out of mercy.
> B. Bernie is not guilty of murder because he killed Wilma at her request.
> C. Bernie is guilty of murder, but not first-degree premeditated murder.
> D. Bernie is guilty of first-degree murder.

ANALYSIS. It works against some people's instincts to decide that a mercy killing can be the highest degree of murder. After all, if vicious killers like Charlie Manson are first-degree murderers, why should we lump poor Bernie in the same category? However, the law is not pegged to the character of the defendant and his motivation for committing the crime. Rather, premeditation depends on his intent. Either a good or bad motive can be used to prove that the defendant acted in a premeditated manner. Thus, even though Bernie wanted to help Wilma end her suffering, he still planned the killing and acted in a premeditated manner. While he may get some type of a break at sentencing, depending on the jurisdiction, he has still met the mens rea requirement for first-degree murder.

Therefore, **A** is a wrong answer. Even if Bernie's motive was to act out of mercy, he still acted with premeditation. Therefore, he is guilty of first-degree murder. Likewise, **B** is wrong. As we learned earlier in this chapter, the victim's consent is not a defense to homicide. In fact, Wilma's request can actually be used by the prosecution to help prove premeditation and explain Bernie's very conscious decision to kill her.

How about **C**? Out of mercy for Bernie, you might be inclined to choose **C** and a jury may ignore the law and do just that. However, technically the facts demonstrate that Bernie killed in a premeditated manner. Therefore, **C** is wrong.

D is the correct answer. Mercy killings can be considered as first-degree murders. See, e.g., *State v. Forest*, 362 S.E.2d 252 (N.C. 1987).

> **QUESTION 8. On the spot.** Marlin and Paul work together in a restaurant. Although they are not enemies, they prefer not to have much to do with each other. Marlin serves the food and Paul proudly prepares it. One day, Paul saw Marlin snacking on a patron's food before serving it to the patron. A stickler for proper health habits, Paul grabbed the nearest kitchen knife and started stabbing Marlin all over. One of the knife wounds hit Marlin's jugular vein and Marlin died as a result of his wounds.

Prosecutors charge first-degree murder. In this jurisdiction, the heightened standard of premeditation is used. Paul is likely to be found

A. guilty of first-degree murder.
B. guilty of murder.
C. guilty of negligent homicide.
D. not guilty of any crime.

ANALYSIS. Now that you have a sense for premeditation, let's quickly go through the options presented by this question. It will be a good review of the premeditation requirement.

First, the facts of this question do not present much, if any, cool, deliberative thought by Paul before he stabs Marlin. Certainly, in a jurisdiction that requires some type of preconceived plan, there is insufficient evidence to support that charge. There is no indication of Paul placing the knife nearby so that he could easily kill Marlin. The manner of stabbing indicates that Paul is flailing more than inflicting a predetermined wound. And, even though there is some type of motive for Paul's acts, it certainly doesn't seem like a motive that has led Paul to premeditating Marlin's death. Be careful to read the facts as given, not as you might write them. Given the facts in this question, there is not enough evidence of premeditation, at least under a standard that requires a preconceived plan to kill. Even under the lower standard, it is doubtful that Paul formed the intent to kill under a cool moment of deliberation. Accordingly, it is highly unlikely that Paul would be found guilty of first-degree murder. **A** is a wrong answer.

However, **B** is still in the cards. As we see in the next section of this chapter, second-degree or plain "murder" is often used as a catch-all category for murders when there is malice but insufficient evidence of premeditation and no legal basis to drop the crime down to manslaughter. Did Paul act with malice? Quickly review the three types of malice: (1) intent to kill; (2) intent to cause serious bodily harm; and (3) gross recklessness. Even though Paul may not have had the intent to kill, he clearly had the intent to cause serious bodily harm. Accordingly, he acted with malice. **B** seems to be a likely answer.

However, before making your final selection, make sure to look at the other alternatives. **C** and **D** are both easier answers to eliminate. Even though we haven't studied negligent homicide in detail (see Chapter 10), your common sense tells you that this was not a situation in which Paul didn't realize he would hurt Marlin. Paul is stabbing at Marlin precisely because he wants to hurt him. Negligent homicides, sometimes referred to as involuntary manslaughter, are reserved for killings in which the defendant does not realize the risk that he will harm the victim, but a reasonable person would have. Here, there is no evidence that Paul did not realize he would hurt Marlin. Therefore, **C** is a wrong answer. Finally, **D** is wrong because there is evidence of malice. Be careful not to choose the "no crime" option just because you are not sure what level of murder is involved in the problem. If there is malice, there is at least murder, even if it is not first-degree murder. **B** is the correct answer.

For another case where the court required proof of "prior calculation and design" before allowing a conviction for first-degree murder, see *State v. Guthrie*, 461 S.E.2d 163 (W. Va. 1995).

2. Murder committed by specific statutory means

In some jurisdictions, like California and New York, first-degree murder includes certain statutorily designated types of intentional killings. If the defendant kills in the manner proscribed by the statute, the defendant is automatically guilty of first-degree murder, regardless of the specific evidence of premeditation. Of course, if one looks at the types of killings ordinarily included in these lists, it wouldn't be difficult to prove premeditation for those crimes. For example, in California, any murder "perpetrated by means of a destructive device or explosive, knowing use of ammunition designed primarily to penetrate metal or armor, poison, lying in wait, [and] torture" is considered first-degree murder. Cal. Penal Code, §189.

In New York, a defendant may be guilty of first-degree murder if she intentionally commits a murder against certain types of victims or while the defendant is trying to escape from custody. N.Y. Penal Code, §125.27. For example, a murder is raised to first-degree if the victim is a police officer or prison guard.

If you are in a jurisdiction that approaches first-degree murder in this manner, your task is relatively easy. Simply determine whether the defendant committed an intentional killing and then check the statutory language to determine whether that particular type of killing is automatically designated as first-degree murder.

> **QUESTION 9. Wrong victim.** Aaron is charged with first-degree murder for killing a police officer during a scuffle on the streets. In that jurisdiction, first-degree murder includes "all intentional murders of police officers." Aaron killed the officer by beating the officer's head on the cement during an altercation over a speeding ticket. Would Aaron be guilty of first-degree murder?
>
> **A.** Yes, if he acted with premeditation.
> **B.** Yes, if he intended to seriously hurt the officer during the altercation.
> **C.** Yes, if he even accidentally killed the officer.
> **D.** Yes, if he intentionally killed the officer by beating his head on the pavement.

ANALYSIS. Don't forget that the designation of a murder as first or second degree (and in some jurisdictions, even third degree) is based on the language of the statute. In this jurisdiction, *all* intentional murders of police officers are first-degree murder. Thus, your task is simply to determine whether Aaron intended to kill the officer.

A is wrong because it doesn't accurately reflect the requirements of the statute. This jurisdiction does not require that a killing be premeditated to be first-degree murder. An alternative way to convict a defendant of first-degree murder is to prove that the defendant intentionally murdered a particular type of victim; here, a police officer.

B is a little trickier. We have learned how malice for murder only requires intent to cause serious bodily harm. However, this statute does not designate any murder of an officer to be first-degree murder. It must be an intentional killing. There is a real question here as to whether Aaron intended to kill the officer or just injure him when he beat the officer's head against the cement. As such, **B** falls short of the standard required for first-degree murder under this statute.

For similar reasons, **C** is clearly wrong. The statute does not provide that accidental killings of officers are sufficient for first-degree murder. When we study felony murder (Chapter 11), you will see that many jurisdictions may designate such killings as murder or even first-degree murder, but the statute here makes no mention of such a category. Based on the statute given in this question, **C** is a wrong answer.

Sometimes the most obvious answer is the correct answer. In this case, that answer is **D**. If the killing of the officer was intentional, by the terms of the statute, Aaron's acts fall within the classification of first-degree murder.

3. First-degree felony murder

We are going to postpone for a moment a detailed discussion of first-degree felony murder. Chapter 11 discusses this subject in more detail. Felony murder refers to a concept by which a defendant is automatically guilty of murder if a death occurs during the commission of a felony. In some jurisdictions, if the death occurs during a particularly serious type of felony, the homicide is automatically designated as first-degree murder, regardless of whether the defendant premeditated the killing or even intended to kill the victim. The felonies that would typically lead to first-degree felony murder include burglary, arson, rape, kidnapping, robbery, and mayhem (BARKRM). However, to really understand how this works, we need to spend some time on the concept of felony murder. In the meantime, here is a quick problem to introduce you to the concept.

QUESTION 10. Botched burglary. Sammy the Snake (all good burglars have a nickname) sneaks into the Jones's house at night to steal their precious painting. He intentionally does not bring a gun so that he won't hurt anyone in the house. Hearing a noise, Mr. Jones jumps out of bed and goes into the living room to investigate. He sees Sammy touch his irreplaceable Rembrandt. Jones has a heart attack and dies. Is Sammy guilty of first-degree murder?

A. Yes, because he acted in a premeditated manner.
B. No, because he did not intend to kill Jones.
C. Yes, because he acted in reckless disregard for human life.
D. No, because Jones's death was accidental.
E. Yes, if felony murder for burglary is considered a first-degree murder.

ANALYSIS.   This is one of those questions where you could easily pick the wrong answer unless you thoroughly review all the possible choices. So, let's take them in order.

A is wrong because there is no evidence that Sammy premeditated Jones's death. In fact, the facts are the opposite. Sammy did not want to hurt anyone so he intentionally did not take a gun into the house. If he didn't intend to kill anyone, he certainly did not act with premeditation.

Does that make **B** correct? No. Under the felony-murder doctrine, even unintentional killings may qualify as first-degree murder. While **B** might be the correct answer if this jurisdiction did not recognize felony murder, if it does, it is irrelevant whether Sammy intended to kill Jones.

C is wrong because it doesn't look like Sammy acted in conscious disregard for human life. Instead, he tried to be the most careful burglar he could be so that he would not harm anyone.

D is wrong for reasons we learn in Chapter 10. The controversial aspect of felony murder is that it does cover accidental killings that occur during the commission of a felony.

Once you understand felony murder, you can see that **E** is the correct answer. Jurisdictions can designate even accidental deaths that occur during certain types of felonies, such as burglary, as first-degree murder. Sammy had better hope that he is not in such a jurisdiction.

D.   Second-degree murder

1. Catch-all murder

In jurisdictions that divide their murders by degree, second-degree or a lesser degree murder is often a catch-all category for any killing that is committed with malice that does not otherwise qualify for first-degree murder. Thus, it includes all intentional killings without premeditation, all killings committed with intent to cause serious bodily harm,[3] and all killings committed by gross recklessness. In other words, it is generic murder.

Consider a case in which a defendant stabs his victim, but the jury does not believe there was sufficient evidence of premeditation. Assuming the defendant cannot argue provocation (an argument that might drop the offense down to manslaughter), the catch-all category for defendant's intentional killing would be a lesser degree of murder, such as second-degree murder.

2. Second-degree felony murder

Jurisdictions are free to use the second-degree designation in any manner they wish. Thus, some jurisdictions, like Pennsylvania, classify their felony murders as second-degree murder. See Pa. Consolidated Statutes, §2502(b). Other jurisdictions, such as California, provide a list of certain felonies that can form the basis for first-degree murder, and all other qualifying murders only lead to second-degree murder. Once again, we should review this in detail when we get to Chapter 11's discussion of felony murder. Meanwhile, you should be aware that a jurisdiction can classify some or all of its felony murders as second-degree felony murder.

As a review of this murder chapter, let's consider second-degree murder in its most common understanding—all murders that do not qualify as first-degree murder.

QUESTION 11. Knife play. Mack and Phil are the best of friends who have some odd hobbies. When they are bored, they like to pretend that they are knife-throwers and throw steak knives at each other. The goal is to come closest to the other person without killing him. Mack throws first. He misses Phil by two feet. Phil, however, is off the mark and hits Mack in the chest. As Mack dies, Phil tells him, "I'm sorry, buddy. I didn't mean to hit you, but you know how competitive I am." Which of the following is true?

A. Phil is guilty of first-degree murder because he acted in callous disregard of Mack's life.

B. Phil is guilty of first-degree murder because he acted in a premeditated manner.

C. Phil is guilty of second-degree murder because he acted with gross recklessness.

D. Phil is not guilty of murder because he did not intend to kill his buddy.

---

3. In New York, killings with intent to cause serious bodily harm are classified as first-degree manslaughter; reckless killings are second-degree manslaughter.

ANALYSIS. By now, this problem should be a cinch. We have learned that there are generally three ways to end up with first-degree murder: (1) premeditated killings; (2) statutorily designated killings; and (3) certain types of felony murder. None of these seems to apply here. If none of these designations apply, the catch-all category is likely to be second-degree murder, or plain murder.

A is the wrong answer because it incorrectly suggests that callous disregard would generally be sufficient to prove first-degree murder. It is not. In jurisdictions that distinguish between first degree and other degrees of murder, it takes at least an intentional, if not premeditated, killing to end up as first-degree murder. Mere malice, as demonstrated by callous disregard, would generally be insufficient.

B is incorrect because there is nothing in the facts that supports a finding of premeditation. Phil didn't have the purpose to kill Mack. He says so directly. Therefore, Phil did not act with premeditation.

This problem asks you to remember the basic standards for malice and murder. Gross recklessness is the lowest level recognized as malice for murder. The question is whether this idiotic game of knife-throwing can be viewed as callous disregard for human life. It can be. Mack and Phil realize the risk of their activity, which is why they engage in it. It gives them a thrill. The risk they are taking is also extreme. There is a high likelihood of harm to another person and there is little or no societal benefit from the activity. Thus, even though they are best friends, Phil can be guilty of murdering Mack by engaging in extremely risky activities that demonstrate wanton disregard for the value of human life. **C** is the correct answer. It is right on the mark in describing the nature of Phil's activities and why they qualify as second-degree murder.

For all the reasons we have discussed, **D** is wrong. For second-degree murder, intent to kill is not necessarily required. In jurisdictions that use it for the catch-all category for all killings committed with malice, gross recklessness is sufficient.

E.   Model Penal Code approach to murder

Under the Model Penal Code, a criminal homicide constitutes murder when the defendant kills purposely, knowingly, or recklessly under circumstances manifesting extreme indifference to the value of human life. Model Penal Code §210(1). There are no degrees of murder under the Model Penal Code. Rather, all murders are considered first-degree felonies that carry a possible sentence of one year to life imprisonment, or death.

The Model Penal Code definition of murder does not include the common law term of *malice*. Nor does it define murder as including an intent to cause grave bodily harm. Rather, the Model Penal Code uses its own language of culpability to describe when a killing is serious enough to constitute murder. If the defendant has as her goal to kill, or knows that a death will be the consequence of her acts, or acts with extreme recklessness, she is guilty of murder.

Using the Model Penal Code's approach to homicide, try the next question.

QUESTION 12. Neighborhood menace. Steve is considered a neighborhood menace. He regularly leaves old junk in his front yard, including automobiles teetering on blocks, old refrigerators, and bins of sharp scrap metal. Several neighbors have complained to Steve that his junk could easily hurt children who play on the block. In fact, there have been several near misses when kids narrowly escaped being injured by one of the cars that fell off its blocks. Steve just ignores his neighbor's complaints.

One day, tragedy strikes. Betty Sue, a young child who lives next to Steve, is killed when one of the cars falls off its block and onto her.

Steve is charged with Betty Sue's murder. In a Model Penal Code jurisdiction, Steve would be

A. not guilty of homicide because the death was an unavoidable tragedy.
B. guilty of first-degree murder because Steve knew children could be killed.
C. guilty of second-degree murder because Steve acted in a grossly reckless manner.
D. guilty of murder.

ANALYSIS. A strong argument could be made that Steve has acted with extreme indifference to human life. He has been warned that his junk poses a danger to the neighborhood children, but he continues to consciously disregard the extreme risk to human life. There is no reason offered to justify Steve's indifference. Rather, Steve is taking a substantial and unjustifiable risk by leaving his junk where he knows the children are likely to be hurt.

As long as you kept in mind the difference between the Model Penal Code approach and the common law approach to murder, this question should have been fairly easy. **A** is wrong for two reasons. First, the tragedy was avoidable. Second, careless behavior may demonstrate an extreme indifference to human life and support a charge of murder under the Model Penal Code.

B and **C** are wrong because the Model Penal Code does not have degrees of murder. If this question asked for the answer under common law, **C** would apply because extreme recklessness is a form of malice.

However, under the Model Penal Code, **D** is the correct answer. Because of his extreme indifference, Steve is guilty of murder.

F.   The Closer: Delighted afterthoughts

Throughout this chapter, we have been discussing how a defendant's level of criminal culpability for a homicide depends on the defendant's mens rea. However, it is important to remember that what is crucial is the defendant's mens rea at the time of the act of killing. Indications of the defendant's mens rea before and after the killing may be helpful in inferring the defendant's mens rea at the time of the offense, but the ultimate decision is *what was the defendant's mental state at the time of killing*? To illustrate this concept, try the following closer question.

QUESTION 13. What a relief! Margo has always hated Nellie. One day, as Margo is approaching her home, Nellie jumps in front of her from nowhere and begins to scream. Margo hits the brakes, but the car still hits and kills Nellie. An investigation shows that Margo was not exceeding the speed limit at the time of the collision, did not anticipate Nellie's actions, and that not even a reasonable person could have anticipated that Nellie would have jumped in front of Margo's car. Nonetheless, prosecutors seek to prosecute Margo because she is so happy that Nellie is killed. In fact, when she was interviewed, Margo just kept on say, "The witch had it coming!" Is Margo guilty of murder?

A. Yes, because she had a motive to kill Nellie.
B. Yes, because driving a car is the equivalent of using a dangerous instrument.
C. Yes, because she had a motive to kill Nellie and she was clearly glad that she had done so.
D. Yes, because she premeditated Nellie's death.
E. No.

ANALYSIS.   The problem in this question is that Margo may have had the intent at some point in her life to kill Nellie, but she didn't have it at the time of the actual accident. To be criminally liable, a defendant must have a culpable mens rea at the time of the criminal actus reus. Otherwise, the defendant's expressed intent at other times is only circumstantial evidence of the defendant's intent at the time of the actual killing.

Under this analysis, **A** is wrong because motive alone does not make a person guilty of murder. The real question is whether motive created an intent in the defendant to kill the victim and that intent existed at the time of the killing. In this case, even though Margo had a motive to kill Nellie, she did not intend to harm her at the time of the accident. In fact, there is not even evidence that Margo acted in a grossly reckless manner. Accordingly, evidence of Margo's motive is insufficient to prove the malice required for murder.

B is wrong because even though automobiles may be dangerous instruments, the issue for murder is still whether the defendant intended to kill, intended to cause grave bodily harm, or even realized the risk that she could kill or seriously harm another. At the time of Nellie's death, there is no evidence that Margo realized that risk. Moreover, because the question states that not even a reasonable person would have realized the risk, Margo may not even be guilty of manslaughter. This part of the homicide analysis is discussed in the next chapter.

For similar reasons, **C** is also wrong. Although it might be coldhearted for Margo to be so happy over Nellie's demise, Margo's attitude still does not prove that at the time her car hit Nellie, Margo intended to harm or kill her, or even knew she was taking the risk of doing so.

Finally, **D** is wrong because there is absolutely no evidence of premeditation unless Margo had some prior indication that Nellie might try to jump in front of her car.

The correct answer is **E**. One need not praise Margo for her callous attitude toward Nellie's death, but unless Margo acted with culpable intent at the time of the collision, she is not guilty of murder. In other words, Margo might generally be a person with a depraved heart, but she is only guilty of murder if she operated with that depraved heart *at the time of the killing.* Being delighted over another person's misfortune is not a crime in itself.

✦ Levenson's Picks:

1. Bad sport	A
2. The enforcer	D
3. Bad dog	C
4. Russian roulette	A
5. Danger below	D
6. Punchy strikes again	B
7. Have some mercy	D
8. On the spot	B
9. Wrong victim	D
10. Botched burglary	E
11. Knife play	C
12. Neighborhood menace	D
13. What a relief!	E

10

Manslaughter

*He had it coming, he had it coming, he only had
himself to blame . . . and if you had been there, I'm sure you would
have done the same.*

— "Jail House Tango" from *Chicago*

CHAPTER OVERVIEW
A. (Voluntary) manslaughter and provoked killings
B. Killing in the sudden heat of passion
C. Requirement #1: Actual heat of passion
D. Requirement #2A: Legally adequate provocation — Categorical approach
E. Requirement #2B: Legally adequate provocation — Reasonable person approach
F. Requirement #3: Insufficient cooling time
G. Model Penal Code approach: Extreme mental or emotional disturbance
H. Involuntary manslaughter and criminal negligence
I. Model Penal Code approach: Reckless and negligent homicides
J. The Closer: Name that homicide
🧭 Levenson's Picks

Now that you have learned what murder is, it is time to examine manslaughter. Simply stated, under the common law *manslaughter is the unlawful killing of another human being without malice.* Like murder, the term *malice* is used for a variety of killings without malice. However, there are generally two types of killings that are included in the manslaughter categories: killings in the heat of passion or under extreme emotional disturbance (often referred to as "voluntary manslaughter") and reckless killings or those committed by grossly negligent behavior (often referred to as "involuntary manslaughter" or "negligent homicide"). To make life easier, we examine each of these types of manslaughter separately. Even if different jurisdictions use different labels for the types of man-slaughters,[1] the concepts are generally the same.

A.   (Voluntary) manslaughter and provoked killings

Believe it or not, not all intentional killings are considered murder. Because the law recognizes the frailty of human behavior, there are some types of intentional killings that are classified as manslaughter and typically carry a lesser penalty than murder. In jurisdictions that differentiate between voluntary manslaughter and involuntary manslaughter, these killings are often referred to as voluntary manslaughter or first-degree manslaughter. However, in many jurisdictions, especially those that follow the Model Penal Code, intentional killings under extreme emotional disturbance are simply labeled "manslaughter." (Model Penal Code §210.3.)

What types of intentional killings are these? Traditionally, (voluntary) manslaughter applied only when a defendant was provoked. However, today jurisdictions apply it when there is: (1) provocation (heat of passion); (2) extreme emotional disturbance; or (3) imperfect self-defense.

The first question you might have is: "Why should the law ever give somebody a break for killing?" It is an excellent question. The heat of passion/provocation doctrine is an increasingly disputed doctrine. At its origins, it was developed for those situations in which society recognized that even reasonable men could be pushed to the point of killing. For example, if a man caught his wife in the middle of an adulterous affair, the courts were willing to mitigate his sentence if he killed in the heat of passion. Likewise, if a man were assaulted, but not to the point where he would be entitled to use lethal self-defense, then too he could intentionally kill but then mitigate his crime with a claim of provoked killing.

Accordingly, voluntary manslaughter developed as a category of killings in which society was willing to partially mitigate the defendant's intentional

---

1. For example, California law recognizes three types of manslaughter: voluntary manslaughter (heat of passion killings), involuntary manslaughter (negligent homicides), and vehicular manslaughter. Pennsylvania has a similar approach, distinguishing between voluntary manslaughter (provocation killings) and involuntary manslaughter (reckless or grossly negligent killings). By contrast, New York recognizes first-degree manslaughter (killings because of extreme emotional disturbance), second-degree manslaughter (reckless killings), and negligent homicide.

killing of the victim. In other words, the defendant does not walk free, but he is subject to a lesser penalty.

The problems with this doctrine should be apparent to you. The last thing that the law wants is to give a bunch of hotheads legal license to kill the person cheating with their wives. Accordingly, the common law developed strict standards as to when the provocation doctrine could be applied. We now examine those requirements. However, before we do so, let's start with an opening problem.

QUESTION 1. Tom and Dick. You wouldn't want either Tom or Dick as your neighbor. Tom recently killed his landlord when the landlord threatened to increase Tom's rent. Dick killed his wife's lover when he found them in bed upon his return from a hard day of work. The prosecutor wants to throw the book at both of them. Which of the following is true?

A. Both Tom and Dick are guilty of murder because all intentional killings are murder.

B. Both Tom and Dick are guilty of murder because they had motives to kill their victims.

C. Neither Tom nor Dick is guilty of homicide because they were provoked to kill their victims.

D. Only Tom is guilty of murder because it is a full defense for Dick to kill his wife's lover.

E. None of the above.

ANALYSIS. Although you haven't yet learned the elements of provocation, the earlier introduction should have been enough for you to answer this question. By doing so, you'll begin to understand the basic principles of voluntary manslaughter. Let's start with **A**. As we stated from the beginning, not all intentional killings are murder. There is a category of intentional killings that is considered a lesser offense, even though the defendant intentionally killed his victim. Therefore, you cannot make a blanket statement like that set forth in **A**.

B is also wrong because not all motives will qualify a killing for manslaughter. As we will see, when a defendant is provoked by a spouse's infidelity or an assault by another, the provocation doctrine may apply. However, killing your landlord because you don't want to pay your rent is not going to be a sufficient basis to claim manslaughter. For similar reasons, **C** is also wrong. Not all types of provocation qualify as a killing for manslaughter. Since there is almost always a reason why a defendant kills his victim, it would make no sense to open up the provocation category to any type of provocation. By doing so, the law would essentially eliminate murder.

Accordingly, as we will learn, the types of provocation that may qualify for manslaughter are relatively narrow in most jurisdictions. Certainly, the request for a rent payment—without more—would not qualify.

D is also wrong although you might have jumped at it because it mentions adultery, a type of provocation that can trigger manslaughter. However, **D** is wrong for reasons you have already learned. Even when provocation is a defense, it is not a full defense. In other words, the defendant will not walk away with no homicide conviction. Rather, provocation is a "partial defense" that mitigates the defendant's intentional killing down from murder to manslaughter.

That leaves **E**—the dreaded "none of the above" as the correct answer. Many students are reluctant to select this option because they think they must have missed something in the other answers. However, if you have carefully analyzed each answer and none is accurate, **E** is the correct one.

B. Killing in the sudden heat of passion

Perhaps the best example of the "heat of passion" doctrine at work is the case of *State v. Thornton*, 730 S.W.2d 309 (Tenn. 1987). In *Thornton*, the defendant came home and found his wife in bed with another man. Thornton shot first and asked questions later. The jury found Thornton guilty of first-degree murder, but the appellate court reversed, holding that Thornton's case was a classic situation of voluntary manslaughter. The court found that as a matter of law, "any reasonable person would have been inflamed and intensely aroused by this sort of discovery" and held that the defendant acted in the heat of passion, and not with malice.

How does the ruling in *Thornton* make sense? The answer lies in the concept of malice. As we learned, malice presumes a depraved and wanton heart, that is, a person who has no concern for human life and kills for that reason. A defendant who is provoked or acts under extreme distress is acting less on reason and more out of pure passion. Even if the law does not completely excuse the defendant's conduct, it is willing to mitigate culpability because society recognizes the "frailty of human nature." Glanville Williams, Provocation and the Reasonable Man (1954). Provocation is therefore considered a partial defense.

Some commentators disagree with the underlying rationale for the provocation defense. In their view, reasonable people do not kill regardless of the provocation. In addition, the provocation doctrine diminishes the value of the victim's life. Even though the victim did not pose a deadly threat to another person, the law allows the defendant to essentially argue, "he had it coming," as if the killing were partially justified.

At common law, there were strict requirements on the use of the provocation doctrine. For a defendant to argue provocation, the evidence must show: (1) the defendant acted in actual heat of passion; (2) there was legally adequate provocation; and (3) there was inadequate time for the defendant to cool off after he was provoked. As in any other area of the law, there are nuances to each of these requirements and we'll use questions to illustrate each. As we discuss these requirements, we use the phrases "heat of passion doctrine" and "provocation doctrine" interchangeably. They refer to the same legal concept.

C.   Requirement #1: Actual heat of passion

If the theory for allowing a partial mitigation of charges is that the defendant is so inflamed that he is not forming intent to kill with a cool, deliberate mind, it makes sense that the defendant must actually be in the heat of passion at the time of the killing. If the defendant is not actually provoked, there is absolutely no reason to reduce the defendant's culpability. Accordingly, the first requirement for the provocation/heat of passion doctrine is that the defendant was actually in the heat of passion at the time of the killing. The next question gives you an idea of how this requirement works and why it is important.

> **QUESTION 2. Debi and Elie.**   Elie returns home after a hard day's work. He catches his wife, Debi, in bed with the gardener. Elie starts laughing hysterically and says to the gardener, "If you want her, you can have her. I'd rather mow the lawn." Elie then heads outside. While he is mowing the lawn, he reconsiders what he said and decides this would be a good opportunity to get rid of his wife and her lover. He heads back into the house, loads his gun, and walks to the bedroom. Coolly, he takes aim and fires. He kills the lover instantly. If Elie claims he killed in the heat of passion, his defense will most likely
>
> **A.** succeed because a reasonable person might be provoked to kill if he finds his wife in bed with another man.
> **B.** succeed if Elie's wife and her lover intentionally provoked Elie.
> **C.** fail because Elie may have been provoked to kill his wife, but not the gardener.
> **D.** fail because Elie was not acting in the heat of passion.

ANALYSIS.   Contrary to what many people think, the mere fact that Elie catches his wife cheating does not give him even a partial excuse to kill her or her lover. Rather, the heat of passion doctrine is only triggered if Elie is actually inflamed at the time he kills his victim. In this case, Elie might have been annoyed by the affair, but he certainly did not act out of the heat of passion. As the facts tell you, he coolly deliberated a plan to kill his victim. Thus, his killing was much more like a premeditated murder than a voluntary manslaughter. Given that analysis, let's look at our answer choices.

A is wrong because it doesn't matter whether a reasonable man would have been provoked if the defendant himself was not actually provoked. The first requirement for the heat of passion doctrine is that the defendant, himself, must actually be in the heat of passion. The doctrine is not a justification for an angry husband to kill his cheating wife.

B is also wrong because the intent of the victims is not the issue. Regardless of whether the wife and her lover intended to provoke the defendant, the heat of passion doctrine does not apply if the defendant was not actually provoked.

C is wrong because it does not accurately reflect the facts of this problem. According to the facts, Elie was not immediately provoked to kill either the wife or the gardener. Moreover, in most jurisdictions, if the defendant is provoked, it doesn't matter whether the defendant kills the cheating spouse or the lover. The heat of passion doctrine would apply in either case.

For all these reasons, **D** is the correct answer. Elie does not get a heat of passion defense because he did not act in the heat of passion. Rather, after some deliberation, he decided to kill his wife and her lover. In fact, not only does the defendant not get his homicide reduced to manslaughter, but he also may very well end up with first-degree murder because the killing was done with premeditation.

D. Requirement #2A: Legally adequate provocation — Categorical approach

Assume, for a moment, that the defendant actually was provoked to kill the victim. Is that sufficient to invoke the heat of passion defense? The answer clearly has to be no. Otherwise, every hot-headed defendant would automatically have a way to reduce a murder he committed to a lesser charge of manslaughter.

The most important requirement in the heat of passion doctrine is that the defendant respond to *legally adequate provocation*. By limiting what is legally adequate provocation, the law can limit how broadly the heat of passion doctrine is used.

There are several approaches to determining whether the defendant has been subject to legally adequate provocation. They include: (1) the categorical approach; (2) the modern "reasonable person" approach; and (3) the Model Penal Code's extreme emotional disturbance approach. Each of these approaches seeks to set limits on how broadly the provocation doctrine may be used.

Historically, the courts recognized limited categories of acts that the law recognized as sufficient to "excite the mind of a reasonable man" to react with lethal force. See *Regina v. Welsh*, 11 Cox Crim. Cas. 336, 338 (1869). These categories included (1) aggravated assaults; (2) observations of adultery by a spouse; (3) illegal arrest; (4) mutual combat; and (5) attacks against a close family member. Unless a defendant was provoked by one of these acts, the defendant could not assert the "heat of passion" doctrine. The next problem is designed to illustrate how this approach worked.

QUESTION 3. Neighborly love.   Ben hears from his best friend, Mike, that Ben's wife has been having an affair with their neighbor. Ben immediately leaves work and gets home in time to see his wife go into the neighbor's house. However, Ben does not see what his wife and the neighbor do in the house. An hour later, the neighbor and Ben's wife come out of the neighbor's house. The neighbor smirks at Ben and says, "she says I'm definitely a better lover than you." The neighbor then flicks a cigarette at Ben. Ben erupts in anger, grabs a brick on the walkway, and throws it at the neighbor and Ben's wife. He kills the neighbor.

If Ben is charged with murder and the categorical approach is applied, Ben can

A. successfully argue heat of passion because his wife was clearly having an adulterous affair.
B. successfully argue heat of passion because the neighbor assaulted Ben with a cigarette butt.
C. successfully argue heat of passion because a reasonable man would have been provoked by Ben's situation.
D. not succeed in asserting a heat of passion defense.

ANALYSIS.   Most people would have no doubt that Ben's wife was having an affair with the neighbor. Nonetheless, the categorical approach allows only very limited situations in which the defendant can argue heat of passion. The two obvious ones in this problem fall short.

First, **A** is an incorrect answer because Ben did not witness his wife's infidelity. He only heard about it. Therefore, under the categorical approach, Ben is not entitled to a heat of passion defense because he did not have legally adequate provocation. Similarly, it is highly unlikely that merely flicking a cigarette at Ben would be construed to be a serious enough "assault" to satisfy the provocation requirement. Therefore, the two most likely categories used for heat of passion are unavailable to Ben. **B** is also a wrong answer.

Many of you might have jumped at **C** because it sounds like a great answer. Indeed, it might be, but not under the standard you are directed to use under the call of the question. In a multiple-choice exam, like an essay exam, always pay attention to the call of the question. In this problem, the question asks whether Ben could argue provocation "under the categorical approach." Therefore, you are not at liberty to apply a more modern standard, such as the reasonable person standard. A further explanation of that standard comes up in the next problem.

Ultimately, the answer to this question is **D.** Under the categorical approach, Ben does not have a heat of passion defense. Hearing about spousal infidelity is not legally sufficient provocation to mitigate a defendant's crime to voluntary manslaughter. Even provocative words are not enough at common law, no matter how insulting or inciteful those words might be. See *Girouard v. State*, 583 A.2d 718 (Md. 1991).

E.   Requirement #2B: Legally adequate provocation — Reasonable person approach

Since the 1860s, there has been a trend away from specific categories of legally recognized provocation. Instead, judges began to ask the jury to determine whether there was an act of provocation that would have inflamed a reasonable person to act at that moment without due deliberation or reflection, but out of passion. See *Maher v. People*, 10 Mich. 212, 81 Am. Dec. 781 (1862) (hearing of a wife's infidelity could be legally sufficient provocation).

Of course, the tricky part of this modern approach is describing the characteristics of the "reasonable person." Does the reasonable person share the defendant's physical traits? How about the defendant's emotional traits? The more the so-called reasonable person is like the defendant, the more likely the jury will find that the defendant was justifiably provoked.

Some courts take a fairly objective approach to determining who is the reasonable person. They allow the defense to argue that a person with the defendant's same physical attributes (age, size, gender) would have been provoked. Thus, in the English case of *Director of Public Prosecutions v. Camplin*, [1978] 2 All E.R. 168, 175, A.C. 705 (Eng. H.L.), the court held that a jury should be permitted to consider a defendant's age and gender in deciding whether a reasonable person with those characteristics would have been provoked.

A minority of courts are willing to use an even more subjective approach to determining whether there has been legally adequate provocation. Not only do they allow the reasonable person to assume the physical characteristics of the defendant, they also frame the provocation issue in terms of whether a reasonable person with the defendant's emotional background would have been provoked. This approach, which borrows from the Model Penal Code approach (see Section G *infra*), is the most pro-defense standard. As long as there is an identifiable reason for the defendant's emotional response, the defendant may succeed at convincing the jury that he was provoked. Of course, this standard is also the most controversial standard because it identifies as "reasonable" an emotional response by the defendant.

The outcome of a case can very much depend on what standard is being used in defining the reasonable person. As a general rule, the defendant wants the reasonable person to share as many as possible of the defendant's physical and emotional characteristics, and life experiences. By contrast, prosecutors generally favor the most objective standard that does not direct the jury to stand as closely in the defendant's shoes. Try the following question to see the difference these standards can make.

QUESTION 4. **Work is no fun.** Bob hates everything about his job. He hates the job he does, he hates his co-workers, and most of all, he hates his boss. Every day, his boss berates Bob in front of his fellow employees. Because of a physical infirmity, Bob uses crutches; his boss calls him "Stump." One day, Bob's boss sees him taking a break to get a drink from the water cooler. The boss tosses a file at Bob that causes him to trip and fall. As the boss and co-workers are laughing and shouting, Bob grabs the letter opener in his pocket and throws it at his boss. It hits him in the heart and kills him.

Under which of the following standards would Bob have the best chance to mitigate the killing to manslaughter because of legally adequate provocation?

A. A categorical approach.
B. A reasonable person approach that takes into account Bob's physical characteristics of being handicapped.
C. A reasonable person approach that takes into account the boss's prior humiliations of Bob.
D. B and C.

ANALYSIS.   First, let's be clear. It is not at all certain that Bob will succeed with any provocation argument. However, the question asks which standard gives him the best chance at success. **A** is wrong because the boss's actions, even though reprehensible, probably still do not constitute a severe assault that would fit into one of the legally adequate provocation categories.

B is better for Bob than **A**, but may not be enough. Under **B**, Bob could argue that a reasonable person with his physical infirmity would have been provoked and therefore he has a defense. However, one could argue that there are many people who struggle with physical infirmities who do not end up stabbing another person to death just because they have been ridiculed. Therefore, **B** is probably not the best answer.

C offers a way for Bob to argue that the jury should take into account his emotional state at the time he is humiliated and set off balance by his boss. If the jury asks whether a "reasonable person who is regularly humiliated" by his employer would have been provoked, he has a better chance at succeeding. However, **C** is still not the best answer. The correct answer is **D** because it allows the jury to step in Bob's shoes as much as possible in deciding whether there has been legally adequate provocation. It is the most subjective standard and therefore the standard that gives him the best chance of success.

F.   Requirement #3: Insufficient cooling time

Traditionally, a defendant was only entitled to argue provocation if he killed immediately after he was provoked. If he waited to kill, the court would find that his actions were not in the heat of passion and therefore there was no basis for mitigating his offense. For example, assume that a defendant came home and saw his wife in bed with another man. Instead of shooting his wife and her lover on the spot, the defendant went out, bought a gun, and returned to kill the man cheating with his wife. Under traditional common law, the defendant could not argue provocation because he had sufficient time to cool off after the events that initially provoked him.

Under the modern approach, some allowances have been made to this strict rule. Principally, the courts have recognized two doctrines that relaxed the traditional cooling time rule. First, some courts allow a delayed response to a provocative act if the defendant can show that his emotions continued to smolder even after the act occurred. If the defendant can show that he had a *long-smoldering reaction*, the defendant may be able to argue provocation regardless of the fact that he did not respond to the provocative act for some hours or even days. Consider, for example, a defendant who has been repeatedly taunted by his victim. In situations in which there has been a "long course of provocating [sic] conduct," courts have been willing to relax the requirement that the defendant's response immediately follow the provocative act. *People v. Berry*, 556 P.2d 777 (Cal. 1976).

Alternatively, some courts have accepted the *rekindling doctrine* by which defendants can argue that even though they may have cooled after the initial provocative act, their heat of passion was rekindled by some kind of reminder of the victim's provocation. For example, consider a defendant who was sexually assaulted by the victim. At the time of the assault, the defendant did not strike back at the victim. However, when the victim taunts the defendant the next day about the prior assault, the defendant lashes back at the victim. A court may be willing to find that the defendant's heat of passion was rekindled, allowing the defendant to argue the provocation doctrine.

There are times when both the long-smoldering reaction and rekindling doctrine may come into play. For example, consider the famous case of *People v. Ellie Nesler*, S056082 (1993). Ms. Nesler shot and killed her son's molester three years after his alleged acts of molestation when she saw him mock her during his molestation trial. Nesler argued that her passion had been long-smoldering and was rekindled when she saw her son's attacker. The prosecutor claimed she was making good on a promise of vengeance. The jury agreed with Nesler and she was found guilty of voluntary manslaughter.

As you try the next problem, consider how the insufficient cooling time rule serves to limit the provocation doctrine and whether it is wise to broaden the use of the provocation defense by allowing defendants to argue that their reaction was either long-smoldering or rekindled.

QUESTION 5. Delayed reaction. For Billy, the day was an absolute nightmare. When he got home, he learned that a man in the park had seriously assaulted his daughter. The assailant was still on the loose. After visiting his daughter in the hospital, Billy joined the hunt for the assailant. He spotted a man in the park hiding behind some bushes. Billy yelled, "Did you do that to my little girl?" The man only grinned and said, "You bet. And, I loved every minute of it." Enraged, Billy lashed out at the man and struck him in the head with a baseball bat. The assailant died and Billy was charged with murder.

If Billy argues that the killing should be mitigated to manslaughter, he will most likely

A. succeed because the assailant had earlier assaulted his daughter.
B. fail, because a grin is insufficient legal provocation.
C. fail because he had sufficient time to cool off after learning about the assault of his daughter.
D. succeed, if the court recognizes the doctrines of rekindling and long-smoldering passions.

ANALYSIS. Be careful with problems like this. Although your sympathies may naturally lie with Billy because of what the assailant did to his daughter, Billy may not be able to mitigate the charges against him down to manslaughter unless his situation meets the requirements of the heat of passion doctrine. The first question, of course, is whether Billy was actually provoked. The question states Billy was "enraged" and "lashed" out at the man. That suggests that he was actually in the heat of passion. The second question is whether there was legally adequate provocation. A serious assault qualifies as legally adequate provocation. It fits one of the categories of traditionally sufficient provocative acts. Under the modern approach, if a person attacks the defendant or someone close to him, one would expect a reasonable person to be provoked.

The problem in this question is that Billy does not kill the assailant at the time of the initial provocation. Rather, he waits, has time to cool down, and then encounters him later. At that point, the law wants to make sure that Billy has not just cooled off and taken the law in his own hands. Rather, Billy is entitled to the heat of passion doctrine only if the jurisdiction allows defendants to argue that their passions were reignited or long-smoldering. With these concepts in mind, let's look at the possible answers.

A is a wrong answer because an earlier assault does not necessarily qualify for the heat of passion doctrine. Rather, it raises the issue of whether there has been too much cooling time and that cooling time has transformed Billy's act into a premeditated act of killing.

B is also not the best answer. Even though it is correct that a grin is ordinarily not sufficient for provocation, it may be enough to rekindle the defendant's passions caused by an earlier, and much more serious, act of provocation.

C initially looks like a good answer. In fact, under the traditional common law approach, it would be the correct answer. However, as always, it is important to consider all the options presented to see if there is a better answer. The better answer is **D**. While **C** may generally be true, **D** is correct because it recognizes the exceptions to the cooling time rule. Note that professors often construct questions that give several answers that are generally true, but only one answer that more specifically addresses the issue in that question. When there is a more accurate answer, it ordinarily makes sense to pick the more specific answer.

G. Model Penal Code approach: Extreme mental or emotional disturbance

The Model Penal Code does not distinguish between voluntary and involuntary manslaughter. Rather, it recognizes two types of killings as manslaughter: (1) recklessly killing another person; or (2) killing another person under circumstances that would ordinarily constitute murder, but which homicide is committed as the result of "extreme mental or emotional disturbance" for which there is a "reasonable explanation or excuse." The first type of manslaughter is addressed in the discussion regarding reckless killings and involuntary manslaughter. The second type of manslaughter under the Model Penal Code — killings under extreme mental or emotional distress — is closely related to the category of killings in the heat of passion and therefore is explained now.

As you recall, common law heat of passion killings require that there be a specific act of provocation that caused the defendant to act in the heat of passion. Model Penal Code §210.3 extends the concept of manslaughter to all killings when the defendant kills because he is suffering from an "extreme mental or emotional disturbance" (EMED) for which there is a "reasonable explanation or excuse." The reasonableness of the explanation or excuse regarding the EMED is "determined from the viewpoint of a person in the actor's situation under the circumstances as he believes them to be."

In other words, the Model Penal Code expands manslaughter beyond those situations in which the defendant is provoked into killing. Rather, it includes any time when the defendant's act is triggered by a mental or emotional disturbance that causes him to act under the equivalent of a heat of passion. Thus, the EMED standard modifies the common law doctrine of heat of passion in several ways. First, it does not require that there be a specific act of provocation. It is enough if the defendant suffered from a condition that caused the defendant to react in an emotional manner. Second, because no specific act of provocation is required, there is no reason to be concerned about whether there was too much "cooling time" before the killing. By definition, the defendant must actually be suffering from the disturbance at the time of the killing. Third, there are no artificial restrictions on evaluating whether an act of provocation was legally sufficient. Because no specific act is required, even words may be enough to trigger the defendant's extreme emotional or mental disturbance.

The tricky part about applying the Model Penal Code approach is determining whether there was a reasonable explanation or excuse for the defendant's EMED. Because the reasonableness of the explanation or excuse for the EMED is "determined from the viewpoint of a person in the actor's situation under the circumstances as he believes them to be," the standard is both objective and subjective. The standard is subjective in that the trier of fact should consider both the defendant's physical and emotional characteristics in determining whether there is a reasonable explanation for the defendant's reaction. However, the standard is also objective in that the trier of fact is directed not to consider the defendant's "idiosyncratic moral values" in making its determinations. In other words, if defense counsel can identify something in the defendant's past that accounts for the defendant's reaction, there may be a ground for EMED. However, if the defendant just lashes out because of a bad personality or abhorrent moral values, the trier of fact may find that that cause is not a reasonable explanation or excuse for the defendant's behavior. See, e.g., *People v. Casassa*, 404 N.E.2d 1310 (N.Y. 1980) (defendant's bizarre behavior was not based on reasonable explanation or excuse, but on defendant's idiosyncratic personality).

If a court finds that a reasonable jury could find that the defendant's behavior meets the legal standards for EMED, it will give the jury an appropriate instruction and let it decide whether to mitigate the killing to manslaughter.

As with many legal concepts, this standard is best understood by looking at concrete examples. Consider, for example, a defendant who was physically and emotionally tormented for years by a man wearing a blue tie. The attacks were brutal and left the defendant with emotional scars. Each attack was accompanied by a tirade of swearing by the defendant's attacker. Years later, the defendant walks by a man in a blue tie who starts swearing. Defendant reacts by attacking and killing the man. Under common law, the defendant's attempt to argue provocation would likely fail. Words alone are insufficient provocation. However, under the Model Penal Code approach, the defendant could attempt to argue that from his viewpoint, in the circumstances as he believed them to be, there was a reasonable explanation or excuse for his extreme mental and emotional disturbance. Accordingly, under the Model Penal Code, the jury could find the defendant guilty of the lesser crime of manslaughter.

By contrast, consider the defendant who hates people of a certain race because he believes that they are inferior. Accordingly, the defendant attacks someone of that race and tries to argue EMED. The defendant's claim is likely to fail because a racist attitude may be considered an idiosyncratic moral value and not a reasonable explanation or excuse for the defendant's emotional disturbance.

With these two examples in mind, try the next problem.

QUESTION 6. Life of hard knocks. Rudy's life has been a nightmare. He has never had a successful social life because of a large, physical deformity on his face. All his life he has been taunted by people calling him names like "Elephant Man" or "Frankenstein." Some have even attacked him. Even after psychological therapy, he rarely has been able to leave his home because the constant ridicule tends to set him off into an uncontrollable rage. One day, Rudy reluctantly ventures out to buy some food at the market. While he is there, a group of people start to point at him and laugh. Scared and furious, Rudy explodes in anger and kills an innocent bystander.

Under the Model Penal Code

> **A.** Rudy has a full defense to murder because he was provoked by the group's laughter.
> **B.** Rudy is entitled to a manslaughter instruction because there was legally adequate provocation.
> **C.** Rudy is entitled to a manslaughter instruction because he suffers from an extreme emotional disturbance.
> **D.** Rudy is guilty of murder.

ANALYSIS. This question makes it pretty clear how the Model Penal Code standard takes a more lenient approach toward manslaughter than traditional common law. Under traditional common law, the group's actions, albeit obnoxious, would not constitute legally adequate provocation. However, the Model Penal Code allows the jury to consider both Rudy's physical deformity and the emotional disturbance he has developed. While there is still no guarantee that the jury will mitigate Rudy's conviction to manslaughter, he has a better chance under the Model Penal Code standard than he does under the common law. By looking at the possible answers, we can see why this is true.

A is wrong because it states that Rudy would have a full defense. Don't be tricked. Provocation, under common law or the Model Penal Code, is never a full defense. It only mitigates the defendant's crime from murder to manslaughter.

B is wrong because merely mocking a person, or pointing at him, is not traditionally legally adequate provocation. Not only does it not fit into any of the categories of legally adequate provocation (e.g., witnessing adultery, an attack, etc.), but a reasonable person is not expected to be so enraged as to kill just because he is embarrassed.

It quickly becomes apparent that the choice is between **C** and **D**. In deciding whether **C** is the correct answer, it must be determined whether Rudy was suffering from an extreme mental or emotional disturbance for which there is a reasonable explanation or excuse. The question gives a historical basis for Rudy's situation. When looking at "the actor's situation," the jury can consider Rudy's physical handicaps and psychological history. Here, the question states that Rudy has been under a psychologist's care and that he carries emotional and physical burdens that may explain why he reacted in the manner that he did. It does not matter that there was not legally sufficient provocation or that he killed an innocent bystander, instead of one of the persons who taunted him. The focus is on whether he had an extreme mental or emotional disturbance for which there is reasonable explanation or excuse. Given Rudy's history, it appears he did.

Accordingly, **C** appears to be the correct answer. Because Rudy would be entitled to a manslaughter instruction under the Model Penal Code, **D** is the wrong answer.

H. Involuntary manslaughter and criminal negligence

Time to switch gears for a minute. Remember that there are two types of cases that are generally treated as manslaughter. The first type, which we have just finished discussing, involves killings related to heat of passion or extreme mental or emotional disturbance. However, there is another type of homicide that traditionally is treated as manslaughter. Homicides caused by mere recklessness or criminal negligence may also be treated as manslaughter or, in some jurisdictions, "negligent homicide." Where jurisdictions differentiate between voluntary and involuntary manslaughter, homicides caused by recklessness or extreme negligence are ordinarily classified as "involuntary manslaughter."

This category of manslaughter is reserved for the clueless defendant. Consider, for example, the defendant who thinks it would be good for his toddler to play unsupervised with a boa constrictor in his crib. The giant snake kills the toddler. Is the defendant guilty of homicide?

Although the lowest mens rea level ordinarily associated with crimes is recklessness,[2] because of the harm caused by a homicide is so serious, the law has created a category of homicide that punishes criminal negligence. The cases in this area use many different and confusing terms to describe the level of mens rea for this type of manslaughter. Some refer to it as "reckless," others as "culpable negligence" or "gross negligence." All of these phrases are being used to describe a level of criminal negligence that is beyond the negligence that leads to mere tort liability. Rather, it is a killing "without due caution and circumspection"[3] to such a degree that the defendant's behavior warrants criminal punishment.

In determining whether the defendant has acted in a criminally negligent manner, the jury may consider the seriousness of the risk that the defendant's behavior posed versus any social utility by the defendant's conduct. Thus, a defendant who drives negligently and kills someone because he is late to a movie is more likely to be found criminally negligent than a defendant who is rushing a sick child to the doctor. In both situations, the defendants have acted negligently because they should have realized the risk posed by their behavior. However, a jury may find the first scenario of negligence more egregious than the second and label it as criminal negligence.

Unfortunately, the newspapers are full of examples of criminally negligent behavior: (1) parents who leave their children in a hot car, causing the

2. See Section 3(B)(2)(c).
3. See 4 Blackstone, Law Dictionary at *192.

children to die;[4] (2) parents not adequately feeding their children;[5] (3) parents failing to get medical care for an ill child;[6] (4) people leaving a loaded gun where children can reach it;[7] or (5) restaurants serving tainted foods. In all these situations, the clueless defendant should have realized the risk to human life by his behavior and not engaged in the risky behavior. Although it depends on all the facts of the case, a jury may find that the level of negligence demonstrated in each of these cases warrants a conviction for manslaughter.

It is important to keep in mind that if the defendant actually realizes the risk of his behavior and still acts in a manner that poses a substantial and unjustifiable risk to human life, the defendant may be guilty of murder. As you recall from Chapter 9, gross recklessness can justify a finding of recklessness for murder. However, if the defendant does not realize the risk, but a reasonable person in the defendant's situation would have realized the risk, the defendant has acted negligently and it is up to the jury to decide whether it is "so gross as to be deserving of punishment." *State v. Hazelwood*, 946 P.2d 875, 877-878 (Alaska 1997).

In deciding whether the defendant acted in an impermissibly negligent manner, some jurisdictions find that the use of a dangerous instrument automatically elevates behavior from mere negligence to criminally culpable negligence. For example, a defendant who negligently operates a car or a gun, and thereby kills someone, may automatically be guilty of manslaughter.

Try the following question to test your understanding of this type of criminal negligence or involuntary manslaughter.

QUESTION 7. Deadly concert. The Roaring Stones play a concert in a crowded nightclub. Many of the attendees realize that anything can happen in a crowded club, but they shove their way in anyway. To please the crowd, the nightclub owner decides to use some indoor fireworks to punctuate the band's performance. The fireworks misfire and cause the curtains in the club to burst into flames. As the customers rush to flee the burning club, several are trampled to death. The nightclub owner is charged with involuntary manslaughter.

The nightclub owner is guilty of involuntary manslaughter if

---

4. See, e.g., *People v. Kolzow*, 301 Ill. App. 3d 1, 703 N.E.2d 424 (1998).
5. See, e.g., *People v. Burden*, 140 Cal. Rptr. 282 (Cal. Ct. App. 1977).
6. See, e.g., *State v. Williams*, 484 P.2d 1167 (Wash. 1971) (allowing manslaughter conviction for ordinary negligence). See also "Christian Scientist" cases in which parents do not seek standard medical attention, but unsuccessfully try to cure their children with prayer. *Walker v. Superior Court*, 763 P.2d 852 (Cal. 1988).
7. See, e.g., *United States v. Irvin*, 369 F.3d 284 (3d Cir. 2004).

A. he was on notice of the risk of using indoor fireworks, but disregarded those risks during the show because he was willing to take any risk to bring in more patrons.

B. he should have realized the risk caused by his extremely negligent behavior, especially when there was no good reason for him to take the risk.

C. he acted in the heat of passion.

D. he premeditated the deaths of the patrons.

E. the victims did not contribute to the negligent behavior.

ANALYSIS. This question is reminiscent of the famous case of *Commonwealth v. Welansky*, 316 Mass. 383, 55 N.E.2d 902 (1944). In that case, the defendant owned a nightclub, the New Coconut Grove. The nightclub had inadequate emergency exits and was generally crowded and unsafe. One night, when the owner was in the hospital, a bar boy accidentally started a fire by lighting a match near some table decorations. The fire quickly spread, killing many patrons and employees trapped in the club. Defendant, the owner, was convicted of manslaughter and sentenced to 15 years of hard labor. The court held that even though the defendant was apparently unaware of the risk at the club and was not even present when the fire occurred, he was grossly negligent in its operation. The conditions under which he operated the club justified criminal punishment. Using this case as a guide, let's evaluate each of the answers proposed.

A is incorrect. If the defendant actually was on notice and subjectively disregarded the risks of his behavior, he will likely be guilty of murder, not manslaughter. Don't forget that conscious disregard of the risk to human life is sufficient for malice and murder.

Skip **B** for a moment while we consider the other options. **C** is incorrect because a heat of passion killing, although a type of manslaughter, is not the type that is ordinarily classified as involuntary manslaughter. Rather, heat of passion killings are typically voluntary manslaughter or manslaughter. Of course, **D** is incorrect because a premeditated killing is first-degree murder, not manslaughter at all. Finally, let's look at **E**. Contrary to tort law, the criminal law does *not* recognize any contributory negligence of the deceased as a defense to homicide. Thus, even if the concert attendees should have known better than to pack into the club, their negligent behavior would not excuse the defendant.

B is the correct answer. The nightclub owner should have realized the risk by his use of fireworks. In fact, if fireworks are viewed as "dangerous instrumentalities," the mere negligent use of them automatically would be sufficient for criminally culpable negligence. In any case, as in *Welansky*, the nightclub owner in this case can expect to be charged and even convicted of involuntary manslaughter.

I.   Model Penal Code approach: Reckless and negligent homicides

The Model Penal Code structures its approach to unintentional killings slightly differently from many common law jurisdictions. A person who kills another recklessly is guilty of manslaughter, unless the defendant demonstrates extreme indifference to human life. Model Penal Code §210.3(1)(a).

The Model Penal Code does not classify negligent killings as manslaughter. Rather, it makes them a separate lesser felony of "negligent homicide." Model Penal Code §210.4. Thus, killings that may be manslaughter under common law would be labeled negligent homicide under the Model Penal Code.

The key under the Model Penal Code is determining whether the defendant consciously disregarded the risk to human life or should have known of the risk. If it is the former, the defendant is guilty of at least manslaughter and possibly murder. If the defendant should have known the risk, the defendant is guilty of negligent homicide.

QUESTION 8. Pet alligator.   Dundee loves his pet alligator. The alligator is so gentle to him that he never even realized that it could hurt another person. However, Dundee is proved wrong when a neighborhood child wanders into Dundee's yard and becomes the alligator's lunch.

Under the Model Penal Code, Dundee should be charged with

A. first-degree murder.
B. second-degree murder.
C. involuntary manslaughter.
D. manslaughter.
E. negligent homicide.

ANALYSIS.   This question is a good review of your knowledge of the categories of homicides under the Model Penal Code. **A** is wrong for several reasons. First, the Model Penal Code does not have different degrees of murder. See Model Penal Code §210.2. Second, murder requires that the defendant either "purposely, knowingly or recklessly under circumstances manifesting extreme indifference to the value of human life" cause the death of another. In this question, clueless Dundee honestly does not believe his pet would hurt another person. For this reason, **B** is also incorrect.

C is the wrong answer because the Model Penal Code also does not have a separate category of "involuntary manslaughter." Rather, all reckless killings are mere manslaughter. Therefore, the question is whether Dundee has acted in a reckless or negligent manner. Given the Model Penal Code's understanding of those terms, it appears as if Dundee has acted negligently. He should have realized the risk to human life, but he did not. Accordingly, **E** is the correct answer and **D** is wrong.

J. The Closer: Name that homicide

In real life, as well as on law school exams, a fact pattern may suggest several different levels of homicide. When this occurs, it is important for the student to focus on the answer that gives both a correct statement of the law and that matches the levels of homicide to that fact pattern. Try this closer to test your ability to match the law with the actual facts of your problem.

QUESTION 9. **Tommy Student.** Tommy Student has survived a semester of criminal law. On the day of his final exam, he arrives at the test site exhausted after studying for 72 hours straight. As he reads the exam, Tommy becomes furious. His professor has humiliated him by using him as the clueless defendant in one of her hypotheticals. Unable to focus, Tommy storms out of the exam room and heads for the professor's office. When he arrives at the office, Tommy begins screaming and gesticulating with his pen. When the professor tells him to put down the pen, Tommy picks up a letter opener on her desk and begins to gesture with it. As he jabs at his professor, Tommy falls forward. The letter opener strikes Tommy's professor in the chest. She dies of a wound to her heart.

Which of the following is correct?

A. If charged with murder, Tommy may use the Model Penal Code to argue that he is only guilty of manslaughter.
B. If charged with first-degree murder, Tommy should be acquitted because he had no motive for the killing.
C. If charged with second-degree murder, Tommy should be acquitted because he only intended to seriously injure, not kill his professor.
D. If charged with negligent homicide, Tommy is not guilty because he did not intend to kill his professor.

ANALYSIS. At first glance, several of these answers might look good. However, it is important to keep focused on whether the answer states both the law and facts correctly, and accurately applies the law to the facts. Let's start with **B**. **B** should be eliminated as an answer right away. First, motive is not required for a first-degree murder conviction, although it is usually helpful to prove premeditation. Moreover, the facts of this problem indicate that Tommy did have a motive to kill. He was angry at his professor for humiliating him. **B** is wrong as to both the law and the facts. **C** is also wrong; it misstates the law. If Tommy had an intent to seriously injure his professor, that would be sufficient for second-degree murder.

Some students will unfortunately jump at **D** simply because it mentions "negligent homicide" and the facts state that Tommy fell forward at the time of the killing. However, read the answer carefully. It doesn't state that Tommy is guilty of negligent homicide. Rather, it states that he is not guilty because he did not intend to kill. Negligent homicides do NOT require an intent to kill.

The only answer that comes close to having both the facts and the law correct is **A**. Under the Model Penal Code, Tommy could argue EMED. He would argue that his physical fatigue, together with the emotional humiliation he suffered, triggered him to kill. If accepted, he would only be guilty of manslaughter.

 ## Levenson's Picks

1. Tom and Dick	**E**
2. Debi and Elie	**D**
3. Neighborly love	**D**
4. Work is no fun	**D**
5. Delayed reaction	**D**
6. Life of hard knocks	**C**
7. Deadly concert	**B**
8. Pet alligator	**E**
9. Tommy Student	**A**

Felony Murder and Misdemeanor Manslaughter (Unlawful Act Doctrine)

There's more than one way to skin a
cat and there's more than one way to prove murder.

Now that you have mastered the mens rea levels required for murder and manslaughter, set aside that approach and take a look at anachronistic short cuts used to prove murder and manslaughter. The felony-murder doctrine allows prosecutors to prove murder simply by showing a death occurred during the defendant's commission of a felony, instead of proving that the defendant acted with malice. Using a legal fiction, prosecutors can substitute the defendant's intent to commit a felony for the ordinary intent required for murder. According to the felony-murder rule, once it is proved that the victim's death occurred during the defendant's commission of a felony, the defendant is automatically guilty of murder, regardless of her mens rea.

In many states, the legislature specifies exactly which felonies qualify for the felony-murder doctrine. In other jurisdictions, the courts must decide which felonies will trigger application of the rule. To do so, the courts not only analyze the general felony-murder rule, but also the limitations on its application.

As you might suspect, the felony-murder doctrine is controversial. It conflicts with criminal law's basic premise that a defendant should be punished according to the harm she intended to inflict. The felony-murder doctrine effectively allows a defendant to be convicted of murder for an unintentional killing.

Despite the controversy, and the Model Penal Code's rejection of the doctrine, the felony-murder doctrine still thrives in the United States. Yet, the criticisms have led many jurisdictions to impose limitations on its use. This chapter discusses the operation of the felony-murder rule and these limitations.

The chapter also discusses a related rule — the "unlawful act doctrine," also known as the "misdemeanor-manslaughter" doctrine. Under the unlawful act doctrine, a defendant is automatically guilty of manslaughter if a death occurs during the defendant's commission of an unlawful act that is not a felony. Once again, because of concerns about its use, some limitations have been created for its application.

A.   Felony murder: The general rule

The felony-murder rule dates back to early British common law.[1] When it was first used, the felony-murder doctrine might have made some sense. In early common law times, it was a capital offense to commit any felony. Thus, if one shot at a neighbor's deer and killed it, the defendant would be guilty of

---

1. For a history of the felony-murder doctrine, see *People v. Aaron*, 409 Mich. 672 (1980).

a capital crime. What would happen, however, if the arrow went astray and killed the neighbor? Even if the killing were accidental, common law would hold the defendant responsible for murder because he was already facing the death penalty for the underlying felony.

Under the felony-murder doctrine, the defendant is guilty of "constructive murder" because the intent to commit the felony substitutes for the intent to kill or cause grievous bodily harm. Traditionally, the felony-murder doctrine is not limited to foreseeable deaths. A felon is strictly liable for all killings committed personally or by an accomplice in the course of the felony.

Today, a classic example of the felony-murder rule would be a bank robber who intends to rob a bank without harming any victims. To that end, the robber uses a toy gun and speaks softly during the robbery. Despite the robber's precautions, one of the bank's customers has a heart attack and dies. Under the felony-murder doctrine, the defendant is still guilty of murder even though she did not intend to kill or harm, or believe that she was taking the risk of harming, the customer.

The rationales offered for the felony-murder rule are (1) it gives added incentive to felons not to participate in felonies or at least to be extra careful in their commission; (2) it vindicates society's additional calls for retribution when a death occurs; and (3) it eases the prosecution's burden of proving malice in cases in which the defendant probably did act in callous disregard of human life, but it may be difficult to prove.

Many modern commentators reject the felony-murder rule. They argue that (1) a person cannot be deterred from committing an accidental act; (2) the rule reflects a "bad luck" principle that punishes defendants who just have the bad luck of having someone unexpectedly die during their commission of a felony; (3) culpability for murder should be tied to a defendant's mens rea; and (4) prosecutors do not need assistance in homicide prosecutions, especially given that statistical evidence shows that homicides occur in felonies at a much lower rate than expected and, when a death occurs, there is usually evidence of the defendant's reckless intent.

At common law, felony murder based on the "big six" felonies of burglary, rape, kidnapping, robbery, arson, and mayhem would automatically lead to a first-degree murder charge. All other qualifying felonies (which meant that the felonies met the limitations discussed in the upcoming subsections of this chapter) would lead to a second-degree murder conviction.

Gradually, England, the creator of the felony-murder doctrine, moved away from its application. In 1957, England abolished the felony-murder rule. However, the rule remains, in one form or another, in nearly every state in the United States. In some jurisdictions, it creates automatic liability for murder. In other jurisdictions, such as Michigan, the rule creates a special category of murders requiring heightened punishment.

The first question of this chapter helps you test your basic understanding of the general felony-murder rule. After that question, we examine the limitations jurisdictions have put on the application of the rule because of the criticisms that have been leveled at it.

QUESTION 1. Accidental murder.   Katie is desperate for money. Her son, whom she adores, wants to go to camp with his friends. However, Katie does not have the money to send him. She decides to get the money she needs by buying insurance on an old boat her family has and surreptitiously burning it to collect the insurance proceeds. Believing her son is at school, Katie goes down to the empty lot where the boat is kept. She looks around to make sure no one is nearby and then lights the boat on fire. After the boat is destroyed, she is horrified to discover that her son skipped school that day and was hiding out in the boat with his friends. The friends survived, but her son was killed during the fire.

Under the felony-murder rule, Katie is

A. guilty of murder because she acted with callous disregard for human life.
B. guilty of murder because she should have realized her son could have been hiding in the boat.
C. guilty of murder because her son died during her commission of a felony.
D. guilty of involuntary manslaughter because a reasonable person would have realized that there is always a risk of harm when one sets a fire.
E. not guilty because she never intended to harm another person.

ANALYSIS.   Don't forget that the felony-murder rule is the "bad luck" rule. Obviously, Katie did not intend to harm her son. She loved him and wanted to get money to send him to camp. Nonetheless, she engaged in a felony (arson) that led to his death. Accordingly, under the traditional common law rule, Katie would be guilty of her son's murder. Let's examine the various options to see which one accurately applies the felony-murder rule to the facts of this question.

A is wrong. Although prosecutors might be able to make a case that Katie knew of the risk to human life and acted in reckless disregard of it, the felony-murder rule does not require proof of malice. Under the felony-murder rule, Katie is guilty of murder *regardless* of whether she acted in callous disregard for human life. In fact, it might be difficult in this case for the prosecution to prove actual malice. Katie is likely to argue that she had no reason to believe anyone would be harmed because the boat is kept in an empty lot, away from other people, and she chose to burn it when she thought her son was safe in school. By using the felony-murder rule, the prosecution could avoid the burden of proving that Katie acted with callous disregard for human life.

B is also wrong because the felony-murder rule does not even require that the defendant should have been aware of the risk. The defendant's responsibility for the murder is automatic, regardless of whether another person would have been aware of the risk to human life. We will address **C** in a moment. Meanwhile, **D** is also wrong. In fact, **D** is wrong for two reasons. First, the felony-murder rule does not require that the prosecution prove any level of mens rea for the homicide. Second, **D** gives the standard for involuntary manslaughter when one is using the mens rea approach to levels of homicide. Felony-murder bypasses that approach.

Our choices are now **C** and **E**. The moment of truth has arrived. Do you understand the basic nature of the felony-murder rule? If you do, you will automatically jump at **C** as the answer. **E** is wrong precisely because the felony-murder rule does *not* require that the defendant intend to harm anyone to be guilty of murder. As **C** states, Katie is guilty of murder because a death occurred during her commission of a felony.

B. Limitation on felony murder: Inherently dangerous felonies

As courts became concerned about the fairness of the felony-murder rule, they developed limitations on its application. These limitations still apply for felonies that are not specifically listed in qualifying statutes for felony murder in the applicable jurisdiction.

The first limitation, adopted by many jurisdictions, is that the defendant be engaged in an "inherently dangerous felony" at the time the victim's death occurs. Consider, for example, a situation in which a defendant is involved in tax fraud. While the defendant is showing his accountant how he plans to scam the Internal Revenue Service, the accountant has a heart attack and dies. Under the traditional felony-murder doctrine, the defendant would automatically be guilty of murder.

Concerned about the harshness of this doctrine, many jurisdictions require that the underlying felony be one that is already inherently dangerous to human life. By adding this requirement, those jurisdictions make it more likely that the defendant actually acted with malice, even though the felony-murder doctrine does not require that actual malice be proved. With such a requirement, the tax cheat would be off the hook for murder because the underlying felony of tax fraud is one that is not likely to be found inherently dangerous to human life.

Although this limitation is fairly easy to understand, there is an added twist you must learn. How do we determine whether a felony is inherently dangerous? Should we look at the *felony in the abstract* and ascertain whether commission of the felony will routinely put victims' lives at risk, or should we look at how the defendant committed the felony in the case at issue and determine whether the *felony as committed* was particularly risky?

As is often the case in the law, the standard you select often makes the crucial difference in whether the felony-murder doctrine applies. Defendants tend to prefer the felony in the abstract approach because it gives them leeway to argue that there are many ways for the underlying felony to be committed in which no one will get hurt. Consider, for example, the felony of grand theft. In the abstract, most of us would say that the felony of grand theft is not one inherently dangerous to human life. There are many ways to commit that felony without anyone being physically harmed. However, what if the grand theft is committed by telling a child's parents that the child, who is suffering from cancer, is best treated with a bogus therapy? As committed, the felony posed a great danger to human life. If the "as committed" test is applied, the felony would be inherently dangerous to human life. See *People v. Phillips*, 414 P.2d 353 (Cal. 1966) (finding the felony of grand theft in the abstract was not inherently dangerous to human life).

For prosecutors, the as committed test is the preferred standard for obvious reasons. The prosecution would not be seeking to apply the felony-murder rule unless somebody has died in the commission of the felony in that case. Thus, as committed, that felony proved to be very dangerous.

Often, the decision of whether the felony-murder rule will survive the first limitation on its application depends on what underlying felony prosecutors choose to anchor the rule and what standard the court uses to determine whether it is inherently dangerous. Go back to our arson case with the accidental death. If prosecutors charge the underlying felony of insurance fraud, it is less likely to be considered inherently dangerous, at least in the abstract, than the felony of arson. Likewise, if the felony is evaluated as committed, it is much more likely to be considered inherently dangerous than evaluating the felony in the abstract.

To see another example of how this first limitation works, try the next question.

QUESTION 2. Shotgun mama. Barbara is an ex-felon. She has been convicted of mail fraud for trying to sell fake gems to unwitting buyers. The police get word that Barbara is back to her old tricks. Therefore, they get a search warrant for her home to see if she has set up another mailing operation to solicit buyers for the fake gems. While executing the warrant, an officer trips over something sticking out from under the couch. As it turns out, Barbara has placed a loaded shotgun under her couch to protect her from intruders. The gun goes off and kills the officer. Barbara is charged with murder.

Under the felony-murder doctrine, Barbara

A. cannot be guilty because mail fraud is not an inherently dangerous felony.
B. cannot be guilty because she never intended to harm the officer.
C. is guilty because the felony of being an ex-felon in possession of a firearm is inherently dangerous in the abstract.
D. is guilty because the felony of being an ex-felon in possession of a firearm was inherently dangerous as committed.

ANALYSIS. Barbara was illegally in possession of a firearm and someone died. Under traditional common law, that would be sufficient to find her guilty of murder under the felony-murder rule. However, the modern approach requires that the court determine whether Barbara's underlying felony was inherently dangerous. To make that determination, it is important to do two things: (1) focus on the correct underlying felony for the felony murder; and (2) properly apply the tests for determining whether a felony is inherently dangerous.

Just because Barbara routinely engages in mail fraud, it would be wrong to assume that the felony-murder charge would be based on the felony of mail fraud. As we have seen, in the abstract, mail fraud is not a particularly dangerous felony. Therefore, it might be best to look for another possible felony to apply the felony-murder doctrine. In this question, Barbara is also guilty of being an ex-felon in possession of a weapon. Perhaps that felony will be a better fit for the doctrine. Let's look at the answers to see.

A would be the right answer if the only possible underlying felony were mail fraud. However, before you pick that answer, it is best to check other possible underlying felonies. Therefore, hold off on selecting **A** until we look at the other choices.

We can quickly eliminate **B**. It is wrong because it completely ignores the felony-murder doctrine. If the felony-murder doctrine applies, it does not matter that Barbara never intended to injure the officer.

How about **C**? **C** is wrong for a different reason. Although we may generally be afraid of ex-felons, it is not accurate to say that being an ex-felon in possession of a weapon is an inherently dangerous crime. There are many ways in which a felon can possess a weapon without creating a high likelihood of killing anyone. For example, an ex-felon may have a collection of old pistols in a locked cabinet. Technically, that still violates the prohibition on ex-felons having firearms, but it certainly is not inherently dangerous. See *People v. Satchell*, 489 P.2d 1361 (Cal. 1971).

That leaves us with **D**. As it turns out, the manner in which Barbara committed the felony of being an ex-felon in possession of a firearm was dangerous in this case. She dangerously left the weapon in a place where someone could trip over it and get hurt. Thus, if the as committed standard is applied, Barbara would be guilty of murder under the felony-murder doctrine.

Accordingly, even though Barbara might not be guilty of felony murder based on an underlying felony of mail fraud, there is another felony that would qualify as inherently dangerous. **D**, not **A**, is the better answer.

By now, you may have figured out that the requirement that the underlying felony be inherently dangerous is designed to limit the felony-murder doctrine to those felonies in which it is more likely that the defendant realized that her actions could hurt another person. The inherently dangerous limitation eliminates the least dangerous felonies from application of the felony-murder doctrine.

Also, there are some felonies that have traditionally satisfied the standards of the felony-murder doctrine. They include the common law felonies of burglary, arson, robbery, kidnapping, rape, and mayhem (BARKRM). In fact, many jurisdictions list these felonies as among those that may trigger first-degree felony murder.

C. Limitation on felony murder: Merger doctrine

There is another limitation on the felony-murder doctrine referred to as the "merger doctrine" or the "independent felony limitation." Just as the inherently dangerous limitation precludes the *least* serious types of felonies from eligibility for the felony-murder doctrine, the independent felony limitation blocks some of the *most* serious felonies from application of the doctrine.

Under the independent felony limitation, if the underlying felony is an "integral part" of the homicide itself, the felony-murder doctrine is not applied. In other words, if the underlying felony is just a step toward causing death, it merges with the resulting homicide. To use the felony-murder doctrine, there must be a separate purpose for punishing the underlying felony.

For example, assume the defendant is charged with assault with intent to kill and felony murder. Prosecutors could not use the assault with intent to kill as the underlying felony for their felony-murder charge. This makes sense for two reasons: (1) prosecutors have to prove intent to kill anyway, so it doesn't make sense to excuse them from proving intent to kill for the murder; and (2) assaulting someone with the intent to kill is just a step toward killing them. The assault literally merges into the murder.

The independent felony limitation serves many purposes. First, it prevents the bizarre result that would occur if any felony could serve as the basis for the felony-murder doctrine. If any felony could qualify, there would never be a crime of manslaughter. Think about it. Manslaughter is a felony. A death occurs during that felony. Automatically, all manslaughters would be murders. That is a bizarre result.

Second, the independent felony limitation prevents jurors from being confused as to when they must find intent and when they need not do so. Going back to our example of assault with intent to kill as the basis for a felony-murder charge, it would be very confusing for jurors to be instructed that they must find intent to kill for the underlying felony, but that they don't have to find malice for the murder.

Finally, one of the rationales for the felony-murder doctrine is that it deters defendants from engaging in dangerous behavior during the commission of a felony. For that rationale to apply, the underlying felony must be one that can be performed violently or nonviolently. For example, a theft can be performed with or without the threat of force. However, if the underlying felony, by definition, always involves the threat to human life, it is absurd to speak of a doctrine that coerces the defendant into committing that felony in a safe manner.

There are several cases that illustrate the operation of the independent felony doctrine. Consider, for example, *People v. Smith*, 678 P.2d 886 (Cal. 1984). In *Smith*, the defendant was charged with felony murder based on the underlying felony of child abuse. The court held that the felony-murder doctrine did not apply because the underlying felony required that the jury determine whether the defendant acted "under circumstances or conditions likely to produce great bodily harm or death." *Id.* at n. 4. In other words, the prosecution was already required to prove that the defendant acted with malice. In such a case, the shortcut of the felony-murder doctrine does not really have a role.

Another famous case is *People v. Ireland*, 450 P.2d 580 (1969). In *Ireland*, the defendant faced felony murder for the death of his wife. The prosecutor tried to use the felony of assault with a deadly weapon to support the application of the felony-murder doctrine. The California supreme court rejected this approach. It held that the underlying felony of assault with a deadly weapon was just a step toward killing the victim and therefore merged with the homicide charge. Prosecutors did not meet the requirement of showing an independent felony supporting the felony-murder charge.

Over the years, the courts have recognized certain felonies as qualifying as independent felonies for the felony-murder doctrine. In most jurisdictions, robbery, burglary, kidnapping, rape, arson, and lewd conduct with a minor qualify as "independent" felonies. However, not all burglaries may qualify. For example, if a burglary is based on an unlawful entry "with intent to kill or assault," that burglary felony may not qualify because it requires proof of malice.

QUESTION 3. Poison pill. Jeanette is charged with felony murder for the death of her husband. The underlying felony for the felony-murder charge is the charge of poisoning. It seems that Jeanette was caught lacing her husband's dinner with arsenic. Poisoning is defined as "willfully administering a toxic substance to another person with the purpose of causing grave illness or death." In those jurisdictions that require that the felony supporting a felony-murder doctrine be an independent felony, Jeanette is likely to be

A. not charged with felony murder because poisoning is an independent felony.

B. not charged with felony murder because only burglary, robbery, rape, kidnapping, and mayhem may serve as the basis for a felony murder.

C. not charged with felony murder because poisoning is not an independent felony.

D. charged with felony murder.

ANALYSIS. The issue raised by this question is whether the underlying felony of poisoning is sufficiently independent to qualify for the felony-murder doctrine. For two reasons, the answer to that question must be no. First, it is fairly clear from the facts of this problem that the poisoning of the husband was just a step toward killing him. There really was no separate purpose for the felony. Second, the elements for the crime of poisoning require that the prosecution prove malice. There can be no conviction for poisoning unless Jeanette had the purpose of causing her husband to become gravely ill or die. It would be extraordinarily confusing to instruct the jury that they need not find malice for murder, when the jury must find malice anyway for the underlying felony charge. With these basic considerations in mind, let's examine the possible answers.

A is wrong because if a felony is an independent felony, it qualifies for the felony-murder doctrine and Jeanette would be charged with felony murder, not exempt from it. Moreover, for the reasons we just reviewed, it is apparent that the felony of poisoning is not independent. Therefore, A is wrong on both the facts and the law.

B is also wrong. Although the felonies listed in that answer will routinely qualify for the felony-murder doctrine, they are *not* the only felonies that qualify. The list of felonies that qualify for felony murder varies by jurisdiction. If you are presented with a felony not routinely used for felony-murder cases, it is important that you understand how each of the possible limitations works and not automatically assume the felony does or does not qualify.

Now, you are faced with the real choice—**C** or **D**? Is poisoning, especially in the circumstances of this case, really an independent felony? Quite clearly, it is not. Poisoning was just the means that Jeanette intentionally took to kill her husband. If the prosecutors can prove poisoning, they don't really need the shortcut of felony murder and it would be very confusing to instruct the jurors that they need not decide whether Jeanette acted in gross disregard for human life.

Therefore, **C** is the correct answer. Jeanette will not be charged with felony murder because the felony of poisoning is not independent. Rather it merges into the crime of murder. **D** is incorrect.

D. Application of felony-murder doctrine: During the commission of the felony

Even if there is a qualifying felony to trigger the felony-murder doctrine, courts will not apply the felony-murder rule unless the charged death occurred "during the commission of the felony." In making this determination, the circumstances of the killing must actually satisfy two conditions: (1) it was sufficiently temporally and geographically related to the commission of the felony; and (2) the felonious conduct was the cause of the death. Some courts refer to this as the *res gestae* rule.

As to the first requirement, it is important when the killing occurred. For example, imagine that some bank robbers robbed a bank, successfully fled, and, after getting home and counting their loot, drove to a local bar to celebrate. While they are driving to the bar, they accidentally hit a pedestrian. Would the felony-murder rule apply? Probably not. By the time the felons hit the pedestrian, the felony had concluded. Instead of being guilty of murder, the felons would likely face a charge of manslaughter.

However, what if the bank robbers have robbed a bank and while they are speeding away to avoid getting caught, they accidentally hit a pedestrian? In that situation, the felony has not yet been completed and the felony-murder rule would apply.

Obviously, the key question is: When do felonies begin and end? *Ordinarily, a felony begins with the preparations for the crime and does not end until the defendants are in custody or have reached a position of "temporary safety."* See *People v. Lopez*, 116 Cal. App. 3d 882 (1981); *People v. Gladman*, 41 N.Y.2d 124 (1976); *People v. Salas*, 500 P.2d 7, 15 (Cal. 1972). Therefore, if one of the bank robbers, in cleaning her weapon to ready it to rob the bank, accidentally causes it to discharge and the bullet hits a passerby, the robbers would be guilty of murder. Likewise, if the robbers cause a customer to have a heart attack when they use her as a shield while escaping from the bank, the felony-murder rule would still be in play. However, if the victim runs into the robber the next day, screams with fear, and dies of a heart attack, the felony-murder probably would not apply.

Try this next question that focuses on when a killing is during the commission of a felony.

QUESTION 4. Cloudy skies. Myra and Margo have plans to kidnap a wealthy businessman, Douglas, and hold him for ransom. After his business closes, Myra and Margo force Douglas into the trunk of their car. They drive him to a remote location and call his wife. Myra and Margo tell his wife, Lori, to leave $100,000 for them at a designated storage locker, and not to call the police. Lori complies. Douglas is then released and returns home. About a week later, Douglas is so stressed about his ordeal that he has a heart attack and dies. Myra and Margo are apprehended a week thereafter.

If Myra and Margo are charged with felony murder, they will most likely

A. be convicted because they kidnapped Douglas and caused his stress.
B. be convicted because they acted with gross recklessness when they kidnapped Douglas.
C. be acquitted because Douglas was never in danger.
D. be acquitted because Douglas's death did not occur during the commission of a felony.

ANALYSIS. Myra and Margo are clearly in trouble for kidnapping, but they may escape prosecution for murder because their felony was complete by the time of Douglas's death. In looking at the options, **A** is wrong because the kidnapping was over, even though the victim continues to experience stress from the ordeal. Had the victim suffered his heart attack during the actual kidnapping, Myra and Margo would be guilty of murder. However, because he had returned to safety and Myra and Margo had completed the kidnapping, the felony-murder rule would no longer apply.

B is also wrong because gross recklessness has nothing to do with the felony murder rule. Remember that the felony-murder rule serves as a substitute for the traditional intent requirements for malice.

C is wrong because it is factually incorrect to state that Douglas was never in danger. In fact, kidnapping is almost always considered a dangerous felony.

Sometimes, the most obvious answer is the correct one. That is the case here. **D** is the correct answer because the death did not occur during the commission of the felony.

E. Felony murder causation issues

In addition to requiring that the felony be linked by time and location to the victim's death, there is also a requirement that the felonious conduct be the "cause" of the victim's death. As Chapter 7 explained, "causation" is shorthand for the determination of whether there was enough of a relationship between the defendant's actions and the harm that resulted such that the defendant should be held responsible. In the felony-murder situation, the issue is whether the felonious conduct was sufficiently related to the death that occurred to hold the felons responsible. As some courts put it, was the death "in furtherance of the felony"?

To determine whether the felony was the cause of the death, courts look at several issues: (1) Who did the killing? (2) Who was killed? (3) Are there any other facts that indicate the killing was not in furtherance of the underlying felony?

1. Who did the killing?

If the death was caused directly by a felon, courts ordinarily have little trouble finding that the felonious conduct was the cause of the victim's death. For example, if three robbers enter a jewelry store and one felon shoots the store owner, the felony-murder rule would hold all co-felons responsible for the victim's murder. However, problems arise when the killing is committed by a non-felon. For example, what if three robbers enter a jewelry store and the owner, meaning to shoot a co-felon out of self-defense, accidentally kills another customer in the store? Who is responsible — the felons or the store owner?

To answer this question, courts apply one of two theories: the agency theory and the proximate cause theory. A majority of jurisdictions apply the *agency theory* of felony murder. Under this theory, a felon is only responsible for the death of a victim if that death was caused directly by one of the felons. If a third party causes the death, the felons are not responsible.

For example, assume that three robbers enter a store. Robber 1 shoots the store owner. Under the agency theory, each felon is an agent of his co-felons so all three felons are responsible for the store owner's murder. However, if instead of a felon shooting the store owner, the felon instead uses the store owner as a human shield and the police accidentally shoot the store owner during a gun battle, the felons are not guilty of felony murder because the death did not occur at the hand of one of the felons. A majority of courts follow the agency approach of felony murder.

The *proximate cause theory* is an alternative approach to determining whether the felony-murder doctrine should apply. Under this theory, a felon is responsible for any death that occurs during the felony regardless of whether the felon directly caused the death so long as the death was sufficiently related to the felons' conduct. This theory was originally created to deal with the "shield cases" in which innocent victims would be killed by police officers during gun battles with the felons. See, e.g., *Taylor v. State*, 55 S.W. 961 (Tex. Ct. App. 1900); *Keaton v. State*, 57 S.W. 1125 (Tex. Ct. App. 1900). In such cases, even though the felon's bullet did not kill the victim, the felon is still responsible for felony murder because the felon's conduct precipitated the death.

There is no set rule identifying exactly when a killing is sufficiently related to the felonious conduct for the defendants to be guilty under the proximate cause theory. Each case depends on its facts. Some courts have described proximate cause thus: "when a felon's attempts to commit a forcible felony set in motion a chain of events which were or should have been within his contemplation when the motion was initiated, he should be held responsible for any death which by direct and almost inevitable consequence results from the initial criminal act." See *People v. Lowery*, 687 N.E.2d 973, 976 (Ill. 1997).

The proximate cause theory has been extended to situations beyond the shield cases. For example, when police officers arrive at a crime scene and the felons begin a gun battle, if one police officer accidentally kills another police officer, the felony-murder doctrine may apply because the death "proximately resulted" from the unlawful activity. See *Commonwealth v. Almeida*, 68 A.2d 595 (Pa. 1949).

2. Who was killed?

In addition to limiting the felony-murder rule by who did the killing or whether the death was proximately related to the felony, some courts do not apply the rule when the victim is a co-felon and not an innocent person. See *Commonwealth v. Redline*, 137 A.2d 472 (Pa. 1958) (felony-murder rule did not apply in proximate cause jurisdiction when police officer killed a co-felon). There are several rationales for this limitation on the application of the felony-murder rule. Felons are not responsible for the death of a co-felon because (1) the killing is viewed as justifiable; (2) co-felons' lives are valued less than those of innocent victims; (3) it is difficult to understand how the death of a co-felon would be "in furtherance of" the felony; and (4) felons assume the risk of dying when they participate in a felony. Although controversial, this exception to the felony-murder rule still survives in many jurisdictions.

3. Did it further the felony?

There is no requirement that the co-felons intend that their victim's death further the felony, but courts may relieve co-felons of responsibility for unanticipated actions by a fellow felon that are not in furtherance of the common purpose of their felony. For example, assume that felons decide to rob a bank. While inside the bank, one of the felons decides to rape one of the customers and then kills her. The other felons could argue that they are not responsible because the death occurred during a separate felony. Some courts use this limitation as a further safety valve to acquit co-felons of murder if one felon's actions are so unpredictable and outside the common purpose of the felony that the co-felons should not be held responsible. See, e.g., *United States v. Heinlein*, 490 F.2d 725 (D.C. Cir. 1973) (co-felon stabbed rape victim when she slapped him; other rapists may not be responsible for murder).

It is time to test your understanding of this last category of restrictions on the application of the felony-murder rule. Remember, the question is ultimately whether the death occurred "during the course and in furtherance of" the felony. Try your hand at the next problem.

QUESTION 5. The botched arson. Manny, Mo, and Jack decide to burn down Jack's dilapidated warehouse to collect the insurance proceeds. At the time they plan to burn it down, they don't realize that two homeless persons (Lou and Larry) have taken shelter in the warehouse. Manny, Mo, and Jack set the warehouse on fire and the structure starts to burn. Firefighters and police respond to an emergency call about the fire. Lou perishes in the fire. However, Larry and Jack are killed when the police accidentally shoot them during their gun battle to apprehend Manny and Mo at the scene.

In this jurisdiction, felony murder only applies for the death of innocent persons. If Manny and Mo are charged with the deaths of Lou, Larry, and Jack, which of the following is true?

A. In an agency jurisdiction, they are automatically guilty of felony murder for the deaths of all three victims.

B. In an agency jurisdiction, they are automatically guilty of the felony murder of Lou and Larry.

C. In a proximate cause jurisdiction, they are automatically guilty of felony murder of all three victims.

D. In a proximate cause jurisdiction, they are automatically guilty of the felony murder of Lou only.

E. None of the above.

ANALYSIS. This question is a little tricky because you have to remember two sets of limitations on the felony-murder rule. First, you must make sure you understand how the agency and proximate cause theories apply. Second, you must keep in mind the limitation for deaths of co-felons. With these principles in mind, let's look at the various options.

A is clearly incorrect because the agency theory only applies when a victim dies "at the hands" of a co-felon. Manny and Mo may be guilty of the felony-murder of Lou because they set the fire, but the direct causes of the deaths of Larry and Jack were the police shootings. Thus, under the agency theory, Manny and Mo are not responsible for those deaths. (*Note:* Under the agency theory, it doesn't matter whether Manny or Mo set the fire. They are responsible for the acts of each co-conspirator.)

B is also incorrect. Some students might be tempted to select this answer because both Lou and Larry are innocent victims in the killings and not co-felons. However, the problem remains that the police shot Larry; he was not directly killed by one of the co-felons.

At this point, you might be tempted to jump at **C** as a correct answer. After all, the proximate cause theory expands culpability to killings that are related to, but not necessarily the direct result of, the felons' actions. However, one of the victims is not an innocent person. Therefore, under the limitation of "who was killed?" during the felony, the defendants are not guilty of Jack's death. **C** is also incorrect.

How about **D**? This answer is also incorrect because it is too limited. Under the proximate cause theory, the defendants are at least guilty of both innocent persons' deaths, not just Lou's death. Therefore, the correct answer for this problem is the dreaded **E** (none of the above). You will only arrive at this answer if you carefully evaluate each possible response for all the rules you have learned about felony murder.

And you are not through yet. There is one more twist on the during the course of and in furtherance of the felony that must be mastered.

F.   Provocative act doctrine

As noted in the prior section, in agency jurisdictions, a felon ordinarily is not responsible for a victim's death unless it was directly caused by one of the co-felons. If the death is at the hands of a third party, felony murder does not apply. However, even in an agency jurisdiction, there may be another doctrine that imposes culpability on the co-felons for deaths at the hands of a third party. It is known as the "provocative act" doctrine. It is often a way around the limitations of the agency theory.

Consider the situation in which felons rob a store and trigger a gun battle with the store owner. The store owner then kills an innocent customer in the store. Under the agency theory, the felons would not be responsible for that death. However, there is a separate theory — apart from felony murder — by which the felons may be responsible. That theory is the provocative act doctrine, which provides that if the actions of a felon create "an atmosphere of malice" that provokes a third party into committing the killing, the felons are guilty of murder. The doctrine is technically not a felony-murder principle because there is an actual finding of malice created by the co-felons' provocative behavior.

The provocative act doctrine was recognized in the famous case of *Taylor v. Superior Court*, 477 P.2d 131 (Cal. 1970). In that case, defendant Taylor acted as the getaway driver in a robbery. While Taylor waited in the car, his co-felons tried to rob a liquor store. After they brandished their guns and repeatedly threatened the victim-owners, the victim-owners shot and killed one of the robbers. Taylor was charged with his co-felon's murder. Because the jurisdiction had adopted the agency theory of felony murder and someone other than one of the felons killed the co-felon, the court had to devise another theory to create liability. Notwithstanding conflicting case law (see *People v. Washington*, 62 Cal. 2d 777, 402 P.2d 130 (1965)), the court held that Taylor was responsible because his co-felon's provocative conduct, as shown by "aggressive actions," caused the death.[2]

Sometimes, the provocative act doctrine is referred to as "vicarious liability" because co-felons are responsible for the atmosphere of malice created by one of their co-felons that results in the death of another person. You'll see how this works in the next question.

QUESTION 6. Running from the law. Mike and Ben, members of the Clips gang, steal a car while an innocent passenger is in the backseat of the car. During the carjacking, Ben and Mike are spotted by the police. Mike starts shooting at the police as Ben tries to speed away. The police shoot back. During the chase, the police accidentally shoot the passenger in the back seat of the car. Mike and Ben are charged with murder.

Assume that the case is charged in a jurisdiction that uses the agency theory of felony murder. Are Mike and Ben guilty of murder?

A. Yes, because of the felony-murder doctrine.
B. Yes, because of the provocative act doctrine.
C. No, because the police shot the victim.
D. No, because only Mike acted with malice.
E. None of the above.

ANALYSIS. As with many questions, the best clue for your answer is in the question itself. When the question states that you are to assume you are in an agency jurisdiction, you should automatically be thinking of the limitations of the agency doctrine approach and ways around it. What that means, of course, is that under the felony-murder rule, felons are only responsible for

---

2. Later, the holding in *Taylor* was overruled by *People v. Antick*, 15 Cal. 3d 79, 539 P.2d 43 (1975) because the death of the co-felon who created the atmosphere of malice was viewed as a suicide, not a homicide. The decision of whether to apply the provocative act doctrine when the co-felon has provoked his own killing varies by jurisdiction.

deaths they directly cause, not deaths caused by third parties. To hold the felons guilty of murder for deaths caused at the hands of third parties, prosecutors have to show malice by using the provocative act doctrine.

A is wrong because the felony-murder rule does not apply because it was not one of the felons who shot the victim. In an agency jurisdiction, in order for the felony-murder rule to apply, the death must be caused directly by one of the co-felons.

B, however, appears to be correct. When Mike started shooting at the police, he created an atmosphere of malice that led to the victim's death. This is the scenario anticipated by the provocative act doctrine. Just to be safe, let's check the other answers to see how they hold up.

C is wrong because it assumes there is no way to hold the defendants responsible for shootings by the police. There is such a way. It is the provocative act doctrine. Therefore, for all the reasons **B** is correct, **C** is the wrong answer.

D is wrong, but for a different reason. Even though we are not applying the felony-murder doctrine, it doesn't mean that felons are not responsible for the acts of their co-felons. As we see in Chapter 14, there is accomplice liability even without the felony-murder rule. Therefore, both Ben and Mike are responsible for the murder, even though it was only Mike whose shooting created the atmosphere of malice that led to the victim's death.

E is wrong because there is a correct answer. The answer is **B** for the reasons noted above.

———————————

Before we move on to another doctrine in this chapter, here is a chart that may help you organize your analysis of felony-murder problems.

Felony-Murder and Provocative Act Doctrines

Basic rule for felony-murder	Death during felony substitutes for proof of malice

Limitations for felony-murder doctrine	1. Inherently dangerous felony
	2. Independent felony
	3. In furtherance of felony
	   a. Duration of felony
	   b. Who caused death?
	      i. Agency theory
	      ii. Proximate cause theory
	   c. Who was killed?
	      i. Does that jurisdiction apply felony murder for death of a co-felon?
	   d. Was the killing outside the scope of the felony?

Provocative act/vicarious liability doctrine	Provocative acts of one felon create malice for all co-felons

G.   Model Penal Code approach to felony murder

The drafters of the Model Penal Code opposed the felony-murder principle because it does not link a defendant's culpability to her intent. However, they did not abolish the rule altogether. Rather, Model Penal Code §210.2(1)(b) provides that if a death occurs during the commission of certain listed felonies, there is a presumption that the defendant acted with recklessness and extreme indifference to human life. The listed felonies include engaging in or being an accomplice in the commission of, an attempt to commit, or flight after committing or attempting to commit robbery, rape, deviate sexual intercourse by threat of force, arson, burglary, kidnapping, and felonious escape.

Therefore, under the Model Penal Code, there is a presumption that a death that occurs during a felony meets the standards for murder, but the defense can rebut that presumption. Under the common law, once a death occurs during a felony, it is automatically murder.

In this next question, try to spot the difference between how felony murder would work under the Model Penal Code approach and the common law approach we studied earlier in this chapter.

QUESTION 7. Late night heist.   Walter breaks into Felipe's home late at night to steal his priceless painting. He does not bring a weapon because he does not want to hurt anyone. He just wants the painting. Hearing his window break, Felipe gets up to investigate. Although it is clear that Walter is not carrying a weapon, Felipe is so startled when he sees Walter that he has a heart attack and dies.

Walter is charged with murder. He is most likely

A. guilty under the common law and Model Penal Code approaches to felony murder.
B. not guilty under the common law approach to felony murder, but guilty under the Model Penal Code approach.
C. not guilty under the Model Penal Code approach to felony murder, but guilty under the common law approach.
D. not guilty under both the Model Penal Code and common law approaches to felony murder.

ANALYSIS.   This question illustrates why the common law approach to felony murder is considered to be harsher than the Model Penal Code approach. Under the common law approach, assuming that burglary is classified as an inherently dangerous felony (which it often is), Walter would be automatically guilty of murder. However, under the Model Penal Code approach, Walter would be allowed to rebut the presumption of extreme indifference by presenting evidence that he intentionally did not carry a weapon because he did not want to hurt anyone.

Accordingly, **A** is wrong because this is a situation in which Walter may be able to rebut the presumption against him. If he can, he is not guilty of felony murder. Also, technically, the Model Penal Code does not have felony murder. It only has murder, which is proved through a presumption.

B is wrong because the common law would impose automatic culpability. This would be a classic example of the reach of the felony-murder rule.

The choice is between **C** and **D**. **C** is the best answer. There is reason to believe that Walter could rebut the presumption against him under the Model Penal Code approach. However, it is very unlikely that he could escape culpability under the common law approach.

H. Unlawful act/misdemeanor-manslaughter doctrine

Just as the felony-murder rule substitutes for proving intent in a murder case, the misdemeanor-manslaughter (or unlawful act) doctrine may be used as a substitute for proving the necessary mens rea for an involuntary manslaughter charge. In many ways, it is analogous to the felony-murder rule. Sometimes, it is called the "misdemeanor-manslaughter" rule. Other jurisdictions refer to it as the "unlawful act" doctrine.

The basic rule is that unintentional killings committed during an unlawful act, not amounting to a felony, automatically constitute manslaughter. The commission of the unlawful act demonstrates that the defendant acted without due caution or circumspection.

For example, assume the defendant is charged with manslaughter when her two Rottweilers kill a passing jogger. The defendant violated a safety ordinance requiring that the dogs be restrained at all times. Because the defendant violated this ordinance, she is automatically guilty of manslaughter. See *State v. Powell*, 426 S.E.2d 91 (N.C. App. 1993).

Like the felony-murder rule, jurisdictions are often uncomfortable with imposing automatic liability on defendants for accidental deaths. Accordingly, the scope of the doctrine is often limited in some manner so that only violations that are likely to lead to serious harms trigger the doctrine. Jurisdictions can choose a variety of limitations to ensure that the unlawful act doctrine is used properly.

Some courts limit the application of the doctrine by requiring that the misdemeanor or unlawful act be "inherently dangerous." Like the inherently dangerous requirement for felonies qualifying for felony murder, this limitation helps ensure that defendants are only guilty of manslaughter in those situations in which it is most likely they did act with criminal negligence.

Other jurisdictions try to accomplish the same goal by requiring that the misdemeanor be *malum in se* ("wrong in itself"). In other words, it must be the type of violation that the law prohibits because the conduct is inherently wrong and could lead to serious harm. If the violation only has a regulatory purpose and is not designed to protect the safety of others, it is often called *malum prohibitum* and cannot trigger the misdemeanor-manslaughter rule. For example, if a defendant speeds down a street with her car and accidentally hits a child who has darted into the street, that defendant may be guilty of misdemeanor manslaughter because a speeding violation is *malum in se*. However, if that same driver is driving at a lawful speed, but with an expired driver's license, this technical violation is nothing more than *malum prohibitum* and would not trigger the misdemeanor-manslaughter doctrine. See, e.g., *Commonwealth v. Williams*, 133 Pa. Super. 104, 1 A.2d 812 (1938).

Finally, some jurisdictions simply state that the violation must be the "proximate cause" of the victim's death. Once again, this limitation is designed to require that there be some significant connection between the type of violation the defendant committed and the death that occurred. This limitation precluded the application of the misdemeanor-manslaughter doctrine in the case of *Todd v. State*, 594 So. 2d 802 (Fla. 1992). In *Todd*, the defendant stole $110 from a church collection plate and took off in his car. He was pursued by several congregants. One of these congregants had a heart attack during the chase, lost control of his vehicle, and died. The defendant was charged with manslaughter on the theory that the victim's death was caused by defendant's petty theft. The court dismissed the indictment because the petty theft did not encompass the kind of direct, foreseeable risk of physical harm that should trigger the misdemeanor-manslaughter doctrine.

If this doctrine seems easier than the felony-murder rule, it is. In part, this is because you have already learned the basic principles from the felony-murder rule. In part, it is because the sole focus of the limitations is on whether the unlawful act was sufficiently bad and related to the harm caused to hold the defendant responsible for manslaughter.

QUESTION 8. Dune-buggy tragedy. Kara loves to race her dune-buggy through the desert. She has been doing so for many years. Recently, state officials passed a law stating: "It is a violation of the law to drive an off-road vehicle in the desert without a permit. Violation of this law is punishable by six months in jail." Kara fails to obtain a permit, but continues to race her dune-buggy. One day, as she drives over a sand dune, she accidentally plows into a hiker and kills him.

Which of the following is true?

A. Kara is guilty of felony murder because her criminal violation led directly to the death of another person.
B. Kara is guilty of misdemeanor manslaughter if driving a dune-buggy without a permit is inherently dangerous.
C. Kara is not guilty of manslaughter because driving a dune-buggy is a *malum in se*, regulatory offense.
D. Kara is not guilty of manslaughter because she did not intend to hit her victim.

ANALYSIS.   This problem should be fairly easy if you read through the answers carefully. **A** is wrong because there is no underlying felony to trigger the felony-murder doctrine. The first step you must take in deciding whether to apply either the felony-murder rule or the misdemeanor-manslaughter doctrine is to determine the nature of the underlying offense. In this problem, you are told that the maximum penalty is six months in jail. Felonies ordinarily require more than a year in jail. Accordingly, the felony-murder doctrine would not apply in this scenario. If anything, it is a candidate for the misdemeanor-manslaughter or unlawful act doctrine.

B seems correct because it identifies the key issue in the problem: Is dune-buggying without a permit inherently dangerous? Ordinarily, simply driving without a permit is considered a regulatory offense. However, if the reason for requiring a permit is to ensure safety during an activity, the unlawful act doctrine may apply.

Luckily, it becomes quite clear after examining **C** and **D** that **B** is the best answer. **C** is almost nonsensical. *Malum prohibitum*, not *malum in se*, is the phrase used to describe regulatory offenses. **C** confuses the two principles and therefore is an incorrect answer. Likewise, **D** is wrong because it misses completely the standard for involuntary manslaughter. Involuntary manslaughter does not require that the defendant intend to harm her victim. Thus, the best answer is **B**.

I.   The Closer: Felony murder and the death penalty

There is rarely much inquiry about application of the unlawful act doctrine. By contrast, the felony-murder rule continues to come under constant criticism. Nonetheless, not only does it still exist in the United States, but it also can be the basis for a death penalty murder conviction.

In *Tison v. Arizona*, 481 U.S. 137 (1987), the Supreme Court held that the felony-murder doctrine can be used in a death penalty case as long as the prosecution demonstrates the defendant's "major participation in the felony committed, combined with reckless indifference to human life." In essence, the Court held that the felony-murder doctrine can establish the defendant's responsibility for the murder, but before the death penalty is imposed, there should also be some further indication by the defendant's participation and reckless indifference to human life that the defendant did indeed act with malice. In effect, there is a heightened felony-murder standard before the death penalty may be constitutionally imposed.

The *Tison* case provides an excellent review of the death penalty. The closer question tests not only your understanding of the general felony-murder rule, but also its application in a death penalty case.

QUESTION 9. Bad boys.   The Tison family is a model family — that is, a model family for antisocial and criminal behavior. The father, Gary Tison, was sentenced to life imprisonment for trying to kill a guard during an earlier prison break. Tison's wife, with their three sons, Donald, Ricky, and Raymond, then planned another escape for Gary Tison and his cellmate, Randy Greenawalt. Using an ice chest, they smuggled weapons into the prison and helped Tison escape. When their getaway car broke down, the group of men flagged down a passing motorist to steal his car. Trying to be Good Samaritans, John Lyons and his young family stopped. The Tisons commandeered the Lyons' car and drove them into the desert. There, Gary Tison ordered his sons to get some water for him.

While the boys were getting the water, they heard John Lyons beg for his life. Then they heard shots. Gary Tison and Randy Greenawalt had mercilessly gunned down the entire family.

Gary Tison escaped into the desert where he subsequently died of exposure, and Donald Tison was killed in a shootout with the police. Randy Greenawalt, Raymond Tison, and Ricky Tison were apprehended by the police.

Which of the following is correct?

A. In all jurisdictions, Raymond Tison, Ricky Tison, and Randy Greenawalt are responsible for the death of their co-felon, Gary Tison.
B. Raymond and Ricky Tison are not guilty of murder because they were not present when the victims were shot.
C. If Raymond and Ricky Tison acted with reckless indifference toward Lyons and his family while the Tisons participated in the Lyons' kidnapping and their father's escape, they could face the death penalty.

> **D.** Only Gary Tison and Randy Greenawalt are guilty of a capital offense since they were the only felons who killed with premeditation.

ANALYSIS. The *Tison* case is truly horrifying. An innocent family was shot down in the desert when they tried to do a good deed. The case demonstrates the operation of the felony-murder rule, as well as whether co-felons can face the death penalty, even if they were not the trigger men.

A is wrong because in many jurisdictions, co-felons are not responsible for the death of a co-felon because that death is viewed as justifiable. Thus, while the surviving felons may all be responsible for the death of an innocent third party, it is not generally true that they are guilty of the death of one of their co-felons.

B is also wrong because it ignores the felony-murder rule. Under the felony-murder rule, it does not matter whether the defendants were actually present when the victims were killed. As co-felons, they are nonetheless responsible for the victims' deaths.

Likewise, **D** is a wrong answer. First-degree felony murder, including felony-murder that qualifies for the death penalty, does not necessarily require that all the felons act with premeditation as to the victims' deaths. Rather, their intent to commit the felony substitutes for the malice and premeditation usually required for the highest level of murder.

That leaves us with **C**. While it is certainly controversial as to whether a defendant who does not order a murder or pull the trigger himself should face the death penalty for a killing by one of his co-felons, the law permits this ultimate sanction if the facts demonstrate the defendant's major participation in a felony, combined with reckless indifference for human life. See *Tison v. Arizona*, 481 U.S. 137, 158 (1987). Though they were ultimately spared from execution, Ricky and Raymond Tison could be tried for a capital offense.

✧ Levenson's Picks

1. Accidental murder	C
2. Shotgun mama	D
3. Poison pill	C
4. Cloudy skies	D
5. The botched arson	E
6. Running from the law	B
7. Late night heist	C
8. Dune-buggy tragedy	B
9. Bad boys	C

Attempt

If at first you don't succeed, try, try again.

E ven an attempt to commit a crime is a crime in itself. The common law recognized the crime of attempt as a misdemeanor. Today, all U.S. jurisdictions prohibit the crime of attempt. Statutory definitions rely heavily on both common law and Model Penal Code concepts of attempt.

There are strong policy reasons to punish someone who attempts but fails to commit a crime. First, a great number of defendants who attempt to commit a crime fail in their efforts only because of circumstances beyond their control. For example, the defendant who tries to rob a bank, but is foiled because he enters just as local police officers are cashing their pay checks, still poses a danger to society. The purposes of punishment still apply to that individual. The robber deserves to be punished because he demonstrated his intent to harm others. There is also a need to deter that individual and others who would try their luck at robbing banks. Unless they are punished, there is no reason for them not to keep trying to rob banks until they succeed. Additionally, a person who attempts to rob a bank is a dangerous individual. It is only a matter of time before he will be successful in harming, financially or otherwise, another person. Finally, society must step in when it can and, if possible, rehabilitate the robber into pursuing law-abiding activities.

Accordingly, the law punishes attempt, although there is a split about how much punishment to impose on a defendant who is only guilty of attempt. That issue is discussed in the general overview of attempt crimes in Section B. Additionally, because the defendant has not actually caused any harm, there is a need to set standards for attempt crimes so that we only punish those defendants who definitely intend to complete the criminal act and have come far enough in their efforts that it makes sense for law enforcement to get involved. Accordingly, the mens rea and actus reus standards for attempt crimes are tailored to ensure that the defendant who is punished for attempt deserves to be marked as a criminal.

Keep in mind throughout this chapter that attempt, like any other crime, requires proof beyond a reasonable doubt of an actus reus and a mens rea. However, unlike crimes such as murder, there is no need to prove that the defendant caused a specific harm.

A. Nature of inchoate crimes

Attempt is an "inchoate crime" because a defendant bears criminal responsibility before the completion of the target offense. In essence, the defendant is punished for trying to commit a crime. The law recognizes other inchoate crimes. For example, solicitation to commit a crime is also an inchoate crime. (See Chapter 13.) A defendant who recruits another person to commit a crime is guilty of an offense whether or not the other person accepts the defendant's proposal. Likewise, conspiracy to commit a crime is an inchoate crime because it punishes a defendant for planning with others to commit a crime, even if that plan never comes to fruition. (See Chapter 15.) Finally, consider the crime of stalking. Stalking is an inchoate crime because the defendant's actions can psychologically and emotionally harm the victim, whether or not the victim is physically harmed.

What do all of these crimes (attempt, solicitation, conspiracy, and stalking) have in common? They punish before the defendant has actually caused the harm he intended. Inchoate crimes provide society with a safety barrier that punishes those who are intent on committing criminal offenses. The remainder of this chapter focuses on attempt. Solicitation and other minor inchoate crimes are discussed in Chapter 13 and conspiracy is addressed in Chapter 15. Although we still need to discuss the details of each of these crimes, try the following question just to give you a quick look at the world of inchoate crimes.

> **QUESTION 1. Too close for comfort.** Mia is furious at her husband, Scott, for having an affair with another woman. Mia approaches her gardener, Jerry, and asks him to help her kill Scott. Jerry declines. Mia then asks Jerry if he'll at least make Scott's life a living hell. Jerry agrees. He follows Scott everywhere he goes. Jerry's actions are designed to, and have the effect of, making Scott extremely anxious and afraid. Meanwhile, Mia puts a deadly snake in the pocket of Scott's suit jacket. However, just before Scott puts on his suit, he notices the snake and calls for help. When the police learn that Mia intended to kill Scott and Jerry intended to harass him, they file criminal charges.
>
> Mia and Jerry are
>
> A. not guilty of any crime because they were never successful at physically harming Scott.
> B. guilty of inchoate crimes because Mia disliked Scott.
> C. not guilty of any crime because Jerry did not commit the crime he was originally asked to commit.
> D. guilty of the inchoate crimes of attempted murder and stalking even if Scott was not physically injured.

ANALYSIS. Although we have not learned the technical requirements for the crimes of attempt, solicitation, and stalking, it should have been clear to you that Mia and Jerry face criminal prosecution even though they were not successful in harming Scott. Therefore, **A** is wrong. Inchoate crimes do not require physical harm.

C can also be eliminated because Mia was guilty of soliciting Jerry to commit murder, regardless of whether Jerry wanted to participate in the scheme. The mere act of asking for Jerry's assistance constituted an inchoate crime.

That leaves you with **B** and **D**. **B** simply states that Mia and Jerry are guilty of some type of crime because Mia had a motive to hurt Scott. However, motive alone is insufficient for any crime. There must be an actus reus and a mens rea, as discussed in detail in the next subsection.

Accordingly, and by process of elimination, **D** is the correct answer. Mia is guilty of attempted murder and Scott of stalking regardless of whether Jerry was physically injured.

B. General overview of attempt crime

Attempt is a separate crime, but if a defendant is successful in his attempt, the crime of attempt merges with the completed crime and the defendant is only guilty of the completed crime. However, if the defendant is unsuccessful in completing the crime, the defendant who has satisfied the applicable mens rea and actus reus requirements is still guilty of the separate offense of attempt.

Initially, the common law recognized attempt as only a misdemeanor. Today, attempt may be charged as a felony, although most jurisdictions punish attempt less severely than the completed crimes. Under the majority approach, attempt carries a lesser punishment than the completed crime because the defendant's acts have caused less harm. However, the minority approach and Model Penal Code approach is to punish attempts the same as the completed crimes, except for crimes punishable by death or life imprisonment. (Model Penal Code §5.05(1).) The rationale for this position is that the defendant still intended to cause harm and therefore still needs to be deterred and punished for his efforts. According to this view, a defendant's punishment should not depend on the good luck or bad luck in completing the plan. The defendant still poses a danger to society. See H.L.A. Hart, Punishment and Responsibility 129-131 (1968).

Understandably, the criminal justice system is hesitant to punish an individual who has not actually caused any harm. There are a variety of policy reasons for setting the standards for attempt crimes high enough so that the court can be sure the defendant intended to harm another and would have done so if the conditions had been different. These policy concerns include:

1. *Police intervention.* At what point does it make sense for the police to intervene? If the police wait too long to intervene, they may fail to

prevent harm. However, if police jump in any time a person takes an innocuous step that could theoretically lead to harm, innocent people could face punishment and law enforcement resources would be wasted.

2. *Not punishing for bad thoughts.* In general, the law does not punish for bad thoughts alone. Rather, a crime requires a criminal intent and a criminal act. Attempt law must be framed in terms that do not punish an individual merely for his bad thoughts.

3. *Chance for abandonment.* Punishment of conduct at too early a stage offers the defendant little reason or opportunity to change his conduct to avoid completing the crime.

4. *Certainty that defendant intended to commit a crime.* Because the defendant has not caused any actual harm, it is important that attempt law require a clear showing of the defendant's intent to commit a crime. It is defendant's intent, in combination with his efforts, that make him blameworthy for the attempt.

Consider these policy considerations in answering the following question. Although policy questions are frequently tested by an essay question, it is possible for your professor to use a multiple-choice question to test your knowledge of the policy considerations underlying a criminal law doctrine.

QUESTION 2. Don't play with matches.   Michael hates his boss. He often fantasizes about burning down his boss's house. Michael has shared these thoughts with his co-workers. One day, Michael goes to the store and buys some matches. One of his co-workers sees him. The co-worker calls 911 and the police come and arrest Michael for attempted arson. Would you expect prosecutors to charge Michael with attempted arson?

A. Yes, because it is immoral to wish harm on another person.

B. Yes, because matches can be used to set a fire.

C. No, because it is never appropriate to punish someone when they haven't caused any actual harm.

D. No, because Michael's conduct is still ambiguous and proceeding against Michael would not be a wise use of police and prosecutorial resources.

ANALYSIS.   This type of question focuses on your understanding of the principles underlying the law of attempt, rather than your actual knowledge of the mens rea and actus reus requirements. However, as with every other area of criminal law, it is critical that you understand the policy reasons underlying the actus reus and mens rea requirements for the crime. This question requires you to show that understanding for the crime of attempt.

A may have seemed appealing at first because it plays to our basic belief that it is wrong to wish harm on another person. However, don't forget that the law does not criminalize everything that is immoral. Not all sins are crimes and not all crimes are necessarily immoral (e.g., regulatory, strict liability offenses). Thus, **A** is wrong. While it may be immoral to fantasize about harming another person, it is not necessarily criminal.

B is also incorrect. While it is true that matches can be used to set a fire, the law does not prohibit all actions that hypothetically could lead to criminal behavior. If it did, the police could arrest potential fraud artists when they buy pens or alcoholics when they buy a car. Either one of these actions could eventually lead to criminal behavior, but it is far too early to commit the resources of law enforcement. It also risks punishing innocent people for equivocal behavior.

C is wrong because it goes too far. The very principle behind inchoate crimes is to allow the law to punish someone who hasn't yet caused any actual harm. The tip-off that this may be the wrong answer is the word *never*. Sometimes it is appropriate to punish people before they cause actual harm; sometimes it is not.

Once again, **D** is the correct answer. In the answer it sets forth the policy reasons for not applying attempt to all preparatory behavior. Rather, as discussed in the next section, lines must be drawn as to when that preparatory behavior is serious enough to justify punishment.

C.   Mens rea requirement for attempt

Like other crimes, attempt requires that the prosecution prove both the actus reus and the mens rea for that crime. While we ordinarily begin by discussing the actus reus for a crime, for inchoate crimes it is not unusual to focus initially on the defendant's intent. Accordingly, we begin with the mens rea requirement for attempt.

1. General Principles

The majority rule is that attempt is a specific intent crime that requires the highest level of mens rea; namely, purposefulness. Therefore, even if a lower mens rea would suffice for prosecuting the completed crime, an attempt of that crime requires a strong showing that the defendant actually intended to complete the offense.

Consider, for example, the crime of attempted murder. As we learned in Chapter 9, the crime of murder only requires that the defendant act with gross recklessness. However, the crime of attempted murder requires that the defendant have the purpose to kill his victim. The rationale behind this difference in mens rea standards is that courts want to be certain of a defendant's intent before they punish him for conduct that has not led to any actual harm.

The case of *People v. Kraft*, 478 N.E.2d 1154 (Ill. App. 1985) is a good example of this principle. In *Kraft*, the defendant shot his gun at victims in another car. When he was apprehended, he claimed he was only trying to scare the victims, not kill them. If the jury believed that explanation, the defendant would not be guilty of attempted murder because he did not act with the purpose to kill. This is true even though he would have been guilty of murder if he had actually hit one of his victims.

Some courts are willing to drop the mens rea requirement for attempt down to knowledge. For example, what if Kraft claimed that he knew it was virtually certain he would hit and kill the persons he shot at, but his purpose in shooting at them was just to scare them? In some courts, this knowledge would be enough to prove attempt.

Even in those courts in which knowledge is not enough to prove the mens rea for attempt, courts permit the prosecution to use a defendant's knowledge of the likely consequences of his acts to help prove intent. For example, imagine a defendant who throws a grenade into a crowded room. Although the defendant may claim that his purpose was just to disperse the crowd, it would not be difficult for the prosecution to argue that defendant's true plan was to thin the crowd by killing many of those inside the room.

Under the Model Penal Code, a defendant who "acts with the purpose of causing or with the belief that [his conduct] will cause" the prohibited result satisfies the mens rea for attempt. Model Penal Code §5.01(1)(b). This standard is more flexible than the common law standard and essentially allows the prosecution to prove the mens rea for attempt in those situations in which the defendant may not wish to cause a particular result but certainly believes that he will. In essence, it allows the mens rea level for attempt to dip down to the "knowingly" standard.

Consider, for example, a defendant who puts a bomb on a competitor's airplane with the purpose of destroying some critical documents being transported on the plane. While the defendant's purpose in putting the bomb on the airplane is to destroy the documents, the defendant undoubtedly believed that he would also kill anyone onboard that plane. If the bomb fails to explode, under the Model Penal Code standard, the defendant would still be guilty of attempt. Under the common law approach, prosecutors would have to argue why the defendant's purpose was really twofold: (1) to destroy the documents and (2) to kill those aboard.

Finally, some jurisdictions uphold attempt convictions if the defendant does not act with purpose, but has the mens rea required for the completed offense. For example, in *People v. Thomas*, 729 P.2d 972 (Colo. 1986), the defendant was charged with attempted manslaughter. In that jurisdiction, a defendant is guilty of manslaughter if he acts recklessly. Even though the prosecution could not prove that the defendant intended to kill or knew he would kill his would-be victims, the defendant was convicted of attempted manslaughter because he acted with recklessness.

Because of the difficulty of proving the high mens rea level ordinarily required for attempt, some jurisdictions have enacted lesser inchoate crimes that do not require that the defendant act with the purpose to cause the prohibited harm. Reckless endangerment is a prime example of such a crime. A defendant who lacks the mens rea of purposefulness for attempt may be guilty of the lesser inchoate crime of reckless endangerment. As the name suggests, the defendant is punished for almost causing another person harm, but the prosecution need only prove that the defendant acted recklessly. Ordinarily, these lesser crimes carry lesser penalties or are misdemeanors.

It is time to try a question to test your understanding of the basic mens rea requirement for an attempt crime. Review the following question with the above principles in mind.

QUESTION 3. Take a dip. Judy and Donna go swimming. Judy is aware that Donna is not a great swimmer. Nonetheless, she takes Donna to a beach with strong currents. She then pushes Donna into the water. Her goal is to frighten Donna a little and show off her own swimming skills. Because of the strong currents, Donna starts to drown. However, before she actually does, Donna is rescued by a lifeguard. Judy is charged with attempted murder.

Under the majority approach, Judy is

A. guilty of attempted murder because she was aware that Donna might be overcome by the currents.
B. not guilty of attempted murder because her goal was to frighten, not kill, Donna.
C. guilty of attempted murder because she acted with malice when she pushed Donna into the water.
D. not guilty of attempted murder because a reasonable person would realize that a lifeguard would probably save Judy.

ANALYSIS. This question focuses on your understanding of the mens rea requirement for attempt. As was discussed, the majority approach requires that Judy have the *purpose* for Donna to drown. Merely knowing that she could drown, or acting negligently, would be insufficient. Your task is to find the answer that best reflects these legal principles.

A is wrong, but it does a wonderful job of highlighting the difference between the mens rea standard for murder and the mens rea standard for attempted murder. Attempted murder requires more than Judy's awareness that Donna might drown; it must be Judy's purpose in pushing Donna into the water to have Donna actually drown. Here, Judy's purpose was to scare, not kill, Donna. Thus, she did not act with the necessary mens rea for the offense. If Donna had actually drowned, Judy probably could have been convicted of murder. However, the mens rea for murder is lower than the required mens rea for attempted murder.

B is the answer that best reflects the mens rea standard for attempted murder. Ordinarily, if a defendant just wants to scare the victim or play a practical joke, there is no attempt even if the defendant comes dangerously close to harming the victim. Under the common law, the defendant must have the purpose (specific intent) to accomplish the crime. Under the Model Penal Code, knowledge of the likely harmful result is sufficient. Here, Judy does not have the purpose to kill Donna. Accordingly, Judy is not guilty of attempted murder and **B** looks like it will be the correct answer.

C is wrong because it assumes that the mens rea standard for attempted murder is the same as for the completed crime of murder. Whereas malice suffices to prove murder, attempted murder requires a higher mens rea, especially when the term *malice* may include merely grossly reckless killings.

Finally, **D** is wrong because it focuses on the reasonable person's mens rea, not the intent of the defendant. The purposefulness standard for attempt is not an objective standard. It is a subjective standard that requires prosecutors to prove that the defendant acted purposefully to cause harm. Accordingly, **D** is incorrect and **B** is the correct answer.

2. Special issues regarding mens rea for attempt

Some tricky mens rea issues can arise in attempt problems. Let's address a couple of the more common ones. First, can one attempt a strict liability crime? The instinctive reaction is no. After all, how does one have the purpose to commit a crime that by definition does not require any mens rea?

Consider, for example, the crime of attempted felony murder. Felony murder applies when a person is accidentally killed during the defendant's commission of a felony. A majority of states do *not* recognize attempted felony murder. See, e.g., *Bruce v. State*, 566 A.2d 103 (Md. 1989). It is illogical to say that the defendant had the purpose to cause an unintentional killing. However, there are some courts that will find the defendant guilty of attempted felony murder even if the defendant did not have the purpose to kill. For example, in *Amlotte v. State*, 456 So. 2d 448 (Fla. 1984), the defendant was held responsible for attempted felony murder when his co-felon shot a guard during their robbery. The guard survived. Even though there was no evidence that Amlotte had the intent for the guard to die, the court upheld a conviction for attempted felony murder.

The second special mens rea issue is related to the first. For attempt, must a defendant act purposely with regard to all the attendant circumstances of a crime, even those that are covered by the strict liability standard for the completed crime? For example, think of the crime of statutory rape. To be guilty of statutory rape, the defendant must intend to have sexual intercourse with a girl under the legal age of consent, but prosecutors need not prove that the defendant knew that the girl was under age. If the defendant intentionally has sex with the girl, and she turns out to be too young, he is strictly liable. What if a defendant tries to have sex with a girl who is under age, but her parents bust in on them before they can complete the act? Is the defendant guilty of attempted statutory rape?

Courts are split on this issue. In some courts, attempt requires that the defendant act purposely with regard to all the attendant circumstances of the crime, even those that may be covered by the strict liability standard for the completed crime. Under this approach, the defendant would not be guilty of attempted statutory rape.

However, most courts take a different approach. They do not require that the defendant act with purpose as to those attendant circumstances of a crime that the defendant would not need to know to be guilty of the completed crime. In these jurisdictions, the defendant would be guilty of attempted statutory rape, regardless of whether it was the defendant's specific intent to have sex with a girl he knew to be underage. See, e.g., *Commonwealth v. Dunne*, 474 N.E.2d 538 (Mass. 1985). The Model Penal Code generally only requires that the mens rea for the attendant circumstances be the same as for the completed crime. See Model Penal Code §5.01. Thus, a person is guilty of attempt if he "purposely engages in conduct which would constitute the crime *if the attendant circumstances were as he believes them to be.*" Model Penal Code §5.01(1)(a) (emphasis added). However, for some statutory rape cases, the Model Penal Code allows for a defense if the defendant "reasonably believed the child to be above the critical age." See Model Penal Code 213.6. If a defendant reasonably believes the girl is an adult, he would not have the mens rea for attempted statutory rape. Some jurisdictions take a middle course for attempts of all strict liability crimes by holding a defendant responsible if he is reckless with regard to any attendant circumstances.

This area is a little tricky, but let's try a question to test your understanding of these special issues arising in the application of the mens rea standard to certain attempt offenses.

QUESTION 4. The feds. Corey faces charges for attempting to kill a federal agent. There is no question that Corey shot at and narrowly missed killing a federal agent. However, Corey's defense is that he may be guilty of reckless endangerment or even attempted murder, but he is not guilty of attempting to kill a federal agent. Attempting to kill a federal agent carries a higher penalty than standard attempted murder. Corey testifies that he did not realize his target was a federal officer; he believed he was shooting at a competing drug dealer.

Under the majority approach, if the jurors believe Corey, they should

A. acquit him of the attempted killing of a federal officer because he did not intend to kill anyone.
B. acquit him of the attempted killing of a federal officer because he did not intend to kill anyone and he did not know the person he shot at was a federal officer.
C. acquit him of attempted murder of a federal agent because he did not have the necessary mens rea for the crime.
D. convict him of attempted killing of a federal agent.

ANALYSIS. This question may remind you of an issue we addressed in Chapter 5 when we discussed mistake of fact. Although it is clear that Corey intended to harm his victim, the key issue is whether Corey needed to have the purpose to kill a *federal* officer. Under the majority approach, Corey would be guilty regardless of whether he believed that he was shooting at a federal officer. With that rule in mind, let's consider the following choices for answers.

A is wrong because Corey admits he tried to shoot a person, he just does not admit he knew the victim was a federal officer. Be careful when selecting an answer that you choose one that is consistent with the facts as they are given to you in the question.

B is wrong for similar reasons. It is quite clear from the problem that Corey did intend to kill someone and, as further analysis will demonstrate, it does not matter if he knew the person was a federal officer.

C is wrong because Corey does not need to know the agent is a federal agent. See *United States v. Feola*, 420 U.S. 672 (1975). The status of the agent as a "federal" agent is considered to be just a jurisdictional element; that is, there is no mistake of fact defense to the completed crime of assaulting a federal officer, even if a defendant does not know the agent's status. Thus, Corey would not need to know the agent's status to be guilty of the attempted assault.

D is the correct answer. As explained above, Corey is no saint and is guilty of attempted murder. It is irrelevant that he does not believe his victim is a federal officer.

D.   Actus reus requirement for attempt

A key issue in attempt is how far the defendant must go with his plans to be guilty of attempt. Consider, for example, a defendant who intends to rob a bank. There are several steps in preparation of this crime that the defendant may take. The defendant may buy a disguise, steal a car, conduct surveillance on the bank, draw a map of the bank, or even call for the bank's hours. Assuming the defendant really has the purpose to rob the bank, at what point has he done enough to be guilty of attempt?

As you recall from the general overview, law enforcement is hesitant to intervene too early in the planning stages of a crime. At the early stages, it is often difficult to determine whether the defendant really has the purpose to commit the crime and whether he has done enough where it makes sense to dedicate law enforcement resources to stop him.

Different courts have promoted different standards to determine when the defendant has crossed the line from "mere preparation" to actual "attempt." They include

- first step
- last step
- physical proximity approach
- dangerous proximity approach
- unequivocality test
- indispensable element test
- probable non-desistance test
- substantial test strong corroborative of intent (Model Penal Code standard).

1. First step test

Courts rarely employ the first step test. Under that test, once it is clear that the defendant has the purpose to commit a crime, anything the defendant does that could lead to the completion of a crime would be a sufficient actus reus to make the defendant guilty of attempt. For example, assume the defendant writes in his diary that he absolutely plans to rob a bank. The first step he takes is to call the bank to find out the bank's hours. Although the defendant has taken the first step toward completing the crime, most jurisdictions would be reluctant to prosecute the defendant for attempt. First, it seems too early to commit law enforcement resources; second, although the defendant has declared his purpose to rob the bank, there is still plenty of time for him to change his mind.

Although courts overwhelmingly reject the first step approach, it has been used in cases of poisoning in which the defendant had the purpose to kill and had administered the first dose of poison to kill his victim. Despite the fact that many more doses would be needed to kill, the court in *Regina v. White*, 2 K.B. 124 (1910), found sufficient evidence of both the defendant's mens rea and actus reus.

2. Last step test

Under early common law, a defendant was not guilty unless he had done all he could to commit a crime and it was only because of bad luck that he was unable to do so. This is sometimes referred to as the *Eagleton* test. See *Regina v. Eagleton*, 6 Cox. Crim. Cas. 559 (1855). For example, assume the defendant wants to kill another person. The defendant pulls the trigger on the gun, but the gun jams or the bullet misses the victim. Here, the defendant has taken the last step toward completing the crime of homicide.

The last step test has been criticized because it delays law enforcement involvement until long after the defendant has manifested his intent and ability to harm another person. Therefore, it puts victims at undue risk. The need to deter and punish a defendant is often apparent long before the defendant commits the last act toward completing a crime.

3. Physical proximity test

Rather than require the defendant reach the last act, some courts hold a defendant responsible for attempt if he is physically near completion of the crime. For example, if a defendant is planning to kill a victim, the defendant would need to be physically near enough to the victim to put the victim at risk, even though the defendant need not have taken the last step of pulling the trigger.

4. Dangerous proximity test

Made famous by Justice Oliver Wendell Holmes, the dangerous proximity test is a traditional test for deciding how close the defendant must have come to completing his dangerous act. Courts favor it over the physical proximity test because it is more flexible in holding a defendant guilty of attempt. The dangerous proximity test focuses both on how much the defendant has done to complete the crime and how much is left to be completed. Some courts seek to clarify the standard by stating that the act must be "very near" or "dangerously near" to completion. However, the standard is necessarily vague because it allows the the trier of fact in each case to determine if the defendant has done enough and has come close enough to causing harm to warrant law enforcement intervention.

To determine whether the defendant's actions fall within dangerous proximity of completing the crime, courts traditionally focus on six factors: (1) how many steps the defendant has taken; (2) how much more action is required for the defendant to complete the harmful act; (3) why the harm never occurred; (4) the amount of harm likely to result; (5) the seriousness of the prospective harm; and (6) the appropriateness of law enforcement interference with the defendant's acts.

Several cases demonstrate how the dangerous proximity standard is applied by the courts. In *Commonwealth v. Peaslee,* 177 Mass. 267 (1901), the defendant was charged with attempting to burn a building. Defendant constructed and arranged combustibles in the building so that they were ready to be lighted. However, the closest the defendant got to actually lighting the materials was driving a prospective accomplice to within a quarter-mile of the building. The court held that the defendant's conduct did not pass the level of mere preparation; he had not come close enough to completing the arson to be charged with attempt.

Likewise, the court in *People v. Rizzo,* 246 N.Y. 334 (1927), found that the defendant was not guilty of attempt when he drove around looking for a particular payroll clerk to rob. Although the defendant was armed and prepared to commit the robbery, the police apprehended him before he could find his prospective victim. Thus, the court found that his acts were mere preparation.

5. Unequivocality test

Instead of assessing how far defendant's conduct has proceeded, the unequivocality test examines whether the defendant's actions, viewed in the abstract, demonstrate an unequivocal intent to commit a crime. Also known as the *res ipsa loquitur* test, a defendant is not guilt of attempt unless his actions unambiguously demonstrate the defendant's intent to commit a crime. See *King v. Barker,* N.Z.L.R. 865 (1924).

For example, if a defendant buys a box of matches, intending to burn a haystack, he still may not be guilty of attempt because there are many lawful explanations for buying matches. The defendant's acts are equivocal and not sufficient for an attempt conviction. See *King v. Barker,* N.Z.L.R. 865 (1924).

The unequivocality test is often criticized as setting too high a barrier to conviction. If the defendant's acts are ambiguous, the defendant cannot be convicted even with conclusive proof of mens rea. Conversely, the un-equivocality test also allows prejudicial assumptions about the way people act to affect the determination of whether there has been an attempt. For example, assume that an African-American man in Alabama in the 1950s was seen following a white woman. If society assumed that an African-American man would only follow a white woman because he wanted to sexually assault her, the defendant's actions would be presumed to show unequivocal evidence of his intent. See, e.g., *McQuirter v. State,* 36 Ala. App. 707 (1953).

6. Indispensable element test

There are several other lesser-used common law tests for attempt. The indispensable element test is a variation of the proximity test. It analyzes whether any indispensable element of the crime still remains to be completed. If all the indispensable elements have been completed, the defendant is guilty of attempt. However, if some indispensable element is incomplete, the defendant is not guilty. For example, if the defendant is charged with attempted murder, but has not yet acquired a weapon for his crime, he is not guilty of the attempt. See *State v. Wood*, 103 N.W. 25 (S.D. 1905).

7. Probable non-desistance test

The probable non-desistance test is another common law test for attempt. As its name suggests, if the defendant goes beyond the point at which someone who wanted to stop would have stopped, the defendant has met the actus reus standard for attempt. For example, if a defendant who plans to rob a bank actually enters the bank and gets to the teller station, the defendant would likely be guilty of attempted robbery, even though it is hypothetically possible that the defendant would never demand money from the teller. The focus of the probable non-desistance test is how much the defendant has already done toward committing the crime, not how much still needs to be done. It requires that a jury think like a criminal and determine when an ordinary person in the defendant's shoes would have done enough that he would not turn back from his criminal activity.

8. Model Penal Code approach

By now, your mind is probably swimming with actus reus standards for attempt and you are begging your instructor to just pick one for you to use on your exam. Most likely, your professor will want you to apply the Model Penal Code approach. More than half of the courts have adopted the Model Penal Code standard for the actus reus of attempt. Model Penal Code §5.01(2) provides that the defendant must take a *"substantial step strongly corroborative of the actor's criminal purpose."* The Model Panel Code also lists certain acts that per se satisfy attempt's actus reus requirement. These include, for example, lying in wait and possessing materials specially designed to commit the crime. Model Penal Code §5.01(2).

In many ways, the Model Penal Code test is a combination of the common law standards you have studied. It focuses both on what the defendant has done toward completing the crime and whether those steps clearly corroborate the defendant's intent. It falls between the first step and the last step test, and includes elements of both the dangerous proximity test and the unequivocality test.

The Model Penal Code test was applied in *United States v. Jackson*, 560 F.2d 112 (2d Cir. 1977). Jackson was charged with armed robbery. Planning to rob a bank, he and his co-conspirators drove to the bank location with guns, robbery tools, and disguises. They also removed their license plate. At that point, they were apprehended by the police. The court held that the defendant's acts both showed a "substantial step" toward committing the crime and corroborated testimony by a cooperating co-conspirator that the defendants planned to rob the bank.

While an improvement over most common law tests, the Model Penal Code approach still does not provide an exact standard as to when the defendant crosses the line from mere preparation to attempt. Each jury must make that decision by looking at what the defendant has already done and whether that indicates a clear intent to commit a crime.

It is time to try a couple of questions applying the actus reus tests for attempt. Question 5 asks you to apply several of the common law standards. Question 6 tests you on the Model Penal Code standard.

> **QUESTION 5. Dirty dumping.**   Max owns a chemical company. It has become very expensive for Max to lawfully dispose of his company's chemical byproducts. Accordingly, Max loads the byproducts into a truck and starts hauling them 50 miles toward a deserted area in the desert, where Max intends to dump the chemicals. Five miles from his destination, and just as he enters restricted lands, Max is apprehended by law enforcement officers. If Max is charged with the attempted dumping of the chemicals, prosecutors are most likely to succeed with proving a sufficient actus reus under
>
> A. the last step test.
> B. the unequivocality test.
> C. the dangerous proximity test.
> D. the probable non-desistance test.

ANALYSIS.   As this question shows, a defendant may be guilty under one common law approach to the attempt actus reus requirement and not guilty under a different approach. Let's consider each of the actus reus tests offered by the possible answers.

A is wrong because Max has not done the *last step* of dumping the chemicals. He is only on his way to do so. In a jurisdiction that requires that last step, Max would not be guilty of attempted dumping even if he had every intention of dumping the chemicals when he arrived at his destination.

B is also wrong because the act of driving chemicals down a desert highway does not pass the *res ipsa loquitur test* of showing that the only reason for Max's action would be to engage in illegal dumping. Even a person who lawfully disposes of chemicals may be required to drive them through the desert. Therefore, Max's actions do not "speak for themselves." They do not satisfy the unequivocality test.

Therefore, there are two choices left. The *probable non-desistance test* asks whether there is still a reasonable chance that the suspect will change his course of action and not engage in the illegal activity. Max is still five miles from his destination. Perhaps when he comes upon the dumping site, he will change his mind. Although this is a close one, it is hard to say with any certainty that Max satisfies the probable non-desistance test. **D** is also a wrong answer.

Ultimately, the best answer is **C**. The *dangerous proximity test* focuses both on how much Max has done toward completing his crime and whether he is close enough to accomplishing his goal that he should be stopped. In this case, Max has loaded the chemicals and has driven 90 percent of the way to his destination. When he is apprehended, he is on restricted lands. While some triers of fact may still want to wait for evidence of him starting to dump the truck, the dangerous proximity test does not require the last step. It would not be unreasonable for a jury to hold that Max has come dangerously close to engaging in the illegal activity.

As this question suggests, it is often difficult under the common law standards to mark exactly when the defendant's actions have crossed from mere preparation to actual attempt. The Model Penal Code approach provides a little more direction in making this decision. Question 6 illustrates use of the Model Penal Code approach.

QUESTION 6. Assassination attempt.   Oswald has decided to kill the Vice President. He buys a high-powered rifle, sets up an ambush spot and waits for the Vice President's motorcade to pass. Oswald has his rifle beside him and is prepared to pick it up at any moment. Less than a minute before the motorcade passes, Oswald is interrupted by a cellular phone call from his mother reminding him to pick up a loaf of bread from the market. Because he is listening to his mother's message, Oswald does not have an opportunity to shoot and kill the Vice President.

Under the Model Penal Code approach, is Oswald guilty of attempted murder?

A. Yes, because he took a substantial step strongly corroborative of his intent to kill.

B. No, because Oswald was not in dangerous proximity of killing the Vice President.

C. Yes, because Oswald had already taken the last step toward killing the Vice President when his phone rang.

D. No, because Oswald's actions did not show his unequivocal intent to kill.

ANALYSIS.   As with many attempt problems, the answer lies in recognizing the wording of the correct standard. You are asked to answer this question under the Model Penal Code. There are two things you must remember: (1) the Model Penal Code requires for the actus reus "a substantial step strongly corroborative of intent"; and (2) certain actions, such as lying in wait, are presumed to satisfy the actus reus requirement. Given these principles, this question should have been fairly easy to answer.

A looks like a textbook answer. It correctly states the Model Penal Code standard. Moreover, Oswald was lying in wait. Even if you had an inclination not to choose **A** because you were wondering whether he took a substantial enough step toward the killing, you would know that such conduct is sufficient to qualify as an actus reus for attempt because it fits one of the per se categories under Model Penal Code §5.01(2)(a). However, before selecting **A**, it is always best to consider the other possible answers.

B is wrong for a couple of reasons. First, it does not cite the correct Model Penal Code standard. Second, it is probably factually incorrect to state that Max was not in dangerous proximity of killing the Vice President. Max was obviously within shooting range and he had probably demonstrated enough reason for law enforcement to get involved.

C is also incorrect because the Model Penal Code does not require that the defendant take the last step toward completing the crime. All that is required is a "substantial step." Here, obtaining a rifle, finding a hiding place, and planning out the shooting would undoubtedly qualify as a substantial step, even though Max never took the last step of pulling the rifle's trigger.

Finally, **D** is wrong because it uses the wrong standard. Unequivocality is one of many common law standards; it is not the Model Penal Code standard. Under the unequivocality test, an argument can be made that Max's actions did not unequivocally demonstrate his intent to kill because if he had such an intent, he would never have answered the phone. By contrast, under the Model Penal Code approach, Max's actions in general were at least strongly corroborative of an intent to kill. Accordingly, the correct answer is **A**.

E.   Attempt defenses: Abandonment and withdrawal

Under the common law's "last step" approach, there are no special defenses for attempt crimes. Because the defendant is not charged until he has taken the last step toward committing the crime, there really is no or little possibility that he would have changed his mind and deserted his criminal activities.

Once courts started using actus reus standards that impose culpability on a defendant before he has done everything he can to commit a crime, a need arose for defenses when defendants voluntarily chose to abandon their criminal schemes. Providing such defenses serves several purposes. First, it prevents the law from punishing those defendants who have undergone a sincere change of heart and who no longer wish to violate the law. Second, an abandonment defense hopefully serves a very practical purpose. It gives defendants an incentive to desist from their criminal behavior. Practically, if a defendant is going to be guilty of attempt even if he abandons his efforts, there is little reason for the defendant to abandon his activities. However, with the possibility of an abandonment defense, a defendant may be willing to have a change of heart.

In formulating the standard for an abandonment defense, it is important that it only be available to those defendants who have a sincere change of heart. It should *not* exonerate those defendants who are just waiting for a better time or more vulnerable victim to harm.

1. Modern common law (abandonment)

Today, there are some courts that recognize an abandonment defense if the defendant *voluntarily and completely stops his criminal efforts*. For the abandonment defense to apply, the defendant must have crossed the line from mere preparation to actual attempt. At that point, the defendant can claim that he had a full change of heart and voluntarily desisted from his criminal activity.

For example, consider a defendant who has grabbed a woman with an intent to rape her. As he is holding her, the defendant realizes that his actions are abhorrent and he releases her. He vows never to attack another woman and the jury believes his story. If the defendant truly had a change of heart and was not just looking for a better opportunity to commit his crime, the defendant could raise an abandonment defense.[1]

However, what if the defendant had grabbed a woman and decided not to rape her because she started to scream? He runs off looking for a smaller woman he can attack in an isolated setting. This defendant would not have an abandonment defense because he has not truly renounced his criminal purpose; he is just looking for a better opportunity to commit his crime.

---

1. Courts have applied the abandonment defense inconsistently in cases charging attempted rape. For example, in *People v. McNeal,* 152 Mich. App. 404 (1986), the court did not allow the abandonment defense when the defendant was convinced by the victim to stop his sexual assault. By contrast, the court in *Ross v. State,* 601 So. 2d 872 (Miss. 1992), was willing to recognize an abandonment defense when the victim convinced the defendant not to rape her because she was pregnant.

2. Model Penal Code (renunciation)

Jurisdictions that allow an abandonment defense generally base it on the Model Penal Code standard. The Model Penal Code refers to the abandonment defense as "renunciation." Under Model Penal Code §5.01(4), it is an affirmative defense if (1) the defendant abandons his effort to commit the crime or prevents it from being committed; and (2) the defendant's conduct manifests a complete and voluntary renunciation of his criminal purpose.

To avail himself of the renunciation defense, a defendant must not only stop his criminal activity, but he must also persuade the trier of fact that he did so because of a sincere change of heart. If the defendant was motivated, even in part, by "circumstances, not present or apparent at the inception of the actor's course of conduct, that increase the probability of detection or apprehension or that make more difficult the accomplishment of the criminal purpose," the defendant cannot assert a renunciation defense. Model Penal Code §5.04. In other words, if the defendant abandoned his efforts because he was afraid of getting caught, or he was looking for more advantageous circumstances under which to commit the crime, he would not be entitled to a renunciation defense.

For example, a defendant starts to rob a convenience store but stops because he hears sirens. The defendant is not entitled to a renunciation defense. There is no showing that the defendant had a full and complete change of heart. Rather, it appears as if the defendant just didn't want to get caught and is simply waiting for a better opportunity to commit his crime.

Other than the name of the defense (abandonment versus renunciation), there is little difference between the modern common law abandonment defense and the Model Penal Code defense. To test your knowledge of the defense in general, try the next question.

QUESTION 7. **X-mas spirit.** Cheryl makes her living by stealing cars. While holiday shoppers are in the mall, she quickly hot-wires their cars and drives them away. One holiday season, Cheryl is sitting inside a beautiful new Mercedes whose lock she has just picked. She has just hot-wired the car when she hears young children singing Christmas carols. Touched by the spirit of the holiday, Cheryl quickly stops the engine and gets out of the car. She catches a bus home and enjoys some warm eggnog. While she is sipping her holiday cheer, the police arrive and arrest her for attempted car theft.

If Cheryl asserts an abandonment or renunciation defense,

A. she will automatically lose because she has stolen many cars before.
B. she will lose if she was just waiting until after the holidays to start stealing cars again.

C. she will automatically win because she did not take the car.
D. she will lose because she was under police surveillance.

ANALYSIS. By now, you should remember the three requirements of an abandonment/renunciation defense: CAV. To successfully assert the defense, the defendant must demonstrate:

C = complete renunciation
A = abandon efforts before the crime is completed
V = voluntarily abandon his or her criminal efforts.

In this situation, the defendant did abandon her efforts before she actually stole the Mercedes. The issue is whether she completely renounced her criminal purposes and whether her renunciation was voluntary. Let's consider the possible answers.

A is incorrect. Although it may be more difficult for a career criminal to convince the jury that she has had a genuine change of heart, her past is not an automatic impediment to asserting an abandonment defense.

B seems to be on the right track. Abandonment or renunciation is not considered complete if the defendant is just waiting for a better opportunity to commit her crime. If all Cheryl is doing is taking a holiday break, she is not entitled to an abandonment/renunciation defense.

C is the wrong answer because it only covers one of the three requirements for an abandonment/renunciation defense. The defendant must abandon her criminal efforts before the crime is completed, but she must do more. She must show her abandonment was complete and voluntary.

D is a red herring and wrong. If Cheryl knew she was under police surveillance and stopped because of her fear of getting caught, she would not be entitled to an abandonment/renunciation defense. However, just being under surveillance does not automatically undermine use of the defense.

Accordingly, **B** is the correct answer. In determining whether Cheryl is entitled to a defense, the trier of fact must determine that Cheryl had a voluntary and permanent change of heart. Yuletide sentiments would not be enough to win her a defense. She would remain guilty of attempted car theft.

F. Attempt defense: Impossibility

Don't be intimidated by the topic of impossibility. Although law students are heard to say, "impossibility is impossible," the defense is not that difficult once you understand its basic premise.

The defense of impossibility arises when a defendant has done everything possible to commit a crime, but unexpected factual or legal circumstances prevent the target crime from being completed. For example, consider the defendant who tries to pick a person's pocket. Assume the defendant actually reaches into the victim's pocket to steal his wallet, only to find that the victim has nothing in his pocket. In this situation, the defendant has clearly committed an attempted theft. He has the necessary mens rea of intending to steal the property and he has even done the last act possible as the actus reus for the crime. There appears to be little reason to give the defendant a defense simply because he tried to pick the wrong pocket. The defendant still deserves to be punished and needs to be deterred from trying to pick pockets in the future.

However, there are situations in which the defendant does everything he can to commit a crime, but is so far from causing actual harm that we would be inclined to excuse him from his attempted crime. For example, consider the defendant who intends to shoot a deer even though it is not hunting season. Defendant shoots what he believes to be a deer. Instead, he hits a decoy. Should the defendant still be punished? Some courts would hold that because it was impossible for defendant to complete his crime, he should not be punished.

The challenge in impossibility cases is to distinguish between those situations in which we still want to punish the defendant — and therefore deny him an impossibility defense — and those cases in which the defendant, regardless of the circumstances, should still be guilty of attempt. The original common law tried to distinguish between the two situations by calling one "factual impossibility," which was not a defense, and the other, "legal impossibility," which is a defense. *The general rule at common law was that "legal impossibility is a defense and factual impossibility is not a defense."*

However, a closer examination shows that this approach is not very satisfying. In reality, the courts used it as a way to slap a label on a given situation depending on whether they believed the defendant should be punished. Many impossibility situations that could be labeled as factual impossibility could also be interpreted as legal impossibility cases.

For example, consider the situation in which a defendant is charged with attempting to receive stolen property. Assume the defendant takes possession of property he believes to be stolen. In reality, the property is not stolen. One could label this situation as factual impossibility because the only reason that the defendant could not receive stolen property was the fact that the property was not stolen. If labeled as factual impossibility, the defendant would not have a defense, but would be guilty of attempted receipt of stolen property. See *People v. Rojas*, 55 Cal. 2d 252 (1961). However, this situation could just as easily be classified as one of legal impossibility. Defendant would argue that it was legally impossible to possess stolen property because the property was not stolen and there is no law against possessing lawful property. If labeled as legal impossibility, the defendant would have a full defense to a charge of attempted possession of stolen property. See *People v. Jaffe*, 185 N.Y. 497 (1906).

While many situations can be labeled as factual or legal impossibility, there are some situations that have been typically defined as one or the other. They are worth a quick examination.

1. Factual impossibility

Factual impossibility is not a defense to criminal attempt. Typically, courts have found the following situations to fall under the category of factual impossibility:

- pickpocket trying to pick an empty pocket;
- pulling the trigger on a weapon that misfires;
- trying to infect another person with a disease even though it turns out the defendant is not infected;[2]
- shooting at a victim who was already dead.[3]

In all these situations, facts arise that make it impossible for the defendant to complete the crime. Yet, the defendant has engaged in activity that is deserving of punishment. He has the mens rea to commit the crime and has taken the last step toward doing so. There is little or no reason not to punish the defendant for attempt.

2. Legal impossibility

By contrast, there are some situations in which the courts traditionally have not deemed it appropriate to punish a defendant for attempt. *Under common law, legal impossibility is considered a full defense to attempt.* However, there really are two types of legal impossibility. The true or *pure legal impossibility* situations occur when a defendant wants to violate the law, but there is no law prohibiting the defendant's behavior. In other words, the defendant does a lawful act with a guilty conscience. For example, consider the defendant who performs an abortion believing it is illegal to do so. In fact, abortion is legal in that jurisdiction. The defendant is not guilty of attempted abortion because it would be legally impossible to be convicted of performing an abortion. Other typical situations of true legal impossibility include:

- smoking marijuana believing it is illegal to do so, but when there is no law prohibiting marijuana in that jurisdiction;
- taking a lawful tax deduction believing it is an unlawful deduction;
- having sex with someone the defendant believes is a minor, but is in fact of legal age to consent.

---

2. See *State v. Smith*, 262 N.J. Super. 487, 621 A.2d 493 (1993).
3. See *People v. Dlugash*, 41 N.Y.2d 725, 363 N.E.2d 1155 (1977).

In all these situations, it is legally impossible for the defendant to be guilty of the completed crime because there is no law prohibiting the defendant's behavior. Under common law, the defendant would have a legal impossibility defense to attempt.

3. Hybrid impossibility

There are some *hybrid situations* that can be classified as either legal or factual impossibility, but are typically treated as legal impossibility. Here, the defendant intends to commit a crime, but some legal characteristic of the attendant circumstances of his conduct make it impossible for him to commit that crime. The classic example would be the one we mentioned before — receiving stolen property. It is possible to be guilty of the crime of receiving stolen property. There is a law prohibiting such conduct. However, a defendant would not be guilty of that crime if the property he possesses and believes is stolen, is not actually stolen. Some courts would be inclined to call this factual impossibility because the fact is that defendant did not possess stolen property. Other courts that do not want to punish the defendant's behavior would affix the label of legal impossibility because there is no crime against possessing non-stolen property.

For the hybrid legal impossibility situations, courts tend to decide ahead of time whether the defendant is deserving of punishment and then affix the label of factual impossibility (no defense to attempt) or legal impossibility (full defense to attempt) according to the result they wish to reach. Some typical situations include:

- shooting a corpse the defendant mistakenly believes to be alive;[4]
- trying to hunt deer out of season when it is in fact still hunting season;[5]
- offering a bribe to a person who turns out not to be a juror.[6]

In these situations, judges can reasonably characterize the defendant's case as either legal or factual impossibility. If the act is legally impossible, the defendant is not guilty of attempt; if it is factually impossible, the defendant is still guilty of attempt.

4. Model Penal Code approach

Because of its commitment to blameworthiness, the Model Penal Code came up with a different approach to the impossibility issue. *Under the Model Penal Code, there is no defense of impossibility.* Rather, a defendant is guilty of attempt if he "purposely engages in conduct which would constitute the

---

4. See *State v. Taylor*, 133 S.W.2d 336 (Mo. 1939) (dictum).
5. See *State v. Guffey*, 262 S.W.2d 152 (Mo. Ct. App. 1953) (defendant shot stuffed deer).
6. See *State v. Taylor*, 133 S.W.2d 336 (Mo. 1939).

crime if the attendant circumstances were as he believed them to be." Model Penel Code §5.01(1)(a).

Once the defendant has the necessary mens rea and actus reus for a crime, the key question to be asked is: "Would there have been a crime had the circumstances been as the defendant believed them to be?" If the answer is yes, the defendant is guilty of attempt. For example, assume the defendant is charged with attemping to receive stolen property. Under the Model Penal Code, if the defendant intended to receive stolen property and took the necessary action to obtain it, he would be guilty of attempted receipt of stolen property, even if the property turned out not to be stolen. The reason for this result is that "had the circumstances been as the defendant believed them to be," that is, had the property been stolen, the defendant would have been guilty of the crime.

Yet, even the Model Penal Code contains an escape hatch for those impossibility situations in which it is so unlikely that the defendant would have caused harm that it makes no sense to convict him of an attempted crime. Model Penal Code §5.05 provides that in situations in which an attempt is "so inherently unlikely to result or culminate in the commission of a crime that neither such conduct nor the actor presents a public danger," the court has the discretion to mitigate the level of the crime or dismiss the prosecution. Thus, pure legal impossibility cases would probably still be dismissed under the Model Penal Code approach, as well as those hybrid cases in which there is very little danger of harm.[7]

For example, consider the situation in which a defendant wants to kill another person by stabbing a voodoo doll. The defendant has the mens rea to kill and has taken what he believes to be the last step toward killing his victim. Under the Model Penal Code, the defendant would be guilty of attempted murder if, had the circumstances been as he believed them to be, that is, if it were possible to kill another person by using a voodoo doll. However, this case might be a prime candidate for the mitigation provisions of Model Penal Code §5.05. There was very little possibility of the defendant causing actual harm. Therefore, the court might mitigate or dismiss his attempted murder charge.

Model Penal Code §5.05 also applies in situations in which your instincts may lead you to apply the defense of legal impossibility. For example, assume that a defendant goes fishing in an area where he believes it is illegal to fish. The defendant carefully drops his line into the waters and catches a fish. However, it turns out that it is not illegal to fish in that area. Rather than decide whether this is factual impossibility (i.e., it was factually impossible for the defendant to illegally catch a fish in that area) or legal

---

7. The Commentary to the Model Penal Code suggests that it did not intend to abolish the pure legal impossibility defense. See American Law Institute, Comment to §5.01, at 318.

impossibility (i.e., it was not illegal to fish in the area), the Model Penal Code would use the following three-step approach:

1. *Did the defendant have the mens rea and actus reus for the crime of attempt?*
   (Yes, the defendant had the purpose to fish illegally and took the last step to do so.)
2. *If the facts were as defendant believed them to be, would the defendant have been guilty of a crime?*
   (Yes, if it had been illegal to fish in those waters, defendant would be guilty of illegal fishing.)
3. *Is there any reason to mitigate or dismiss the attempt charges?*
   (Yes, the fact that lawmakers did not make it illegal to fish in that area is a clear indication that defendant really poses no threat of harm.)

5. *Last thought: Mistake of law and fact versus factual and legal impossibility*

One last thought before you try a question regarding impossibility. Do not confuse mistake of law and mistake of fact with factual impossibility and legal impossibility. In fact, they are opposites of each other. In mistake of fact situations, the defendant makes a factual mistake that prevents him from having the requisite mens rea for the crime. Thus, mistake of fact is generally a defense. However, the opposite is true for factual impossibility. Factual impossibility is generally not a defense. Likewise, the general rule is that mistake of law is not a defense; however, legal impossibility is a defense.

Keep these distinctions in mind:

Mistake of fact	=	Defense
Factual impossibility	=	No defense
Mistake of law	=	No defense
Legal impossibility	=	Defense

It is time to apply your knowledge of impossibility to a couple of questions. Remember, in each situation, the defendant has attempted to do something the defendant believes is illegal but has been prevented from doing so by facts or circumstances the defendant has not anticipated. When should the defendant still be guilty of attempt and when should the defendant have a full impossibility defense?

QUESTION 8. Wrong briefcase.   Austin Powers intends to steal trade secrets from his competitor at a trade conference. He intentionally buys a briefcase that looks identical to his competitor's so that he can swap briefcases during their meeting and obtain valuable information. However, Austin accidentally picks up his own briefcase and leaves the meeting. He is charged with attempted theft of the trade secrets.

Which of the following is correct?

A. Powers has a mistake of fact defense because he mistakenly picked up the wrong briefcase.

B. Powers has a pure legal impossibility defense because it is not illegal to take one's own property.

C. Powers has no impossibility defense under the Model Penal Code because if the circumstances were as he believed them to be, he would have taken his competitor's briefcase.

D. Powers is not guilty of attempt because it was factually impossible for him to steal his own briefcase.

ANALYSIS. Hopefully, you found this question to be very straightforward. It is helpful to approach an impossibility question the same way you would approach any attempt problem. First, ask whether the defendant had the necessary mens rea for the crime of attempt. Here, the defendant had the purpose to steal another person's property. Therefore, the mens rea requirement is satisfied. Second, ask whether the defendant has satisfied the actus reus requirement for attempt. The defendant took the last step toward committing the crime — he grabbed what he believed to be the other person's briefcase. Accordingly, the defendant has met all the requirements to be guilty of attempted theft.

The next step is to ask whether the defendant is entitled to an attempt defense. If the situation is one of factual impossibility, the defendant will not have a defense; if the defense is legal impossibility, the defendant would have a defense under common law. Under the Model Penal Code, the defendant would only be entitled to mitigation of his attempt charge if he was not likely to cause harm. With those basic concepts in mind, let's examine the possible answers.

A should be ruled out immediately. This is *not* a mistake of fact situation. Mistake of fact would apply if the defendant thought he was taking his own property, but mistakenly picked up the property of another person. If that were the case, the defendant would have a full defense because he did not have the purpose to take another person's property. However, in this case, Powers intends to take someone else's property. Thus, he has the necessary mens rea for the crime. Mistake of fact does not apply.

B is also wrong. Pure legal impossibility would only apply if it were not a crime to take another person's property. However, it is a crime to take another person's property. Accordingly, this is not a situation of pure legal impossibility.

The choice comes down to **C** and **D**. **C** correctly states the Model Penal Code standard for deciding whether there has been an attempt. If the facts were as Powers believed them to be, that is, that he had grabbed someone else's suitcase, he would have been guilty of theft. Accordingly, he is guilty of attempted theft and does not have an impossibility defense.

Finally, **D** is wrong for the simplest of reasons — factual impossibility is *not* a defense under common law or the Model Penal Code. Once the act is labeled as factual impossibility, Powers is still guilty of the crime of attempt.

Impossibility is a challenging topic. Try another question to help you feel comfortable with the doctrine.

QUESTION 9. Scalping tickets. Malone is apprehended outside the sports stadium selling basketball tickets. Malone believes that it is illegal to scalp tickets, but he is willing to take the risk because he can make so much money reselling tickets. An officer charges him with attempted scalping of tickets. In researching the law, Malone's lawyer discovers that the jurisdiction repealed its scalping laws ten years ago. He argues that Malone is not guilty of attempted scalping because it was impossible for him to commit that crime.

Under the common law, Malone should

A. succeed because he did not intend to violate the law.
B. succeed because it was legally impossible to scalp tickets.
C. fail because he tried to violate the law.
D. fail because he is guilty of attempted scalping.

ANALYSIS. In this situation, Malone has the purpose to commit a crime and has taken what he believes to be all the steps necessary to commit that crime. However, this is an example of a pure legal impossibility situation. No matter how hard Malone tries, he cannot violate a law that has been repealed. Therefore, we need only find the answer that reflects this legal principle.

A is wrong because Malone did intend to violate the law. Make sure in analyzing answers that you find one that reflects the facts of your actual problem. **B** is the one most directly on point. You have to be confident in your understanding of legal impossibility to select **B**, but if you are, you have found the right answer. This is a situation of true legal impossibility. No matter what he does, Malone cannot violate a law that does not exist.

C is wrong because impossibility always applies when the defendant thinks he may be engaging in conduct that will violate the law. Nonetheless, in the legal impossibility cases, a defendant's mistaken belief is not enough even if he tries to break a law that does not exist.

Finally, **D** is wrong because Malone cannot be guilty of attempting something that is not a crime. Perhaps he is guilty of trespassing or some other minor offense, but he is not guilty of attempted scalping.

G.   The Closer: The disappearing attempt

Attempt is challenging enough without creating an artificially difficult closer question. However, there is one other aspect of attempt that must be kept in mind. What if a defendant attempts to commit a crime and then, in a manner he did not anticipate, is actually successful in his attempt? How should the defendant's culpability be evaluated?

Ordinarily, if an attempt succeeds, the defendant is only guilty of the completed substantive crime. Attempt *merges* with the completed substantive crime. A defendant cannot be guilty of both attempt to commit a crime and commission of that crime.

Here is your closer:

QUESTION 10. Love hath no fury.   Bethany and Marcy love the same man. Marcy loves him so much that she would be willing to kill Bethany if it came to that. However, she would prefer if Bethany would just get sick or leave town. Marcy comes up with an elaborate plan to drive Bethany from her life. Knowing that Bethany hates snakes, Marcy drops scores of lethal snakes in Bethany's yard. When Bethany returns home, she is bitten by one of the snakes. She rushes to the hospital where they give her an antidote in time to save her. However, when Bethany returns home, she is bitten by another snake and dies before emergency help can arrive. Marcy is charged with attempted murder and murder. When interviewed by the police, all she can say is, "I knew that one of them would eventually get her."

Marcy is

A. guilty of murdering Bethany.
B. guilty of attempted murder and murdering Bethany.
C. guilty of only the attempted murder of Bethany.
D. not guilty of murder or attempted murder.

ANALYSIS.   This is a tricky one because the answer depends on whether the court finds that the snake attacks are all part of one act or are separate acts. If the first bite is separate from the second bite, Marcy could be guilty of both attempted murder and murder. However, if it is one continuous plan that finally succeeds, Marcy is only guilty of murder. Let's look at the options.

A is correct if there was a continuing plan to have snakes bite Bethany until she dies. If that is the case, the first bite was part of an ongoing attempt to kill Bethany. When Bethany finally dies, the attempts merge into the completed murder. **B** is correct if the first snake bite is a separate incident. **C** is incorrect for the simple reason that Bethany eventually dies. Likewise, **D** is wrong because there is no way that Marcy will not be charged with some crime.

The better answer is **A** because of Marcy's comments to the police. By stating that she knew the snakes would eventually kill Bethany, Marcy made it clear that there was a continuing attempt to kill the victim. In such a case, the attempt would merge into the murder and Marcy would be guilty of murder, not attempted murder and murder.

 # Levenson's Picks

1. Too close for comfort	**D**
2. Don't play with matches	**D**
3. Take a dip	**B**
4. The feds	**D**
5. Dirty dumping	**C**
6. Assassination attempt	**A**
7. X-mas spirit	**B**
8. Wrong briefcase	**C**
9. Scalping tickets	**B**
10. Love hath no fury	**A**

13

Solicitation and Other Inchoate Offenses

Give every man thy ear, but few thy voice.
— William Shakespeare

CHAPTER OVERVIEW
A. Solicitation — General principles
B. Solicitation versus attempt
C. Using another as an instrumentality of crime versus solicitation
D. Solicitation, accomplice liability, conspiracy, and merger
E. Model Penal Code approach
F. Defenses to solicitation
   1. Renunciation
   2. First Amendment defense
G. Other inchoate crimes
H. The Closer: Bad taste or illegal?
⬥ Levenson's Picks

There are many inchoate crimes. We have already learned about attempt and we are about to learn about conspiracy. Those are the inchoate crimes most commonly charged. However, there are other inchoate offenses on the books. In particular, this chapter focuses on solicitation and stalking. Occasionally, they are used by prosecutors when a defendant has taken a step toward committing an offense, but has not crossed the line to attempt.

A.   Solicitation — General principles

Say the word *solicitation* and inevitably one image comes to mind — a "john" asking a prostitute for sex. While the prostitution scenario may be one of the most common examples of criminal solicitation, it is not the only one. The crime of solicitation can apply whenever a defendant recruits, encourages, directs, counsels, or induces another person to commit a crime. As an inchoate crime, the offense of solicitation is complete even if no further steps are taken toward commission of the target offense. *Just asking another person to commit a crime is a crime in itself.*

At common law, solicitation was a misdemeanor even if the defendant solicited another to commit a felony crime. There was no general crime of solicitation. Rather, states generally had statutes that banned the solicitation of specific types of crimes, such as prostitution and murder. Today, most states have a general criminal solicitation statute that makes it illegal to solicit any crime.

Like other crimes, solicitation requires both an actus reus and mens rea. The actus reus for solicitation may be purely verbal. It includes any command, request, or encouragement to another to commit a crime.

As for mens rea, solicitation is a specific intent crime. The defendant must have the purpose to promote or facilitate the commission of a crime. Therefore, if the defendant is just kidding when he makes the request, or doesn't expect the person solicited to take the request seriously, the defendant is not guilty of solicitation.

Consider, for example, a situation in which law students complain to one another about how much work they face. Jokingly, one student says to the other, "Do us all a favor — blow up the school. That way none of us will have any work." The defendant would not be guilty of solicitation if she did not actually intend that her colleague blow up the school.

With these principles in mind, try this basic solicitation question.

QUESTION 1. Yabadaba doo. Fred and Wilma have had a tumultuous marriage. After years of fighting with his wife, Fred asks his neighbor, Barney, "to beat some sense into Wilma." Fred thinks Barney will talk to Wilma and get her to stop complaining. Instead, Barney goes to the police and tells them that Fred has solicited him to beat up his wife.

Is Fred guilty of soliciting an assault?

A. Yes, because words alone are enough for solicitation.
B. Yes, because a reasonable person would understand that Fred wanted Barney to beat Wilma.
C. No, because Barney went to the police and never attacked Wilma.
D. No, because Fred did not have the mens rea for solicitation.

ANALYSIS.   This is a straightforward solicitation question. Certainly, Fred has satisfied the actus reus requirement by approaching Barney and asking him "to beat some sense into Wilma." Remember that words alone are enough for solicitation. However, the problem here is with the mens rea. Fred does not have the specific intent (purpose) for Barney to actually beat Wilma. Accordingly, he is not guilty of solicitation, even if Barney interprets his words in that manner. Given that analysis, let's look at the answer choices.

A is incorrect even though it is correct to state that words alone are enough to satisfy the actus reus requirement of solicitation. The problem with A is that it ignores the mens rea requirement for the crime.

B is wrong because it again ignores the mens rea requirement for solicitation. Solicitation is not a negligence crime. If it were, perhaps B would be the correct answer. However, solicitation requires that Fred have the purpose of having Barney actually beat his wife.

C is incorrect because it does not give the correct rationale for why Fred is not guilty of soliciting assault. A defendant is guilty of solicitation even if the person solicited does not take any further step toward committing the crime. The defendant's crime is complete once he encourages another to commit a crime, regardless of whether that crime is actually committed. Therefore, it is irrelevant that Barney went to the police and never attacked Wilma.

D is the correct answer because it focuses on the shortcoming in the evidence in this case. Fred thinks that Barney will only talk to his wife, not beat her. Therefore, he does not have the purpose of having Barney commit a crime against his wife. Without the necessary mens rea, Fred is not guilty of solicitation.

B.   Solicitation versus attempt

Attempt and solicitation are two different crimes. Attempt requires that a defendant take substantial steps toward completing the crime. Solicitation is complete as soon as a defendant asks another person to participate in a crime.

There are actually three key differences between attempt and solicitation. First, attempt requires that some act be taken toward commission of the crime. Usually, that act must be a "substantial step" toward completion of the crime. Solicitation can occur at a much earlier stage when a plan to commit a crime is just beginning. Second, solicitation involves a third party who is recruited to participate in a crime. Attempt may be done by the defendant alone. Third, attempt generally carries a heavier sentence than solicitation because the defendant has done more toward completing a crime, thereby putting the victim at greater risk.

Consider the case of *State v. Davis*, 319 Mo. 1222 (1928). In *Davis*, the defendant wanted to have her husband killed to collect his life insurance. The defendant approached a prospective "hit man" for the job, but the plan went no further because the hit man decided to contact the police. Given that jurisdiction's standard for attempt at that time, the defendant did not do enough to be guilty of attempted murder. However, the defendant's conduct, together with her intent to have her husband killed, would support a charge of solicitation to commit murder.

In a rare case, it is possible for the solicitation itself to constitute a "substantial step" toward commission of a crime. For example, in *United States v. Church*, 29 M.J. Rptr. 679 (C.M.R. 1989), the defendant was found guilty of attempted murder of his wife when he recruited a person to kill her and actually paid for the hit man's services. Unfortunately for the defendant, the person he recruited was an undercover officer. Contracting an agent to murder and paying him when he believed the job would actually be performed constituted a "substantial step toward commission of the crime." As the court stated, it was as if the defendant armed a missile (the hired assassin) and fired it toward his intended victim. However, many states adhere to the view expressed in the Model Penal Code commentaries that "no matter what acts the solicitor commits, he cannot be guilty of attempt because it is not his purpose to commit the offense personally." Model Penal Code Commentaries, Comment to §5.02. Thus, so long as the person solicited does not take further steps toward commission of the crime, the defendant will not be guilty of attempt or another completed offense.

Let's attempt a solicitation problem now. Keep in mind the differences between solicitation and attempt when you try the next question.

QUESTION 2. It's cheaper to steal.   Joanie desperately wants a new blouse. However, the blouse is far more expensive than she can afford to pay. Joanie approaches her best friend, Mary, and asks her to hide the blouse under her clothes. Mary is dressed in several layers, whereas Joanie is wearing a shirt that would not conceal the blouse. A salesperson overhears this conversation as she passes by the dressing room. Joanie is arrested.

Joanie can be properly charged with

A. solicitation to steal.
B. attempt to steal.
C. solicitation and attempt to steal.
D. none of the above.

ANALYSIS.   This question should highlight for you the differences between attempt and solicitation. Under almost every test for attempt, Joanie has not gone far enough to be guilty of attempted theft. All she has done is to ask someone else to take something. It is the third person, Mary, who takes the steps to steal the item. However, the mere act of asking, with the intent that the other person assist in the crime, is enough to be guilty of solicitation. Once you understand this, the answer is obvious.

B is wrong because Joanie did not do enough for an attempt. Moreover, under the Model Penal Code, Joanie could never be guilty of attempt in this situation because she never intended to commit the offense personally and Mary never tried to smuggle the blouse out of the store.

C is wrong for the same reason that **B** is. Joanie has not done enough to be guilty of attempt. However, it is clear that we want to punish Joanie. She is the real instigator here and the crime is being performed for her benefit. None of these facts are required to find solicitation, but they certainly help in proving Joanie's mens rea.

Accordingly, **A** is the correct answer. Just by asking her friend Mary to steal, Joanie has committed the inchoate crime of solicitation. It is irrelevant that Mary takes no steps toward committing the crime before she is arrested. The crime of solicitation is completed once the defendant asks, encourages, or commands another person to commit a crime.

C.   Using another as an instrumentality of crime versus solicitation

We now need to discuss the only tricky issue regarding solicitation. What happens if a defendant uses another person to commit a criminal act, but that person does not realize that she is participating in criminal activity? In this situation, the defendant has not solicited a crime, but is using an "innocent instrumentality" to commit her crime. The defendant is responsible for any crime committed by that person on the defendant's behalf.

Let's take an easy example. Assume Joe Smuggler in South America wants to smuggle some drugs into the United States. To do so, he asks a friend who is traveling to the United States to take some clothes for him up to the United States. Unbeknownst to his friend, the clothes have drugs sewn into their linings. In this situation, Joe Smuggler is guilty of illegally importing the drugs. It is not solicitation because the friend he asks has no idea that he is helping with the commission of a crime.

The next question tests your understanding of the difference between solicitation and using an innocent person (instrumentality) to commit a crime.

QUESTION 3. Driving Ms. Daisy. Daisy needs a new car badly. In fact, she wants one so much that she is prepared to steal it. Daisy goes to the fanciest restaurant in town. When she comes out, she points to the shining Mercedes in front and asks the valet to go get her car. Believing Daisy is telling the truth, the valet goes and delivers the car to her. Daisy is arrested before she can drive off in the car.

Which of the following is true?

A. Daisy is guilty of solicitation and the valet is guilty of theft.
B. Daisy is guilty of solicitation and the valet is guilty of attempted theft.
C. Daisy is guilty of solicitation, but the valet is not guilty of any crime.
D. Daisy is guilty of attempted theft.

ANALYSIS. Even though Daisy has asked the valet to give her someone else's car, she has not solicited a crime. Rather, Daisy is using an innocent person to assist her in committing a crime. In this situation, Daisy is guilty of the actual crime of attempted theft, rather than just solicitation.

A is therefore wrong on both accounts—Daisy is not guilty of solicitation and the valet is not guilty of theft. Daisy is not guilty of solicitation because she is actually guilty of the substantive crime that the valet unwittingly helped her commit. The valet is not guilty of any crime because he did not have the specific intent to steal.

B is wrong for the same reasons as A. Once again, Daisy is not guilty of solicitation, but she is guilty of the substantive crime committed with the valet's help. Some of you may have chosen B because the plot is stopped before Daisy can drive off in the car and it therefore looks like an attempt. But, the valet is not guilty of the attempt because the valet did not know that the car did not belong to Daisy.

Finally, C is wrong. Daisy is not guilty of solicitation. She is guilty of attempted theft. D is the correct answer. Although the valet may innocently assist her with her scheme, she alone is guilty of the theft.

D.   Solicitation, accomplice liability, conspiracy, and merger

In the next chapter, you learn about accomplice liability. Accomplice liability refers to a defendant's responsibility for a crime she helps to take place. One way a defendant can help a crime to take place is to solicit someone to commit it. Accordingly, solicitation is not just an inchoate crime. It is also a theory of liability that makes the defendant guilty of any crime that the person she solicits ends up committing. Therefore, if a defendant solicits a person to kill her husband, and the hit man does his job, the defendant is guilty of murder as an accomplice. For sentencing purposes, the crime of solicitation merges into the completed crime and the defendant will be punished only for the more serious offense.

Similarly, if a defendant asks another person to commit a crime and that person agrees but does not actually commit the crime, the defendant is guilty of solicitation and conspiracy. Conspiracy is an agreement between two or more persons to commit a crime. (See Chapter 15.) Even if the target offense is never completed, the participants are still guilty of conspiracy.

Solicitation is an invitation to join a conspiracy. It pushes criminal liability to the earliest possible point. For that reason, it is a controversial doctrine and not all courts enforce it. When a defendant is guilty of soliciting a person to assist in a crime and that person agrees, the court will not punish the defendant for both solicitation and conspiracy. Rather, as with solicitation and the completed offense, solicitation and conspiracy merge for purposes of sentencing.

All of this will make a little more sense in the next few chapters when we study accomplice liability and conspiracy in detail. Meanwhile, consider their basic differences when answering the next question.

QUESTION 4. Criminal alliances. Tommy Terrorist is trying to recruit people to assist with a terrorist plot against a major business in town. Tommy asks Ernie to help him make a pipe bomb and plant it in the company's headquarters. Ernie agrees and makes a bomb. However, before the bomb can be detonated, Tommy and Ernie are apprehended.

Which of the following is incorrect?

A. Tommy is guilty of solicitation, conspiracy, and attempted destruction of property.
B. Tommy is an accomplice to attempted destruction of property.
C. Tommy may be punished for solicitation and conspiracy, but not attempted destruction of property.
D. Tommy is guilty of solicitation, conspiracy, and attempted destruction of property, but his crimes of solicitation and conspiracy will merge for purposes of sentencing.

ANALYSIS. This problem may seem a little intimidating because we have not yet studied conspiracy and accomplice liability in detail. Nonetheless, you already understand them enough to answer this question. If, as explained, a conspiracy is an agreement by two or more persons to commit a crime, Tommy would appear to be in a conspiracy with Ernie. Tommy is also responsible for Ernie's acts as an accomplice. Finally, Tommy clearly asked Ernie to participate in the criminal activity. Therefore, he is also guilty of solicitation. **A** is a correct statement, but the call of the question asks you to identify the "incorrect" statement. **A** is a wrong answer.

B is a correct statement as well. Tommy would be an accomplice to the attempted destruction of property. Accordingly, **B** is the wrong answer.

C, however, misstates the law. As was explained, solicitation and conspiracy merge for purposes of sentencing. Thus, even without knowing the law of conspiracy in detail, it is apparent that **C** is an incorrect statement and therefore could be the correct answer to this question. Moreover, as we discussed, if a defendant solicits another person to participate in a crime, and that crime is committed, the solicitor is guilty of the crime as well. Here, Ernie committed an attempt. Therefore, Tommy is responsible for the attempt because he solicited Ernie to commit it.

Finally, **D** is a correct statement and therefore the incorrect answer to the question. Solicitation merges with conspiracy, but not with the substantive crime. In the final analysis, **C** is the correct answer.

E. Model Penal Code approach

Under the Model Penal Code, a person is guilty of solicitation to commit a crime if (1) the actor's purpose is to promote or facilitate the commission of a substantive offense; and (2) with such purpose, he commands, encourages or requests another person to engage in conduct that would constitute the crime, an attempt to commit it, or would establish the other person's complicity in its commission or attempted commission. Model Penal Code §5.02(1).

The Model Penal Code definition is broader than traditional common law because (1) it applies to all crimes — misdemeanors and felonies, not just felonies; (2) it specifically recognizes a solicitation to commit an attempt; (3) it does not require that the person solicited be the actual perpetrator of the crime; and (4) it makes an uncommunicated solicitation a solicitation in itself, not just attempted solicitation.

A couple of examples will show you how common law solicitation and Model Penal Code solicitation law differ. Consider defendant Doe who plans to ask his best friend to commit a crime. He writes out the following request and slips it into his friend's coat: "Dear Buddy, I think we should try and shoplift those great sports videos today. I don't want you in harm's way, so why don't you give your roommate Charlie your coat and ask him to hide the videos in there?" When Charlie puts on his coat, he feels something in the pockets. Thinking it is an old receipt, he throws the note away without reading it. Is Doe guilty of solicitation?

Common law jurisdictions would differ on whether the defendant is guilty of solicitation. First, if shoplifting the videos is a misdemeanor, some jurisdictions do not recognize a solicitation to commit a misdemeanor. Second, even assuming that shoplifting is a felony, the defendant did not plan on having his friend actually commit the shoplifting. Rather, he was going to help another person to commit it. Finally, the note was never communicated. At common law, this would be an attempted solicitation; under the Model Penal Code, it is a type of solicitation.

To test your understanding of the differences between Model Penal Code solicitation and common law solicitation, try the next question. It should not be too difficult.

QUESTION 5. No smoking.   Barry is looking to buy some marijuana, but he is too afraid to ask a dealer to sell it to him. Instead, he leaves a phone message on his friend Don's cell phone asking him if he'll ask around and find someone to sell them some marijuana. Don doesn't get the message because he loses his phone. Campus police learn of the phone message and arrest Barry. In that jurisdiction, it is a misdemeanor to buy or sell marijuana.

Which of the following is true?

A. Under the Model Penal Code and traditional common law, Barry is guilty of solicitation.
B. Under the Model Penal Code, Barry is guilty of attempted solicitation.
C. Under common law, Barry is guilty of attempted solicitation.
D. Under the Model Penal Code, Barry is guilty of solicitation.

ANALYSIS.   This question tests on the differences between common law and Model Penal Code approaches to solicitation law. Note that there are three key facts in the question that highlight the differences between the two approaches. First, the crime being solicited is a misdemeanor. Already, that is an indication that only the Model Penal Code would apply. Second, Barry is not asking Don to actually buy the marijuana. Rather, he wants Don's help in finding someone to buy it. Third, Don does not actually receive the message. Therefore, at most, this would be an attempted solicitation under common law; the Model Penal Code calls the same crime solicitation.

Now, let's take a look at the answers. **A** is wrong because it holds Barry guilty under traditional common law. For all three reasons we identified, traditional common law would not apply. How about **B**? **B** is a little trickier.

Indeed, Barry would be guilty under the Model Penal Code, but not of attempted solicitation. Rather, the Model Penal Code finds even attempted solicitations to be solicitation.

C is also wrong. Once again, under common law, solicitation only applied to felonies. Moreover, Barry is not asking Don to actually commit the crime. Rather, he is using Don to solicit another person's involvement.

Finally, and almost by process of elimination, **D** is the correct answer. Barry has asked another to facilitate the commission of a crime. Under the Model Penal Code, that is all that is needed for Barry to be guilty of solicitation.

F.   Defenses to solicitation

Very few defenses exist to a solicitation charge. Under the common law, once the defendant made initial contact with the person she sought to solicit, the defendant was guilty of solicitation and abandonment was not a defense. However, the Model Penal Code takes a different approach. It recognizes a defense of renunciation if a defendant takes the necessary steps to prevent the crime she has solicited.

1. Renunciation

Under Model Penal Code §5.02(3), it is an affirmative defense if the defendant, after soliciting another person to commit a crime, persuades that person to abort the plan or the defendant otherwise prevents the commission of the offense. *To assert the defense, the defendant must (1) completely and voluntarily renounce her criminal intent; and (2) either persuade the solicited party not to commit the offense or otherwise prevent him from committing the crime.*

The rationale behind the renunciation defense is that it gives an incentive to defendants to stop their criminal behavior before it leads to actual harm. Consider, for example, a defendant who asks a friend to help her burglarize a home. After making the request, the defendant realizes that it would be a grave error to turn to a life of crime. Accordingly, the defendant rushes to her friend and tells him that she really doesn't want either one of them to commit burglary. Both the defendant and the friend agree that they will not commit the crime. In this situation, because the defendant has voluntarily and completely renounced her criminal intentions and has been successful in aborting the criminal plans, she would not be guilty of solicitation. She no longer needs to be punished or deterred because she has voluntarily turned away from criminal behavior.

There are situations in which a defendant aborts a criminal plan only because she is afraid she will get caught or she wants to wait for a better opportunity to commit the crime. In these cases, renunciation is not a defense because the defendant has not completely and voluntarily renounced her criminal intent. For example, if a defendant asks her friend to burglarize a home, and then tells him the plans are off because it looks like the occupants will be home for the evening, the defense of renunciation does not apply. The defendant is just waiting for a better opportunity to commit the crime.

The next problem tests your understanding of this concept of renunciation. It is important to understand this concept because it applies to other crimes, such as attempt and conspiracy.

QUESTION 6. Kill the boss. Catherine is fed up with her boss. He keeps harassing her and making her life miserable. Catherine asks her friend, Erwin, if he will kill her boss for her. Erwin agrees to do so for a modest fee. The night of the planned killing, Catherine gets word that her boss will be having dinner with the chief of police. Catherine calls Erwin and says she wants him to call off the killing. If the victim hears of their plot, and Catherine and Erwin are arrested before he can kill the boss, can Catherine successfully assert a renunciation defense to solicitation? Assume that the case is being handled in a jurisdiction that recognizes the Model Penal Code's standards for a renunciation defense.

A. Yes, because Erwin never came within dangerous proximity of killing her boss.

B. Yes, because she had the intent to stop Erwin from killing her boss.

C. No, because she did not fully and voluntarily renounce her intention to have her boss killed.

D. No, because Catherine had already completed the necessary actus reus and mens rea for solicitation.

ANALYSIS. Catherine may have called off the killing for that evening, but she is not entitled to a renunciation defense unless she completely and voluntarily renounces her criminal purpose. In this question, Catherine appears to be calling off the killing because the time is not right to kill her boss, not because she has renounced her criminal purpose.

A is a wrong answer because it ignores that a solicitation occurred the minute Catherine asked Erwin to kill her boss, regardless of whether Erwin came within dangerous proximity of accomplishing that task. Once again, it is important not to confuse solicitation law with the law of attempt.

B is also wrong because a fair reading of the facts indicates that the reason Catherine called off the killing of her boss was not that she had renounced her criminal purpose, but that she was waiting for a better opportunity for her boss to be killed. As such, she did not completely and voluntarily renounce her criminal purpose.

The choice then comes down to **C** or **D**. **C** is the better choice because it explains why the renunciation defense does not apply in this scenario. **D** would be the correct answer in a jurisdiction where renunciation is not a defense. As under the common law, once the actus reus and mens rea for solicitation were completed, the defendant would automatically be guilty of solicitation, regardless if she changed her mind and thwarted the crime she had solicited. Because renunciation can be a defense in this jurisdiction, but Catherine did not meet its requirements, **C** is the correct answer.

2. First Amendment defense

Solicitation is a crime whereby speech itself can be enough to satisfy the actus reus of the crime. Occasionally, a defendant may try to raise a First Amendment defense to a charge of solicitation. In general, there is no First Amendment defense for speech that otherwise constitutes criminal conduct. See *Rice v. Paladin Enterprises* ["Hit Man" case], 128 F.3d 233, 242 (4th Cir. 1997). However, abstract advocacy of lawlessness may be protected by the Fourth Amendment if it is not intended or likely to produce imminent lawless action. See *Brandenburg v. Ohio*, 395 U.S. 444 (1969).

When solicitation is directed at a specific, unlawful act, there is no First Amendment defense. For example, in *People v. Rubin*, 96 Cal. App. 3d 968 (1979), the court rejected a First Amendment defense for a defendant who offered to "pay anyone who kills a member of the American Nazi party." However, if a defendant gives a speech criticizing tax laws as unconstitutional, the defendant would not be guilty of solicitation unless her words called for the immediate violation by certain individuals of the tax laws. See *United States v. Buttorff*, 572 F.2d 619, 623-624 (8th Cir. 1978) (holding that general tax evasion speeches had First Amendment protection because they do not incite imminent lawless activity). The case may be different if the defendant not only speaks against the tax laws but gives specific instructions as to how to violate them. In that situation, the First Amendment defense does not apply. See *United States v. Fleschner*, 98 F.3d 155 (4th Cir. 1996).[1]

Your constitutional law course will probably cover First Amendment defenses in more detail. For purposes of a basic criminal law course, it is sufficient to know that there is generally no First Amendment defense to criminal activity, including soliciting another person to commit a crime. The only time there might be such a defense is when a defendant gives a speech that does not seek to prompt immediate, unlawful action.

---

1. Compare *United States v. Freeman*, 761 F.2d 549 (9th Cir. 1985) (suggestions as to how to prepare false tax returns were abstract enough and far enough removed from criminal act to warrant First Amendment defense).

QUESTION 7. Bad chat. Michael is frustrated with the ongoing war in Iraq and participates regularly in a chat room discussion on the Internet Service regarding the war. In his latest posting, Michael has stated, "It's time to say no. Tear up those Selective cards. Or go AWOL. Don't let the government push us around anymore." Michael hopes his comments will generate more discussion regarding the problems with the war. When a government agent surveying the chat room reads Michael's comments, he has him arrested for soliciting violations of the Selective Service laws.

If Michael seeks a First Amendment defense, he will most likely

A. succeed because his words were not intended to incite imminent violations of the law.
B. succeed because words alone cannot be the basis for criminal conduct.
C. fail because his words could prompt a person to disobey the Selective Service laws.
D. fail because there is never a First Amendment defense to the crime of solicitation.

ANALYSIS. This question should have been relatively easy for you because (1) the question is a prime example of when a First Amendment defense may apply; (2) some of the proposed answers state absolutes (e.g., "never" or "always") and are therefore not as likely to be the correct answer. With those warnings in mind, let's look at Michael's conduct and the various available answers.

Michael is engaging in fairly classic First Amendment activity. He is speaking out against the war and is doing so in a general forum. Although he uses words that in another context might be solicitation, because they are general advocacy and do not threaten imminent unlawfulness, they would seem to qualify for a First Amendment defense.

This is definitely one of those situations in which going through the various answer options helps. At first read, **A** looks promising. It is a true statement that Michael has a First Amendment defense if his "words were not intended to incite imminent violations of the law." In fact, Michael's actions and intent may not meet the basic requirements for solicitation unless he had the purpose of encouraging or promoting a crime.

By contrast, **B** goes too far. Words can be the basis for criminal conduct. In fact, that is exactly what the law of solicitation is all about. Words alone are often the actus reus for solicitation.

C is also incorrect. Just because words might prompt someone to violate the laws does not mean that the defendant intended that they do so. In criminal law, the focus is on the mens rea of the defendant, not the person who responds to her conduct or words.

Finally, **D** is wrong because it asserts that a First Amendment defense is "never" a defense to the crime of solicitation. It is rarely a defense, but the word *never* goes too far.

In the last analysis, **A** is the best answer. There is no clear line as to when speech turns from advocacy to criminal behavior. However, the court will focus on the defendant's intent. General advocacy is insufficient to constitute solicitation; advocacy directed at specific individuals with the purpose of causing imminent lawless behavior can suffice.[2]

G.   Other inchoate crimes

In addition to solicitation, there are other inchoate offenses that seek to punish a defendant before she has caused actual injury. The crime of stalking is a prime example.

Stalking is defined as the repeated and intentional harassment of another person in a manner that makes a credible threat putting that person in fear of her safety. Stalking is a controversial crime because it punishes a defendant long before he does anything that physically hurts the victim. Thus, it is a typical inchoate crime. However, because law enforcement authorities do not want to wait until it is too late to apprehend the defendant, they criminalize menacing behavior.

As with other inchoate crimes, stalking requires proof of the highest level of intent. A defendant must purposely and maliciously harass his victim. Moreover, the defendant must make a "credible threat" of harm. The threat may be written or verbal. It must be of a nature that a reasonable person in the target's situation would fear for her safety.

As with solicitation, defendants sometimes try to argue a First Amendment defense to stalking. However, there is no First Amendment right to threaten another person. Accordingly, a First Amendment defense will not prevail.

> **QUESTION 8. Peeping Tom.**   Tom is fascinated with movie stars, especially Shannon Stone. One day, he sees her in the grocery store and starts to stare at her. He follows her up and down the aisles. Tom gives Stone the creeps. She calls the authorities to prosecute Tom for stalking. Stone tells the authorities that even though Tom has never spoken a

---

2. For an interesting discussion of federal laws criminalizing solicitations of illegal activity on the Internet, see Bruce Braun, Dane Drobny & Douglas C. Gessner, *www.commercial_terrorism.com: A Proposed Federal Criminal Statute Addressing the Solicitation of Commercial Terrorism Through the Internet*, 37 Harv. J. on Legis. 159 (2000).

> word to her, he makes her uncomfortable and she fears that next time they run into each other in the market, he will snap and hurt her.
>
> Is Tom guilty of stalking?
>
> **A.** Yes, because he made Stone feel uncomfortable.
> **B.** Yes, because he followed Stone in the store.
> **C.** No, because Tom has not come dangerously close to harming Stone.
> **D.** No, because Tom does not pose a credible threat to Stone.

ANALYSIS. We all have a natural tendency to want to stop creepy behavior. However, that urge should not be confused with the law on inchoate offenses. Before we punish a defendant who has not yet harmed another person, it is important to make sure that the defendant had the purpose to harm and poses a credible threat. In this question, Tom is definitely an annoyance but there are insufficient facts to prove that he poses a credible, imminent threat to Stone.

Accordingly, **A** is the wrong answer. Merely making a victim uncomfortable does not constitute the crime of stalking. The defendant must pose a credible threat and there must be evidence of his intent to harass. Stalking entails more than just making the victim feel uncomfortable. There must be evidence of a purpose to harass and harm.

For similar reasons, **B** is wrong. It is not a crime to intentionally follow another person unless there is the intent to cause fear in the victim by one's behavior. Here, Tom probably felt that it was flattering for Stone to be followed. Moreover, there is no evidence that a reasonable person would have felt in fear of her safety from Tom's behavior. A reasonable person would not be thrilled, and may even be a bit annoyed, but there is insufficient evidence of a credible threat in this hypothetical.

C is wrong because it confuses the law of attempt and the law of stalking. The Holmes standard for attempt, discussed in Chapter 12, requires that the defendant come in dangerous proximity of completing the crime. Stalking punishes behavior that may not reach the threshold for attempt.

Therefore, it becomes clear that **D** is the correct answer. The crime of stalking only applies when there is a credible threat of harm to the victim. Tom's behavior, although it makes Stone uncomfortable, has not demonstrated a credible threat of harm.

H.   The Closer: Bad taste or illegal?

The study of solicitation and other inchoate crimes is designed to demonstrate the tension between protecting victims from possible harm and safeguarding the freedom of individuals to act without government interference. Solicitation law pushes the criminal law to the earliest stages of preparatory criminal behavior. It therefore poses a threat to a person's right to act. The last question of this chapter provides an overview on the limits of criminalizing inchoate crimes.

QUESTION 9. **Organ sales.** Marvin runs a science laboratory in a local university. Recently, there have not been enough donated cadavers for Marvin's experiments. Therefore, Marvin puts an ad in the local newspaper stating the following: "Wanted—Dead only! Five Human Cadavers. Looks Don't Matter. Will pay top dollar. Contact (888) 387-9800." In that jurisdiction, Model Penal Code §606 makes it illegal to sell human remains. When the advertisement is brought to the attention of local authorities, the district attorney files criminal charges against Marvin for soliciting a violation of §606. Marvin asserts several defenses to these charges. First, he claims that the law violates his First Amendment rights. Second, he claims that he did not really intend to buy the cadavers. He just wanted to get the names of those with cadavers to sell so that he could solicit them for a donation. Finally, Marvin claims that he never took a substantial step toward obtaining the cadavers, other than taking out an advertisement. In fact, he claims that he told his research assistant to withdraw the advertisement and inform everyone who calls that it is illegal and wrong to sell cadavers.

Despite these arguments, the prosecutor charges Marvin with solicitation. Assuming that Marvin is believed, which of the following defenses are most likely to succeed?

I. First Amendment defense
II. Lack of intent
III. No substantial step toward completion of crime
IV. Renunciation

A. All of the above.
B. None of the above.
C. I and II.
D. II and IV.

ANALYSIS. This question provides a good review of the law of solicitation and the defenses to that crime. It also requires you to do something that might be contrary to your instincts. You must assume the jury believes Marvin. You might not personally believe him, but for the purposes of this question, you must assume that his facts are true and make your selection accordingly. Using that standard, evaluate each of the possible defenses.

I. Is Marvin entitled to a First Amendment defense? The answer is no. Remember the general rule that the right of free speech does not protect speech that is designated as criminal behavior. Soliciting a violation of the law is a prime example of speech that is not protected.

II. Does Marvin have a defense of lack of intent? The answer here is yes. If the jury actually believes Marvin's story, he did not have the purpose of encouraging, promoting, or facilitating a crime.

III. Is it a defense that Marvin did not take a substantial step toward completing the crime? The answer is no. Even if Marvin did not take a substantial step, his mere act of soliciting through the advertisement could be enough if all the requirements for the crime were met.

IV. Finally, is Marvin entitled to a renunciation defense? If it is true that he told his research assistants to tell people he had no intention of buying the cadavers and that they should not sell any, under the Model Penal Code approach he would have a renunciation defense.

Now that you have analyzed each option, it should be easy to pick the answer. If Marvin has a defense under II and IV, **D** is the answer to the question.

✦ Levenson's Picks

1. Yabadaba doo	**D**
2. It's cheaper to steal	**A**
3. Driving Ms. Daisy	**D**
4. Criminal alliances	**C**
5. No smoking	**D**
6. Kill the boss	**C**
7. Bad chat	**A**
8. Peeping Tom	**D**
9. Organ sales	**D**

14

Accomplice Liability

He is my friend, and he is me.
— Abraham Lincoln

CHAPTER OVERVIEW

A. General overview of accomplice liability
1. Common law distinctions
a. Prinicipal in the first degree
b. Principal in the second degree
c. Accessory before the fact
d. Accessory after the fact
2. Modern approach
3. Accessory after the fact
4. Using another person as an instrument to commit a crime
B. Mens rea requirement for accomplice liability
1. Purposeful standard
2. Mens rea standard for strict liability crimes
3. Mens rea standard for reckless or negligent crimes
C. Actus reus requirement for accomplice liability
D. Liability for foreseeable offenses
E. Relationship between the parties
1. Public authority justification defense
2. Protected class of persons
3. Culpable-but-unconvitable principal
4. Acquitted principal

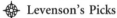

U nder both common law and by statute, a defendant may be accountable for committing a crime even if he simply helps another in its commission. At common law, there were distinct categories to identify the roles of individuals participating in a crime. Today, all individuals who assist in the commission of a crime are accomplices and are jointly responsible for the offense committed.

For the most part, the terms *accomplice* and *aider and abettor* are now interchangeable. These terms refer to those individuals who assist in the commission of a crime.

This chapter outlines those elements that must be proven to establish accomplice liability. As you go through this chapter, keep one very important concept in mind. *Accomplice liability is not a separate crime. It is a theory by which a defendant is guilty of a crime because he is responsible for another person's criminal behavior.*

Rather than discuss the Model Penal Code approach to accomplice liability in a separate section in this chapter, differences between it and the common law are discussed throughout the chapter. As you will see, the Model Penal Code also holds a person responsible for personally committing a crime or assisting in a crime, although its standards for accomplice liability are somewhat different. Model Penal Code §2.06.

A. General overview of accomplice liability

It's worth repeating: Accomplice liability is not a separate crime; it is a theory by which a defendant is guilty of a specific substantive offense committed by another person. The defendant is guilty because he purposely did something to help with the commission of that crime.

For example, assume that Patty has agreed to help her boyfriend rob a bank. Patty will act as the getaway driver. Her boyfriend goes into the bank, puts a gun in the teller's face, and takes the cash. Certainly, the boyfriend is guilty of bank robbery. How about Patty? She, too, is guilty of bank robbery. As an accomplice, she is guilty of the substantive crime she helped her boyfriend commit. She is not guilty, however, of being an "accomplice."

The basic premise of accomplice liability is that all persons who assist in the commission of a crime should be held accountable, to some degree, for that offense. The doctrine of complicity recognizes that one individual's actions may influence whether or how another person acts. The involvement of more than one person in the criminal activity generally means that there is more likelihood of the participants achieving their goal. For this reason, all participants are guilty of the substantive crime they help commit, regardless of whether it was originally their idea to commit the crime or they played a primary role.

QUESTION 1. Firebug. James and Martin are friends and business partners. Both of them realize that their business is going down the tubes and they are about to lose their entire investment. James comes up with a plan. He tells Martin that they should torch the business and collect on their insurance policy. Martin loves the idea and agrees to set the fire. After Martin burns the business to the ground, James submits an insurance claim and collects the proceeds. They are both charged with insurance fraud.

Which of the following is true?

A. James is guilty of being an accomplice.
B. Only Martin is guilty of insurance fraud.
C. James and Martin are both guilty of insurance fraud.
D. Martin is guilty of arson and James is guilty of being an accomplice.

ANALYSIS. You should be able to answer this question, even though we have not yet studied the formal requirements for accomplice liability. Do it the old-fashioned way: Review each possible answer to see if it comports with your understanding of the basic nature of accomplice liability.

A is clearly wrong. There is no crime of "being an accomplice." Either James is guilty of insurance fraud or he is not guilty. He may be guilty of insurance fraud because of accomplice liability, but his actions do not make him guilty of being an accomplice.

B is wrong because everyone who helps to commit a crime, with the proper mens rea, is guilty of that offense. Thus, assuming James purposely helped with the insurance fraud by submitting the insurance claim, he too is guilty of insurance fraud.

C looks like a much better answer. Both of the defendants are guilty of the crime because they both assisted in its commission. As we will learn, it does not matter that Martin burned the building and James submitted the insurance forms. Accomplice liability does not depend on which role the defendant performed as long as the defendant acted with the purpose of helping to commit the crime. Also, don't be thrown off because this answer doesn't state that Martin would also be guilty of arson. That may be true, but

C is correct because James and Martin are at least both guilty of insurance fraud.

Before we select **C**, take a quick look at **D**. Like **A**, it gives the faulty option of having James guilty of being an accomplice. James may be an accomplice, but he is guilty of the substantive crime of insurance fraud.

1. Common law distinctions

At common law, there were distinct categories and labels that applied to participants in crimes. These labels helped to identify the role of each participant and the likely range of sentencing that defendant faced. Going from the most culpable to the least culpable, they included the following.

a. Principal in the first degree   This was the actual perpetrator of the crime. For example, in a bank robbery, the principal in the first degree was the defendant who actually entered the bank and demanded money from the teller.

b. Principal in the second degree   This was the person who aided and abetted the principal by being present, or nearby. For example, in a bank robbery, the lookout or getaway driver was the classic principal in the second degree.

c. Accessory before the fact   This was the person who helped prepare for the crime. For example, in a bank robbery, the person who cased the bank or purchased the disguises, but did not participate in the actual robbery, was considered an accessory before the fact.

d. Accessory after the fact   This was the person who, knowing that a felony had been committed, received, relieved, comforted, or assisted the felon. For example, in a bank robbery, a person who learned that his friend had just committed a robbery but offered to hide the defendant and his loot until the police had called off their search was considered an accessory after the fact.

Here is a quick question to test your understanding of these categories. Today, all of the participants, except for an accessory after the fact, are equally liable for the crime. However, at common law they were sometimes treated differently.

QUESTION 2. Who's in charge?   Ray and his buddies are cocaine distributors. Ray is the brains behind the operation. He keeps lists of customers, obtains the cocaine from a wholesaler, and divides up the distribution duties to his buddies. Jan delivers the actual cocaine to the customers while Karl acts as a bodyguard. During one of their recent deliveries, Jan and Karl needed a quick way to escape when witnesses called the police. Jan's cousin, Fenton, gave them his car to use to flee.

If the old common law approach is applied, which of the following classifications is correct?

A. Ray is the principal in the first degree, Jan is the principal in the second degree, Karl is the accessory before the fact, and Fenton is the accessory after the fact.

B. Ray is the principal in the first degree, Karl is the principal in the second degree, Jan is the accessory before the fact, and Fenton is the accessory after the fact.

C. Jan is the principal in the first degree, Ray is the principal in the second degree, Karl is the accessory after the fact, and Fenton is an accessory before the fact.

D. Jan is the principal in the first degree, Ray is an accessory before the fact, Karl is a principal in the second degree, and Fenton is an accessory after the fact.

ANALYSIS. This problem requires that you correctly label each defendant's participation under the old common law standards. Let's start with Ray. Ray is behind the scenes. Although he is the mastermind, he is not on the scene when the cocaine is distributed. Accordingly, he would not be the principal in the first degree, even though he is the brains behind the operation. Rather, he is an accessory before the fact.

Jan is the on-the-spot perpetrator. He is the one who actually delivers the drugs. Accordingly, he is the principal in the first degree, although he is not the mastermind behind the crime. As the bodyguard, Karl is nearby when the drugs are delivered. As such, he plays the role of a principal in the second degree. Finally, there is Fenton. Because Fenton becomes involved after the drugs have been distributed, he plays the role of an accessory after the fact.

Before selecting the correct answer, make a simple list of your players and roles. From there, it is easy to select the right answer.

Jan	—	principal in the first degree
Karl	—	principal in the second degree
Ray	—	accessory before the fact
Fenton	—	accessory after the fact

The only answer that reflects these designations is **D**. All the others have confused the roles of the players.

As the next section discusses, modern statutes have generally eliminated the common law categories and hold all the participants to a crime, apart from the accessory after the fact, liable for the offense. However, it is still helpful to know the different roles that accomplices may play in an offense because courts will occasionally use common law language in their descriptions of the defendants' participation in crimes.

2. Modern approach

Most modern statutes no longer rely on the common law categories for accomplices to a crime. Rather, all those who assist the principal in the commission of a crime, either before or during its commission, are considered accomplices or aiders and abettors.

Generally, all participants in a crime are subject to the same punishment, except for an accessory after the fact. For example, in a bank robbery, the robber, getaway driver, and the person who planned the robbery would all be subject to the same punishment. The court may not actually impose the same punishment, but theoretically each defendant is equally responsible for its commission.

The rationale behind holding accomplices to the same level of culpability as principals is that a person who plans a crime should not escape punishment because he hides behind the scenes. When a crime is the combination of more than one person's efforts, each defendant is contributing to the overall commission of the crime. While judges may have the discretion to tailor sentences, there should be no arbitrary classifications limiting the punishment that can be imposed.

Here are some sample statutes reflecting the modern approach.

California law. "All persons concerned in the commission of a crime, whether it be felony or misdemeanor, and whether they directly commit the act constituting the offense, or aid and abet in its commission, or, not being present, have advised and encouraged its commission . . . are principals in any crime so committed." Cal. Penal Code, §31.

Federal law. "Whoever commits an offense against the United States or aids, abets, counsels, commands, induces or procures its commission is punishable as a principal." 18 U.S.C. §2(a).

Model Penal Code. "A person is guilty of an offense if it is committed by his own conduct or by the conduct of another person for which he is legally accountable, or both." Model Penal Code §2.06.

The modern approach has led to several important rules regarding accomplice liability.

Rule #1:   Principals need not be convicted   Under modern statutes, the prosecution need only prove that a crime was actually committed and the accomplice participated before or during its commission. The accomplice's liability does not depend on whether the principal is apprehended or convicted. For example, consider a case in which the evidence proves there were three participants in a robbery—the robber, lookout, and planner. Only the lookout is apprehended. So long as the prosecution proves that the robbery occurred, the lookout can be convicted even if his co-participants are never convicted.

Rule #2:   No need to charge specific form of complicity   Instead of charging defendants under a specific common law label, all defendants, other than accessories after the fact, may be charged directly with the substantive crime committed.

The next question tests your understanding of the modern approach of accomplice liability. Just remember, criminal law is a real democracy. Everyone who participates can be (and is) guilty of the crime.

QUESTION 3. Betsy and Ross.   Betsy sees Ross trying to steal an antique flag from a nearby shop. She intentionally distracts the store owner so Ross can steal the flag. Ross escapes with the flag, but Betsy is turned into the police when she brags to a neighbor how she helped Ross steal the flag. Betsy is charged with stealing the flag.

If Betsy challenges the charges, she should

A. succeed because Ross stole the flag and she was only an accessory.
B. succeed because Ross was not apprehended.
C. fail because Betsy helped Ross steal the flag.
D. fail because Betsy did not plan the theft of the flag.

ANALYSIS.   This question should raise several red flags (sorry!). Under the common law approach, prosecutors would have had to designate Betsy as a principal in the second degree. She would only be guilty if Ross was guilty. Under the modern approach, the rules of pleading are more flexible and Betsy is guilty regardless of whether Ross is apprehended and convicted. Let's look at the possible answers.

A is wrong because accessories are also guilty of the crime they helped commit. Even though Ross stole the flag, Betsy assisted. Accordingly, she can also be guilty of the substantive offense.

B is wrong because there is no longer a requirement that the principal in the first degree be arrested and convicted. So long as prosecutors can prove that the crime actually took place, it is irrelevant whether the principal is ever apprehended and convicted.

How about **C**? Yes, it seems right on point. Betsy helped steal the flag so her challenge should fail. It doesn't matter whether she was the principal, or if the principal was convicted — she is responsible. It also doesn't matter whether she came up with the plans for the crime. As an aider and abettor, she is guilty. **D** is also wrong.

3. Accessory after the fact

Earlier, we mentioned that accessories before the fact are treated as accomplices and generally subject to the same punishment as principals. However, accessories after the fact are still treated differently. Under both common law and modern statutes, accessories after the fact are treated as less culpable than principals or accessories before the fact. The rationale for this approach is that the after-the-fact accessories are slightly less culpable because they did not become involved until after the crime was completed. As such, they are typically subject to a lesser penalty. At common law, spouses could not even be charged as accessories after the fact.

For example, in a bank robbery, a person who agrees to conceal a robber and his loot, even though that person did not know in advance that there was going to be a robbery, is an accessory after the fact. Although it is wrong to help criminals at any point in their activities, we give the accessory after the fact a break because he had no role prior to commission of the offense.

QUESTION 4. **You did what?!**   Marlene is surprised by a knock at her door. Her best friend, Alfie, arrives with blood on his hand and a knife in his pocket. He admits that he just stabbed a police officer and is hiding from the law. He asks Marlene if she can help him get to the border. Marlene gives Alfie $500 cash and tells Alfie to bury his knife in her backyard. Alfie escapes. Bloodhounds find Alfie's knife in Marlene's backyard. She is charged with being an accomplice to the murder.

Marlene is

A. guilty as an aider and abettor.
B. guilty as an accessory after the fact.
C. guilty as a principal.
D. none of the above.

ANALYSIS.   Given the nature of Alfie's crime, you may be ready to throw the book at him and Marlene. However, because Marlene did not know about the killing until after it was completed, she is technically only an accessory after the fact. She is in that category of accomplices that is still treated differently than those participants who assist a crime before it is completed.

Is Marlene an aider and abettor? No. Although she helps Alfie, she is only an accessory after the fact. She is therefore not guilty of murder. She is guilty, instead, of the separate crime of being an accessory after the fact to murder. She may also be guilty of other statutory crimes that we will not study in detail, including concealing evidence or assisting in an escape. **A**, however, is an incorrect answer.

As we've discussed, Marlene is an accessory after the fact and she is guilty of being so. **B** is the correct answer. **C** is wrong because Alfie would be the principal in this example. **D** is wrong because **B** is the right answer.

4. Using another person as an instrument to commit a crime

Before we study the actus reus and mens rea requirements for accomplice liability, it is important to consider one more issue that can be raised when more than one person participates in a crime. In each of the examples above, the accomplice or accessory knew that he was participating in a criminal activity. However, what if a person unknowingly or unwittingly participates in a crime? Is that person still an accomplice?

No. If a person unknowingly or unwittingly participates in a crime, that person is not an accomplice but is considered a mere instrument by which the actual perpetrator committed the offense. For example, *A* asks *B* to deliver a sealed envelope to a bank teller. Inside the envelope is a note demanding the bank's money and threatening harm if it is not produced. *B* is an innocent agent and not an accomplice to the crime.

Animals and objects may also be used as instruments. For example, a defendant may train a dog to enter another person's house to steal an item or use a remote control device to accomplish the same. In these situations, the defendant, not the dog or device, is responsible for the crime.

The concept of using another person as an instrumentality to commit a crime is expressed in federal law. Title 18, United States Code, Section 2(b) states: "Whoever willfully causes an act to be done which if directly performed by him or another would be an offense against the United States is punishable as a principal."

At common law, there were some crimes that one could not cause another person to do on one's behalf. For example, perjury traditionally required that the convicted person be the one who actually testified falsely. An accomplice could encourage or dupe another into testifying falsely, but the accomplice would still not be lying under oath. Modern statutes, however, would hold a defendant responsible for "causing" an act that, if done by the defendant, would constitute a crime.

Let's try one problem dealing with the issue of when a defendant causes another person to commit a crime.

QUESTION 5. Lend a hand. Tyrone wants to steal the beautiful Porsche parked on the street in front of his home. He calls a locksmith and tells him that he has lost the key to his car. The unsuspecting locksmith arrives and makes a new key for Tyrone. Tyrone then drives off in the Porsche. When he is apprehended, he and the locksmith are charged with stealing the car. Both plead not guilty.

Which of the following is incorrect?

A. Tyrone is not guilty because he could not have stolen the car without the locksmith's help.
B. The locksmith is an accomplice to the theft.
C. Tyrone and the locksmith are both guilty of theft.
D. All of the above.
E. None of the above.

ANALYSIS.   In this situation, Tyrone is using the unsuspecting locksmith to help him commit a crime. Because the locksmith is unaware that he is assisting in a crime, he is being used as an instrument by Tyrone and is not an accomplice. Therefore, a correct answer should have Tyrone as guilty because he used the locksmith as an instrument, and the locksmith as not guilty because he was not a knowing accomplice in the crime.

A is certainly an incorrect statement. A defendant can be guilty even if he could not have committed the crime without someone else's help. So long as the defendant participates in the commission of the crime, the defendant is guilty. Since the call of the question asks you to mark the incorrect statement, a check should temporarily go next to **A**.

However, **B** also looks like it will fit the call of the question. The locksmith is not an accomplice to the theft because he did not knowingly participate in a crime. As we discuss further in the section on mens rea, only defendants who have the purpose in having a crime succeed are considered accomplices.

C is also an incorrect statement because only Tyrone will be guilty of theft; the locksmith is Tyrone's instrument to commit that crime.

This is one of those situations in which "none of the above," as designated in **E**, is the correct answer. Every statement in the answers to this question is incorrect. None of them correctly reflects that the locksmith is John's instrument to commit a crime. John is the dupe and Tyrone is the thief.

B. Mens rea requirement for accomplice liability

Although it is not a separate crime, accomplice liability requires both a mens rea and an actus reus for the defendant to be guilty of the underlying substantive crime. The actus reus for accomplice liability is an act of encouragement. The mens rea requirement is that the defendant acted (helped) with the purpose to have the crime succeed.

1. Purposeful standard

The classic case used to teach the standards of accomplice liability is *Hicks v. United States*, 150 U.S. 442 (1893). In *Hicks*, the defendant was accused of murder for allegedly encouraging his friend, Stand Rowe, to kill the victim, Andrew Colvard. In the version of the facts adopted by the court, Rowe and Hicks had a confrontation with the victim. At some point during their conversation, Colvard said something that led Hicks to laugh and caused Rowe to direct his rifle at Colvard. Hicks then took off his hat and hit his horse with it. He stated to Colvard, "Take off your hat and die like a man." At that point, Rowe shot and killed Colvard. Hicks then rode off with Rowe. Later, Hicks testified that he left with Rowe because he feared him and had separated from him as soon as he could. The judge instructed the jury that "[i]f the deliberate and intentional use of words [had] the effect to encourage one man to kill another, he who uttered the words is presumed by law to have intended that effect, and is responsible therefore."

The appellate court reversed Hicks's conviction because the jury instruction misstated the law. To be an aider and abettor, it is not enough that one does something that assists with a crime. *The prosecution must prove that the defendant spoke or acted with the purpose to encourage or assist another in the commission of a crime.* The focus must be on the defendant's purpose when uttering the words, not the effect of the defendant's conduct on the principal.

Judge Learned Hand expressed the mens rea requirement for accomplice liability as follows: To be guilty as an accomplice, a defendant must not only know that his acts may assist the commission of a crime, but must also have the specific purpose of having the crime succeed. *United States v. Peoni*, 100 F.2d 401 (2d Cir. 1938) (Learned Hand, J.).

There are many ways to establish a purpose to aid and abet. The primary method is to demonstrate that the accomplice had a "stake in the venture." The more the defendant benefits from the principal's actions, the more likely the defendant acted with the purpose to assist the principal. See *People v. Lauria*, 251 Cal. App. 2d 471 (1967).

Some courts refer to a requirement that there be a "nexus" between the defendant's actions and the principal's criminal actions. This label is another way of describing the requirement that the accomplice intend to assist the principal's commission of a crime.

Originally, the Model Penal Code was drafted to allow accomplice liability to be proven with knowing participation in a crime. However, the final draft of the Model Penal Code now requires that the actor have "the purpose of promoting or facilitating" the commission of the crime. Model Penal Code §2.06(3)(a).

Before trying to apply the mens rea requirement for accomplice liability, take a moment to think about the rationale for the high mens rea standard. In today's society, there are many ways that people might accidentally assist another in a criminal act. For example, imagine that a mattress salesman has a well-known prostitute enter his store. The prostitute states that she is interested in buying a bed that can stand a lot of wear. The mattress salesman may have his suspicions about how the bed is to be used, but his primary interest is in selling a mattress. If the mattress salesman sells the bed to the prostitute, is he an accomplice to prostitution? No. The mattress salesman is just trying to make a sale. He has no real nexus to the prostitute's business. His purpose in making the sale is not to promote prostitution, but to sell the bed. Accordingly, he is not an accomplice to prostitution. Both the Model Penal Code and common law set the mens rea requirement at "purpose" in order to ensure the maximum autonomy for individuals in a laissez-faire society.

In some jurisdictions, the mattress salesman's case may qualify for a separate, lesser crime of *criminal facilitation*. Rather than make a defendant an accomplice to the substantive crime he helps, a jurisdiction may have a statute that prohibits a defendant from knowingly providing aid to another person who commits a crime.

In analyzing the next question, keep in mind the high mens rea standard for accomplice liability. It is only when a defendant helps with the purpose of having a crime succeed that the defendant is guilty of that crime as an accomplice.

QUESTION 6. Fill'er up.   Wylie works as a gasoline station attendant. There has been a rash of late afternoon bank robberies in the area. At 4:30 P.M., a car with no license plates and a driver dressed suspiciously pulls into the station. Although Wylie is fairly sure that the driver is the serial bank robber, he fills up the car with gas. The driver then proceeds to rob Security Pathetic Bank.

Is Wylie guilty of bank robbery?

A. No, because he was not present at the time that Security Pathetic Bank was robbed.

B. Yes, because he profited by the bank robber's purchase of gasoline.
C. No, because his purpose in selling gas was not to facilitate robbery.
D. Yes, because he suspected the car driver was a serial bank robber.

ANALYSIS. This question tests your understanding of the mens rea requirement for most accomplice situations. Suspicion is not enough. The mens rea requirement is set at purposeful so that innocent persons who may tangentially assist criminals are not caught up in the criminal justice system. We might not be thrilled that Wylie has sold gas to the robber, but his actions, without the necessary mens rea, do not make him an accomplice to robbery.

However, you still must be careful in selecting an answer. Although you can be fairly certain from the facts that Wylie is not guilty of bank robbery, it is also important to select the answer that offers the correct rationale. For example, **A** is incorrect even though it states that Wylie is not guilty of bank robbery. The reason it is a wrong answer is that it gives the wrong rationale. As we learned earlier in this section, a person can be an accomplice even if he is not at the scene of the crime. Therefore, the rationale offered in **A** is incorrect.

B is wrong because it assumes that everyone who profits from a crime is automatically an accomplice. Although profits may be one way of proving that a defendant had enough of an interest to want a crime to succeed, it does not by itself prove purpose. In this case, the small amount of profit that Wylie made from his sale of gasoline does not establish that he has a stake in the robber's illegal activities.

C looks like the best answer. In this hypothetical, there does not seem to be sufficient evidence that Wylie had the purpose to help in a bank robbery, even if he did sell gasoline to the robber. Charging Wylie with bank robbery would cast the net of accomplice liability too broadly given all the ways in which people may inadvertently assist in a crime.

Before circling **C** as your final answer, take a look at **D**. **D** is wrong because it states the wrong mens rea standard for accomplice liability. Suspicion is not enough. Wylie must have the purpose to promote or facilitate the bank robbery.

CAVEAT: Before we look at some special mens rea situations, you should be aware that there are some jurisdictions that use a more relaxed mens rea standard for serious crimes. For example, in *United States v. Fountain*, 768 F.2d 790 (7th Cir. 1985), the defendant lifted his shirt to reveal a knife, which another inmate seized and used to stab a guard. Because of the seriousness of the crime, the court held that knowing assistance was sufficient to prove accomplice liability. The issue may just be one of semantics. The less legitimate reasons there are for a defendant's actions, the more likely his purpose was to assist in furthering a crime if he knew how his actions would likely help.

2. Mens rea standard for strict liability crimes

In many jurisdictions, the prosecution must prove a higher level of mens rea for the accomplice than it is required to prove for the principal of a strict liability crime. Recall that to be guilty of strict liability crimes, the principal need not have any mens rea as to attendant circumstances. The same is not true of an accomplice. Often, the courts require that the accomplice at least know that his actions are helping in a criminal endeavor.

For example, in *Johnson v. Youden,* 1 K.B. 544 (1950), defendants were charged with aiding and abetting a builder who was selling a house at a price in excess of that permitted by law. Selling a house at an unlawful price is a strict liability crime. Although the builder could be convicted of the unlawful sale even if he did not know that he was charging an unlawful price, the defendants (who were lawyers for the builder) could not be convicted as accomplices unless they knew the builder was charging an excessive price.

The Model Penal Code is ambiguous on what level of culpability is required for an accomplice to a strict liability offense. Model Penal Code §2.06(3)(a) requires that the defendant act with purpose as to the "commission of the offense." This clause is intentionally ambiguous as to whether the accomplice must have knowledge or purpose as to the elements of a crime for which the principal is strictly liable. Either way, an accomplice may require more mens rea than the defendant who would be strictly liable for his actions.

A good example of this principle is a case in which the defendant is charged with being an accomplice to statutory rape. Ordinarily, the defendant would be guilty if he has sex with a minor, even if he is unaware of the girl's age. If a person helped the defendant arrange his date with the minor, that person could only be charged with being an accomplice to statutory rape if he knew that the girl was underage.

It is relatively rare for a person to be charged as an accomplice to a strict liability offense. However, when that rare situation occurs, whether it is on an exam or in life, keep in mind the unique mens rea requirement for accomplices to strict liability offenses.

QUESTION 7. **Dirty dumping.** Zak is charged with being an accomplice to the illegal dumping of hazardous waste. Zak's friend, Marshal, had asked Zak if he could use Zak's truck to take some used chemicals to the desert where they could be disposed of safely. Zak readily agreed. As it turns out, Marshal dumps the chemicals in an illegal dumping site.

Is Zak guilty of the strict liability offense of illegal dumping?

A. Yes, because Zak assisted a strict liability offense.

> **B.** Yes, if Zak knew that the desert site was an illegal dumping site.
> **C.** No, if Marshal believed that it was legal to dump the chemicals at the desert site.
> **D.** No, because a person can never be an accomplice to a strict liability offense.

ANALYSIS.   You are told in the question that Zak is charged with being an accomplice to a strict liability offense. Ordinarily, strict liability offenses do not require that the defendant know the circumstances that make his conduct wrong. However, for the accomplice, many jurisdictions require such knowledge. Assuming such a jurisdiction, prosecutors must prove more than that Zak loaned his truck for an illegal activity. Even if illegal dumping charges would be warranted against Marshal, the government must prove that Zak knew he was assisting with illegal activities.

Let's look at the possible choices for answers. **A** is wrong because merely assisting with a strict liability offense does not automatically make the accomplice liable. Some mens rea requirement is still needed. Answer **B** reflects the better approach. Indeed, if Zak did know the illegal nature of the activity, he would be guilty.

C and **D** offer some red herrings that are worth examining. **C** is tempting if you don't read the answer carefully. It refers to Marshal's state of mind, not Zak's. Moreover, it is wrong even as to Marshal. Because he is the principal, Marshal may very well be guilty of the strict liability offense even if he honestly believed his dump site was legal. The same is not true for Zak.

Finally, **D** is wrong because it overstates the situation. A person can be an accomplice to a strict liability offense, but there is a heavier burden on prosecutors than there ordinarily is in strict liability offenses. The prosecutor must prove that the accomplice knew those circumstances that made the principal's conduct unlawful.

It probably won't surprise you too much to learn that there are also some special rules on accomplice liability when it comes to reckless or negligent crimes. Let's take a quick look at them.

3. Mens rea standard for reckless or negligent crimes

Ordinarily, the mens rea requirement for accomplices is purposeful. However, by definition, it is impossible to intend a negligent result. If the defendant intended the harm, the result would have been purposeful, not negligent. Therefore, accomplice liability for negligent crimes requires that the defendant (1) had the purpose to assist the principal; and (2) was negligent regarding the results.

Consider some examples. In *State v. McVay*, 47 R.I. 292 (1926), the defendants were the captain and engineer of a steamer. When the boilers of the steamer burst and killed passengers, the defendants were charged as accomplices to involuntary manslaughter because they fired up the boilers. Even though the defendants did not intend to kill anyone, they were guilty of the negligent homicides that resulted, because they had the purpose to assist the ship's operation and, like the principal, acted negligently in doing so.

Drag racing cases often raise the issue of what level of mens rea is required for the racer who is charged with aiding in deaths caused by his competitor. In *People v. Abbott*, 445 N.Y.S. 2d 344 (N.Y. App. Div. 1981), Abbott was drag racing when his opponent careened out of control and killed passengers in an oncoming car. The defendant was held to be guilty of criminally negligent homicide because he purposely encouraged and participated in the activity that negligently resulted in the deaths.

The Model Penal Code takes a similar approach to analyzing the culpability required to be an accomplice to a negligent crime. Pursuant to Model Penal Code §2.06(4), a defendant need only act with the kind of culpability that is sufficient for commission of the offense. Thus, if an offense only requires a negligent state of mind, proof of negligence is sufficient to convict the accomplice.

Here is a quickie question dealing with accomplice liability for negligent crimes. A similar approach is taken for offenses that require mere recklessness.

QUESTION 8. Gun shy. George is charged with aiding and abetting involuntary manslaughter. George sells guns at swap meets. He sold a handgun to a minor who accidentally shot and killed a friend while displaying the gun. Is George an accomplice to the involuntary manslaughter?

A. Yes, if he should have known that the minor might accidentally shoot someone with the gun.

B. No, because he did not have the purpose for the minor to accidentally kill his friend.

C. Yes, if it was a strict liability offense to sell the handgun to the minor.

D. No, because only the minor was responsible for the shooting.

ANALYSIS. As we have been learning criminal law, we have also been learning how to take multiple-choice exams. One technique that works quite well, especially in tricky areas, is process of elimination. Rather than looking for the right answer, look for what is wrong with the other answers. That technique should work quite well with this question. It is a question based on the case of *State v. Ayers*, 478 N.W.2d 606 (Iowa 1991).

Is there anything wrong with **A**? No. Because he is charged with being an accomplice to a negligent crime, George is guilty if he acted with the same kind of culpability required for the substantive offense, that is, negligence. The trick to answering this question is remembering that involuntary manslaughter ordinarily requires negligent conduct. If the defendant intends or knows he is going to kill someone, the crime charged would most likely be murder.

By contrast, there are problems with each of the other possible answers. **B** is wrong because it would be impossible to have the purpose to cause a negligent result. By definition, the crime of negligence means that the defendant did not realize that the victim would be hurt or die. It would be unrealistic to make purposefulness the mens rea requirement for being an accomplice to a negligence crime. It is sufficient that the defendant act with the same kind of culpability required for commission of the negligence offense.

C is wrong because it requires too little to prosecute George as an accomplice. Merely selling the weapon is not enough. It may be enough for a strict liability crime such as the unlawful sale of a weapon to a minor, but it is not enough to be an accomplice to involuntary manslaughter.

Finally, **D** is wrong because a person can be an accomplice to a negligence offense. In this situation, George's negligence facilitated the tragedy. As such, he is guilty.

Let's look now at the easier element for accomplice liability — actus reus. As you will see, if the defendant has the necessary mens rea, almost any act, even a verbal one, is sufficient to satisfy the actus reus requirement for accomplice liability.

C. Actus reus requirement for accomplice liability

The rule is easy: *To be an accomplice, the defendant must provide an act of assistance.* The actus reus for accomplice liability may be either a positive act or an omission when there is a duty to act. See Model Penal Code §2.06(3)(a)(iii). It may be any aid or encouragement provided by the accomplice.

Although there are an infinite number of ways for an accomplice to help, here are a few classic examples. In a bank robbery, the lookout, getaway driver, and master planner are all accomplices to the robber who actually asks the teller for the money. Likewise, a police officer who stands idly by and does not intervene with the robbery, even though he has a duty to do so, may be an accomplice by omission if he has the purpose of allowing the robbery to occur.

In analyzing whether there was a sufficient actus reus for accomplice liability, keep in mind the following rules.

Rule #1:   Speech alone may be a sufficient actus reus for accomplice liability if it is intended to encourage or help the principal commit the crime   Consider a situation in which the defendant sees another person beating up his enemy. The defendant yells, "Hit him harder." Those words are a sufficient actus reus for accomplice liability.

Rule #2:   Mere presence is insufficient for an actus reus unless it is offered as a form of encouragement   Consider a situation in which the defendant sees another person beating up his enemy. The defendant stands by and watches the assault. The defendant is not an accomplice unless he has arranged with the assailant to be there to give him moral support. Because the general rule is that there is no duty to rescue, merely being present is an insufficient actus reus for accomplice liability without a showing that it was a form of encouragement.

Rule #3:   The accomplice's help need not contribute to the criminal result   A person is guilty of aiding and abetting even if the criminal result would have occurred anyway and the defendant's actions had no actual impact on the outcome. Consider the situation in *State v. Tally*, 102 Ala. 25 (1894). In that case, a group of men set out to kill the victim. The defendant took steps to prevent the victim from receiving warning of the attack. Even if the victim would have been killed regardless of the defendant's actions, the defendant is still an aider and abettor to the murder.

Rule #4:   The principal need not be aware of the accomplice's acts   A person can aid and abet a crime even though the principal is unaware of the accomplice's help. Consider a situation in which a principal decides to rob a store. While the principal is taking money from the store owner, the accomplice, who dislikes the owner but does not know the principal, cuts the wires of the store's security system. Even though the principal and accomplice do not know each other and have not coordinated their efforts, the accomplice is guilty of the robbery as an aider and abettor.

Rule #5:   The accomplice's acts must be capable of assisting the principal   This is a tricky one. Consider the situation in which a defendant sees the principal about to kill the victim. The defendant yells words of encouragement to the principal, but the principal is deaf and unaware of the defendant's presence. Under the traditional common law, there is no accomplice liability. However, under the Model Penal Code, there is accomplice liability if a person aids, or attempts to aid, another's commission of a crime. Model Penal Code §2.06(3). The Model Penal Code focuses on the defendant's actual blameworthiness, not the fortuity of success.

These basic rules should help you deal with most of the accomplice liability situations you encounter. Try them with the next couple of questions.

QUESTION 9. Third wheel. By sheer accident, Shirley learns of a plot to kidnap the President and hold him for ransom. She overhears the conversation when she picks up the wrong phone line. Shirley has always hated the President so she does not report the plot to the police. At the designated time of the kidnapping, Shirley stands by as the President is abducted into a car. As the car is pulling away, the Secret Service ask her which way the abductors are headed. Shirley points in the wrong direction. The abductors get away even though some of the Secret Service agents do manage to go in the right direction to chase them. Shirley has never met the abductors.

After the ransom is paid and the President is released, the abductors are charged with kidnapping. Shirley is charged as an accomplice to the kidnapping. Does she have a sufficient actus reus for the crime?

A. Yes, because Shirley failed to report the kidnapping plot.
B. Yes, because Shirley pointed in the wrong direction.
C. No, because Shirley did not know the kidnappers.
D. No, because Shirley's wrong directions did not actually help the plot.

ANALYSIS. This question should be fairly easy for you. It tests many of the basic rules we discussed in this section on actus reus. As we go through each answer, you can see those rules at play.

First, **A** is wrong because an omission is only an actus reus when the defendant has a duty to act. There are no facts indicating that Shirley had a duty to report the kidnap plan. If she had been a law enforcement officer, perhaps she would have had such a duty, but an ordinary citizen can stand by as a crime is committed without thereby becoming an accomplice.

Before we go to **B**, take a look at **C** and **D**. **C** is wrong because an accomplice need not know the principal to be an aider and abettor to his crime. If Shirley did know the kidnappers and had agreed to assist them, she would be a co-conspirator (see Chapter 15). However, Shirley could be an accomplice if she purposely helped in the commission of a crime, regardless of whether the principals are aware of her help.

D is also wrong because it is not necessary that the accomplice's help actually make a difference. As long as it was capable of helping, as pointing the police in the wrong direction would be, it is a sufficient actus reus.

By now, it is apparent that **B** is the correct answer. The mere act of pointing, if done with the purpose of facilitating a crime, is sufficient for accomplice liability.

Let's try a slightly trickier question that is based on an actual case.

> **QUESTION 10. Don't clap.** Jed is a jazz magazine publisher. He hears that a foreign saxophonist who is illegally in the country and does not have a work permit will be performing in a one-night concert. Nonetheless, Jed buys a ticket to the concert and attends. Jed wants to see if the saxophonist is really as great as everyone says. Jed is impressed. He claps as the saxophonist takes the stage and writes a favorable review of the concert.
>
> Jed is charged with aiding and abetting the saxophonist's violation of the immigration labor laws prohibiting foreign musicians from performing without work permits. Which of the following actions would be sufficient to hold Jed guilty of the crime charged?
>
> **A.** Attending the concert.
> **B.** Writing a favorable review.
> **C.** Clapping at the concert.
> **D.** None of the above because the saxophonist would have played regardless of Jed's actions.

ANALYSIS.   If this case strikes you as implausible, take a look at *Wilcox v. Jeffrey*, 1 All E.R. 464 (1951). Believe it or not, a defendant may be an accomplice by the smallest acts of encouragement. Let's look at our possible answers.

A is a bit tricky. Although attending an event can be a form of encouragement, it generally runs afoul of the "mere presence" rule unless there is specific evidence showing that it was done to encourage the principal to engage in criminal activity. At the time Jed attends the concert, he is not there to encourage or discourage the musician. He is a mere observer. Jed could argue that he was merely present at the time of the offense and should not be considered to be an accomplice. **A** is wrong, but is a close call.

B is also tricky. Read the question carefully. The musician is only playing in one concert. By the time that Jed writes his review, the concert is completed. The review does nothing to assist in the one concert in which the musician performed. Accordingly, **B** is wrong.

Clapping isn't much, but it would be enough of an actus reus for accomplice liability if Jed has the purpose to encourage in his violation of the law. Therefore, **C** is correct and **D** is wrong.

D.   Liability for foreseeable offenses

Now that you understand what actus reus and mens rea are required for accomplice liability, let's look at some related issues that can arise. The first issue is what crimes an accomplice is responsible for once he has helped the principal. What if the accomplice thinks he is helping one crime, but the principal uses that assistance to commit a different offense? Is the accomplice still guilty for the substantive offense?

The general rule is that an accomplice is only responsible for those crimes he purposely helps to succeed. However, a majority of jurisdictions now extend accomplice liability to both intended crimes and those criminal harms that are "reasonably foreseeable" or those that are "the natural and probable consequence" of the defendant's acts.

For example, consider the case of *People v. Luparello*, 187 Cal. App. 410 (1987). Luparello asked friends to help him obtain information regarding his former lover "at any cost." Although Luparello never indicated that he wanted his friends to kill to get the information, nor even considered that they would do so, they ended up doing just that. Luparello was convicted as an accomplice to murder because the killing was reasonably foreseeable given his request.

The natural and probable consequence rule of accomplice liability is subject to criticism because it can be inconsistent with fundamental principles of criminal law. It allows a conviction even when the defendant does not have the required mens rea for that crime. For example, although it may be correct to say that Luparello was guilty of involuntary manslaughter for enlisting the help of his friends and not realizing how far they would go to fulfill his request, he would not ordinarily be guilty of murder unless the prosecution could prove that he had considered the risk that his friends would take his request as a direction to kill. However, under the natural and probable consequence rule, Luparello became an accomplice to murder, not manslaughter.

If the principal engages in a "separate frolic" during the commission of a crime, the accomplice may be able to escape liability by arguing the separate crime was not foreseeable. For example, assume that a defendant agrees to help his friends rob a store. While inside, one of the other robbers decides to rape one of the store attendants. The defendant would be an accomplice to the robbery, but not to the rape because it was the other robber's separate frolic. However, if the defendant knew that the typical modus operandi by his fellow robber was to rob and rape, prosecutors may be able to argue for accomplice liability.

It is up to the jury to decide when an offense is close enough to the one that the defendant anticipated that it should be considered "reasonably foreseeable." If the jury decides it is, the defendant is guilty as an accomplice to that offense, even though it may be slightly different than the one the defendant intended to assist.

Try this next question to test your understanding of this principle.

QUESTION 11. **Crime spree.** Billy Bob and Mary Sue are on a small crime spree. Together they have robbed three convenience stores. Mary Sue serves as the getaway driver while Billy Bob robs the convenience store owners at gunpoint. On their fourth robbery attempt, Billy Bob changes his mind when he realizes that the convenience store is conveniently located next to a bank. Much to Mary Sue's surprise, Billy Bob goes into the bank and robs the tellers. He also steals the purse of a woman standing in the bank. On his way out, Billy Bob shoots out the tires on a police car parked nearby.

When Billy Bob and Mary Sue are apprehended, they are both charged with bank robbery, destroying government property, and purse snatching. If Mary Sue claims she is not guilty, she is likely to

A. succeed because her purpose in being a getaway driver was to help Billy Bob rob convenience stores.
B. fail because all the crimes were reasonably foreseeable and the natural and probable consequences of their crime spree.
C. succeed as to the charge of bank robbery, but not to the charges of destruction of government property and purse snatching.
D. fail because Mary Sue is automatically responsible for all crimes committed by a person she agreed to aid and abet.

ANALYSIS. In truth, the issue of whether a crime was reasonably foreseeable lends itself much better to an essay question than a multiple-choice question. Nonetheless, professors find a way to include it in objective questions. Half the battle is to recognize the correct standard to apply. Once this is done, you should be able to select the correct answer, even if the concept of reasonably foreseeable is somewhat flexible.

Many of you will have selected **A** because it accurately reflects the mens rea standard for accomplice liability, but it is an incorrect answer. Mary Sue cannot claim she is not guilty simply because she thought she was only helping the robbery of convenience stores. She is also responsible for all reasonably foreseeable offenses. The robbery of another type of establishment would seem to meet that standard. Therefore, at minimum, Mary Sue would be guilty of robbing the bank.

B is a definite possibility because an argument can be made that all the crimes were reasonably foreseeable and a natural consequence of Mary Sue's decision to help Billy Bob commit robberies. Certainly, it is not that unexpected that a robber would try to avoid apprehension or steal from other easy targets at the scene. It does not matter that Mary Sue did not foresee the additional crimes. The standard is an objective one: Would the reasonable person in Mary Sue's position foresee the principal committing the charged offense(s)?

In comparison, **B** is a better choice than **C**. There is no logical reason that the court would decide that the bank robbery was not a reasonably foreseeable offense, but the destruction of property and purse snatching were.

Finally, **D** is wrong because Mary Sue is not automatically responsible for all crimes committed by the principal. The limiting principle is whether they were reasonably foreseeable. Once again, beware of the answers that are too absolute.

E.   Relationship between the parties

Although an accomplice is responsible for crimes committed by the principal, an accomplice's culpability is not dependent on whether the principal is convicted. Even if the principal is not caught or convicted, an accomplice may still be guilty of the crimes. Accomplice liability depends on proof that a crime was committed and the defendant assisted in the commission of the crime; it does not depend on the prosecution and conviction of the principal. Principals and accomplices may be excused from crimes for many reasons.

1. Public authority justification defense

Sometimes a principal cannot be prosecuted because he was working for law enforcement. For example, in *Vaden v. State*, 768 P.2d 1102 (Alaska 1989), the defendant was charged with aiding and abetting the illegal hunting of foxes. Vaden piloted a plane chartered by an undercover agent for the illegal hunt. Although the officer would not be prosecuted because he was acting in a law enforcement role, Vaden was still culpable as an accomplice. The Model Penal Code would also impose liability on an accomplice, even though he helps an innocent or irresponsible party engage in criminal conduct. Model Penal Code §2.06(2)(a).

2. Protected class of persons

Similarly, an accomplice may be immune from charges because he is within the class of persons protected by the charged statute. See Model Penal Code §2.06(6)(a) (victims cannot be liable as accomplices). For example, children who contract their services in violation of child labor laws cannot be prosecuted under those laws because the laws were designed to protect them. However, a defendant who helps to engage the services of children in violation of this law could be charged as an accomplice or even as a principal.

3. Culpable-but-unconvictable principal

An accomplice may be guilty of aiding and abetting even though the principal has a policy-based defense to the crime. For example, the principal may have diplomatic immunity, a claim of entrapment, or other types of immunity from prosecution. The principal's defenses do not automatically shield an accomplice from prosecution.

4. Acquitted principal

Even the acquittal of a principal does not shield an accomplice from prosecution. If the principal and the defendant are tried in separate proceedings, the acquittal of the principal does not preclude the conviction of the accomplice. Inconsistent verdicts are permitted. See *United States v. Standefer*, 447 U.S. 109 (1980).

5. Different degrees of culpability

Accomplice liability is usually viewed as derivative liability. The accomplice is guilty to the same degree as the principal. Some courts, however, gauge the relative culpability of the parties based on their individual mens rea. For example, imagine that a defendant is so angry at his cheating spouse that he hires a hit man to kill her. The hit man faces murder charges. However, the defendant may be able to reduce his culpability to voluntary manslaughter if he can convince the jury that he acted in the heat of passion.

6. Feigned accomplice

Finally, a person who acts as an accomplice in an effort to apprehend the principal during the commission of a crime is not guilty of aiding and abetting the offense. The person does not act with the purpose of having the crime succeed, but with the purpose of stopping the criminal activity.

QUESTION 12. Visiting dignitary. Barclay works in a foreign consulate in Washington, D.C. Barclay teams up with two other consulate workers, Saji and Hanif, to smuggle narcotics in diplomatic pouches. Barclay's role is to hide the small narcotics bags inside the diplomatic pouches that are carried in and out of the country. Eventually, they are caught. Saji is a foreign diplomat so he is not prosecuted. Hanif is prosecuted first and acquitted. If Barclay is then prosecuted for being aiding and abetting narcotics smuggling, he should be

A. acquitted because neither principal was convicted.
B. acquitted because diplomats are protected classes of persons under the narcotics laws.

C. acquitted because he should be no more responsible than the principals.
D. convicted if he had the purpose to smuggle drugs.

ANALYSIS. This question should have been fairly easy for you. You just have to remember that an accomplice can be guilty regardless of whether the principal is convicted. The issue is whether a crime occurred and the defendant had the necessary mens rea and actus reus for accomplice liability. In this question you are told that Barclay helps by secreting the narcotics in the pouches. You just need to be sure to pick an answer that accurately reflects whether he has the necessary mens rea to be an accomplice.

A is the wrong answer because it incorrectly states that the principal needs to be convicted for Barclay to be guilty. In fact, the opposite is true. So long as a crime was committed, and Barclay purposely assisted with that crime, he is guilty.

B is also wrong, but for a slightly different reason. Diplomats may be protected from prosecution, but not because the narcotics laws make them a protected class. Narcotics laws are not like child labor laws that are designed to protect children. Rather, diplomatic immunity stems from policy reasons for not prosecuting foreign officials. If you are looking for other examples of protected class statutes, think about the Mann Act (which protects women from being transported across state lines for immoral purposes) or statutory rape laws (where the girl would not be an accomplice because the laws are designed to protect her from harm).

C is wrong because it misstates the basic law regarding accomplice liability. Accomplices can be liable, even when principals are not convicted. Accomplices can also be liable to a different degree than they might ordinarily be if they were not judged by derivative liability.

The correct answer is **D**. If Barclay had the necessary mens rea for accomplice liability (i.e., purpose), he is guilty regardless of whether the people who actually smuggled the drugs are convicted.

F.   Abandonment and withdrawal defense

As we learned in Chapters 12 and 13, there is an abandonment defense that can be applied to some crimes. Under rare circumstances, and in some jurisdictions, a defendant can claim an abandonment defense to accomplice liability if the defendant withdraws from involvement before the principal completes the crime. In some jurisdictions, this is known as a "withdrawal" defense.

At common law, a majority of jurisdictions did not recognize an abandonment defense to accomplice liability. Some jurisdictions, however, have added a statutory defense when a defendant voluntarily and completely renounces involvement in a crime and makes substantial efforts to prevent it. See, e.g., N.Y. Penal Code §40.10(1).

The Model Penal Code recognizes an abandonment defense if the defendant terminates his complicity prior to the commission of the offense and either (1) wholly deprives it of effectiveness; or (2) gives timely warning to law enforcement authorities or otherwise makes proper efforts to prevent the crime. See Model Penal Code §2.06.

Since you have dealt with abandonment before, let's try a question regarding the defense as it relates to accomplice liability.

QUESTION 13. Bound and gagged. Marnin breaks into Sylvia's home with his two friends, Brad and Jonathan. Marnin gags Sylvia, but decides to leave without taking anything. He tells Brad and Jonathan that he doesn't want anything more to do with the robbery. After he leaves, Brad and Jonathan take Sylvia's belongings. At trial, Marnin claims an abandonment defense. If Marnin is charged with being an accomplice to the robbery in a Model Penal Code jurisdiction, he should

A. be acquitted because he has an abandonment defense.

B. be acquitted because he left without taking anything and told Brad and Jonathan that he did not want to continue his involvement in the robbery.

C. be convicted because he did not voluntarily withdraw from his criminal activities.

D. be convicted because he did not meet the requirements of an abandonment defense.

ANALYSIS. You may instinctively want to give Marnin a break because he didn't take anything during the robbery, but he is only entitled to an abandonment defense if he meets the requirements for that defense. In this case, the Model Penal Code requirements apply. While it appears that Marnin voluntarily withdrew from the robbery, he did not wholly deprive it of its effectiveness, give timely warning to law enforcement, or otherwise prevent the crime. Accordingly, he still is going to be on the hook as an accomplice to the robbery by Brad and Jonathan.

Given this analysis, **A** is wrong because Marnin does not have an abandonment defense under the Model Penal Code. He has not met all of its requirements. Likewise, **B** is the wrong answer because it was not enough that Marnin did not take anything during the robbery. Once he helped as an accomplice by binding and gagging Sylvia, he became responsible for the criminal acts of the principals, Brad and Jonathan.

C is incorrect because it is factually wrong. It appears that Marnin did voluntarily withdraw from the robbery. That was not the problem with his abandonment defense. The problem was that he did not make enough effort to stop the principals from completing the offense.

Therefore, **D** is the correct answer. Marnin did not meet the requirements of an abandonment defense under Model Penal Code standards. If the question had asked whether he met the requirements under common law standards, the answer may have been very much the same. First, there was ordinarily no abandonment defense under the common law. Second, when there is one, there is usually a requirement that the defendant make a substantial effort to prevent the crime he has assisted.

G.   The Closer: Finding the purpose

Of all the issues that arise regarding accomplice liability, the one that your professor is most likely to concentrate on is whether the defendant had the necessary mens rea to be an accomplice. Let's go back to the *Hicks* case and test your understanding of this principle in a slightly more difficult fact pattern.

QUESTION 14. "Die like a man." Hicks has heard that Rowe has set out to kill his old enemy, Colvard. When Hicks sees Rowe approach Colvard, Hicks yells to Colvard, "Take off your hat and die like a man." As Colvard starts to take off his hat, Rowe shoots him dead. Rowe is then shot by the police and Hicks is prosecuted for Colvard's murder as an accomplice.

Hicks is most likely

A. guilty because his words may have had the effect of encouraging Rowe to shoot Colvard.
B. guilty if he intended his words to encourage Rowe to shoot Colvard.
C. guilty if Rowe would not have shot Colvard unless Hicks had yelled his words.
D. not guilty because mere words are not enough to aid and abet a murder.

ANALYSIS.   This last question raises the interesting issue of whether words spoken to the victim can be enough to establish accomplice liability. As we learned, words alone may be enough but they must (1) be intended as encouragement; and (2) be capable of providing assistance. Thus, it is hypothetically possible that Hicks's comments could be enough to aid and abet the murder. Examine the answers to see if any of them meet the requirements for words to trigger accomplice liability.

A is wrong because the focus should be on what Hicks intended, not the effect of his words. The effect of words may be one clue as to what the defendant intended, but there must be proof of the defendant's purpose. Therefore, **B** appears to be the better answer.

Before settling on **B**, examine **C** and **D**. **C** is wrong because it is not necessary that the accomplice's actions or words be the sole or primary cause of the accomplice's actions. Any efforts that are capable of helping are sufficient. Therefore, **D** is also wrong. Mere words are enough to aid. Do not confuse "mere words" with "mere presence."

B turns out to be the correct answer. Focus on the defendant's intent. Did he have the purpose to help? If so, odds are that you'll find a sufficient actus reus, even if it is just words.

Levenson's Picks

1.	Firebug	C
2.	Who's in charge?	D
3.	Betsy and Ross	C
4.	You did what?!	B
5.	Lend a hand	D
6.	Fill'er up	C
7.	Dirty dumping	B
8.	Gun shy	A
9.	Third wheel	B
10.	Don't clap	C
11.	Crime spree	B
12.	Visiting dignitary	D
13.	Bound and gagged	D
14.	"Die like a man"	B

Conspiracy

Conspiracy is stronger than witchcraft.
— Haitian proverb

Conspiracy is a unique and controversial crime. Like attempt, it is an inchoate crime. It punishes behavior before it has harmful effects. However, unlike attempt, it does not require a substantial step toward completing the crime. The gist of the offense of conspiracy lies in the unlawful agreement. A mere agreement to commit a crime is conspiracy. Conspiracy laws allow prosecutors to strike at the special danger posed when groups of people come together to commit crimes.

This chapter examines the crime of conspiracy. In addition to reviewing the elements of the crime, we also examine the scope of conspiracy, how it imposes vicarious liability, limits on how it can be charged, and possible defenses. Finally, the chapter ends with a discussion of "super-conspiracies," also known as RICO charges.

Whenever there are more than two defendants in a scenario, you should automatically examine the problem for a possible conspiracy or accomplice liability, or both. Conspiracy is a favorite of prosecutors and therefore an important crime to master in criminal law.

A.   General overview of conspiracy law

Conspiracy is a crime separate from the underlying offense. For example, a defendant who conspires to rob a bank and then actually robs it, is guilty of both conspiracy and bank robbery. Unlike attempt and solicitation, the conspiracy charge does not merge into the completed offense.

Conspiracy law is premised on the assumption that group crime poses an extra risk to safety and compliance with the laws. The more people involved in the planning and execution of a crime, the more likely the crime will succeed. Conspiracy allows more complex crimes, and the group's moral support and peer pressure add to each member's perseverance in the assigned task. Because of these added dangers, conspiracy is treated as a separate crime with serious consequences.

Prosecutors favor the conspiracy charge for several reasons:

1. it is a separate crime carrying its own penalties;
2. it allows the apprehension of potential criminal conduct at an earlier stage than attempt;
3. members of a conspiracy are vicariously responsible for the criminal acts of their co-conspirators, even without proof of accomplice liability;
4. conspiracy allows the apprehension and prosecution of large groups of individuals;
5. conspiracy is a continuing offense that gives prosecutors a longer time to file charges;

6. venue for conspiracy charges exists anywhere in which an act of the conspiracy occurred; and

7. a hearsay exception allows the admission of co-conspirators' statements.

A conspiracy is defined as "an agreement by two or more persons to commit a crime." To be guilty of conspiracy, a defendant must (1) agree to commit a crime; (2) with the intent to have the crime succeed. In some jurisdictions, there is a third requirement: (3) one of the conspirators must have committed an "overt act" toward the commission of the crime.

The punishment for conspiracy depends on the jurisdiction. In federal court, most conspiracies are punishable by five years' imprisonment. 18 U.S.C. §371. Under the Model Penal Code, the punishment for conspiracy is the same as provided for the most serious offense that the parties conspired to commit. Model Penal Code §5.05(1).

Each conspiracy must have a goal to commit a crime. This goal is referred to as the "object" of the conspiracy. The law no longer recognizes conspiracies "to offend public morals." Compare *Shaw v. Director of Public Prosecutions*, [1962] A.C. 220 (House of Lords). However, some jurisdictions still recognize a conspiracy to pursue some noncriminal but harmful objective, such as a conspiracy "to cheat or defraud another person." See 18 U.S.C. §371 (recognizing conspiracy to defraud the United States). A conspiracy may have more than one objective.

One of the most important consequences of being a member of a conspiracy is that each conspirator is responsible for the criminal acts of fellow co-conspirators in furtherance of the conspiracy. This is referred to as "co-conspirator liability" and is discussed in more detail in the next section.

These are the basics of conspiracy law. Here is your first basic question.

QUESTION 1. Manny, Moe, and Jack. Manny, Moe, and Jack decide that they need some additional cash so they agree to rob a liquor store. Manny gives Jack a gun to use in the robbery, Moe steals the getaway car, and Jack actually robs the bank. All three are apprehended. What crimes can Manny be charged with?

A. Conspiracy to rob a bank.
B. Conspiracy to rob a bank and bank robbery.
C. Conspiracy to rob a bank, car theft, and bank robbery.
D. None of the above.

ANALYSIS. Even with the very brief introduction of this section, you should be able to select the correct response to this question. Manny has purposely agreed with at least one other person to commit a crime. Therefore, he has met the requirements for conspiracy. Moreover, the bank robbery actually occurs. As a co-conspirator, Manny is vicariously responsible for the crimes of his co-conspirators. Accordingly, Manny is guilty not only of the completed bank robbery crime, but also of the car theft that was in furtherance of the conspiracy.

A is wrong because it is only partially correct. Yes, Manny is guilty of conspiracy to rob a bank, but he is responsible for more. He is also guilty of the actual bank robbery and the car theft. Therefore, **B** and **D** are incorrect as well. The correct response is **C**. Because he joined the conspiracy, Manny will get the book thrown at him, even though he was never present for the actual bank robbery and he didn't personally steal the car. Now you can see the power of a conspiracy charge.

Let's look in detail at the consequences of being a member of a conspiracy before we analyze the intricacies of each element of the crime.

B. Consequences of a conspiracy charge

"A conspiracy is a partnership in crime." *Pinkerton v. United States*, 328 U.S. 640, 644 (1946). As such, it has some unique substantive and procedural consequences.

1. Substantive consequences

There are four major substantive consequences of being charged with conspiracy: (1) conspiracy is a separate crime; (2) conspiracy punishes preparatory conduct; (3) conspirators have co-conspirator liability; and (4) under federal law, conspiracy aggravates the degree of the crime.

First, as we discussed in the first section, *conspiracy is a separate crime.* Thus, if two or more persons agree to commit a crime and commit it, each person is guilty of at least two crimes: conspiracy and the completed substantive offense. In this regard, the Model Penal Code diverges from common law. Under the Model Penal Code, the crime of conspiracy merges with the completed target offense unless the prosecution proves the conspiracy involved the commission of additional offenses not yet committed or attempted. Model Penal Code §1.07(1)(b); ALI Comment to §1.07, at 109.

Second, *conspiracy punishes preparatory conduct.* The mere act of agreeing to commit a crime is sufficient for the conspiracy even if there is no substantial step toward completing that crime. Conspiracy is an inchoate crime that punishes behavior at the earliest stage of planning.

Third, *conspirators have co-conspirator liability.* Once a defendant joins a conspiracy, she is responsible for all acts of the co-conspirators done within the scope of the conspiracy, even if there is no evidence of accomplice liability. Co-conspirator liability is discussed in more detail in Section F.

Fourth, *under federal law, conspiracy aggravates the degree of the crime.* Conspiring to commit a misdemeanor is a felony even though the target offense, when accomplished, would only be a misdemeanor. Conspiracy aggravates the degree of the crime because of the risks accompanying group criminality. Many states reject this approach and a conspiracy to commit a misdemeanor is only a misdemeanor in itself.

2. Procedural consequences

A conspiracy charge also gives prosecutors many procedural advantages: (1) a conspiracy charge joins multiple defendants for trial; (2) a conspiracy charge can extend the statute of limitations; (3) venue for a conspiracy charge is proper anywhere acts of the conspiracy occurred; and (4) there is a hearsay exception that allows the introduction of co-conspirators' statements. Let's examine each of these advantages in more detail.

First, a *conspiracy charge joins multiple defendants for trial.* By doing so, prosecutors can present a broad view of the defendants' criminal activities for the jurors. Seeing a group of defendants sitting together for trial, jurors are more likely to believe that "birds of a feather flock together," that is, all that the defendants who are charged in the conspiracy were jointly involved in criminal activity.

Second, *a conspiracy charge can extend the statute of limitations.* Conspiracy is a continuing offense that does not end until the objectives of the conspiracy have succeeded or failed. Accordingly, the statute of limitations for conspiracy does not begin to run until the last act of the conspiracy. By charging conspiracy, prosecutors can extend the statute of limitations beyond that which would apply if the focus was on a specific act by a specific defendant. For example, defendants *A* and *B* agree to rob a series of banks. The statute of limitations for the first bank they rob has run out, but because their conspiracy has continued, the first robbery can be charged as part of the conspiracy.

Third, *a conspiracy charge allows prosecutors greater latitude in selecting venue.* Venue is proper anywhere a conspiratorial act occurred. For example, defendants *A* and *B* agree to bribe a popular local politician. Defendant *A*, who lives in a different state, arranges for the bribe money. Prosecutors may charge the conspiracy in *A*'s jurisdiction where there will be less popular support for the politician and the defendants.

Finally, *a conspiracy charge offers a major evidentiary advantage.* An established exception to the hearsay rules is the admissibility of co-conspirator statements. See Fed. R. Evid. §801(d)(2)(E). The statement of one conspirator is deemed to be a vicarious admission by an agent of the other partners to the conspiracy. To introduce a co-conspirator's statement, there must be independent proof that a conspiracy existed, the defendant was connected with it, and that the statement was made in furtherance of the conspiracy. If there is, a defendant may be convicted on the words of a fellow co-conspirator. For example, defendants *A* and *B* are charged with conspiring to rob a bank. As part of their case against *B*, prosecutors are allowed to introduce a hearsay statement by *A* to friend *C* that *A* and *B* are planning to rob a bank and they want *C* to join them in their criminal venture.

The following question is one way that your professor may examine your understanding of the substantive and procedural advantages of bringing a conspiracy charge.

QUESTION 2. Time to decide.   Polly Prosecutor is trying to decide whether to file conspiracy charges against Darlene Defendant. Darlene was only a peripheral player in the alleged narcotics conspiracy. While her co-conspirators would deliver drugs in 20 states, Darlene merely sat in California as a contact person in case any of the conspirators needed help. The police learned about Darlene when one of her fellow co-conspirators told an undercover officer posing as a buyer that "Big D could handle anything if there were problems with the delivery."

Darlene has been charged with conspiracy and the distribution of narcotics in 20 states. Which of the following arguments would be a defense to the charges against her?

A. Darlene never even went to the 20 states where delivery occurred.
B. The statements by her fellow co-conspirators were inadmissible hearsay.
C. Darlene never attempted herself to deliver narcotics.
D. None of the above.

ANALYSIS.   Darlene is in trouble. Even though she was just a bit player in a large narcotics conspiracy, she is now saddled with the acts and statements of her co-conspirators.

A is wrong because each conspirator is responsible for the acts of the other co-conspirators in other venues. Conspiracy is a form of partnership that ties each co-conspirator to the acts of fellow conspirators, wherever they may occur.

B is wrong because co-conspirator statements may be used to incriminate Darlene. You will learn more about this exception in your evidence course, but suffice it to say that statements by fellow conspirators during the course of and in furtherance of a conspiracy may be used to convict all members of a conspiracy.

C is wrong because conspiracy is an inchoate crime that does not require that the defendants actually take a substantial step toward completing the crime. The mere agreement is illegal. Then, if the crime is actually committed, each defendant is responsible for both conspiracy and the completed substantive crime.

    D is the correct answer. This question should give you a pretty good idea of why the conspiracy crime is referred to as the "darling" of the prosecution.

C.   Actus reus requirement of conspiracy

Now that you have a sense of the consequences of a conspiracy charge, let's examine in more detail the elements of a crime of conspiracy. Recall that conspiracy requires "an agreement by two or more persons to commit a crime." *The actus reus of conspiring is "to agree" to commit a crime.*

    An agreement to commit a crime may be expressed or implied. It is relatively rare for conspirators to openly agree to commit a crime. Accordingly, one must look to circumstantial evidence to determine whether there has been such an agreement. Words, actions, similar motives, and even gestures like a nod, wink, or handshake are enough to demonstrate an agreement.

    One of the most frequently used arguments is that the conspirators demonstrated their agreement through *concerted action.* For example, assume that the defendant is present at a drop site where a large quantity of cocaine is being unloaded from an airplane. The cocaine is hidden in refrigerator boxes. Prosecutors may argue that the defendant's presence at the illegal activity is a strong indication that the defendant agreed to participate in the narcotics conspiracy. See, e.g., *United States v. Alvarez,* 625 F.2d 1196 (5th Cir. 1981).

    Mere presence at a crime scene is not necessarily enough to prove that the defendant agreed to commit a crime, but it can be an indication. For example, assume that *A* and *B* independently decide to rob the same store. *A* and *B* have no contact with each other before they try to rob the store. As *A* enters through the front door, *B* enters through the back door. They rob the store at the same time. In this situation, the defendants' parallel actions do not necessarily prove that they had an agreement. See, e.g., *People v. McChristian,* 18 Ill. App. 3d 87 (1974) (members of a gang began shooting simultaneously at a rival gang member; because there was no evidence the participants planned the meeting or shooting, the court reversed the conspiracy conviction).

    A defendant need not know all the members of the conspiracy or have contact with them. It is sufficient if a defendant knows he is agreeing with others to commit a crime. Accordingly, there are many conspiracies that charge a defendant with conspiring with "persons known and unknown" to commit a crime. For example, a defendant agrees to help in a narcotics conspiracy. The defendant need not know the identity of the supplier or distributors, yet the defendant is still a co-conspirator with those individuals.

Finally, not all conspirators must join the conspiracy at the same time. When a defendant joins an ongoing conspiracy, prosecutors may use actions by co-conspirators prior to when the defendant joined the conspiracy as evidence in the conspiracy charge against him.

QUESTION 3. Come join the band. Leland and Jane have a casual conversation about how great it would be if they had as much money as their boss. Leland tells Jane, "It wouldn't be that hard to share his money. All we would need to do is to take it out of the safe when he goes home for the day." Jane, just nods her head in response. At the end of the work day, Jane sneaks into her boss's office. Inside, she sees Leland emptying the safe. Jane helps him by stuffing some of the money into her clothes and carrying it out of the business. Leland has arranged for Myron to act as a lookout for the theft.

When their boss discovers the loss, he checks the film from a video camera hidden above the safe. It shows Leland, Jane, and Myron in his office. They are all charged with conspiring to steal from the boss. Jane claims that she never agreed to participate in a conspiracy. Jane's argument is likely to

A. succeed because she never said she would help Leland steal from her boss.
B. succeed because she never knew that Myron was in the conspiracy.
C. fail because the three of them engaged in concerted action.
D. succeed, because a nod of the head is insufficient to show membership in a conspiracy.

ANALYSIS. Whether or not she ever said, "Yes, I'd love to join your conspiracy," Jane is probably on the hook because she showed in every other way that she was part of the criminal partnership. A nod of the head may be enough to show agreement. However, if there was any doubt, Jane's actions when she goes into her boss's office shows that she is aligned with Leland's plan.

Accordingly, **A** is the wrong answer because it is not required that a conspirator expressly agree orally or in writing to be a member of a conspiracy. A co-conspirator can show in many different ways, including concerted action, that she has joined a conspiracy.

B is also wrong because it is not required that the defendant know all of the members of the conspiracy. Not all conspirators must join at the same time. A defendant who joins an ongoing criminal conspiracy is automatically responsible for the actions of everyone in the conspiracy who acts in furtherance of that conspiracy.

That leaves **C** or **D**. You can get this right either by "picking" the correct answer or eliminating the wrong answer. Let's eliminate the wrong answer. **D** is wrong because the nod of a head can be enough of an actus reus for conspiracy. Therefore, **C** is correct. By engaging in concerted action, Jane demonstrated that she was joining the conspiracy.

Yet, as you can surmise, it is not enough for a defendant to do something that might help other conspirators. As with other crimes, the key element for conspiracy is the mens rea requirement. Because conspiracy law can punish someone before she ever causes any harm, it is important to be sure that the defendant has a culpable mental state.

D.   Mens rea requirement of conspiracy

Conspiracy actually requires two mens rea: (1) an intent to agree (i.e., join the conspiracy); (2) with the purpose to commit a crime.

The first mens rea requirement is simple. It simply means that the defendant intended her actions to signal her decision to join the conspiracy. For example, if a defendant nods to another person, it can sometimes be a mere greeting and other times serve as an indication that the defendant agrees. To be guilty of conspiracy, the jury must find that the defendant's words or actions indicated that the defendant intended to join the conspiracy.

Second, the defendant must have another level of mens rea. In addition to intending to join a group, the defendant must be doing so with the purpose of having a crime succeed. Thus, as with accomplice liability, conspiracy requires that the defendant have the purpose to commit a crime. For example, assume *A* asks *B* and *C* to help her package white powder that *A* knows to be cocaine and plans to sell on the streets. *B* and *C* are only guilty of conspiracy to distribute cocaine if their purpose is to assist in the distribution of drugs. They are not guilty if they believe that they are helping *A* store baby powder for his own use. If this were the case, they would not have the purpose for a crime to succeed.

When purpose is the required mens rea, knowledge alone is insufficient to convict a defendant of conspiracy. The reason for this rule is illustrated by the famous case of *People v. Lauria,* 251 Cal. App. 2d 471 (1967). In *Lauria,* the defendant ran a telephone answering service used by prostitutes. The defendant knew that prostitutes used the service because he engaged them himself. The court held that knowledge alone was insufficient to establish the mens rea for conspiracy. Rather, prosecutors needed to prove the defendant had a stake in the venture or otherwise had the purpose to facilitate prostitution.

The rationale for the high mens rea standard for conspiracy is the same as that for accomplice liability. Judges are worried that conspiracy charges can be used as a dragnet to charge all those who have been associated with illegal activities to the slightest degree. For example, condom manufacturers, mattress salesmen, and negligee outlets know that some of their customers are prostitutes, but society does not want to charge these otherwise legitimate businesses with conspiracy to commit prostitution.

Although the mens rea standard for conspiracy is high, there are many ways a jury may infer a defendant's purpose to have a crime succeed. In *Lauria,* the court held that a manufacturer or service provider's purpose may be inferred when

- a defendant has a stake in the illegal venture, as demonstrated by her inflation of rates charge for the illegal use of her business;
- a defendant provides goods or services that serve no legitimate use; and
- the volume of business the defendant conducts with those buyers who engage in illegitimate activities is grossly disproportionate to any legitimate demand and use of the defendant's services or products.

Moreover, there are some crimes where knowledge is sufficient. Overall, the more serious the crime, the more likely the courts will recognize that a defendant who knowingly participates with those who commit such a crime had the necessary mens rea for conspiracy.

Finally, conspiracy law generally requires that the defendant need only know of those attendant circumstances the defendant would need to know for the substantive crime. Thus, if the defendant agreed with others to attack a person, but did not know that person was a federal officer, the defendant would still satisfy the mens rea requirement because the status of the victim was not a material element for the assault or conspiracy charge. The exception to this is when the defendant agrees to do an act that is otherwise "innocent in itself." In that situation, the court may require proof that the conspirators acted with the purpose to commit an illegal act. For example, if *A* and *B* decide to have consensual sex and *C* drives them to a motel, *C* is not guilty of conspiracy to commit statutory rape unless *C* knows *B* is a minor. There must be an agreement to engage in prohibited conduct.

Time to try a couple of mens rea questions. Keep in mind the two requirements of mens rea for the special crime of conspiracy.

QUESTION 4. Just kidding.   Manuel asks Franco to help him burn down city hall. Franco thinks Manuel is kidding and answers flippantly, "sure." A police officer, who overhears the conversation, immediately arrests both of them and charges them with conspiracy to commit arson. Is Franco guilty of conspiracy?

A. Yes, because he agreed to burn down city hall.
B. Yes, because he was on notice that Manuel wanted to burn down city hall.
C. No, because it only takes one person to burn down city hall.
D. No, because Franco was just kidding when he answered, "sure."

ANALYSIS. In this question, you are told that Franco was just kidding when he responded to Manuel. Because he was just kidding, even if he said "sure," he didn't have the purpose to join a conspiracy to burn down city hall. In finding the correct answer, don't just focus on Franco's words. Focus on his intent.

A is wrong because even if Franco said "sure," and Manuel understood that to be an agreement, if Franco did not have the intent to join the conspiracy or have Manuel burn down city hall, he is not guilty of conspiracy.

B is also wrong because the standard for conspiracy is not negligence or recklessness or even knowing conduct. In most jurisdictions, the defendant must act purposely.

C is wrong because it doesn't really matter if the co-conspirator is needed or does anything to help the conspiracy. Conspiracy criminalizes the unlawful agreement itself.

Therefore, **D** is the correct answer. If Franco was just kidding when he responded to Manuel, he did not intend to join the conspiracy and burn down city hall.

Try the next question that raises a slightly different issue regarding the necessary mens rea for conspiracy.

QUESTION 5. Pass the sugar. Falcone sells a sugary substance called lactose. Lactose can be used to supplement baby formula or as a cutting agent to dilute drugs. Approximately 75 percent of Falcone's sales are to Gordy who, as Falcone knows, uses the lactose to dilute and package illegal drugs. Falcone knows he can charge Gordy a little more than other customers because he isn't likely to complain to the authorities. Thus, over the course of a year, Falcone makes numerous sales of large quantities of lactose to Gordy.

Gordy and Falcone are charged with conspiracy to distribute drugs and distribution of drugs. Is Falcone guilty of the conspiracy?

A. Yes, because he had the necessary mens rea for conspiracy.
B. No, because it is not per se illegal to possess or sell lactose.
C. Yes, because he was reckless in selling lactose to a drug dealer.
D. No, because he was in an official partnership with Gordy.

ANALYSIS. This question raises the *Lauria* issue of when a defendant's knowing participation with someone involved in illegal activity establishes that the defendant acted purposely with regard to joining a conspiracy.

Remember the three indicators from *Lauria* that a defendant may be purposely involved in a conspiracy as shown by his stake in the venture: (1) inflation of rates for illegal activities; (2) services that don't have much legitimate use; and (3) disproportionate number of sales for illegal use. These indicators are not the only ones that can be used to prove purpose, nor is it required that all three be present. Rather, they are a guide toward establishing whether the defendant had the necessary purposeful intent when he joined the conspiracy.

For this question, there is certainly reason to believe that Falcone has crossed the line into having a stake in Gordy's venture, enabling prosecutors to argue that he has the purpose for his lactose to be used for illegal purposes. Before we select **A** as an answer, let's see what the other choices offer.

B is wrong because even the sale of a lawful product can create a stake in an illegal venture, although it requires more of a showing of purposefulness. However, there is no requirement that a co-conspirator provide something that is illegal in all settings.

C is also wrong because the standard, even in these circumstances, is not mere recklessness. As we discussed, the ordinary standard is purposefulness. Even when it dips down, it does not fall lower than knowingly.

Finally, **D** is a red herring. There is no requirement that co-conspirators be in a formal partnership. By its nature, criminal activity involves clandestine activities. The legal status of the partnership is not important; the defendant's intent is!

———————————

For all the other crimes we have studied so far, we would be done with the elements of the crime after discussing actus reus, mens rea, and, perhaps, causation. For conspiracy, there is no causation requirement because a conspiracy need not lead to a harmful result. However, there is one more requirement to discuss — an overt act.

E.   Overt act requirement

At common law, the only elements required for conspiracy were the actus reus (agreeing) and mens rea (intentionally joining with the purpose of having the crime succeed). Most modern conspiracy statutes now have added an overt act requirement, but they generally do not require it for conspiracies to commit the most serious offenses. For example, the general federal conspiracy statute (18 U.S.C. §371) requires an overt act, but the federal crimes of conspiring to distribute illegal drugs (21 U.S.C. §846) and conspiring to launder money (18 U.S.C. §1956(h)) do not require an overt act. See also Model Penal Code §5.03(5) (general requirement of an overt act for conspiracies, but no overt act requirement for most serious crimes).

What is an overt act? An overt act is any legal or illegal act done by any of the conspirators to set the conspiracy into motion. For example, *A* and *B* decide to rob a bank. *A* calls the bank to see what time it opens. *A*'s act is sufficient to be an overt act for both *A* and *B*.

As you can see, it doesn't take much to satisfy the overt act requirement for conspiracy if there is one. Its only point is to show that the conspiracy has gotten off the ground and proceeded beyond the mere idea stage into action. Accordingly, it may include otherwise innocuous acts and only one conspirator need commit one overt act.

Oftentimes, indictments provide a lengthy list of overt acts. The prosecutor does *not* need to prove all those overt acts for the jury. It is sufficient if he proves one. The purpose of laying out so many overt acts is to give jurors a step-by-step guide of what the conspiracy did and the conduct of each conspirator. However, at the time of deliberations, the jurors are instructed that they only need to find that one conspirator committed one overt act.

Let's see if you can spot all the elements of conspiracy, including an overt act.

QUESTION 6. Weather report. Joshua illegally smuggles aliens across the border. His partner, Maria, gives Joshua the names of aliens who are willing to pay to be brought across the border. They share the fee paid by the aliens. Maria has recently come to Joshua with the names of more potential customers. Joshua checks the weather report to see when the moon will be new because it is easier to smuggle people without any moonlight. Maria and Joshua are arrested before either one of them can do anything else.

Are Maria and Joshua guilty of conspiracy?

A. No, because they have not actually started to transport the aliens.
B. No, because they have not taken a substantial step toward transporting the aliens.
C. No, because it was not illegal for Joshua to check the weather reports.
D. Yes, because they both agreed to smuggle the aliens and there was at least one overt act in furtherance of that conspiracy.

ANALYSIS. This should have been an easy question. Not much is needed for an overt act and only one conspirator need commit it. Joshua checking the weather report would be more than enough.

Accordingly, **A** is wrong because it is not required that the conspiracy progress to the point where the conspirators are actually transporting the aliens. An overt act can be any step after there has been an agreement to commit a crime. Likewise, **B** is incorrect. "Substantial step" is the standard for attempt. For an overt act, "any act" to further the conspiracy would qualify.

C is wrong because it is not required that the overt act be illegal in itself. It can be a totally lawful act and still qualify as an overt act. **D** is correct. Both defendants had all the necessary elements for the crime of conspiracy, including the simple overt act of checking the weather report.

F. Co-conspirator liability (The Pinkerton rule)

One of the most important consequences of belonging to a conspiracy is that a conspirator is responsible for all acts of her co-conspirators during the course of and in furtherance of the conspiracy, even if the conspirator is unaware these acts are being committed. As discussed below, this is referred to as the "Pinkerton rule." The rationale for the Pinkerton rule is that co-conspirators are considered each other's agents. Moreover, without such a rule, a conspirator behind the scenes could insulate herself from liability for those acts that help the conspiracy succeed.

In 1946, the United States Supreme Court decided a pair of cases establishing the rule of co-conspirator liability. In the first of these cases, *Pinkerton v. United States,* 328 U.S. 640 (1946), the Court recognized that conspirators are responsible for each other's criminal acts even if they don't directly participate in them. This case established the basic Pinkerton rule. In the second case, *Kotteakos v. United States,* 328 U.S. 750 (1946), the Court narrowly defined what constitutes one conspiracy and thereby limited the impact of the Pinkerton co-conspirator liability rule. The limitations on the size and configuration of conspiracies, and thus the impact of the Pinkerton rule, are discussed in the next section.

The *Pinkerton* case itself gives you a good idea of how co-conspirator liability works. Daniel Pinkerton was charged with conspiring with his brother, Walter, to commit violations of the Internal Revenue Service code relating to their manufacture and sale of whiskey. Daniel was also charged with the substantive tax fraud counts relating to the conspiracy, even though he was in prison when his brother committed these offenses. Because the tax offenses were during the course of and in furtherance of their conspiracy, Daniel was liable for the substantive criminal acts of his brother, even though he could not be charged as an aider and abettor.

Co-conspirator liability is broader than accomplice liability because it applies even if the co-conspirator is unaware that the crime is being committed and has done nothing to help the commission of the crime. Instead, co-conspirator liability occurs when a co-conspirator commits a crime during the course of the conspiracy that somehow furthers the conspiracy. The defendant need not anticipate that a co-conspirator would commit that crime. It is sufficient if the crime committed was reasonably foreseeable and was a natural consequence of the conspiracy. For example, assume that *A*, *B*, and *C* decide to rob a bank. Without telling his co-conspirators, *B* steals a car to use in the robbery. *A* and *C* are responsible for that theft even though it was not the object of their conspiracy. See also *State v. Bridges*, 133 N.J. 447 (1993) (defendant was responsible for shooting when a person he had asked to accompany him to a fight shot an onlooker; shooting was a reasonably foreseeable and a natural consequence of their conspiracy).

The Pinkerton rule has been the subject of a great deal of criticism because it imposes punishment even when a defendant is not personally culpable for a crime. *The Model Penal Code has rejected the Pinkerton rule.* A conspirator is only guilty of the substantive crime of a co-conspirator if there is evidence of accomplice liability.

Even when the Pinkerton rule applies, it is not applied retroactively. In other words, a conspirator is not guilty of substantive offenses committed by co-conspirators prior to his joining the conspiracy, although those acts by the co-conspirators may be used as evidence to prove the general conspiracy charge. See *Levine v. United States*, 383 U.S. 265, 266 (1965); *United States v. Blackmon*, 839 F.2d 900, 908-909 (2d Cir. 1988).

Let's try a problem involving the Pinkerton rule. Assume you are not in a Model Penal Code jurisdiction when you answer the next question.

QUESTION 7. High as a kite. Sonny and his girlfriend, Cher, illegally sell prescription painkillers. Unbeknownst to Sonny, Cher gets the painkillers by forging a physician's signature on prescription pads and filling the different prescriptions at different pharmacies. When Sonny and Cher are apprehended, Sonny is charged with conspiracy to sell drugs, forgery, and the illegal purchase of prescription drugs. Sonny contests the charges. Sonny is

A. guilty of conspiracy and the unlawful purchase of prescription drugs.
B. guilty of conspiracy, the unlawful purchase of prescription drugs, and forgery.
C. guilty as an accomplice to all of Cher's crimes.
D. not guilty of any of the crimes because Cher did not tell him about the forgeries.

ANALYSIS. You can see from this question that co-conspirator liability works quite differently from accomplice liability. Not only did Sonny not do anything to help Cher, he didn't even know that Cher was committing the forgeries. Yet, under the Pinkerton rule, Sonny is responsible for those forgeries because they were committed during the course of the conspiracy and in furtherance of it.

Therefore, **A** is incorrect because it does not hold Sonny responsible for the forgeries. Under the Pinkerton rule, Sonny is responsible for the crimes committed by his co-conspirator, Cher. Let's skip to **C** for a minute. Even though it states that Sonny is guilty of all of Cher's crimes, it provides the wrong rationale. Sonny is not responsible because he is an accomplice. He does not have the mens rea or actus reus for accomplice liability. Rather, Sonny is guilty only under co-conspirator liability. **C** is wrong because it provides the wrong rationale for the result. **D** is completely off base. Regardless of whether a conspirator knows of his co-conspirator's crimes, the conspirator is guilty if the crimes were during the course of and in furtherance of the conspiracy. In this case, Sonny and Cher would not have been able to acquire the drugs to engage in their illegal sales unless Cher had obtained the drugs. It is reasonably foreseeable and a natural consequence of the conspiracy that Cher would use any means, legal or illegal, to obtain the painkillers. Accordingly, **B**, which holds Sonny responsible for all the crimes, is the correct answer.

G.   Scope of the agreement — Single or multiple conspiracies

Because members of the same conspiracy are liable for each other co-conspirator's acts, where we draw the boundaries of each conspiracy is crucial. If a defendant is charged with the acts of another conspirator, she can avoid liability if it can be shown that they were members of different conspiracies. Thus, defendants frequently argue that there were multiple small conspiracies, rather than one large one that dragged them into its net of co-conspirator liability.

In analyzing the boundaries of conspiracies, it can be helpful to think of two basic models of conspiracy. Some conspiracies may have aspects of both models, but it is still helpful to understand the basic configuration of conspiracies.

1. Wheel conspiracy

First, there is the wheel conspiracy. In a wheel conspiracy, all the conspirators are tied together through the same middleman or "hub." Although the individual conspirators do not know each other, they are all connected to the same conspiracy because they are operating through the same middleman. If the separate spokes of this wheel have a vested interest in the success of one another's illegal conduct, there is a single wheel conspiracy and each individual member is responsible for the crimes of every other member of the conspiracy. However, if the only connection among the spokes is that they know the same middleman, there are multiple small conspiracies and the spokes of the wheel are not liable for one another's acts.

In *Kotteakos v. United States*, 328 U.S. 750 (1946), the companion case to *Pinkerton*, the Court described the operation of a wheel conspiracy and the problems in using it to impose co-conspirator liability. Kotteakos was one of 32 defendants charged with using the same loan broker, Simon Brown, to obtain false loans. Other than using Brown as their broker, the individual borrowers had no other connection. The government sought to try all the defendants in one conspiracy and charge them with the substantive crimes of one another. The Supreme Court held that the defendants were involved in smaller individual conspiracies and not the one large conspiracy charged by the government. In order to charge them with being in one big conspiracy, the government would have to connect the individual spokes of borrowers by showing that they had a common interest in a single venture.

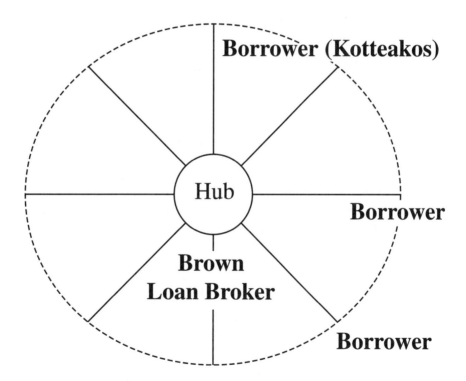

One way to show a common interest tying spokes together is to prove that the individual conspirators relied on the success of each other in succeeding in their plan. For example, if the individual borrowers used part of the proceeds obtained by the others' loans as the down payments for their loans, a common venture would be shown.

In *Anderson v. Superior Court*, 78 Cal. App. 2d 22 (1947), the court was willing to put all the defendants together in a single, wheel conspiracy.

Anderson was one of several persons paid to refer women to an illegal abortionist. Although the defendants argued that they were independent operators working with the same abortionist as the hub, the court found that they were all tied together as spokes of the wheel because they shared a common interest in keeping the abortionist in business. Although this is a stretch for a wheel conspiracy, some courts are willing to be extremely flexible in finding a stake in a common venture.

2. Chain conspiracy

In a chain conspiracy, conspirators participate in a single conspiracy by performing different roles along a single distribution line. Each conspirator plays a different role at her stage of the criminal plan. The classic example is the sale of narcotics. The manufacturer, middleman, and distributor are all on the chain of one conspiracy to distribute drugs. Although they might not know each conspirator's identity, they know that there must be someone at the various stages to ensure that the scheme works.

- Manufacturer
  |
- Wholesaler
  |
- Distributor

3. Combined conspiracy

In reality, many conspiracies have elements of both wheel and chain conspiracies. There may be a line of distribution, but parties along that line may also have multiple customers who operate more like a wheel conspiracy. For example, in *United States v. Bruno*, 105 F.2d 921 (2d Cir. 1939), the government charged 88 people with one conspiracy to import, sell, and possess narcotics. The court found that there was one conspiracy for importation because each defendant knew he was working along a chain of individuals engaged in a scheme to distribute drugs. The importers, middlemen, and retailers were tied together in a single chain. However, the multiple retailers were the spokes of mini-wheel conspiracies. Because they were more competitors than collaborators, the court was unwilling to hold the retailers responsible for each other's sales transactions.

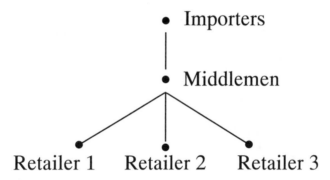

4. Multiple objectives to one conspiracy

In figuring out the scope of a conspiracy, do not be misled by the fact that there may be multiple objectives to a single conspiracy. If a conspiracy has its goal to commit several crimes, it is still ordinarily viewed as one conspiracy. See *United States v. Braverman*, 317 U.S. 49 (1942). For example, defendants might agree to import and distribute illegal drugs. This conspiracy has two objectives (to import and to distribute), but it is still one conspiracy.

The next question focuses on whether there is one or multiple conspiracies. As we discussed, the difference can be crucial. If it is one conspiracy, a defendant may face liability for the acts of many co-conspirators. If the defendant can isolate herself as being involved in a smaller conspiracy with limited parties, she faces less Pinkerton liability.

QUESTION 8. Red hot goods. Aaron is a petty thief. He spends his time burglarizing homes and stealing their possessions. Then, he has to pawn them off with his favorite "fence," Steve. Steve buys stolen goods from several people and resells them. Aaron has sold stolen goods to Steve three times. He heard about Steve from Ross, who also periodically sells stolen goods to Steve. Among the stolen goods that Steve resells are guns. Aaron has never sold a gun to Steve, but he would if he could steal some.

As the result of an undercover operation, police discover Steve's fencing operation and arrest him. Steve confesses to doing business with Aaron, Ross, and ten other burglars who regularly sell stolen goods to him. Based on Steve's testimony, the grand jury returns a massive indictment charging Steve, Aaron, Ross, and the ten other individuals with conspiracy to possess stolen goods and 100 counts of possession of stolen guns. Twenty of those counts involve the possession of stolen guns that carries a higher penalty than other counts of possession of stolen goods.

Aaron moves to dismiss, claiming that he has been mistakenly charged in one conspiracy when there were multiple conspiracies. Aaron claims that he is only responsible for his own conspiracy with Steve and he is not guilty of any of the substantive counts related to Steve's possession of stolen goods from other individuals.

Aaron's claim is

A. with merit because he never met most of the persons who fenced stolen goods with Steve.
B. without merit if Aaron knew that Steve's ability to fence goods for him depended on his ongoing illegal activities for other burglars.
C. with merit because Steve never fenced a stolen gun.
D. without merit because Steve was the hub for a large, illegal operation.

ANALYSIS. This question should have reminded you of *Kotteakos* and the issues raised by that case. As a person who fences stolen goods, Steve is the hub of a wheel conspiracy. The real issue is whether the spokes of the wheel, represented by Aaron, Ross, and the other burglars, were sufficiently connected to constitute a single venture. If they were, Aaron would be responsible for all of the co-conspirators' crimes, not just the ones he committed with Steve. It doesn't even matter if, in some sense, the burglars are competitors. Nor does it matter that they haven't met each other. What matters is if they are tied together by a common interest in a single venture.

A is wrong because it doesn't matter if a conspirator has met his co-conspirators. A person can join a conspiracy without knowing all the members of the conspiracy.

Although couched in general language, **B** seems to be a pretty good answer. As in *Anderson*, Aaron may have been in a common venture with the other burglars if the success of his business with Steve depended on his ongoing business with the other burglars. Before selecting **B**, check the other answers. You can eliminate **D** because it does not contain the entire rule for wheel conspiracies. Just because there is a hub, it doesn't mean there isn't one conspiracy. There still is one conspiracy if the spokes are connected with a rim of common interest in the venture.

That leaves us with **B** or **C**. **C** is incorrect because Aaron's conspiracy with Steve was broader than what he is trying to claim now. Aaron agreed to sell stolen goods to Steve, including stolen guns if he could get them. He never limited his conspiracy to stolen goods except guns. The answer to this problem, whether on a multiple-choice question or an essay, depends on the extent of Aaron's interests in the success of Steve's work for the other burglars. If they had sufficient common interest, there is one conspiracy. If not, there are separate conspiracies between each co-conspirator and Steve. **B** turns out to be the best answer.

Questions in this area can be rather challenging. Many courts think that *Anderson* went too far and they want to see a more concrete relationship among all of the co-conspirators. For example, they would be reluctant to find one conspiracy among Steve and all his burglars unless they had more direct dealings or financial connections. However, so long as you understand that the spokes must be connected in a common interest, you should be able to find the right answer in the options given to you on a multiple-choice question.

H.   Rules regarding parties to conspiracy

Another way that defendants may challenge a conspiracy is to argue that the agreement was not between two or more persons that qualified as conspirators under the law. Depending on the jurisdiction, certain individuals may not qualify as parties to a conspiracy. There are three rules to learn in this area: the Gebardi rule, the Wharton rule, and the bilateral versus unilateral conspiracy rule.

1. Gebardi rule

In *Gebardi v. United States*, 287 U.S. 112 (1932), a man and woman were charged with conspiring to violate the Mann Act because they agreed to cross state lines to have sex. The Mann Act was designed to protect women. Accordingly, a woman who consents to cross state lines for sex cannot be charged with conspiring to violate the act.

Therefore, *the Gebardi rule stands for the principle that a person who is protected by the law that the defendants are conspiring to violate cannot be a valid party to the conspiracy.* There must be at least two other persons who do qualify as conspirators for there to be the basis of a conspiracy charge.

For example, consider the child labor laws. Assume that Milo hires children to work in his sweatshop. He is charged with conspiring with the children to violate the labor laws. The conspiracy charge could not stand in those jurisdictions that follow the Gebardi rule because the children, who are supposed to be protected by the child labor laws, do not qualify as co-conspirators. If, however, Milo had an assistant, Jerry, who helped him hire the children, there would still be a conspiracy regardless of the children being ineligible parties to the conspiracy. Milo and Jerry would qualify as co-conspirators and two qualified conspirators is enough to sustain a conspiracy charge.

2. Wharton rule

Some jurisdictions follow another rule limiting parties who qualify as co-conspirators. *The Wharton rule holds that if it is impossible to commit the substantive offense without cooperative action, the preliminary agreement between the parties to commit the offense is not an indictable conspiracy.* The Wharton rule prohibits "double-counting" the conspiracy and the substantive offense.

For example, the crime of dueling requires two people. Under the Wharton rule, the government could not charge the two duelers with conspiracy to duel and dueling. Many crimes necessarily involve two people. They include dueling, bigamy, adultery, incest, gambling, and buying and selling contraband. Therefore, if the only two persons involved in a bribe are the giver and recipient, they are guilty of bribery but could not also be charged with conspiracy to bribe. However, if there are more persons who help them set up the crime, they could qualify and there could still be two qualified persons for the conspiracy count.

Today, courts generally defer to the legislatures to determine whether the Wharton rule applies to an individual crime. If legislative intent clearly allows both a conspiracy charge and a substantive charge for a particular group activity, the Wharton rule will not be applied. See *Iannelli v. United States*, 420 U.S. 770 (1975). Although the Model Penal Code does not specifically recognize the Wharton Rule, see Commentaries, Comment to §5.04, at 482-483, Model Penal Code §2.06(6)(b) provides that a defendant is not an accomplice if the conspiracy is "inevitably incident" to the commission of his crime.

3. Bilateral rule

Finally, there is a third rule that may affect whether there are sufficient parties for a conspiracy charge. *At traditional common law, a conspiracy requires at least "two guilty minds," that is, at least two persons who can actually be prosecuted for conspiracy.* This is also called the *plurality requirement.* Thus, if one of two persons charged with a conspiracy could not be prosecuted for the crime, there is no conspiracy.

There are many reasons that a conspirator may not be prosecutable or convicted.[1] The most common scenario is the *feigned conspirator*. Under the bilateral rule, a defendant could not be convicted for conspiring with a police informant or undercover officer. The rationale for the bilateral rule is that a conspiracy with a government agent is not likely to create the same risk as those collective actions conspiracy law is designed to prevent. See *United States v. Escobar de Bright*, 742 F.2d 1196 (9th Cir. 1984). However, some jurisdictions, including those under the Model Penal Code, have adopted the "unilateral" concept of conspiracy. Thus, if the defendant believes he is conspiring with another to commit a crime, he is guilty of conspiracy regardless of whether the other person can be convicted. Model Penal Code §5.04(1).

The acquittal of all co-conspirators does not necessarily bar the conviction of a defendant for conspiracy, even in a bilateral jurisdiction. If the other conspirators are acquitted in the *same* trial as the defendant, the defendant has a strong argument that there was no conspiracy because the jury did not find two guilty minds. However, if the acquittals came in different trials, the court may still uphold the defendant's conspiracy conviction because inconsistent verdicts are permitted.

Finally, corporations can be members of a conspiracy but there must be at least two human beings involved in the conspiracy. A corporation cannot conspire solely with its own agents.

Let's try a question that quizzes you on these specific rules regarding who qualifies as a party to a conspiracy. In real life, it depends on the statutes and case law of the jurisdiction. For the next question, assume that all three rules—the Gebardi rule, Wharton rule, and bilateral rule—are applicable.

QUESTION 9. Drugs and wives.   Barbara is trying desperately to get rid of her husband, Trent. To build up the courage to kill him, Barbara starts to use drugs. She buys her drugs from Darren, a local drug dealer. Barbara then approaches Ira and asks him to kill her husband. Barbara thinks Ira is a "hit man," but he is actually an undercover police officer.

Assuming the Gebardi, Wharton, and bilateral rules apply in the jurisdiction, which of the following crimes is Barbara guilty of?

A. Conspiracy to buy drugs.
B. Conspiracy to murder.
C. Conspiracy to buy drugs and conspiracy to murder.
D. None of the above.

---

1. Common reasons co-conspirators may not be prosecuted or may be acquitted include diplomatic immunity, insanity, or spousal relationship.

ANALYSIS.   This may be Barbara's lucky day. Under the rules that limit the parties to a conspiracy, Barbara may escape prosecution for her conspiracies. Keep in mind that she will still be guilty of the substantive crimes of buying drugs and solicitation to murder, but the conspiracy offense may not apply.

A is wrong because Barbara can argue the Wharton rule. A conspiracy to buy drugs necessarily involves a buyer and seller. Under the Wharton rule, if there are only two parties involved in a crime that requires cooperative action, the conspiracy charge is not brought. Barbara could gain a windfall through this rule.

B is wrong because in a bilateral jurisdiction, there must be two guilty minds. Since this conspiracy only involved Barbara and an undercover officer, she would not be guilty because there was only one guilty mind — hers. In a Model Penal Code jurisdiction that follows the unilateral approach, Barbara could be charged and convicted of conspiracy to murder.

C is obviously wrong because A and B are wrong. The correct answer is D. Barbara may luck out of being charged with conspiracy because of the limitations imposed by these rules.

I.   Duration of conspiracy and abandonment/withdrawal defense

Given that a defendant is responsible for all acts by co-conspirators during the course of and in furtherance of a conspiracy, it is often important to know when a conspiracy begins and ends. *A conspiracy begins the minute two or more persons agree to commit a crime. It lasts until it has been abandoned or its objectives have been achieved.* A conspiracy is generally considered to be abandoned when none of the conspirators is engaging in any action to further the conspiratorial objectives.

The Supreme Court has held that unless the parties originally agreed prior to the commission of the offense that they jointly would make efforts to conceal their criminal activity, an act of concealment is *not* considered part of a conspiracy. See *Grunewald v. United States*, 353 U.S. 391 (1957).

In many jurisdictions, a conspirator may limit her liability by withdrawing from a conspiracy and renouncing her involvement. There are two basic approaches to renunciation. Under the common law approach, a co-conspirator could end her Pinkerton liability for the future crimes of co-conspirators by withdrawing from the conspiracy. However, the defendant would still be on the hook for the original crime of conspiracy. Once committed, a conspiracy could not be "uncommitted." To withdraw from a conspiracy, a defendant would have to take "affirmative action" to announce her withdrawal to all the other conspirators. In some jurisdictions, the defendant would also have to notify law enforcement officials or otherwise thwart the plot.

The Model Penal Code offers a different approach. Under Model Penal Code §5.03(7)(c), the statute of limitations for conspiracy begins to run once the defendant has either informed her co-conspirators or notified the authorities that she is terminating her association with the conspiracy. Defendant could argue that at that point, she is no longer a member of the conspiracy and should not be responsible for her co-conspirators' acts. However, under Model Penal Code §5.03(6), it is also an affirmative defense to the crime of conspiracy if the defendant successfully thwarts the success of the conspiracy, under circumstances manifesting a complete and voluntary renunciation of her criminal purpose. If a defendant actually thwarts the criminal acts of the conspiracy, she can avoid liability for even the initial conspiracy she joined.

QUESTION 10. "I quit!" Alexander, Polly, and Quentin have conspired to rob a bank. As they are driving to the robbery, Polly gets cold feet. She tells Alexander and Quentin to drop her off on their way to the bank because she has changed her mind about the robbery. After they drop her off, Alexander and Quentin proceed to rob the bank. However, they are foiled in their attempt when the police happen upon the robbery and stop it.

Alexander, Polly, and Quentin are charged with conspiracy to rob the bank and attempted robbery. Polly claims she withdrew from the conspiracy so she is not guilty of any of the crimes. Assuming Polly voluntarily and completely withdrew from the conspiracy, which of the following is true?

A. Under the Model Penal Code, Polly is not guilty of any crime because she withdrew from the conspiracy.
B. Under the common law approach, Polly is not guilty of any crime because she withdrew from the conspiracy.
C. Under the Model Penal Code, Polly is only guilty of conspiracy, but not guilty of the attempted robbery.
D. Under both the Model Penal Code and common law, Polly is guilty of conspiracy and attempted robbery.

ANALYSIS. Under the common law, there was no way out of a conspiracy once a defendant joined. At best, a defendant could limit her liability for co-conspirators' crimes. Under the Model Penal Code approach, a defendant may be able to renounce a conspiracy and avoid criminal liability if she prevents its commission.

In this case, even assuming that Polly voluntarily and completely withdrew from the conspiracy, she would still be guilty of the conspiracy to rob the bank because she did nothing to thwart the conspiracy. All she did was to drop out. Accordingly, **A** is the wrong answer. At minimum, Polly is still guilty of conspiracy, even under the Model Penal Code approach.

B is also wrong because the common law was even stricter in its standard. Even if a defendant withdrew from a conspiracy, she would still be guilty of the original crime of the conspiracy.

Polly's best hope is under **C**. By withdrawing from the conspiracy, Polly could limit her co-conspirator liability for the attempted robbery, but she is still guilty of the conspiracy because she did not thwart the attempt. It was coincidental that the police stopped her co-conspirators from robbing the bank.

D is incorrect because Polly did enough to withdraw from the conspiracy and terminate co-conspirator liability. However, she did not do enough to escape liability altogether. **C** is the correct answer.

J. Criminal enterprises and RICO

A quick word about super-conspiracies. It is doubtful that you will learn about criminal enterprises and the Racketeer Influenced and Corrupt Organizations (RICO) Act in your basic criminal law course. Yet, most states now have enacted some type of RICO statute or anti-gang statute that is aimed at punishing criminal conduct by ongoing criminal enterprises. The key aspect of RICO laws is that the defendant must be associated with an "enterprise," which is defined as a legal or illegal organization engaging in ongoing activities. If the defendants engage in a pattern of racketeering activity (defined as two or more crimes of a certain type, such as murder, gambling, narcotics dealing, or fraud) through or affecting the enterprise, the defendants are guilty of a RICO violation. RICO crimes typically carry a much heavier penalty than ordinary conspiracies.

RICO is different from traditional conspiracies because there is no need under RICO to fit defendants into a wheel or chain conspiracy. Multifaceted, diversified conspiracies are covered by the statutory concept of the "enterprise." It is enough that defendants associate for the purpose of making money through repeated criminal activity. See *United States v. Elliott*, 571 F.2d 880 (5th Cir. 1977). Thus, the two key differences between RICO and traditional conspiracies are (1) activity that would be viewed as multiple conspiracies under traditional law may be charged together under RICO as a pattern of racketeering activity; and (2) evidence of other conspirators' crimes that are unrelated to a specific racketeering activity are admissible against a RICO defendant.

Anti-gang statutes work in much the same way as RICO statutes. They typically enhance the penalty for crimes by showing that there is ongoing criminal behavior in a particular organization or gang of individuals.

Although these are just the basics of RICO and criminal enterprise crimes, at least you have some idea that such statutes exist and expand on traditional notions of conspiracy law. Below is a question on the basics of RICO law.

QUESTION 11. Don't cross the family. Robert and Marlon belong to a Mafia family that has a wide variety of criminal enterprises. Some of the family members run prostitution rings, some sell drugs, and some run illegal gambling operations. Which of the following is incorrect?

A. Robert and Marlon cannot be charged with RICO unless the same persons who run the gambling operations also run the prostitution rings.
B. Robert and Marlon cannot be charged with RICO unless their activities are conducted through or affect a RICO enterprise.
C. Robert and Marlon can be charged with RICO if they have a pattern of racketeering activity that affects their criminal enterprise.
D. A Mafia family may be considered an enterprise for purposes of RICO law.

ANALYSIS. The RICO laws were originally enacted to deal with the problems of investigating and prosecuting organized crime. Accordingly, it is likely that the law would apply to Robert and Marlon's activities.

A is an *in*correct statement and therefore is a *correct* answer. The key way that RICO differs from general conspiracy law is that it can combine into one charge many different conspiracies whose operation constitutes a pattern of racketeering activity. As a super-conspiracy, RICO can combine different conspiracies into a pattern of racketeering activity constituting a criminal enterprise.

B is a correct statement of one of the requirements for RICO. A defendant's activities must affect or be conducted through an enterprise. Likewise, **C** and **D** are correct statements of the law. **C** defines the essence of RICO charges. Defendants can be charged if they have a pattern of racketeering activity that affects a criminal enterprise. **D** also states that many types of operations, including a Mafia family, may qualify as an enterprise under RICO. Because the call of the question asks for the incorrect statement, **A** is the answer to this question.

K. The Closer: Felony murder and co-conspirator liability

Now that you have learned conspiracy law, it is time to think strategically about how conspiracy questions may arise on an examination and how conspiracy law relates to other areas of law you have learned. Whenever you see multiple defendants, and a person dies, at least three legal doctrines should come to mind: co-conspirator liability, accomplice liability, and felony murder. This is not to say that all three principles will apply, but they could. Therefore, analyze the problem with these concepts in mind.

For example, what happens if defendants conspire to rob a bank, rob the bank, and kill a security guard during the robbery? Surely, all the defendants are guilty of conspiracy and robbery. Are they also guilty of the murder of the security guard? Yes, they are. Both felony murder and co-conspirator liability would hold them responsible for the death of the security guard if it was during the course of and in furtherance of the robbery conspiracy.

The closer question asks you to apply your knowledge of these multiple doctrines to a problem in which there may be alternative means of convicting the defendants for a variety of crimes.

QUESTION 12. Busted deal. Karl and Donald have arranged to deliver cocaine to Laura. Karl drives the car as Donald directs him to the delivery point. As they approach the drop-off point, Karl senses that Laura has arranged to rip off the cocaine and leave Karl and Donald with nothing. Karl backs up quickly to get away. As he does, he accidentally hits Molly, a little old lady who had the misfortune of crossing the road at that moment. Molly dies.

Under the common law approach, what crimes is Donald guilty of?

A. Murder only.
B. Only conspiracy to murder and conspiracy to distribute cocaine.
C. Attempted distribution of cocaine, conspiracy to distribute cocaine, and murder.
D. Accomplice liability, attempted distribution of cocaine, and conspiracy to distribute cocaine.

ANALYSIS. Before looking at the answers, let's consider Donald's possible criminal liability. First, Donald conspired with Karl. Remember, it is not important that there be an express agreement. There might have been one in this case, but we know for sure there was concerted action that demonstrates a conspiracy. It was also Donald's purpose to distribute cocaine. Therefore,

Karl is guilty of conspiracy to distribute cocaine. As an accomplice, Karl is also guilty of the attempted distribution of cocaine. Karl and Donald have taken a substantial step toward delivering the cocaine. They are close to the drop-off point and their intent is clear. Therefore, as an accomplice, Donald is guilty of the substantive offense. How about the murder? The murder was an accidental killing during the course of a felony. Conspiracy to distribute cocaine and attempted distribution of cocaine are both felonies. Either one of them supports a charge of felony murder. Accordingly, even if Donald could argue that the killing was not "in furtherance of" the conspiracy, it still met the qualifications of felony murder.

With those principles in mind, let's look at the proposed answers. **A** is incorrect because it does not state that Donald is also guilty of conspiracy. **B** is incorrect because it does not recognize that Donald has accomplice liability for the attempted distribution of cocaine and liability under felony murder for the death of Molly. Our choices are therefore **C** and **D**. Look at **D** first. It is wrong because it holds that Donald is guilty of accomplice liability. Remember that accomplice liability is NOT a separate crime. Rather, it is a theory by which Donald would be guilty of a substantive crime.

C is the correct answer. Donald is guilty of conspiracy, attempted distribution, and murder. Using a combination of accomplice liability, conspiracy law, and felony murder, a defendant may face a multitude of charges from one criminal activity.

 ## Levenson's Picks

1. Manny, Moe, and Jack	**C**	
2. Time to decide	**D**	
3. Come join the band	**C**	
4. Just kidding	**D**	
5. Pass the sugar	**A**	
6. Weather report	**D**	
7. High as a kite	**B**	
8. Red hot goods	**B**	
9. Drugs and wives	**D**	
10. "I quit!"	**C**	
11. Don't cross the family	**A**	
12. Busted deal	**C**	

Introduction to Defenses, Self-defense, and Defense of Another

Let me assert my firm belief that the only thing we have to fear is fear itself.
— Franklin D. Roosevelt

CHAPTER OVERVIEW

A. Introduction to defenses
   1. Justification defenses
   2. Excuse defenses
B. General principles of self-defense
C. Elements of self-defense
   1. Honest and reasonable fear
      a. Honest fear
      b. Reasonable fear
      c. Model Penal Code approach
   2. Immediate, imminent, and unlawful threat
   3. Proportional response
   4. Initial aggressor rule
   5. Duty to retreat
D. Imperfect self-defense
E. Model Penal Code approach
   1. Honest belief by actor that force is necessary

I n practice, the first defense raised in a criminal case is a challenge to the government's case-in-chief. Defendants will argue that the prosecution has not proved every element of the crime beyond a reasonable doubt. However, defendants may also offer what are known as "affirmative defenses." These defenses contend that even if the prosecution has proved the elements of a crime, there is a justification or excuse for the defendant's behavior and therefore the defendant is not guilty of the offense charged.

In this chapter, we review the general concept of justification and excuse defenses. Then we focus on the most common justification defense — self-defense. In Chapter 17, we discuss the other justification defenses. Excuse defenses are discussed in detail in Chapters 18 to 20.

A.   Introduction to defenses

Once the prosecution has proven the elements of the crime, the defendant may assert what are traditionally known as affirmative defenses. There are two types of affirmative defenses: justification and excuse.

1. Justification defenses

Justification defenses are premised on the belief that the law cannot and does not anticipate all the difficult situations a defendant may confront. Rather, there are some situations in which the defendant faces a difficult choice, but the right choice is actually to engage in conduct that would be a crime in other circumstances. For example, it is ordinarily impermissible to kill another person. However, if the person has a knife at your throat, you are permitted to kill in self-defense. From society's perspective, your actions are "justified" given all of the circumstances. Justification defenses include

- necessity (choice of evils)
- self-defense
- defense of others
- protection of property
- law enforcement

2. *Excuse defenses*

There are also a number of defenses that excuse a defendant's otherwise unlawful behavior. An excuse defense differs from a justification defense in that the excused conduct is socially undesirable, but the defendant is not criminally responsible. An excuse defense is typically allowed when the defendant acts under some disability that renders him free of blame or subject to less blame. In other words, excuse defenses recognize that people are only human and, under certain circumstances, people commit bad acts for which they are not blameworthy. The traditional excuse defenses include

- duress (coercion)
- insanity
- diminished capacity
- intoxication
- infancy
- entrapment
- mistake of law
- imperfect self-defense

For example, assume that a third party threatens to kill the defendant's child if the defendant does not rob a bank. The defendant robs a bank. Although it was wrong to rob the bank, the defendant's behavior is excused because of the coercive circumstances.

The first multiple-choice question of this chapter focuses on your understanding of the theoretical difference between justification and excuse defenses. Before you answer it, keep in mind that we have actually already studied other types of "defenses" that may come into play in a criminal case. For example, mistake of fact may undermine the prosecution's case, or the Wharton rule may excuse defendant from being guilty of conspiracy. Now, we are moving beyond those defenses to the traditional justification and excuse defenses.

QUESTION 1. Crazy Tom. Tom is a paranoid schizophrenic. He often hallucinates, seeing people and objects that do not exist. On one occasion, Tom imagined that he was being attacked by the devil. Accordingly, Tom shot at his attacker. It turned out to be the little boy from next door who simply rang the doorbell. If Tom is able to successfully assert a defense, it will be because

A. insane defendants are justified in their acts.
B. insane defendants are excused from their behavior.
C. self-defense excused his acts.
D. Tom's actions were justified by the circumstances.

ANALYSIS.   This question will be much easier once you have studied both self-defense and the insanity defense. However, you should be able to answer the question just using the introductory material.

A is incorrect. Although we excuse insane persons' behavior, we do not do so because we think they made the correct decision and therefore were justified in their actions. Rather, we recognize their frailty and excuse their behavior. **A** is wrong because it states that insane defendants are "justified" in their acts. If anything, they are "excused" for their acts. Therefore, **B** appears to be the correct answer. Before selecting **B**, though, consider the alternatives.

C is wrong because Tom really wasn't acting in self-defense. Tom wasn't actually being attacked. The little boy next door simply rang the doorbell. Moreover, self-defense is not an excuse defense. It is a justification defense. Therefore, there were at least a couple of clues indicating that **C** was incorrect.

D is also incorrect. Tom's actions may have been justified in his own mind, but they were not actually justified by the circumstances. Justification defenses assume that society would countenance the defendant's behavior and label it as correct under the circumstances. No one would say that it was right to shoot a boy for ringing the doorbell.

B is the correct answer. Insane defendants are excused from, not justified in, their behavior.

Now that we have touched on the theory of defenses, let's spend the remainder of the chapter focusing on one of the primary justification defenses — self-defense. Defenses, like crimes, have required elements. In other words, to successfully assert the defense, the defendant must show that each requirement of the defense was met. At this stage, we do not worry about who has the burden of proving these elements. Often times, the burden falls on the defense to prove affirmative defenses, although some jurisdictions require prosecutors to disprove them. Regardless, the defense has the burden of demonstrating how the facts of the case support the basic requirements for self-defense.

B.   General principles of self-defense

Under both the common law and the Model Penal Code, a defendant is justified in using force to protect himself from the threat of immediate and unlawful force. The rationale behind self-defense is that under the law, human life holds the highest value. When someone's life is threatened, he may take necessary steps to protect his life and well-being. Although a defendant may assert self-defense to a non-homicide crime (e.g., assault), the more difficult issues are raised when a defendant claims to have killed in self-defense. Accordingly, that is the focus of much, but not all, of our discussion.

Both excuse and justification theories support the doctrine of self-defense. At early English common law, self-defense was treated as an excuse. The defendant's act of killing was excused because the law would not blame a person for acting on instinct to protect his life.

By contrast, today self-defense is considered a justified act. From a utilitarian viewpoint, if someone must die, it is better that it be the aggressor who has behaved in an antisocial manner. Moreover, self-defense can, over time, save many lives as aggressors are deterred from attacking others who are allowed to defend themselves. From a moral perspective, one might argue that the aggressor forfeits his life by attacking another or that the right of an innocent person to life is morally superior to an aggressor's right to life.

Self-defense has long been recognized at common law. When all the elements of the defense are met, the defendant enjoys a *full defense* to the crime. Even when the defendant has not satisfied all the requirements for the defense, a partial defense may be available. See Section D, *infra*.

Although the definition varies by jurisdiction, in general the elements of self-defense are

- an honest and reasonable fear of death or great bodily harm;
- from an imminent and unlawful threat;
- proportional response to that threat; and
- defendant was not the initial aggressor.

Some jurisdictions have a fifth requirement:

- duty to retreat.

Once a defendant has presented sufficient facts to make a claim of self-defense, most jurisdictions place the burden on the prosecution to disprove self-defense beyond a reasonable doubt. However, a minority of courts impose the burden on the defense to prove each element of self-defense by a preponderance of the evidence.

In the next few subsections, we review each of these elements in detail. Before we do, however, you can become familiar with the requirements by trying the following simple question.

QUESTION 2. Not too fast.   Glen and Howard are co-workers. Glen is jealous that Howard received a raise when Glen did not. Therefore, Glen says to him during the lunch break, "You jerk. One of these days I'm going to kill you." Glen is unarmed when he makes the remark. Howard responds by taking out a gun and shooting Glen dead. If Howard claims self-defense, he is likely to

A. succeed because it was wrong for Glen to say he was going to kill Howard.

B. succeed because he was justified in his actions.
C. succeed because Howard had a right to kill anyone who threatened him.
D. fail because the threat to him, if any, was not imminent.

ANALYSIS.   Good common sense and a basic knowledge of the requirements for self-defense will get you through this question. As you probably surmised, not every threat justifies self-defense. It needs to be a plausible, imminent threat. In this situation, Glen makes a verbal threat, but it is vague, non-immediate, and not accompanied by any show of force. Therefore, in all likelihood, Howard would not have the right to kill in self-defense. Given that quick analysis, let's look at the possible answers.

A is wrong. Although it may have been morally wrong for Glen to threaten Howard, that did not automatically trigger the right of self-defense. If it did, there would be a lot of needless killings in this world. **B** is a little more challenging. It is the correct answer only if Howard has met all of the requirements of self-defense. In your quick review of the requirements presented earlier, at least one should stand out. The threat of harm is not imminent. Therefore, Howard was not justified in his actions. **B** is incorrect. For similar reasons, **C** is incorrect. Just because someone threatens you, it does not mean you have the right to kill. The threat must meet all the requirements of self-defense. As we discussed, this threat was vague and not imminent.

Accordingly, **D** is the best answer. It reflects that the threat was vague and not imminent. Howard went overboard in shooting Glen.

You will understand this question a lot better after a detailed review of all the elements of self-defense, the subject of the following five subsections.

C.   Elements of self-defense

1. Honest and reasonable fear

Self-defense may only be used when a defendant both honestly and reasonably fears the use of unlawful force. Before deadly force may be used in self-defense, a defendant must fear death or grave bodily harm.

The key case used to study self-defense is *People v. Goetz*, 68 N.Y.2d 96 (1986). In this famous case, Bernhard Goetz, a subway rider in New York, shot four young men he claimed were going to rob and kill him. A closer examination of the facts revealed that the men, although menacing, had not actually physically assaulted Goetz. Nonetheless, he claimed he was in actual fear for his life and entitled to use self-defense. The grand jury wondered whether it was sufficient for Goetz to have an honest fear for his life or whether that fear also had to be reasonable. Goetz claimed that his past experiences with the New York subways and African-American youth made him fear for his life and that he was therefore entitled to use self-defense. The prosecution argued that Goetz, who is white, was overly sensitive and racist; the prosecution further claimed that Goetz's fear was not reasonable.

In the end, the trial jury agreed with Goetz and acquitted him of the homicide charge. Although the court held that a defendant claiming self-defense must have both an honest and reasonable fear of death, grave bodily harm, or the commission of a serious felony, the case vividly demonstrates that it is not so easy to decide what is reasonable.

a. Honest fear   Let's examine each requirement more closely. First, in order to claim self-defense, a defendant must show that he *honestly feared* the use of unlawful force. Self-defense is not an excuse to kill for illicit purposes. For example, suppose A and B are in a bar together. A is annoyed at B for flirting with A's date so he shoots B. It turns out that B was carrying a gun, but A didn't know that. A cannot claim self-defense, even though B had a gun, because A was not in fear of B when he shot him.

The jury decides whether the defendant was honestly in fear of the victim. Other motives for the killing, the relationship between the parties, the defendant's demeanor, and remarks made at the time of the assault are all factors the jury considers. In the end, if the jury decides that the defendant honestly feared his victim, the defendant has met part of the requirement for self-defense.

If the defendant uses deadly force, he must generally fear death or grave bodily harm. Under the Model Penal Code and in many jurisdictions, a defendant may also use deadly force if he honestly and reasonably fears becoming the victim of a serious felony crime, such as rape, kidnapping, or robbery. See Model Penal Code §3.04(2)(b).

Before we go on to the requirement that the defendant's fear also be reasonable, let's try a quick question regarding the requirement of a sincere, honest fear.

QUESTION 3. Shrimp cocktail. Arthur and Kirk are at a cocktail party when Kirk says to Arthur, "the time has come for me to kick your butt." Arthur starts to laugh and says, "You shrimp. There's no chance you can hurt me." As Kirk looks the other way, Arthur kicks him in the rear. If Arthur is charged with assault and he claims self-defense, his defense will likely

A. fail because he did not fear Kirk.
B. succeed because Kirk threatened him first.
C. succeed because he honestly feared Kirk.
D. fail because Kirk did not threaten imminent harm.

ANALYSIS. The key to answering this question is to decide whether Arthur honestly feared Kirk when he assaulted him. If he did, he might meet the first requirement of a self-defense claim. However, if he didn't, it doesn't even matter if someone else might have been frightened. Arthur does not get to claim self-defense.

From all the facts, it seems overwhelmingly clear that Arthur did not fear Kirk. In fact, he was bent on humiliating him. **B** and **C** are therefore wrong. **B** is wrong because it doesn't matter that Kirk threatened Arthur first. If that threat did not cause Arthur any fear, Arthur cannot claim self-defense. **C** is wrong because the facts indicate that Arthur did not fear Kirk. First, he says, "[t]here's no chance you can hurt me." Second, Kirk is actually walking away at the time that Arthur kicks him. Therefore, there does not seem to be a factual basis for claiming that Arthur honestly feared Kirk.

That leaves two choices: **A** and **D**. **D** is a little trickier. **D** is wrong because, factually, Kirk did threaten imminent harm. He says, "the time has come" for Kirk to kick Arthur. The problem is not that the threat is not imminent; the problem in claiming self-defense is that the threat doesn't cause any fear in Arthur. **A** is the correct answer. If Arthur does not fear Kirk, he is not entitled to claim self-defense.

Now that we have looked at the first part of the requirement that there be an honest and reasonable fear, let's examine the part that usually raises the most issues for law students and courts: Did the defendant have a reasonable fear of harm from the victim?

b. Reasonable fear   In most jurisdictions, having an honest fear is not enough to claim self-defense. The defendant must also have a *reasonable fear* of unlawful force. An objective reasonableness requirement means that the defendant's conduct is justified only when society, as represented by the jury, agrees with the defendant. Without a reasonableness requirement, each individual would have license to hurt another whenever his aberrational or bizarre beliefs dictate that he should do so.

For example, assume defendant sees his long-time enemy (and boss) waving a plastic knife at the company picnic. Because of previous run-ins with his boss, the defendant believes that his boss may actually try to attack him. The defendant therefore shoots him. Assuming defendant had an honest fear of injury, his fear was unreasonable. The only threat was a plastic knife and it did not warrant the use of deadly self-defense.

Although the defendant's fear must be reasonable, it need not be correct. For example, a defendant sees a person point a gun at him and shoots first to avoid injury. The gun turns out to be a starter pistol. If a reasonable person would have made the same mistake, it is irrelevant that there was no actual threat of harm.

A major issue in applying the elements of self-defense is determining what standard should be used to define the "reasonable person." How objective is the reasonableness standard? You will soon come to realize that the reasonableness standard is not as "objective" as some would claim. In fact, the trend is to make it ever more subjective.[1]

In *Goetz*, the court noted that deciding whether the defendant's fear was reasonable required evaluating the "circumstances" facing the defendant. Specifically, the jury could consider

- the physical attributes of the persons involved;
- the defendant's prior experiences; and
- the physical movements and comments of the potential assailant.

Thus, if you have a small defendant who has been assaulted before in the subway, the jury can be asked whether a "reasonable person with the defendant's background and in the defendant's circumstances" would have feared an attack. In evaluating the reasonableness of the defendant's fear, the jury would be entitled to take into account that the defendant faced an attacker much bigger than him and that the defendant had been attacked before.

A difficult issue that arises in analyzing whether a defendant's fear was reasonable is whether the jurors may take into account the race of the attacker. For example, was it reasonable for Goetz to fear the subway youth because they were African Americans? Many commentators have argued that even if racial fear is *typical*, it should not be considered *reasonable*, and courts should therefore exclude race evidence from trial.

There is no set rule as to which factors constitute objective factors the jury may consider in deciding whether the defendant had a reasonable fear of harm. However, courts are more likely to allow the jurors to consider the physical circumstances of the defendant's situation than whether a defendant with the same emotional, psychological, or cultural background as the defendant would have reasonably feared harm from the victim. Courts and commentators continue to debate to what extent the victim's background, such as that of a battered spouse, should factor into the evaluation of whether the victim had an honest and reasonable fear of the defendant.

Let's try a question that challenges you to decide whether the defendant had a reasonable fear entitling him to use self-defense.

QUESTION 4. Big, bad, and brown. Jenny's car breaks down at night in a dangerous part of the city. She does not have a cell phone, and no other motorists stop to help her. Jenny decides to walk to the nearest gas

---

1. Remember the difference between objective and subjective standards: Subjective standards focus on the characteristics of the defendant and his situation; objective standards focus on the hypothetical "reasonable" person.

station for help. As she walks through the dark streets, Jenny sees a large, Hispanic man approach her. Jenny, who is Caucasian and petite, becomes alarmed. She has heard that the area she is in hosts one of the meanest Hispanic gangs in town. The man starts to yell at Jenny, but she does not understand what he is saying. However, based on his tone, she believes that he is threatening her with harm. Jenny takes a knitting needle out of her purse. As the man walks toward Jenny, appearing to hold something in his jacket pocket, she plunges the knitting needle into his chest. The needle hits his heart and the man dies. As it turns out, neighbors who heard the man (Carlos) yell said that he was telling Jenny in Spanish that he could help her if she would just slow down. Carlos did not have a weapon. Instead, he was holding a radio that he keeps in his pocket.

Jenny is charged with murder. If she asserts self-defense, she is likely to

A. succeed because she honestly believed that Carlos was going to harm her.
B. succeed because it is reasonable to believe that a Hispanic man in a gang area is threatening harm.
C. fail because Carlos was not armed.
D. fail unless a small woman in Jenny's situation would have reasonably believed, as Jenny did, that Carlos threatened her with grave bodily harm, death, or a serious felony.

ANALYSIS. On an essay test, your instructor would want you to discuss in detail whether Jenny had an honest and reasonable fear for her life. However, multiple-choice questions give your professor less flexibility in examining these types of issues. At most, your professor can give you a basic fact scenario to see if you can identify the appropriate standard to be used in evaluating that scenario.

In this situation, **A** is wrong because an honest fear is insufficient for a self-defense claim under the common law approach and the approach followed in most jurisdictions. Rather, the defendant must have both an honest and reasonable fear of harm. There is no question that Jenny was afraid of Carlos. The real question is whether she was reasonably afraid. Beware of those answers that, though correct, only get you halfway there.

B is wrong because it relies on gross racial stereotypes to define a reasonable fear. It may be typical, but it is not reasonable, to believe that all Hispanic men in a gang area are gang members threatening harm. If the problem gave more facts indicating that Carlos was a gang member (e.g., visible tattoos or gang apparel), race might be one factor in determining the reasonableness of Jenny's fear. However, courts are reluctant to allow race to be the sole or even primary factor in finding that a fear was reasonable.

C is wrong because it doesn't matter whether Carlos was actually armed if Jenny reasonably believed he was. Even mistaken beliefs may be reasonable and support a claim of self-defense.

D turns out to be the correct answer. It best encapsulates the standard for self-defense. Jenny must honestly and reasonably believe that Carlos would threaten her. It usually would be permissible to take into account Jenny's size and circumstances, even though this adds a subjective element to the objective reasonable person test.

The issue of how much of the defendant's situation (past history, mental and emotional qualities, etc.) is considered in deciding whether the defendant had a reasonable fear is important in cases involving battered spouses. We explore that issue in detail in sections C(2) and G. First, however, let's look at the Model Penal Code approach and the remaining common law requirements for self-defense.

c. Model Penal Code approach   The Model Penal Code takes a more subjective approach to self-defense than the common law does. Under Model Penal Code §§3.04 and 3.09(2), a defendant's subjective belief that force was necessary is sufficient for self-defense unless the defendant is charged with a crime requiring a mens rea of only recklessness or negligence. Proponents of the subjective standard argue that it is fairer and more realistic than the objective reasonableness standard because no person is reasonable when he believes death or severe bodily harm is imminent. Under such circumstances, a person's actions are governed by emotion, not reason. "Detached reflection cannot be demanded in the presence of an uplifted knife." *Brown v. United States*, 256 U.S. 335, 343 (1921) (Holmes, J.).

Accordingly, under the Model Penal Code approach, "the use of force upon or toward another person is justifiable when the actor believes that such force is immediately necessary for the purpose of protecting himself against the use of unlawful force by such other person on the present occasion." Model Penal Code §3.04. Thus, a defendant like Goetz would have a better chance at successfully asserting self-defense if charged with intentional murder because the law would focus on his subjective intent, not on whether a reasonable person would have the same reaction to African-American youth.

However, even the Model Penal Code standard is not completely subjective. Model Penal Code §3.09 provides that an honest, but unreasonable fear, is a defense if Goetz is charged with a crime that requires purposeful, knowing, or extremely reckless conduct. Accordingly, if Goetz were charged with murder, he could assert a claim of self-defense as long as his use of self-defense was not extremely reckless. But, if Goetz were charged with only negligent homicide, he could not claim self-defense unless his fear was reasonable.

QUESTION 5. Pea shooter. Marty is taking a walk around the neighborhood when he runs into his old nemesis, Biff. When they were children, Biff terrorized Marty. However, Biff and Marty are now grown men with families and businesses of their own. Biff starts to show Marty a new BB gun that Biff has purchased. Marty assumes that Biff will use the weapon to kill him and quickly draws his own gun and shoots Biff. In fact, the BB gun was empty and Biff planned to give it as a holiday gift to his son.

Marty is charged with Biff's death. Under the Model Penal Code approach, which of the following is accurate?

A. If Marty is charged with negligent homicide, he can claim self-defense.
B. Marty cannot claim self-defense under any circumstances because a reasonable person would know that Biff was not threatening Marty.
C. Marty can claim self-defense if he is charged with intentional murder and he honestly believed that Biff would kill him.
D. Marty can claim self-defense for any charge because Biff had always been a threat to Marty.

ANALYSIS. Recall that under the Model Penal Code approach, a defendant can claim self-defense so long as he believes that the force he uses is needed to protect himself from unlawful force. Thus, the starting point in the analysis is that a subjective fear alone may be sufficient to trigger a self-defense claim. However, as Model Penal Code §3.09 clarifies, if Marty is negligent or reckless in his mistaken belief that Biff was a threat, he cannot claim self-defense if charged with an offense for which recklessness or negligence suffices for culpability. How does this all play out in this question? After understanding the basic fact pattern, the best thing you can do is study each proposed answer to determine the nature of the charges Marty faces and how they affect his claim of self-defense.

First, Marty tries in **A** to claim self-defense even though he is charged with negligent homicide. An honest, but negligent, fear would not provide a defense to negligent homicide. Here, Marty assumes that because Biff was a bully as a child and is now carrying a pea shooter, he automatically wants to kill Marty. Such a belief is not reasonable. Marty is negligent in having such a belief. Accordingly, he would not be able to claim self-defense to an offense that only requires negligence.

B is wrong because it goes too far. There are some circumstances under which Marty could claim self-defense. For example, if Marty were charged with intentionally killing Bill, he could claim that he honestly believed that Bill was a threat. Even though that fear may not be reasonable, Marty is charged with an offense that requires more than negligence or recklessness. Accordingly, a subjective, honest fear would be sufficient. **C** accurately reflects that analysis and is the correct answer.

D is wrong because it assumes that once a victim has been a threat, he remains a threat forever. Prior altercations with a victim may be one factor in deciding whether the defendant had an honest and reasonable fear, but it does not give a license to kill in self-defense anytime the defendant runs into the victim in the future.

2. Immediate, imminent, and unlawful threat

Self-defense is limited to situations in which the defendant faces an immediate, imminent threat. It is only in those situations that there are no alternatives to using force against the other person. If the threat is not imminent, there are usually alternative, lawful measures available.

For example, *A* tells *B* that when *A* gets back from his vacation in two weeks, he is going to kill *B*. *B* responds by shooting *A* on the spot. The imminency requirement has not been met. *B* had plenty of alternative means to stop *A* from killing him. *B* would not be entitled to argue self-defense.

At common law, a strict, objective standard was used to determine whether the defendant faced a threat of imminent harm. For many courts, the threat had to be present at the very moment that the defendant shot his attacker. However, that standard has been relaxed. Now, the jury ordinarily decides whether a reasonable person would believe the threat from the victim was imminent.

The Model Penal Code further relaxes the imminency requirement for self-defense. Under Model Penal Code §3.04(1), it is sufficient that the actor reasonably believed the use of defensive force was "immediately necessary . . . on the present occasion."

Difficult issues arise in *battered spouse cases* because the deceased may have been killed when he was not posing an immediate threat to the defendant, such as when the abuser is sleeping. Under the traditional approach, battered spouses may not be able to claim self-defense because preemptive strikes are not allowed and the defendant did not pose an immediate, objective threat. See, e.g., *State v. Norman*, 324 N.C. 253 (1989) (self-defense instruction denied because battered wife killed husband in his sleep). However, the more modern approach allows the jury to view the imminency of the threat through the subjective eyes of the defendant. Thus, because abused spouses may feel constantly threatened, the jury may find a reasonable belief that the threat was imminent. See, e.g., *State v. James*, 121 Wash. 2d 220 (1993).

It should be apparent that prosecutors tend to favor the objective standard for the imminency requirement and defendants prefer that the jury use the subjective standard and "step in the defendant's shoes" when deciding whether the defendant faced an immediate threat. The next question tests your understanding of the differences between these two approaches.

QUESTION 6. **He had it coming.**   Sally was in a terrible marriage. Her husband, Marc, constantly beat and humiliated her. In front of the children, he would threaten to kill her and them. Over the course of their ten-year marriage, Marc had broken Sally's arm, ribs, and fractured her skull. Yet, she could not escape him. Even when she went to a battered women's shelter, he would find her. One horrible day, Marc came home from work and told Sally, "You've got 20 minutes to live, you slut." He then grabbed a beer and sat down in his favorite chair, with a shotgun by his side. As he was drinking the beer, Marc fell asleep. While he was sleeping, Sally quickly grabbed the gun and shot Marc in the head. She was charged with murder.

If Sally claims self-defense, she is likely to

A. succeed under the traditional approach to self-defense.
B. succeed because Marc deserved to die.
C. fail under the traditional approach to self-defense, but may succeed under a subjective approach to the imminency requirement.
D. fail under any standard because she could have called the police while her husband slept.

ANALYSIS.   The horrible thing is that this type of situation arises all too frequently in real life. Let's take a look at how it would be analyzed on a multiple-choice test. First, to review, consider whether Sally had an honest and reasonable fear of her husband. Given his constant abuse of her, and his latest threat, it appears she did have an honest and reasonable fear. Second, was the threat of death or serious bodily harm imminent? The answer depends on which approach you adopt. Under the purely objective approach, it is difficult (although not impossible) to find that a sleeping person poses an imminent harm. However, such a finding is much easier if one views the situation through Sally's eyes. From Sally's perspective, she was always under threat of death from Marc, even when he was sleeping.

A is wrong because the traditional approach would require that the threat to Sally be objectively imminent. Here, Marc was asleep. Although her fear remained, it is not reasonable to believe that a person is going to be killed while the attacker is asleep.

B is wrong but highlights an important policy discussion regarding self-defense and the imminency requirement. One of the reasons for the imminency requirement is to prevent defendants from using "self-help" and extracting their own justice from an abuser. It may have been wrong for Marc to beat his wife, but self-defense is not a license for vigilante justice. Whether or not Marc deserves to be punished, let alone die, is not a decision that society lets an individual make.

This leaves us with the choices of **C** and **D**. **D** states that under any standard Sally's defense would fail. However, Sally would have a decent (although not guaranteed) chance for self-defense under the more subjective standard. Under a subjective standard, the jury would be directed to consider Sally's entire situation and past in determining whether, from her perspective, the threat from Marc was imminent. Because the threat was omnipresent and she had never been able to escape him, she would be more likely to have a successful argument under the subjective standard. **C** is the correct answer.

3. Proportional response

A person may only use that force which is necessary to protect himself from attack. In other words, the defendant's use of force must be proportional to the threat he faces; no excessive force is permitted. Therefore, a defendant who faces a threat of non-deadly force may only respond with non-deadly force. Before a defendant can use deadly force, he must be faced with deadly force or the risk of serious bodily injury.

For example, imagine that *A* threatens to punch *B* in the arm. *B* cannot respond by shooting *A* in the heart. The response would be disproportional to the threat.

Model Penal Code §3.04(2)(b) limits the use of deadly force to cases in which the threatened danger is "death, serious bodily harm, kidnapping, or sexual intercourse compelled by force or threat." This provision extends the use of lethal force in self-defense to cases in which the defendant faces those crimes (kidnapping, rape) in which serious harm is most likely to occur.

Generally, self-defense only authorizes the use of force against one's attacker; it is not a justification for using force against a third person. However, if a defendant acts in self-defense against an attacker and an innocent party is accidentally injured, the defendant may be excused from causing the injury unless the defendant acted negligently or recklessly with regard to that third person. See Model Penal Code §3.09(3). For example, a rival gang member shoots at the defendant. The defendant then shoots back at the gang member, but the bullet passes through the attacker's body and hits an innocent third party. Defendant is not responsible for shooting the third party. However, if the defendant runs behind a park bench occupied by several children and starts shooting at the gang member, the defendant would be responsible for the negligent homicide of the children if he accidentally shoots them while responding to the threat from the gang member.

Time for a question on this third requirement for self-defense.

QUESTION 7. "I'll show you." Harland is approached by Stan, who threatens to shoot him in the head. Harland responds by yelling, "You want a piece of me? I'll show you." Harland then kicks Stan, causing him to drop his gun. Stan is injured by the blow and Harland is charged with assault.

If Harland argues self-defense, he is likely to

A. fail because the threat was not imminent.
B. fail because he did not have a reasonable fear of death or serious injury.
C. fail because he responded with a different type of force than the force Stan had threatened.
D. succeed.

ANALYSIS. Common sense goes a long way in criminal law. This question is a little odd because the defendant uses *less* force than may have been justified, but don't be confused. A defendant may use non-lethal force to respond to a threat of non-lethal force or lethal force. However, a defendant can only use lethal force when confronted with the threat of death, serious bodily injury, or a crime that could lead to such consequences.

A is wrong because Harland was faced with a real, imminent threat. **B** is also wrong because Harland could reasonably fear serious injury from someone who threatens to shoot him in the head.

The choice is again between **C** and **D**. To make the right choice, you need to understand the basic rule articulated above. If a defendant is confronted with lethal force, he may use lethal *or non-lethal* force to respond. Legally, it is not a problem that Harland used less force than he was entitled to use in self-defense. **D** is the correct answer.

4. Initial aggressor rule

Ordinarily, self-defense is not allowed if the defendant was the initial aggressor in the altercation. For example, assume *A* attacks *B* with a knife. *B* responds by pulling a gun. *A* takes out his own gun and shoots *B* first. In this situation, *A* is not entitled to use force because he was the one who created the deadly situation. In other words, one cannot create his own necessity to use self-defense.

Consider the case of *United States v. Peterson*, 483 F.2d 1222 (D.C. Cir. 1973). In *Peterson*, the defendant spotted the victim trying to remove windshield wipers from one of the defendant's junked cars. The defendant protested and went back into his house to get a gun. The victim was about to leave when the defendant threatened to shoot. The victim then grabbed a lug wrench and headed toward the defendant. When the victim would not stop, the defendant shot him. The court held that the defendant was not entitled to assert self-defense because he had provoked the threat of deadly force.

As you can see from *Peterson*, it is sometimes a sticky question as to who is the initial aggressor. Was it the victim who began the situation by trying to steal windshield wipers or the defendant who first threatened deadly force? Many courts try to draw a distinction between instigators and aggressors. The victim in *Peterson* was certainly an instigator, but it was the defendant who introduced deadly force. Accordingly, Peterson was seen as the initial "aggressor."

Moreover, a defendant who has reached a safe haven and then intentionally returns to a scene of violence is ordinarily viewed as an aggressor not entitled to use self-defense. For example, in *Laney v. United States*, 294 F.3d 401, 412 (2d Cir. 1923), the defendant escaped from a mob into a safe backyard. Rather than remain in a place of safety, the defendant loaded his gun and went out to confront the mob. The defendant's actions deprived him of the opportunity to invoke self-defense. See also *Rowe v. United States*, 370 F.2d 240 (D.C. Cir. 1996) (defendant left scene of argument, went home to load his gun, and returned; defendant not entitled to argue self-defense).

An initial aggressor may reclaim the right to use self-defense by communicating to his adversary his intent to withdraw and then by attempting to do so in good faith. If his adversary continues to pursue him, the defendant may then protect himself with force.

The Model Penal Code takes a more flexible approach to the initial aggressor rule. Under Model Penal Code §3.04, an initial aggressor only loses the privilege of self-defense if he provokes the use of force *with the initial purpose of causing death or serious bodily harm*. Therefore, if an initial aggressor only threatens a moderate, non-deadly use of force and the victim escalates the encounter into one involving the threat of deadly force, the defendant may defend himself against the deadly attack. The defendant may be guilty of the initial, non-deadly attack, but he does not lose the right to assert self-defense when the situation escalates.

QUESTION 8. Macho, macho man. Frankie is a member of the Sharks gang. He hears that members of the rival Jets gang will be meeting at a particular park. Knowing that he would be unwelcome in the park, Frankie nonetheless goes to that location. True to their colors, the rival gang members threaten Frankie with deadly force, to which he responds by killing one of the Jets.

Is Frankie entitled to claim self-defense?

A. No, because Frankie provoked an altercation.
B. Yes, because he was threatened with deadly force.
C. No, because Frankie left a place of safety to go to a dangerous area.
D. Yes, because Frankie was a member of a rival gang.

ANALYSIS. In this situation, Frankie may have done an unwise thing, but he was not necessarily an initial aggressor. Rather, he was more of an instigator and being an instigator does not necessarily deprive a defendant of the right to use self-defense. Using that as the starting point for our analysis, look at the various answer options.

A is wrong because the only provocative thing that Frankie did was go to a park. This was not enough to make him an aggressor. Accordingly, **A** is the wrong answer.

Before examining **B**, take a look at **C**. **C** is wrong, although it may have tempted you by its reference to a "place of safety." Remember, that issue only arises if a defendant leaves a place of safety and provokes the use of deadly force by himself threatening deadly force. In this question, there are no facts to suggest that Frankie ever drew a gun on any of the rival gang members, until after he was threatened with deadly force.

The choice is between **B** and **D**. Can you see why **B** is the better answer? A gang member does not have a general license to kill rival gang members. Rather, he may only do so when threatened with deadly force. So, **B** is the correct answer.

5. Duty to retreat

At traditional common law, a person did not have a duty to retreat before resorting to deadly force. A man could stand his ground. However, many jurisdictions have added this duty as a prerequisite to asserting self-defense in order to preserve life as much as possible. In jurisdictions with this requirement, a person has the duty to retreat, if possible, before resorting to deadly force. Even in these jurisdictions, however, there is generally no duty to retreat before using non-deadly force.

The duty to retreat is applied only when the defendant knows he can retreat with complete safety. If the defendant cannot safely retreat, there is no duty to do so. See Model Penal Code §3.04(2)(b)(ii).

A majority of jurisdictions that impose a duty to retreat make an exception when the defendant is attacked in his own home. This is often referred to as the "castle rule." A man is the king of his castle and should not have to retreat when he is there. (Also, where is he going to go?) Accordingly, if a defendant is attacked in his home, he may use lethal self-defense without first attempting to retreat.[2]

Under the Model Penal Code, a defendant does not have a duty to retreat from his home or place of work, unless he is the initial aggressor or is assailed in the workplace by someone he knows to be a co-worker. Model Penal Code §3.04(2)(b)(ii)(1).

---

2. Some jurisdictions modify this rule by requiring the defendant to retreat if the attacker is another lawful occupant of the home, but do not require the defendant to retreat if the attacker is an intruder.

Let's finish up the basic requirements for self-defense with this last question relating to the duty to retreat.

QUESTION 9. Subway escape.   Assume that in the *Goetz* case, Goetz is confronted with four youths wielding knives. At just that moment, subway police come running up from behind Goetz, although he does not see or hear them. They easily outnumber the attackers and could subdue them and escort Goetz to safety. Before Goetz can see the officers, he shoots the attackers.

If Goetz is in a jurisdiction that applies the duty to retreat rule, is he entitled to use self-defense?

A. No, because the arrival of the police eliminated the need to use lethal force in self-defense.

B. No, because Goetz could have retreated with complete safety.

C. No, because Goetz had a duty to retreat because he was not in his own home.

D. Yes.

ANALYSIS.   Before using lethal force in self-defense, Goetz must retreat if he can. However, this depends on Goetz knowing that he can retreat with complete safety. In this question, even if Goetz could safely escape, he did not realize it because the officers were behind him. Accordingly, the duty to retreat probably does not apply.

Let's check each of the answers. First, **A:** It is not altogether clear that the arrival of the officers eliminated the need for self-defense. It would be helpful to know more facts, such as how quickly the officers would be able to subdue the youths and whether Goetz could be harmed before this could be accomplished. Moreover, **A** does not acknowledge that Goetz did not know about the police. Once again, the duty to retreat arises only when the defendant is aware that he can retreat with safety.

B is wrong for the same reason. We don't know if Goetz could have retreated with complete safety and, more important, he did not know if he could retreat with complete safety.

C is the biggest red herring of this question. While it is true that the duty to retreat arises outside of the home, location is not the only factor in deciding whether the duty applies.

Thus, **D** is the right answer. It is a little tricky because it doesn't explain why he had the right to use self-defense. Rather, you have to be confident enough in your understanding of why he did not have a duty in this case to select **D** as the correct answer.

D.   Imperfect self-defense

Throughout this chapter, you probably have been wondering what happens to a defendant who meets some of the requirements for self-defense, but not all of them. For example, what if a defendant honestly fears he is in mortal danger, but a reasonable person would not agree? In some jurisdictions, the defendant can argue *imperfect self-defense.*

Imperfect self-defense ordinarily gives the defendant a *partial defense* to a charge of homicide. A defendant who has an honest, but unreasonable, fear of his victim can reduce his charge from murder to manslaughter. In some jurisdictions, the reduced charge is voluntary manslaughter, on the theory that an unreasonable fear "provoked" the defendant into killing. Other jurisdictions reason that the defendant was reckless or criminally negligent in killing because of his unreasonable fear, and therefore reduce the charge to involuntary manslaughter. The Model Penal Code favors this approach. It holds that a mistake as to the need for force is a defense *except* for offenses that only require recklessness or negligence. See Model Penal Code §3.09(3).

In the infamous case of the Menendez brothers, Eric and Lyle Menendez argued that they shot their parents out of self-defense. At the time of the shooting, the parents were sitting on the couch, eating ice cream, and filling out college applications for their boys. It is hard to see that as an immediate threat. However, because of alleged abuse by their parents in the past, the Menendez brothers argued that they honestly believed their parents were about to kill them. If the jury believed that (which it did not!), the defendants would have been entitled to a lesser manslaughter conviction.

Try to come up with the perfect answer to the following imperfect self-defense question.

QUESTION 10. Blue tie.   When he was young, Michael was repeatedly beaten by a man who always wore a blue tie. The beatings were severe and Michael almost died from one of them. One day when Michael was an adult, a man with a blue tie accosted Michael on the street, yelling at him and clenching his fist. Michael responded by pulling out a gun and killing the man. Michael has been charged with murder.

Assuming we are in a jurisdiction that recognizes imperfect self-defense, which of the following is correct?

A. Michael is not guilty of any crime.

B. Michael is guilty of manslaughter, not murder.

C. Michael is guilty of murder because he intended to kill the victim.

D. Michael is guilty of murder if he was negligent in shooting his victim.

ANALYSIS.   From all the facts, it appears that Michael honestly feared the man in the blue tie. However, a reasonable person probably would not have feared imminent death. Under the all-or-nothing approach, Michael would be guilty of murder if his fear was not reasonable. By contrast, in jurisdictions that recognize imperfect self-defense, Michael would have a chance at conviction on a lesser charge. Since this jurisdiction recognizes imperfect self-defense, let's look at the options with that in mind.

A is incorrect because no jurisdiction adopts a purely subjective approach to self-defense. To do so would give paranoid defendants a license to kill. If imperfect self-defense applies, **B** is the correct answer. The charge is reduced to manslaughter. However, let's check out the other options before selecting a final answer.

C is wrong because an imperfect self-defense claim reduces the charge from murder to manslaughter, and this jurisdiction recognizes imperfect self-defense. Finally, **D** is completely off the mark. If a person is negligent, he is not guilty of murder. The applicable charge is involuntary manslaughter or negligent homicide. Therefore, **B** is the correct answer.

E.   Model Penal Code approach

Throughout this chapter, we have mentioned the Model Penal Code approach to the elements of self-defense. This section summarizes the differences between the Model Penal Code and the traditional common law approach to self-defense.

In general, the Model Penal Code takes a more flexible approach to the requirements of self-defense. In particular, Model Penal Code §3.04(1) allows for self-defense when "the actor believes such force is immediately necessary for the purpose of protecting himself against the use of unlawful force by such other person on the present occasion."

1. Honest belief by actor that force is necessary

As you can see, the Model Penal Code standard is very subjective. Yet it too has limitations. If the defendant is reckless or negligent in his belief that force is necessary, he cannot claim self-defense for a reckless or negligent offense, such as manslaughter or negligent homicide. Model Penal Code §3.09(2). But the same defendant could still reduce a murder charge on an imperfect self-defense theory. Model Penal Code §3.09(3).

2. Relaxed immediacy requirement

The immediacy requirement is also more relaxed. Under the Model Penal Code, the immediacy of the threat facing the actor is viewed from the actor's standpoint, with the usual limitation that if the actor is recklessly or negligently mistaken, he does not have a defense to crimes requiring recklessness or negligence. Model Penal Code §3.09(2).

3. No excessive force

The Model Penal Code allows deadly use of force in self-defense when the defendant is confronted with deadly force, the risk of serious bodily injury, or a serious crime such as kidnapping or violent rape that often lead to serious injury. This is slightly broader than the traditional common law approach.

4. Initial aggressor rule

The Model Penal Code recognizes the initial aggressor limitation on the use of self-defense. The Model Penal Code's initial aggressor rule differs from that of the common law in that (1) the actor is only considered an initial aggressor if he initially had the *purpose* of causing death or serious bodily harm; and (2) the right to use self-defense can be regained if the initial aggressor does not use it in the same part of the encounter in which he was the provoker.

5. Duty to retreat

Finally, Model Penal Code §3.04(2)(b)(ii)(1) recognizes a duty to retreat before using deadly force if the defendant knows he can do so with complete safety. However, there are three situations in which the actor is *not* obliged to retreat: (1) he is in his dwelling and is not the initial aggressor; (2) he is in his workplace and the other person is not a co-worker; or (3) he is a public officer using force in the performance of his duty.

Law professors are famous for using multiple-choice questions to test the differences between the common law and Model Penal Code approaches. Try the next question to see how you would do on such a question relating to self-defense.

QUESTION 11. Richard the Lamehearted.   Richard is tired of working as a grunt associate at a law firm. He decides to take a few months off to explore the world. His first stop is a convention of Hell's Angels motorcycle members. The men at the convention are big, covered in menacing-looking leather outfits with chains, and obviously strong. One of them spots Richard and yells, "Hey, grunt! You'd better run before I put tracks down your back." Richard starts to quake as he quickly flashes back to the high school bully who had knocked Richard over with a bicycle. Richard grabs a nearby crowbar and throws it at the biker's head. It hits the man's bare skull and immediately kills him. Another biker yells at him, "What the heck did you do? He was just kidding you. The guy was harmless as a flea." Richard is charged with negligent homicide, but argues self-defense.

Which of the following is correct?

A. In a Model Penal Code jurisdiction, a defendant is entitled to a full self-defense whenever he honestly fears for his life.
B. In a Model Penal Code jurisdiction, Richard is guilty of murder because he was at least negligent in killing the victim.
C. In a common law jurisdiction, Richard had a duty to retreat before using deadly force and the threat of force was not imminent enough to support self-defense.
D. In a Model Penal Code jurisdiction, Richard is guilty of negligent homicide if he should have realized that his victim did not pose a true risk.

ANALYSIS. In this question, Richard may have honestly feared for his life, but his fear appears unreasonable and not based on a threat of imminent death. Under the common law approach, this would not have been enough for self-defense. Under the Model Penal Code approach, defendants can argue self-defense, but not if Richard is charged with a crime that requires only negligence or recklessness.

Therefore, **A** goes too far. It is the wrong answer because the Model Penal Code approach, although more subjective, does not create a purely subjective standard for self-defense to all crimes. Here, Richard is charged with negligent homicide. If he is negligent in assessing the risk of harm to him, he cannot argue a full self-defense.

B is wrong because negligence does not support a charge of murder under either the common law or the Model Penal Code. Don't forget — if a defendant is negligent in assessing the risk, he is guilty of a crime that only requires negligence. Murder requires much more.

C is a bit tricky. Although common law probably would have found the threat not to be imminent enough to allow self-defense, it is not true that there was a duty to retreat under common law. Therefore, **C** is partially incorrect.

D is the right answer. If Richard acted negligently with regard to the nature of the threat or its imminence, he is guilty of negligent homicide.

F. Defense of another

Once you understand self-defense, defense of another is actually quite easy. There are two primary approaches to this issue. The majority approach is that a defendant may use force in defense of a third person if he reasonably believes such force is necessary to defend that third person from imminent unlawful attack. The minority approach requires that the defendant "stand in the shoes" of the person being defended and that the defense fails unless the person under attack would have had the right to use self-defense.

For example, imagine a situation in which the defendant comes upon two men struggling. *A* has *B* on the ground and is pummeling him. The defendant rushes in on *B*'s behalf and attacks *A*. It turns out that *A* is an undercover police officer trying to subdue *B*.

Under the general approach, as long as the defendant was reasonable in his belief that *B* had the right to use self-defense, the defendant will be justified in defending *B* by using force against the officer. From the defendant's perspective, *B* was faced with a serious, imminent threat and could either defend himself or have someone help defend him.

However, under the minority approach, the defendant must be correct about *B*'s right to use self-defense. Since suspects do not have the right to hit officers, *B* would not have had a right of self-defense and the defendant could not argue defense of another. See *People v. Young*, 210 N.Y.S.2d 358 (1st Dept. 1961), *rev'd*, 11 N.Y.2d 274 (1962). These courts do not want to encourage people to take the law into their own hands.

Model Penal Code §3.05 allows defense of another when the defendant believes the use of force is necessary. The standard is a subjective one, although the defendant is responsible for any reckless or negligent offense if he is wrong in his assessment of the situation. Model Penal Code §3.09(2).

As we near the end of this chapter, let's try a question regarding the defense of another. It is a good way of recalling the general requirements of self-defense because, at minimum, the person who defends another must believe that the person he is helping would have the right to defend himself.

QUESTION 12. Damsel in distress. Daniela is a skilled karate master and drug dealer. Solly is the neighborhood Good Samaritan; he does not know Daniela or her background. One day, Solly sees Daniela struggling with two men. Honestly believing the men are trying to mug Daniela, Solly rushes to her rescue. He pounces on the men and injures them. As it turns out, the men are undercover narcotics officers and they were trying to arrest Daniela but she was resisting with her fancy karate moves.

If Solly is charged with assaulting the officers in a jurisdiction that follows the majority approach

A. he can argue defense of another.

B. he can argue self-defense.

C. he cannot argue defense of another because Daniela did not have the right to resist the officer.

D. he cannot argue defense of another because Daniela was not under an immediate threat of harm.

ANALYSIS. Stop for a minute and think. Do we really want to punish Solly because he honestly (and reasonably) believed he was helping a woman who was being mugged? Your common sense tells you no and so does the general rule regarding defense of another. If Solly honestly and reasonably believed that Daniela was entitled to use self-defense, he can come to her aid. Let's look at the options.

A is looking very good. However, make sure to look at all the options before selecting your final answer. **B** is wrong because Solly was not defending himself; he was defending another person. **C** is wrong because even though Daniela may not have had a right to defend herself, Solly could reasonably believe that she had the right to defend herself. If he did, he could still argue defense of another. Finally, **D** is wrong because it does not accurately reflect the facts of the case. Daniela was under an immediate threat of harm. It may not have been an unlawful harm, but it was a harm. Therefore, based on what Solly knew, she would have been entitled to argue self-defense. **A** is the correct answer.

G.   The Closer: Expert testimony in self-defense cases

To what extent should expert testimony be allowed to support a defendant's claim of self-defense? Consider, for example, a battered woman who killed her abuser while he was sleeping. Jurors are apt to believe that the threat was not imminent and she did not act reasonably because her abuser was incapacitated at the time that he was killed. Defense counsel routinely request that they be allowed to introduce expert testimony explaining "battered woman's syndrome" (BWS) and how it supports the defendant's self-defense claim.

Initially, courts were reluctant to admit this type of expert testimony for fear that it would usurp the function of the jury. However, courts have been increasingly willing to allow expert testimony regarding BWS and related claims. In some jurisdictions, courts limit expert testimony to whether the defendant suffers from BWS and the general effects of that syndrome. Other courts allow the expert to state an opinion as to whether the defendant believed using deadly force was necessary. Finally, some courts allow an expert to testify that not only did the defendant believe she was under an immediate threat, but given the nature of BWS, such a belief was reasonable. See, e.g., *People v. Humphrey*, 91 P.2d 1 (Cal. 1996).

Although courts now admit expert testimony on various syndromes, including BWS, there remains a concern that the law will begin to officially sanction self-help by victims of abusive relationships. It is one thing to feel some compassion toward the abused and be willing to excuse her behavior, but it is another thing to recognize these killings as justified because the abuser no longer deserved to live.

The closer challenges the reaches of self-defense by applying it to a syndrome case and considers the effects of allowing expert testimony in such cases.

QUESTION 13. Battered law students.   Havi feels miserable. Her professor, Laurie, has emotionally and physically abused her during Havi's first year of law school. Havi thought she could get ahead by working for Laurie; however, she soon became Laurie's slave. Laurie repeatedly berates Havi and threatens to block her graduation from law school if she ever complains about Laurie's actions. When Laurie is really agitated, she points a gun at Havi and tells her she must finish her assignments. As a result of Laurie's abuse, Havi has stopped sleeping and eating. One day, when she cannot take it anymore, and Laurie is deep in thought, Havi hits Laurie over the head. When Havi is charged with assault, she claims self-defense.

In her defense, Havi wants to call an expert on battered law-student syndrome. The prosecutor objects to such testimony. Which of the following rulings would help Havi the most?

A. The expert is allowed to testify as to the general miserable conditions of law students.
B. The expert is allowed to testify as to a syndrome called "battered law-student syndrome" and how it makes law students feel like they are under a constant threat.
C. The expert is allowed to testify that insomnia and lack of appetite are symptoms of battered law-student syndrome.
D. The expert is allowed to testify that Havi honestly and reasonably believed that Laurie would hurt her and that such beliefs are consistent with battered law-student syndrome.

ANALYSIS.   My daughter, Havi, forced me to write this question. Although a bit strained, it makes the point. There can be all types of syndromes relating to self-defense. The goal for the defendant is to get the jury to believe the defendant's claim that she feared the decedent and to find that such a fear was reasonable under the circumstances.

In the closer, each of the answers presents testimony that would help the defendant. However, only one would help the most. **A** gives the jurors some background on the defendant's situation, but does not explicitly address why her fears of imminent harm were sincere and reasonable. **B** gives the defense a little more credibility by giving a label to Havi's condition. **C** further helps the jurors see that Havi is not lying when she describes the effects of Laurie's actions on her. However, **D** is the best answer because it goes straight to the legal standard for self-defense — under the circumstances, did Havi have an honest and reasonable fear of imminent harm?

 # Levenson's Picks

1. Crazy Tom	**B**
2. Not too fast	**D**
3. Shrimp cocktail	**A**
4. Big, bad, and brown	**D**
5. Pea shooter	**C**
6. He had it coming	**C**
7. "I'll show you"	**D**
8. Macho, macho man	**B**
9. Subway escape	**D**
10. Blue tie	**B**
11. Richard the Lamehearted	**D**
12. Damsel in distress	**A**
13. Battered law students	**D**

17

Defense of Property, Law Enforcement Defenses, and Necessity

Necessity alters the law. — Russian proverb
Necessity became a law. — American proverb
Necessity has no law. — English proverb
Necessity is stronger than choice. — Welsh proverb

CHAPTER OVERVIEW
A. Defense of property/Defense of habitation
B. Law enforcement defenses
    1. Right to arrest
    2. Use of force for crime prevention
    3. Use of force for apprehension and arrest
C. Necessity
    1. Choice of evils
    2. No apparent alternatives
    3. Imminent threat
    4. Defendant chose the lesser harm
    5. Not self-created
    6. No contrary legislative intent
    7. Model Penal Code versus common law approach
    8. Special necessity cases — Prison escapes

D. The Closer: Marijuana and medical necessity

⊕ Levenson's Picks

T his chapter addresses some additional justification defenses, including the key justification defense of necessity. Remember, as justification defenses, the theory behind each of these defenses is that the defendant has actually made the right decision by her actions, even though she ordinarily would be guilty of violating the law.

A. Defense of property/Defense of habitation

At common law, deadly force could be used to prevent any type of felony, including burglary. However, the rule evolved over time. Now, only limited force may be used to defend property. Property is not as valuable as human life, so deadly force may *not* be used *solely* to defend property. But, deadly force may be used to protect a resident when her home is being invaded. Therefore, if lives could be at risk, deadly force may be used against an intruder in self-defense. If the home is unoccupied, deadly force cannot be used.

These rules are well illustrated by the famous case of *People v. Ceballos*, 12 Cal. 3d 470 (1974). In *Ceballos*, the defendant set up a spring gun in his garage to protect his property. Two unarmed youths broke into the garage and the spring gun went off and shot one in the face. The defendant was charged with assault with a deadly weapon. The defendant argued defense of property, but this defense was denied because potentially lethal force may not be used to defend property.

Ceballos also claimed self-defense because he lived above the garage. He argued that it was just coincidence that he was not home when the youths broke into the garage. The court rejected this claim as well. Because the defendant was not home, there was no immediate threat to his personal safety. The only threat was to his property, and that did not justify the use of the spring gun.

Would Ceballos be entitled to argue self-defense if he had been home and the burglars were breaking into his bedroom? Probably, yes. If a burglary occurs when a resident is present, and the resident fears for his life, self-defense may apply. However, there is no right to shoot burglars just because they might steal something. Life is always more valuable than property.

The Model Penal Code offers very detailed rules for the use of force in defense of property. Model Penal Code §3.06. These rules allow deadly force when

- a person is being dispossessed of her dwelling; or
- an intruder is committing a felony against the defendant's property (like burglary or arson) and has used deadly force against the defendant; or
- attempting to use force, other than deadly force, to prevent a felony would expose the defendant to substantial risk of serious bodily harm.

Each jurisdiction must decide when deadly force may be used in protection of a residence. The general rule is that deadly force may not be used to protect property alone; it is permissible, however, to protect a person in her dwelling when it is unclear whether the threat is to the person or the possessions. In fact, some jurisdictions recognize a presumption that a home intrusion poses a threat to the safety of the occupant.

QUESTION 1. Not the Monet.   Rodney lives in a mansion with a fabulous art collection. He uses two pit bulls to protect his home. When Rodney is on vacation, Charlie tries to break into the home to steal one of Rodney's priceless Monets. Charlie is mauled to death by the pit bulls; Rodney is charged with homicide.

Which of the following is incorrect?

A. Pit bulls are like spring guns—they cannot be used to protect property alone.
B. Rodney could use the pit bulls because he has a right to protect his possessions.
C. Rodney could have used the pit bulls if he had been home when the break-in occurred.
D. The use of pit bulls was not justified even though Charlie was burglarizing Rodney's home.

ANALYSIS.   This question often trips up law students because the use of protection dogs is so common and students are tempted to apply tort concepts, such as "assumption of the risk," to the analysis of the criminal case. In fact, you should think of the dog as a spring gun. Dogs have no judgment; they just spring on their attackers. Unlike a defendant who uses self-defense after determining that he is under attack, dogs simply react to any threat. Because deadly force is not allowed to prevent the theft of property, it is improper to use vicious dogs when no people are present.

This question is also tricky because it asks which of the answers is *in*correct. Here, **A** correctly states how pit bulls are viewed. They are like spring guns and cannot be used to protect property alone. **A** is a correct statement and thus not the answer to this question.

By contrast, **B** is an incorrect statement of the law. A defendant may not use lethal force to protect possessions. As an incorrect statement of the law, **B** appears to be the right answer to this question. A quick check of **C** and **D** verifies that **B** is the right answer. Rodney could have used deadly force if he had been home because then he would have been protecting both his person and his possessions. **D** is also an accurate statement of the law and helps highlight why we do not allow a defense in these situations. We do not allow the use of lethal force in response to any wrongdoing; rather, it is only justified when human life is at risk. **B** is an incorrect statement of the law, but the correct answer to this question.

B. Law enforcement defenses

We sometimes must determine whether a police officer was justified in her use of force or crossed the line separating law enforcement from criminal behavior. Certainly, police have greater authority to use force than the average citizen. However, that authority is not unlimited. Police officers violate the law when they use force in an unjustifiable manner.

The phrase "law enforcement defenses" actually covers a myriad of situations. We examine (1) the rights of police and others to restrain a person; (2) the rights of police and others to use force in crime prevention; and (3) the rights of police and others to use force to apprehend a person.

1. Right to arrest

Police officers have the right to arrest a defendant for a felony or misdemeanor if the arrest is based on probable cause. Felony arrests can be made with or without a warrant, regardless of whether the officer witnessed the crime. However, misdemeanor arrests can only be made if the officer witnessed the offense. If a police officer makes a lawful arrest, he has a full defense to a charge of false imprisonment.

Private persons have common law authority to make "citizen's arrests." A citizen may arrest another person if (1) the offense was a felony or a misdemeanor involving breach of the peace; (2) the crime actually occurred; and (3) the citizen making the arrest reasonably believed that the suspect committed the offense. As with the police's authority, citizen arrests for misdemeanors are only lawful when the citizen witnessed the offense. A lawful citizen's arrest is a full defense to a charge of false imprisonment.

The issue that sometimes arises in these cases is whether the citizen still has a law enforcement defense if she is wrong about whether a crime has occurred or the arrestee has committed it. Under common law, a crime must have occurred or there is no defense. However, if a crime occurs, and the defendant makes a reasonable mistake as to who committed that crime, the defendant still has a law enforcement defense to false imprisonment.

2. Use of force for crime prevention

Both police officers and private citizens may use force to prevent a crime from being committed, so long as the force used is necessary to prevent the commission of the crime. If the force was necessary, the intervening individual cannot be charged with assault.

Deadly force may not be used to prevent a misdemeanor; however, it is allowed to prevent a felony. In most jurisdictions, the right to use deadly force is limited to the prevention of certain particularly dangerous felonies. For example, a defendant could use deadly force to prevent a rape or robbery, but not to prevent a shoplifter from escaping with the goods. In some jurisdictions, deadly force is justified anytime the defendant reasonably believes that the person is about to commit a felony and deadly force is necessary to prevent the felony.

3. Use of force for apprehension and arrest

Throughout the early days of common law, law enforcement officers had the right to use deadly force against anyone reasonably believed to have committed any felony. The officer could use deadly force even if the circumstances did not require her to do so to apprehend the suspect. This approach was countenanced because felons lost all rights (including to their lives) once they committed the felony. Moreover, the approach made some sense at the time because all felonies were capital offenses.

Under modern common law, an officer can only use deadly force if the suspect is attempting to escape after a felony and the use of such force is necessary to apprehend him. Many jurisdictions have limited this rule further by allowing deadly force only to apprehend a felon who has committed a dangerous felony.

Private persons have even less of a right to use deadly force in apprehending a felon. To prevent vigilantism, a private person generally can only use deadly force to apprehend a felon when the felony was dangerous, the felon was warned, and the private person is correct in her assessment that the suspect committed the crime and deadly force was necessary.

It is relatively rare for people to be charged with homicide for the unlawful use of force during an apprehension. However, if such a charge is brought, the appropriate defense to raise is the law enforcement defense.

There is a constitutional dimension to the law enforcement defense as applied to police officers. (Private individuals are not subject to constitutional restrictions.) In *Tennessee v. Garner*, 471 U.S. 1 (1985), officers responded to a call that there had been a break-in at a home. When they arrived, an officer saw someone run into the backyard. The officer gave chase and the 15-year-old suspect then tried to scale a fence. Although the officer could see that the suspect had no weapon in his hands, the officer shot him anyway and killed him. The boy's family then sued.

The Supreme Court held that the use of deadly force in that situation was unreasonable under the Fourth Amendment, even though Tennessee law allowed the use of deadly force to arrest suspected felons. The Supreme Court established the rule that deadly force can only be used to effectuate an arrest if the officer reasonably believes the fleeing suspect poses a threat of death or serious bodily injury to others and such force is necessary to prevent escape. For example, if a suspect has a weapon and threatens either the officer or someone else, deadly force can be used.

The bottom line is that non-deadly force may always be used to arrest a fleeing suspect. However, deadly force may only be used if the suspect poses a threat of serious harm or death to others.

Time to try a law enforcement defense question. Keep *Tennessee v. Garner* in mind when you answer the question.

QUESTION 2. High school stunt.   Pablo and his friend, Marisa, decided to play a prank on their high school teacher. Dressed like Bonnie and Clyde and carrying fake machine guns, they went over to the teacher's house. First, they appeared to plant a grenade near the door of the house. (It turned out to be a fake.) Then, they started to hotwire the teacher's car to steal it. The teacher spotted the intruders and called the police. When the police arrived, they drew their guns and warned Pablo and Marisa to freeze. Instead, Pablo and Marisa panicked and started to run away in the direction of the local school. Fearing that the thieves would hurt the school children, Officers Ron and Don shot Pablo and Marisa, killing them both. When it was discovered that Pablo and Marisa were just engaged in a prank, were carrying fake weapons, and had planted a fake grenade, Officers Ron and Don were charged with negligent homicide.

If Ron and Don raise a law enforcement defense, they are likely to

A. win because Pablo and Marisa had committed a felony by attempting to steal their teacher's car.

B. win because the officers reasonably believed that Pablo and Marisa posed a serious danger and had just committed a dangerous felony.

C. lose because *Tennessee v. Garner* prohibits the use of deadly force against underage suspects.

D. lose because they were wrong when they concluded that Pablo and Marisa posed a serious risk to others.

ANALYSIS.   The key to doing well on this question is realizing that officers still have a law enforcement defense even if their assessments are wrong, so long as they are reasonable in making those assessments. However, officers do not have a blank check to shoot any fleeing felon. Let's see which answer best reflects the modern common law rules, as informed by *Tennessee v. Garner*.

A is wrong because it goes too far. Officers cannot shoot and kill a suspect just because she has committed a felony. Deadly force may only be used when the suspect continues to pose a danger to others.

B seems to incorporate all the elements of the law enforcement defense. First, it states that the officers believed Pablo and Marisa had committed a dangerous felony *and* continued to pose a serious danger. Second, it allows for the fact that officers can have a law enforcement defense even when they are wrong in their assessments, as long as their beliefs are reasonable. In this question, when the suspects appear to have grenades and machine guns, and are running toward a school, it is probably reasonable to believe that the suspects have committed a dangerous felony and continue to pose a serious danger. **B** is the correct answer.

C is wrong because *Tennessee v. Garner* does not establish a per se rule prohibiting the use of deadly force against children. The suspect in that case happened to be 15 years old, but that was not the decisive factor. The decisive factor was that the officer had ascertained that the suspect did not have a weapon, but shot him anyway.

Finally, **D** is wrong because the law enforcement defense does not require that the officers' assessment be correct. It only has to be reasonable.

C. Necessity

A person who commits a crime because it is the lesser of two evils can invoke the "necessity" defense. The necessity defense is also called the "choice of lesser evils" defense. Self-defense, which we studied in Chapter 16, is actually a type of necessity defense because the defendant is allowed to commit what would otherwise be a wrongful act (killing someone) in order to save her own life. However, the defense of necessity has broader reach than self-defense cases. It applies to a myriad of situations in which the defendant faces two evils and chooses the better alternative.

For example, consider a mountain climber who is caught in an unexpected snowstorm. To avoid certain death, she breaks into a cabin to seek shelter during the storm. Ordinarily, breaking into someone else's cabin would be the crime of trespass. However, because it was the lesser evil in this situation, and the defendant did not have any other alternatives, her actions were justified and she will be afforded a necessity defense.

The rationale for the necessity defense is that even well-drafted statutes cannot account for every real-life situation. Sometimes, unexpected circumstances force people to engage in illegal behavior. If a defendant faces a choice of evils and chooses the one least harmful to society, the defendant is not deserving of punishment. She is not blameworthy and does not need to be deterred since she made the right choice. As you can probably infer, jurors in necessity cases act as supplemental lawmakers. By applying the necessity defense, they are essentially saying that had the legislature known the precise facts of the defendant's case, it probably would have made an exception to the law's general prohibition against this conduct.

There are many situations in which a necessity defense may arise. Some typical ones include distributing needles to prevent HIV transmission; stealing food to avoid starvation; violating traffic laws to speed a patient to the hospital; breaking a dam to avoid the flooding of a village; and, in the eyes of some courts, escaping from prison to avoid intolerable conditions. Throughout this chapter we examine these and other examples of necessity cases.

To avoid allowing all defendants to argue necessity, strict requirements are imposed on asserting this defense. Under common law, there were four requirements for a necessity defense:

1. Defendant faces a choice of evils.
2. There are no apparent legal alternatives.
3. There is an imminent harm.
4. Defendant chooses the lesser evil.

Additionally, the courts impose the following restrictions on the use of necessity:

5. Defendant did not create the necessity.
6. There has been no legislative decision to prohibit the necessity defense in that situation.

We examine each of these requirements and how they apply in a necessity defense case.

1. Choice of evils

Necessity applies only when a defendant confronts a choice of evils. The choice is ordinarily between suffering immediate physical harm and committing a crime. For example, imagine the captain of a ship caught in an unexpected storm. To prevent his ship from sinking and the crew from dying, he illegally docks in an embargoed port. The captain could successfully argue a necessity defense.

In your casebook, you might find even more extreme examples of necessity. For example, in the famous case of *Regina v. Dudley & Stephens,* 14 Q.B.D. 273 (Eng. 1884), the defendants argued necessity when accused of eating a fellow raft-mate while trying to survive in a lifeboat. Although the defendants did not prevail with their necessity defense, they were undoubtedly faced with a choice of evils.[1]

---

1. Several explanations have been given as to why the defendants failed in their necessity argument in *Regina v. Dudley & Stephens.* Some commentators argue that the case stands for the principle that the defense of necessity may never be used in homicide cases. P.R. Glazebook, *The Necessity Plea in*

Economic necessity alone is insufficient to justify the commission of a criminal act. For example, a defendant who has lost his job cannot argue necessity to justify stealing money from his neighbor.

Recognizing that the defendant faced a choice of evils is the first step toward deciding if a necessity defense is applicable. Try the following question to see if you are confident about this first step.

QUESTION 3. Color TV.   Herman is addicted to television. He watches sports on television whenever he can. Herman is very excited about the upcoming Super Bowl game; he plans to be glued to the television. An hour before the game, Herman's television goes on the fritz and he loses the signal. Desperate to watch the game, Herman breaks into his neighbor's house and plants himself in front of his neighbor's television. When the neighbor learns of what Herman has done, he has Herman prosecuted for trespass.

Can Herman claim a necessity defense?

A. Yes, because he was desperate to watch the Super Bowl.
B. Yes, because he did not destroy anything in his neighbor's house.
C. Yes, because he had no other choices at the time.
D. No.

ANALYSIS.   Even though Herman may love to watch sports, his situation does not qualify for a necessity defense. His inability to watch the Super Bowl does not qualify as the type of harm that triggers a necessity defense. In fact, it is even less than an economic harm, which also would not qualify.

Accordingly, **A**, **B**, and **C** are incorrect answers. **A** is wrong because no matter how desperate Herman was to watch the Super Bowl, missing the game does not really qualify as an "evil" for purposes of a necessity defense. **B** is also incorrect because trespass is a crime, regardless of whether Herman destroyed anything in his neighbor's home. **C** is wrong because there was another choice. He could have read a book! By now you get the point. The necessity defense is reserved for when a defendant faces serious harm. **D** is the correct answer.

2. No apparent alternatives

For the necessity defense to apply, the defendant must not have any lawful alternative. Necessity is a defense of "last resort." If there is a lawful alternative, the defendant must select it.

English Criminal Law, 30 Cambridge L.J. 87 (1982). Others suggest that the seamen had other options, such as drawing lots to decide who would die. Cf. *United States v. Holmes*, 26 F. Cas. 360 (C.C.E.D. Pa. 1842). Finally, some suggest that the harm was not sufficiently imminent. No cases, however, argue that the sailors did not face some extreme choice of harms.

For example, imagine that a defendant's wife is very ill. Rather than taking her to the emergency room, he breaks into a local pharmacy for drugs. Because the defendant had a lawful alternative, the defense of necessity does *not* apply.

Of course, a defendant needs to know that there is a lawful alternative. For example, imagine that a defendant is in a remote location when a medical emergency arises. The defendant thinks that the only thing he can do is administer a controlled substance to his wife, even though it would ordinarily be unlawful for him to do so. As it turns out, a doctor is camping nearby and could have lawfully administered the drugs. In this situation, there was an alternative, but it was not *apparent.*

Issues regarding the existence of apparent alternatives often arise in conjunction with whether the threat is immediate. However, before we get to that discussion, let's try a question regarding this second requirement for a necessity defense, that there be no lawful alternative.

QUESTION 4. No need for war. Puya is an activist against the war. He feels that every day the war threatens to kill more innocent victims. In an effort to try to stop the war, Puya decides to organize a group of protestors to break into the local ROTC office and destroy the equipment inside. When he is apprehended, Puya argues that he was faced with a choice of evils. He could either allow the killing of innocent people or destroy the ROTC office in protest.

Puya's necessity defense is likely to

A. succeed if the government is fighting an unjust war.
B. fail because he could have protested the war by writing to his Congressional representative.
C. succeed if he chose the lesser of the two evils.
D. succeed because the alternatives might not be as effective as what he did.

ANALYSIS. Necessity is often raised in civil disobedience cases. For several reasons, the defense usually is not successful. One of the key reasons it fails is because the protestor always has the alternative of working for change through the legislative process. This process offers a lawful alternative to the defendant's illegal acts.

Therefore, **A** is the wrong answer. Disagreement with government policy does grant one a license to violate the law.

C and **D** are also wrong because they do not adequately address the issue of whether there were apparent lawful alternatives. **C** is wrong because even if Puya is right and the war is a greater evil, he should be seeking change through the normal democratic processes. **D** is also incorrect, although it is a little trickier than **A** and **C**. A defendant is required to choose a lawful alternative over an unlawful alternative, even if the defendant does not believe it would be as effective as breaking the law. Unless it is so ineffective that it is really no alternative at all, the legal option comes first.

B is the correct answer. If Puya disagrees with the war, he should write his Congressional representative. Later in this chapter we return to civil disobedience cases. However, you can already see why it is difficult to raise a necessity defense in those cases.

3. Imminent threat

To succeed with a necessity defense, the defendant must face an immediate threat. If the threat is in the future, the defendant likely has time to find another alternative.

For example, the defendant hears on the radio that a hurricane with torrential rains and flooding will hit in the next 72 hours. The defendant has time to evacuate, but instead she runs to her neighbor's house and steals his plywood and boat. After the storm, the defendant is charged with trespass and theft. She is not likely to prevail with a necessity defense because the threat was not imminent enough when she engaged in her illegal conduct. The defendant had a lawful alternative to her illegal actions; she could have evacuated.

Now, try this next question on whether the threat facing the defendant was sufficiently imminent that the defendant did not have any apparent alternatives to her illegal actions.

QUESTION 5. Mountain man. Donald is hiking in the mountains when he learns that a storm is headed his way. Donald has time to hike down the mountain and avoid a dangerous situation. However, Donald does not choose that option. Instead, he breaks into a cabin to shelter himself from the coming storm. When he is charged with trespass, Donald tries to argue a necessity defense.

Donald's necessity defense is likely to

A. fail because the threat of physical harm was not imminent.
B. fail because he had a lawful alternative.
C. fail because Donald was not under an imminent threat and he had a lawful alternative.
D. succeed because Donald was faced with a choice of evils.

ANALYSIS. This question is not particularly difficult if you have good multiple-choice test-taking skills. It is critical when answering any multiple-choice question that you examine ALL of the answers before selecting your answer. In this question, there are two reasons why Donald's defense will not succeed. Therefore, the best answer to the question is the answer that includes both reasons.

Donald's necessity defense will not succeed, in part, because at the time he broke into the cabin, the harm he faced was not imminent. Accordingly, **A** is partially correct. However, **B** is also partially correct because Donald had a lawful alternative. He could have hiked down the mountain. So, neither **A** nor **B** is the correct answer to this question. Rather, **C** includes both rationales and is therefore better. Donald is going to lose because the threat was not imminent and he had a lawful alternative. Once you understand that, it is apparent that **D** is wrong. **D** wrongly assumes that whenever a defendant is faced with a choice of evils, the defendant automatically gets to argue necessity.

4. Defendant chose the lesser harm

By far, the most important element of necessity is that the defendant, when confronting the choice of evils, chose the lesser harm. The defendant's actions can only be justified if society agrees that she made the right decision under the circumstances.

The defendant's selection is evaluated by an objective standard. In other words, it is insufficient that the defendant honestly believed that she picked the lesser evil. Society, as represented through the jury, must agree as well.

It is not always an easy task to decide whether a defendant has chosen the lesser evil. However, there are a few guidelines to help with this decision. First, loss of life is a greater evil than loss of property. Therefore, if a defendant needs to destroy property to save lives, she may very well be able to argue a necessity defense. For example, assume a defendant sees a small child suffocating in the back of a car. In order to save the child, the defendant breaks the windows of the car. The defendant would have a full defense to a charge of damaging the car.

Second, many jurisdictions do not allow a necessity defense in homicide cases. It is simply too difficult to decide which of two lives is more valuable. However, even when courts do allow a necessity defense in homicide cases, they only do so when a defendant risks fewer lives to save more lives.

Even this calculus is not simple. For example, assume four mountain climbers are roped together. One falls. Unless she is cut loose, all of them will die. One way you could look at this situation is that one hiker must be sacrificed to save the others. However, there is another way to look at the situation. Instead of three versus one, you could think of it as "every man for himself." In other words, each hiker stakes his life against the hiker who will be sacrificed. In that case, the calculus is one versus one three times. Since one life is not more valuable than another, necessity would not be allowed. Because of the difficulties inherent in allowing necessity in homicide cases, many jurisdictions completely reject its application.

QUESTION 6. Breaking dike. Margaret realizes that the dam at the top of the hill is about to break. If it breaks one way, it will kill many people in the town. However, if Margaret dynamites the dam to break in another direction, it will flood Perry's farmlands and destroy all his crops, but no people. Margaret dynamites the dam, knowing full well that Perry's crops will be destroyed. She wishes she had had time to talk to Perry before taking action, but the dam was going to break at any minute.

If Margaret is charged with destroying Perry's property, she

A. has no defense because she did not have Perry's consent to flood his lands.
B. has no defense because the threat was not imminent.
C. has a defense because she saved the lives of the townspeople.
D. has a defense because Perry is unlikely to complain.

ANALYSIS. Since this question did not require you to apply necessity in a homicide situation, it should be pretty straightforward. The townspeople's lives are more important than Perry's crops. (*Note:* It would be an interesting twist if Perry were to starve to death without those crops. Then, you would have to fall back on whether, in that jurisdiction, one innocent life can be sacrificed to save others.) The threat was imminent (the dam was about to break) and there did not appear to be any lawful alternatives. In fact, Margaret appears to have made the right choice. The lesser evil is to flood the crops.

Accordingly, **A** is wrong. While ordinarily it would be a crime to destroy property without the owner's permission, the whole point of a necessity defense is to allow a defense when the defendant is forced to choose the lesser of two evils and does so. Intuition should tell you that Margaret is not a criminal; she is a heroine.

B is also wrong. Don't fight the facts of a question. The facts dictate that the dam could break at any moment. Accordingly, there was an imminent threat.

It must be **C** or **D**. Between those two, **C** is much better. If Margaret is not entitled to argue necessity, she has committed a crime, regardless of whether the victim chooses to prosecute. However, **C** accurately reflects the correct necessity ruling in this case. Margaret is allowed the necessity defense because she chose the lesser of two evils.

5. Not self-created

A defendant cannot create her own necessity to violate the law and then rely on the necessity defense to justify her actions. For example, assume that a defendant negligently starts a fire. The only way to stop the fire from burning down the entire neighborhood is to divert the fire toward his neighbor's vacant guest house. If the defendant were charged with arson for burning down the guest house, under common law, the defendant could not assert the necessity defense.

The Model Penal Code approach to this element is slightly different. Under Model Penal Code §3.02, a defendant who creates her own necessity does not lose the right to assert the defense for intentional crimes. She may, however, be prosecuted for reckless or negligent offenses if she was reckless or negligent in creating the situation. Model Penal Code §3.02(2). Thus, the defendant in the above hypothetical has a necessity defense to arson (if defined as the intentional destruction of a structure), but he could still be charged with criminal mischief for his negligent act of starting the fire.

The discussion in this area may remind you of the initial aggressor rule under self-defense (see Chapter 16). Self-defense is a type of necessity defense. The necessity is created to kill one's attacker. However, if a defendant provoked the deadly attack as the initial aggressor, she created her own necessity and is not entitled to argue self-defense.

The following question focuses on this element outside the self-defense context. The same basic principle applies — the defendant cannot create her own necessity.

QUESTION 7. Back to the mountain. Let's return to the "Mountain man" hypothetical of Question 5. This time, however, imagine that Donald knew before he started climbing the mountain that a storm was fast approaching. Disregarding the danger, Donald hiked up the mountain anyway. When the storm hit, Donald broke into the cabin to save his life.

Under the common law, is Donald entitled to a necessity defense?

A. Yes, because he was faced with an imminent threat of death.
B. Yes, because the threat to his life was caused by a natural phenomenon.
C. No, because once the storm hit, he did not choose the lesser harm.
D. No, because he brought the necessity upon himself.

ANALYSIS. Although Donald was eventually threatened with deadly harm if he did not violate the law, he is still *not* entitled to argue necessity because he brought the problem upon himself.

A is wrong because it ignores the fact that there would have been no threat of imminent death if Donald had not gone up the mountain. He knew a violent storm was approaching; he brought the danger upon himself.

B is wrong, although it does raise an interesting point. Necessity cases, as opposed to duress cases (see Chapter 18), usually involve a threat from an act of nature. However, they need not do so. A threat created by another person may trigger a necessity defense. Moreover, just because a natural phenomenon creates a threat, it does not mean that there is an automatic necessity defense. The defendant can argue necessity only when he has met all the requirements of the defense. In this question, the defense fails because Donald created his own necessity.

Even though **C** denies Donald the defense, it is incorrect because it offers the wrong rationale. Once the storm hit, saving his life by breaking into the cabin was the lesser harm. But Donald has no defense because he brought the problem upon himself. **D** is the correct answer.

6. No contrary legislative intent

If there has already been a legislative judgment that a particular necessity does not outweigh society's support for a particular law, the defendant may not argue necessity in violating that law. For example, assume that a defendant wants to distribute clean needles to addicts in a city park in order to stem the spread of HIV. The city has an ordinance prohibiting the distribution of needles in a public place. If the legislative history of that ordinance indicates that the city rejected the argument that more harm is prevented by distributing the needles than by banning distribution, the defendant is not entitled to argue necessity.

The problem of contrary legislative intent often arises in *civil disobedience cases.* Defendants in civil disobedience cases often claim that violating the law is justified by an interest in preventing a greater harm to society. The necessity defense does not usually work in these cases. In addition to the fact that the defendant can seek to change the law through the legislative process, there has already been a decision by society that the "evil" the defendant seeks to prevent is not an evil at all or, at least, not a lesser evil.

For example, assume a defendant wants to protest a war. He chooses to do so by violating the Selective Service laws and not registering. Necessity is not a defense because there has already been a legislative judgment (by congressional declaration of war) that it is a just war.

As we discuss in the closer, contrary legislative intent may also undermine claims of medical necessity to use certain illegal drugs. If there is a debate in society over the legality of a practice, it is up to the legislature, not an individual defendant, to resolve the question.

Some courts have suggested that there is a difference between direct and indirect civil disobedience. *Direct civil disobedience* occurs when a defendant violates the very law he is protesting. For example, when African Americans in the 1960s violated segregation laws, they were engaging in direct civil disobedience. Some courts are more willing to allow a necessity defense in those cases because the legislative system cannot be counted on to fairly assess society's wrongs. Most courts, however, are not receptive to the necessity defense in that situation because it still undermines legislative intent.

Certainly, a defendant is unlikely to prevail with a necessity defense if she only engages in an act of *indirect civil disobedience.* For example, if a person obstructs the operations of the Internal Revenue Service to protest an unpopular war, the criminal action is not directly related to the harm the defendant is seeking to prevent and so necessity is not a defense. See *United States v. Schoon,* 971 F.2d 193 (9th Cir. 1991).

Although defendants may not satisfy all the requirements for a necessity defense, they may still try to argue it in hopes of getting *jury nullification.* Jury nullification occurs when the jury acquits a defendant out of sympathy for her cause, regardless of whether the evidence demonstrated that the defendant had a valid defense. Accordingly, in civil disobedience cases, the prosecutor often files a pretrial motion to prohibit the defendant from raising a necessity defense so that the jury will not be misled into believing the defendant's acts were justified.

The next question focuses on the last element of necessity. Don't forget that the necessity defense is designed for those situations in which the law has not anticipated the defendant's predicament and the defendant therefore may commit a lesser evil to prevent greater harm.

QUESTION 8. Katya's caper. Katya objects to the government's use of satellites in military operations. She fears that the satellites have helped the military target and kill thousands of Iraqis through the use of so-called smart bombs. To prevent more killing, Katya sneaks into a military base and destroys one of its computers. As it turns out, the computer she destroys is not one that controls global positioning of the satellites.

Does Katya have a necessity defense?

A. Yes, because destroying property is a lesser harm than killing thousands of people.
B. Yes, because Katya honestly believed that by destroying the computer she would save human lives.
C. No, because the government had decided that the war was justified.
D. No, because war is the lesser harm.

ANALYSIS. You immediately should have identified this question as a civil disobedience question in which it is unlikely that the defendant will be able to succeed with a necessity defense. One of the reasons such a defense would be unsuccessful, although clearly not the only reason, is that there has been a legislative judgment that the war is in the United States' best interest.

Accordingly, **A** is wrong. Even if destroying property is a lesser evil than killing thousands of people, a necessity defense is not permitted if there has been a legislative judgment that the war serves a greater good. **B** is also wrong. Katya's sincerity is not at issue. Even if she acts in good faith, this is not a decision for her to make.

The choice comes down to **C** and **D**. When you get to this point, it should be easy. Few people would say that war is the lesser harm. However, the government has already decided the war is justified. Accordingly, **C** is the correct answer.

Let's try another question outside of the war protestor arena. Although different, you should be able to recognize some of the common issues that arise in necessity defenses.

QUESTION 9. Save the pets.   People Adoring The Animals (PATA) has been lobbying the legislature for years to ban the use of animals in testing drugs and cosmetics. So far, PATA has not been successful. To keep the pressure on, PATA stages a raid on a local cosmetic company's test lab. Several members of PATA break in and release the animals from their cages. As the animals run free, they damage the equipment in the laboratory. Some of the equipment is broken, but no one is hurt.

The PATA members are prosecuted for malicious mischief. If they raise a necessity defense, they are likely to be found

A. guilty because they created their own necessity.
B. guilty because experimenting on animals is not evil.
C. guilty because they should not have taken the law into their own hands.
D. Not guilty.

ANALYSIS.   If you found this question a little more challenging, it is probably because the answers did not have the magic language you were looking for: "defendant's actions were barred by legislative intent." Yet, even without this obvious answer, you should have been able to pick the right answer.

A is wrong because there is no indication that the PATA members created their own necessity. They are not the ones who decided to harm the animals. **B** is also wrong because experimenting on animals may be evil. The real question is whether society finds it to be the greater evil.

The reason the PATA members cannot avail themselves of the necessity defense is that they should not have taken the law into their own hands. Their efforts to get the law changed have failed. Until they are successful in their legislative efforts, they must obey the laws. The correct answer is **C**.

7. Model Penal Code versus common law approach

There are several ways that the Model Penal Code approach to necessity is different. Model Penal Code §3.02 provides that a defendant may engage in criminal conduct to avoid harm if (1) the harm avoided is greater than the harm done; (2) there is no specific prohibition to the use of a choice of evils defense for this offense; and (3) there is no clear legislative purpose to exclude the choice of evils defense in the defendant's situation. Generally, the Model Penal Code necessity defense is broader than the common law defense in three ways:

1. There is no imminency requirement. Imminency of harm is one factor to be considered in deciding whether the defendant had a lawful alternative.
2. There is no absolute prohibition on self-created necessity. A defendant does not lose her necessity defense even if she created the situation. Instead, the defendant is only responsible for any crimes of recklessness or negligence caused by her actions.
3. Necessity is available in homicide prosecutions. While most common law jurisdictions do not allow the necessity defense in homicide situations, the Model Penal Code does not have this limitation.

Here is a quick question to test your understanding of the differences between the Model Penal Code and common law approach to the necessity defense.

> **QUESTION 10. Plane crash.** Four people survive a plane crash in a remote section of the snowy Andes Mountains. For two weeks, they have not spotted any help. In all likelihood, they will all die within days unless they eat something. One of the four is much weaker than the others and is likely to die even if he eats something. The other three decide to kill him and feed on his flesh so that they can survive. They do so and survive until they are rescued a couple of weeks later.
>
> When charged with murder, can the survivors argue a necessity defense?
>
> A. Yes, under both the common law and the Model Penal Code.
> B. Yes, under common law, but not under the Model Penal Code.
> C. Yes, under the Model Penal Code, but not under the common law.
> D. No, under the Model Penal Code or common law.

ANSWER. This question is a prime example of the differences between the common law rules of necessity and those under the Model Penal Code. First, because this is a homicide case, most common law jurisdictions would not allow the defendant to assert necessity. Second, there is a problem with imminency. The question states that the defendants would die in several days. It is unclear whether that is imminent enough to meet the common law standards.

The best answer to this question is **C**. The Model Penal Code would allow the defendants to argue necessity. They acted to save more lives by sacrificing one life and the threat of death was imminent under the relaxed Model Penal Code standard. **A** and **B** are wrong because a common law jurisdiction would probably not allow a necessity defense in this situation; **D** is wrong because the Model Penal Code would allow such an argument to be made.

8. Special necessity cases — Prison escapes

It is not uncommon when an inmate escapes from intolerable prison conditions for her to argue that she acted out of necessity. There is a debate in the legal community as to whether escape cases really fall under the doctrine of necessity or if they are covered by duress (discussed in Chapter 18). Some courts favor the use of a duress analysis because they don't want to send the message that escape is ever justified; other courts allow the necessity approach because they agree that the defendant made the choice of lesser evils. Of course, the defendant couldn't care less about the theoretical basis for her defense. She just wants to avoid an escape conviction. Because many courts do view escape cases as a special type of necessity defense, we analyze them in this chapter.

Defendants who escape from custody may argue that they needed to do so because they faced a choice of evils (intolerable conditions versus escape) and had no apparent lawful alternatives (because any attempts to complain would be ignored or result in retaliation). To ensure that prisoners will choose the lawful alternative if and when it is available, an extra requirement is added to escape cases. *The rule is that a defendant must surrender herself immediately upon reaching a place of safety. United States v. Bailey*, 444 U.S. 394 (1980) (adopting surrender rule of *People v. Lovercamp*). If a defendant does not immediately surrender herself, she cannot argue necessity, regardless of the threat faced by staying in custody.

The surrender requirement was added to prevent a flood of inmates from escaping from prison and arguing that bad prison conditions forced them to do so. Inmates can justify escape under this standard, but only to prevent immediate harm. However, the necessity defense is not a "get out of jail free" card for inmates.

QUESTION 11. Jail house blues. Wally is a prisoner in Lompoke Prison. He has been repeatedly and brutally sexually assaulted by bigger inmates at the prison. Although he has complained to the prison authorities, they have not been able to prevent the ongoing attacks. Wally's attackers are now threatening to kill him because he snitched. At dinner, one of them said,

"By the end of tonight, you will wish you were never born." Wally knows he cannot stay so he sneaks out of prison on a laundry truck that evening. He then starts hitchhiking his way back to his home across the country. He stays with various friends along the way. Three weeks later, Wally is picked up by the authorities. He is charged with escape.

Does Wally have a necessity defense?

A. Yes, because he faced intolerable conditions.
B. Yes, because he contacted the authorities when he was in prison.
C. No, because he brought the situation upon himself by ending up in prison in the first place.
D. No, because he failed to surrender to the authorities immediately after he escaped.

ANALYSIS.   Be careful. Even though you may feel a great deal of sympathy for Wally, he does not necessarily have a necessity defense. He must meet all the requirements of a necessity defense, including surrendering himself *immediately* upon reaching a place of safety. In this question, Wally makes the cardinal error of failing to surrender immediately after he escapes. By staying with his friends three weeks without surrendering, Wally loses the right to argue a necessity defense.

Therefore, **A** is wrong because even if Wally faced intolerable conditions, he did not meet all the requirements for a necessity defense in a prison escape case. **B** is also wrong because the rules required that Wally contact the authorities *right after* his escape, not just when he was in prison.

There is an interesting choice between **C** and **D**. Some students are tempted to select **C** because they argue that prison isn't meant to be a comfortable place. Even if that is the case, being sentenced to prison should not and does not mean that an inmate should be sentenced to sexual abuse or death. **C** is therefore incorrect. The correct answer is **D**. By failing to surrender himself immediately after his escape, Wally became ineligible for the necessity defense.

D.   The Closer: Marijuana and medical necessity

One of the hottest issues in the courts right now is whether a defendant who uses marijuana for medicinal purposes should be allowed to argue necessity. The Supreme Court has rejected a federal medical necessity defense. See *United States v. Oakland Cannabis Buyers' Coop.*, 532 U.S. 483, 121 S. Ct. 1711, 149 L. Ed. 2d 722 (2001). See also *Gonzales v. Raich*, 125 S. Ct. 2195

(June 6, 2005) (federal prohibitions override more liberal state drug laws). However, there may still be a chance for defendants in state marijuana prosecutions to argue necessity. By trying the closer, you can see the difficulties in using a necessity defense to argue that the medicinal use of marijuana is justified.

QUESTION 12. Clearing the smoke. Jane suffers from a terrible and incurable disease that leaves her in perpetual pain. She has tried all kinds of conventional medicines, but none of them helps. Finally, she decides to use some marijuana. The marijuana gives her some relief. There is an effort to legalize marijuana in her state, but so far the law has not been reformed.

Which of the following issues is likely to pose the greatest problem for Jane in arguing a necessity defense to illegal possession of a controlled substance?

A. Jane did not face a choice of evils.
B. The legislature has not legalized marijuana use.
C. Jane did not face immediate harm.
D. Jane brought the necessity upon herself.

ANALYSIS. As this question starkly highlights, the greatest problem in securing a necessity defense to marijuana charges is the legislative decision to criminalize marijuana use, regardless of its medicinal effects. **A** is wrong because Jane did face a choice of evils. She could stay in perpetual pain or use an illegal drug. **C** is wrong because the harm to Jane was constant and therefore always immediate. Of course, **D** is wrong because Jane did not bring the disease upon herself. However, Jane will still lose because the legislature has thus far rejected legalizing marijuana use. Notwithstanding the poignancy of her situation, Jane does not have the right to take the law into her own hands. **B** is the correct answer.

Despite the fact that Jane's situation does not meet the legal requirements for necessity, her counsel is still likely to try to argue her situation to the jury. In essence, the defense would be seeking jury nullification of a law it feels is being unfairly applied in Jane's case. In response, prosecutors can be expected to argue for a court ruling barring the defense argument.

 # Levenson's Picks

1. Not the Monet	**B**
2. High school stunt	**B**
3. Color TV	**D**

4.	No need for war	B
5.	Mountain man	C
6.	Breaking dike	C
7.	Back to the mountain	D
8.	Katya's caper	C
9.	Save the pets	C
10.	Plane crash	C
11.	Jail house blues	D
12.	Clearing the smoke	B

18

Duress

We are free up to the point of choice; then the choice controls the chooser.

—Mary Crowley

CHAPTER OVERVIEW

I n Chapters 16 and 17, we discussed justification defenses. For those defenses, the law forgives the defendant because he has made a choice that society believes is the most beneficial under the circumstances.

There is a second category of defenses known as the *excuse defenses.* Excuse defenses rest on a different theoretical framework. The defendant may not have made the right choice by committing a crime, but we excuse his behavior because he was not fully able to control his behavior. Excuse defenses include duress, intoxication, insanity, diminished capacity, infancy, and entrapment. In this chapter, we focus on the first of these — the duress defense.

A.   Introduction to duress defense

If a defendant is compelled to commit a crime by another person's use of force or threat to use force, the defendant may claim the defense of "duress." Another name for the duress defense is "coercion."

A very simple example helps to illustrate the duress defense. Assume *A* threatens to shoot *B* if *B* does not burn *C*'s car. If *B* goes ahead and destroys *C*'s car, *B*'s actions may be excused because he acted under duress.

The rationale behind the duress defense is that the defendant has acted without a fair opportunity to exercise free will and therefore is not deserving of punishment. The defendant was forced by another to commit the crime.

The duress defense differs from the necessity defense in two key ways. First, defendants who act under duress may not necessarily have chosen the lesser evil, but we nonetheless excuse their behavior. For example, assume that *A* threatens to break *B*'s leg if he does not sell drugs to neighborhood kids. We may not be able to determine whether a broken leg for *B*, or drugs for the children, is the lesser harm. However, the defendant would still be permitted to use the duress defense because he was forced to commit the crime.

Second, the duress defense differs from the necessity defense because the duress defense ordinarily applies when a *person* has forced the defendant to commit a crime. Most (but not all) necessity defenses arise when defendants are forced to choose to commit a lesser evil because of an act of nature.

There are strict limitations on use of duress defenses. Also, the elements of the defense differ under the common law and Model Penal Code. First, we review the common law requirements of duress. Then, we compare them to the Model Penal Code requirements.

B.   Common law requirements

There are six elements of duress under common law:

1. A threat of death or serious bodily harm
2. Imminently posed
3. Against the defendant or a close friend or relative

4. That creates such fear that an ordinary person would yield
5. The defendant did not put himself in the situation; and
6. The defendant is not seeking to raise the defense to a homicide.

1. Threat of death or serious bodily harm

The common law only allows a duress defense when there is a threat of death or grave bodily harm. For example, assume that a person threatens to kill the defendant unless he carries drugs onto a plane. This threat would satisfy the first requirement of a duress defense. Compare, however, a defendant who receives a cryptic phone call threatening to make the defendant's life "very unpleasant" if he refuses to carry the drugs. Under the common law, this threat would be too vague to qualify for a duress defense, although threats of lesser harms may qualify under the Model Penal Code approach.

Threats of economic harm never qualify for a duress defense at common law or under the Model Penal Code. For example, if an employer threatens to fire the defendant unless she participates in a fraud scheme, the defendant is *not* entitled to argue "economic necessity."

Let's try a question that focuses on this first element of a duress defense.

QUESTION 1. Bank or burn.   Patrick lives by himself in a small home. Keenan threatens to burn Patrick's house down while Patrick is at work if Patrick does not help Keenan commit a bank robbery. Assuming that Keenan is ready and able to carry out this threat, does Patrick have a duress defense if he helps Keenan commit a bank robbery?

A. Yes, because Keenan has coerced Patrick into helping with the robbery.
B. Yes, because Keenan has threatened Patrick with severe harm.
C. No, because Keenan's threat does not create a duress defense.
D. No, because duress is not a defense to property crimes.

ANALYSIS.   Although you may feel sorry for Patrick, empathy alone does not create a duress defense; the defendant must act under threat of death or serious bodily harm. In this question, you are told that Keenan is going to set fire to Patrick's house when Patrick is at work. Accordingly, the only threat made is one of damage to the defendant's property. A threat of damage to a person's property is insufficient to raise a duress defense. With this thought in mind, let's look at the answers.

A is wrong because it allows Patrick a duress defense. Don't forget that the word *coercion* is a term of art with the same legal meaning as *duress.* Coercion does not encompass all forms of pressure put on a defendant to commit an offense.

B is also wrong. "Severe harm" is not the same as specifying that the harm will be physical harm or death. Read the words carefully before selecting an answer.

C seems to be on target because it states there is no duress defense available, but we must examine D before selecting our final answer. As it turns out, D is wrong. Duress may certainly be a defense to a property crime. However, in order to be a valid defense, there must be a threat of serious bodily injury or death. That was missing here, so C is the correct answer.

2. Imminence

At common law, the threatened harm must be imminent. In other words, a threat that "someday I'll get you" would not qualify for a duress defense at common law. The threat must be of immediate harm, as gauged by the court and jury.

For example, imagine a situation in which a defendant is told that if he does not smuggle drugs, his family will have a terrible accident "real soon." Under common law, the threat of future harm would probably be too distant to qualify for a duress defense. The law expects a defendant to find another way to deal with the threat — such as going to the authorities — rather than just agreeing to commit a crime.

> **QUESTION 2. Tony Toscano.** An anonymous caller tells Tony Toscano that if he does not help with a fraud scheme, he and his wife "will have to jump at every shadow" because one day the caller will catch up with them and break every bone in their bodies. Fearing for both his safety and that of his wife, Tony helps with the fraud scheme.
>
> Is Tony entitled to assert a duress defense at common law?
>
> A. Yes, because it was reasonable for him to be in fear for his life.
> B. Yes, because it was inevitable that he would be attacked.
> C. Yes, because the crime he committed was not violent.
> D. No.

ANALYSIS. As we will see later, Tony may do better under the Model Penal Code standard that does not require strict imminence. However, under the common law standard, Tony has a problem. Although it may be inevitable that he and his wife will be attacked, the attack is not imminent. The law therefore expects Tony to respond in another way, such as by calling the authorities. Tony would not be entitled to argue duress.

A is wrong because even if Tony reasonably feared for his life, the actual threat of harm was not imminent. Accordingly, the duress defense would not apply. **B** is wrong because an "inevitable" threat is not the same as an "imminent" threat.

C is wrong, although many students select it because they think different rules of duress apply for different types of crimes. Under the common law, imminency is a requirement for a duress defense to all types of crimes. Under the Model Penal Code, imminency is only one factor in determining whether the duress defense is available. The more dangerous the crime that the defendant committed, the more immediate and serious the harm he faced must be. Since this question specifically asks the reader to answer under common law, **D** is the correct answer.

3. Threat against defendant or close friend

Under early common law, the defendant himself had to be threatened to trigger a duress defense. Later, the common law included threats to close friends or relatives of the defendant. The Model Penal Code allows threats to any person to trigger duress.

For example, imagine that a defendant receives word that his neighbor will be seriously injured unless the defendant participates in a scheme to defraud the telephone company. Under common law, the defendant would not have a duress defense because the threat was not against him or a close family member. The goal of this limitation is to restrict the use of duress. The defense is reserved for those extreme situations in which a defendant is concerned about the welfare of those nearest and dearest to him.

QUESTION 3. Poor teacher. Azadeh has a great deal of admiration for her professor. Although she doesn't socialize with her professor, Azadeh recognizes the contributions that he makes to society. Earl approaches Azadeh and tells her that he will harm Azadeh's professor unless Azadeh helps Earl break into the registrar's office.

If Azadeh helps Earl, does she have a duress defense under common law?

A. Yes, because Earl has threatened someone Azadeh respects.

B. No, because Azadeh is not related to or close friends with her professor, nor is there an indication that the threatened harm was imminent.

C. Yes, because Earl is the person who should be punished.

D. No, because Earl did not make a serious threat.

ANALYSIS. This question should have been relatively easy for you. Admiration and respect for someone do not create the type of relationship that triggers a duress defense at common law. Therefore, Azadeh will not have a duress defense, even though she felt some responsibility for her professor. As we see later in the chapter, the answer to this question might be very different under the Model Penal Code.

A is wrong because it is not enough that Azadeh respects the person being threatened. Common law looks for an ongoing, close relationship — the type of relationship that would drive most people to commit a crime to safeguard that person.

B looks like the right answer, but let's check **C** and **D**. **C** is a red herring. Although Earl should be punished, that doesn't mean that Azadeh is off the hook. Both defendants may have some criminal responsibility for the break-in. At sentencing, the court can take into account their relative culpabilities.

D is wrong because Earl did make a serious threat — he threatened to harm the professor. Nothing in the facts indicates that he was not sincere about this threat. Make sure not to add facts into your multiple-choice questions.

The correct answer is **B**. Azadeh may have believed she was doing a noble thing, but technically she did not meet the common law requirements for duress.

4. Fear created would cause an ordinary person to yield

The most important factor in a duress defense is the one we are about to discuss. Both the common law and Model Penal Code impose a reasonableness requirement on the duress defense. The common law standard is usually more objective than that of the Model Penal Code. Under the common law, the threat to the defendant must induce **"such a fear as a man of ordinary fortitude and courage might justly yield to."** *United States v. Haskell,* 26 Fed. Cas. 207 (Pa. Cir. Ct. 1823). Jurisdictions differ on how much the jury is to consider the defendant's individual conditions and circumstances in making this decision.

For example, imagine a battered woman whose abusive spouse tells her that he will beat her up unless she steals some groceries before he returns from work. The ordinary person would simply leave the home before the person who has made the threat returns. However, a battered woman may find it reasonable to believe that she has no choice but to commit the crime to protect herself, and often her children, from harm. Under a strict common law approach, the battered woman will have difficult time asserting a duress defense. She must convince the court to change the standard from whether a "man of ordinary fortitude and courage" might yield, to the more subjective standard of whether a "reasonable woman in the battered woman's situation" might yield.

The common law has been reluctant to relax this standard for fear it will give everyone an excuse to succumb to threats. Society's preference is that persons resist pressures to commit crimes. Common law wants to reserve duress for those situations in which defendants truly have no choice but to succumb to a threat.

QUESTION 4. Tony Toscano again. Let's return to the hypothetical about Tony Toscano.[1] As you may recall, an anonymous caller warns Tony that if he does not assist with a fraud scheme, he and his wife will be "jumping at shadows" because the caller will one day track them down. This time the caller adds, "Tony, buddy, forget about my last call. Just help us out and believe me, you'll be a lot happier." Tony still trembles when he thinks about the call.

If Tony does not call the police, but instead helps with the fraud scheme, will he have a duress defense under common law standards?

A. Yes, because Tony feared immediate use of force against a loved one.
B. Yes, because he did not commit a serious crime.
C. No, if Tony's fear was not reasonable.
D. No, because it is never justified to put one's interest ahead of society's interests.

ANALYSIS. This question, like its predecessor, shows the weaknesses in Tony's duress defense. He still has the problem of a vague threat. Now, however, it is not just that the threat is not imminent. It also appears that Tony's fear may not be reasonable. The caller has said that Tony would be a lot happier if he committed the fraud, but he has backed off from threatening any harm. Let's look at the choices.

At first, **A** looks like a good choice because Tony's trembling demonstrates that he is honestly afraid of the caller. However, it is missing the very element that we have been studying in this subsection. It is not enough that the defendant fear the use of force — this fear must be reasonable. Therefore, **A** is not the right answer.

B is wrong because the level of crime committed does not determine whether a defendant's fear must be reasonable. The Model Penal Code approach has a sliding scale under which a defendant may be able to commit a lesser crime based on a lesser showing of duress. However, the requirements of the common law duress defense are firm, regardless of the crime the defendant is accused of committing.

D is wrong and it should have been simple for you to see why. It has one of those absolute words that should alert you to be careful before selecting this answer. Rarely are answers that include "always" or "never" correct. In this case, **D** is incorrect because one can occasionally put one's interests

---

1. Both this question and Question 2 are loosely based on the facts of *State v. Toscano*, 378 A.2d 755 (N.J. 1977).

ahead of society's. That is exactly how the duress defense is different from necessity. In duress cases, even if the defendant did not act in a way that maximized the benefits to society, we may still excuse his behavior because he was not in full control of his free will.

C is the correct answer. To have a valid duress defense, Tony must honestly fear the threat and it must be the type of threat that would cause a reasonable person to respond as Tony did.

5. Defendant did not put himself in situation

As with the necessity defense, a defendant cannot create the need to fall back on a duress defense. Under the common law, a defendant who negligently puts himself into a situation in which he is forced to commit a crime forfeits any duress defense.

For example, assume that a defendant joins a gang. He knows when he joins this gang that they routinely engage in illegal behavior. The head of the gang approaches the defendant and asks him to help the gang rob a liquor store. Defendant refuses. The leader then threatens to hurt the defendant's family if the defendant does not participate. Under the common law, the defendant cannot assert a duress defense to the robbery because by joining the gang, he voluntarily put himself into a situation in which he would be pressured to participate in the robbery.

Try the next question and determine whether the defendant forfeited his right to argue duress.

QUESTION 5. **Get rich too quick.** Barry and Michael are good friends and securities brokers. Barry has known Michael for years and knows that he is a schemer. In fact, Barry has learned that Michael has recently been doing some questionable trades for Mafia members. Barry asks Michael if he can "get in on some of the action." Michael puts Barry in contact with his client. Michael warns Barry, "These guys play hardball." Barry responds, "Don't worry about me. I can handle it."

Barry then calls Michael's Mafia connection. They tell him about some illegal trades they want Barry to make. When Barry balks, the Mafia members say, "Don't make us hurt you. We know where you live and where you work. One false move and you and your family are dead."

Barry goes ahead and puts together the illegal transactions. When he is caught, he argues duress. Based on these facts, Barry is likely to be

A. guilty, because he is not entitled to argue duress.
B. not guilty, because he and his family were threatened with death.
C. not guilty, because he and his family were threatened with imminent death.
D. not guilty, because he and his family were threatened with imminent death and a reasonable person would have succumbed to the threats as well.

ANALYSIS.   This question can be a little tricky if you don't know what to look for in the answers. Unlike some of the other questions you have answered in this book, this question does not give a specific answer that articulates the precise reason it is the correct answer. Rather, it has three distracters and then the correct answer. The three distracters are **B**, **C**, and **D**. From reading just those answers, you would think that the focus of the question is on whether there was an imminent threat that the defendant honestly and reasonably believed he must yield to by committing illegal behavior. However, the text of the question indicates why none of these answers is correct. Even if Barry faced an imminent threat of death that a reasonable person would have yielded to, this defendant loses the privilege to argue duress because he brought the situation upon himself. He voluntarily put himself in a situation in which he could be pressured to commit the crime.

B, **C**, and **D** are wrong answers because none of them deals with the true issue raised by the question — did Barry forfeit his duress defense by putting himself in a situation in which he would be pressured to commit a crime? Only **A** answers that question, even though the specific reason Barry does not get the duress defense is not articulated in the answer. **A** is the correct answer.

6. Homicide situations

The common law strictly precludes the use of a duress defense in murder cases. For example, assume a man has taken several people hostage. He approaches one of the hostages and threatens to kill her small child unless the woman takes a knife and slits the throat of yet another hostage. If the woman slits the throat of the other hostage, she does not have a duress defense to murder, even though it is understandable why she decided to comply.

In a few jurisdictions, the defendant may argue *imperfect duress* in a homicide case to mitigate murder to manslaughter on the theory that a defendant who kills under duress lacks malice and is acting under extreme emotional distress. See, e.g., *Wenworth v. State*, 349 A.2d 421, 427-428 (Md. Ct. Spec. App. 1975); but see *People v. Son*, 93 Cal. Rptr. 2d 871 (Cal. App. 2000). However, most courts simply reject any type of duress defense in a homicide case.

Courts are divided as to whether duress is a defense to *felony murder*. For example, imagine that a defendant is compelled to participate in a robbery. During the robbery, one of the other robbers accidentally shoots a bystander. In many courts, if the defendant can successfully argue that he is not guilty of the robbery because he acted under duress, he is not guilty of the felony murder. See, e.g., *State v. Hunter*, 740 P.2d 554 (Kan. 1987). Other courts do not recognize a duress defense to the felony murder. See, e.g., *State v. Rumble*, 680 S.W.2d 939 (Mo. 1984).

QUESTION 6. Terrible decisions. For Gary, it is a terrible nightmare. Intruders have seized him and his family. They have affixed bombs to each of the restrained victims and threaten to detonate them if Gary does not drive with an intruder to the mayor's office and assassinate the mayor. Gary feels like he has no choice. Reluctantly, he goes with the assailants to the mayor's office. He can hear his wife and kids sobbing on a walkie-talkie that the assassins have brought with them. He hears the intruders guarding his family starting to count down, "10, 9, 8, 7, 6, 5, 4 . . ." Finally, Gary kicks open the mayor's door and shoots him.

Gary is charged with murder. He argues that he acted out of duress. Alternatively, he argues a necessity defense. Which of the following is true under the majority common law approach to both of these defenses?

A. Gary would have a necessity defense, but not a duress defense.
B. Gary would have a duress defense, but not a necessity defense.
C. Gary would have both a duress and necessity defense.
D. Gary would have neither a duress nor necessity defense.

ANALYSIS. Once again, you are presented with a situation in which your instincts may tell you that Gary should not be convicted, but the law takes a harsher stand. Recall that in most jurisdictions, a necessity defense is not available in homicide cases, even when a greater number of people are saved by sacrificing a lesser number of innocent lives. Likewise, no duress defense is permitted for a homicide. Gary's best hope would be in a jurisdiction that recognizes an imperfect duress defense. If the court allowed such a defense, Gary might be able to reduce his charge to manslaughter. Alternatively, Gary could argue for leniency at sentencing or for the prosecutors to exercise their discretion by choosing not to charge him with murder in the first place.

The answer to this question is **D**. For homicides, Gary would have neither a duress defense nor a necessity defense.

C. Additional issues: Mistaken threats and brainwashing

Before we compare the Model Penal Code approach to the common law approach to duress, it is worth considering a couple of issues that may arise in a discussion of or a test on duress.

1. Mistaken threats

First, there is the issue of whether there must have been an actual threat or whether it is sufficient that the defendant honestly and reasonably believed that there was a threat. For example, imagine a case in which a caller tells the defendant that captors have his wife and will kill her unless the defendant immediately robs the local bank. The defendant robs the bank. In fact, the caller turns out to be a practical joker. So long as it was reasonable for the defendant to believe there was a threat, and a reasonable person would have yielded as well, the defendant can assert a duress defense even though, in fact, it was a false threat.

2. Brainwashing

Second, the question sometimes arises as to whether brainwashing may substitute for a specific threat against the defendant and thereby trigger a duress defense. In some jurisdictions, brainwashing is recognized as something that deprives a defendant of his free will like a physical threat does. The defendant is coerced through indoctrination, rather than by specific threats. Other jurisdictions, however, tend to view brainwashing cases simply as situations in which the defendant changed loyalties and, therefore, brought the coercive situation upon himself. Generally, it is very difficult for a defendant to prevail with a brainwashing theory of duress.

QUESTION 7. Patty Hertz. Patty Hertz is the heiress to a financial empire. She is kidnapped by radicals who oppose the policies of the establishment and hope to use her to convince others to rebel against traditional social and financial institutions. For 20 hours each day, the radicals lecture Patty on the evils of her family's financial empire. They lock her in a closet and do not let her out until she shouts at the top of her lungs, "Down with capitalist pigs. The money belongs to the people!" Desperate to get out of the closet, Patty yells the statement several times each day. After months of this treatment, Patty is told that she has a chance to prove her loyalty to her principles by helping with a bank robbery. Patty agrees, but she is arrested when the attempted bank robbery fails.

If Patty tries to mount a duress defense, she will most likely

A. succeed, because she was brainwashed into helping with the robbery.
B. succeed, because she honestly believed that she needed to help with the robbery to avoid confinement.
C. fail, because she was not threatened with serious bodily harm or death if she did not assist with the robbery.
D. fail, because she acted with complete free will at the time of the robbery.

ANALYSIS. This question demonstrates how brainwashing, like traditional physical coercion, acts to deprive a defendant of free will. However, courts are much more reluctant to allow brainwashing as a defense than they are to allow evidence of physical threats.

In this situation, Patty probably will not succeed with her brainwashing defense. Regardless of whether she honestly believed that she needed to help with the robbery to avoid confinement, unless that confinement brought the risk of serious bodily harm or death, traditional duress law would not allow for a duress defense. **A** and **B** are wrong answers.

Patty would likely fail with a duress defense. Of **C** and **D**, **C** is the much better answer. **D** is wrong because Patty did not act with complete free will at the time of the robbery. Nonetheless, because she did not face the kind of threat ordinarily necessary for a duress defense, she probably will not prevail. **C** gives the specific reason that common law will bar her defense. Quite simply, she did not face death or serious bodily harm at the time she committed her offense, notwithstanding the brainwashing.

D.   Model Penal Code approach

Throughout this chapter, we have noted that the Model Penal Code takes a slightly different approach, which makes it easier for defendants to succeed with a duress defense. In this section, we summarize the differences between the common law and Model Penal Code approaches and highlight how the Model Penal Code approach is more lenient.

Duress under the Model Penal Code (§2.09) is broader than under the common law in several ways.

First, the Model Penal Code abandons the deadly force and imminency requirements. Rather, the type of force threatened and its imminence are factors to consider in deciding whether a person of reasonable firmness in the defendant's situation would have committed the offense. Under the Model Penal Code, a threat of "unlawful force" is all that is required for a defendant to raise a duress defense. Conceivably, this may even include some of the techniques used in brainwashing. Under the Model Penal Code, the more serious the crime the defendant committed, the more serious and imminent the threat must have been for the defendant to be entitled to a duress defense.

Second, the Model Penal Code recognizes a threat to any person. Under the common law, the defendant must react to a threat to himself or to a close relative. Under the Model Penal Code, the threat may be to any person.

Third, the Model Penal Code's reasonableness requirement examines aspects of the defendant's situation. Specifically, the Model Penal Code allows the trier of fact to consider subjective factors in assessing reasonableness, including the defendant's emotional condition and previous experiences. Therefore, battered women mounting duress defenses will typically fare better under the Model Penal Code.

Fourth, a defendant under the Model Penal Code does not necessarily lose the defense if he contributed to creating the situation that ended up being coercive. *Under the Model Penal Code, the defendant retains a duress defense, unless he recklessly places himself into a situation in which it is probable he will be pressured into committing a crime.* However, if a defendant joins a gang, erroneously believing that it only engages in minor offenses, he may be able to argue duress if forced to commit a serious offense. See Model Penal Code §2.09(2).

Finally, the Model Penal Code duress defense can be applied in homicide cases. Under the Model Penal Code, there is no prohibition against using duress as a defense to murder or manslaughter.

The following chart summarizes the differences between the common law and Model Penal Code approaches to duress.

Duress Defense

Requirements	*Common Law*	*Model Penal Code*
	1. Threat of death or SBH	1. Threat of "unlawful force"
	2. Imminently posed	2. No separate imminency requirement
	3. Against defendant or close relative	3. Against any person
	4. Ordinary person would yield	4. Person of reasonable firmness in defendant's situation would yield
Limitations on Defense	1. Defendant did not put himself in situation	1. Defendant did not recklessly put himself in duress situation (if charged with crime of negligence, no duress defense if defendant negligently put himself in duress situation)
		2. Allows for application in homicide cases
	2. Not available in homicide cases	

Use this chart to help you answer the next question.

QUESTION 8. **Taxi madness.** Johnnie is a taxi driver and his job has given him no end of trouble. He has been robbed ten times in the last year. One day, he picks up a man with a stocking cap and bulge in his pocket who asks to be taken to the First National Bank. A voice inside of him tells Johnnie the man may be up to no good, but Johnnie wants the fare, so he figures he will take his chances.

When the cab pulls up in front of the bank, the man suddenly shoves a gun into Johnnie's hands and tells him to rob the bank. The stranger tells Johnnie that if he doesn't come out in ten minutes with the loot, the man will shoot the next three pedestrians he sees. Not sure if the guns are real, Johnnie decides that he'd better go in and rob the bank. When the teller resists Johnnie's demands, Johnnie pushes the teller and grabs her money. Unfortunately, the teller falls, hits her head, and dies. Johnnie is eventually charged with bank robbery and negligent homicide. (There is no felony murder law in the jurisdiction.) As it turns out, the gun being held by the man waiting in the taxi was a fake.

Which of the following is true?

A. Under the Model Penal Code and common law approaches, Johnnie would have a defense to bank robbery and negligent homicide.
B. Under the Model Penal Code approach only, Johnnie has a defense to bank robbery, but not to negligent homicide.
C. Under the Model Penal Code approach, Johnnie has a defense to negligent homicide, but not to bank robbery.
D. Johnnie has no duress defense to bank robbery or negligent homicide under either the Model Penal Code or common law standards.

ANALYSIS. Johnnie is in trouble if he needs to argue duress. Under either the common law or the Model Penal Code, he will have difficulty meeting the standards for a duress defense.

Under the common law, Johnnie is likely to fail in arguing duress because the threat was not to his close family or friends, and the case involves a homicide. Under the Model Penal Code standards, Johnnie also faces obstacles. While its requirements are generally more lenient, the Model Penal Code denies the duress defense to any defendant who recklessly puts himself into situations in which it is probable he will be coerced into illegal action. If the defendant is charged with a crime of negligence—such as in this problem—the defendant cannot claim duress if he negligently placed himself into the situation. Johnnie, because of his greed, has done just that.

Accordingly, it appears that **A** is wrong. Certainly, under the common law, Johnnie would not be entitled to argue duress. There had been no threat to him directly and it is unclear whether an ordinary person would yield to the type of the threat posed. Since **A** requires that Johnnie have a duress defense under common law, **A** is already a wrong answer.

B is also wrong, because even under the Model Penal Code Johnnie has problems with his duress defense. When Johnnie picks up the stranger, he considers the risk that the man could be dangerous, but he takes the risk because he wants the fare. By recklessly putting himself in a situation in which he might have to claim duress, Johnnie forfeits the defense.

If **B** is wrong, **C** is also wrong. Under the Model Penal Code, if a defendant is charged with a crime that only requires negligence, even negligently placing oneself in a situation in which there might be duress precludes the defendant from arguing duress. Model Penal Code §2.09(2).

D is the correct answer. Most likely, Johnnie will have a difficult time succeeding with a duress defense under either the Model Penal Code or common law standards.

E.   The Closer: Revisiting prison escapes

Finally, let's come full circle and, as we did with the defense of necessity, ask whether duress can be a (and might be the more appropriate) defense for prison escape cases. Recall from Chapter 17 that some courts prefer not to state that a defendant was justified in escaping from prison. If they did, the courts would be holding that it is a positive social good for the inmate to escape. Rather, they feel more comfortable stating that the defendant is excused from being prosecuted for the escape because he was forced by intolerable conditions to flee. Determine for yourself whether duress is an appropriate theory of defense for a prison escape case.

QUESTION 9. The great escape.   Steve is an inmate in Alcajazz Prison. He has already been brutally assaulted by fellow inmates in the prison. When he complained, the guards just laughed and turned the other way. Now, his assailants have said they will kill him because he complained to the guards. At dinner, Steve sees one of his tormentors hide a knife in his pants. Again, Steve tries to complain to the guards, but they are too busy eating. Steve hides in the dining room until everyone is gone. Then, he follows an abandoned sewage tunnel out of the prison. Steve is recaptured when he calls the local police and surrenders to them.

If Steve is charged with escape, which of the following is true?

A. He can argue a duress or necessity defense.
B. He can argue a necessity defense only.
C. He can argue a duress defense only.
D. He does not have a duress or necessity defense.

ANALYSIS. As you will see, an escape from intolerable prison conditions may satisfy the requirements for both a necessity and duress defense. The necessity defense requirements are satisfied if the defendant faced an imminent threat, he chose the lesser harm, he had no lawful alternatives, and he promptly surrendered himself to the authorities. However, the defendant may also have a duress defense. He faced a threat of serious bodily injury, it was against him directly, the threat was imminent, a reasonable person would likely yield, and so long as being convicted of a crime is not the same as putting oneself in a situation to be killed, Steve has satisfied all the duress requirements as well.

Accordingly, the answer to the closer is **A**. In real life, defendants will argue as many defenses as they can. It is not necessarily important to them whether the court finds a justification or excuse. The bottom line is the same. If the defendant is successful, he avoids a criminal conviction for a crime he was forced to commit.

Levenson's Picks

1. Bank or burn	**C**
2. Tony Toscano	**D**
3. Poor teacher	**B**
4. Tony Toscano again	**C**
5. Get rich too quick	**A**
6. Terrible decisions	**D**
7. Patty Hertz	**C**
8. Taxi madness	**D**
9. The great escape	**A**

19

Insanity

Your prodigal son has left again to exercise some demons.
—John W. Hinckley, Jr.

CHAPTER OVERVIEW

A. Competency to stand trial
B. The insanity defense
    1. Rationale for insanity defense
    2. Insanity as a legal standard
    3. "Disease or defect" of the mind
    4. Major tests for legal insanity
        a. Traditional M'Naghten test
        b. Deific command exception
        c. Irresistible impulse test
        d. *Durham* product rule
        e. Model Penal Code standard
C. Diminished capacity
D. The Closer: Covering the bases
✤ Levenson's Picks

I n a criminal case, the defendant's mental condition can be at issue in several ways. This chapter focuses on three: competency to stand trial, the insanity defense, and diminished capacity. In any given case, one or all of these may arise. As you will learn, each one has a different rationale and different requirements. Insanity and diminished capacity are excuse defenses. In principle, the defendant is seeking to be excused from her criminal behavior because of some defect in her thought processes. Competency also focuses on a defendant's mental condition, but the issue is *not* whether the defendant is culpable. Rather, the issue is whether the defendant is mentally fit — competent — to stand trial.

A.   Competency to stand trial

Before we discuss the "mental defenses," let's take a moment to understand the issue of competency to stand trial. Unlike insanity and diminished capacity, which focus on the defendant's mental state at the time of the crime, competency focuses on the defendant's mental status at the time of trial.

Time of crime - Time of trial
[Insanity and diminished capacity]   [Competency issues]

If a defendant is mentally incompetent at the time of trial, she may not be tried. Typically, the defendant is committed to a mental facility until she regains competence.

Under certain conditions, a defendant may be forcibly medicated in order to make her competent to stand trial. The Supreme Court held in *Sell v. United States*, 539 U.S. 166 (2003), that the government can only forcibly medicate a defendant to render her competent if doing so would further important government interests and is medically appropriate. Compelling government interests include the government's need to deal with the defendant's dangerousness or to ensure a fair and timely trial on serious charges. The trial court must also find that the medication is unlikely to have side effects that interfere with the defendant's ability to assist in her defense. The *Sell* decision left undisturbed a previous holding that courts must explicitly make these findings before forcibly medicating a defendant to render her competent, or refusing to allow a defendant to stop taking her medication during a trial. See *Riggins v. Nevada*, 504 U.S. 127 (1992). If a defendant is unlikely to become competent, criminal prosecution is ordinarily dropped and the authorities seek civil commitment of the defendant.

A defendant is mentally competent to stand trial if she has sufficient ability (1) to consult with her attorney and (2) to rationally understand the proceedings. *Dusky v. United States*, 362 U.S. 402 (1960). This is known as the Dusky standard.

For example, assume that a defendant is babbling and hallucinating when she is arrested for murder. The defendant may or may not have been in this condition when she allegedly committed the murder, but she certainly is in no condition to assist her lawyer in preparing for or presenting a defense at trial. If the court believes (ordinarily based on the testimony of experts) that the defendant either does not understand the proceedings or is not able to communicate with counsel, or both, the court may deem the defendant incompetent for trial.

A defendant who suffers from total amnesia, but is otherwise in full command of her faculties, presents an interesting question. Is she competent to stand trial? Most courts say she is, even though the defendant is able to do little to assist defense counsel. See, e.g., *State v. Wynn*, 490 A.2d 605 (Del. Super. 1985).

Ethically, defense counsel, as well as the prosecutor, has a responsibility to bring to the court's attention any concerns regarding the defendant's competency to stand trial. See, e.g., *Evans v. Kropp*, 254 F. Supp. 218 (E.D. Mich. 1966). The court also has a responsibility to *sua sponte* (i.e., on its own motion) address any issues regarding a defendant's competency. See *Pate v. Robinson*, 383 U.S. 375, 385 (1966).

This first question focuses on a defendant's competency for trial. To be able to answer it, you must first memorize the Dusky standard for assessing mental competency.

QUESTION 1. Where am I?   The police respond to a 911 call that a man, dressed only in shorts and talking to himself, is walking down the street. As they approach the man, they recognize him as Martin Doe, who is wanted for a string of recent, particularly bizarre rapes. The police apprehend Doe and arrest him for the rapes. At his arraignment, Doe claims he has no idea why he is in court and says he must be released immediately because he is late for tea with the Queen. Doe's lawyer requests a few minutes to talk to his client. Twenty minutes later, the lawyer comes back to the courtroom very frustrated. Doe refuses to cooperate unless the lawyer promises to use a strategy that the lawyer believes could harm Doe's case. Doe tells the court, "Okay, so I'm wanted for some rapes. That doesn't mean I should have to work with this fool. Get me a lawyer I can trust! I'll talk his ear off."

Based on this evidence alone, and without a mental competency examination, is Doe incompetent to stand trial?

A. Yes, because he thinks he has an appointment for tea with the Queen of England.
B. No, because he understands the nature of the proceedings and has the ability to assist in his defense.
C. Yes, because he committed bizarre crimes and was found walking down the street talking to himself.
D. Yes, because he may not be willing to cooperate with his new lawyer.

ANALYSIS.   Doe may have mental problems and not the greatest working relationship with his lawyer, but he is probably competent to stand trial. He appears to understand the charges and has his own view of how they should be handled.

"Competency" for the defendant does not refer to his legal abilities or judgment. It refers only to whether he is capable of having rational thought processes to assist in his defense. The standard for legal incompetency is set very high to prevent defendants from manipulating the legal system by feigning incompetency. In this case, Doe is deeply disturbed, but he is not necessarily incompetent. There is probably enough here for the court to order an expert competency examination, but this record alone is not enough under *Dusky* to require a finding of incompetence.

Therefore, **A**, **C**, and **D** are wrong. **A** is wrong because his claim to have an appointment with the Queen of England may be enough to trigger a competency inquiry, but alone is not enough to meet the Dusky standard. You must consider the other facts of the question before deciding whether Doe is competent. Later in the question, Doe states that he is willing to work with another lawyer and that he understands the charges against him. His initial comments in court do not indicate that he is per se incompetent.

C is also wrong for two reasons. First, it focuses on the wrong time period. Although a defendant's behavior at the crime scene may suggest that he continues to be mentally deranged, incompetency is concerned with his mindset at the time of the legal proceedings. Thus, a defendant may be insane at the time of a crime, but legally competent for trial. Second, merely walking around talking to oneself is not per se incompetency. Heck, many law professors have been known to act in a similar manner.

D is wrong because it is speculative. Doe has indicated that he is willing to try a new lawyer. Moreover, disagreement with a lawyer's strategy does not indicate that Doe is incompetent. Rather, it indicates that he understands and can participate in his defense, but is stubborn in his positions. Recalcitrance is not the same as incompetence.

B is the correct answer. Doe understands he is charged with rape and has the ability to assist in his defense. That is the bare standard established by *Dusky* for competency.

Once competency is established, we can consider whether the defendant has any mental defenses to the charges against him. That inquiry focuses on the two key affirmative mental defenses to crimes: insanity and diminished capacity.

B.   The insanity defense

Insanity, if proved, is a full defense to a criminal charge. An insane person is not responsible for her actions. While she may be committed to a mental institution, she is not punished under the criminal justice system.

In studying the defense of insanity, keep in mind that plenty of defendants have mental problems. Only the most severe cases qualify for an insanity defense. Depending on the standards used, it may be difficult for even an obviously disturbed individual to successfully invoke an insanity defense.

For example, you may recall the famous case of Andrea Yates, the Texas housewife who drowned her five young children. Yates had been diagnosed with acute postpartum psychosis, a condition that caused her to suffer paranoia, hear voices, and hallucinate. Despite this verified medical condition, Yates did not initially prevail with her insanity defense. Estimates are that less than 2 percent of defendants who raise an insanity defense do so successfully.

Also, keep in mind that insane persons can form mens rea; it is only that that their intent was generated by a diseased mind. The insanity defense, unlike the diminished capacity defense discussed *infra*, does not focus on whether the defendant formed the mens rea for the offense. Rather, it addresses whether a defendant whose diseased mind has caused her to form criminal intent should be punished.

1. Rationale for insanity defense

There are several reasons that the insanity defense is recognized as an excuse for criminal conduct. First, a person who does not know what she is doing or cannot control her acts cannot be deterred. It is therefore illogical to punish her. Second, while we want to incapacitate a criminally insane person, we can do so by committing her to a mental institution without adding the stigma of classifying her as a criminal. For the safety of the insane individual, as well as that of other inmates, it is better for her to be confined in a hospital, not a prison. Third, the spectacle of punishing a person who does not have control over her reason is tantamount to punishing an animal or infant who is incapable of reason. Fourth, there are historical reasons for the insanity defense. In the days of the ecclesiastic courts, insane persons were not held responsible for their actions. Fifth, and foremost, the underlying principle of criminal law is that the defendant exercises free will. The insane are deprived of free will by their mental disease or condition. Without free will, they cannot be morally responsible for their actions.

2. Insanity as a legal standard

Insanity is a *legal* standard. Although medical findings are considered in making the legal determination, ultimately, whether a person is excused because of insanity is an independent legal, social, and moral determination. In constructing legal standards for insanity, courts and legislatures consider both the standard's fairness to the defendant and the defense's impact on society. Over the past 30 years, the pendulum has swung back and forth regarding the appropriate standard for an insanity defense.

Prior to the attempted assassination in 1984 of President Ronald Reagan by John W. Hinckley, Jr., many jurisdictions had liberal insanity defense standards. However, after that incident the standards became stricter. Not only did many jurisdictions return to the traditional common law rules regarding insanity, but they also shifted the burden of proof, requiring the defendant to prove that she is insane, rather than requiring the prosecution to prove that she is sane.

3. "Disease or defect" of the mind

All the insanity tests have the same initial requirement: A defendant must suffer from a mental disease or defect of the mind. "Mental disease or defect" is also a legal, not a medical, concept. Not all diseases recognized as insanity for medical purposes qualify for an insanity defense.[1] Legal mental diseases are defined by their impact on the defendant's behavior rather than by their scientific characteristics.

A mental disease or defect is generally defined as "any abnormal condition of the mind which substantially affects mental or emotional processes and substantially impairs behavior controls." *McDonald v. United States*, 312 F.2d 847, 851 (D.C. Cir. 1962). Because this definition is vague, courts often look to a number of factors in deciding whether to classify an abnormal condition as a legal mental disease. These factors include the following:

- Does the condition have clear symptoms?
- Do the medical and scientific communities support the recognition of this condition as a criminal defense?
- Is this a condition defendants are likely to bring upon themselves?
- Is this condition easily feigned?
- How frequently will this condition be invoked for an insanity defense?
- Are there policy reasons to exclude or include this condition as a disease?

For example, compare a defendant who has paranoid schizophrenia, a well-recognized mental disease, with one who claims to be suffering from compulsive gambling disorder. Courts are more inclined to recognize schizophrenia as a mental disease or defect because it has clear symptoms, it is biologically and genetically based so defendants don't generally bring it upon themselves, it is difficult to feign, it does not involve overwhelming numbers of defendants, and the medical community supports the recognition of the condition. By contrast, courts have been reluctant to recognize compulsive gambling disorder as a mental disease or defect

---

1. This principle is illustrated well in *State v. Guido*, 40 N.J. 191 (1963), where a psychiatrist changed his mind as to whether the defendant suffered from a mental disease because of the different legal standards adopted by the court.

because there is not strong scientific consensus on its status as a disease, it potentially applies to many defendants, it is easy to feign, and gamblers are often blamed for bringing the condition upon themselves by initially choosing to gamble.

Over the years, the courts have recognized a wide variety of conditions as mental diseases or defects, including premenstrual syndrome (PMS), postpartum syndrome, multiple-personality disorder, post-traumatic stress disorder (PTSD), and general psychosis. Courts have been more reluctant to recognize battered spouse syndrome, compulsive gambling disorder, alcohol and drug addiction (unless prolonged use has permanently affected the defendant's brain), personality disorders, and psychopathy (a long history of antisocial conduct). (See Model Penal Code §4.01(2).)

Question 2 applies these initial concepts regarding the insanity defense. Keep in mind that insanity is a legal, not strictly medical, concept.

QUESTION 2. Road rage syndrome. A.J. Hoyt is charged with murder for shooting a fellow motorist on the freeway. A.J. has been in and out of therapy for mental problems. As a child, he was diagnosed as hyperactive. In defense of the murder charge, A.J.'s lawyer wants to argue insanity. He claims that A.J. suffers from a disease known as "road rage syndrome." The symptoms are that the driver is easily startled and is unable to control his temper when driving. A.J. even has a driving expert who will testify to the existence of a road rage condition and that A.J. suffers from it.

Is the court likely to allow A.J. to raise an insanity defense to the murder?

A. Yes, because he has an expert who will testify that he has a disease or defect.

B. Yes, because he was clearly enraged at the time of the killing.

C. No, because he has not proved he was schizophrenic.

D. No, because his condition does not likely meet the legal standards for mental disease or defect.

ANALYSIS. Creative lawyers seek to have the court recognize new mental conditions that excuse their clients' conduct. Here, the lawyer wants the court to consider "road rage" as a mental condition that excuses the defendant's behavior. However, the likelihood of success depends on whether the factors we identified earlier in this section support a finding that road rage is a mental disease or defect that supports an insanity defense.

There are several reasons a court would be reluctant to find road rage to be a mental disease or defect. First, it could affect many cases. Unfortunately, it is not unusual to find angry drivers on our freeways. The courts do not want to open the floodgates and let scores of drivers excuse their behavior because of their inability to control their anger while driving. Second, the medical community has yet to support the classification of this condition as a mental disease or defect. Even though A.J. may be able to find a driving expert to support his claim, the medical community as a whole does not. Third, there is an argument that drivers bring this condition upon themselves by choosing to drive in stressful situations. Fourth, it is a condition that is easily feigned. Finally, there are strong policy arguments against recognizing the syndrome. In essence, it allows defendants who are already engaged in a dangerous activity (i.e., driving) to have a ready-made defense if they lose control.

However, A.J. does have a couple of things going for him. First, he has a history of mental problems. Second, he did manage to find a behavioral expert who supports his contention. Nonetheless, it will be a challenge for A.J. to get the court to recognize his condition as a mental disease or defect.

Let's look now at the answers. **A** initially looks good. After all, A.J. was able to get an expert to testify in support of his defense. However, experts are often available for hire to support a defendant's (or prosecutor's) arguments. The mere fact that a driving expert states there is a condition called "road rage" does not mean that the court must recognize it as a mental disease or defect. **A** is wrong.

B is also wrong. Being angry is not the same as being insane. Under the heat of passion doctrine, angry defendants may be able to partially mitigate their crimes. However, it is not a per se reason for finding them insane.

The choice comes down to **C** or **D**. **D** is the better answer. **C** is wrong because a finding of schizophrenia is not a prerequisite for claiming insanity. It is only one example of a recognized disease or defect. **D** better captures the reasons A.J.'s defense will fail. After considering all the factors of the mental disease or defect test, it is unlikely that the court will recognize road rage as a legal mental disease or defect.

4. Major tests for legal insanity

Assume that the defense team is able to identify a specific mental disease or defect that is supported by the defendant's insanity argument. The next step is to determine whether, given that condition, the defendant meets the standards for legal insanity. There are several different standards for legal insanity. Each jurisdiction selects the standard it wants to apply.

a. Traditional M'Naghten standard   The traditional legal insanity test is referred to as the M'Naghten test. Under this test, a defendant is presumed sane. To prove insanity, the defendant must demonstrate

- at the time of the commission of the offense;
- the defendant was laboring under a defect or disease of the mind; and
- the defendant did not know

- the nature and quality of his acts; or
- that his acts were wrong.

See *M'Naghten's Case*, House of Lords, 10 Cl. & F. 200, 8 Eng. Rep. 718 (1843).

The M'Naghten standard emerged after a jury returned a verdict of "not guilty on the ground of insanity" in a famous case. The defendant, M'Naghten, admitted he had come to London to murder the Prime Minister, Sir Robert Peel, but mistakenly killed the Prime Minister's secretary, Edward Drummond. M'Naghten claimed he murdered Drummond because the Tories (a British political party) were persecuting him. M'Naghten hired the best psychiatrists of his day and convinced the judge to give a general jury instruction authorizing an acquittal if the defendant did not know he was doing a wicked act. When the jury acquitted, Queen Victoria ordered the House of Lords to set more definitive standards for an insanity defense. The result was the M'Naghten test.

Under the M'Naghten test, a defendant is insane if he has a mental disease or defect that caused him not to know the nature and quality of his acts or that his acts were wrong. For example, assume that a defendant thinks that he is chopping open a watermelon. In fact, he is hallucinating and he is really chopping open a person's skull. This defendant would meet the M'Naghten standard.

Likewise, if a defendant knew that he was chopping open a person's skull, but could convince a jury that because of his mental disease or defect he had no idea that his conduct was wrong, he too would have an insanity defense under the M'Naghten standard.

When the law speaks of the defendant not knowing his acts were "wrong," it means that the defendant did not know that they were either legally or morally wrong. Moral wrong is judged by society's morals, not the defendant's own deviant moral system. Thus, a defendant who claims to belong to an extreme religious sect that allows him to kill his unfaithful wife cannot argue that he did not know his conduct was morally wrong. It is the morality of society in general, not the defendant's aberrant sense of morality, that governs. See, e.g., *State v. Crenshaw*, 98 Wash. 2d 789 (1983) (defendant killed his wife on their honeymoon because he claimed she had been unfaithful and his "Moscovite" religion supported his actions; insanity defense not recognized because defendant made up his religion and he must be judged by society's general morals).

In responding to the questions posed to them, the judges in M'Naghten discussed the situation of defendants who claim to have "partial delusions." These are defendants who hypothetically have partial delusions, but are otherwise completely sane. Most courts do not treat this as a separate aspect of the M'Naghten standard because they reject the notion that a defendant could be delusional enough to satisfy the standard while, in all other aspects, be completely sane. However, if there is such a situation, the M'Naghten judges held that the defendant should be treated according to his responsibility if the delusions were real. This is referred to as the "insane delusions test." For example, if the defendant has a delusion that she is being attacked by aliens (who turn out to be her family members), she is exempt from punishment because of her demented belief that she needed to use self-defense. However, if the defendant, even in a delusional state, only believed that the aliens were threatening to tease her and she killed them in response, she still would not have a defense.

The M'Naghten test is considered the strictest of all the insanity tests because it only allows an insanity defense when a defendant has a mental disease or defect that makes it impossible for the defendant to know what she is doing or that it is wrong. If the defendant knows what she is doing and that it is wrong, but still cannot control herself, an insanity defense will fail.

To get a better sense of the application of the M'Naghten test, try the next question.

QUESTION 3. Insane Ted. Ted is a former professor who has dropped out of society and lives in a primitive shack in the woods. Occasionally, he leaves his secluded surroundings and ventures to the city where he makes mail bombs and sends them to his former colleagues. He is so notorious that he has been labeled the "Bombmaster." After Ted sends his bombs, he usually sends a note ranting about the imperialist, capitalist empire. In the notes he states, "I'm sorry that people will have to die, but the world is evil, not me." When Ted is apprehended and charged with several attempted murders, he raises an insanity defense. Ted is diagnosed as a paranoid schizophrenic.

Does Ted have an insanity defense under the M'Naghten standard?

A. Yes, because he has been diagnosed as a paranoid schizophrenic.
B. Yes, because a mental disease caused him to believe that he was right and society was wrong.
C. No, because he is not legally insane.
D. No, because he is charged with serious crimes.

ANALYSIS. Clearly, Ted is a very disturbed individual. In fact, he may even be medically insane. However, he is not legally insane unless he meets the requirements of the applicable insanity standard. In this situation, he is being judged under the strict M'Naghten standard: (1) Does Ted know what he is doing? and (2) Does he know it is wrong? As we examine the possible answers, we will see that Ted does not meet the M'Naghten insanity test because his statement reveals that he knows the nature of his acts (that he may kill people) and that his acts are considered wrong by society.

Therefore, **A** is wrong. Even though Ted has been diagnosed as a paranoid schizophrenic, he is not legally insane because this disease did not prevent him from knowing either the nature or quality of his acts or that his acts were wrong. **B** is also wrong. Ted does not have the right to act according to his own moral standards. As long as he knows that society would view his actions as wrong, he is not legally insane under M'Naghten.

The choice comes down to **C** or **D**. **D** can be eliminated because the insanity defense can apply to any crime. In this case, Ted does not get an insanity defense because, despite his mental problems, he knows the nature and quality of his acts and that they are wrong. His statement, "I'm sorry . . ." indicates that he knows he has something to be sorry for because society would condemn his actions. He also indicates that he knows the consequences of his acts, that is, that people will die. Accordingly, Ted does not meet the requirements for legal insanity under the M'Naghten standard.

b. Deific command exception   There are other standards for legal insanity that may be applied in place of or in addition to the traditional M'Naghten standard. One of the earliest additions to the insanity standard was the "deific command." Most jurisdictions now allow an insanity defense when the defendant, due to a mental disease or defect, believes that God or a supreme being ordered her to commit the crime. In such cases, the defendant may know her actions are contrary to society's morals and legally wrong, but believes that a deific command has overridden society's morals.

For example, imagine that a mentally ill woman hears what she believes to be the voice of God. The voice tells her to kill the next person she sees. Although the woman knows it is unlawful to kill, she follows the command. If her delusional state is due to a mental disease or defect; she is entitled to assert the insanity defense.

You may be wondering what prevents every defendant from claiming that God or Satan told her to commit a crime. Two things keep this defense in check: (1) the defendant must have a mental disease or defect; and (2) the jury must believe the defendant.

Moreover, keep in mind that the deific command defense is different from a defendant who claims that her religious convictions forced her to commit a crime. The latter does not fall within the deific command.

For example, David Koresh led a cult of religious fanatics in Waco, Texas. He indoctrinated them in his religious beliefs that included the religious duty to commit incest and child abuse. Koresh's followers could not avail themselves of the deific command because they were choosing to follow religious beliefs. They did not claim to hear the "voice of God" directly, although Koresh did claim to be God's messenger.

QUESTION 4. **Woman's bathrobe.** Cameron is apprehended after he stabs his stepmother 70 times and leaves her in a bathtub. Immediately after the stabbing, Cameron hits the road. When the police catch up with him, he is wearing only a pair of women's stretch pants and a housecoat. He tells the officers that God commanded him to kill his stepmother because she was practicing sorcery. Cameron claims that he is the Messiah and that he was compelled to follow God's command, even at the risk of being arrested.

If Cameron asserts an insanity defense, and assuming he has a mental disease or defect, he is likely to

A. succeed under the deific command test.
B. fail because he knew he was killing and that it was wrong to kill.
C. succeed because he meets the requirements of the M'Naghten test.
D. fail under the deific command test.

ANALYSIS. This question is based on the case of *State v. Cameron*, 674 P.2d 650 (Wash. 1983). Cameron indeed stabbed his stepmother 70 times and tried to escape by walking from Oregon to California in only women's stretch pants and a robe. There was very little question that Cameron suffered from a mental disease or defect. The real question is whether he met the legal standards for insanity.

If restricted to the M'Naghten standard, Cameron would likely *not* succeed with his defense. He knew that he was killing and that he could get in trouble for doing so. His real argument is that he had to follow God's command. Under the deific command exception, Cameron would have an insanity defense.

Accordingly, **A** is the right answer. **B** is wrong because it merely states the M'Naghten test. If that were the only standard available, Cameron would fail. However, in this problem, another legal alternative exists. **C** is wrong because Cameron does not meet the M'Naghten standard. He knows that he is killing and that it is wrong. Under the M'Naghten standard he would not be legally insane. Finally, **D** is wrong because Cameron has met the requirements of the deific command test. He has a mental disease or defect and he committed his offense because a deity commanded him to do so. Also, you should note that since **A** and **D** are opposites, there was a good chance that one of them would be the correct answer. For this question, **A** is the correct answer.

c. Irresistible impulse test Another extension of the insanity test is the "irresistible impulse" or "policeman at the elbow" test. Under this test, an accused is legally insane if, due to a mental disease or defect, she would have been unable to stop herself even if there had been a policeman at her elbow at the time she committed the crime. Insanity has destroyed the defendant's power to choose between right and wrong.

For example, consider a defendant with a long history of mental disease. In front of hundreds of people, she attacks a speaker at a conference. The defendant knows what she is doing and that her conduct is wrong; she is not hearing voices from God. Nonetheless, she may be able to get an insanity defense in jurisdictions that apply the irresistible impulse test, because she cannot control herself.

Many courts reject the irresistible impulse test because it is difficult for experts to distinguish between offenders who could not control themselves and those who chose not to control themselves. Courts that reject this test do not want to give criminals an easy excuse to not control their behavior.

Judge for yourself whether the defendant in the next problem would satisfy any of the standards for legal insanity that we have discussed thus far.

QUESTION 5. Klepto Katy. Katy has a history of mental disease and a lengthy criminal record for theft crimes. To defend her on the latest charge of attempted theft, her lawyer raises an insanity defense. He claims that Katy must be insane because she tried to steal a radio out of the police car when the police stopped to talk to her and her husband about prowlers in their neighborhood. While the officers' attention was directed toward her husband, Katy cased their car. She then waited until their heads were turned and then quickly reached into the back window of the cruiser and grabbed the radio. She almost got away with the theft, but the radio went off. Katy said, "I thought I was more careful this time. Something in me just wanted me to have that radio."

Under which, if any, of the following standards is Katy likely to have an insanity defense?

A. M'Naghten test.
B. Deific command exception.
C. Irresistible impulse test.
D. None of the above.

ANALYSIS. If you thought this question was too easy, it is because you missed something. Certainly, the irresistible impulse test seems to jump out at you in this question. However, if you look carefully at the facts, you will see that Katy does not meet any of the legal standards for insanity.

First, **A** is wrong because Katy clearly knows what she is doing and that it is wrong. **B** does not apply because Katy never claims that she was hearing divine voices. However, you probably jumped at **C** as the right answer, even though it is wrong.

Katy cannot avail herself of the irresistible impulse test. Certainly she has a compulsion to steal, but her actions and statement indicate that it is not an irresistible impulse. It is not irresistible because she resisted the urge to steal until the officers were talking to her husband. This fact indicates that the impulse is not irresistible. **D** is the correct answer.

d. _Durham_ product rule   In _Durham v. United States_, 214 F.2d 862 (D.C. Cir. 1954), Judge Bazelon proposed an insanity rule that eliminates the "right-wrong" dichotomy of the traditional M'Naghten standard. According to the _Durham_ test, a defendant is excused by reason of insanity "if his unlawful act was the product of mental disease or defect." This test has not been widely accepted because it fails to give the fact-finder any clear standards for evaluating the defendant.[2] As long as a psychiatric expert makes some connection between the defendant's acts and a mental disease, that defendant can be adjudged insane.

For example, assume that Mary suffers from a mental disease that causes her to believe she will become the president of a major corporation if she kills its current president. Mary acts on this belief and kills the company president. Under the _Durham_ rule, Mary has an insanity defense even though she knew what she was doing, knew it was wrong, and could have controlled herself. As long as an expert testifies that the killing was the product of her delusional thoughts, she has a _Durham_ insanity defense.

In the next problem, consider whether the _Durham_ test gives a different result than the other insanity tests we have reviewed so far.

QUESTION 6. Presidential delusions. Oswald suffers from a mental disease that causes him to believe that the President is conspiring with the military to draft Oswald. To stop the President, Oswald decides to shoot him. Oswald waits until the perfect time when the presidential motorcade is passing Oswald's hiding place, then shoots. Oswald injures the President and is charged with attempted murder. He argues an insanity defense.

Under which standard would Oswald be most likely to have a successful insanity defense?

A. Irresistible impulse test.
B. _Durham_ product rule.
C. M'Naghten test.
D. Deific command test.
E. Insane delusions test.

---

2. In fact, the D.C. Circuit has subsequently rejected the _Durham_ rule. See _United States v. Brawner_, 153 U.S. App. D.C. 1 (D.C. Cir. 1972).

ANALYSIS. This simple question highlights why the *Durham* test is considered the most liberal common law standard for insanity. Oswald would not have a defense under the irresistible impulse test because he was able to control his impulses until the most opportune time to shoot arose. **A** is wrong. Also, under the M'Naghten test, Oswald would have no chance of prevailing. Oswald knew what he was doing (i.e., he was going to kill the President to stop the conspiracy) and he knew it was wrong (which is why he hid when he shot). **C** is also wrong. The question also offers no suggestion that Oswald was hearing voices at the time of the crime, so **D** is wrong. Finally, Oswald would not even prevail under the insane delusions test because there would be no right to use self-defense to prevent being drafted. The correct answer is **B**. Only under the *Durham* product rule could Oswald argue insanity by showing that his illegal action was the product of his mental disease or condition.

e. Model Penal Code standard   The last insanity standard we examine is set forth in Model Penal Code §4.01. The Model Penal Code standard for insanity is more lenient than the traditional M'Naghten approach, although not as vague as the *Durham* rule. Under Model Penal Code §4.01, a person is not responsible for her criminal conduct if she *lacks substantial capacity to either appreciate the criminality (wrongfulness) of her conduct or to conform her conduct to the requirements of the law.*

How, then, is the Model Penal Code standard different from the M'Naghten approach? First, it relaxes the requirement that a defendant "know" the difference between right and wrong. It focuses instead on whether a defendant "lacks *substantial capacity* to appreciate" the nature and con-sequences of his acts. Under the traditional M'Naghten test, the issue is black and white: Either the defendant is so seriously mentally ill that she does not know the nature or wrongfulness of her acts, or the defendant is sane. This M'Naghten test requires an impairment so extreme that few defendants qualify. However, as the Model Penal Code recognizes, there are many seriously mentally ill people who are sometimes aware of their acts and sometimes not.

Second, while an insane person might know what she is doing, she might not "appreciate" why it is wrong. For example, if a defendant hits a child in the head with a hammer, she may know she is breaking the child's skull and she may even know it is illegal. However, because of a mental condition, she may not understand why it is wrong to break the child's skull. The appreciation standard of the Model Penal Code requires that the defendant have an emotional understanding of the consequences of her acts.

Third, the Model Penal Code *incorporates both the deific command test and the irresistible impulse test.* A defendant who hears God's voice probably has a good argument that she lacked substantial capacity to appreciate the nature of her acts. Finally, the Model Penal Code expressly states that a defendant who is unable to "conform her conduct" to the requirements of the law because of a mental disease or condition has an insanity defense.

As you can now see, prosecutors tend to favor the strict M'Naghten standard. However, defense counsel often urge the courts to follow the Model Penal Code standard because it offers greater opportunity for a defendant to be successful with an insanity defense.

QUESTION 7. Breaking point. Sadly, for the last five years, Lacey has not been able to work as a bank teller because of her experience in a very traumatic, violent bank robbery. The doctors have diagnosed Lacey as suffering from post-traumatic stress syndrome, a recognized mental condition. Whenever Lacey sees someone who looks like the robber, she tends to overreact. One day, while Lacey is walking down the street, a homeless person sticks out his hand and says, "Come on, lady, give me your money." Lacey reacts by taking out a gun and shooting the man. As she shoots, she shouts: "I'll never be a victim again! The heck with the laws, take this!"

At trial, Lacey argues that she is not guilty by reason of insanity.

Will Lacey succeed with her insanity defense?

A. Yes, under the M'Naghten standard, if she did not appreciate the consequences of her acts.
B. Yes, under the irresistible impulse test, if she did not appreciate the consequences of her acts.
C. Yes, under the Model Penal Code, if she didn't have substantial capacity to appreciate the consequences of her acts.
D. No, because she knew that shooting was against the law.

ANALYSIS. In some ways, insanity multiple-choice questions can be easy. Because it is too difficult to write a short question that delves into all the elements of the defense, professors will often test to see if the student can match the right definition to the right standard. In this case, only one insanity standard — the Model Penal Code standard — allows for an insanity defense if the defendant does not have "substantial capacity to appreciate the consequences of her acts."

A is wrong because M'Naghten rejects the insanity defense if the defendant realizes at all that her actions are wrong. There is no requirement that the defendant merely not appreciate the consequences of her acts. M'Naghten is more stringent than that.

B is also wrong. A person may fully appreciate the consequences of her acts, but still not be able to control her behavior.

C is the right answer. Under the Model Penal Code, Lacey could have a defense if she did not have "substantial capacity to appreciate the consequences of her acts." If she lacks that capacity, she is not guilty by reason of insanity, even if she knew that shooting was against the law. Therefore, **D** is also wrong.

We have now covered the basic standards for an insanity defense. As you review them, keep in mind that a defendant found not guilty by reason of insanity is not released into custody. Rather, that person is committed after acquittal. In fact, a defendant acquitted by reason of insanity may be hospitalized for longer than she might have served in prison had she been convicted. *Jones v. United States*, 463 U.S. 354 (1983).[3]

In addition to the insanity defense, there is another mental defense that is used in some jurisdictions. The next section of this chapter discusses the controversial defense of "diminished capacity."

C. Diminished capacity

Diminished capacity is a controversial defense, and has been abandoned by many jurisdictions. It is fundamentally different than the insanity defense. It allows a defendant who does not have a full insanity defense to argue that she was not able to form the intent for the crime charged because she had diminished mental capacity.

For example, assume the defendant is charged with first-degree murder requiring premeditation. The defendant may argue that she suffers from a mental disease or condition that prevents her from being able to form the necessary mens rea for first-degree murder. She is incapable of premeditation. Rather, the defendant is responsible, at most, for second-degree murder because it requires a less sophisticated degree of thinking.

The diminished capacity defense is criticized because it can allow a defendant to evade criminal responsibility on the basis of vague psychiatric testimony and nebulous standards for mental disabilities. For example, you may have heard of the "Twinkie defense" case. In 1978, Dan White shot and killed the first openly gay city supervisor of San Francisco and the city's mayor. At trial, he argued that he had diminished capacity in part because he had eaten too many Twinkie cupcakes and had a chemical imbalance in his brain. The defense convinced the jury to reduce White's conviction from murder to manslaughter because White did not form the necessary mens rea for murder in California.

Different jurisdictions take different approaches to diminished capacity. Some jurisdictions reject it altogether. Especially when the jurisdiction uses a

---

3. A not guilty by reason of insanity verdict should not be confused with a verdict of "guilty but mentally ill" (GBMI) used in some jurisdictions. In these jurisdictions, if the defendant does not qualify for an insanity defense, the jury may still be instructed as to what types of mental illness would allow for a GBMI verdict. If the jury returns a GBMI verdict, the defendant is sentenced as if there had been an unqualified guilty verdict. However, psychiatrists will examine the defendant and determine whether she will serve her sentence in a mental health facility instead of a prison. Unlike a not guilty by reason of insanity verdict, a GBMI verdict limits a defendant's commitment to the maximum time of her sentence, unless she is also civilly committed.

flexible standard for insanity, it is less necessary to have an alternative mental defense. Also, some jurisdictions bar the defense, but do permit the court to consider mental illness as a mitigating factor during sentencing.[4]

Those courts that recognize a diminished capacity defense tend to limit its use to specific intent crimes that have lesser-included general intent crimes. In other words, a defendant can argue that her diminished capacity prevented her from forming the intent for the more serious specific intent crime, but she would still be guilty of a lesser-included general offense. For example, a defendant may argue that she was not able to think clearly enough to premeditate a murder. If the jury accepted the argument, the defendant would not be guilty of first-degree murder, but she is still guilty of a lesser degree of murder.

Finally, a few jurisdictions follow the Model Penal Code approach, which allows a defendant to raise a diminished capacity defense. Even if there is no lesser-included defense, under the Model Penal Code, a successful diminished capacity argument may result in the defendant being found not guilty of any crime. For example, if a defendant is charged with reckless driving (a "general intent" offense) and she claims that because of her mental condition she could not and did not realize the risks posed by her driving, she would escape punishment altogether for her acts.

Although defendants are always free to argue that they did not form the necessary mens rea, a diminished capacity defense gives the defendant the opportunity to also call an expert to attest to her mental condition. Worried that these experts have too much influence on the jury's evaluation of the defendant's mens rea, many legislatures, especially after the Twinkie case, banned the diminished capacity defense.

QUESTION 8. Frankie Fraud. Frankie is a loan officer. He is charged with helping customers obtain loans based on false loan applications. Frankie claims that he suffers from a stress disorder (acute stress syndrome). He plans to call an expert to testify about the condition and how it confuses Frankie so much that he is unable to think clearly about his work.

Which of the following is untrue?

A. In a Model Penal Code jurisdiction, Frankie will be able to present his expert and argue diminished capacity.

---

4. The focus here will be on the traditional diminished capacity defense, not the "partial responsibility" defense that allows a defendant to avoid punishment even if she displays the requisite intent for the crime. That defense has been largely discredited and abolished by most jurisdictions. See Peter Arenella, *The Diminished Capacity and Diminished Responsibility Defenses: Two Children of a Doomed Marriage*, 77 Colum. L. Rev. 827 (1977).

> **B.** In a jurisdiction that allows diminished capacity for specific intent crimes, Frankie will be able to call his expert if there is a lesser-included crime.
> **C.** Under the common law approach, Frankie has a full defense to any crime if he suffered from diminished capacity.
> **D.** If Frankie is tried in a jurisdiction that does not recognize diminished capacity, he may argue that he lacked intent, but he cannot call his expert witness or get a diminished capacity jury instruction.

ANALYSIS. This question requires that you understand the various approaches to diminished capacity. Let's go through each of them to see if you are clear on the details. Remember, we are looking for the statement that is *un*true.

A is a true statement. The Model Penal Code has the most generous approach and Frankie would be able to call an expert to argue diminished capacity for any type of crime. Because it is true, **A** is a wrong answer.

B is also a true statement. Most jurisdictions that recognize a diminished capacity defense only do so for specific intent crimes that have lesser-included offenses. In such situations, the expert can help explain why the defendant did not and could not form the specific intent for the offense. As a true statement, **B** is a wrong answer.

C, however, is an incorrect statement and therefore the right answer. Under the common law, Frankie would not have a full defense. Rather, his diminished capacity could be used only to reduce his level of culpability. The answer to this question is **C**.

Finally, take a look at **D**. It is actually a true statement. Even in jurisdictions that do not recognize diminished capacity, a defendant may still argue that he did not form the intent for the crime. He just cannot blame it on a syndrome and use an expert to make his case. **D** is a wrong answer to this question.

D.   The Closer: Covering the bases

In most cases in which the defendant has a mental problem, counsel will want to try both insanity and diminished capacity defenses. However, there may be strategic reasons for forgoing an insanity defense. For example, a defendant may wish to avoid the lengthy involuntary hospitalization she faces if the defense is successful. A diminished capacity defense may lead to conviction on lesser charges, resulting in an earlier release of the defendant.

Any given set of facts may lead to the possibility of both the insanity and diminished capacity defenses being raised. In the closer, we use a style of multiple-choice question many professors use to test the range of issues raised by mental defenses: two questions based on one set of facts.

The following facts apply to both Questions 9 and 10:

QUESTIONS 9 and 10. **Battle fatigue.** Bob had suffered long enough. For three years, he had been subjected to the indignities and pressures of law school. He could no longer eat or sleep; he suffered from constant headaches. The doctors were unclear as to the precise nature of his condition, but were willing to analogize it to "battle fatigue," also known as post-traumatic stress disorder (PTSD).

On the day before his Remedies final, Bob saw another student's outline sitting on a library table. Bob grabbed it and ate it page by page to "digest" the knowledge it contained. Bob was charged with stealing the outline. The elements of stealing are (1) knowingly taking an object; (2) without permission; and (3) with the specific intent of depriving the owner permanently of it.

When confronted with his acts, Bob said, "I knew that I would get in trouble, but I couldn't help myself. After studying law so much, it is hard to tell the difference between right and wrong."

QUESTION 9. **Mentally ill law students.** Assuming the above facts, what is likely to be Bob's greatest obstacle in asserting that he has a mental disease or defect?

A. He is in law school.
B. He has no clear symptoms.
C. He is one of many law students who may suffer from the same condition.
D. He is asserting PTSD for a condition other than true battle fatigue.

ANALYSIS. This question focuses on the first paragraph of facts given for Questions 9 and 10. Bob is claiming that an unusual condition is a mental disease or defect. The mere fact that it is not traditional PTSD, however, does not disqualify it from being a legitimate mental disease or defect. Therefore, **D** is wrong. Additionally, just because he is in law school doesn't mean that he couldn't have a mental disease or defect. Therefore, **A** is wrong. **B** is wrong because Bob does have clear symptoms — he can no longer eat or sleep, and he suffers from headaches. The best answer is **C**. The court may be reluctant to recognize Bob's condition because it would open the floodgates to many sufferers of school pressure.

QUESTION 10. Insane or diminished?   Assuming the court decides Bob has a mental disease or defect, what would be the most effective argument for Bob to make in his defense?

A. Bob is clearly disturbed so he should be civilly committed, not convicted.
B. Under the M'Naghten test for insanity, Bob is insane because it was hard for him to tell the difference between right and wrong.
C. Under the Model Penal Code test, Bob did not understand that he would not gain knowledge by eating an outline.
D. Bob has a diminished capacity defense because he had a severe mental disturbance that prevented him from controlling his urges.

ANALYSIS.   To answer this question, you must understand both the insanity tests and the diminished capacity tests. As in real life, both issues are in play with this set of facts.

A is wrong because it is not specific enough. A defendant cannot simply argue that he was disturbed and therefore should not be punished. The defendant must meet the specific standards for insanity and diminished capacity discussed in this chapter.

B is also wrong, although it at least alludes to the correct legal standard. **B** is wrong because the strict M'Naghten test requires that Bob not *know* he was doing wrong. Here, Bob admits that he knew he could get into trouble. This statement shows that he knew what he was doing was wrong, although it was difficult for him to determine that.

Finally, there are **C** and **D** to consider. **C** has a good chance of being the right answer, if only because the Model Penal Code is the most lenient insanity standard. However, we should check **D** before selecting a final answer. Diminished capacity could very well be a defense for someone like Bob, but not because the defendant couldn't control his urges. Rather, diminished capacity, when properly applied, examines whether the defendant had the necessary mens rea for the crime, not whether the defendant had volitional control. In **D**, Bob is not arguing that diminished capacity prevented him from knowing the outlines belonged to anyone else, or from forming the intent to permanently deprive the owner of his outlines. Therefore, **D** is a wrong answer and **C** is correct.

◈ Levenson's Picks

1.	Where am I?	**B**
2.	Road rage syndrome	**D**
3.	Insane Ted	**C**
4.	Woman's bathrobe	**A**
5.	Klepto Katy	**D**
6.	Presidential delusions	**B**
7.	Breaking point	**C**
8.	Frankie Fraud	**C**
9.	Mentally ill law students	**C**
10.	Insane or diminished?	**C**

Intoxication, Infancy, and Entrapment

Young men are as apt to think themselves wise enough, as drunken men
are to think themselves sober enough.
—Lord Chesterfield, letter to Philip Stanhope (Nov. 24, 1747)

This chapter focuses on several additional excuse defenses. As expected, each has its own requirements. The only common theme is that they are all excuses. In other words, even though the defendant committed an unjustified, criminal act, he is not punished because intervening circumstances relieve him of some or all of the blame.

A. Intoxication

In criminal law, there are two types of intoxication defenses. Involuntary intoxication provides a complete defense to a crime. Voluntary intoxication generally does not completely excuse a defendant's actions; rather, it reduces culpability. The term *intoxication* covers both alcohol use and drug use.

1. Involuntary intoxication

Involuntary intoxication is a complete defense if it causes the defendant to commit a crime he would not have otherwise committed. In some cases, involuntary intoxication may also cause legal insanity by rendering a defendant unable to know what he is doing or know that it is wrong.

For example, assume that while the defendant is not looking, someone slips a drug into his drink. After drinking the doctored beverage, the defendant hallucinates and commits a crime. The defendant has a full defense to the crime if, in the hallucinated state, he was unaware of the criminal nature of his acts.

Involuntary intoxication takes three forms: (1) unwitting intoxication; (2) coerced intoxication; or (3) pathological effect intoxication. *City of Minneapolis v. Altimus*, 238 N.W.2d 851 (Minn. 1976).

Unwitting intoxication occurs when a person is unaware that he is ingesting alcohol or a drug. For example, a defendant is involuntarily intoxicated when another person spikes his drink or medication. However, if the defendant is aware that his drink is altered, but does not know what the effects will be of the adulterant, the defendant cannot claim involuntary intoxication. He chose to take the risk that his actions would be altered and he remains responsible for his conduct.

Coerced intoxication occurs when a person is forced to ingest a drug or alcohol. For example, if a defendant is forced at gunpoint to swallow LSD, the defendant's intoxication is involuntary.

Pathological effect refers to medication or alcohol producing an unexpected grossly excessive effect. For example, a defendant takes an aspirin. However, the defendant has an unnatural reaction to the aspirin, and it has the same effect on him as LSD would have on others. The defendant may be able to argue involuntary intoxication because of the unexpected, extreme mind-altering effect of the aspirin.[1]

As with unwitting intoxication, a defendant may not argue involuntary intoxication if he has had a reaction, but knew at the time he took the drug

---

[1] Model Penal Code §2.08(4)(c) defines "pathological intoxication" as "intoxication grossly excessive in degree, given the amount of intoxicant, to which the actor does not know he is susceptible."

that its effects were unpredictable. For example, take the case in which a defendant is offered a little "sunshine" pill at a party. He accepts the pill and ingests it. If it turns out to be LSD, he cannot claim involuntary intoxication on the grounds that he did not know what the effect of the unknown substance would be on him.

The Model Penal Code, like the common law, recognizes a full involuntary intoxication defense. See Model Penal Code §2.08. Intoxication that is not self-induced or is pathological can serve as a full defense if it has the same impact as insanity, that is, it causes the actor to not know what he is doing or to lose the ability to conform his conduct to the law.

Try this initial intoxication problem to test your understanding of involuntary intoxication.

QUESTION 1. Laced marijuana.   Valerie, Patsy, and Barbara go to a party. Barbara gets a headache and asks for a glass of soda. Unbeknownst to her, someone spikes her soda with a hallucinogen. Patsy takes a bite of the "special brownies" that are being served. Patsy assumes the brownies have a little marijuana in them. What she doesn't know is that they are also laced with LSD. Finally, Valerie tells her host that she does not drink or take drugs because she is afraid of the potential effect. The host pokes her in the rear end with a little needle that he tells her is a "pick-me-up." It turns out to be heroin. Minutes later, Valerie, Patsy, and Barbara are found setting fire to guests' cars in the front of the house.

Which of the defendant(s) could successfully claim involuntary intoxication?

A. Only Barbara, because she did not know her soda had been spiked.
B. Patsy and Barbara, because they did not anticipate they might ingest a drug.
C. Barbara and Valerie.
D. None of them because there is always a risk of becoming intoxicated at a party.

ANALYSIS.   The easiest way to answer this question is to assess each defendant's chances of arguing involuntary intoxication. Barbara seems to be in a good position because she did not realize she was taking an intoxicant. This is an example of unwitting intoxication. By contrast, Patsy probably does not have a good argument for involuntary intoxication because she realized that the brownies would probably have some mind-altering effect on her, even though she may not have realized how much of an effect. Finally, Valerie seems to have a good claim of involuntary intoxication because she did not voluntarily ingest a drug; it was forced upon her. Therefore, it appears that Barbara and Valerie can argue involuntary intoxication.

Accordingly, **A** is wrong because it does not recognize Valerie's valid argument of involuntary intoxication. **B** is wrong because Patsy cannot claim involuntary intoxication even though she did not know the brownies had been laced with LSD. Because she knew that the brownies would have some mind-altering effect, she cannot complain that the effect was more dramatic than she anticipated. See *People v. Velez*, 221 Cal. App. 631 (1985) (defendant "voluntarily" intoxicated after smoking marijuana cigarette laced with PCP).

Finally, **D** is wrong because it goes too far. Of course, there are risks anytime a person goes to a party, but that act alone does not negate a claim of involuntary intoxication. Patsy's actions are the type of risk assumption that negate a claim of involuntary intoxication. **C** is the correct answer: Barbara and Valerie can argue involuntary intoxication.

2. Voluntary intoxication

The common law takes a more restrictive approach to voluntary intoxication. Some jurisdictions bar a voluntary intoxication defense altogether. The Supreme Court has held that a defendant is not constitutionally entitled to raise a voluntary intoxication defense. See *Montana v. Egelhoff*, 518 U.S. 37 (1996).

At early common law, intoxication was never a defense. However, as courts became more lenient, they began to recognize a limited voluntary intoxication defense. Today, in jurisdictions in which a voluntary intoxication defense is allowed, it is ordinarily permitted only to reduce specific intent crimes (i.e., crimes requiring a particular purpose, motive, or sophisticated mental state) to lesser offenses. In this way, voluntary intoxication works very much like the defense of diminished capacity. A defendant can argue that because he was intoxicated, he could not form the necessary mens rea for the crime charged.

The distinction between specific-intent crimes (when intoxication can be argued) and general-intent crimes (when there is typically no intoxication defense) is an elusive one. Sometimes it helps to start with an example. In *Roberts v. People*, 19 Mich. 401 (1870), the defendant was charged with assault *with intent to murder*. The defendant claimed that he was too drunk at the time of the assault to form the intent to murder. Although intoxication is generally not a defense to assault (after all, how much lucid thought is needed to hit someone?), it was held to be a defense to assault with intent to murder. Because Roberts was charged with a specific-intent crime, prosecutors needed to prove that he not only wanted to assault his victim, but specifically wanted to kill him.

Generally, voluntary intoxication is not allowed as a defense to a crime that requires only a reckless act. For example, drunk driving and even vehicular homicide are considered general-intent crimes. Therefore, the drunk driver cannot claim a defense based on intoxication. Battery and assault are considered classic examples of general-intent crimes for which voluntary intoxication is not a defense.

However, if a defendant is charged with a crime that requires an intent to defraud or premeditation (which requires cool deliberate thought), voluntary intoxication may be used to argue that he did not form the high level of mens rea required for the crime. For example, assume the defendant is charged with burglary with the intent to steal. The defendant admits breaking into the victim's house, but claims he was too drunk to intend to steal anything because he was too drunk to figure out why he was in the building. If the jury believes the defendant, he would have a voluntary intoxication defense to this specific-intent crime. Because of his intoxication, he could not form the intent to steal. The defendant may be guilty of some other crime, such as trespass or breaking and entering, but he is not guilty of burglary with the intent to steal.

Some courts have rejected an approach that requires them to distinguish on a crime-by-crime basis whether the charged offense is a specific- or general-intent crime. Instead, they have adopted rules that limit the voluntary intoxication defense to specific crimes, such as first-degree murder. Alternatively, they only allow this defense when the effects of intoxication are permanent and the defendant now has a mental condition or disease that allows him to argue insanity. See *State v. Stasio*, 396 A.2d 1129 (N.J. 1979). There are a few courts, however, that allow intoxication as a defense to any crime, including reckless offenses.

The Model Penal Code allows voluntary intoxication to negate the mens rea of any crime, except for crimes requiring recklessness or negligence. Model Penal Code §2.08(2). For example, assume a defendant is charged with recklessly damaging a building by lighting a fire. Although voluntary intoxication might be a defense to the crime of intentionally burning a building, it is not a defense to the form of the crime that only requires the defendant to act recklessly.

Finally, it is important to note that a defendant who forms the intent to commit a crime and then drinks to give himself courage to complete the task is not entitled to claim intoxication. The defendant formed the intent for the crime before becoming intoxicated and his intoxication does not negate that preformed intent.

It is time to try a second question involving intoxication. This time, we focus on a situation in which a defendant has voluntarily impaired his sense. Is he entitled to an intoxication defense?

QUESTION 2. Tipsy taxpayer. Calvin is a chronic alcoholic. Seldom does a day pass when he doesn't end up drunk by lunchtime. As a result of his problem, Calvin has had some encounters with law enforcement. In particular, he is facing charges for breaking a beer bottle over a security officer's head, willfully evading his taxes, and driving without a license.

For which of these crimes, if any, is Calvin likely to be able to argue an intoxication defense?

A. Willful tax evasion.
B. Assaulting the security officer.
C. Driving without a license.
D. All of the above.

ANALYSIS. In deciding whether Calvin has an intoxication defense, the most important thing to do is determine whether you are dealing with a specific-intent crime that requires a sophisticated level of intent or a general-intent crime that is on par with the recklessness and negligence standards of the Model Penal Code.

In this question, the only specific-intent crime Calvin faces is tax evasion. How, you might ask, should you know that tax evasion requires specific intent? First, recall our discussions of mens rea and mistake of fact. Willfully in the tax context generally means at least knowingly or intentionally. Second, you might be able to get to the correct answer even without knowing the elements of willful tax evasion. It is clear that **B** is wrong because assault does not require specific intent. Assault is a classic general-intent crime. **C** is wrong because driving without a license is generally a strict-liability crime. Because **B** and **C** are wrong, **D** cannot be true. The answer to this question is **A**.

3. Degree of intoxication

The mere intake of alcohol or drugs is insufficient to demonstrate intoxication. There must be a "prostration of the defendant's faculties" such that the defendant is incapable of forming the mens rea necessary for the crime. See *State v. Cameron*, 104 N.J. 42 (1986).

To determine whether the defendant has ingested enough alcohol or drugs to be intoxicated, courts consider the following factors: quantity consumed; time period of consumption; blood-alcohol content; defendant's conduct, as perceived by others; and defendant's ability to recall significant events.

QUESTION 3. **Liquid courage.** Warner and his buddy, Trent, have decided to rob the bank. Warner is very nervous about the caper, so Trent suggests that they drink a few beers before they get started. By the time they rob the bank, nothing is bothering Warner. Boosted by his liquid courage, Warner robs the bank.

Is Warner entitled to an intoxication defense?

A. Yes, because he might not have robbed the bank if he had been sober.
B. Yes, because Trent was the one who suggested that they drink before the robbery.
C. No, because he had already formed the intent to rob before he drank.
D. No, because voluntary intoxication is never a defense.

ANALYSIS. Even though he felt more daring after drinking, Warner formed the intent to rob before he drank. His liquid courage does not negate his intent for the crime. Even with a few drinks, there is no indication that Warner has had a complete prostration of faculties that makes it impossible for him to form the intent to rob.

A is the wrong answer. The mere speculation that Warner would not have otherwise robbed the bank does not create an intoxication defense. **B** is also wrong. Warner is a grown man; he could have declined Trent's offer to drink. By agreeing to drink, especially as part of his plan to build up the courage to rob, Warner loses any intoxication defense.

Now, your choice should be fairly easy. You know that **D** is wrong. Voluntary intoxication can be a defense, but it is not in this case because Warner voluntarily drank after he had formed the intent to rob. Once again, beware of answers with the words "never" or "always."

C is correct. If Warner had already formed the intent to rob, merely blunting his senses by drinking would not be enough to trigger an intoxication defense.

B.   Status defenses

Although a person who has been drinking can be prosecuted for crimes he commits, a person cannot be prosecuted merely for being an addict or alcoholic. In *Robinson v. California,* 370 U.S. 660 (1962), the Supreme Court held that a defendant could not be convicted of being a narcotics addict. People may be punished only for their acts, not their status. Thus, a narcotics addict may be prosecuted for buying, possessing, or selling drugs. Likewise, an alcoholic may be prosecuted for drunk driving or being drunk in public.

The next problem illustrates the difference between a defendant who cannot be punished because of his status and a defendant who can be punished because of his acts related to that status.

> **QUESTION 4. Satan worshipper.** Sally is a Satan worshipper. When she can, she likes to engage in various rituals to worship Satan. The police arrest Sally for sacrificing her neighbor's dog to Satan.
>
> If Sally claims that she cannot be prosecuted because she is a Satan worshipper, she will most likely
>
> A. lose because she had no right to kill her neighbor's dog.
> B. lose because she has unpopular beliefs.
> C. win because she cannot be prosecuted for her religious status.
> D. win because she cannot be prosecuted for her religious acts.

ANALYSIS. As you might have guessed, the law is not going to go out of its way to make things easier on Satan worshippers. While a defendant cannot be prosecuted just for her First Amendment beliefs, she can be prosecuted for illegal acts taken in the name of those religious beliefs. Thus, Sally is likely to lose. **C** is wrong because Sally is not being prosecuted just for her religious beliefs. She is being prosecuted for her acts. **D** is wrong because Sally *can* be prosecuted for acts related to her status as a Satan worshipper.

Between **A** and **B**, **A** is definitely the better answer. The popularity of a defendant's beliefs do not determine whether she is guilty of a crime. If Sally did not violate the law, she would have been able to assert her beliefs all that she wanted. **B** is wrong. In the end, **A** is the correct answer. Sally will lose because she had no right to kill the neighbor's dog.

C.   Infancy

The law excuses the acts of children it deems too young to be criminally responsible for their actions. Children under a certain age are presumed incapable of forming the intent required for a criminal offense, but different jurisdictions choose different ages for the defense of infancy. Furthermore, some jurisdictions treat infancy as an automatic full defense, whereas others hold infancy provides a rebuttable presumption that the defendant was too young to commit the crime.

Under the common law, three arbitrary age limits were placed on the prosecutions of minors. First, the common law conclusively held that a child under the age of seven years did not have the cognitive capacity to form the mens rea for any crime. The presumption was not rebuttable. Second, a minor between the ages of 7 and 14 years was presumed incapable of committing a crime, but the prosecution could rebut this presumption by demonstrating that the youth was capable of understanding the nature and consequences of his acts and of distinguishing right from wrong. *In re Devon T.*, 85 Md. App. 674 (1991). Finally, a youth over 14 years had no infancy defense.

Although the common law approach has had a significant influence on how states draft their infancy defense statutes, many jurisdictions, like California, have eliminated the common law's first category, the conclusive presumption. Even very young minors may be prosecuted if the prosecution can prove the child's mens rea for the crime. Minors are typically tried in juvenile court. The Model Penal Code also favors this approach. Under Model Penal Code §4.10, a person under the age of 16 years at the time of the offense must be tried in juvenile court. The Model Penal Code does not set forth an age at which a defendant is not responsible for his acts.

In many jurisdictions, minors aged 14 years and older may be transferred to the adult criminal justice system if they are charged with particularly serious offenses. Otherwise, criminal charges against minors are typically handled in the juvenile courts.

QUESTION 5. Baby Face Nelson. Nelson and Bart are arrested for kicking an infant to death. Nelson is eight years old; Bart is six years old. Both boys were previously arrested for assault and shoplifting, but they were released to the supervision of their parents. The prosecution wants to charge both boys with murder.

Under the common law approach, the prosecution will be

A. successful in pursuing charges against both boys.
B. unsuccessful in pursuing charges against both boys.
C. more likely successful in pursuing charges against Nelson than against Bart.
D. more likely successful in pursuing charges against Bart than against Nelson.

ANALYSIS. This one should have been easy. Because he is under seven years old, the common law conclusively presumed that Bart was not responsible for his acts. He cannot be prosecuted for the crime. **D** is wrong. However, Nelson is a different story. There is only a rebuttable presumption that he did not have culpability for the crime. If the prosecutor can overcome that presumption, Nelson can be prosecuted. Here, Nelson's prior record and the seriousness of the crime would be strong evidence that he is capable of understanding the nature and consequences of his acts, and that his actions are wrong.

Therefore, **A** is wrong because the common law would have given Bart a full excuse defense. **B** is also wrong because the prosecutor could pursue a prosecution against Nelson by using his age and prior record to show that he could have formed the mens rea for the crime. **C** is the correct answer.

D.   Entrapment

Entrapment is another type of defense that defendants use to excuse their behavior. Entrapment allows a defendant to be excused because the government unfairly induced the defendant to commit the crime. There are two primary standards used to determine if a defendant has been entrapped: (1) the subjective ("predisposition") standard and (2) the objective ("government inducement") standard. Entrapment is a full defense to a crime.

The entrapment defense serves two important purposes. First, it discourages the police from using overreaching tactics. Second, it helps ensure that only persons who are inclined to commit crimes, and not those pressured by the authorities to do so, are convicted.

To successfully invoke the entrapment defense, the defendant must first demonstrate that he was induced by a government official or informant to commit a crime. Typically, the defendant argues that an undercover agent or government snitch induced him to participate in a crime. A defendant cannot be entrapped by a third party who is not working for or with the government.

However, even if the defendant proves he was approached by a government official, the defendant cannot argue entrapment unless he meets a second requirement. This second requirement differs by jurisdiction. In some jurisdictions, the defendant must show that he was not predisposed to commit a crime. This subjective standard focuses on the defendant's mindset and is used in federal court and many state courts. However, some jurisdictions use a more objective standard. The defendant has an entrapment defense if, regardless of his predisposition, a law-abiding person would have been induced by the police conduct to commit a crime.

1. Federal approach: Predisposition test

In federal court and several state courts, the test for whether a defendant was entrapped is the subjective predisposition test. If the defendant was predisposed to commit the crime and law enforcement agents only offered him the opportunity to do so, there is no entrapment defense. See *United States v. Russell*, 411 U.S. 423 (1973) (adopting *Sorrells/Sherman* subjective approach).

For example, assume that the defendant asks his friends for cocaine. An undercover officer hears the defendant's request and offers to sell the defendant cocaine. The defendant was *not* entrapped; he had a predisposition to purchase cocaine. Even before the government official offered, the defendant had indicated that he wanted to purchase cocaine.

In deciding whether a defendant was predisposed to commit a crime, the jury may consider a variety of circumstances, including defendant's prior criminal behavior; defendant's statements regarding his attitude toward committing the offense; defendant's motive for participating in the illegal conduct; who instigated the criminal behavior; and defendant's level of involvement in the crime. Prosecutors generally favor the predisposition standard because it allows them to introduce evidence of the defendant's prior bad acts to prove that the defendant was predisposed to commit a crime.

Even under the predisposition approach, there are limits on the type of behavior the government may engage in to induce a defendant to commit a crime. First, a defendant may move to dismiss a case on due process grounds if the government has engaged in outrageous misconduct. Dismissals under this theory are rare and occur only when the government constructs the crime from beginning to end. See, e.g., *Greene v. United States*, 454 F.2d 783 (9th Cir. 1971).

Second, it is not enough that the government demonstrate that the defendant was predisposed to engage in marginally acceptable social behavior. In *Jacobson v. United States*, 503 U.S. 540 (1992), the Supreme Court held that a government sting operation that lured a defendant interested in legal adult pornography into buying child pornography constituted entrapment.

Using the predisposition test, determine whether the defendant in the next question has an entrapment defense.

QUESTION 6. John Z.   Defendant John Z. Dellorian is charged with attempting to sell unlicensed firearms. Undercover officers approached Dellorian after they heard that he was peddling different types of illegal weapons. In checking Dellorian's criminal record, they noted that he had been arrested twice with illegal weapons although he was never convicted on those charges.

Posing as a prospective buyer, one of the officers called Dellorian and said that he had heard that Dellorian was a man with connections. The undercover officer then began lying, telling Dellorian that he too sold illegal firearms and that maybe they could do better if they combined their business. Dellorian believed the officer and agreed to do a deal with him. The two met. The officer brought a couple of guns with silencers, and Dellorian brought an unregistered automatic rifle. The officer then introduced Dellorian to a prospective buyer who, unbeknownst to Dellorian, was also an undercover officer. Dellorian offered to sell the prospective buyer his illegal automatic rifle. The officers then arrested Dellorian and charged him with the attempted sale.

If Dellorian raises an entrapment defense in federal court, he is likely to

A. win, because he was induced by the undercover officer to try to sell an illegal weapon.

> **B.** win, because he was not predisposed to engage in a crime.
> **C.** lose, because the government created the crime from beginning to end.
> **D.** lose, because he was predisposed to sell the illegal guns.

ANALYSIS. Under the predisposition standard, Dellorian is going to lose. Overall, the facts indicate that Dellorian was inclined to engage in illegal activity, despite his lack of prior convictions. His prior arrests show his predisposition, he had illegal weapons with him, and he jumped at the opportunity to sell to a prospective buyer. Here, the government merely provided the opportunity for Dellorian to engage in the illegal sale.

Therefore, **A** is a wrong answer. Even though the undercover officer proposed the illegal sale, Dellorian is still guilty if he was predisposed to take the officer up on his offer. **B** is wrong because the facts do suggest Dellorian was predisposed. The officer did not have to beg him or threaten him to participate in the transaction. He willingly came with his illegal weapon in hand.

C is wrong for two reasons. First, factually the government did not create the crime from beginning to end. Dellorian already had in his possession illegal weapons. Second, if the government did create the crime from beginning to end, Dellorian would win, not lose, on a motion to dismiss.

The correct answer is **D**. Dellorian was predisposed. Therefore, he is not entitled to an entrapment defense under the predisposition test.

2. Alternative approach: Overreaching government tactics

Some jurisdictions use an objective standard to determine whether there has been entrapment. Rather than focusing on whether the defendant was predisposed to commit a crime (a subjective standard that focuses on the defendant's state of mind), the government misconduct test focuses on the nature of the government's conduct. For example, in *People v. Barraza*, 23 Cal. 3d 675 (1979), the defendant was charged with selling heroin to undercover narcotics agents. An undercover agent had approached the defendant while he was in a detoxication center. The female decoy constantly pressured the defendant to find and sell her some heroin. The court found that *"the government's conduct was likely to have induced a law-abiding person to commit the crime."* As such, it constituted entrapment.

Although the government misconduct test focuses primarily on the nature of the government inducement and whether it would induce a law-abiding person to commit a crime, it would be misleading to see it as a totally objective standard. In practice, the jury looks at the defendant's circumstances in determining whether law enforcement used proper investigative and apprehension techniques. Thus, officers may have more leeway if the defendant has a criminal background.

Try the next question to see how the government misconduct test works in comparison to the predisposition test for entrapment.

QUESTION 7. Simple Sonya. Sonya is approached by undercover officers who believe she is helping to smuggle illegal aliens into the United States. The officers tell Sonya that there is a family desperate to get to the United States to secure medical treatment for their seriously ill child. The officers further say that if the child is not smuggled in immediately, the child will die. To further convince Sonya to participate, the officers tell Sonya, "Look, you are probably in trouble just for having these discussions with us. You might as well go the whole way and help this kid get treatment. Imagine what will happen to you when we tell the family, and their friends in the United States, that you wouldn't help. I wouldn't want to be in your place when they find out."

Sonya reluctantly agrees to help. She contacts some of the people who had helped her smuggle her family into the United States years ago. She then drives a van to the border to meet the family. When she gets there, the officers pretend to introduce her to illegal aliens. It turns out that they are actually more undercover officers. Sonya is arrested for attempted smuggling.

Would Sonya have an entrapment defense in a jurisdiction that follows the government misconduct test?

A. No, because she was predisposed to help with the smuggling operation.

B. No, because she had smuggled on a prior occasion.

C. Yes, because the officer's conduct would have induced a law-abiding citizen to engage in the illegal conduct.

D. Yes, because the officers first approached Sonya.

ANALYSIS. Under the facts of this question, Sonya will fare better in a jurisdiction that uses the government misconduct test than one that uses the predisposition standard. Because she has prior experience with smuggling, the government would be able to argue that she was predisposed to commit this crime. However, if the facts are looked at from the perspective of whether the government's action would have induced a law-abiding person to commit the crime, Sonya has a good argument that the government's approach was so heavy-handed that it constituted entrapment.

Looking at the answers, we can quickly eliminate **A** as a wrong answer because it sets forth the wrong legal standard. In a jurisdiction that follows the government misconduct test, the focus is on the government's misconduct, not the defendant's predisposition. **B** is wrong because a person can be entrapped, especially under the government misconduct test, even if she has previously committed the same crime.

Between **C** and **D**, **C** is the better answer. **C** sets forth the correct legal standard. **D** is incorrect. It is not true that just because an officer makes the first approach that the defendant has an entrapment defense under either the predisposition or the government misconduct test.

3. Model Penal Code approach

Finally, there is the Model Penal Code approach to entrapment. The Model Penal Code incorporates the objective government misconduct test, but it leaves the determination as to whether there was entrapment to the court, not the jury. See Model Penal Code §2.13. The rationale behind this approach is that judges are less inclined to be offended by undercover methods because they are more familiar with investigative techniques. Under the Model Penal Code, the entrapment defense is unavailable in cases involving serious bodily injury. Model Penal Code §2.13(3).

E.   The Closer: Consent and contributory negligence

The final defense we explore in this chapter is "consent." Ordinarily, consent is not a defense to a criminal charge. For example, a defendant cannot claim that he is not guilty of murder because the victim wanted to die. However, as discussed in Chapters 21 (Rape) and 22 (Theft Crimes), there are some crimes for which the prosecution must prove lack of consent in order to establish its prima facie case. For example, rape may be defined as "sexual intercourse without consent" and theft as "the unlawful taking of the property of another without consent."

Likewise, criminal law does not recognize "contributory negligence" as a defense. Even if a victim is reckless in getting himself into a situation in which he could be the victim of a crime, the victim's behavior does not excuse the defendant's criminal conduct.

The closer focuses on this last aspect of criminal defenses.

> **QUESTION 8. No seat belts.**   When Alex asked his friend Bruce to go for a ride in Alex's new sports car, Bruce quickly agreed. The two of them went speeding down the coastal highway. Bruce did not wear his seatbelt. As they were driving, Alex asked Bruce if it was okay if they drag-raced with other drivers on the highway. Bruce responded, "Sure, I'm up for it." They

then raced against a car owned by Colin. During the race, Alex lost control when Colin's car bumped his. Bruce was ejected from the car and killed; Alex suffered severe injuries but probably would have survived if he had agreed to a blood transfusion. However, he refused a transfusion for religious reasons and died.

Colin has been charged with the murders of both Alex and Bruce. Which, if any, of the following arguments can Colin successfully raise in his defense?

A. Alex contributed to his own death by not agreeing to a blood transfusion.

B. Bruce consented to ride in Alex's car.

C. Colin is excused from the murder because it was Alex's idea to drag race.

D. None of the above.

ANALYSIS. As this question demonstrates, Colin cannot escape criminal liability by blaming the victims for their own injuries. As discussed in Chapter 7 (Causation), a victim's refusal to have a blood transfusion generally does not excuse a defendant's criminal conduct. **A** is a wrong answer. Also, consent is not a defense, so **B** is wrong. Finally, **C** is wrong because it does not matter who originally came up with the idea for the illegal activity. The law does not excuse a defendant who freely chooses to engage in the unlawful acts, even if they are proposed by another person. The correct answer to the closer is **D**.

Levenson's Picks

1. Laced marijuana	C
2. Tipsy taxpayer	A
3. Liquid courage	C
4. Satan worshipper	A
5. Baby Face Nelson	C
6. John Z.	D
7. Simple Sonya	C
8. No seat belts	D

[T]he deeper problem is the rape law's assumption that rapes involve honest men and violated women.

— Prof. Catharine A. MacKinnon

CHAPTER OVERVIEW
A. Types of rape
B. Elements of rape
  1. Sexual intercourse
  2. Unlawful
  3. Without consent
  4. By force or fear
  5. Or deception
C. Mistake as a defense
D. Rape reform legislation and rape shield laws
E. Model Penal Code approach
F. Statutory rape
G. The Closer: Fear versus threat
  ✦ Levenson's Picks

Rape is an example of a crime against a person, as are assault, battery, and homicide. However, because of public attitudes regarding the relationships between men and women, rape raises unique issues. Common law rape laws were influenced by a concern that women would make unfounded allegations of rape. Today, the concerns are the opposite.

There is a fear that traditional rape laws make it too difficult for victims of rape to come forward and accuse their attackers.

In this chapter, we review various rape laws. As we do, keep in mind that men and women may view the crime of rape somewhat differently. Although both may agree that forcible intercourse by a stranger constitutes rape, there can be less agreement as to whether aggressive sexual conduct by an acquaintance constitutes a criminal offense.

A.   Types of rape

Historically, the law defined at least two different types of conduct as rape. The first type of rape is "forcible rape." It is defined as "unlawful sexual intercourse with a woman without her consent by force, fear or fraud." See *Regina v. Morgan*, [1976] A.C. 182. Today, acquaintance rape is considered a type of forcible rape in which the victim knows her attacker. The second type of rape is "statutory rape." It traditionally refers to sex with an underage female, which is rape because the victim was too young to legally consent.

The law of rape is strongly influenced by its historical roots in ancient male concepts of property. A woman was viewed as the chattel of her husband or father. Thus, rape was a property offense involving an unlawful taking and a husband couldn't be guilty of raping his wife.

In modern times, the law of rape has had to struggle with the social stigma associated with the crime. Society tends to blame the rape victim (because of her dress, relationships, mannerisms, etc.) for her plight. As a result, rape is the most underreported crime. It is estimated that fewer than 50 percent of female rape victims report the crime to police. The law of rape struggles to deal with the concern that rape is a crime easily alleged, but difficult to prove. It is also a challenge to construct a law that deals with the reality of how men and women communicate, and do not communicate, during sexual relationships.

Even without studying the details of rape law, you probably have some instincts regarding the key issue that arises in these cases. The first question of this chapter helps you identify that issue.

QUESTION 1. "No means no." Harry has been dating Sally for two weeks. After dinner, Harry drives Sally back to her apartment. He says to her, "Wow, you look amazing. A woman would only dress like that if she wanted to have sex with me." As Sally said, "Are you out of your mind?" Harry responded by telling her, "Don't bother to say no. I know you mean yes." Harry then locked the doors of the car, pinned Sally against the back seat, put his hand on her throat, and had sex with her. When she could finally get out of the car, Sally ran to her apartment and called a girlfriend. A couple of days later, Sally finally called the police.

Which of the following is correct?

A. Harry had the right to assume that no meant yes.
B. Harry had the right to assume that Sally's attire indicated she wanted to have sex.
C. Sally's failure to report the incident immediately means she was not raped.
D. Harry committed rape by forcing her to have sex with him if it was clear she had not consented.

ANALYSIS.   The key issues in a rape case are: (1) Did the victim consent to the sex? and (2) Should the defendant have understood that the victim had not consented? In this case, it is clear (in fact, clearer than it is in many other cases) that the victim did not consent. The key issue will be whether Harry should have understood that she had not consented and that he was forcing her to have sex. The prosecutor will argue that this is a situation in which Harry understood that Sally didn't want to have sex, but he just didn't want to take no for an answer. The fact that Harry had to lock Sally in the car, pin her against the seat, and use force is a further indication that he was aware that he was acting without her consent.

Therefore, **A** is wrong. Men do not have the right to assume that no means yes. However, there may be cases in which all of the circumstances, including a woman's words, gave the defendant an erroneous signal that the victim had consented.

B is also wrong. There is no license to have sex with a woman just because of the way she dresses. Once again, the defendant will have to argue that he believed, based on the victim's words and actions (and not her attire), that she was consenting to the sexual act.

Failure to report a rape does not mean that a rape did not occur. The defendant may claim that the failure to report indicated that the woman didn't believe she had been raped, but there are many reasons women do not report this crime. **C** is wrong.

The correct answer is **D**. If it is clear that Sally had not consented and Harry was forcing her to have sex, he has committed rape. Although Harry may plead ignorance, there are many facts in this question that indicate that Harry knew, but didn't care, that his victim was not willingly having sex with him.

B.   Elements of rape

Although each jurisdiction may have its own statutory definition of rape, the common law defined rape as "unlawful sexual intercourse with a woman without her consent by force, fear or fraud." Thus, the elements of the crime of rape included (1) sexual intercourse; (2) unlawful in nature; (3) without the woman's consent; (4) by fear, force, or fraud. In many jurisdictions, the prosecution was also required to prove that the woman resisted.

Let's evaluate each of these elements and the challenges it poses for proving a crime of rape.

1. Sexual intercourse

The actus reus for the crime of rape is "sexual intercourse" or "carnal knowledge." The slightest penetration is sufficient; there need not be completion of the sexual act. Many states now have statutes that prohibit many other types of sexual assaults. Thus, the crime of sexual assault can encompass more than forced heterosexual intercourse.

2. Unlawful

At common law and under Model Penal Code §213.1, a husband cannot be guilty of raping his wife. Women were considered the property of men and marriage constituted per se consent to intercourse. Today, some jurisdictions have laws that prohibit the rape of one's spouse, although they often place additional procedural burdens on the prosecution.

3. Without consent

Sex without consent is rape if the defendant is aware or should be aware that he is acting without the victim's consent. If the defendant has a mistaken belief that his victim has consented, he may still have a defense. In England, an honest but unreasonable mistake as to consent would be sufficient to claim a mistake of fact defense, so long as the defendant was not reckless in forming that belief. (See Section C *infra*.) However, in the United States, a defendant is generally guilty of rape unless he honestly and reasonably believes his victim has consented.

Although the victim may originally agree to sex, it is rape if the victim withdraws consent during the act of intercourse. See *People v. John Z.*, 29 Cal. 4th 756 (2003). The key question is whether the victim made it clear that she was withdrawing consent. In some jurisdictions, the defendant is entitled to a "reasonable time in which to act after consent is withdrawn and communicated to the defendant" (see *State v. Bunyard*, 133 P.3d 14 (Kan. 2006)), but in other jurisdictions the defendant must cease the sexual act immediately.

4. By force or fear

It surprises many law students to learn that rape is not ordinarily defined simply as "sex without consent." Rather, because of the difficulty in ascertaining when a woman has consented, common law also included a requirement that the prosecution prove that the intercourse was accomplished by force, fear, or fraud.

There is no set amount of force that must be used for a defendant's acts to constitute rape. Prosecutors typically encourage the jury to evaluate the defendant's threats from the victim's perspective. Thus, in an acquaintance rape situation, a defendant who engages in rough sex play with the victim, or blocks a victim's departure, may meet the requirements. See, e.g., *State v. Rusk*, 424 A.2d 720 (Md. 1981).

Some rape situations do not require proof of force. For example, the law presumes that an unconscious, mentally incompetent, or underage victim is incapable of giving consent. No showing of force is required in these cases.

To ensure that a defendant is not charged with rape simply because a woman regrets her decision not to decline a man's sexual advances, the common law required that the prosecutor prove that the victim *resisted* to corroborate the allegation that the defendant had sex by force. Many modern jurisdictions have abandoned the resistance requirement because it is unrealistic (many women freeze and cannot resist) and also puts women at peril (some studies show that women who resist are injured more severely than women who submit).

There are also rape cases in which the defendant does not use force, but uses *threats* to get his victim to submit. Ordinarily, laws require that the defendant threaten some type of force. Thus, a court refused to hold it was rape when a girl submitted to sex because her principal threatened to prevent her from graduating if she refused him. See *State v. Thompson*, 792 P.2d 1103 (Mont. 1990). However, some jurisdictions take a broader approach to what constitutes a threat and include abuse of authority as the basis for a rape charge.

Let's try a question that focuses on the means by which a defendant in an acquaintance rape situation might get his victim to succumb.

QUESTION 2. Nowhere to go. Luke meets Diane in a bar and offers her a ride home. When they get to her house, Luke follows her in. Diane becomes afraid because she barely knows Luke and she does not want him in her house. However, she tries to play it cool by offering him a quick beer before he leaves. Luke drinks the beer and then starts to hug Diane. She freezes and does not respond. Luke then starts to remove her clothes. Diane just starts to cry. Luke says, "Oh, I feel the same way too." Diane then tries to push Luke away. He responds by saying, "Oh, you like to play rough, heh? Well, I don't mind that game," and he grabs Diane, throws her on the bed, slaps her a few times, and tears her clothes off. By this time, Diane is struggling, but she is too scared to scream. Luke proceeds to have sex with her.

Is Luke guilty of rape?

A. Yes, if Luke realized that Diane did not want to have sex and forced her into it.

B. Yes, because Diane did not expressly state that she wanted to have sex with Luke.

C. No, because Diane should not have accepted Luke's offer to drive her home.

D. No, because Diane never said no to Luke's advances.

ANALYSIS. This question focuses on an unfortunately all-too-common scenario. Men and women do not communicate well about sex and often put their own interests ahead of those of their partners. In this situation, the jury will have to decide whether Diane consented to sex and whether Luke realized she had not consented.

You would probably do best on this question by trying to eliminate wrong answers first. **B** is wrong because the law does not require that a defendant get express permission before having sex. Perhaps such a law would be a good idea, but it is not realistic given the manner in which parties interact in an intimate situation.

C is also wrong because merely agreeing to a ride home is not an invitation to sex. Likewise, **D** is wrong because there can be a rape even when the victim is too scared to say no.

The correct answer is **A**. If Luke realized Diane did not consent, and he used force to have sex with her, he is guilty of rape, regardless of whether they were acquaintances.

5. Or deception

Finally, in some jurisdictions, a defendant may also *rape by deception.* The deception must go beyond the defendant's false proclamations of love and commitment or failure to disclose the true reason for wanting to have sex. For example, in *People v. Evans,* 379 N.Y.S.2d 912 (N.Y. App. Div. 1975), a young college student alleged rape because she was tricked into having sex with a man who performed a psychological experiment on her and intimidated her into having sex. The court held that the deception in that case was inadequate to support a charge of rape. However, *if the defendant deceives a victim into believing she is not actually having sex* by, for example, telling her that he is a doctor placing a medical instrument into her, it is rape if he uses that opportunity to have intercourse with the woman.

QUESTION 3. Sleep with me or die! Dr. Boro meets with his new patient, Sandra, and tells her that she has a terrible disease that can only be cured by having sex with someone with healthier genes who can transmit his DNA to her through his semen. Reluctantly, Sandra agrees to the "treatment." Dr. Boro then proceeds to have sex with Sandra. When Sandra learns that Boro's claims were a hoax, she reports him for rape.

Is Dr. Boro guilty of rape under the traditional definition of rape?

A. Yes, because Sandra was tricked into having sex.
B. No, because Sandra knew she was having intercourse with Dr. Boro.
C. Yes, because Dr. Boro forced Sandra into having sex.
D. No, because rape can only be committed by the threat of physical violence.

ANALYSIS. Although Dr. Boro has acted despicably, he is not guilty of rape. Under rape law, deception only counts if the victim somehow doesn't realize she is actually having sex. There are some states that have statutorily broadened the deception category to include situations in which deception is used to create a fear of unlawful physical injury. See, e.g., Cal. Penal Code §266c. However, under the traditional approach to rape, the type of deception in this case does not establish the crime of rape. See *Boro v. Superior Court*, 163 Cal. App. 3d 1224, 210 Cal. Rptr. 122 (1985).

Thus, **A** is wrong. Not every time a victim is tricked into having sex is the defendant guilty of rape. **C** is also wrong because the victim was not forced into having sex; she chose to do so because of misrepresentations. However, **D** goes too far. Rape does not require the threat of physical violence, but this is not a case in which the deception rule applies. The correct answer is **B**. The victim knew she was having sex with Dr. Boro, so technically this is not rape.

C.   Mistake as a defense

The most difficult issue that arises in rape cases is whether a defendant, who mistakenly believes his victim has consented, is still guilty of rape. Is an honest mistake of fact enough to exculpate the defendant or should the defendant's mistake also have to be reasonable?

Historically, some courts have held that an honest mistake as to consent could constitute a defense to rape because it demonstrated that the defendant did not have the necessary mens rea for the crime. In *Regina v. Morgan*, [1976] A.C. 182, defendant Morgan and his three friends were charged with raping Morgan's wife. While out drinking, Morgan suggested to his co-defendants that they go to his home and have sexual intercourse with his wife. He described her as "kinky" and preferring to struggle during sex. The men took Morgan up on his suggestion and returned to have sex with Morgan's struggling wife. When charged with rape, they claimed that they honestly believed the victim had consented. The trial court rejected the defense because the belief was not reasonable. The appellate court held, however, that an honest belief in consent, even if not reasonable, is a defense to rape because it negates the defendant's mens rea for the crime.[1]

In response to the *Morgan* decision, the British Parliament enacted a statute that made reckless disregard of whether there was consent a sufficient mens rea for rape. Many U.S. courts followed suit by requiring that the defendant have both an honest and reasonable belief that the victim had consented. If a reasonable person would have realized that the victim was not consenting, the defendant is guilty of rape regardless of what he thought. See *People v. Williams*, 841 P.2d 961 (Cal. 1992) (honest and reasonable mistake required for defense to rape); *Commonwealth v. Sherry*, 437 N.E.2d 224 (Mass. 1982) (recognizing general rule in American courts that mistake of fact for rape requires that the defendant act in good faith and with reasonableness).

From the next question, you can see how important the standard for mistake of fact is in determining whether there has been a rape.

QUESTION 4. **Friend of a friend.**   Paul's friend sets him up on a date with Kathy. His friend tells him that Kathy is a lot of fun and can enjoy herself without expecting a wedding band. Kathy and Paul go out for a nice dinner. At the dinner, Kathy is very flirtatious. On the ride home, Kathy tells Paul that she had a great time and she hopes that they will become closer friends. Paul drops Kathy off at her home. An hour later, Kathy realizes that she left her wallet in Paul's car. She does not know his phone number, but she knows where he lives. Kathy goes over to his house and pounds on the door. Paul answers the door and says, "Wow, my friend was right. That was fast." He then grabs Kathy and starts to kiss and fondle her. She is so shocked that she cannot move. She tries to tell Paul that she has just come for her wallet, but he puts his hand on her mouth and starts to remove her clothes. By the time Kathy can tell Paul why she is there, he has already penetrated her.

Under the approach to mistake of fact in rape cases reflected in *Regina v. Morgan*, is Paul guilty of rape?

A. Yes, because it was unreasonable for Paul to believe that Kathy wanted to have sex with him on their first date.

---

1. However, the appellate court still refused to reverse the defendants' convictions because it found that no reasonable jury could have found that the defendants made a sincere, honest mistake of fact.

> **B.** Yes, because he did not ascertain Kathy's true intentions.
> **C.** No, because Kathy initiated the contact.
> **D.** No, if Paul honestly believed Kathy was consenting to sex.

ANALYSIS.   As you can see from this question, it can be critical whether the mistake of fact standard is an honest mistake or an honest *and reasonable* mistake as to whether the victim has consented. Clueless Paul may be able to convince a jury that he made an honest mistake, but prosecutors could likely argue that his mistake was unreasonable.

Looking at the possible answers, **A** can be eliminated immediately because it states the wrong standard for mistake. Under rape law as reflected in *Morgan*, an honest mistake was enough. **B** is also wrong because it is another way of stating that Paul could not have a mistake defense. Now, the choice should be much easier. The mere fact that Kathy initiated the contact does not give Paul the right to have sex with her. **C** is wrong. The correct answer is **D**. If Paul honestly believed Kathy was consenting, even if he was mistaken, he would have had a defense to rape.

Today, Paul would not have such an easy defense. He would be entitled to a mistake defense only if his mistake as to her consent was honest and reasonable.

D.   Rape reform legislation and rape shield laws

Although courts continue to strive to treat victims better, reform legislation has had little effect on rape victims' reporting behavior. The prevailing view among academics continues to be that rape law is still based on male perspectives and stereotypes of male-female behavior, and that the real changes that need to be made are related to society's attitudes, not just the legal standards for rape.

Nonetheless, some rape law reforms include

- elimination of the resistance requirement;
- elimination or relaxation of the force requirement;
- elimination of the marital exemption;
- elimination of a mistake defense;[2] and

---

2. Many scholars are troubled by this proposal because it would have the effect of holding the defendant strictly liable for rape, regardless of whether a reasonable person would have believed the victim had consented. Every defendant would have to be correct that his victim did, in fact, consent to the sexual intercourse.

- admission of expert testimony on rape trauma syndrome to explain the victim's reaction to the sexual assault.

To encourage more rape victims to come forward, legislatures enacted rape shield laws. Rape shield laws limit the scope of cross-examination of a rape victim to prevent the woman and her sexual past from being put on trial. Typically, rape shield laws prohibit the admissibility of the victim's prior sexual history. Yet these laws are subject to exceptions, as well. For example, under Federal Rule of Evidence 412(a), a woman's sexual behavior is generally not admissible. However, if the issue is consent, her prior sexual conduct with the defendant is admissible. Fed. R. Evid. 412(b)(1)(B). Or, if the issue is the source of the woman's injuries or the semen found in her, the woman's other sexual acts are admissible. Fed. R. Evid. 412(b)(1)(A). Finally, the Constitution can require that a victim's other sexual conduct be admitted in order to prove, for example, bias on the part of a woman using allegations against the defendant to hide a sexual affair with another person. Fed. R. Evid. 412(b)(1)(C); see *Olden v. Kentucky*, 488 U.S. 227 (1988).

Try a quick question relating to the use of rape shield laws.

> **QUESTION 5. Foul moves.**   Cody Bryant is charged with rape. According to the prosecution, the first time Cody met the victim he forced her into having sex. Cody wants to introduce evidence that the alleged victim is an extremely promiscuous young woman and consented to his sexual advances. In particular, he wants to introduce evidence that the alleged victim had sex with 20 different partners before meeting Cody. The prosecution has moved to bar the introduction of this evidence.
>
> Under the rape shield law, the court should
>
> A. deny the motion because the woman's sexual behavior is relevant to whether she consented.
> B. grant the motion because the woman's prior sexual acts did not involve Cody.
> C. deny the motion because Cody has a constitutional right to defend himself.
> D. grant the motion because a woman's sexual past is never relevant in a rape trial.

ANALYSIS.   Although you might think that the woman's past is relevant to whether she was raped, the legislature has made a determination that her sexual history is not admissible. Accordingly, **A** is wrong. Even if the evidence is probative, the prejudicial impact on the victim, and the likelihood that jurors might simply rule in favor of the defendant because they don't like the woman's sexual conduct, has led the legislature to pass a rape shield law barring this evidence.

C is also wrong. Do not be confused by the "constitutional exception" to the rape shield law. It does not apply every time the defendant claims he has a constitutional right to defend himself. It is limited to situations in which the victim is using her allegations against the defendant to hide another relationship.

Thus, the motion should be granted. Between **B** and **D**, **B** is the better answer. **D** is wrong because a woman's sexual past can be relevant in a rape trial. It just is not relevant in this case because her prior sexual acts did not involve Cody and the issue is consent. **B** is the correct answer.

E.   Model Penal Code approach

Like the criminal codes of many states, the Model Penal Code does not have one rape law. Rather, it sets forth many different types of sexual acts that can constitute criminal offenses. They range from indecent exposure to sexual assault to rape. See Model Penal Code Article 213: Sexual Offenses.

The crime of "rape" under the Model Penal Code is a felony. A defendant commits rape by purposely, knowingly, or recklessly having sexual intercourse with a female under any of the following circumstances: (1) the female is less than 10 years old; (2) the female is unconscious; (3) the female is compelled by force or threat of death, grievous bodily harm, extreme pain, or kidnapping; or (4) the defendant intoxicates the victim. Model Penal Code §213.1(1).

The Model Penal Code recognizes a partial marital exemption. If a man and a female not his wife live together, the man may not be charged with rape, although he may be guilty of gross sexual imposition. Model Penal Code §213.1(2)(a). Gross sexual imposition requires that the defendant use a "threat that would prevent resistance by a woman of ordinary resolution," or that the defendant knows that the victim suffers from a mental disease or defect that makes her unable to appraise the nature of her conduct. It also applies in situations in which the defendant fraudulently represents himself to be the victim's husband.

Many jurisdictions follow the Model Penal Code's approach to rape. It should be a fairly easy standard for you to apply.

QUESTION 6. Slipped her a mickey. Walter invites Marion to his house for dinner. During dinner, he slips a narcotic into her drink. Marion remains conscious, but she loses all her inhibitions and frankly does not even know what Walter is doing until he is already on top of her and they are having sex. The next day, Marion claims she was raped.

Walter is most likely

A. not guilty, because Marion remained conscious.
B. not guilty, if Marion did not say no to Walter's advances.
C. not guilty, because Marion lost her inhibitions.
D. guilty.

ANALYSIS.   This one should be easy. Walter intoxicated Marion with the narcotic. Having sex with an intoxicated person, even if she is not unconscious, is defined as rape under the Model Penal Code and in many jurisdictions.

A is wrong because an intoxicated person is incapable of giving consent under the Model Penal Code approach, even if she is conscious. **B** is wrong because Walter has taken away Marion's ability to refuse his advances. Likewise, Walter cannot rely on Marion losing her inhibitions as a defense to rape, because he caused her to do so by intoxicating her. **C** is therefore wrong.

The correct answer is **D**. Walter is guilty of rape by intoxication.

F.   Statutory rape

By statute, jurisdictions prohibit sexual intercourse with a person under a certain age, often 16 years old. The law conclusively presumes that a person under that age is incapable of consent. No showing of force, fraud, or intimidation is required.

In most jurisdictions, the defendant's mistake of fact as to his victim's age is irrelevant. If the defendant has sex with a person under the age of legal consent, the defendant is automatically guilty of statutory rape. Some jurisdictions, however, allow a reasonable mistake defense, if a reasonable person would also have believed the victim was of lawful age to consent. See Model Penal Code §213.6(1).

QUESTION 7. **Young sweet thing.**   Ron meets Honey at a bar. Honey is drinking and smoking. As they get to know each other better, Honey tells Ron that she is a college student, 20 years old. In fact, Honey is only 15 years old, a fact that she does not reveal to Ron until after they have slept together. Upset that their daughter is having sex, Honey's parents report the incident to the police and Ron is charged with statutory rape.

In most jurisdictions, Ron is

A. guilty of rape, because he had sex with Honey.
B. guilty of rape, because he forced himself upon Honey.
C. not guilty of rape, because Honey lied to him about her age.
D. not guilty of rape, because it was reasonable for Ron to believe that a girl who is drinking and smoking is not a minor.

ANALYSIS. Statutory rape is a type of strict-liability crime. Once the defendant has sex with an underage victim, the defendant is automatically guilty regardless of whether he made a good faith mistake as to the victim's age. Ron is guilty even if he honestly and reasonably thought Honey was 20 years old.

B is wrong because it does not even accurately reflect the facts of the problem. There is no allegation that Ron forced himself on Honey. If the law did not presumptively hold that Honey is incapable of giving consent, this would not be a rape case. However, Honey cannot give lawful consent because of her age.

C is wrong because it does not matter whether Ron was misled as to Honey's age. Although some jurisdictions recognize a good faith defense, most jurisdictions do not. Under the majority approach and traditional common law, Ron is strictly liable for having sex with an underage victim. Therefore, **D** is also wrong. It doesn't matter that Ron made an honest and reasonable mistake; mistake is ordinarily not a defense to statutory rape.

A is the correct answer. Ron is guilty of rape — statutory rape — because he had sex with Honey, an underage person.

G.   The Closer: Fear versus threat

Recall that one basis for the charge of forcible rape is that the defendant instilled fear in the victim. What if the victim is truly afraid of the defendant, but the defendant has not actually threatened her? Is that still rape?

The short answer is no. It is not enough that the victim fears the defendant. There must be an actual threat (verbal or physical) that causes the fear. However, if a defendant preys on a victim's self-created fear, that may be enough for rape. For example, if a victim conveys to the defendant that she will submit only because the defendant will kill her if she doesn't, the defendant commits rape if he does not disabuse the victim of this false fear.

The closer presents a difficult case that raises the question of how much of a threat a defendant must present to be guilty of rape.

QUESTION 8. **Molly and Perry.** Molly and Perry are at a party together. They start having sex, but a minute into their sexual relations, Molly decides she wants to stop. She starts to pull away, but she doesn't do so completely because Perry doesn't disengage. For five more minutes, Perry continues to have sex with Molly. Molly reports the incident and Perry is charged with rape. When she is asked why she didn't yell stop or more forcefully resist Perry, she said that she was too afraid that he might get mad at her for leading him on and hurt her.

Under traditional rape law, will Perry be found guilty of rape?

A. Yes, because Molly tried to pull away.
B. Yes, because Perry could have hurt Molly if she resisted.
C. No, because Molly consented to sex.
D. No, because Perry did not use force or a threat of force.

ANALYSIS.   This is a challenging problem. Molly initially consented to sex. However, she later withdrew that consent. The problem is whether she adequately conveyed that withdrawal to Perry and whether he then used force or a threat to continue the sexual encounter.

When you are reading a tough question, sometimes the proposed answers can make the problem a little easier. Let's start with **A**. Molly withdrew consent by pulling away, but it is unclear whether Perry used or threatened force at any point to continue the encounter. Therefore, a key ingredient for rape is missing—the threat or use of force. **A** is an incorrect answer.

B is also incorrect. Even though Perry hypothetically could have hurt Molly, he never suggested that he would. It was Molly's self-created fear that caused her to believe this. Traditionally, this was insufficient for rape.

Now, we have a tough choice between **C** and **D**. **C** is a bit ambiguous. Molly did, in fact, consent to sex, although she later tried to withdraw her consent. However, it is unclear whether she adequately conveyed that withdrawal of consent to Perry. Moreover, even after Molly pulled away, Perry did not use any force or threat of force to get Molly to continue. Accordingly, between the two, **D** is the better answer.

✦ Levenson's Picks

1. "No means no."	**D**	
2. Nowhere to go	**A**	
3. Sleep with me or die!	**B**	

4. Friend of a friend   **D**
5. Foul moves   **B**
6. Slipped her a mickey   **D**
7. Young sweet thing   **A**
8. Molly and Perry   **D**

Theft Crimes

It's not for stealing that you are punished, but for getting caught.
— Russian proverb

CHAPTER OVERVIEW

A. Larceny
  1. Trespassory taking
  2. Property in the possession of another
  3. Intent to permanently deprive owner
B. Robbery
C. Extortion and blackmail
D. Misappropriation and embezzlement
E. Fraud crimes
  1. False pretenses
  2. Larceny by trick
F. Modern theft and fraud crimes
G. The Closer: Defenses to theft crimes
✣ Levenson's Picks

The law of theft crimes concerns itself, to a significant degree, with the historical evolution of crimes against property. Historically, the courts recognized a long litany of theft-type crimes. Today, many statutes lump these crimes into two broad categories: "theft" and "fraud." Nonetheless, the courts still rely on common law principles regarding the elements of theft crimes to interpret modern laws.

Theft crimes are crimes against property. Like crimes against persons, they have three components: actus reus, mens rea, and circumstances. The actus reus varies with the type of theft crime. The minimum mens rea requirement is an intent to perform that act by which the property is acquired. However, there may be an additional mens rea requirement, such as an intent to permanently deprive the owner of the property. Finally, the key circumstance in these crimes is that the defendant's actions concern the property of another. Thus, it is important to analyze the meaning of "property" under various theft laws.

The law of theft did not develop smoothly. Originally, only theft crimes that posed physical danger to others (e.g., robbery) were punishable. Gradually, both the courts and lawmakers expanded the law of theft to cover other types of offenses, such as larceny, embezzlement, and obtaining property by false pretenses (fraud).

In this chapter, we examine a wide variety of theft crimes, ranging from robbery to modern forms of fraud.

A.   Larceny

Larceny was the most basic theft crime at common law. Although many jurisdictions still retain the term *larceny,* the modern equivalent is *stealing.*

Larceny is defined as "the trespassory taking and carrying away of the personal property of another with intent to permanently deprive that person of the property."

The elements of larceny are

- intentional taking and carrying away
- personal property
- in the possession or presence of another
- without consent [trespassory taking]
- with intent to permanently deprive another of his property.

1. Trespassory taking

To apply these elements, it is important to understand some of the key terms. First, what is trespassory taking? A taking is trespassory when the person who lawfully possesses the property does not consent to the taking. For example, if a defendant takes a purse off a woman's lap without her permission, he has engaged in a trespassory taking.

The crime of larceny is satisfied by any slight movement of the taken property; the defendant need not transport the property far nor succeed in permanently depriving the victim of her property. The act of carrying away the property is also known as "asportation."

For example, assume John Doe is a pickpocket. He picks up an item from a store counter when the shopkeeper is not looking and heads for the door. Even if he is caught before he can leave the premises, he is still guilty of larceny because he took the property without permission and moved it away from its owner.

A thief may also use an instrument or third party to help with the taking. For example, a defendant can ask an innocent third person to retrieve a piece of property for him. If the defendant knows that he does not have a right to the property, it doesn't matter that the third person was an innocent instrument; the defendant is still guilty of larceny.

The Model Penal Code has relaxed the requirement that the defendant actually move the property away from its owner. Under Model Penal Code §223.2(1), it is sufficient if the defendant "exercises unlawful control" over the moveable property. Thus, if a defendant affixes a "sold" tag to an item he knows he has not purchased, the defendant is guilty of theft even if he does not remove the item.

The key issue in deciding whether a taking was trespassory is ascertaining whether the victim consented to the defendant's removal of the property. If the victim has agreed to give the property to the defendant, there is no larceny.

Let's use our first larceny question to test your understanding of a trespassory taking.

QUESTION 1. Sweater snatch. Joannie and Sally regularly borrow each other's clothes at school. After gym class, Joannie sees Sally's sweater lying on the bench. Thinking that she can borrow it, Joannie puts on the sweater and leaves to go to class. The gym teacher sees this and has Joannie charged with larceny.

What is Joannie's best defense?

A. She did not carry away the sweater.
B. She believed she had Sally's consent to wear the sweater.
C. She could always return the sweater if she were caught.
D. Joannie has no defense.

ANALYSIS. There is no question that Joannie intentionally took a sweater that she knew belonged to another. However, for this to be a trespassory taking, Joannie must realize that she does not have consent to take the sweater, and she must take and carry it away.

A is wrong because Joannie did carry away the sweater, even if only a short distance. Under common law, the slightest movement was sufficient; under the Model Penal Code, no movement is necessary if the defendant has exercised unlawful control.

Joannie would have a much better defense under **B**. Although she knew the sweater belonged to Sally, Joannie thought she had permission to take the sweater. Therefore, she committed a taking, but it was not "trespassory" (i.e., unlawful), because she had the owner's permission.

C is wrong because if Joannie had stolen the sweater, merely being willing to return it is not a defense to larceny. **B** is the right answer. Joannie has a defense of consent, making **D** a wrong answer.

Let's continue to look at the other elements of larceny and the specialized meanings of some key terms.

2. Property in the possession of another

Traditional theft laws covered only the taking of *tangible personal property.* Tangible personal property included money, objects, fixtures or crops severed from the land, and animals. It did not include real estate, services, or intangible rights, like guarantees or copyrights. For example, unauthorized use of computer services would not constitute larceny. See *Lund v. Commonwealth*, 232 S.E.2d 745 (Va. 1977).

The Model Penal Code takes a broader view of property, including anything "of value," from real estate to tangible personal property.

Larceny also applies only when the property is taken from the possession of another, even if the defendant is the rightful owner of that property. Thus, if a defendant takes his car in to be repaired, but uses an extra key to drive it off the lot without paying the repair bill, the defendant is guilty of the larceny of the money he owed for his car repairs.

Because the common law crime of larceny applied only when a defendant took property out of the lawful *possession* of another, the issue would arise as to what crime would apply if a defendant were given short-term custody over an item and decided to keep it permanently. For example, assume a store owner asks his delivery girl to deliver a box of merchandise to another store. Instead, the delivery girl keeps the box of items. Although the delivery girl would try to argue that she had possession of the goods and therefore could not be guilty of larceny, the court would most likely hold that she had *mere custody* of the items and by deciding to keep them, she indeed took them out of the possession of the owner.

Finally, abandoned property is considered not to be the property of anyone and a defendant cannot be guilty of larceny if he finds and keeps truly abandoned property. However, under the Model Penal Code and the laws of many states, if a person finds property and knows it belongs to another person, but doesn't know who that person is, the defendant must make reasonable efforts to return the item.

It is time to try a question that focuses on the property element of larceny.

> **QUESTION 2. Repair man.** Shellie's television has broken. Fortunately for Shellie, she purchased an extended warranty so that she can call the repairman whenever her set needs service. Shellie calls the repairman, who says he will be out in the afternoon to fix her set. Later, the repairman arrives, but he goes to the wrong house. Shellie's neighbor, Byron, has the repairman fix his television instead.
>
> Under traditional common law, is Byron guilty of larceny?
>
> A. Yes, because he had not paid for the repair service.
> B. Yes, because his actions involved personal property.
> C. No, because he was in mere custody of his television.
> D. No, because he did not take the property of another.

ANALYSIS. For this question, it is crucial that you recall the common law definition of property — it has to be tangible, personal property. It is not larceny if a person steals services. Under modern statutes, Byron's actions may be criminal, but they are not larceny under traditional common law.

Therefore, **A** is wrong. Stealing services did not constitute larceny under common law. **B** is also wrong. Be careful with this one. Although his television constitutes personal property, the crime of larceny requires the trespassory taking of another person's property. Byron did not take Shellie's television set. Therefore, he is not guilty of larceny.

The choice comes down to **C** or **D**. **C** can be quickly eliminated for two reasons. First, Byron does not have mere custody over the television; it is actually his television. Second, the issue of mere custody only arises when the defendant is charged with temporarily having someone else's items in his possession. In this situation, Byron has his own television, not that belonging to Shellie.

The correct answer is **D**. Under the strict common law definition of property, Byron did not take the property of another. He may be guilty of some other statutory offense, but he is not guilty of common law larceny.

Finally, let's look at the intent element for larceny. As you will soon see, merely "borrowing" an item without permission is not larceny. The crime of larceny requires more.

3. Intent to permanently deprive owner

A defendant is not guilty of larceny unless he intends to permanently deprive another person of his property. Merely borrowing an object is insufficient for the requirements of the common law crime of theft. For example, if the defendant decides to borrow his neighbor's lawnmower without permission, he may have trespassed onto the defendant's property, but he has not committed larceny.

Some jurisdictions hold that a defendant who takes an object and abandons it, or recklessly exposes it to loss, or uses up the value of the item, meets the intent requirement, even if the defendant claims he did not intend to permanently deprive the owner of the property. See, e.g., N.Y. Penal Law §155.00(3). Thus, if a defendant borrows his neighbor's electric razor without permission, and then uses it to shave a buffalo or just leaves it in a yard, he is still guilty of theft, even if he always intended to return the razor.

If the defendant takes an object with the intent to keep it, it does not matter if he later changes his mind and decides to return the object. The crime of larceny is completed when the defendant originally takes and carries away the object with the intent to permanently deprive the owner of it.

Here is the last question regarding the crime of larceny.

QUESTION 3. Going for a joyride.   Bryan decides to take his neighbor's Ferrari for a joyride. He sneaks in the car when his neighbor is not looking and starts it with a spare set of keys kept in the glove compartment. While Bryan is cruising, the police pull him over on a traffic violation. Because the car's registration is not in Bryan's name, the officer arrests Bryan for stealing the car.

Is Bryan guilty of larceny?

A. Yes, because he took the car without permission.
B. Yes, because he intended to permanently deprive his neighbor of the car.
C. No, because the car had an extra set of keys in it.
D. No, because he was only going for a joyride.

ANALYSIS.   This problem should not be too difficult if you know what it means to go on a "joyride." The bar examiners certainly expect you to know this term because this problem is a favorite on the Multistate Bar Examination. A joyride is when a defendant borrows a car without permission. By definition, it does not involve the intent to permanently deprive the owner of his property. Accordingly, **A** is wrong because even if Bryan did not have permission to take the car, he only intended to borrow it. **B** is wrong because it is counter to the facts you are given. Remember, don't fight the facts on multiple-choice questions. If it is a joyride, the defendant intends to use the object and then return it.

C is also off track. Remember, criminal law does not blame the victim. Thus, even if it was negligent for the neighbor to keep an extra set of keys in the car, so long as the victim has not given consent to Bryan, the victim's negligence is irrelevant.

The correct answer is **D**. If Bryan was only going for a joyride, he did not intend to permanently deprive his neighbor of his car. Accordingly, he is not guilty of larceny.

B.   Robbery

In addition to basic theft crimes, there are also aggravated theft offenses. To protect victims from the physical danger presented by certain thefts, the common law developed the crime of robbery.

Robbery is the taking of property from another person with force or intimidation. Its elements include

- taking of property
- from the victim's person or presence
- by force or intimidation
- with intent to permanently deprive.

As its definition suggests, robbery is a combination of the crimes of larceny and assault. The crime is like an assault because the property must be forcefully taken from the victim's person or presence. For example, if the defendant threatens to shoot the victim unless he steps away from his motorcycle and lets the defendant drive it away, and the defendant then takes the motorcycle, the defendant has committed robbery.

In discussing larceny, we discussed the elements of "property" and "with intent to permanently deprive." *The unique aspect of robbery is that the taking must be by force or threat of force.* The defendant need not cause actual injury to the victim; using slight force is sufficient. If a threat is used, it must be of immediate and unlawful injury. Threats of future injury constitute a different crime: extortion.

For example, assume the defendant approaches the victim and threatens to shoot her unless she gives him her jewelry. The victim complies. Defendant's threat of immediate and unlawful injury satisfies the requirement of robbery. Words like "snatched" or "grabbed" often indicate that the defendant took the property against the victim's will.

Determine which crime, if any, applies to the facts of Question 4.

> **QUESTION 4. Rolling the bum.** Hank sees an unconscious drunk on the sidewalk and cautiously approaches him. Hank can see that the man has a wallet in his pocket. Hank carefully reaches into the victim's pocket and pulls out his wallet. Hank checks the wallet for identification, but when he finds none, he puts the wallet in his own jacket and walks away.

> Although Hank is carrying a concealed weapon at the time of the encounter, he never displays it while he is taking the wallet. Hank is apprehended shortly thereafter.
>
> Which crime(s), if any, is Hank guilty of?
>
> **A.** Robbery.
> **B.** Larceny.
> **C.** Robbery and larceny.
> **D.** No crime.

ANALYSIS. Hank certainly took the drunk's property without his permission, but the key issue is whether Hank used force or the threat of force. Although Hank is carrying a weapon, he never displays the weapon or otherwise threatens force. Rather, he carefully slips the wallet out of the bum's pocket. Because he does not use any force, or the threat of force, **A** is a wrong answer. Hank is not guilty of robbery.

However, Hank is guilty of larceny. He took the property of another with the intent to permanently deprive him of that property. This question is a little tricky because an argument could be made that at the time Hank initially removed the wallet, he did not intend to keep the wallet but only took it to look for identification. However, even if that had been the case, by the time Hank walked away he had the intent to permanently deprive the victim of the wallet.

C and **D** are wrong because the crime that fits here is larceny, not robbery. **B** is the correct answer.

C.   Extortion and blackmail

If robbery is the taking of property by threat of present violence, *extortion is the taking of property by threat of future violence*. It sometimes goes by the name of *blackmail*. Its elements include

- taking of property
- from another
- by threat of future violence.

Although common law originally required the threat of future violence, today many jurisdictions define extortion as including the threat of other types of harms, such as the exposure of secret or embarrassing information, the filing of criminal charges, or other official action against the victim. However, courts will not expand the list indefinitely. For example, extortion law is not meant to cover remarks such as, "Give me a raise, or I will quit!"

Modern laws have also relaxed the requirement that there be an actual taking of property. In some jurisdictions, the mere threat for the purpose of obtaining property is sufficient, even if the defendant never actually takes the property.

Finally, extortion law is incorporated under the federal Hobbs Act, 18 U.S.C. §1951, which prohibits government officials from requesting or receiving quid pro quos in exchange for their official actions.

QUESTION 5. "Or else!" Sammy, a local politician, is scared. Danny called him and threatened to "rub him out" and tell Sammy's wife about his affair with his secretary unless Sammy transfers $10,000 to Danny's bank account and votes in favor of a new development bill. Feeling he had no choice, Sammy votes in favor of the bill and transfers $10,000 to Danny's bank account.

Under modern state and federal extortion laws, what, if any, crimes(s) is Danny guilty of?

A. Hobbs Act violation.
B. Robbery.
C. Extortion.
D. A and C.

ANALYSIS. This question should have been fairly easy for you. First, the call of the question gives a hint that you will want to use both state and federal extortion laws. Second, and most important, Danny is threatening future harm. Finally, Danny wants an elected official to take official action in response to the threat.

Accordingly, Danny is guilty of a Hobbs Act violation, but he is also guilty of more. He is not guilty of robbery because the threat is not of immediate violence. However, he is also guilty of ordinary extortion. Accordingly, **D** is the correct answer. **A** and **C** are only partially correct. **B** is wrong because the threat is of future violence and revelations of Sammy's improprieties.

D.   Misappropriation and embezzlement

Courts and lawmakers have expanded theft crimes to include the conversion of property that is already in the defendant's possession. Such conversion is called "misappropriation" and is the criminal act at the heart of the crime of "embezzlement."

Embezzlement is the unlawful conversion of another's property that is already in the possession of the defendant. Its elements are

- a fraudulent
- conversion of ("misappropriation")
- the property of another
- that the defendant already possesses.

For example, assume that the defendant works as a teller at a bank. When no one is looking, he pulls some money out of his teller drawer and puts it in his pocket. Under traditional larceny law, it may be difficult to convict the defendant because he did not take the money out of the possession of another person. Rather, he had possession of the funds, but abused his position of trust by converting the money to his own use.

It is easy to keep the concepts of larceny and embezzlement separate. If property is taken from the possession of another, the crime is larceny. If the defendant already has possession of another's property and converts it to his own use, the crime is embezzlement. In many jurisdictions, a general theft statute covers both offenses.

Originally, embezzlement was used only for a narrow category of individuals who by their status had possession of another's property. This primarily included servants who were entrusted with their masters' property, clerks, brokers, bankers, attorneys, and trustees.

There are many ways the defendant may misappropriate or convert the victim's property to his own use. For example, the defendant may spend it, use it for collateral for a loan, hide it, destroy it, or make it a gift. Typically, if you see a "bailee" who starts to use the property he is supposed to be safeguarding, you should think of the crime of embezzlement.

QUESTION 6. Attorney payments.   Ginger is a lawyer who represents Irene in a lawsuit against Irene's landlord. The parties agree to settle and the landlord sends a settlement check to Ginger for her client. Instead of forwarding the money to her client, Ginger puts the money in a client trust account and begins to use it for Ginger's own purposes.

What crime(s) is Ginger guilty of?

A. Embezzlement.
B. Extortion.
C. Larceny.
D. No crime.

ANALYSIS.   This is a classic embezzlement case. Ginger was not the rightful owner of the money sent to her; she had the responsibility of holding it for her client, Irene. Instead, she misappropriates it by using it for her own purposes. It is not larceny because Ginger did not take the money out of the possession of another. It is also not extortion because Ginger does not have to make threats to obtain the money. Accordingly, **A** is the correct answer. **B** and **C** name the wrong crime and **D** is wrong because the crime of embezzlement does fit these facts.

E.   Fraud crimes

In addition to unlawfully taking property from another by threat, force, or conversion, a person may cheat another out of property. Fraud occurs when a person knowingly gives property to another, but does so because of false representations. Common law divided fraud crimes into two different technical offenses: (1) false pretenses and (2) larceny by trick. We discuss both of these offenses and then try a problem that determines if you know the difference between the two.

1. False pretenses

The crime of false pretenses occurs when a defendant obtains title *to goods or money through acts of deceit or misrepresentation.* The elements are

- taking title and possession of the property of another
- by knowingly making false representations with regard to material facts
- with an intent to defraud.

Here is a simple example: Assume that you go to your car mechanic, who tells you that your transmission needs to be replaced. You pay the mechanic $2,000 to replace the transmission. As it turns out, the mechanic was lying. There was nothing wrong with your transmission. He has obtained your money by false representations and thus is guilty of the crime of false pretenses.

In some jurisdictions, paying with a bad check is also considered false pretenses because title to the goods obtained passes with the presentation of the check. However, in other jurisdictions, in which title does not pass until a check clears, the crime is not false pretenses. Rather, it is larceny by trick. As you are about to learn, larceny by trick applies when a defendant obtains possession, not title, by the use of deceit.

A defendant is guilty of fraud only if he makes a false representation as to a material fact. Puffing about the value of an item is not considered a misrepresentation. Thus, if the defendant tells his victim that the watch he is selling him is a real treasure and extremely valuable, it is not false pretenses if it turns out that the watch is not so special. However, if the defendant tells the victim that the watch is solid gold, and it turns out to be made of tin, the defendant has made a specific misrepresentation to obtain the victim's money and is guilty of false pretenses.

2. Larceny by trick

Larceny by trick is another offshoot of traditional larceny. *It is larceny by trick when a defendant* obtains possession, *not title, because of misrepresentations or acts of deceit.* The elements of larceny by trick are

- taking possession of the property of another
- by knowingly making false representations as to material facts or making false promises
- with an intent to defraud.

Here is a simple example of larceny by trick. The defendant offers to hold a person's ring while she goes for a swim. When she jumps in the water, he disappears with the ring. The defendant knows that he does not have rightful title to the ring. Rather, he has possession because he tricked the victim into believing he would hold it for her.

Both false pretenses and larceny by trick require intent to defraud. A defendant's intent to defraud can be inferred from his statements, actions, and the results of his actions. For example, in *Nelson v. United States,* 227 F.2d 21 (D.C. Cir. 1955), defendant offered to give a car that he said he only owed $55 on as security for a debt. In fact, he owed more than $3,000 on the car. The court held that it was proper for the jury to infer from the defendant's false statements and acts that he had intent to defraud.

Now it is time to check your understanding of these two common law fraud crimes.

QUESTION 7. Car swap.   Darnell agrees to sell his car to Jamie. Darnell tells Jamie that his car has only 60,000 miles on it. In fact, Darnell has rolled back the odometer on the car from 140,000 miles. Jamie pays Darnell $12,000 for the car. The car falls apart shortly thereafter.

What crime, if any, has Darnell committed?

A. Embezzlement.
B. Larceny by trick.
C. False pretenses.
D. Highway robbery.

ANALYSIS.   Let's go through each of the possible answers to see which one is correct. Sometimes it is easiest to eliminate the obviously wrong answers first. **D** falls into that category. Darnell's actions are not robbery. He has not used force or the threat of force to obtain property. **A** is also incorrect. Embezzlement only applies when the defendant misappropriates property already in his possession.

That leaves the choice of **B** (larceny by trick) or **C** (false pretenses). Remember that false pretenses applies when the defendant obtains title to the property through deceit. In other words, if the victim thinks that he is giving something to the defendant forever, the crime involved is false pretenses. If the defendant only gets possession because the victim does not know he is giving up something forever, larceny by trick is the applicable crime. Here, Jamie knows he is giving money permanently for this car. In other words, Darnell will obtain "title" to the money. Accordingly, the applicable crime is false pretenses. **C** is the correct answer; **B** is wrong.

F.   Modern theft and fraud crimes

Modern statutes tend to group different types of theft crimes together, and create broad categories of fraud crimes. By doing so, they avoid arcane distinctions that lead to technical loopholes. For example, under the Model Penal Code, theft crimes are all treated as a type of "larceny" or simply as "theft." Even fraud is included as a theft.

Many jurisdictions, including the federal codes, bar schemes to defraud. For jurisdictional purposes, the federal offense requires the use of the mail or interstate wires to commit the fraud.

Modern statutes have also expanded the definition of "property" that may be stolen. In many jurisdictions, property now includes services, the unauthorized use of property, intangible property, jointly owned property, and secured and unsecured property.

The next question gives you an idea of how the modern fraud statutes expand on traditional notions of theft.

QUESTION 8. McNally's folly. John McNally is a public official engaged in a kickback scheme. In exchange for financial kickbacks, he uses his power to select the companies who win government contracts. The government charges McNally with a scheme to defraud the citizens of his jurisdiction out of their intangible right to honest government.

Which of the following is correct?

A. McNally is guilty of traditional larceny by trick.
B. McNally is guilty of traditional embezzlement.
C. McNally is guilty of traditional false pretenses.
D. McNally may be guilty of modern fraud.

ANALYSIS. This question is based on the Supreme Court case of *McNally v. United States*, 483 U.S. 350 (1987), and the changes it prompted in the federal fraud statutes. In *McNally*, the Court examined the federal mail and wire fraud statute and found that it did not cover theft of intangible rights, such as the right to fair and honest services. In response, Congress passed an additional statute to expand the definition of property to include such rights. See 18 U.S.C. §1346. Accordingly, now McNally may be guilty of modern fraud. However, **A**, **B**, and **C** are wrong because under traditional theft law, this type of property was not covered. **D** is correct because, depending on the jurisdiction, it may now be covered by the fraud statutes.

G.   The Closer: Defenses to theft crimes

As with other offenses, a defendant charged with a theft crime can both contest the evidence of the prima facie case and raise affirmative defenses. In contesting the prima facie case, defendants most often claim (1) the alleged property taken does not qualify as "property" under the law; (2) the owner consented to the taking; and (3) the defendant did not intend to permanently deprive the owner, but was simply borrowing the object without permission. Remember, though, that intent to repay or return the property is not a defense if it is formed after the defendant takes the property.

There are also affirmative defenses to theft crimes. The key affirmative defense is the "claim of right" defense. On rare occasions, a defendant charged with a theft crime can claim that he is the true owner of the goods or money, and that he was just trying to reclaim his right to it. Claim of right generally is not a defense to a theft crime that involves violence or the threat of violence, such as robbery or extortion. The Model Penal Code recognizes an affirmative defense to theft if the defendant reasonably believed that he was recovering property that was owed to him. Model Penal Code §223.1(3).

Use the closer to review how the theft crimes work and what, if any, defenses you think could apply.

> **QUESTION 9. Laptop Larry.** Bernice asked Larry to loan her his laptop. Larry agreed. After using it awhile, Bernice sends Larry $500 with a note, "Dear Larry. Thanks for the laptop. It is working beautifully." Larry cashes the check, but then decides that he really needs his laptop back. He goes over to Bernice and asks her to return his laptop. When she balks and tries to explain that she had paid him for it, Larry reaches over, pushes her away, and grabs the laptop. Before he can walk away, he is arrested by a police officer who has been watching the encounter.

> Which crime, if any, is Larry guilty of?
>
> **A.** Larceny.
> **B.** False pretenses.
> **C.** Robbery.
> **D.** No crime.

ANALYSIS. This question may have been a bit challenging. Not only do you need to remember the different categories of theft crimes, you also need to understand how the claim of right defense works. Let's take it step by step.

A is wrong because this is not a larceny case. Larry did far more than just grab someone else's property. In fact, if that were all that he had done, he might have been able to raise a claim of right argument, although he would probably lose on that as well because he had been paid for the laptop. Also, if larceny were charged, there would be the issue of whether he sufficiently moved the object to be guilty of the offense.

B is wrong because he did not use any misrepresentations to take the property. He simply grabbed it. The choice comes down to robbery or no crime. **C** is correct. This is a robbery situation. Larry used force to obtain the property. Even if he had a claim of right, he would not be entitled to use force to exercise that claim of right. **D** is a wrong answer.

✦ Levenson's Picks

1. Sweater snatch	**B**
2. Repair man	**D**
3. Going for a joyride	**D**
4. Rolling the bum	**B**
5. "Or else!"	**D**
6. Attorney payments	**A**
7. Car swap	**C**
8. McNally's folly	**D**
9. Laptop Larry	**C**

23

Other Crimes Against Person and Property

~

If there has been any crime, it must be prosecuted.
—Calvin Coolidge

~

CHAPTER OVERVIEW
A. Assault
B. Battery
C. Burglary
D. Arson
E. Kidnapping
F. The Closer: Felony murder revisited
✥ Levenson's Picks

In prior chapters, we focused on many of the traditional crimes taught in a law school course. However, a few others may arise either during your criminal law class or as you study for the bar examination. They usually arise when you are asked to apply the misdemeanor-manslaughter doctrine or felony-murder law. To do so, you may need to know a variety of crimes against persons and property, including those examined in this chapter.

A. Assault

Assault is typically defined as an *attempted battery*, which is the unlawful and offensive touching of another person. *There are typically two ways to commit assault: (1) the defendant can attempt to batter the victim; or (2) the defendant can put the victim in apprehension of an imminent battery.*

Simple assault is generally considered to be a misdemeanor. However, there are a variety of statutes that increase the penalty for different types of aggravated assaults. For example, defendants today may be charged with assault with a deadly weapon, assault on school property, assault against a police officer, or assault with the intent to cause serious bodily injury.

To constitute assault, it is not necessary that the defendant cause any actual injury. In fact, if injury is inflicted, the defendant may be charged with battery. (See Section B *infra.*)

The actus reus for assault is any action, other than words alone, that threatens to injure the victim. As for the mens rea requirement, assault is a specific-intent crime because it requires that the defendant intend to harm the victim or to create apprehension in the victim that she will be harmed. If a defendant is charged with an apprehension battery, the prosecution must prove that the defendant intended to create reasonable apprehension in the mind of the victim of imminent bodily harm.

Using this information, consider the following problem.

QUESTION 1. Gotcha. Eric and Carol have been getting on each other's nerves at work. Carol decides she needs to liven things up by playing a practical joke on Eric. When Eric arrives at work, Carol pretends to throw a baseball at his head. However, unbeknownst to Eric, the ball is attached to a string and rebounds to Carol before it hits Eric. Nonetheless, Eric is extremely startled and upset by the incident.

Is Carol guilty of assault?

A. Yes, because Carol acted recklessly.
B. Yes, because Carol intended to and did create a reasonable apprehension in Eric that he would be hit by the ball.
C. No, because Carol never intended to hit Eric with the ball.
D. No, because Eric suffered no physical injury.

ANALYSIS. Don't forget that there are two types of basic assaults recognized in criminal law: (1) attempted battery; and (2) attempt to cause apprehension of imminent bodily harm. In this situation, Carol is not guilty of the first type of assault, but she is guilty of the latter. Even if she meant it as a joke, she intentionally created a reasonable apprehension in Eric that he would be hit in the head by the baseball.

A is a bit tricky. It is not the right answer because even though Carol may have acted recklessly, she needed to intend to cause reasonable apprehension in the mind of the victim.

Skipping **B** for the moment, take a look at **C** and **D**. **C** is wrong because a defendant can be guilty of assault even if she never intends to physically harm the victim. An intent to cause reasonable apprehension of imminent physical harm is sufficient. **D** is wrong because it doesn't matter for an assault charge whether the victim is actually injured. If the victim is injured, the defendant can be charged with battery.

B is the correct answer. If Carol intended to create a reasonable apprehension in Eric that he would be hit by the ball, she is guilty of (apprehension) assault.

B. Battery

Battery is the unlawful application of force to another person resulting in either bodily injury or an offensive touching. As with assaults, many jurisdictions have passed statutes creating different degrees of battery. A battery that results only in an offensive touching is usually treated as a misdemeanor and labeled as "simple battery." However, if the defendant causes severe bodily harm, the defendant may be charged with a felony. If the defendant touches the victim with the purpose of sexual arousal, sexual gratification, or sexual abuse, the defendant may be charged with sexual battery.

The elements of battery are straightforward. The actus reus is a harmful or offensive touching. For example, if a defendant gropes a victim without the victim's consent, the defendant has committed a battery. The touching need not injure the victim, leave a mark, or even be painful. A defendant may commit a battery through direct contact with the victim, such as by hitting, tripping, or slapping the person; or indirectly, by, for example, spraying the victim with chemicals, throwing a cup of urine in the victim's eyes, or unleashing a dog on the victim.

Battery is considered a general intent crime because the defendant need only intend to do the physical act that results in an offensive or harmful touching. The defendant need not act with an intent to violate the law or injure the other person.

You often hear the phrase, "assault and battery." However, now you understand that they are actually two different offenses: Assault is the attempted battery; battery is the actual unlawful touching. The next question illustrates the differences between the two offenses.

> **QUESTION 2. Kiss it goodbye.** Ralph has always had a crush on Ellie, but she has never responded to his advances. Even though he knows she will be furious, Ralph goes ahead and gives her a kiss as they are riding in a crowded elevator. Ellie reports him to the police and Ralph is charged with battery.
>
> Which of the following is correct?
>
> **A.** Ralph is not guilty unless he hurt Ellie with his kiss.
> **B.** Ralph is guilty because he touched Ellie in an offensive manner.
> **C.** Ralph is not guilty because he never assaulted Ellie.
> **D.** Ralph is guilty because others in the elevator saw him kiss Ellie.

ANALYSIS. Even a kiss can be a criminal act if it is an offensive touching. In this situation, Ellie has made it clear that she would be offended by Ralph's advances. Accordingly, Ralph has committed a battery on Ellie, even if she is not injured.

A is wrong because a battery does not require injury. C is also wrong. Assault and battery are two different offenses. Assault is an attempted battery. However, once the unlawful touching has occurred, the defendant is guilty of battery. In many jurisdictions, assault merges into the crime of battery for purposes of sentencing.

D is wrong because Ralph's kiss would have been offensive to Ellie even if others did not witness it. The correct answer is B. Ralph is guilty of battery because he touched Ellie in an offensive manner.

C. Burglary

Burglary is a special type of property crime. It does not have to involve theft. *The common law definition of burglary is "breaking and entering of the dwelling house of another at nighttime with the intent to commit a felony inside."* Thus, a burglary is committed if the defendant enters a dwelling with the intent to commit any felony, not just when he intends to steal something from the house.

The elements of common law burglary include

- breaking and
- entering
- the dwelling house of another
- at nighttime
- with intent to commit felony inside.

Each of these elements has a specific meaning and application.

First, *breaking* covers the opening of a door or window of a dwelling, even if it was unlocked or already partially opened. If the defendant opened it wider, or defrauded another into opening a residence, the requirement is met. However, if the entry is completely consensual and without fraud, there is no burglary. Some courts have recognized types of constructive breakings. They include gaining entrance by threat, fraud, or misrepresentation, or by exceeding the scope of entry to which there was consent.

Second, there must be actual *entering* for there to be a burglary. Traditionally, burglary was a crime inside a home. The law's greatest concern is for the safety of individuals inside their homes. The defendant doesn't even need to completely enter the dwelling—reaching into a window that the defendant has opened is good enough. Moreover, there is even an entry if the defendant uses a physical instrument to help him reach inside the home. See, e.g., *People v. Tragni*, 449 N.Y.S.2d 923 (1982) (entry made by inserting grabbing instrument through hole in the wall).

Third, at common law, burglary covered only *residential buildings*, but statutes have now expanded burglary to include commercial buildings. Even under modern law, though, a person may not be guilty of burglary for breaking and entering into her own residence.

Fourth, at common law, an illegal entry was burglary only if it *occurred at night*; otherwise, it was only trespass. Today, many jurisdictions have eliminated the nighttime requirement.

Fifth, the mere entry of a home does not constitute burglary. Burglary occurs only when the defendant *enters with intent to commit a crime inside,* such as larceny, rape, kidnapping, murder, or arson. If the defendant does not have such intent, she may be guilty of trespassing, but she is not guilty of burglary. Because burglary requires the *specific intent* to commit a crime inside the residence, the defendant may be able to raise defenses such as intoxication that allow her to argue that she was not capable of forming the specific intent for the crime.

Finally, you must remember that burglary is separate from any crime the defendant may actually commit in the residence. For example, assume that the defendant breaks into a home with the intent to steal. Even if she does not steal, she is still guilty of burglary. However, if she does steal, she is guilty of two crimes: burglary and theft.

Modern statutes have modified the common law of burglary in various jurisdictions. For example, there are specialty crimes for burglarizing motor vehicles and injuring occupants during a burglary. However, for purposes of the next two questions, we continue to focus on the common law requirements of burglary that we just discussed.

QUESTION 3. Shiny ring. Marybelle has seen her neighbor wearing the most beautiful diamond ring. Marybelle decides that she just must have it. As she walks past her neighbor's home one evening, Marybelle sees the ring on the inside of her neighbor's windowsill. Seeing that nobody is home, Marybelle tries to open the window. It is already open a crack and Marybelle is able to open it enough to reach her hand inside. However, the ring is just out of her reach. Marybelle runs home and grabs some tongs, then uses them to reach inside the window. She grabs the ring and runs. However, she is later arrested when her neighbor sees Marybelle wearing her ring around town.

Which of the following crimes(s) can Marybelle be charged with?

A. Larceny.
B. Burglary.
C. Robbery.
D. A and B.
E. All of the above.

ANALYSIS. To make this question more challenging, you are offered five options. However, success is simply a matter of going through each option and deciding whether the elements of that crime have been met.

First, Marybelle is guilty of larceny. She took the personal property of another with the intent to deprive that person permanently of the property. **A** looks feasible, but you must wait to make your final selection until after you look at the other possible responses.

How about burglary? Let's review the elements. Marybelle broke into the home by opening the window, even though it was already partially opened. Then, she entered the residence by reaching inside. It doesn't matter that her entire body did not go into the home or that she used tongs to help her reach inside. Her actions were enough to constitute an entry. There is also no problem with the other elements. The incident happened at night, it was a residence, and at the time she reached inside, she had the intent to commit a felony, namely, to steal the ring. Therefore, **B** also looks like a feasible answer.

How about robbery? In everyday parlance, people often say they have been "robbed." For example, a person who finds her home broken into may tell the police that she has been "robbed." In truth, she has been burgled. As you recall, robbery requires a taking with the threat of force. There was no threat of force in this question. Therefore, **C** is wrong.

Now, let's pick the right answer. Since Marybelle is guilty of both larceny (**A**) and burglary (**B**), the correct answer to this question is **D**. **E** is wrong because Marybelle is not guilty of robbery.

Let's try a different type of burglary question, just so you feel comfortable with this very important offense.

QUESTION 4. Culligan man. Oleg works as a utility repairman. After getting a call regarding a possible gas leak in Bryna's home, he goes over there and tells her that he is there to check for the gas leak. Once inside, Oleg sees that Bryna is alone and he proceeds to sexually assault her. He then leaves without taking anything from Bryna's home.

Assuming that the jurisdiction does not require that a burglary occur at night, what, if any, crimes has Oleg committed?

A. Burglary.
B. Trespass.
C. Rape.
D. A and C.

ANALYSIS. This question may be a bit trickier than the first one. Although Oleg does something terrible once he is in Bryna's home, the key issue for burglary is whether he had the intent to commit a felony at the time of the entering. **A** is wrong because Oleg did not break into Bryna's home and he did not have the intent to commit a felony until after he was inside. He formed the intent to rape *after* he was already in the home. As a result, he is not guilty of burglary.

B is also wrong. Oleg did not trespass. He was invited into Bryna's home to check the gas. In some jurisdictions, overstaying your welcome can vitiate consent and convert a lawful entry into a trespass, but the better answer for this question is **C**. Oleg is definitely guilty of rape. **D** is wrong because Oleg is not also guilty of burglary.

D.   Arson

Arson is another common law offense that is typically mentioned in some fashion in criminal law courses. For example, if a defendant burns down his neighbor's house and a firefighter accidentally dies, the arson may be the basis of a felony-murder charge.

The common law definition of arson is "the malicious burning of the dwelling of another." The elements of common law arson include

- burning
- the dwelling house
- of another
- with malice.

As with burglary, each of the common law elements of arson has a specific meaning and application.

First, the actus reus of the crime of arson is *burning*. Common law required that there be an actual burning of some part of the structure. Damage to property inside the structure was insufficient. Likewise, smoke damage to the building itself was insufficient. There had to be actual charring of the structure. Modern arson statutes often relax this requirement by allowing smoke damage or damage to the contents of a building to satisfy this requirement.

Second, at common law, arson applied only to a *residential building*. Once again, most jurisdictions have statutorily expanded arson to include commercial buildings.

Third, like burglary, common law arson required that the dwelling burned be *in the possession of another*. An owner of a building could be guilty of arson, however, if at the time of the fire, the building was lawfully occupied by the tenant. Under modern statutes, arson now generally applies to even the burning of one's own home, business, or other property.

Finally, the mens rea requirement for arson is *malice*. Like the malice required for murder, there is no requirement that the defendant act with ill will. Rather, it is sufficient if the defendant acted purposely, knowingly, or with gross recklessness. Thus, if a person sets a fire, realizing there is a high risk that the structure will burn, the defendant has acted with malice and may be guilty of arson.

With this understanding of the common law requirements for arson, try the next question.

QUESTION 5. Firefly Freddy.   Freddy loves the Fourth of July and fireworks. He buys a variety of fireworks for the holiday and takes them over to show his neighbor. To demonstrate how they work, Freddy sets off one of the sparklers. His neighbor's couch catches fire and burns. Freddy apologizes for the considerable smoke damage to his neighbor's home, saying, "Gee, I knew that could happen, but I always love to see those fireworks go off." Freddy is charged with arson.

Under common law standards, is Freddy guilty of arson?

A. Yes, because he maliciously burned his neighbor's property.
B. No, because he did not act maliciously.
C. Yes, because he negligently burned his neighbor's property.
D. No, because he did not maliciously burn his neighbor's property.

ANALYSIS.   Take a close look at the facts of this question and the common law requirements for arson. Freddy meets two of the requirements, but he does not meet all of them. **A** is wrong because under the common law, causing smoke damage or burning the contents of a home was not considered arson. Thus, it was insufficient for arson that the neighbor's couch burned and that he had smoke damage.

B is wrong because Freddy did act maliciously. Although he had no ill will toward his neighbor, Freddy's comment that he knew what would happen indicated that he realized the risk and took it anyway. Gross recklessness is one form of malice.

C is also wrong. If Freddy acted only negligently, he would not be guilty of arson. Mere negligence is an insufficient mens rea for the crime. The defendant must act with at least gross recklessness to show malice.

The correct answer is **D**. I'm sure that Freddy's neighbor is none too pleased with Freddy and will sue him for the damage to his home, but under common law requirements, Freddy is not guilty of arson.

E.   Kidnapping

The final common law crime we cover in this chapter is kidnapping. *Kidnapping is traditionally defined as the "unlawful confinement and movement of a victim by threat or use of force, or by deception."* Its elements are

- intentional unlawful confinement
- movement of the victim
- threat or use of force, or deception.

Unlawful confinement takes place when a person is held without her consent. It can be the physical restraint of the victim or the confinement of the victim by the use of physical barriers. Thus, if a defendant locks her victim in a car, she has unlawfully confined the victim. However, the confinement must be *intentional.* Thus, if the defendant accidentally locks the victim in the car, there is no kidnapping.

At common law, kidnapping also required some *movement* of the victim. The victim did not need to be moved far. For example, a defendant could come up to a victim, put a gun at her back, and tell her to move toward the door. Even if the victim took only a step or two, there would be sufficient movement for kidnapping.

Finally, the defendant must confine the victim without her consent. Kidnappers usually use *coercion, threats,* or *force.* However, *deception* can also be used. For example, if the victim is lured into a car by false representations and then held there against her will, the defendant would be guilty of kidnapping.

Here is a question to review these elements of common law kidnapping.

> **QUESTION 6. Going home.** Abram offers to give Emma a ride home. She accepts his offer and hops in his car. Abram, however, is a seriously disturbed individual who never has anyone to talk to or keep him company. Therefore, he makes Emma ride around with him in the car for two hours before he drops her off.
>
> If Abram is charged with kidnapping, he will likely be
>
> A. acquitted, because he ultimately let Emma go.
> B. acquitted, because he never intended to hurt Emma.
> C. acquitted, because he did not use force against Emma.
> D. convicted, because he took Emma against her will.

ANALYSIS. Even though Abram only temporarily confined Emma against her will, his actions were sufficient for kidnapping; he intentionally confined her, there was more than enough movement to satisfy the legal requirements, and Abram used deceit to lure Emma into his car.

In going through the possible answers, you should note that **A** is wrong because it does not matter that Abram ultimately released his victim. He had already completed the crime of kidnapping by the time she was released.

B is also wrong because there can be a kidnapping without physical injury to the victim. In fact, if Abram had also hurt her, he would be responsible for both crimes — the kidnapping and the assault.

C is wrong because use of force is only one way that kidnapping can be committed. Threat of force, or the use of deceit, are alternative means.

The correct answer is **D**. Abram confined and moved Emma against her will. Even though he might have believed he had a good reason for doing so, he still acted intentionally. He is guilty of kidnapping.

F. The Closer: Felony murder revisited

As has been suggested throughout this chapter, the felonies discussed in this and the previous chapter are often used as predicate offenses for felony murder. Felony murder is discussed in detail in Chapter 11. Recall that if the defendant is not guilty of the underlying felony, he is not guilty of felony murder. Thus, it is crucial to know the requirements for these underlying felonies. You also need to remember that an attempt to commit a felony is also a felony. (See Chapter 12.)

The closer requires you to apply your understanding of the elements of common law crimes to determine whether the defendant is guilty of felony murder.

QUESTION 7. **Catch Kate.**   Jerome has been hired to grab Kate and return her to her ex-husband. Jerome waits until Kate goes to sleep and then uses a key the ex-husband gave him to enter her home. Jerome goes inside to grab Kate. He finds her in bed with her new lover. Using a gun that he took from Kate's car before he entered her home, Jerome tells Kate to get out of bed. She does. Jerome then starts to reach for some of Kate's jewelry as "compensation" for his hard work. Just then, Kate's cat jumps on Jerome and he accidentally fires the gun. Jerome kills Kate's son, who has come into the room to see what is happening.

Which, if any, of the following crimes has Jerome committed?

  I. Burglary
 II. Kidnapping
III. Murder
IV. Larceny

A. None of the above.
B. I and III.
C. I, II, and III.
D. All of the above.

ANALYSIS.   One short fact pattern can trigger many crimes. As you would do on an essay exam, it is critical in evaluating a multiple-choice question to look carefully at each element of the offenses to determine whether that specific crime has been committed.

First, has Jerome committed burglary? Yes. He broke into the home. Although he had the key, he did not have consent to enter. It was nighttime and Jerome had the intent to kidnap Kate. Therefore, he met all the requirements for burglary. I applies.

Second, Jerome is also guilty of kidnapping. He used the threat of force to get Kate out of bed. That mere movement is sufficient for kidnapping, even though Jerome never took Kate from the residence. II applies.

Third, Jerome may also be guilty of murder. Even though accidental killings usually result in involuntary manslaughter convictions, or no charge, here Jerome accidentally killed someone during the commission of two felonies—burglary and kidnapping. The felony-murder doctrine would apply, and so III applies as well.

Finally, is Jerome guilty of larceny? Here, he may get a break. Although he intended to take the jewelry, he never started to carry it away. If attempted larceny had been offered as an option, it might have applied. But, on these facts, Jerome does not qualify for conviction of larceny, and so you should cross IV out.

Jerome is guilty of burglary, kidnapping, and murder. **C** is the correct answer.

Levenson's Picks

1. Gotcha	**B**	
2. Kiss it goodbye	**B**	
3. Shiny ring	**D**	
4. Culligan man	**C**	
5. Firefly Freddy	**D**	
6. Going home	**D**	
7. Catch Kate	**C**	

Sentencing and the Death Penalty

"No, no!" said the Queen. "Sentence first—verdict afterwards."
— Lewis Carroll, *Alice in Wonderland*

CHAPTER OVERVIEW

A. Sentencing
   1. Revisiting purposes of punishment
   2. Types of sentencing schemes
   3. Eighth Amendment limitations on sentencing
B. Death penalty
   1. Constitutionality of the death penalty
   2. Procedures for death penalty cases
   3. Equal protection challenges
   4. Execution issues
C. The Closer: The *Apprendi* revolution
◈ Levenson's Picks

A crucial question in any criminal case is the defendant's sentence. Different jurisdictions handle sentencing differently. Some use an indeterminate sentencing scheme that gives the judge broad discretion; others use a determinate sentencing scheme that sets mandatory sentences or provides more specific sentencing guidelines. This chapter addresses the nature of these sentencing schemes and constitutional limits on them.

This chapter also looks at the ultimate punishment — the death penalty. Capital punishment remains controversial and is not used in all jurisdictions. Presently, federal law and a majority of states do authorize the death penalty. This chapter examines the nature of the death penalty and constitutional restrictions on its imposition.

A.   Sentencing

1. Revisiting purposes of punishment

In Chapter 2, we examined the purposes of punishment underlying criminal law. Those purposes of punishment not only affect the definitions of crimes, but also the punishments imposed at sentencing. The four purposes of punishment we discussed were retribution, deterrence, incapacitation, and rehabilitation. As a quick review, try this question about the purposes of punishment that may be served by incarcerating a defendant.

QUESTION 1. **Set an example.**   Michael pleads guilty to failing to file his income tax returns. At sentencing, he throws himself on the mercy of the court. He tells the judge that he has learned his lesson and is incredibly sorry that he broke the law. He further informs the court that he has paid all his back taxes and has given some extra to charities to make up for his transgression. The judge believes Michael when he says that he will never break another law and that he has already become a model citizen. Nonetheless, the judge sentences Michael to one year in prison because "others need to learn from your mistake."

Which purpose of punishment most likely accounts for Michael's sentence?

A. Retribution.
B. Deterrence.
C. Incapacitation.
D. Rehabilitation.

ANALYSIS.   The judge's stated purpose in sending Michael to prison is that he wants others to learn from Michael's mistake. That is the language of deterrence. In this situation, **A** appears to be wrong because there is nothing to indicate that the judge wants to punish Michael simply because Michael deserves punishment. In fact, it is clear that Michael has done plenty to repay his debt to society. **C** is also incorrect because Michael does not pose a danger to society. By paying his back taxes and avowing that he will never break another law again, Michael has demonstrated that he has already been rehabilitated. Thus, **D** does not seem to apply. The judge's stated reason for punishment is to send a message to others that they must file their tax returns. This indicates that general deterrence is the primary reason for punishing Michael. **B** is the correct answer.

2. Types of sentencing schemes

The two primary models of sentencing schemes are *indeterminate sentencing* and *determinate sentencing.*

Indeterminate sentencing schemes give judges a great deal of discretion to decide on an appropriate sentence. For example, a statute may provide that the defendant's offense is punishable by up to a maximum of 20 years. Under such a system, the judge has the discretion to impose any sentence from probation to the maximum of 20 years. Sometimes this is referred to as a "discretionary" sentencing scheme. The chief benefit of such an approach is that it gives the court a great deal of power to tailor a sentence to the individual defendant. It can also give power to a parole board to decide when the defendent should be released. The downside is that it can lead to inconsistency in sentencing. One judge may give probation for a crime while another judge regularly imposes the maximum sentence for the very same crime.

Determinate sentencing schemes limit the court's sentencing discretion. Sometimes, jurisdictions have mandatory sentences for certain crimes, or for recidivists. For example, mandatory minimum sentences are a type of determinate sentencing. So are "three strikes" laws that require life imprisonment after a conviction for a serious or violent felony. There are also systems that limit a judge's discretion by requiring the court to impose a sentence within certain guidelines established by a sentencing commission or the legislature. These systems have more flexibility than mandatory sentencing schemes, but still limit discretion by requiring that sentences ordinarily fall within the guideline range.

Since 1987, the federal courts have been required to impose sentences in accordance with the Federal Sentencing Guidelines. However, in 2005, the United States Supreme Court held in *United States v. Booker*, 543 U.S. 220 (2005), that the guidelines should only be considered advisory. They no longer control a federal judge's sentencing decisions.

Look at the next question and determine what kind of sentencing scheme is being used by the court.

QUESTION 2. No mercy. Margaret is convicted of unarmed bank robbery. Desperate for money to feed her children, Margaret walked into a bank and told the teller, "Give me all of your money. I'm a desperate woman and I'll do desperate things." The teller gave Margaret $500. Before Margaret got to the bus stop to catch a ride home, she was apprehended by the police.

> At sentencing, the judge tells Margaret, "I can really feel for your situation. If I had my way, I'd send you home to take care of your kids. But, my hands are tied. The guidelines for your sentence require three to five years in prison. I hereby impose a four-year sentence."
>
> Under what kind of sentencing scheme has Margaret been punished?
>
> **A.** A determinate sentencing scheme.
> **B.** An indeterminate sentencing scheme.
> **C.** A fully discretionary scheme.
> **D.** A mandatory statutory punishment.

ANALYSIS. Clearly, the judge would have preferred to have given Margaret a different sentence, but he was locked in by the controlling guidelines. As such, he is operating under a determinate sentencing scheme. **A** is the correct answer. **B** is incorrect because the judge does not have broad discretion to impose a sentence. For the same reason, **C** is also wrong. Indeterminate sentencing schemes are discretionary schemes. **D** is wrong, however, because it goes too far in the other direction. This was not a mandatory sentence. The court had leeway to impose a sentence anywhere between three and five years.

3. Eighth Amendment limitations on sentencing

In addition to any statutory limitations on a court's sentencing power, the Eighth Amendment to the United States Constitution prohibits the infliction of "cruel and unusual punishment." The Supreme Court has interpreted the Eighth Amendment as prohibiting the imposition of grossly disproportional sentences. In the landmark cases of *Rummel v. Estelle*, 445 U.S. 263 (1980) and *Solem v. Helm*, 463 U.S. 277 (1983), the Court addressed whether life sentences for career offenders are unconstitutional. In *Solem*, the Court set forth three factors to be examined in determining whether a sentence is unconstitutionally disproportional: (1) the gravity of the offense compared to the severity of the penalty; (2) penalties imposed for similar offenses in the same jurisdiction (intra-jurisdictional analysis); and (3) penalties imposed in other jurisdictions for the same offense (inter-jurisdictional analysis).

In *Rummel*, the Court rejected the defendant's argument that his life sentence for being a petty criminal violated the Eighth Amendment, noting that Rummel was sentenced to life imprisonment with the possibility of parole. However, the Court in *Solem* accepted the defendant's argument that as a nonviolent, petty criminal, his sentence violated the Eighth Amendment because he was sentenced to life imprisonment without the possibility of parole.

It would be a mistake, however, to believe that any defendant sentenced to life without the possibility of parole can automatically succeed with an

Eighth Amendment challenge to his sentence. In 1991, the Supreme Court decided the case of *Harmelin v. Michigan*, 501 U.S. 957 (1991). Harmelin had received a mandatory sentence of life imprisonment without possibility of parole after he was convicted of his first offense of possessing 972 grams of cocaine. The Supreme Court held that the sentence did not violate the Eighth Amendment because of the serious nature of the offense. The key vote in the decision was by Justice Kennedy, who emphasized in his concurrence that the most important prong of the *Solem* test was the seriousness of the offense. Two justices, Chief Justice Rehnquist and Justice Scalia, noted that they would overrule *Solem* because they believe the Eighth Amendment only prohibits certain modes of punishment and does not provide a guarantee against disproportionate sentences.

Since *Harmelin*, the Supreme Court has upheld three strikes statutes that impose life sentences for recidivists, even for relatively minor crimes. In *Ewing v. California*, 538 U.S. 11 (2003) and *Lockyer v. Andrade*, 538 U.S. 63 (2003), the Court upheld the California three strikes law against challenges that it was unconstitutional. Generally, courts must defer to legislative judgment as to the appropriate sentence for offenses. It is only in the rarest of cases that a defendant can successfully claim that his sentence is disproportional.

QUESTION 3. Erwin's bad day. Erwin is caught shoplifting several children's videos from a store. He has two prior convictions: one for robbery and one for sale of cocaine. Erwin has never actually hurt anyone during his crimes. Nonetheless, under the recidivist law in his jurisdiction, he receives a life sentence. He will not be eligible for parole until he is 85 years old. In that same jurisdiction, only arson, robbery, murder, and rape would also require the type of sentence Erwin received. Moreover, only two other states have similar punishments for recidivists.

Is Erwin's sentence unconstitutional?

A. Yes, because it is the equivalent of life imprisonment without the possibility of parole.
B. Yes, because his last offense was a relatively minor one.
C. No, because the Eighth Amendment does not prohibit grossly disproportionate sentences.
D. No, because his sentence is not necessarily grossly disproportionate.

ANALYSIS. This question is similar to the facts of *Lockyer v. Andrade*, 538 U.S. 63 (2003), in which the Supreme Court upheld the defendant's sentence. Although your initial reading of the facts may suggest that the sentence imposed was unduly harsh, you must read through all the answers to determine if Erwin really has a viable constitutional challenge.

A is wrong, although it is a bit tricky. While it is true that sentences that carry life imprisonment without the possibility of parole are more likely to succeed with an Eighth Amendment challenge, the Court's rulings in *Harmelin* and *Andrade* make clear that a defendant will not automatically succeed just because he faces the equivalent of life without the possibility of parole.

B is also wrong. Although Erwin's last crime was a minor one, he is being sentenced as a recidivist. Accordingly, Erwin can face a much harsher sentence, as did the defendants in *Rummel, Andrade,* and *Ewing.*

The choice comes down to **C** or **D**. As always, you should avoid broad pronouncements of the law. The law, particularly in this area, is more subtle. Therefore, **C** is a wrong answer. The Eighth Amendment still prohibits grossly disproportionate sentences, although it is often very difficult to prove that a sentence meets that standard. **D** is the correct answer. Erwin's sentence, although harsh, is not necessarily grossly disproportionate. Rather, it is a harsh sentence, dictated by the legislature, for a repeat offender. Given Erwin's prior convictions for serious crimes like robbery and narcotics sales, he is unlikely to succeed with a constitutional challenge to his sentence.

B.   Death penalty

The death penalty is the punishment reserved for the most serious offenses. Capital punishment remains controversial and is not used in all jurisdictions. Presently, federal law and the laws of 37 states authorize the death penalty. Both its justification and its administration raise many important issues.

1. Constitutionality of the death penalty

In *Furman v. Georgia*, 408 U.S. 238 (1972), the Supreme Court held that the death penalty is constitutional and does not violate the Eighth Amendment prohibition against cruel and unusual punishment if implemented properly. However, the Court has put certain limitations on the use of the death penalty. First, it must be procedurally applied in a manner that does not lead to arbitrary or discriminatory decisions. Accordingly, it is unconstitutional to have mandatory death penalty statutes. See *Woodson v. North Carolina*, 428 U.S. 280 (1976). Second, it is unconstitutional to execute a defendant who is under the age of 18 at the time of the offense. *Roper v. Simmons*, 543 U.S. 551 (2005). Third, the Court has held that it is cruel and unusual punishment to execute severely mentally retarded defendants. *Atkins v. Virginia*, 536 U.S. 304 (2002). Finally, the Court has struck down the death penalty as excessive when applied as a punishment for non-homicide crimes, such as rape, see *Coker v. Georgia*, 433 U.S. 584 (1977), or child rape, *Kennedy v. Louisiana*,

554 U.S. ___, 128 S. Ct. 2641 (2008). The Court has not ruled on whether the death penalty may be constitutionally applied to serious offenses other than murder, such as treason or espionage.

In deciding whether the death penalty is constitutional in these contexts, the Supreme Court looks to evolving standards of decency to determine what constitutes cruel and unusual punishment. Thus, the more that states and foreign countries reject the death penalty in certain circumstances, the more likely it is that the Supreme Court will also strike down its application in those circumstances under the Eighth Amendment. *Roper v. Simmons*, 543 U.S. 551 (2005).

2. Procedures for death penalty cases

To ensure that the death penalty is constitutionally applied, all capital trials use bifurcated proceedings. In the "guilt phase," the trier of fact determines whether the defendant is guilty of the charged offense. In many jurisdictions, a jury must find that a murder involved "special circumstances" in order to qualify it for the death penalty. Special circumstances may include multiple murders, murder of a law enforcement officer, murder for profit, murder of a witness, murder by explosive device or torture, or certain types of felony-murders. See *Tison v. Arizona*, 481 U.S. 137 (1987) (only felony murderer who has substantial involvement in murder and shows reckless disregard is eligible for death penalty).

Following the guilt phase, the jury decides the "penalty phase" of the case. In the penalty phase, the jury weighs the aggravating and mitigating circumstances of the case and decides whether it is appropriate to apply the death penalty. Jurisdictions may adopt lists of aggravating and mitigating circumstances. These lists guide judges and juries in applying the death penalty in that jurisdiction. See *Gregg v. Georgia*, 428 U.S. 153 (1976). Common aggravating factors include number of victims, method of killing, identity of the victim, defendant's prior criminal record, defendant's age at the time of the crime, defendant's level of participation, and defendant's likelihood for future violence. Additionally, jurors may consider victim impact evidence. Although such evidence is naturally emotional, it is not inconsistent with the deliberative process in death penalty cases. See *Payne v. Tennessee*, 501 U.S. 808 (1991).

Generally, jurors may consider any aspect of the defendant's character or the crime as mitigating factors. See *Lockett v. Ohio*, 438 U.S. 586 (1978). Specifically, they may look at a defendant's lack of criminal record, a defendant's age at the time of the crime, whether the defendant was provoked or coerced into participating in the killing, a defendant's mental and emotional state, a defendant's role in the offense, and the defendant's behavior while in custody.

Unless waived by the defendant, a jury, not a judge, must decide those facts necessary to find the aggravating circumstances warranting the death penalty. *Ring v. Arizona*, 536 U.S. 584 (2002). In some jurisdictions, the jury recommends a death sentence and the court formally imposes it. In other jurisdictions, the jury actually returns a death verdict that the court reviews at the time of sentencing.

The Model Penal Code does not take a position on whether the death penalty should be authorized for murder, as reflected by the brackets around Model Penal Code §210.6. Instead, the Model Penal Code outlines how those jurisdictions that have adopted the death penalty should impose it. See Model Penal Code §210.6.

There are special rules for the selection of jurors for a death penalty case. The court must seat a "death-qualified" jury. Specifically, jurors are eligible to sit on a death penalty case only if they agree that they would be willing to impose the death penalty under proper circumstances. If a juror indicates that he could never impose the death penalty, that juror should be excused for cause.

3. Equal protection challenges

Although there is a great deal of empirical evidence that the death penalty is applied disproportionately to African-American defendants who kill white victims, the Supreme Court has thus far rejected attempts to prove that capital punishment violates the Equal Protection Clause of the Fourteenth Amendment. See *McCleskey v. Kemp*, 481 U.S. 279 (1987). For there to be an equal protection violation, the defendant must show clear evidence of purposeful discrimination and not just proof of discriminatory impact.

4. Execution issues

The execution of a murderer who has lost his sanity while on death row is unconstitutional. See *Ford v. Wainwright*, 477 U.S. 399 (1986). However, it may be constitutional to forcibly medicate an inmate to render him sane enough to be executed. See *Singleton v. Norris*, 319 F.3d 1018 (8th Cir. 2003), *cert. denied*, 540 U.S. 832 (2003).

While the Eighth Amendment prohibits cruel and unusual punishments, the Supreme Court has not found any particular method of execution to be unconstitutional under this standard. In fact, the Supreme Court has recently upheld lethal injection as a constitutional method of execution. See *Baze v. Rees*, 553 U.S. ___, 128 S. Ct. 1520 (2008). Individual states, however, have found some forms of capital punishment to be cruel and unusual under their state constitutions. See, e.g., *Dawson v. Georgia*, 554 S.E.2d 137 (Ga. 2001) (finding death by electrocution violates state constitution's prohibition against cruel and unusual punishment).

Obviously, this is not an exhaustive discussion of the death penalty. However, it gives you a basic overview of the laws governing its implementation. The next question tests your understanding of these basic principles.

QUESTION 4. **'Til death do we part.** Gary and Maria have been married for 20 years when she suddenly discovers he is having an affair. When Maria confronts Gary with her discovery, Gary decides that the easiest way to resolve the problem is to kill her. After checking her life insurance policy, Gary loosens the wheels on her car. As planned, Maria's car goes off the road while she is driving the kids to school, killing herself and their three children.

In that jurisdiction, the death penalty may be imposed only if the jury finds that a defendant committed an intentional killing with special circumstances. Special circumstances include killing multiple victims and killing for profit.

Which of the following is true?

A. A death-qualified jury must impose the death penalty because Gary committed a killing for profit.
B. Gary is not subject to the death penalty because he obviously had to be mentally ill at the time of the offense.
C. The prosecution can call Maria's parents to testify tearfully as to whether they believe Gary should get the death penalty.
D. Gary's reason for killing his wife is irrelevant to the jury's determination of whether he should receive the death penalty.

ANALYSIS. This should have been a fairly simple question for you. It highlights the most basic death penalty rules. First, **A** is wrong because mandatory death sentences are unconstitutional. See *Woodson v. North Carolina*, 428 U.S. 280 (1976). Gary may receive the death penalty for his crime, but even a death-qualified jury is not required to impose the death penalty.

B is wrong for two reasons. First, mere mental illness is not enough to protect a defendant from the death penalty. In *Atkins*, the Court held that only a narrow category of defendants who suffer from mental illness can avoid the death penalty. Second, there is no real evidence that Gary is mentally ill. Resist the temptation to assume that people only kill when they are mentally ill. Tragically, many defendants in full control of their faculties kill as well.

As stated, **C** is the correct answer. Witness impact testimony is permissible, even though it is highly emotional and appeals to the jurors' sympathies, not reason. **D** is wrong because a defendant's reason for killing his wife may be relevant as either an aggravating factor or mitigating factor in a death penalty case.

C.   The Closer: The *Apprendi* revolution

Perhaps the most important development in sentencing law in the last few decades has been the Supreme Court's decision in *Apprendi v. New Jersey*, 530 U.S. 466 (2000). In *Apprendi*, the Court held that any fact that makes a defendant eligible for a sentence beyond the statutory maximum must be found by a jury on proof of evidence beyond a reasonable doubt. Failure to do so violates a defendant's due process rights. The *Apprendi* decision was followed by the Court's decision in *Blakely v. Washington*, 542 U.S. 296 (2004), in which the Court held that any fact that subjects a defendant to a sentence above the ordinary sentence for that offense should also be found by a jury. As a result of these cases, there is a greater burden on prosecutors to charge and prove to the jury facts that may have an impact on sentencing, other than a defendant's prior criminal record. Finally, the Court held in *Booker* that guidelines that dictate sentences without having the necessary facts pled and proved to a jury violate due process.

The last question integrates your knowledge of sentencing in general with this new procedural development.

QUESTION 5. 150 more kilos.   Monica is charged with having 300 grams of cocaine for sale. After she pleads guilty to this offense, the prosecutor argues at sentencing that Monica is really a major narcotics dealer who is responsible for selling hundreds of kilos of cocaine on a regular basis. To make this argument, the prosecutor presents the testimony of an informant who testifies that he has regularly seen Monica with large shipments of cocaine.

After hearing the evidence and deciding that Monica is probably a major drug dealer, the judge imposes the maximum sentence of 20 years in jail. Monica is stunned. Based on guidelines in that jurisdiction, the appropriate sentence for 300 grams of cocaine is three years in custody. Monica objects to her sentence.

Monica's best argument is:

A. The purposes of punishment do not apply to her case because she pled guilty to the charged offense.
B. A 20-year sentence for 300 grams of cocaine is cruel and unusual punishment.
C. Monica was denied her due process rights in sentencing.
D. Indeterminate sentencing schemes overly restrict a judge's discretionary powers at sentencing.

ANALYSIS. The closer requires that you remember some of the sentencing principles we learned earlier in this chapter, as well as the *Apprendi* principles we just discussed. Let's look at each possible answer.

Just because a defendant pleads guilty, it doesn't mean that the purposes of punishment no longer apply. Even if the defendant has demonstrated remorse, the court may still feel that the defendant deserves to be punished and needs to be so she won't commit the offense in the future. Additionally, Monica may continue to be a danger unless she is incarcerated and rehabilitated. **A** is wrong.

B is also wrong. Recall that under *Harmelin v. United States,* even a life sentence is not unconstitutional for a drug offense. Monica's sentence may be harsh, but is not unconstitutional.

Once again, **C** is looking promising. The problem with Monica's sentencing procedure is that the prosecutor is taking a shortcut in proving facts that dramatically affect her sentence. She was convicted of being a small-time drug dealer and is being sentenced for being a major narcotics offender. The procedures used in Monica's case violate due process and the principles of *Apprendi, Blakely,* and *Booker.*

You can check that answer by noting that **D** is wrong. It incorrectly describes indeterminate sentencing. Indeterminate sentencing schemes do not restrict a judge's discretionary powers the way that determinate sentencing schemes do.

✳ Levenson's Picks

1. Set an example	**B**
2. No mercy	**A**
3. Erwin's bad day	**D**
4. 'Til death do we part	**C**
5. 150 more kilos	**C**

25

Closing Closers

I have climbed to the top of the greasy pole!
— Benjamin Disraeli, commenting on the meaning of success
(Sir William Fraser, *Disraeli and His Day*, 2d ed. p. 52 (1891))

This chapter is different from the others. It includes 25 questions without introductory discussion of the black-letter law. The questions are intended to serve two purposes. First, they are a review of the principles discussed throughout this book. Second, unlike the questions in each chapter, these questions often involve multiple issues. The questions in this book are designed to be similar to those you are likely to see on your exams.

I have included short analyses of the questions at the end of the chapter. You will get more out of these analyses if you have worked through the questions ahead of time. If you find any ambiguities or problems with them, feel free to e-mail me so those problems can be addressed.

Finally, before you begin, let's take the opportunity to review some basic good rules on taking multiple-choice examinations.

Rule 1: Don't look for the right answer; look for what is wrong with the other answers. It is critical to consider each answer before selecting your response. If you jump at what you believe to be the right answer, you will often miss something.

Rule 2: Beware of absolutes. Be very wary of selecting an answer that includes the words "never" or "always." As you have seen, the law is ordinarily more complex than these answers would suggest.

Rule 3: Be sure you are applying the correct legal standard. Check the question to determine which standard applies. In criminal law, professors love to use multiple-choice questions to test on the differences between the Model Penal Code and common law approaches to issues.

Rule 4:   Make sure that each word of the answer is correct. In a multiple-choice exam, you do not receive partial credit. The answer is either right or wrong.

Now, you are ready to begin. Here goes.

QUESTION 1. Island of the blue dolphins.   Cori Anderson has been charged with a violation of the Modern Marine Act (MMA). Section 4 of the MMA provides: "It is a felony to knowingly kill or injure a blue dolphin." Anderson was arrested when Coast Guard officials found him shooting at dolphins near his fishing nets. Anderson claimed that the dolphins had been destroying his livelihood by pulling apart the nets. Although he confessed to shooting at the creatures, he claims that he believed he was shooting at blue sharks.

What is Anderson's best defense at trial?

A. Necessity.
B. Mistake of fact.
C. Self-defense.
D. Factual impossibility.

QUESTION 2. Thanks, neighbor!   During a fire in the neighborhood, Luke Skiwalker decides to break into his neighbor's house to take some hoses and shovels that might help Luke save his home. When he enters his neighbor's home, he is confronted by Darth who has also gone to the neighbor's house for tools. They both grab for the shovel. Darth gets the shovel first and starts swinging at Luke's face. Luke grabs a hammer and throws it at Darth's head, immediately killing him. He then runs off with the shovel and hoses to save his house. When Darth is discovered, Luke is charged with murder and larceny.

What is Luke's best defense to the larceny?

A. Self-defense.
B. Duress.
C. Temporary insanity.
D. Necessity.

QUESTION 3. Eliminating the competition.   Bob Brains, a student at Byola Law School, studies in the law library. Brains is a very competitive student. He is currently number two in the class. Late one night before finals, Brains sees the number one student, Alvin Einstein, have an asthma attack in the library. Brains just stands there and watches. He makes no effort to call for help or administer artificial respiration. Rather, Brains is delighted that his competition is being eliminated. For five minutes, Brains just stares at the gasping Einstein. Finally, Einstein collapses and dies. Brains is charged with homicide.

Which of the following is correct?

A. Brains is guilty of first-degree murder because there was sufficient time for him to deliberate over Einstein's death.
B. He is guilty of first-degree murder because he watched with malice.
C. He is guilty of negligent homicide because the benefit of being number one in law school is outweighed by the costs.
D. He is not guilty.

QUESTION 4. Assaulting the presidency.   George M. Shugah is furious at the President over some of his recent policies. Shugah writes complaint letters to his senator, who responds with the following note:

> Dear Faithful Citizen:
>
> You're right. The President has to go. Ultimately, America's freedom is up to you. If you take action, you can take back the White House. The law is what the people say it is!
>
> Sincerely,
> Your Senator

After reading this note, George decides to kill the President. He buys a high-powered rifle, travels to Washington, D.C., and stands in line to get into the White House. A Secret Service agent spots George's rifle and arrests him for attempting to kill the President. As it turns out, even if George had shot at the White House, the President was in another state giving a campaign speech.

At trial, what is George's best defense to the charge of attempted murder?

A. Mistake of law.
B. Insufficient mens rea.
C. He has not come within dangerous proximity of killing the President.
D. Factual impossibility.
E. Entrapment.

QUESTION 5. Too much partying. Defendant Herman Ferrari is charged with reckless driving. Ferrari claims that he did not intend to drive in a reckless manner, but did so only because he had a few too many drinks during a celebration after his criminal law final. Ferrari felt peer pressure to have a few drinks at the celebration.

In the majority of common law jurisdictions, does Ferrari have an intoxication defense?

A. No, because voluntary intoxication is not a defense to the crime with which Ferrari has been charged.
B. No, because voluntary intoxication is never a defense.
C. Yes, if Ferrari was intoxicated, he could not form the intent for the crime.
D. Yes, because Ferrari was suffering from involuntary intoxication.
E. Yes, because duress is a common law defense.

QUESTION 6. Double robbery. Mary decides to rob a bank because she needs money to buy holiday gifts. She buys a mask, gets a toy gun, and plans the robbery. Unbeknownst to Mary, Joan also needs money for gifts and decides to rob the same bank on the same day. On that day, Mary enters through the front door of the bank while Joan enters through the rear. Mary robs the tellers; Joan loots the vault. Neither sees the other and each runs out to her respective car to escape.

What may Mary and Joan each be charged with?

A. Bank robbery, conspiracy, and aiding and abetting each other's bank robberies.
B. Bank robbery only.
C. Aiding and abetting the other's bank robbery.
D. Conspiracy and bank robbery.
E. No crime because neither one was the but for cause of the robbery.

QUESTION 7. Illegal transports. Linette asks Angela to help her smuggle illegal aliens across the border. Out of friendship, Angela agrees and they set a date for the smuggling. Linette rents a van to transport the aliens, recruits two other people to help, and calls Angela. Angela tells Linette that she has changed her mind. Linette goes ahead anyway and transports the illegal aliens across the border.

If Angela is charged in a Model Penal Code jurisdiction with both conspiracy to transport the illegal aliens and the substantive charges of transporting illegal aliens, what will she likely be found guilty of?

A. Guilty of conspiracy only.
B. Guilty of conspiracy and the substantive charges of transporting illegal aliens.
C. Not guilty of any crime because she abandoned the conspiracy.
D. Not guilty of any crime because she did not commit an overt act.
E. Not guilty of any crime because she did not reach an explicit agreement with all members of the conspiracy.

QUESTION 8. Still fighting.   Max Melvin is a collector of war memorabilia. His friend, Shawn Thomas, visits Melvin one day and offers to buy some of the memorabilia. They stand in the open doorway of Melvin's home and try to negotiate a sale. Melvin, however, is not interested in selling. Melvin grabs an old Civil War sword and yells, "Get out, you scoundrel. I'm going to kill you. How dare you try to part me from my precious collection!" Melvin then starts flailing at Thomas. Thomas, believing that Melvin is going to kill him, pulls out a gun and shoots Melvin. Melvin dies and Thomas is charged with murder.

Under traditional common law, if Thomas raises self-defense, will his defense fail or succeed?

A. Likely fail because he was the initial aggressor.
B. Likely fail because he had a duty to retreat before using deadly force.
C. Likely fail because he did not have an honest and reasonable fear for his life.
D. Likely fail because there was no immediate threat of violence.
E. Likely succeed.

QUESTION 9. Wrong house.   Defendant Carl Gata-Kilher is angry at his neighbor because his neighbor kicked Carl's dog. Carl buys a gun and shoots at his neighbor through his window. The bullet ricochets off his neighbor's window frame and kills a passerby.

Under the common law, what is Carl guilty of?

A. No crime because he did not intend to kill the passerby.
B. Murder.

C. Manslaughter.
D. No crime because he did not have a motive to kill the passerby.
E. Attempted murder only.

QUESTION 10. BWS. Bea Victum is charged with killing her abusive husband. Bea claims that at the time of the killing she was suffering from battered women's syndrome. For her entire ten-year marriage, Bea's husband beat and humiliated her. She never wanted to complain to the police because her husband was a prominent doctor in town. Instead, she hid in her house and suffered the beatings. When she heard that her husband was about to leave her for a younger woman, Bea decided she would not take it anymore. One night, she waited for her husband by the door and stabbed him in the heart with a scalpel when he came home from work.

Under traditional common law, Bea is likely to be

A. acquitted of murder because she had an honest and reasonable fear for her life.
B. acquitted of murder because a reasonable battered woman would do the same as she did in the circumstances.
C. convicted of voluntary manslaughter because she had an imperfect self-defense claim.
D. convicted of murder.

QUESTION 11. Forbidden fruit. Officer Mike Jensen and his friend, Shant Mardian, had an unusual way of having fun. On their days off, they would play "William Tell." Mike would try to shoot an apple off Shant's head with his service revolver. In turn, Shant would use a bow and arrow to shoot at apples from under Mike's armpits. Both Mike and Shant were expert shots. One day, while Shant was shooting at the apples under Mike's arms, Shant was distracted by the whistle of a nearby spectator. His arrow hit Mike in the side. Shant rushed to Mike's side and took him to the hospital. At the hospital, Mike developed an infection and died.

Under the Model Penal Code approach, Shant is most likely

A. guilty of murder because he was aware that he might miss and kill Mike.
B. guilty of involuntary manslaughter because he did not have the intent to kill Mike.

C. not guilty of homicide because he was not the actual cause of Mike's death.

D. not guilty of homicide because Mike consented to the dangerous activity.

QUESTION 12. Suitable felonies. The following crimes are considered felonies:

I. Bombing
   —Defined as: "knowingly using an explosive device to destroy occupied residential property."
II. Poisoning
   —Defined as: "knowingly using a toxin with intent to kill or cause great bodily injury."
III. Grand theft
   —Defined as: "knowingly taking the property of another without force or threat of violence."
IV. Assault with a deadly weapon
   —Defined as: "using a deadly weapon with the intent to kill another."

Which of the above felonies is most likely to qualify for application of the felony murder doctrine in those jurisdictions that apply the most common limitations on the use of the felony-murder rule? In analyzing the felonies, examine the offenses in the abstract.

A. I, II, and IV.
B. II and IV.
C. I only.
D. I and III.
E. IV only.

QUESTION 13. Dangerous liaisons. Tim McRay approaches his old army buddy, Terry Nikos, and asks his help in bombing a local government building. Nikos really doesn't want to help but he is afraid of McRay. Nikos remembers from his army days that McRay could go crazy if he didn't get his way. Nikos, who has two young children, is afraid that McRay may hurt them if Nikos doesn't go along with his plan. McRay has once threatened to stomp on anyone who wouldn't stick by him.

Nikos keeps his involvement to a minimum. When McRay asks, Nikos rents a storage unit to which McRay has access. On the day of the bombing,

Nikos has no contact with McRay. He doesn't go near the bomb site and doesn't help McRay prepare the bomb. In fact, Nikos heads in the other direction. When Nikos hears that McRay has actually set off the bomb, killing several people, he goes directly to the authorities to cooperate in their investigation.

Under traditional common law, Nikos is

A. guilty of conspiracy, attempted murder, and accomplice liability.
B. guilty of conspiracy and murder.
C. not guilty of conspiracy because he abandoned the conspiracy.
D. not guilty of any crime because he acted under duress.
E. guilty of conspiracy but not murder because he did not take a substantial step toward completion of the crime.

QUESTION 14. High stakes. Tom Playlock is hooked on gambling. He gambles day and night, even at work. In fact, he gambles away all the money he needs to pay his taxes. He has become so obsessed with gambling that he thinks the "chips" are something to eat and that IRS stands for "isn't roulette sensational!" When charged with tax evasion, Playlock claims that he should have a defense based on his gambling addiction. According to his experts, Tom doesn't realize that he has any tax responsibilities because he doesn't realize the consequences of his gambling. The crime of tax evasion requires "an intent to willfully evade paying taxes." The lesser crime of failure to file income tax returns only requires that a "defendant fail to file tax returns in a timely manner."

Under the Model Penal Code

A. Tom's gambling problem is irrelevant.
B. Tom's gambling problem may only be considered for sentencing.
C. Tom's gambling problem can be a defense to tax evasion.
D. Tom's gambling problem is irrelevant because he is charged with general intent crimes.
E. Tom's gambling problem is not a defense unless he was legally insane.

QUESTION 15. Bad date. Andrew and Emma had been dating for years when she suddenly ended their relationship. Upset by her decision, Andrew broke into Emma's apartment with the intent to convince her to get back together with him. When Emma disagreed, Andrew threatened to kill himself. At that point, Emma said, "No, Andrew. You know I care about you too much to let you hurt yourself." She then gave him a hug. Andrew mistakenly took her actions as a signal that Emma wanted to get back together. He grabbed her. At that point, Emma didn't know what to do. If she refused his advances, she worried Andrew would kill himself. However, she really didn't want to have sex with him. Yet, she felt she had no choice, so she did not resist his advances. The next morning, when she threw him out for good, Emma called the police and reported Andrew for rape. When the police arrested him, the police found on Andrew some valuables he had taken from Emma's home because he wanted her to "pay" for what she had done to him.

In most jurisdictions, Andrew is

A. guilty of larceny and rape.
B. guilty of burglary, larceny, and rape.
C. guilty of rape only.
D. guilty of larceny and rape.
E. guilty of larceny only.

QUESTION 16. March On. Mark Militant is tough on crime. Following law school, he takes a job as the head of a boot camp. Parents of difficult boys send their children to the camp so Mark can mold them into young men. Mark decides that what delinquent teenagers really need is more discipline. In order to instill that discipline, Mark forces the teens to march every day for 10 miles. Although the teens complain, they have always found a way to complete their task.

One day, a new teen arrives at the boot camp. He is a real whiner. He complains about everything from making his bed to clearing his dishes. During the 10-mile march, the teen starts to complain about chest pains. Without examining the boy, Mark decides the teen is faking it. He orders the teen to continue to march. After another 100 yards, the boy collapses. Mark hovers over him and orders him to get up. When the boy doesn't do so, Mark continues to march on with the group. He leaves the boy there all night. When he returns, the boy is dead. An autopsy reveals that the boy has died from cold and exposure. Mark is shocked. He honestly didn't believe there was any chance the boy would die.

Based upon his conduct, Mark is most likely

A. guilty of voluntary manslaughter because the boy provoked Mark's conduct.
B. guilty of involuntary manslaughter because of his callous and wanton disregard for human life.

C. guilty of involuntary manslaughter because he had a duty to help the teen.

D. not guilty of homicide because he was not the proximate cause of the teen's death.

E. not guilty of homicide because he was not the actual cause of the teen's death.

QUESTION 17. Make me an offer. Tiffany Tsuris is charged with conspiracy to bribe and bribery. The evidence at trial is that Tsuris and the Mayor agreed that Tsuris would pay the Mayor $50,000 in exchange for the Mayor's promise to use his influence to award Tsuris' company the city contract. Tsuris moves to dismiss the conspiracy charge.

Under which rule would Tsuris have the best argument for dismissal?

A. *Lambert* rule.

B. *Wharton* rule.

C. *Pinkerton* rule.

D. *Kotteakos* rule.

E. *Luparello* rule.

QUESTION 18. Boom. Kabinski is out to kill his old nemesis, Prof. I. M. Genius. He prepares a package of explosives and mails it to Prof. Genius. Instead, it is misdelivered to Prof. Ian Nobel. Nobel, who liked to snoop into Genius's affairs, peeked into the package. It then went off, killing him.

If charged with murder, Kabinski is

A. not guilty because he did not intend to kill Nobel.

B. not guilty because Nobel contributed to his own death.

C. not guilty because he had no malice toward Nobel.

D. not guilty because he made a mistake of fact.

E. guilty.

QUESTION 19. Diamond ring. Jorge sees a woman sleeping on a blanket at the beach. On her hand is a gigantic, shimmering diamond ring. Jorge, a former diamond dealer, is drawn to it immediately. He wants to get a better look at it, although he plans to get it back to the woman before she wakes. Without waking the woman, Jorge gently slips the ring off her hand. He is apprehended by a lifeguard as he is trying to put the ring back on the woman's finger. Jorge is charged with stealing (i.e., taking the property of another person with the intent to permanently deprive that person thereof).

Assuming that Jorge was slightly drunk at the time, what would be his best defense?

A. Voluntary intoxication.
B. Irresistible impulse.
C. Lack of mens rea.
D. No use of force.
E. Abandonment.

QUESTION 20. Bulls-eye.   Aaron has just returned home from a date when he notices a light on in his house. He is suspicious because he turned off all the lights before leaving on his date. Aaron then sees a figure exit the side door of his house with what appears to be a television set. Aaron grabs his bow and arrow and shoots at the figure as it is walking away from him. The arrow finds the mark, killing the intruder.

If charged with homicide for the death of the intruder,

A. Aaron has full defense because he acted in self-defense.
B. Aaron can assert the law enforcement defense.
C. Aaron is guilty of murder.
D. Aaron has a full defense because he was protecting his home.
E. Aaron had a duty to retreat.

QUESTION 21. Kiss the gun.   Gus has a problem with alcohol and women. Whenever he gets drunk, he gets violent with women. He forces them to play a game called "Kiss the Gun," in which the woman must kiss the front of the barrel of a loaded gun before she is allowed to leave his house. Several of the women have told him he is crazy and that he is going to kill someone one day, but Gus just laughs and says, "Let's have fun. I think we can take our chances."

Sure enough, when it is Marcy's turn to play the game, the gun goes off and kills her. The evidence is disputed as to who pulled the trigger, although Gus admits that they were playing "Kiss the Gun."

If Gus is charged with murder, he is most likely

A. guilty because he was told the gun could kill someone.
B. not guilty because there is not proof beyond a reasonable doubt that he pulled the trigger.
C. guilty because no reasonable person could believe the gun was safe.
D. not guilty because Marcy committed suicide.
E. guilty of negligent homicide.

QUESTION 22. Killer barbeque. Salar is freezing in his home, but he cannot afford to buy a new heater for his family. In order to keep them warm, he lights a barbeque in his living room. The family goes to sleep. Tragically, the fumes from the barbeque kill everyone but Salar. When the police arrive, Salar is sobbing hysterically. He tells them, "No one could have loved his family more than I did. I've read about these tragedies, but I never thought it would happen to us. I can't believe how stupid I was. You have to believe me. It is a mistake I'll have to live with my whole life."

In a Model Penal Code jurisdiction, and assuming that the jury believed Salar, he is most likely guilty of

A. manslaughter.
B. first-degree murder.
C. murder.
D. felony murder.
E. negligent homicide.

QUESTION 23. Holiday rush. Kevin is very excited about the upcoming holiday sales. He wants to buy several special gifts for his loved ones. In anticipation of the great sales, Kevin lines up in front of the Wal-Mart at midnight. He stands in the freezing cold rain, with only a bottle of whiskey to keep him warm. As he waits and drinks, he becomes increasingly anxious. Thousands of people are in line with him and he is worried that they will get the sale items before him.

The store is scheduled to open at 6:00 a.m. At 5:30 a.m., the crowd starts to push and shove. Kevin hears people talking about grabbing the very items he wants to buy. Meanwhile, the security guard at Wal-Mart starts to taunt him by looking at his watch, grabbing a few items for himself and laughing. However, the guard knows that he is protected by the big glass doors, so he is not worried.

At 5:45 a.m., the crowd really starts to get unruly. There is plenty of pushing and shoving. Kevin can't stand it anymore. Together with others in the line, he pushes down the door, crushing the security guard as he rushes in to shop.

If Kevin is charged in a common law jurisdiction with killing the security guard, which of the following is true?

A. He is not guilty of any crime because the guard's death was just a tragic accident.

B. He is not guilty of manslaughter because he was intoxicated at the time of the crime.

C. He is guilty of murder if he didn't care whether the guard died so long as he could get his gifts.

D. He is guilty of involuntary manslaughter because others in the line were also responsible for killing the guard.

E. He is guilty of voluntary manslaughter because he was provoked by the security guard.

QUESTION 24. **Hotel surprise.**   Sampson is angry because some friends, Mike and Jay, have stolen his personal items, including family mementos. Sampson asks his buddy, Greg, to go over to Mike's house to help him recover the items. Sampson asks Greg to bring his gun just to scare Mike a little. However, he asks Greg to unload the gun before he takes it over so no one will get hurt.

When Sampson and Greg get to Mike's house, they ring the doorbell and Mike lets them in. Greg pulls out the gun and orders Mike and Jay not to move. Sampson grabs the memorabilia and starts to leave. Jay has a heart attack and dies.

Assuming all common law principles apply, which of the following crimes may be charged against Sampson?

A. Accomplice to kidnapping and burglary.

B. Robbery, felony-murder, and murder.

C. Solicitation to commit robbery, accomplice to robbery, and robbery.

D. Conspiracy, assault, burglary, robbery, and murder.

E. Accomplice, burglary, kidnapping, robbery, and murder.

QUESTION 25. **Last lethal question.**   Under current Supreme Court law, when is it unconstitutional to apply the death penalty?

A. When the defendant was under age 21 at the time of the killing.

B. When the defendant was convicted of felony-murder.

> **C.** When the defendant was mentally retarded at the time of the offense.
> **D.** When the defendant raped and killed his victim.
> **E.** When the execution will be by lethal injection.

 Levenson's Picks

1. **Island of the blue dolphins.** **B** is the best answer. Anderson's best defense is mistake of fact. Anderson will argue that knowing he is killing a dolphin is a material element of the crime, especially since the statute requires that he "knowingly" kill the animal and it carries felony penalties. **A** is incorrect because economic necessity is never a defense; **C** is incorrect because the dolphins did not threaten Anderson with physical harm. **D** is a red herring in this sea of legal problems. Factual impossibility only applies when a defendant is unsuccessful in his intended illegal acts. Here, Anderson did not intend to commit an unlawful harm, although he actually did kill the dolphins.

2. **Thanks, neighbor!** **D** is correct, but only because this is a tricky question. Although Luke is charged with both murder and larceny, the question calls only for the best defense to larceny. Therefore, **A** is wrong. For the murder, self-defense is a viable option. However, it makes no sense with regard to the larceny. **B** is wrong because no one was forcing Luke to steal the tools; he was faced with the lesser of two evils. The defense that applies in such situations is necessity. You should note that if the question asked about a defense to the murder, necessity would not be the correct answer under common law because it is not a defense to a homicide. However, under the Model Penal Code, it could be a defense. Finally, although Luke is under extreme stress, it does not mean that he is insane. **C** is a wrong answer.

3. **Eliminating the competition.** **D** is right. Many multiple-choice exams include this type of question. It lulls you into thinking the question is about the degree of homicide the defendant faces; in fact, the real issue is whether the defendant has committed the necessary actus reus. Brains had no duty to help Einstein. Therefore, the general rule applies that an omission does not fulfill the actus reus requirement for a crime. **A**, **B**, and **C** are incorrect because there was no actus reus for the crime.

4. **Assaulting the presidency.** **C** is the best answer. Even though a senator told George it was important for him to take action, George

could never claim a mistake of law defense or entrapment. There was no official judicial or administrative authorization of his behavior, nor was there an attempt to get George to do something illegal. Moreover, George appears predisposed to shoot the President. Therefore, **A** and **E** are wrong. **B** is wrong because George had every intent to kill the President. **D** is wrong because factual impossibility is not a defense under the common law. Under the Model Penal Code, impossibility is not a defense if the defendant would have been guilty had the circumstances been as he believed them to be. **C** is the best answer. Although George could probably be charged with some other crime, such as trespass, if the President was out of town, he would have a strong argument that he was not in dangerous proximity of killing the President.

5. **Too much partying.**   Pick **A** as your answer. Remember, voluntary intoxication is not a defense to a crime requiring only recklessness. Ferrari has been charged with reckless driving. **B** is incorrect because voluntary intoxication can be a defense to specific intent crimes. This answer is too absolute. **C** is wrong because recklessness can be formed even when a defendant is intoxicated. **D** and **E** are wrong because peer pressure does not make intoxication involuntary or under duress.

6. **Double robbery.**   Choose **B**. Each defendant is responsible for her own robbery, but because the defendants were unaware of the other's crime, there is no conspiracy or accomplice liability. **A**, **C**, and **D** are incorrect because there was no agreement between the defendants nor purpose to help each other commit a crime. **E** is wrong because each defendant caused the bank to suffer a loss. Causation analysis does not require that a defendant be the only cause of harm.

7. **Illegal transports.**   **A** is the correct answer. This question is relatively easy if you remember that the Model Penal Code rejects the notion of automatic co-conspirator liability. Rather, in order to hold Angela responsible for the substantive transportation charge, the prosecution would have to prove that she aided and abetted that offense. **B** is incorrect because Angela has done nothing to help with the transportation of the aliens. **C** is wrong because even if Angela abandoned the conspiracy, she is still responsible for the conspiracy charge because she did not thwart the conspiracy. **D** is wrong because an overt act may be committed by any defendant. **E** is incorrect because conspiracy agreements need not be express.

8. **Still fighting.**   Almost every multiple-choice exam will have a self-defense question. Here, **E** is the correct answer because the defense is likely to succeed. With Melvin flailing at him with a sword and

threatening to kill him, Thomas appears to have an honest and reasonable fear that his life is in imminent danger. Thomas was not the initial aggressor and under common law, he did not have a duty to retreat. Accordingly, **A-D** are incorrect.

9. **Wrong house.**   **B** is right. In essence, this is a fancy transferred intent problem, combining a causation issue with intent issues. **A** and **D** are wrong because Carl's intent transfers from his intended victim to the actual victim; his motive is irrelevant except to prove intent. **C** is wrong under the common law, although some modern jurisdictions would only hold Carl responsible for the reckless killing of the unintended victim. Carl would not be entitled to claim voluntary manslaughter under common law because kicking a dog would not likely be adequate legal provocation. **B** is correct because Carl had the intent to kill and did kill, albeit the wrong victim.

10. **BWS.**   Choose **D**. It is very difficult to use a multiple-choice question to examine on battered women's syndrome, but it can be done. The professor can set forth a question to determine if you know the correct legal standard to be applied. Here, although Bea is very sympathetic, she would not likely meet the common law requirements for self-defense. Bea engaged in a preemptive strike. At the time she killed, the threat was not yet imminent. **A** is wrong because fear is just one element of self-defense. **B** is wrong because the traditional reasonable person standard ordinarily does not frame the question in terms of the "reasonable battered woman." Imperfect self-defense is a statutory creation, making **C** incorrect. Under the traditional common law, Bea is guilty of murder.

11. **Forbidden fruit.**   **A** is right. This question requires that you know the Model Penal Code approach to homicide and causation. The Model Penal Code recognizes gross disregard for human life as a basis for a murder charge, regardless of whether the defendant had the intent to kill the victim. Certainly, participating in a game of shooting arrows at each other is an action that could be considered grossly reckless. **B** is wrong because the Model Penal Codes does not have categories of voluntary and involuntary manslaughter. **C** is wrong because Shant is certainly a link in the causation that leads to Mike's death, even if Mike did develop an infection. Finally, **D** is wrong because consent is not a defense to homicide and there is no indication that Mike wanted help to commit suicide.

12. **Suitable felonies.**   **C** is your best bet. This type of question may make you a little nervous because it is slightly different from the standard multiple-choice format. However, it is easy to answer if you just go through I-IV to determine if the felony, as described,

meets the two main limitations on felony murders; that is, it is inherently dangerous and independent of the actual killing. Only one felony in this list meets both requirements. Even in the abstract, bombing an occupied residence is inherently dangerous. The felony also appears to be independent because it does not require that the defendant act with the intent to kill. By contrast, poisoning (II) and assault with a deadly weapon (IV) require intent to kill and are therefore not independent felonies. As defined, grand theft (III) is not an inherently dangerous felony. Unless the jurisdiction applied the "as committed" standard, grand theft would not meet the felony-murder requirements.

13. **Dangerous liaisons.** **B** is the best answer. I included this question because it addresses issues from almost every area of the book— offenses, inchoate crimes, and defenses. To answer it, first evaluate the facts to see if the defendant committed any crimes. If so, determine whether he has any defense. By agreeing to help McRay, Nikos has committed conspiracy. Once his co-conspirator commits a crime in furtherance of that conspiracy, Nikos is also guilty of that offense under traditional common law. Here, McRay would be guilty of murder. However, there is no separate crime of accomplice liability. Therefore, **A** is wrong. **C** is wrong because Nikos did not formally abandon the conspiracy by notifying McRay or the police. He also does not have a duress defense because the threat is too vague so **D** is a bad choice. Finally, **E** is wrong because Nikos need not take a substantial step to be guilty of a co-conspirator's crimes.

14. **High stakes.** Pick **C**. Tom may have an unusual mental condition, but if it actually exists, it could play a major role in Tom's case. It certainly would not be irrelevant as **A** states. Moreover, under the Model Penal Code, a mental condition that prevents the defendant from forming the necessary intent for the offense may be considered. **B** is wrong because Tom's condition affects whether he is guilty of the offenses charges, not just the issue of sentencing. **D** is wrong because Tom is not charged with only general-intent crimes. Finally, **E** is wrong because even if Tom is not insane, he still may not have been able to form the mens rea for tax evasion.

15. **Bad date.** **E** is the answer. Andrew was probably trespassing when he broke into Emma's apartment, but he is not guilty of burglary because he did not have the intent to commit a felony inside at the time of his entry. He is also not guilty of rape. Andrew did not force Emma into sex, even though she did not really want to have sex with him. This question highlights the difference between sex without consent and nonconsensual sex by means of force, intimidation, or

threat. Essentially, Emma is guilted into having sex with Andrew. Finally, Andrew is guilty of larceny. Even though he did not have the intent to steal at the time of his entry, he did take Emma's property with the intent to permanently deprive her of it. The final count? Andrew is guilty of larceny only.

16. **March on.**   **C** is the best answer. Take a moment to analyze this problem. In a homicide question, always consider whether the defendant satisfied the actus reus, mens rea, and causation requirements for the crime. Mark is accused of homicide. As for the actus reus, he leaves the boy to die. Therefore, this is a question involving an omission. Here, because Mark has assumed the responsibility for the boys, he has a duty to help them. Given the facts, this duty may be contractual, by status relationship, or he assumed the care. Then, the question is what was Mark's mens rea. The facts indicate that Mark believes the boy is "faking" it. If that is Mark's mental state, then Mark "should realize" that the boy might die, but he does not. Mark does not have "conscious disregard" for the life of another person. The malice requirement for murder requires a subjective disregard for the life of another. Assuming the jury believes Mark, he may be negligent, but he is not reckless in how he treats the boy. Finally, there is the question of causation. Certainly, Mark's failure to help is a link in the chain of causation. Therefore, there would be actual cause. Moreover, because it is foreseeable that failing to help the boy would lead to his death, and acts of nature generally do not break the chain of causation, Mark would be the proximate cause. With these thoughts in mind, take a look at the options. **A** is clearly wrong because the boy's whining does not even come close to legally adequate provocation. **B** is wrong because if Mark actually had "callous and wanton disregard," he would be guilty of murder, not involuntary manslaughter. **D** and **E** are wrong because, as we saw, Mark is both the actual and proximate cause of the boy's death. Therefore, **C** is the best answer. Because Mark had a duty to help the boy, he is responsible for the boy's death. It is manslaughter so long as Mark was not subjectively aware of the risk to the boy. What is tricky about this question is realizing that Mark was unaware of the risk to the boy. On an essay exam, it would not be too difficult to argue that Mark "must have been aware" of the risk and therefore acted in a callous and wanton disregard. However, if a question tells you that he honestly did not realize the risk, look for manslaughter instead of murder.

17. **Make me an offer.**   Pick **B**. Sometimes, your professor will want you to know criminal law rules by the names of the cases establishing those rules. We've talked about several of these rules throughout the book. The one that applies here is the *Wharton* rule. **A** is wrong because the

Lambert rule applies to mistake of law questions. As you'll recall, Mrs. Lambert avoided conviction because she was unaware that she had to register as a felon when she entered a new jurisdiction. **C** is wrong because *Pinkerton*, which relates to conspiracy law, actually establishes co-conspirator liability. It would not be a basis for dismissal. **D** is wrong because *Kotteakos* relates to the scope of conspiracies. Nothing about this question seems to focus on whether multiple parties belonged to the same conspiracy. **E** does not work because *Luparello* focuses on whether accomplices are responsible for foreseeable crimes. By the process of elimination, we can see that **B** is the right answer. The *Wharton* rule prohibits a conspiracy charge from being brought when the underlying crime requires two persons for its commission.

18. **Boom.**   You don't have to be a Nobel Prize winner to realize that **E** is the right answer. On its face, the question is another example of the transferred intent doctrine. Kabinski intended to kill one victim, but accidentally killed another. **A** is, therefore, incorrect because it doesn't matter whether Kabinski kills another victim. **B** is wrong because contributory negligence does not apply. Criminal law is reluctant to blame the victim, even if the victim was snooping into other people's affairs. **C** is wrong because malice transfers to the new victim. Moreover, malice does not mean that the defendant has ill will toward a particular person. Rather, as you'll recall, it means whether the defendant had the intent to kill, intent to cause great bodily harm, or acted with gross recklessness. **D** is wrong because mistake of fact does not apply. It is often tempting to pick this answer when the defendant makes a mistake, but mistake of fact applies only when the defendant accidentally commits a crime. Here, the defendant wanted to commit murder. He had the intent to kill another human being, and that is all that the definition of murder requires. Kabinski is guilty of murder and **E** is the correct answer.

19. **Diamond ring.**   **C** is the correct answer. Even if you don't cover theft crimes in your criminal law class, your professor may give you a question like this. Everything you need to answer it is within the question. Jorge is charged with stealing. The question tells you that stealing requires "intent to permanently deprive that person" of her property. This is the same as the common law definition of larceny. The question tells you that Jorge planned to give the ring back to the woman when she wakes up. Therefore, he does not have the mens rea for the crime. That makes **C** the right answer. Take a look at why the other answers are wrong. **A** is wrong because the question tells you that Jorge is only "slightly drunk" at the time he takes the ring. He clearly can form the intent to take another person's property, even though he had something to drink. Don't automatically select the intoxication

defense just because a problem indicates the defendant has been drinking. **B** is wrong because irresistible impulse is not a defense unless you have the facts to support an insanity defense. For an insanity defense, you must have a disease or defect of the mind. The question does not refer to any such disease or defect. **D** is wrong because use of force may be required for robbery, but it is not a defense to larceny or stealing. Finally, **E** is wrong because the woman did not abandon her property. She may have been careless in leaving it exposed on a beach blanket, but that is not an invitation to have someone steal it. **C** is the best answer.

20. **Bulls-eye.** **C** is again the correct answer. The intruder should not have been stealing from Aaron, but that does not give Aaron license to kill the intruder. This question focuses on the rules of self-defense. **A** is wrong because the suspicious figure at his home is walking away at the time Aaron shot him. The first requirement for self-defense is that the victim poses a physical threat to the defendant. In this question, the victim did not pose such a threat. **B** is wrong because not even law enforcement can shoot a fleeing felon unless there is evidence that the suspect poses a threat to other persons. **D** is wrong because lethal force cannot be used to protect property. Finally, **E** is wrong because Aaron did not have a duty to retreat. While some jurisdictions have such a duty, generally it does not require a defendant to retreat in his own home or "castle." Aaron should have called the police instead of shooting the thief. He is guilty of murder and **C** is the correct answer.

21. **Kiss the gun.** **A** is the best answer. This is an "implied malice" question. Gus may not intend to kill Marcy, but he consciously and callously takes the risk. It is very similar to the Russian Roulette question in Chapter 9 of the book. First, it doesn't matter whether Gus pulled the trigger. He encouraged Marcy to do so, and that is a sufficient actus reus for the crime. **B** is a wrong answer. **C** is also wrong, but for different reasons. Murder requires that the defendant realize the extreme risk to human life. **C** focuses only on the reasonable person. **D** is wrong because there is no evidence that Marcy intended to commit suicide. **E** is wrong for the very reason that **A** is right. If Gus was unaware that the gun might go off and kill Marcy, then **E** would be the right answer. Here, however, he was on notice that the gun could kill someone. In fact, that was the thrill of the game. **A** is the better answer.

22. **Killer barbeque.** Pick **E**. Some professors prefer to focus on the Model Penal Code standards for homicide. If yours does, this is the type of question you are likely to see. The question screams with negligent homicide. It indicates the defendant "never thought" such a

tragedy would happen to him, that he was "stupid," and that he made a tragic "mistake." Whereas such clueless behavior would be manslaughter under common law, the Model Penal Code refers to it as negligent homicide. Therefore, **A** is wrong because the Model Penal Code requires reckless disregard or extreme emotional disturbance for manslaughter. **B** is wrong because the Model Penal Code does not have degrees of murder. **C** is wrong because murder requires extreme indifference to human life. Here, Salar loves his family and did not consciously disregard the risk. Finally, the Model Penal Code also rejects felony murder as automatically making the defendant guilty of murder. Rather, it creates a presumption that the defendant acted with extreme indifference to human life. Here, Salar did not. Therefore, even if you thought Salar was guilty of arson (which he is not because there was no fire damage to the structure), felony murder would still not apply. **D**, therefore, is wrong. **E** is the correct answer.

23. **Holiday rush.**   **C** is the best pick. Sadly, the newspapers can provide you with plenty of examples for practicing your knowledge of criminal law. In this question, Kevin has acted with callous disregard in trampling the security guard to death. It was a tragic accident, but it was also much more. **A** is wrong because Kevin acts in an extremely reckless manner by pushing into the store. **B** is wrong because intoxication is not a defense to murder unless it is a high level, such as the first degree, that requires premeditation or some type of sophisticated thought. **D** is wrong because the culpability of other persons does not reduce Kevin's culpability. Finally, **E** is wrong because the security guard did nothing to provoke the killing.

24. **Hotel surprise.**   **D** is the correct answer. This question is designed to test your knowledge of multiple crimes and culpability theories. When you see a question like this, check to see if the elements for each crime listed are satisfied. Then, review the question for theories of culpability. Let's start with kidnapping. Under common law principles, kidnapping requires both intentional unlawful confinement *and* movement of the victim. There was no movement, so you can eliminate kidnapping and **A** as an answer. How about **B**? Sampson does meet the requirements for common law robbery and felony murder. As an accomplice, he took property by force or intimidation. This is robbery. It does not matter that he sought to reclaim his own property. The requirement is only that he took the property from the victim's person or presence. One does not have the right to reclaim property by use or threat of force. How about felony-murder? A death occurred during the robbery, so Sampson would also be guilty of felony-murder. **B** is looking pretty good until you notice that both murder and felony-murder are listed. Sampson is

not guilty of murder and felony-murder. It is all one crime. **B** is wrong. How about **C**? **C** is also wrong. One is not guilty of being an accomplice to robbery and robbery. Accomplice liability is how Sampson is guilty of the robbery. Moreover, solicitation merges with the completed crime of robbery. **D** requires you to analyze whether Sampson is guilty of the additional crimes of conspiracy, assault, and burglary. He is guilty of conspiracy because he agreed with Greg to rob his victims. He is guilty of assault because they intentionally put their victims in apprehension by drawing the gun. Finally, Sampson is guilty of burglary because he broke into Mike's house with the intent to commit a felony inside the dwelling. Therefore, Sampson is guilty of all of the crimes listed in **D**. As for **E**, it can be quickly eliminated. It has one glaring problem: Sampson is not guilty of being an accomplice. Accomplice liability is the theory by which he is guilty of the crimes listed in **D**. Therefore, **D** is the best answer.

25. **Last lethal question.** **C** is the dead-bang right answer. This question tests recent developments in death penalty law. **A** is wrong because it is only unconstitutional to commit minors who were under 18 years old (not 21 years old) at the time of the offense. Felony-murder may result in the death penalty if there was major participation and reckless indifference. Therefore, **B** is wrong. **C** is tricky, but wrong. The Supreme Court has held that the death penalty for rape is cruel and unusual punishment; **D** also states that the defendant killed his victim. **E** is wrong because the Supreme Court recently upheld execution by lethal injection. **C** is the correct answer. As the Supreme Court held in *Atkins*, it is unconstitutional to impose the death penalty on a mentally retarded defendant.

Congratulations, you have climbed that greasy pole! I hope this book has been helpful in your efforts. It has been my pleasure and honor to write it for you.

Index